Supervision

Concepts and Skill-Building

Supervision

Concepts and Skill-Building   Sixth Edition

Samuel C. Certo
Steinmetz Professor of Management
Rollins College

McGraw-Hill
Irwin

Boston   Burr Ridge, IL   Dubuque, IA   Madison, WI   New York   San Francisco   St. Louis
Bangkok   Bogotá   Caracas   Kuala Lumpur   Lisbon   London   Madrid   Mexico City
Milan   Montreal   New Delhi   Santiago   Seoul   Singapore   Sydney   Taipei   Toronto

McGraw-Hill
Irwin

SUPERVISION: CONCEPTS AND SKILL-BUILDING

Published by McGraw-Hill/Irwin, a business unit of The McGraw-Hill Companies, Inc., 1221 Avenue of the Americas, New York, NY, 10020. Copyright © 2008 by The McGraw-Hill Companies, Inc. All rights reserved. No part of this publication may be reproduced or distributed in any form or by any means, or stored in a database or retrieval system, without the prior written consent of The McGraw-Hill Companies, Inc., including, but not limited to, in any network or other electronic storage or transmission, or broadcast for distance learning.

Some ancillaries, including electronic and print components, may not be available to customers outside the United States.

This book is printed on acid-free paper.

3 4 5 6 7 8 9 0 QPD/QPD 0 9 8

ISBN: 978-0-07-340500-1
MHID: 0-07-340500-0

Editorial director: *John E. Biernat*
Senior sponsoring editor: *Kelly H. Lowery*
Editorial assistant: *Megan Richter*
Developmental editor I: *Kelly Odom*
Project manager: *Marlena Pechan*
Lead production supervisor: *Michael R. McCormick*
Designer: *Jillian Lindner*
Lead media project manager: *Cathy L. Tepper*
Typeface: *10/12 Palatino*
Compositor: *International Typesetting and Composition*
Printer: *Quebecor World Dubuque Inc.*

Library of Congress Cataloging-in-Publication Data

Certo, Samuel C.
    Supervision : concepts and skill-building / Samuel C. Certo.—6th ed.
        p. cm.
    Includes index.
    ISBN-13: 978-0-07-340500-1 (alk. paper)
    ISBN-10: 0-07-340500-0 (alk. paper)
    1. Supervision of employees. I. Title.
    HF5549.12.C42 2008
    658.3'02—dc22   2006035826

www.mhhe.com

To Sarah and Drew . . .
Watching how you face everyday challenges is a true encouragement to me. Your strong faith and everyday tenacity constantly keep you moving in the right direction. Full speed ahead!

Preface

The critical contribution that modern supervisors make in generating organizational success is undeniable. Topics contained in this new edition continue to represent both traditionally proven and cutting-edge supervision concepts that serve as practical tools for meeting present-day supervision challenges. The key thrust for this new edition is to enhance the text's usefulness by providing students with a rich mix of practical supervision ideas as well as real-life examples that illustrate how modern supervisors solve contemporary problems. Carefully studying supervision concepts and examples throughout this text will greatly enhance your chances of success and personal rewards as a supervisor.

This new edition, like previous editions, prepares students to be supervisors. Reflecting on the complexities of the supervisor's job, *Supervision: Concepts and Skill-Building* helps students learn what it takes to be a successful supervisor. Overall, this book focuses on discussing important supervision concepts *and* providing fundamental skills necessary for applying these concepts.

The continuing success of this text continues to reaffirm my belief that a high-quality supervision text must contain important theoretical material as well as facilitate the student-learning and instructional processes. The following sections outline in detail how this new edition presents supervision theory and facilitates these processes.

OVERVIEW OF TEXT DEVELOPMENT

The Foundation

This sixth edition, like all previous editions, is built on a solid theoretical foundation. To generate this foundation, surveys were mailed to instructors of supervision courses as well as supervisors nationwide to gather information about what would be needed to develop the highest quality supervision learning package available in the marketplace. The main themes generated from the results of this survey were summarized and presented to focus groups around the country for refinement and expansion. Supervision professors and practicing supervisors then acted as individual reviewers to help fine-tune the book plan, and they served as final advisers before writing began. Figure A depicts the focus of various professionals during the development of this text.

The Sixth Edition—A Successful Tradition Continues

Supervision: Concepts and Skill-Building is divided into five main parts: "What Is a Supervisor?" "Modern Supervision Challenges," "Functions of the Supervisor," "Skills of the Supervisor," and "Supervision and Human Resources." Each part concludes with an exercise that is linked to instructor-accessible videos called the "Manager's Hot Seat Video." The following sections describe the parts and chapters of the sixth edition.

Part One, "What Is a Supervisor?" consists of the first chapter, "Modern Supervision: Concepts and Skills." Chapter 1 aims at providing the student with a thorough introduction to supervision before embarking on a more detailed study of the supervision process. Revision highlights for this chapter include a new opening vignette about gaining acceptance as a new supervisor, with a reflective end-of-chapter case and a new section expanding the discussion about supervisory skills.

FIGURE A   *Supervision:* The Professional Team

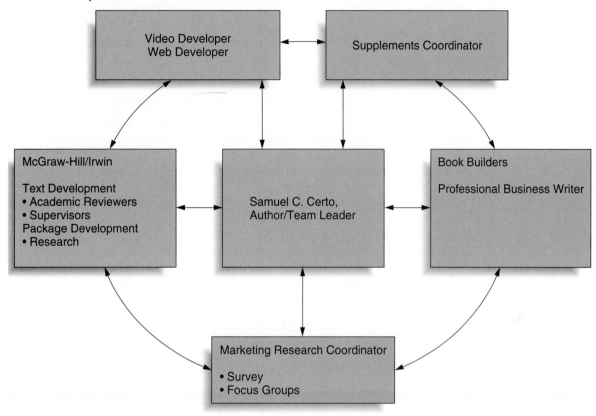

Part Two, "Modern Supervision Challenges," covers areas in which supervisors will have to meet important contemporary organizational challenges. Chapter 2, "Ensuring High Quality and Productivity," depicts how quality and productivity can affect supervision in organizations. Both Chapter 3, "Teamwork: Emphasizing Powerful Meetings," and Chapter 4, "Meeting High Ethical Standards," have been updated for this edition. There is added coverage of team building and relationships in Chapter 3. In Chapter 4, coverage of ethics in today's business world has been added. Chapter 5, "Managing Diversity," is an important chapter that focuses on how diversity can affect the supervision process. Major topics include defining diversity, prejudice, stereotypes, sexism, and ageism. New coverage has been added regarding the growing number of female leaders in business, the increase of disabled workers in the workforce, and the improvements made to communication technology.

Part Three, "Functions of the Supervisor," contains four chapters. Chapter 6, "Reaching Goals: Plans and Controls," combines the planning and control functions of a supervisor. For this edition, an array of new chapter examples, including a focus on banking, goal setting, and planning in the field of construction, have been added to improve the chapter's richness and pragmatism. Chapter 7, "Organizing and Authority," emphasizes organizing and delegating. This chapter includes new examples of flexibility and supervisor delegation. Chapter 8, "The Supervisor as Leader," has added coverage on the differences between a manager and a leader. Chapter 9, "Problem Solving, Decision Making, and Creativity," gives students insights about the kinds of problems and decisions that supervisors face, as well as possible steps for solving problems and making decisions. A new opening vignette about problem solving as a 911 dispatcher has been added to this edition.

Part Four, "Skills of the Supervisor," discusses important abilities that supervisors must have to be successful. These abilities include "Communication" (Chapter 10), "Motivating Employees" (Chapter 11), "Problem Employees: Counseling and Discipline" (Chapter 12), "Managing Time and Stress" (Chapter 13), and "Managing Conflict and Change" (Chapter 14). For this edition, Chapter 11 has been revised to demonstrate creative motivation techniques for employee retention with an emphasis on high standards. Chapter 12 has been improved with more coverage of how constructive criticism and creative solutions can positively affect problem employees. More focus on time management and handling stress characterize this revision of Chapter 13, and a focus on organizational politics and changes in work scheduling is addressed in Chapter 14.

Again in this edition, "Appendix A: Organizational Politics" follows Part Four. This appendix continues to provide students with a special and unique vehicle for learning about the impact of politics on supervision in modern organizations. The material provides a clear definition of organizational politics and discusses various levels of political action as well as political tactics. Also emphasized is a related topic called impression management, along with special coverage of how to manage organizational politics.

The text concludes with new organization in Part Five, "Supervision and Human Resources." Chapter 18, from the fifth edition, is now Appendix B, which is discussed subsequently. Chapter 15, "Selecting Employees," focuses on the process of choosing the right person to fill an open position and the sources, methods, and legal issues that must be considered. Chapter enhancements for this revision include an additional focus on hiring practices and skills for interviewing job candidates. Chapter 16, "Providing Orientation and Training," discusses the process of orienting new employees, developing skills in employees, and evaluating training methods. This edition's improvements to Chapter 16 include a new opening vignette about the importance of the manager's commitment to training, along with updated training techniques and tips. Chapter 17, "Appraising Performance," discusses the importance of a systematic performance appraisal and provides several appraisal methods. Edition enhancements include an added focus on the effectiveness of personal development plans, how different companies use appraisal data, and the relationship between appraisal feedback and performance.

The text ends with Appendix B (new to this edition) and Appendix C, formerly Appendix B. Appendix B, "Supervision Laws: Health and Safety, Labor Relations, Fair Employment" focuses on practical legal information relevant to successful supervision. Appendix C, "Finding a Career Path That Fits," is a rich career resource for students regarding finding that first job, perhaps a supervision job, as well as managing a career. It emphasizes important topics such as setting career goals, preparing for a job search, and interviewing essentials. Internet resources are pinpointed from which students can get help with self-assessments of their personality and skills, résumé building, job hunting resources, and how to evaluate a good job offer. This appendix is designed to be a vital topic for course discussion as well as a valuable reference guide as students actually begin and manage their careers.

OVERVIEW OF TEXT LEARNING SYSTEM

Each chapter in this edition continues the tradition of making the study of supervision interesting, enjoyable, effective, and efficient. As you will see, new pedagogy elements have been added to this edition to further enhance the power of the overall pedagogy. Each pedagogy component is described in the following sections.

Chapter Quotations

New quotes that begin each chapter are drawn from business experts, historical figures, and company policies. Quotes have been chosen specifically to help frame the topics presented in the chapters and are followed by the identities and affiliations of those quoted to help students see the relevance of their study of supervision. For example, the quote that opens Chapter 5 (on managing diversity) reads as follows:

> Diversity [is] the art of thinking independently together.
> —Malcolm Stevenson Forbes, publisher (1919–1990)

Chapter Outlines

The chapter outlines provided at the beginning of each chapter are tools students can use to preview the chapters and review the materials before testing. These outlines also can be used to help students understand the relationship of certain topics to other chapter topics.

Learning Objectives

The key points of the chapter's content form the basis for the learning objectives. The learning objectives serve as a guide for studying the material and as a means of organizing the material in both the summary at the end of the chapter and the instructor's manual.

A Supervisor's Problem

New to this edition, each chapter opens with a vignette, entitled "A Supervisor's Problem," which is an episode about an actual supervisor on the job. As an example of a "Supervisor's Problem," Chapter 1 opens with a story about Tyrone Dugan, a new supervisor in a new environment working hard to prove himself as a capable leader to his employees. Each "Supervisor's Problem" has a corresponding discussion exercise section at the end of the chapter entitled "You Solve the Problem" (see below for details) and an additional exercise, available online to instructors as a follow-up, entitled Appendix D, "How Supervisors Solved Their Problems."

Margin Definitions

Key terms are defined in the margins. Students can use these definitions to test their understanding of the terms and find the places where important concepts are discussed.

Learning Highlights

Several real-world examples depicting supervisors meeting daily challenges are nested within each chapter. These examples have been carefully chosen and placed within chapters to help make learning via this text more interesting, more applicable, and more lasting. As a result of this highlights program, this book is rich with real-world supervisory experiences. In addition, these highlights have been extensively updated for this edition. The types of highlights appearing throughout the book are described below:

Supervision and Ethics

This feature is designed to illustrate the vital role that ethics plays in being a supervisor. Virtually every phase of supervisory activity can be affected by ethical issues. For example, the new "Supervision and Ethics" feature in Chapter 5 talks of the ethical complications of romantic pursuits between supervisors and subordinates.

Supervisory Skills

This feature shows students how supervisors use skills to meet current challenges as they conduct their work. These boxes are designed to give students the most current examples available. For instance, the new box in Chapter 7 focuses on the art of supervisory delegation.

Tips from the Firing Line

In each chapter, this feature highlights practical guidelines that can help students be successful supervisors. Chapter 12 contains a fresh and thorough look at constructive criticism and how to bestow it effectively as a supervisor.

Supervision and Diversity

Each of these features illustrates an important diversity issue related to the chapter content and emphasizes how modern supervisors can deal with the issue. A new example in Chapter 15 discusses Bertucci's Brick Oven Ristorante's actions to attract diverse employees with its commitment to developing employees and promoting from within.

Supervision across Industries

This feature illustrates how the textual content relates to various industries. These boxes, which are spread throughout the text, ensure that students get a full, rich understanding of how supervision concepts can be applied to many different situations. As examples, the text emphasizes real companies in industries like automobiles (Honda Motor Company), construction (Grayson Homes), and supermarkets (Whole Foods).

Summary

Learning objectives are recapped at the end of each chapter in brief summaries of the chapter concepts. This unique format allows students to review what they've learned from each learning objective.

Figures and Tables

Illustrations and tables are used extensively to clarify and reinforce text concepts.

Key Terms

Each chapter includes a list of key terms. Reading this list can help students review by testing their comprehension of the terms. The number of the page on which a term is first defined is also included in the glossary at the end of the book. These terms are highlighted throughout the book as margin definitions.

Review and Discussion Questions

These questions test understanding of the chapter concepts. They can be used independently by students or by instructors as a method of reviewing the chapters.

Skills Module

Skills modules at the end of each chapter reflect an expanded commitment in this edition to emphasize student skills in applying supervision concepts. Each module contains a number of elements that instructors can use as a formal part of a course to develop students' application abilities. Students also can use the elements independently. Each skills module is divided into two parts: concepts and skill-building.

Part One: Concepts

This skills module section focuses on helping students clarify and retain the supervision concepts studied in the chapter. The section contains a summary organized by chapter learning objectives, a list of key terms along with reference page numbers where students can review the meanings of the terms, and review and discussion questions that students can study independently or that instructors can use as the basis for classroom discussion.

Part Two: Skill-Building

This section focuses on helping students develop abilities in applying chapter concepts to solve supervision problems. This section contains:

You Solve the Problem. New to this edition, this activity asks students to respond to questions by applying the chapter's concepts to the opening scenario. For instance, the opening scenario for Chapter 3, "Supervising Duplisea's Sales Team Is a Long-Distance Effort," is based on a company called CheckFree. The "You Solve the Problem" feature for this chapter asks students to discuss whether team characteristics can be present in a "virtual" team, such as CheckFree.

Problem-Solving Case. Next, each chapter contains a short case that further applies the chapter's concepts to various supervision situations. Specially designed questions for each case ask students to focus on solving a supervision problem. For example, a new case in Chapter 12, "Suspensions of Lexington, Kentucky, Police Officers," asks students to determine the right of the police department to discipline its officers for misconduct while they are off duty.

Knowing Yourself. Each chapter contains a short, engaging self-assessment quiz, which helps students see the kinds of supervisors they can be. For example, Chapter 5, "Managing Diversity," presents a questionnaire students can use to explore their age bias. Discussion questions accompanying the quizzes help students more fully explore the self-assessment results to build better insights about themselves. In the Chapter 5 skills module, for example, students are asked to generate a list of common prejudices people might have against older workers.

Skills Exercises. A skills exercise is an activity specifically designed to help students develop supervision skills. Each skills module contains two exercises that vary in format and design. Some exercises are designed to be completed by individuals, whereas others are designed to be completed as groups. Most exercises can be used either in class or out of class. For example, the skills exercises for Chapter 6 focus on developing goal-setting skills and controlling skills.

Manager's Hot Seat Videos. In today's business world, it is important for a supervisor to be aware of situations that may arise with employees. These 10 segments show how a real manager handles difficult, unscripted situations in the workplace. These improvised scenarios reveal how issues such as diversity in hiring, sexual harassment, organizational change, and project management really shape the way business is done. Teaching notes in the Group & Video

Resource Manual (information below) provide background information and extensive teaching ideas, and the video questions at the end of each part in the text are helpful for students to test their knowledge of the chapters pertaining to the segments. These videos are the perfect way to expose students to the interpersonal side of supervisory work in organizations. New to this edition, adopting instructors can access this feature online. Also offered as a package, students can purchase special access to the scenarios. Students are able to view the segments and answer integrated questions as they watch. Contact your McGraw-Hill rep for details and to set up an account.

Glossary

Terms and definitions are gathered from each chapter and listed at the end of the book in the glossary, which provides ready reference for students and instructors. To encourage student review, the text pages on which the terms are defined and discussed are included.

ANCILLARIES

I am extremely pleased with the ancillaries that accompany this new edition. These ancillaries focus on enhancing the student-learning process as well as the capabilities of instructors using this book. A description of each ancillary follows.

Online Learning Center

The sixth edition's Online Learning Center (OLC) (www.mhhe.com/certo6e) gives both students and professors access to a wealth of knowledge. Use our links to professional resources, job-search aids, student questions, video teaching notes, and video case answers. The material from the OLC also can be exported for use in WebCT, Blackboard, and PageOut.

New to this edition's OLC is an additional video section. Our goal is to provide instructors with diverse pedagogy to facilitate the student's learning experience. Included are 10 new videos coupled with each part of the text, complete with thorough teaching notes.

Also new is a resource entitled "How Supervisors Solved Their Problems." This segment contains answers to all of the chapter opening vignettes ("A Supervisor's Problem") and student-generated hypotheses in the end-of-chapter section "You Solve the Problem."

The Group & Video Resource Manual: An Instructor's Guide to an Active Classroom (in print 0073044342 or online at www.mhhe.com/mobmanual)

Authored by Amanda Johnson and Angelo Kinicki, the Group & Video Exercise Resource Manual was created to help instructors create a livelier and more stimulating classroom environment. The manual contains interactive in-class group and individual exercises to accompany the chapters in this text.

This valuable guide is paired with the Manager's Hot Seat Video Web site and includes information and exercises to help instructors integrate the Hot Seat scenarios into their classrooms. For each exercise, the manual includes learning objectives, unique PowerPoint slides to accompany the exercises, and comprehensive discussion questions to facilitate enhanced learning.

Access to the manual can be acquired via the same Web site as the Hot Seat segments. As indicated above, please contact your McGraw-Hill rep for more details.

Instructor Resource CD-ROM (IRCD)

This edition's IRCD is the instructor's one-stop shop to access course materials, including the Test Bank, Instructor's Manual, and Power Point Slides. The IRCD is free to all adopting instructors; talk to your McGraw-Hill rep to get a copy.

The development of a high-quality test bank to accompany the sixth edition of *Supervision* was of the utmost importance. The test bank, written by Dr. Amit Shah of Frostburg State University, includes more than 2,000 questions and is available in both CD-ROM and computerized form on the OLC. Each chapter includes multiple-choice questions, short essay questions, and matching questions. In addition, a prepared quiz is provided for each chapter and can be duplicated or used as a transparency. Each question in the test bank includes the answer, the corresponding text page on which the answer can be found, and the rationale for the answer. All questions are graded according to their level of difficulty and organized according to the learning objectives, for consistency with the entire teaching package.

Instructor's Manual

Each chapter of the instructor's manual is organized according to the text learning objectives. Part One provides a quick summary for each chapter. Part Two, "Teaching the Concepts by Learning Objectives," includes the following resources for each learning objective:

1. Key terms and their definitions from the text.
2. Teaching notes that describe the focus of the text section in which the learning objective is discussed.
3. Examples not used in the text, frequently supported by supplementary handouts.
4. An exercise, plus details on using the exercise and the anticipated results.

Part Three, "Notes on the Boxed Features," provides a synopsis of the "Supervisory Skills," "Tips from the Firing Line," "Supervision across Industries," "Supervision and Ethics," and "Supervision and Diversity" boxes. Some teaching tips are also included regarding how to utilize these materials in your lectures.

Part Four, "Answers to Review and Discussion Questions," provides the answers or suggested answers for each question.

Part Five provides answers and solutions to the end-of-chapter exercises and cases, including the Knowing Yourself quizzes and exercises.

Dr. Amit Shah of Frostburg State University is also the author of the instructor's manual.

PowerPoint Slides

This text comes with a full suite of color PowerPoint slides, created by Dr. Amit Shah of Frostburg State University, that distill key concepts and objectives from each chapter in the book. Professors may present these slides as they lecture to reinforce key themes and/or distribute them as lecture notes. The slides are available on both the instructor's CD-ROM and the OLC.

ACKNOWLEDGMENTS

For the author, the many years of success of *Supervision: Concepts and Skill-Building* have been very gratifying. As with any book, however, the success of this book has been due, in very large part, to the hard work and commitment of many respected colleagues. I am pleased to be able to acknowledge the input of these professionals. A special thanks to the experts who have provided feedback over the years:

Raymond Ackerman
Amber University

Rex Adams
Southside Virginia Community College, Daniels

Musa Agil
Cape Fear Community College

Linda Alexander
Southeast Community College, Lincoln

Gemmy Allen
Mountain View College

Scott Ames
North Lake College

E. Walter Amundsen
Indiana University Southeast

Paul Andrews
Southern Illinois University

Lydia Anderson
Fresno City College

Solimon Appel
College for Human Services

Bob Ash
Rancho Santiago College

Glenda Aslin
Weatherford College

Bob Baker
Caldwell Community College

James Bakersfield
North Hennepin Community College

L. E. Banderet
Quinsigamond Community College

Robert Barefield
Drury College, Springfield

Laurence Barry
Cuyamaca College

Perry Barton
Guinnett Area Technical College

Lorraine Bassette
Prince George Community College

Vern Bastjan
Fox Valley Technical College

Becky Bechtel
Cincinnati Technical College

Kenneth Beckerink
Agricultural and Technical College

Gina Beckles
Bethune-Cookman College

Jim Beeler
Indiana Vocational and Technical College, Indianapolis

Robert Bendotti
Paradise Valley Community College

Jim Blackwell
Park College

David Bodkin
Cumberland University

Arthur Boisselle
Pikes Peak Community College

Robert Braaten
Tidewater Community College

James Brademas
University of Illinois, Urbana

Suzanne Bradford
Angelina College

Richard Braley
Eastern Oklahoma State College

Janis Brandt
Southern Illinois University

Stanley Braverman
Chestnut Hill College

Duane Brickner
South Mountain Community College

Dick Brigham
Brookhaven College

Arnold Brown
Purdue University North Central

Eugene Buccini
West Connecticut State University

Gary Bumbarner
Mountain Hope Community College

Kick Bundons
Johnson County Community College

Bill Burmeister
New Mexico State University

Randy Busch
Lee College

Oscar S. Campbell
Athens State College

Marjorie Carte
D. S. Lancaster Community College

Joseph Castelli
College of San Mateo

Win Chesney
St. Louis Community College at Meramac

James Chester
Cameron University

William Chester
University of the Virgin Islands

Michael Cicero
Highline Community College

Jack Clarcq
Rochester Institute of Technology

Charles Clark
Oklahoma City Community College

Sharon Clark
Lebanon Valley College

Virgil Clark
Sierra College

Jerry Coddington
Indiana Vocational and Technical College, Indianapolis

Bruce Conners
Kaskaskia College

Ronald Cornelius
University of Rio Grande

Gloria Couch
Texas State College Institute

Darrell Croft
Imperial Valley College

Joe Czajka
University of South Carolina

Beatrice Davis
Santa Fe Community College

James Day
Grambling State University

Richard De Luca
University of Hawaii, Kapiolani Community College

Edwin Deshautelle, Jr.
Bloomfield College

Richard Deus
Louisiana State University at Eunice

Ruth Dixon
Sacramento City College

Mike Dougherty
Milwaukee Area Technical College

Leroy Drew
Diablo Valley College

Janet Duncan
Central Maine Technical College

Ron Eads
City College of San Francisco

Acie B. Earl, Sr.
Black Hawk College

Patrick Ellsberg
Labette Community College

Earl Emery
Lower Columbia College

Tracy Ethridge
Tri-County Technical College

Roland Eyears
Baker College, Flint

Tom Falcone
Central Ohio Technical College

James Fangman
Wisconsin Technical College

Medhat Farooque
Central Arizona College

Jim Fatina
Indiana University

Dr. Anthony Favre
Mississippi Valley State University

Janice M. Feldbauer
Austin Community College

Jack Fleming
Triton College

Lee Fleming
Moorpark College

Charles Flint
San Jacinto College Central

Toni Forcioni
Montgomery College, Germantown

Laurie Francis
Mid State Technical College

Cheryl Frank
Inver Hills Community College

Connie French
Los Angeles City College

Larry Fudella
Erie Community College South

William Fulmer
Clarion University of Pennsylvania

Carson Gancer
Kalamazoo Valley Community College

Autrey Gardner
*Industrial Technology Department,
Warren Air Force Base*

David Gennrich
Waukesha County Technical College

Brad Gilbreath
New Mexico State University

Sally Gillespie
Broome Community College

Catherine Glod
Mohawk Valley Community College

Tim Gocke
Terra Technical College

Richard Gordon
Detroit College of Business, Dearborn

Greg Gorniak
Pennsylvania State University, Behrend

William G. Graham
Palm Beach Community College

Valerie Greer
University of Maryland

James Grunzweig
Lakeland Community College

James Gulli
Citrus College

Peter J. Gummere
Community College of Vermont

Thomas Gush
College of DuPage

Bill Hamlin
Pellissippi State Technical College

Willard Hanson
Southwestern College

James Harbin
East Texas State University

Carnella Hardin
Glendale College

Scott Harding
Normandale Community College

Louis Harmin
Sullivan County Community College

LeeAnna Harrah
Marion Technical College

Lartee Harris
West Los Angeles College

Edward L. Harrison
University of South Alabama

Paul Hedlund
Barton County Community College

Dr. Douglas G. Heeter
Ferris State University

Kathryn Hegar
*Indiana Vocational and Technical,
Terre Haute*

J. Donald Herring
State University of New York—Oswego

Charles A. Hill
UC—Berkeley Extension

Gene Hilton
Mountain View College

Jean Hiten
Brookhaven College

Roger Holland
Owensboro Community College

Larry Hollar
Cerritos College

Russ Holloman
Catawba Valley Community College

Joshua Holt
Ricks College

Tonya Hynds
Augusta College

Robert Ironside
Indiana University at Kokomo

Ruby Ivens
Lansing Community College

Ellen Jacobs
North Lake College

Debbie Jansky
Milwaukee Area Technical College

Bonnie Jayne
College of St. Mary

Bonnie Johnson
Fashion Institute of New York

Sue Jones
Odessa College

Iris Jorstad
Waubonsee Community College

Vincent Kafkaa
Effective Learning Systems

Ronald C. Kamahele
University of Alaska—Anchorage

Jack E. Kant
San Juan College

Sarkis Kavooyian
Bryant & Stratton

Bernard Keller
Delaware Technical and Community College

Robert Kemp
Pikes Peak Community College

James Kennedy
Angelina College

Howard Keratin
Peralta Laney College

James Kerrigan
Fashion Institute of Technology

Scott King
Stonehill College

Jay Kingpin
EI Centro College

Edward Kingston
University of South Florida

Ronald Kiziah
Piedmont Virginia Community College

Mary Lou Kline
Caldwell Community College

Russell Kunz
Collin County Community College, Spring Creek

Sue Kyriazopoulous
DeVry Institute of Technology

Bryan Lach
Alamance Community College

Joyce LeMay
Saint Paul College

Les Ledger
Central Texas College

Allen Levy
Macomb Community College Center

Corinne Livesay
Mississippi College

Thomas Lloyd
DeVry Institute of Technology

Barbara Logan
Westmoreland County Community College

Rosendo Lomas
Albuquerque Technical-Vocational Institute

Frances Lowery
Lawrence Technical University

Henie Lustgarten
Brewer State Junior College

Paul D. Lydick
Paul D Camp Community College

Alvin Mack
University of Maryland

Jon Magoon
Everett Community College

Marvin Mai
Santa Rosa Junior College

John Maloney
College of DuPage

Joseph Manno
Empire College

Gary Marrer
Glendale Community College

Lynda Massa
Santa Barbara Business College

Noel Matthews
Front Range Community College

Edward Mautz
Montgomery College

Ron Maxwell
EI Camino College

Kim McDonald
IPFW

Robert McDonald
Central Wesleyan College

Tim McHeffey
Suffolk County Community College

William McKinney
University of Illinois, Urbana

Joseph McShane
Gateway Technical Institute, Kenosha

Raymond Medeiros
Southern Illinois University

Unny Menon
California State Polytechnic University

Dorothy Metcalfe
Cambridge Community College Center

Eugene Meyers
Fashion Institute of Design and Merchandising, Los Angeles

Charles Miller
Western Kentucky University

Dr. Diane Minger
Cedar Valley College

David Molnar
NE Wisconsin Technical College

Daniel Montez
South Texas College

Dominic A. Montileone
Delaware Valley College

Wayne Moorhead
Delaware Valley College

Peter Moran
Brown Mackie College

Ed Mosher
Wisconsin Indianhead Technical College

Donald Mossman
Laramie County Community College

John Mudge
Concordia College

James Mulvihill
Mankato Technical Institute

David W. Murphy
Madisonville Community College

Hershel Nelson
South Central Technical College

John Nugent
Polk Community College

Randy Nutter
Montana Technical College

Sylvia Ong
Scottsdale Community College

Cruz Ortolaza
Geneva College

Smita Jain Oxford
Commonwealth College

Joseph Papenfuss
Catholic University of Puerto Rico

Mary Papenthien
Westminster College, Salt Lake City

John Parker
Milwaukee Area Technical College

Robert Payne
Baker College

James Peele
Manchester Community College

Joe Petta
Carl Sandburg College, Galesburg

Bonnie Phillips
Regis College

David A. Phillips
Purdue University

Martha Pickett
Casper College

Sarah T. Pitts
Christian Brothers University

Steven Pliseth
University of Wisconsin, Platteville

Barbara Pratt
Sinclair Community College

Robert Priester
Community College of Vermont

Barbara Prince
Madison Area Technical College

John Pryor
Northern Nevada Community College

Marcia Ann Pulich
University of Wisconsin—Whitewater

Margaret Rdzak
Cardinal Stritch College

William Redmon
Western Michigan University

Arnon Reichers
Ohio State University

Charles Reott
Western Wisconsin Technical Institute

Peter Repcogle
Orange County Community College

Richard Rettig
University of Central Oklahoma

Harriett Rice
Los Angeles City College

Robert Richardson
Iona College

Charles Riley
Tarrant County Junior College

Richard Riley
National College

Michael Rogers
Albany State College

Robert Roth
City University, Bellvue

Larry Runions
North Carolina Vocational Textile

Henry Ryder
Gloucester County College

Larry Ryland
Lurleen B. Wallace Junior College

Mildred Sanders
Jefferson State Community College

Don Saucy
University of North Carolina—Pembroke

Duane Schecter
Muskegon Community College

S. Schmidt
Diablo Valley College

Ralph Schmitt
Macomb Community College South

Irving Schnayer
Peralta Laney College

Greg Schneider
Waukesha County Technical College

Arthur Shanley
Muwaukee School of Engineering

Margie Shaw
Lake City Community College

Allen Shub
Northwestern Illinois University

Pravin Shukla
Nash Community College

Clay Sink
University of Rhode Island

Dr. Leane B. Skinner
Auburn University

Ron Smith
DeKalb Institute of Technology

Steve Smith
Mid State Technical College

Wanda Smith
Ferris State University

Carl Sonntag
Pikes Peak Community College

Marti Sopher
Cardinal Stritch College

Jerry Sparks
St. Louis Community College at Florissant Valley

David Spitler
Cannon International Business College

Richard Squire
Central Michigan University

Dick Stanish
Northwest Technical College

Gene Stewart
Tulsa Junior College

George Stooks
State University of New York—Oswego

John Stout
Brookhaven College

Art Sweeney
University of Scranton

Sally Terman
Troy State University

Sherman Timmons
Scottsdale Community College

Don Tomal
University of Toledo

Donna Treadwell
University of Arkansas at Little Rock

Ron Tremmel
Johnson County Community College

Guy Trepanier
Rend Lake College

John Tucker
Iona College

Bill Tyer
Purdue University

Robert Ulbrich
Tarrant County Junior College

Diann Valentini
Parkland College

Steven Vekich
Fashion Institute of Technology

Susan Verhulst
Des Moines Area Community College

Michael Vijuk
Washington State Community College

Charles Wall
William Rainey Harper College

Joyce Walsh-Portillo
Broward Community College

Kathy Walton
Bakersfield College

John P. Wanous
Ohio State University

David Way
Galveston College

Robert Way
Salt Lake City Community College

Vincent Weaver
Greenville Technical College

Rick Webb
Milwaukee Area Technical College

Ronald Webb
Johnson County Community College

Rick Weidman
Prince George Community College

Alan Weinstein
Messiah College Grantham

Bill Weisgerber
Canisius College

Julia Welch
Saddleback College

Floyd Wente
University of Arkansas Medical School

Ron Weston
Contra Costa College

Charles Wetmore
California State University, Fresno

Jerry Wheaton
North Arkansas Community College

Luther White
Central Carolina Community College

Michael R. White
University of Northern Iowa

Timothy G. Wiedman
Thomas Nelson Community College

Stephen L. Winter
Orange County Community College

Michael White
University of Northern Iowa

Sara White
University of Kansas Medical Center

Barbara Whitney
St. Petersburg Junior College

Tim Wiedman
Thomas Nelson Community College

Stephen Winter
Orange County Community College

Arthur Wolf
Chestnut Hill College

Barry Woodcock
Tennessee Technological University

Michael Wukitsch
American Marketing Association

Catalina Yang
Normandale Community College

Charles Yauger
Arkansas State University

Morrie Yohai
New York Institute of Technology

Teresa Yohon
Hutchinson Community College

James Yoshida
University of Hawaii, Hawaii Community College

Allan Young
Bessemer State Technical College

Marilyn Young
Waukesha County Technical College

Richard Young
Pennsylvania State University

Dan Yovich
Purdue University North Central

Fred Ziolkowski
Purdue University

Karen Zwissler
Milwaukee Area Technical College

Obviously, the professionals at McGraw-Hill deserve special recognition. I was fortunate enough to have two fine editors on this project. Kelly Lowery was the editor on this project before being interrupted by maternity leave. Kelly's tenacity and fortitude certainly helped this edition become a reality. John Weimeister, the other editor, did an outstanding job. John's market savvy and support were much appreciated characteristics of his publishing personality. Megan Richter, the editorial assistant, was the indispensable coordinator of this new edition project. Megan monitored all project activities and ensured their timely completion. Several others at McGraw-Hill were indispensable in making this edition a reality. These professionals include Kelly Odom, Marlena Pechan, Michael McCormick, Jillian Lindner, Cathy Tepper, Elisabeth Nevins Caswell, and Tammy Eiermann.

Orlando businessman Charles Steinmetz, a longtime leader in the pest-control industry, has taught me many practical lessons about supervision over the years.

Chuck and his wife, Lynn, recently established the Steinmetz Chair in Management to bolster scholarship at the Roy E. Crummer Graduate School of Business at Rollins College. I feel much honored to be the first holder of the Steinmetz Chair of Management and hope to relate to students the keen business acumen and high moral and ethical standards that have made Charles Steinmetz a world-class entrepreneur and manager. I would like to thank Dr. Craig McAllaster, Crummer Dean, for creating an educational climate in which professionalism in textbook writing can grow and flourish.

From a personal viewpoint, without the love and support of a caring family, I would never be able to complete daunting projects of this nature. My wife, Mimi, is a very special person who is always interested in what I do. She continually reminds me of how important a spiritual, family, and professional balance is to a worthwhile life. Other family members, Brian, Matthew, and Lizzie, Sarah and Drew, and Trevis and Melissa, always show unconditional support. Through Skylar and Lexie, the beginning of our family's next generation, I am continually reminded of the true purpose of our existence.

Samuel C. Certo

About the Author

Dr. Samuel C. Certo is professor of management and former dean at the Roy E. Crummer Graduate School of Business at Rollins College. He has been a professor of management for over 20 years and has received prestigious awards, including the Award for Innovative Teaching from the Southern Business Association, the Instructional Innovation Award granted by the Decision Sciences Institute, and the Charles A. Welsh Memorial Award for outstanding teaching at the Crummer School. Dr. Certo recently received the Bornstein award at Rollins College for the significant contribution of his scholarship in enhancing the national reputation of Rollins College. His numerous publications include articles in journals such as *Academy of Management Review, Journal of Experiential Learning and Simulation,* and *Training.* He also has written several successful textbooks, including *Modern Management.* Professional books published include *The Strategic Management Process* and *Digital Dimensioning: Finding the E-Business in Your Business.* A past chairman of the Management Education and Development Division of the Academy of Management, he has been honored by that group's Excellence of Leadership Award. Dr. Certo also has served as president of the Association for Business Simulation and Experiential Learning, as associate editor for *Simulation & Games,* and as a review board member of the *Academy of Management Review.* His consulting experience has been extensive, with notable experience on boards of directors.

Brief Contents

Contents

What Is a Supervisor?

1. Modern Supervision: Concepts and Skills

Successful Supervisors Plan, Organize, Staff, Lead, and Control
Digital Vision/Getty Images

Chapter **One**

Modern Supervision: Concepts and Skills

Learning Objectives

After you have studied this chapter, you should be able to:

1.1 Define what a supervisor is.

1.2 Describe the basic types of supervisory skills.

1.3 Describe how the growing diversity of the workforce affects the supervisor's role.

1.4 Identify the general functions of a supervisor.

1.5 Explain how supervisors are responsible to higher management, employees, and co-workers.

1.6 Describe the typical background of someone who is promoted to supervisor.

1.7 Identify characteristics of a successful supervisor.

Work hard, have high standards, and stick to your values, because somebody's always watching.

—*Ivan Seidenberg, Chairman and CEO, Verizon*

When you become a supervisor, no one can guarantee that the employees in your group will be as thrilled as you are. In fact, you may have to convince them—as well as your own manager—that you're ready and able to tackle the challenges of your new job.

That's what happened to Tyrone Dugan when he was hired to be assistant manager at the Qdoba Mexican Grill in Florissant, Missouri. Qdoba is a nationwide chain of almost 200 fast-food casual Mexican restaurants, where food is prepared as customers watch. Although the company describes its work environment as "casual" and "fun," the casual dress and hands-on interaction between supervisors and employees do not necessarily translate into a simple job. Supervisors working closely with their employees must figure out how to meet goals while maintaining a positive environment.

Charged with leading a staff of 10 employees, Dugan quickly realized that some of them were waiting to see if he could prove himself as their supervisor. Listening and watching carefully, Dugan learned that employees were observing his performance and commenting to his manager if they thought he fell short in some way, such as not starting a process on time. One employee in particular seemed to question Dugan's leadership, though none of the employees expressed their opinion to him directly.

Reflecting on the challenges of this transition, Dugan believes that at first he was "too passive" with his employees. With experience, he discovered that he got better results by setting clear standards and following up with employees to be sure they were meeting those standards.

Dugan also worked hard to establish positive communications with his employees. He explains, "I just started talking to them." Recognizing that envy can fuel resentment of a supervisor, he assured the employees that "they could have the same opportunity [for promotion] that I had if they were willing to work hard." His encouragement evidently succeeded. Several of Dugan's employees eventually took on supervisory positions at other Qdoba locations.

New supervisors sometimes face the problem of proving to their employees that they are capable and ready to assume new responsibilities, as Tyrone Dugan did.

1. What sort of job-related skills can help Dugan demonstrate he has the knowledge to handle the job?
2. What type of people skills can help him in his new position?

Source: Based on Sonja D. Brown, "Congratulations, You're a Manager! Now What?" *Black Enterprise,* April 2006, downloaded from Business & Company Resource Center, http://galenet.galegroup.com; Qdoba Mexican Grill Web site, www.qdoba.com, accessed June 29, 2006.

Tyrone Dugan's experience of learning to be a good supervisor is significant because supervisors are critically important to their organizations. Supervisors like Dugan inspire employees to do their best. By motivating employees to perform at their peak, the supervisor enables an organization to benefit from their commitment, talent, and enthusiasm.

supervisor
A manager at the first level of management

A **supervisor** is a manager at the first level of management, which means the employees reporting to the supervisor are not managers. Many different kinds of organizations need supervisors. Figure 1.1 reprints actual want ads for a variety of supervisory jobs.

The basic job of a manager is to see that an organization meets its goals, yet there are distinctions. For the top executives of an organization, managing is about making sure that the organization's vision and business strategy will allow it to meet its goals through the years ahead. Managing at the supervisory level means ensuring that the employees in a particular department are performing their jobs so that the department will contribute its share to accomplishing the organization's goals. Usually, supervisors focus on day-to-day problems and goals to be achieved in one year or less. This chapter introduces what supervisors do and what skills and characteristics they need to be effective.

FIGURE 1.1
A Sampling of
Supervisory
Positions to
Be Filled

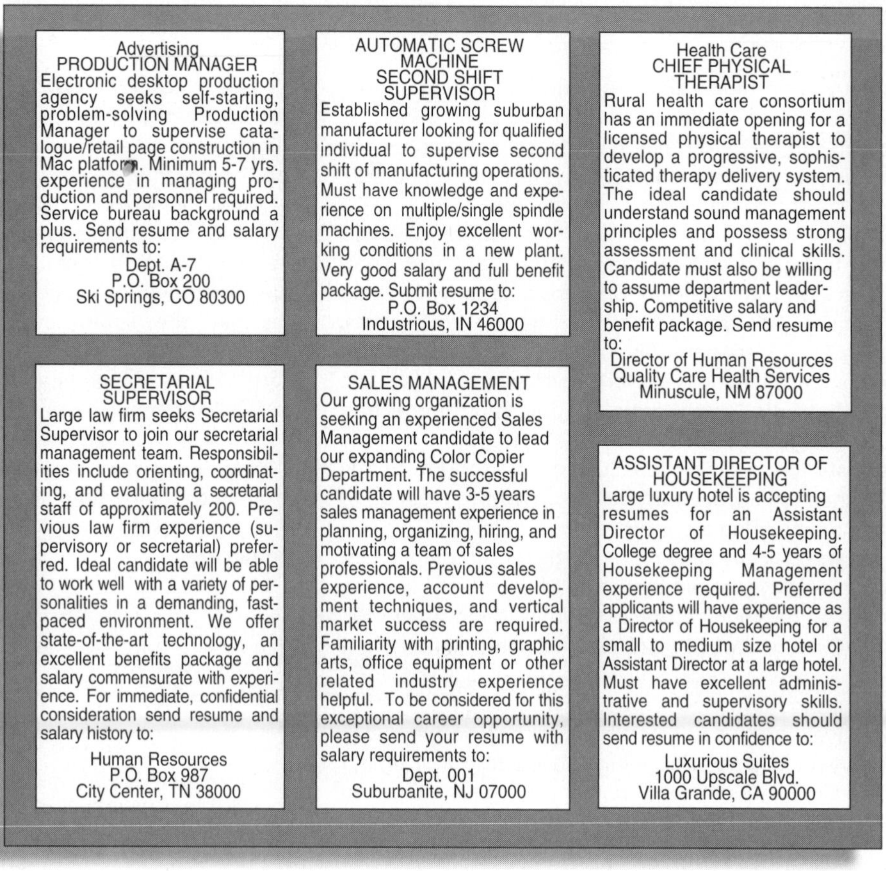

Advertising
PRODUCTION MANAGER
Electronic desktop production agency seeks self-starting, problem-solving Production Manager to supervise catalogue/retail page construction in Mac platform. Minimum 5-7 yrs. experience in managing production and personnel required. Service bureau background a plus. Send resume and salary requirements to:
Dept. A-7
P.O. Box 200
Ski Springs, CO 80300

AUTOMATIC SCREW
MACHINE
**SECOND SHIFT
SUPERVISOR**
Established growing suburban manufacturer looking for qualified individual to supervise second shift of manufacturing operations. Must have knowledge and experience on multiple/single spindle machines. Enjoy excellent working conditions in a new plant. Very good salary and full benefit package. Submit resume to:
P.O. Box 1234
Industrious, IN 46000

Health Care
**CHIEF PHYSICAL
THERAPIST**
Rural health care consortium has an immediate opening for a licensed physical therapist to develop a progressive, sophisticated therapy delivery system. The ideal candidate should understand sound management principles and possess strong assessment and clinical skills. Candidate must also be willing to assume department leadership. Competitive salary and benefit package. Send resume to:
Director of Human Resources
Quality Care Health Services
Minuscule, NM 87000

**SECRETARIAL
SUPERVISOR**
Large law firm seeks Secretarial Supervisor to join our secretarial management team. Responsibilities include orienting, coordinating, and evaluating a secretarial staff of approximately 200. Previous law firm experience (supervisory or secretarial) preferred. Ideal candidate will be able to work well with a variety of personalities in a demanding, fast-paced environment. We offer state-of-the-art technology, an excellent benefits package and salary commensurate with experience. For immediate, confidential consideration send resume and salary history to:
Human Resources
P.O. Box 987
City Center, TN 38000

SALES MANAGEMENT
Our growing organization is seeking an experienced Sales Management candidate to lead our expanding Color Copier Department. The successful candidate will have 3-5 years sales management experience in planning, organizing, hiring, and motivating a team of sales professionals. Previous sales experience, account development techniques, and vertical market success are required. Familiarity with printing, graphic arts, office equipment or other related industry experience helpful. To be considered for this exceptional career opportunity, please send your resume with salary requirements to:
Dept. 001
Suburbanite, NJ 07000

**ASSISTANT DIRECTOR OF
HOUSEKEEPING**
Large luxury hotel is accepting resumes for an Assistant Director of Housekeeping. College degree and 4-5 years of Housekeeping Management experience required. Preferred applicants will have experience as a Director of Housekeeping for a small to medium size hotel or Assistant Director at a large hotel. Must have excellent administrative and supervisory skills. Interested candidates should send resume in confidence to:
Luxurious Suites
1000 Upscale Blvd.
Villa Grande, CA 90000

TYPES OF SUPERVISORY SKILLS

Although a supervisor in a Pizza Hut restaurant and a supervisor in a Ford Motor Company factory work in very different environments, the skills they need to be successful fall into the same basic categories. These categories of skills are used by all levels of managers in all kinds of organizations. Skills developed during a beginning supervisory job will prove useful in every job held throughout a management career.

Classic Understanding of Management Skills

For many years, experts have considered managers' success dependent on three basic categories of skills: technical, human relations, and conceptual. In addition, the application of those skills requires a fourth skill: decision making.

technical skills
The specialized knowledge and expertise used to carry out particular techniques or procedures

Technical skills are the specialized knowledge and expertise used to carry out particular techniques or procedures. A United Way fundraiser's ability to persuade executives to write big checks is a technical skill. A mechanic's ability to bring an automobile engine back to life relies on technical skills. Other technical skills may involve bookkeeping, selling, and many other types of work. To be "technical," skills do not have to be mechanical or scientific; they can involve any work-related technique or procedure.

human relations skills
The ability to work effectively with other people

Human relations skills are the skills required to work effectively with other people. These skills include the ability to communicate with, motivate, and understand

FIGURE 1.2
Relative Importance of Types of Skills for Different Levels of Managers

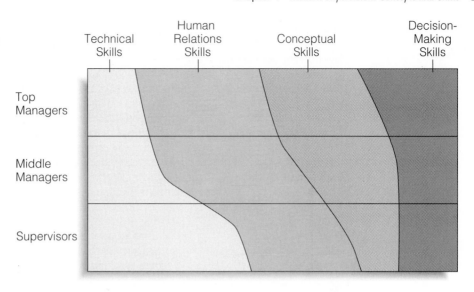

people. Supervisors use their human relations skills to impress their superiors, inspire employees, defuse conflicts, get along with co-workers, and succeed in many other ways.

conceptual skills
The ability to see the relation of the parts to the whole and to one another

Conceptual skills involve the ability to see the relationship of the parts to the whole and to one another. For a supervisor, conceptual skills include recognizing how the department's work helps the entire organization achieve its goals and how the work of various employees affects the performance of the department as a whole.

decision-making skills
The ability to analyze information and reach good decisions

Decision-making skills involve the ability to analyze information and reach good decisions. Someone with strong decision-making skills can think objectively and creatively. Chapter 9 provides a more detailed look at how to make decisions effectively.

The relative importance of each type of skill depends on the level of management. As shown in Figure 1.2, human relations skills are important at every level of management. However, supervisors rely more on technical skills than do higher-level managers because employees who have a problem doing their jobs go to the supervisor and expect help. Also, top managers tend to rely more on decision-making skills simply because they tend to make more complex decisions.

Modern View of Management Skills

Expanding on the classic view of management skills, current thinkers have taken a fresh look at the activities a manager typically performs.[1] This way of thinking starts with a list of activities and then identifies the skills required to carry out those activities successfully. The typical manager's activities fall into three groups:

1. *Task-related activities:* Efforts to carry out critical management-related duties, such as planning, setting objectives for employees, and monitoring performance.
2. *People-related activities:* Efforts to manage people, such as by providing support and encouragement, recognizing contributions, developing employees' skills, and empowering employees to solve problems.
3. *Change-related activities:* Efforts to modify components of the organization, such as monitoring the environment to detect a need for change, proposing new tactics and strategies, encouraging others to think creatively, and taking risks to promote needed changes.

TABLE 1.1
Skills of Successful Managers

Clarifying roles	Assigning tasks; explaining job responsibilities, task objectives, and performance expectations
Monitoring operations	Checking on the progress and quality of the work; evaluating individual and unit performance
Short-term planning	Determining how to use personnel and other resources to accomplish a task efficiently; determining how to schedule and coordinate activities efficiently
Consulting	Checking with people before making decisions that affect them; encouraging participation in decision making; using the ideas and suggestions of others
Supporting	Being considerate; showing sympathy and support when someone is upset or anxious; providing encouragement and support when a task is difficult or stressful
Recognizing	Providing praise and recognition for effective performance, significant achievements, special contributions, and performance improvements
Developing	Providing coaching and advice; providing opportunities for skill development; helping people learn how to improve their skills
Empowering	Allowing substantial responsibility and discretion in work activities; trusting people to solve problems and make decisions without getting approval first
Envisioning change	Presenting an appealing description of desirable outcomes that the unit can achieve; describing a proposed change with enthusiasm and conviction
Taking risks for change	Taking personal risks and making sacrifices to encourage and promote desirable change in the organization
Encouraging innovative thinking	Challenging people to question their assumptions about the work and consider better ways of doing it
External monitoring	Analyzing information about events, trends, and changes in the external environment to identify threats and opportunities for the work unit

To carry out these activities, supervisors and other managers rely on a diverse set of skills, including those listed in Table 1.1. Situations vary, so individual supervisors may need skills beyond those listed here.

To develop the variety of skills needed to be a good supervisor, you should learn and practice the concepts discussed in this book. Get to know good supervisors and managers and observe how they handle situations. Supervisors who continually develop their skills in each area are the ones most likely to be promoted to higher levels of management.

Supervising a Diverse Workforce

Good human relations skills are especially important in today's environment because of the increasing diversity of the U.S. workforce. In 1980, just over half (51 percent) of the workforce consisted of white men; this group's share of the workforce is expected to fall to 43 percent by 2012.[2] While the share of white men in the workforce declines, the share of black, Hispanic, and Asian workers is expected to rise. (See the accompanying "Supervision and Diversity" to learn more about Hispanics, the largest ethnic group.) Women are entering the workforce at about the same rate as men, and they now make up more than 46 percent of the adult labor pool, holding a majority of the jobs in 151 occupations.[3] In addition, the

SUPERVISION AND DIVERSITY

THE LARGEST ETHNIC MINORITY GROUP

Hispanics—immigrants and descendants of immigrants from Latin America—have become the largest ethnic minority group in the United States. In two more generations, members of this group are expected to represent almost one-fourth of the U.S. workforce. That means many supervisors will have Hispanic employees in the coming years.

A wide variety of Americans wear the label *Hispanic.* Their origins are diverse, and they include both well-paid professionals and entry-level workers at the low end of the wage scale. Currently, the majority come from Mexico.

The timing and geography of this wave of immigration distinguish it from earlier patterns in U.S. history. Mexican immigrants can readily drive back to their country of origin, so it is easier for them to maintain ties with that culture. And in our modern economy, media and marketers target messages to this group, so they can more readily maintain their use of the Spanish language. The majority of Mexican immigrants and most of their children speak both Spanish and English, a valuable talent in many organizations.

Statistically, the rate of high school graduation among Hispanics trails the U.S. average. Hispanic immigrants tend to have a very strong work ethic, and teens rush to get jobs before graduating. For supervisors, this situation may indicate required areas for the training and development of this important segment of the labor force.

Source: Based on Brian Grow, "Hispanic Nation," *BusinessWeek*, March 15, 2004, downloaded from Infotrac, http://web5.infotrac.galegroup.com.

---

segment aged 65 years and over is expected to represent more than 16 percent of the U.S. population by 2020.[4]

Opportunities and Challenges

Together, these changes mean that supervisors can expect to have more employees who are female, nonwhite, and experienced—perhaps senior citizens holding a job after retirement. Consider Al Aurilio, who supervises workers sorting scrap materials that arrive at the warehouse of Pacific Iron and Metal Company, located in Seattle, Washington. With more than 60 years of experience at the company, Aurilio has become an expert in the metal composition of the items to be sorted, and he willingly shares his knowledge with employees.[5] As described in subsequent chapters, this growing diversity enables supervisors to draw on a greater variety of talent and gain insights into more perspectives than ever before.

Diversity is not a new issue. During the 1800s, for example, immigrants from Germany settled in the region from Pennsylvania west to Minnesota. They opened schools and businesses for their communities and published German-language newspapers. The working-class town of Cicero, Illinois, was once populated mostly by people of Czech, Polish, and Slovakian heritage. Today, Cicero is dominated by a growing share of Mexican immigrants, who have opened shops, taken jobs in factories, and elected Ramiro Gonzalez, a Mexican immigrant, town president (equivalent to mayor).[6] In other towns and cities, immigrants may come from Bosnia, Somalia, Congo, or Ethiopia, like the employees of Robinwood Inc., a Boston maker of candles and giftware. Company co-founder Philip Celeste works with the International Rescue Committee to hire and train refugees.[7]

Although diversity is not a new issue, the even greater diversity expected in the U.S. workforce of the future—coupled with laws and policies intended to ensure fair treatment of various groups—requires supervisors to work successfully with a much wider variety of people.

Subtle Discrimination

Today hardly anyone would say that it is all right to discriminate or that a manager should be allowed to give preference to employees of the manager's race or sex. However, subtle forms of discrimination persist in every workplace, and everybody holds some stereotypes that consciously or unconsciously influence their behavior. The subtle discrimination that results may include ignoring the input from the only woman at a meeting or mistaking an African-American professional for someone with a less prestigious job.

Supervisors and other managers can use several tactics to improve attitudes:

- Have employees work with someone who is different, which gives the employees a chance to educate themselves about the customs and values others hold.
- Use the kind of behavior they expect employees to exhibit, including demonstrating respect for others.
- Question negative stereotypes. When an employee makes an offensive comment, point out the damage it does and ask the employee to avoid such remarks in the future.

Unfortunately, many supervisors still work for organizations that fail to see the advantages of hiring and developing a diverse workforce. Even in an organization whose management is not committed to these goals, supervisors can provide advice and coaching to female and nonwhite employees, helping them get along in the organization. Supervisors also can make a point of learning about the individual employees in the department, such as what motivates them and what their career goals are. Throughout this book, you will find more specific ideas for meeting the diversity challenge as it relates to the chapter topics.

GENERAL FUNCTIONS OF THE SUPERVISOR

Jennifer Plotnick is a supervisor of her city's board of education. Her responsibilities include ensuring that the employees in her department are doing a good job, preparing a budget for her department, making sure not to spend more than the budgeted amounts, explaining to employees what they are expected to do, and justifying to her manager why she needs to add people to her department in the following year. In contrast, supervisors in other settings may spend most of their time enabling employees to do their jobs and handle fewer responsibilities than Plotnick.

Although settings and degrees of responsibility may differ, supervisors and other managers carry out the same types of functions. To describe these common activities, management experts categorize them as planning, organizing, staffing, leading, and controlling. The management functions are illustrated in Figure 1.3, which shows that all of the activities should be directed toward enabling employees to deliver high-quality goods and services, whether to customers of the organization or to colleagues in another department.

Planning

planning
Setting goals and determining how to meet them

Common sense tells us that we do our best work when we know what we are trying to accomplish. The supervisor's job includes determining the department's goals and the ways to meet them. This is the function of **planning.** Sometimes a supervisor has a substantial say in determining the goals themselves, whereas another supervisor must focus on how to achieve goals set by higher-level managers.

FIGURE 1.3
**Functions of
Supervisors and
Other Managers**

As mentioned previously, the supervisor's job is to help the organization meet its goals. Organizational goals are the result of planning by top managers. The purpose of planning by supervisors, then, is to determine how the department can contribute to achieving the organization's goals. This includes planning how much money to spend—and, for a retailer or sales department, how much money to bring in—what level of output to achieve, and how many employees will be needed. Computer technology has made new planning tools possible as well. Chapter 6 discusses planning in greater detail.

Organizing

Once the supervisor figures out what needs to get done, the next step is to determine how to set up the group, allocate resources, and assign work to achieve those goals efficiently. This is the function of **organizing.**

organizing
Setting up the group, allocating resources, and assigning work to achieve goals

Somebody has to decide how to set up the overall organization, creating departments and levels of management. Of course, few supervisors have much of a say in those kinds of decisions. At the supervisory level, organizing usually involves activities such as scheduling projects and assigning duties to employees (or, as will be discussed subsequently, enabling employees to carry out these organizing tasks). In addition, modern supervisors are increasingly responsible for setting up and leading teams of workers to handle special projects or day-to-day operations. Virtual teams rely on electronic communication to function effectively when team members and supervisors are widely separated. Chapter 7 discusses organizing in greater detail, and Chapter 3 addresses leading a team.

Staffing

The supervisor needs qualified employees to carry out the tasks that he or she has planned and organized. The activities involved in identifying, hiring, and developing the necessary number and quality of employees are known as the function of **staffing.** Whereas an operative (nonmanagement) employee's performance is usually judged on the basis of the results that the employee has achieved as an individual, a supervisor's performance depends on the quality of results that the supervisor achieves through his or her employees. Therefore, staffing is crucial to the supervisor's success. The various activities of the staffing function are addressed in Chapters 15–17.

staffing
Identifying, hiring, and developing the necessary number and quality of employees

Leading

Even if the supervisor has the clearest and most inspired vision of how the department and its employees should work, this vision will not become a reality unless employees know and want to do their part. The supervisor is responsible for letting employees know what is expected of them and inspiring and motivating employees to do good work. Influencing employees to act (or not act) in a certain way is the function of **leading.** Good leadership is even more important for supervisors in this time of rapid change, fueled by the widespread use of the Internet and other technologies.

leading
Influencing people to act (or not act) in a certain way

Organizing draws heavily on the supervisor's conceptual skills, but leading requires good human relations skills. The supervisor needs to be aware of and use behaviors that employees respond to as he or she desires. Chapter 8 includes a more detailed discussion of leading. Other chapters discuss the ways in which supervisors influence employees to act, such as by communicating (Chapter 10), motivating (Chapter 11), and disciplining (Chapter 12).

Controlling

The supervisor needs to know what is happening in the department. When something goes wrong, the supervisor must find a way to fix the problem or enable employees to do so. Monitoring performance and making needed corrections is the management function of **controlling.**

controlling
Monitoring performance and making needed corrections

In an increasing number of organizations, the supervisor is not supposed to control by dictating solutions. Instead, the supervisor is expected to provide employees with the resources and motivation to identify and correct problems themselves. In these organizations, the supervisor is still responsible for controlling, but he or she works with others to carry out this function. Chapter 6 discusses these and more traditional principles of controlling in more detail. Now the control function can also include the use of e-mail controls that monitor employees' use of the computer and "e-supervision technology," which uses both the Internet and audio-video technology to monitor store operations for safety, customer service, stock levels, and other supervisory details.[8]

Relationships among the Functions

Notice that Figure 1.3 shows the management functions as a process in which planning comes first, followed by organizing, then staffing, then leading, and finally controlling. This order occurs because each function depends on the preceding function or functions. Once the supervisor has planned what the department will do, he or she can figure out the best way to organize work and people to accomplish those objectives. Then the supervisor needs to get the people in place and doing their jobs. At that point, the supervisor can direct their work and inspire their efforts. The results are then evaluated by the supervisor to ensure that the work is getting done properly. During the controlling function, the supervisor may wish to revise some goals, at which point the whole process begins again.

Of course, real-life supervisors do not spend one week planning, then one week organizing, and so on. Instead, they often carry out all the management functions during the course of a day. For example, a patient care coordinator in a hospital might start the day by checking the nurses' performance (controlling), then attend a meeting to discuss the needs of the patients (planning), then help resolve a dispute between a nurse and a physical therapist (leading). Thus, Figure 1.3 is a very general model of managing that shows how the functions depend on one another, not how the supervisor structures his or her work.

Typically, supervisors spend most of their time leading and controlling, because they work directly with the employees who are producing or selling a product or providing support services. Planning, staffing, and organizing take up less of a supervisor's time. In contrast, higher-level managers are responsible for setting the overall direction for the organization; thus, they spend more time on planning and organizing.

RESPONSIBILITIES OF THE SUPERVISOR

A supervisor with a poor understanding of his responsibilities once accompanied a boom truck operator into a storage yard to pick up a piece of equipment called a crusher liner. Under and near an electric power line, they worked together, with the truck operator watching the supervisor, who handled the lift line. Tragically, the boom swung into the power line, and the powerful current killed the supervisor. Carl Metzgar, a safety expert who analyzed this incident, points out that the accident occurred because the supervisor was not supervising. A supervisor who had focused on observing, coaching, and following up on work would have observed the arrangement of the equipment and the power line and directed the employee to perform the task in a safe manner. In Metzgar's words, "A supervisor should be in charge of the big picture."[9] An employee who becomes a supervisor assumes all the responsibilities listed in Table 1.2. In summary, though supervisors have more power than nonmanagers, they also have many responsibilities—to higher management, to employees, and to co-workers.

Types of Responsibilities

Supervisors are responsible for carrying out the duties assigned to them by higher-level managers. This includes giving managers timely and accurate information for planning. They also must keep their managers informed about the

TABLE 1.2
Responsibilities of Supervisors

Sources: Nolo.com, "When You're the Boss," reprinted at www.workingwoman.com/wwn/article.jsp?contentId=513&ChannelID=210; Rona Leach, "Supervision: From Me to We," *Supervision*, February 2000, p. 8.

- Recognize the talents of each subordinate.
- Share your vision of where the organization wants to go.
- Treat employees with dignity and respect.
- Conduct necessary meetings efficiently and ensure they accomplish their intended tasks.
- Keep your staff informed and up to date.
- Be accessible to those under your supervision.
- Conduct periodic evaluations of your group's progress.
- Provide an opportunity for employees to evaluate you.
- Praise your staff for their accomplishments.
- Keep in touch with your industry.
- Be able to perform the duties of those you supervise.
- Keep a sense of humor.
- Be fair.
- Follow proper hiring practices.
- Know the law as it applies to your company and your job.
- Adhere to workplace safety rules and regulations.
- Keep accurate employee records.
- Avoid sexual harassment and discrimination based on gender, age, race, pregnancy, sexual orientation, or national origin.
- Know how to fire an employee without violating his or her rights.

department's performance. Supervisors are expected to serve as a kind of linch-pin, or bridge, between employees and management. Thus, their responsibilities include building employee morale and carrying employee concerns to the relevant managers.

Some supervisors may question the notion that they have a responsibility to their employees. After all, the employees are responsible for doing what the supervisors say. Nevertheless, because supervisors link management to the employees, the way they treat employees is crucial. Supervisors are responsible for giving their employees clear instructions and making sure they understand their jobs. They must look for problems and correct them before employees' performance deteriorates further. They also need to treat their employees fairly and speak up for their interests to top management.

Finally, supervisors are responsible for cooperating with their co-workers in other departments. They should respond promptly when a co-worker in another department requests information. They should share ideas that will help the organization's departments work together to accomplish common goals. And supervisors should listen with an open mind when co-workers in other departments make suggestions about improving the way things are done. When supervisors learn from one another's ideas, the whole organization benefits, and the supervisors have the satisfaction of working together as members of a team.

Responsibilities in a Changing Organization

As technology continually advances and international trade grows, organizations have had to become experts in rapid change. They have needed to change to reflect competition from businesses in other countries and benefit from technologies such as the Internet. Today's supervisors have to be skilled in online as well as face-to-face communication, and they have to be prepared to change as fast as their employers do.

Organizations can meet stiff competition by making their structures more efficient. Many organizations have eliminated layers of management, transferring more decision-making authority to supervisors and their employees.[10] Dell Inc., for instance, has succeeded in the difficult business of selling personal computers by operating more efficiently than the competition. The company recently underwent an effort to cut annual expenses by $1.5 billion. Supervisors were among those who presented cost-cutting strategies directly to the company president.[11] Today, supervisors often have responsibilities that only a few decades ago would have been assigned to middle management. Supervisors work closely with employees and now also handle much of the planning and organizing once done by middle managers.

In addition, the organization may expect operative employees to play an active role in traditional management tasks such as setting goals, allocating work, and monitoring and improving quality. An old-fashioned "command-and-control" approach to supervision in this setting would not be effective. It stifles the very creativity and empowerment that this kind of reorganization seeks to foster.

As a result, the supervisor's role in such situations is to make it easier for employees to carry out their broad responsibilities. This role is based on the recognition that employees' knowledge and commitment are among an organization's most valuable assets. Edward E. Lawler III, an expert in organizational effectiveness and professor at the University of Southern California, says an organization is most successful when it hires talented employees and "treats them right." According to Lawler, when management motivates and enables employees to perform well, the organization creates a "virtuous spiral," in which the organization and its people achieve more and more of their goals.[12] Treating employees right includes a leadership style that is respectful, fair, and ethical. Employees expect to be treated with dignity, which includes listening to them and displaying consideration for their individual differences. They want their supervisor to be fair when making decisions and to include them in decision making when possible. And they expect their supervisor to be ethical and behave in ways that are consistent with his or her words.[13]

These responsibilities rely heavily on interpersonal skills. Thus, the changes occurring in today's workplace require supervisors to rely less on their technical expertise and more on their ability to understand, inspire, and build cooperation among people. If a supervisor is used to telling others what to do and then checking the way the work gets done, this new style of supervision may feel awkward. However, many supervisors find that employees can, and do, contribute ideas and commitment that put their organization in a virtuous spiral. In Hamilton, Ontario, steel company Dofasco expects teams of line workers to make many types of decisions and maintain quality standards. These empowered employees and their supervisors have helped the company remain profitable even during recent years, when a manufacturing slowdown hurt competitors.[14]

In addition, technology is changing supervisors' jobs in many ways. Information technology has made it easier for employees to work in many locations, so supervisors need to motivate and control employees they may not see face to face every day. Many employees want to telecommute, or work on a computer from a remote location such as their home. Telecommuting makes the supervisor's job both more important and more challenging.

Responsibilities and Accountability

accountability
The practice of imposing penalties for failing to adequately carry out responsibilities and providing rewards for meeting responsibilities

Whatever the responsibilities of a particular supervisor, the organization holds the supervisor accountable for carrying them out. **Accountability** refers to the practice of imposing penalties for failing to carry out responsibilities adequately, and it usually includes giving rewards for meeting responsibilities. Thus, if customer service supervisor Lydia Papadopoulos effectively teaches the telephone representatives on her staff to listen carefully to customers, the company might reward her with a raise. In contrast, a higher-level manager who gets frustrated with a supervisor who fails to provide information about what is happening in the department might eventually fire the supervisor for not carrying out this responsibility.

BECOMING A SUPERVISOR

Most supervisors start out working in the department they now supervise. Because technical skills are relatively important for first-level managers, the person selected to be supervisor is often an employee with a superior grasp of the technical skills needed to perform well in the department. The person also might have more seniority than many other department employees. Good work habits and leadership skills are also reasons for selecting an employee to be a supervisor. Sometimes a company will hire a recent college graduate to be a supervisor, perhaps because the person has demonstrated leadership potential or a specialized skill that will help in the position.

Unfortunately, none of these bases for promotion or hiring guarantee that a person knows how to supervise. A hotel employee promoted to a supervisory position, for instance, might be at a loss for ways to motivate those who now report to her. Gene Ference, president of HVS/The Ference Group of Weston, Connecticut, suggests that coaching is a more effective means of encouraging performance and development than simply saying, "Do your best." According to Ference, coaching means asking questions such as, "How do you think we can apply these culinary principles to our new spa menu?" and "The guest corridors in the west wing were exceptionally clean today. How can we ensure that happens all of the time?"[15]

Becoming a supervisor marks a big change in a person's work life. The new supervisor suddenly must use more human relations and conceptual skills and devote more time to planning ahead and keeping an eye on the department's activities. Also, a change occurs in the supervisor's relationships with the employees in the department. Instead of being one of the crowd, the supervisor becomes a part of management—even the target of blame or anger when employees resent company policies. All these changes are bound to lead to some anxiety. It is natural to wonder whether you are qualified or how you will handle the problems that surely will arise.

Preparing for the Job

One way to combat the anxiety is to prepare for the job. A new supervisor can learn about management and supervision through books and observation. He or she can think about ways to carry out the role of supervisor. More important than friendliness are traits such as fairness and a focus on achieving goals. A supervisor can also strive to learn as much as possible about the organization, the department, and the job. To see what awaits a new supervisor, refer to Figure 1.4.

FIGURE 1.4
What Awaits the New Supervisor?

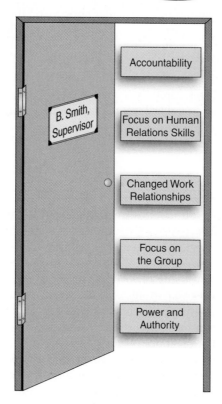

Once on the job, a supervisor needs to continue the learning process. More important than understanding the layout of the workplace is knowing about the employees in the department or work group. Who are the quiet but productive workers, for example, and who are the unofficial leaders? To get to know employees, a supervisor can talk to his or her own manager and read performance appraisals, but the most reliable sources of information are the employees themselves. Particularly in the early days on the job, a supervisor should take time to discuss goals with employees and observe their work habits.

A supervisor may learn that one or more employees had been candidates for the supervisor's job and therefore may be jealous. One constructive approach that a supervisor might take to this problem is to acknowledge the other person's feelings, ask for the employee's support, and discuss his or her long-term goals. An important aspect of this approach is that the supervisor is helping employees meet or exceed their own goals. For example, a sales supervisor can help a potentially jealous salesperson increase sales. Most employees will regard someone who helps them make more money as a better manager.

Obtaining and Using Power and Authority

To carry out his or her job, a supervisor needs not only knowledge but also power (the ability to do certain things) and authority (the right to do certain things). To acquire power upon assuming the job of supervisor, it may help to have the new supervisor's boss make an official announcement of the promotion. When accepting the job, a supervisor can ask his or her boss to announce the promotion at a meeting of the employees. There the supervisor can take the opportunity to state his or her expectations, desire to work as a team, and interest in hearing about work-related problems.

A new supervisor should not rush to make changes in the department but instead should first understand how the department works and what employees expect. Making changes quickly and without seeking their input can alienate employees and put them on the defensive. The supervisor can build support for change by introducing it gradually after inviting suggestions when appropriate.

For more ideas on becoming a supervisor, see "Tips from the Firing Line." Also, many chapters in this book will provide ideas that will help with this transition. For example, Chapter 7 discusses the delegation of authority, and Chapter 14 covers the sources and types of power, along with more information about managing change.

CHARACTERISTICS OF A SUCCESSFUL SUPERVISOR

Unfortunately, many of us have worked for someone who seemed to stifle our best efforts or angered us with unfair decisions. Many of us also have worked for a supervisor who taught us new skills, inspired us to do better than we thought possible, or made us look forward to going to work each day. What is behind the success of this second category of supervisors? Figure 1.5 illustrates some characteristics of successful supervisors. Complete the Knowing Yourself exercise on page 22 to see whether supervising is a good fit with your current traits and interests.

A successful supervisor has a *positive attitude*. Employees tend to reflect the attitudes of the people in charge. When the supervisor's attitude toward work and the organization is positive, employees are more likely to be satisfied with and interested in their work. In addition, managers and co-workers alike prefer working with someone who has a positive attitude.

TIPS FROM THE FIRING LINE

BECOMING A SUPERVISOR

Often, a new supervisor takes on his or her position as the result of a promotion. That means the supervisor's relationships with others in the department will change. How do you maintain positive working relationships with people when you are now responsible for ensuring they get their work done correctly and efficiently? Here are some suggestions for making the transition smoothly:

- *Set limits on your behavior.* Some kinds of behavior that co-workers commonly engage in—gossiping, grumbling about work, choosing friends—will interfere with your role as supervisor. Employees are counting on you to be fair and objective. If some employees expect favors based on friendship, they are not true friends.

- *Don't be a "rescuer."* Instead of jumping in to get the work done whenever a problem arises, teach the employees in your group to do the tasks you once handled. Training can be harder than doing the job yourself, but it builds a stronger work group.

- *Figure out how to measure success.* How can you tell if each person is succeeding in terms of quality, cost, and timeliness? As a supervisor, you need to see when employees are on track toward meeting their goals and when you need to step in.

- *Communicate with everyone.* Make a point of talking to each member of your work group so that you can understand each person's goals and everyone knows what your expectations are. Show employees how each person's efforts benefit the whole group.

- *Be firm.* Sometimes employees "test" a new supervisor to see if rules and standards will be enforced. If that happens, you will need to make it clear that you are serious about the whole group's success.

- *Learn from others.* Get to know other supervisors and managers who will share the wisdom gained from their experience.

Sources: Based on Brandi Britton, "Making the Move from Peer to Supervisor," *Los Angeles Business Journal,* October 10, 2005; Ed Lisoski, "From Peer to Supervisor," *Supervision,* May 2005, both downloaded from Business & Company Resource Center, http://galenet.galegroup.com.

FIGURE 1.5
Characteristics
of a Successful
Supervisor

Successful supervisors are *loyal.* As a part of the management team, they must take actions that are best for the organization. This responsibility may include making decisions that are unpopular with employees. In such situations, supervisors must recognize that taking on a supervisory job means they cannot always be "one of the gang."

Successful supervisors are *fair.* Supervisors who play favorites or behave inconsistently will lose the support and respect of their employees and not be able to lead effectively. Also, when supervisors make assignments and decisions on the basis of whom they like best, they will not necessarily make the assignments and decisions best suited to the organization. Another aspect of being fair is to follow the rules yourself. The supervisor can set a good example, for instance, by being on time and refraining from doing personal tasks on the job or taking supplies home.

Supervisors also need to be *good communicators.* Employees and bosses alike depend on the supervisor to keep them informed of what is happening. Employees who receive clear guidance about what is expected of them will not only perform better but also be more satisfied with their jobs. Good communication also includes making contact with employees each day and listening to what they have to say. Chapter 10 takes an in-depth look at the communications skills that supervisors need to develop.

To be successful, supervisors must be *able to delegate,* that is, give their employees authority and responsibility to carry out activities. Since supervisors tend to have excellent technical skills, delegating may be a challenge. They may resist giving an assignment to an employee who may not carry it out as easily or as well as they, the supervisors, could do. Nevertheless, supervisors cannot do the work of the whole department. So, they must assign work to employees. Equally important, a supervisor should give employees credit for their accomplishments. This, in turn, makes the supervisor look good; the employees' successes show that the supervisor is able to select and motivate employees as well as delegate effectively. Chapter 7 discusses delegation in greater detail.

Finally, a successful supervisor must *want the job.* Some people are happier carrying out the technical skills of their field, whether it is carpentry, respiratory therapy, or financial management. People who prefer this type of work to the functions of managing will probably be happier if they turn down an opportunity to become a supervisor. In contrast, people who enjoy the challenge of making plans and inspiring others to achieve goals are more likely to be effective supervisors. For an example of such a supervisor, see the "Supervision across Industries" box.

ABOUT THIS BOOK

This book introduces the many kinds of activities supervisors must carry out to accomplish their overall objective of seeing that employees contribute toward achieving the organization's goals. Part One is devoted to a broad view of the supervisor's role. Chapter 1 serves as an introduction to the general activities and responsibilities of supervisors.

Part Two describes the challenges modern supervisors face in meeting their responsibilities. The ever higher expectations of customers, business owners, and the general public have made high quality at low cost a necessary concern of employees at all levels, including the supervisory level. Therefore, Chapter 2 addresses how supervisors can understand and carry out their role in maintaining and constantly improving quality and productivity. Chapter 3 covers groups and teamwork, reflecting the increasingly common role of the supervisor as a

SUPERVISION ACROSS INDUSTRIES

AUTO INDUSTRY SUPERVISOR DEPENDS ON PEOPLE SKILLS

Arthur Little started his career with Honda Motor Company as an assembler at the company's plant in Marysville, Ohio. One of the major requirements was physical endurance. Although Little was young (in his early twenties) and fit from two years of active duty in the Navy, he found the experience of assembling vehicles exhausting. But his co-workers encouraged him, and he became used to the demands of the job. He began to think of Honda's employees as "kind of a family"—the part of the job he liked best.

Little was eager to learn, so he next took a position at the Honda plant in which he learned several jobs and rotated among them. In that way, he became familiar with procedures in various parts of the Marysville plant. He began substituting occasionally for the plant's supervisors, called *team leaders*. By taking these assignments, Little earned points in Honda's system of rewarding workers for their work experience.

Eventually, a supervisor's position became vacant, and Little applied for the job. The points he had earned helped him win the slot.

Now that Little is a supervisor, he has to focus on his role of ensuring that workers are safe and productive. He continues to see Honda's workers as one of the company's assets, saying their attitude makes his work almost easy: "You don't have a bunch of guys waiting around for something to happen."

Senior staff engineer Brad Alty agrees with the priority Little places on human relations, saying that the main skill needed in a Honda team leader is to be a "people person." He explains, "You have to be willing to work with others, you have to be motivated and believe in teamwork, and you have to have honesty and integrity."

Source: Based on James Cummings, "Ohio Plant Supervisor Builds on Experience to Rise through Ranks at Honda," *Dayton (Ohio) Daily News,* May 23, 2005, downloaded from Business & Company Resource Center, http://galenet.galegroup.com.

team leader. Supervisors (and others in the organization) also must consider the ethical implications of their decisions, the topic of Chapter 4. The value of diversity is the topic of Chapter 5.

Part Three takes a deeper look at the supervisory functions introduced in this chapter. Chapter 6 discusses how supervisors use planning and controlling to enable their work groups to reach goals and objectives. Chapter 7 covers the function of organizing, including supervisors' use of delegation to share authority and responsibility. Chapter 8 examines the supervisor's role in carrying out the management function of leading. Chapter 9 explains how supervisors can be effective at creatively solving problems and making decisions.

Part Four describes the skills needed by supervisors in all kinds of organizations. Individual chapters cover the ways supervisors can communicate, motivate their employees, supervise "problem" employees, manage time and stress, and handle conflict and change. These skills are important at all levels of management and in all types of organizations. A special appendix follows this part and emphasizes how supervisors can negotiate and handle organizational politics.

The last part of this book addresses activities related to managing the organization's human resources: its employees. Chapter 15 covers the supervisor's role in selecting new employees. Chapter 16 discusses the process of training new and current employees. Chapter 17 describes how supervisors appraise employees' performance.

Finally, an end-of-book appendix introduces some of the many government laws and regulations that guide supervisors' roles and decisions with regard to human resources. It focuses on health and safety issues, labor relations, and fair employment practices.

Throughout the book, the chapters include special features designed to help you apply the principles of supervision to the practice of supervising real people in a real organization. These features include "Tips from the Firing Line" and "Supervisory Skills," which discuss actual examples of modern supervisory challenges—creativity, innovation, and teamwork—as well as provide practical tips for effective supervision. "Supervision and Diversity" boxes demonstrate how the diverse workforce of the future is already affecting the lives of supervisors. "Supervision across Industries" boxes demonstrate the applicability of supervision practices in a wide variety of business areas. "Supervision and Ethics" boxes illustrate how supervisors are able to meet the demands of their job in an ethical manner. Chapter-opening cases and end-of-chapter cases show how real supervisors and organizations have approached the issues covered in the chapter and solved common problems in the workplace.

An end-of-book notes section, divided by chapter, provides source and additional reading material for various topics covered within the chapters. The glossary at the end of this text provides a quick reference to all key terms. For review, each definition is followed by the number of the page where the boldfaced key term is defined.

The Skills Modules at the end of each chapter contain self-assessments, skill-building exercises, role-playing exercises, information applications, and miniature case studies. These exercises allow you to use the concepts from the text and develop leadership abilities.

SKILLS MODULE

PART ONE: CONCEPTS

Summary

1.1 Define what a supervisor is.

A supervisor is a manager at the first level of management. That is, the employees reporting to the supervisor are not themselves managers.

1.2 Describe the basic types of supervisory skills.

According to the classic model, the basic supervisory skills are technical, human relations, conceptual, and decision-making skills. Technical skills are the specialized knowledge and experience used to carry out particular techniques or procedures. Human relations skills enable the supervisor to work effectively with other people. Conceptual skills enable the supervisor to see the relation of the parts to the whole and to one another. Decision-making skills are needed to analyze information and reach good decisions. A more recent model identifies skills needed to succeed in task-related, people-related, and change-related activities. These skills include clarifying roles, monitoring operations, and planning for the short-term; consulting, supporting, recognizing, developing, and empowering employees; and envisioning change, taking risks, encouraging innovative thinking, and monitoring externally.

1.3 Describe how the growing diversity of the workforce affects the supervisor's role.

Compared with the current makeup of the U.S. workforce, an increasingly large share of employees will be female, nonwhite, and older. As a result, supervisors in the future will typically manage a more diverse group of employees. This reality means that supervisors can benefit from a greater variety of talents and viewpoints, but it also requires them to draw on more sophisticated human relations skills than in the past.

1.4 Identify the general functions of a supervisor.

The general functions of a supervisor are planning, organizing, staffing, leading, and controlling. Planning involves setting goals and determining how to meet them. Organizing is determining how to set up the group, allocate resources, and assign work to achieve goals. Staffing consists of identifying, hiring, and developing the necessary number and quality of employees. Leading is the function of getting employees to do what is expected of them. Controlling consists of monitoring performance and making needed corrections.

1.5 Explain how supervisors are responsible to higher management, employees, and co-workers.

Supervisors are responsible for doing the work assigned to them by higher management and for keeping management informed of the department's progress. They link higher management to employees. Supervisors are responsible for treating employees fairly, making instructions clear, and bringing employee concerns to higher management. Organizations that have undergone restructuring or reengineering often make supervisors responsible for empowering and enabling employees instead of focusing on command and control. Supervisors also are responsible for cooperating with co-workers in other departments. Organizations hold supervisors accountable for meeting these various responsibilities.

1.6 Describe the typical background of someone who is promoted to supervisor.

Most supervisors begin as employees in the department they now supervise. They usually have superior technical skills and may have seniority or demonstrate leadership potential.

1.7 Identify characteristics of a successful supervisor.

A successful supervisor is usually someone who has a positive attitude, is loyal, is fair, communicates well, can delegate, and wants the job.

Key Terms			
	supervisor, *p. 3*	decision-making	leading, *p. 10*
	technical skills, *p. 4*	skills, *p. 5*	controlling, *p. 10*
	human relations	planning, *p. 8*	accountability, *p. 13*
	skills, *p. 4*	organizing, *p. 9*	
	conceptual skills, *p. 5*	staffing, *p. 9*	

Review and Discussion Questions

1. What are some ways that a supervisor's job is similar to those of managers at other levels? How does a supervisor's job differ from those of other managers?

2. Imagine that you have just been promoted to supervise the cashiers in a supermarket. List the specific technical, human relations, conceptual, and decision-making skills you think you might need to succeed at this job. How might you develop them continually to achieve the job of store manager?

3. Identify whether each of the following skills relates most to task-related, people-related, or change-related activities.

   a. The ability to communicate well with one's manager.

   b. The ability to evaluate whether sales clerks are delivering polite and timely service.

   c. The ability to plan a safety training program for the housekeeping staff.

    d. The ability to involve employees in making good scheduling decisions to accommodate their vacation preferences.

    e. The ability to see how new technology can help the department meet its goals.

    f. The ability to teach an employee how to machine a part without unnecessary changes in the setup of equipment.

4. Population trends suggest that the workforce will become increasingly diverse. What are some advantages of greater diversity? What challenges does it pose to the supervisor?

5. What are the basic functions of a supervisor? On which functions do supervisors spend most of their time?

6. As the controlling function changes in many organizations, supervisors should no longer control by dictating solutions. How do they carry out the controlling function instead?

7. What responsibilities do supervisors have to each of these groups?

    a. Higher management.

    b. The employees they supervise.

    c. Co-workers in other departments.

8. Emma has just been promoted to an office manager position in a small real estate office. Some of the people she will supervise are her former peers; she is aware that one of them also applied for the office manager's job. How can Emma prepare for her new position? What might be the best way to approach the co-worker who did not get the manager's job?

9. What are some ways a new supervisor can use power and authority effectively?

10. List the characteristics of a good supervisor. In addition to the characteristics mentioned in the chapter, add any others you believe are important. Draw on your own experiences as an employee and/or supervisor.

PART TWO: SKILL-BUILDING

YOU SOLVE THE PROBLEM

Reflecting back on page 3, consider the challenges faced by Tyrone Dugan. List the skills that you consider most important for establishing authority and a positive work environment. Which of these skills did Dugan use? What additional advice can you give Dugan for establishing himself as a successful new supervisor? With your group, prepare a report offering your recommendations.

Problem-Solving Case: *Refereeing the Referees of the Atlantic Coast Conference*

When basketball teams from Duke, Georgia Tech, and the other 10 members of the Atlantic Coast Conference (ACC) play, most eyes are on the players and the scoreboard. Some avid fans also watch the referees, sometimes challenging their calls. Few would notice one important observer: John Clougherty, supervisor of the ACC's officials.

To carry out his job, Clougherty attends dozens of games every season and watches the rest on DVDs at home. At the ready is a legal pad, on which he takes notes about the number of fouls called on each team and data about particular calls he needs to discuss later with individual officials. When they make a mistake, Clougherty lets them know right after the game. In fact, quick feedback is one of this supervisor's priorities. Right after he became supervisor, he began requiring that each game be recorded on DVD and that a disc be delivered to the officials minutes after the end of the game. If there is a disagreement about a call and Clougherty is at the game, he might review the recording immediately with the officials. The information also helps him communicate effectively with team coaches.

Clougherty uses his DVD recordings as an important resource for teaching the referees. Occasionally, they also provide a record in support of disciplinary actions. During a recent game between Florida State and Duke, a crew of officials improperly called a technical foul on a Florida State basketball player and then failed to review the play on the courtside monitor. Clougherty responded with a suspension.

In addition to training and discipline, Clougherty is also responsible for hiring. He has brought several new officials to ACC games. For his hiring expertise, he draws on his extensive experience: "After 30 years [as a college referee], I think I have a pretty good idea for talent." In fact, he has plenty of firsthand experience. During those 30 years of officiating, Dougherty worked at a dozen Final Four games and four national title games.

1. Which supervisory skills seem to be most important to Clougherty's job? Why?
2. What types of responsibilities does he undertake?
3. How important do you think Clougherty's experience as a referee was in preparing him to be a supervisor? Other than that work experience, what experiences and qualities do you think would be important for someone to succeed in Clougherty's job? Do those experiences and qualities apply to most supervisory jobs?

Sources: Ed Miller, "ACC Official Supervisor, a Relatively Thankless Job," *(Norfolk, Va.) Virginian-Pilot*, March 6, 2006, downloaded from Business & Company Resource Center, http://galenet.galegroup.com; Atlantic Coast Conference, "This Is the ACC," ACC Web site, www.theacc.com, accessed June 29, 2006.

Knowing Yourself

Is Supervising Right for You?
Answer each of the following questions Yes or No.

	Yes	No
1. Do you consider yourself a highly ambitious person?		
2. Do you sincerely like people and have patience with them?		
3. Could you assume the responsibility of decision making?		
4. Is making more money very important to you?		
5. Would recognition from others be more important to you than taking pride in doing a detailed job well?		
6. Would you enjoy learning about psychology and human behavior?		
7. Would you be happier with more responsibility?		
8. Would you rather work with problems involving human relationships than with mechanical, computational, creative, clerical, or similar problems?		
9. Do you desire an opportunity to demonstrate your leadership ability?		
10. Do you desire the freedom to do your own planning rather than being told what to do?		
Total		

Give yourself 1 point for each Yes answer. If your score is 6 or more, you might be happy as a supervisor. If your score was 5 or less, you should think hard about your preferences and strengths before jumping into a supervisory job.

Source: From *Supervisor's Survival Kit: Your First Step,* by Elwood N. Chapman. Copyright © 1993 Pearson Education Inc. Reprinted by permission of Pearson Education Inc., Upper Saddle River, NJ.

Class Exercise

Recognizing Management Skills

Which of the five management functions would you rely on in each of the following situations? Discuss your choices in class.

1. One of your employees is chronically late for work.
2. Your department has switched to a new word-processing program and some people are having difficulty making the change.
3. Your manager has asked you to have your staff complete a special project without incurring any overtime.
4. It is time to prepare your department's budget for the coming year.
5. Your team's productivity is not meeting the standards the team set.

Building Supervision Skills

Defining Your Role as Supervisor

Instructions

1. Imagine you are the supervisor in each scenario described below, and you must decide which supervisory function(s) you would use in each.
2. Many of the scenarios require more than one function. The "Answers" column lists the number of functions your answer should include. Mark your answers using the following codes:

Code	Supervisory Function	Brief Description
P	Planning	Setting goals and determining how to meet them
O	Organizing	Determining how to set up the group, allocate resources, and assign work to achieve goals
S	Staffing	Identifying, hiring, and developing the necessary number and quality of employees
L	Leading	Getting employees to do what is expected of them
C	Controlling	Monitoring performance and making needed corrections

3. As a class, compare and discuss your answers and the reasoning you used in determining them.

Scenarios

Your group's work is centered on a project that is due in two months. Although everyone is working on the project, you believe that your subordinates are involved in excessive socializing and other time-consuming behaviors. You decide to meet with the group to have the members help you break down the project into smaller subprojects with mini deadlines. You believe that this will help keep the group members focused on the project and that the quality of the finished project will then reflect the true capabilities of your group.

Answers
(four functions)
1. _____

Your first impression of the new group you will be supervising is not too great. You tell your friend at dinner after your first day on the job: "Looks like I got a babysitting job instead of a supervisory job."

(three functions)

2. _____

Your boss asks your opinion about promoting Andy to a supervisory position. Andy is one of your most competent and efficient workers. Knowing that Andy lacks leadership skills in many key areas, you decide not to recommend him at this time. Instead you tell your boss you will work with Andy to help him develop his leadership skills so that the next time an opportunity for promotion occurs, Andy will be prepared to consider it.

(one function)

3. _____

You begin a meeting of your work group by letting the members know that a major procedure the group has been using for the past two years is being significantly revamped. Your department will have to phase in the change during the next six weeks. You proceed by explaining the reasoning management gave you for this change. You then say, "Take the next 5 to 10 minutes to voice your reactions to this change." The majority of comments are critical of the change. You say, "I appreciate each of you sharing your reactions; I, too, recognize that *all* change creates problems. However, either we can spend the remaining 45 minutes of our meeting focusing on why we don't want the change and why we don't think it's necessary, or we can work together to come up with viable solutions to solve the problems that implementing this change will most likely create." After 5 more minutes of an exchange of comments, the consensus of the group is that they should spend the remainder of the meeting focusing on how to deal with the potential problems that may arise from implementing the new procedure.

(three functions)

4. _____

You are preparing the annual budget allocation meetings to be held in the plant manager's office next week. You decide to present a strong case to support your department's request for money for some high-tech equipment that will help your employees do their jobs better. You will stand firm against any suggestions of budget cuts in your area.

(one function)

5. _____

Early in your career you learned an important lesson about employee selection. One of the nurses on your floor unexpectedly quit. The other nurses pressured you to fill the position quickly because they were overworked even before the nurse left. After a hasty recruitment effort, you made a decision based on insufficient information. You regretted your quick decision during the three months of problems that followed, until you finally had to discharge the new hire. Since that time, you have never let anybody pressure you into making a quick hiring decision.

(two functions)

6. _____

Source: This team-building exercise was prepared by Corinne Livesay, Belhaven College, Jackson, Mississippi.

Building
Supervision
Skills

Leading a Team

In Chapter 1 ("Modern Supervision: Concepts and Skills"), you learned two ways to categorize the different skills that supervisors use to decide which skills apply in any given situation. Here, you will apply your knowledge of the classic skill categories to several team-building situations.

Instructions

Imagine that you are the supervisor in each of the following situations. Decide which of the following skills will best help you build a team: technical, human relations, conceptual, decision making. Each situation requires more than one skill.

1. As the supervisor of a group of production workers in a plant that manufactures parts for telephones, you have been asked by upper management to join a team of supervisors from different departments. Your objective will be to investigate ways to improve the time required to fill large orders from major customers. Which two skills do you think will be most important to you on this team?

2. You supervise 20 telephone operators on the night shift at a mail-order catalog company. You used to be an operator yourself, so you know a great deal about the job. Management has been pressing you and other supervisors to reduce the amount of time operators spend on the telephone for each order. You believe that a potentially negative situation for your employees can be solved with a friendly competition between two teams of operators. There are no punishments for the team that comes in second, but there is a reward for the team that wins. Team members are encouraged to find new ways to reduce telephone time without reducing customer satisfaction. Which two skills do you think would be most important as you get your teams up and running?

3. You are a supervisor in the engineering department and a member of a team that includes people from production, finance, marketing, and engineering. After conducting marketing research, your team must determine whether to recommend that your company expand its operations overseas. Which three skills do you think would be most important in your contribution to the team?

Part One Video Cases

MANAGER'S HOT SEAT VIDEO 1: "VIRTUAL WORKPLACE: OUT OF THE OFFICE REPLY"

Changing technologies in the workplace present new possibilities and challenges for both the supervisor and employee. For example, employees now have the freedom to work from home or another location than the office if approved by their employer. Read the following scenario describing the video selection "Virtual Workplace: Out of the Office Reply," then watch the video selection. Next, answer the three questions that pertain to the specific challenges in this supervisor–employee situation.

SCENARIO

Three months ago, Ralph Ramos assigned a number of employees to work as telecommuters to alleviate the lack of space in their office building. Among them was Angela Zononi, an employee and friend for more than four years, who was delighted to work from home since her commute to the office was particularly time consuming. Although things went relatively smoothly for the first six weeks, since then, communication and performance have taken a steady downturn. Angela has biweekly meetings with Ralph in his office. Lately they have had unprecedented arguments and frequent misunderstandings.

QUESTIONS

1. The characteristics of a successful supervisor are (a) a positive attitude, (b) loyalty, (c) fairness, (d) good communication, (e) the ability to delegate tasks, and (f) enjoyment of the job. How does Ralph specifically show (or not show) each of these qualities in the meetings he has with Angela?
2. Refer to Table 1.2 on page 11. Which responsibilities of a supervisor does Ralph exhibit? Which others could he have integrated that would have contributed to a positive outcome throughout the whole situation?
3. If you had been Ralph, what would you have handled differently in setting up the work situation? Could you have avoided the problem issues with Angela? How?

MANAGER'S HOT SEAT VIDEO 2: "LISTENING SKILLS: YEAH, WHATEVER"

In the previous video case, we could see that as a supervisor, Ralph felt that listening to Angela was one of his most important priorities. This video, "Listening Skills: Yeah, Whatever," shows a supervisor handling an employee who does not listen effectively. Read the following scenario describing the video selection, then watch the sections "The Meeting" and "Afterthoughts." Next, answer the three questions that pertain to the specific challenges in this supervisor–employee situation.

SCENARIO

At Midnight Visions, account managers oversee four to six accounts at any given time. Some of Miguel Valentino's (the young creative director) current accounts are Jezebel, Antonioni, and HotSpot. This is the first time Miguel has had three high-profile accounts at the same time—a result of shifting schedules and production slow downs. Pilar Grimault (senior account manager) has a lot of confidence in Miguel, but because Miguel has had less experience than most, she watches over him more closely. In addition to reviewing the account reports, she has casually checked in with some team members and clients about Miguel's performance—most of the news is great with a few things that could and should have been handled better. This is really a positive review, and the trouble spots at this stage of the game are minor. But they still need to be addressed. The trouble spots she is most concerned with involve the Jezebel

(continued)

account—Miguel went $11,000 over budget and then charged the client for overages without checking with or warning it. The company was thrilled with the end media and accepted the overages, but not the process. Today is the review.

QUESTIONS

1. It is clear in the first meeting that Miguel is distracted and at some points disrespectful to Pilar in not listening to what she is saying to him. Still, Pilar does not do anything to draw him back to the point of the meeting. What should Pilar have done to take control of the situation?

2. Table 1.1 on page 6 categorizes the skills of a supervisor. Applying this modern view of management skills, choose one of the skills described in the table. Then analyze Pilar's performance in both meetings in terms of that skill. How was she a success or failure?

3. If you had been in Pilar's shoes, what would you have done in the first meeting immediately after Miguel began to focus on things other than your intent for the meeting?

Part Two

Modern Supervision Challenges

Successful Supervisors Ensure Quality and Productivity through Teamwork
The McGraw-Hill Companies, Inc. / Lars A. Niki, photographer

Chapter **Two**

Ensuring High Quality and Productivity

Learning Objectives

After you have studied this chapter, you should be able to:

2.1 Describe the consequences suffered by organizations as a result of poor quality work.

2.2 Compare product quality control and process control.

2.3 Summarize techniques for quality control.

2.4 Identify ways organizations measure their success in continuous quality improvement.

2.5 Identify constraints on productivity.

2.6 Describe how productivity and productivity improvements are measured.

2.7 Identify ways productivity may be improved.

2.8 Explain why employees have fears about productivity improvement and how supervisors can address those fears.

If you forget the customer, nothing much else matters.
—*Anne Mulcahy, CEO, Xerox Corporation*

A Supervisor's Problem: Contributing to Better Quality and Productivity at Hayward Pool Products

Business success has made efficiency an important challenge for the supervisors, employees, and management of Hayward Pool Products. The company, which makes swimming pool equipment, defines its main objective as "perfect pool water." Hayward equipment, including filters, heaters, and pumps, is designed to meet top standards for energy efficiency. Hayward's quality standards have helped the company grow.

In the 1990s, Hayward acquired a manufacturing facility in Nashville, Tennessee, making 15,000 pool heaters a year. As the company's sales grew to more than 25,000 heaters, it appeared Hayward would need to spend millions of dollars for a bigger facility. But first the company brought together employees and managers to see if they could make better use of what they already had.

Hayward adopted an improvement technique called *kaizen*, in which teams evaluate manufacturing processes, changing them to meet goals for quality and efficiency. Hayward set up teams of 10 to 12 people drawn from management, the shop floor, and support functions such as human resources and finance. Each team studied a manufacturing process from start to finish, looking for ways to make the physical setup more efficient, reduce waste, and lower the amount of parts the company had to keep in inventory. Team members also suggested ways to make workers' jobs safer and less physically stressful.

In launching this effort, the company considered workers as well as the bottom line. Before beginning the *kaizen* process, Hayward made sure all employees knew the company intended that no one would be laid off as a result of greater productivity. If a particular job was no longer needed, that employee would be assigned different responsibilities.

Thanks to the *kaizen* process, Hayward doubled its production in the existing Nashville facility. By putting off its expansion plans, the company saved the $8 million cost of a new facility—all without compromising on its "perfect pool water" objective. But did it do so at the expense of its supervisors? Isn't it up to supervisors to figure out how employees can work more efficiently and deliver better quality?

Sources: "Creativity before Capital," *Industry Week*, January 2004, downloaded from InfoTrac, http://web4 .infotrac.galegroup.com; Hayward Pool Products, "About Us," downloaded from the Hayward Web site, www .haywardnet.com, June 29, 2004.

Hayward Pool Products delivers customer value—high quality at good prices. Hayward's Web site states the quality emphasis: "Our main objective is perfect pool water." And the company minimizes costs by making production efficient. At Hayward and other companies, supervisors have a major role in helping keep quality high and costs low.

This chapter looks at the supervisor's role in ensuring high quality and productivity. Quality has different meanings depending on the kind of business and the customers served. However, a logical way to understand the meaning of *high quality* is to think of it as work that meets or exceeds customers' expectations. Table 2.1 describes eight possible measures for the quality of goods or services. **Productivity** is the amount of results (output) an organization gets for a given amount of inputs (see Figure 2.1). Thus, productivity can refer to the amount of acceptable work employees do for each dollar they earn or the number of acceptable products manufactured with a given amount of resources.

Many of the supervisor's activities, including planning, leading, and controlling, are directed toward improving quality and productivity. This chapter considers

productivity
The amount of results (output) an organization gets for a given amount of inputs

FIGURE 2.1
The Productivity Formula

$$\text{Productivity} = \frac{\text{Outputs}}{\text{Inputs}}$$

TABLE 2.1
Dimensions of Quality

Source: Adapted from David A. Garvin, "Competing on the Eight Dimensions of Quality," *Harvard Business Review,* November–December 1987.

Dimension	Explanation
Performance	The product's primary operating characteristic, such as an automobile's acceleration or the picture clarity of a television set
Features	Supplements to the product's basic operating characteristics—for example, power windows on a car or the ceremony with which a bottle of wine is opened in a restaurant
Reliability	The probability that the product will function properly and not break down during a specified period; a manufacturer's warranty is often seen as an indicator of reliability
Conformance	The degree to which the product's design and operating characteristics meet established standards, such as safety standards for a baby's crib
Durability	The length of the product's life—for example, whether a stereo lasts for 5 years or 25 years
Serviceability	The speed and ease of repairing the product—for example, whether a computer store will send out a repairperson, service the computer in the store, or provide no maintenance service at all
Aesthetics	The way the product looks, feels, tastes, and smells, such as the styling and smell of a new car
Perceived quality	The customer's impression of the product's quality, such as a buyer's belief that an Audi is a safe and reliable car

the supervisor's role in making these improvements. It begins with a description of the consequences of poor quality and then introduces types of quality-control efforts. The chapter explains how managers at all levels can measure whether they are improving quality and meeting high-quality standards. Next, this chapter takes a deeper look at the meaning and measurement of productivity. It concludes by describing ways that supervisors can participate in efforts to improve productivity.

CONSEQUENCES OF POOR QUALITY

Like employees at all levels, supervisors must care about quality. They must care because poor quality limits the organization's access to resources and raises its costs.

Limited Resources

When the quality of an organization's goods or services is poor, the whole organization suffers. As word spreads about problems with the product, customers look for alternatives. The organization develops a negative image, which drives away customers and clients. The organization loses business and therefore revenues, and it also has more difficulty attracting other important resources. An organization with a poor reputation has a harder time recruiting superior employees and borrowing money at favorable terms.

Many firms know that the potential for lost business is a major reason to invest in quality. Dell established itself as a market leader by selling high-quality computers at a low cost, thanks to its efficient operations. Unfortunately, the drive to be efficient began to move the company away from customer satisfaction. In particular, many customers became frustrated with Dell's call centers. One reason: Many service reps were trained to solve only one category of a problem, so almost 45 percent of calls had to be transferred from the agent who answered the call to someone with the knowledge needed to help the customer. Richard L. Hunter, brought in to improve Dell's customer service, called the situation "terrible," explaining that it was comparable to "delivering materials to the wrong factory 45 percent of the time." Worse, to slow the tide of calls from customers, Dell tried removing its toll-free service number from its Web site. Customers' reactions showed up in Dell's declining market share and slumping customer satisfaction ratings. To improve the situation, Hunter is borrowing factory methods such as giving each call center employee a colored flag to raise whenever he or she needs help, along with training to equip service reps to solve a wider range of problems.[1]

Higher Costs

Poor quality work can also lead to high costs. Some managers might think it is expensive to ensure that things are done right the first time. But the reality is that businesses spend billions of dollars each year on inspections, errors, rework, repairs, customer refunds, and other costs to find and correct mistakes. Attracting new customers costs several times more per customer than keeping existing customers satisfied, so marketing costs are higher too. Thus, poor quality often results in much wasted time and materials, in addition to requiring that unacceptable items be fixed or discarded. If the problems remain undetected until after the goods have been sold, the manufacturer may have to recall its products for repair or replacement. In addition, poor goods and services may result in lawsuits by disgruntled or injured customers.

Quality programs may carry some start-up costs, but the cost of poor quality is higher. When General Electric set out to improve its quality in 1995 with its now-famous Six Sigma initiative, it spent $300 million. But the program was an investment that reaped savings between $400 and $500 million. It also permitted an additional $100–$200 million in indirect savings.[2]

Even more costly, in terms of money, reputation, injury, and death, was the recall of millions of Firestone tires in 2000 and 2001. Ford Motor Company, which had used the tires on its Ford Explorer sport utility vehicles, blamed Firestone for failure rates of up to 450 per 1 million tires. Firestone insisted that the vehicle's design was partly to blame for more than 100 deaths involving Explorers. Both companies endured the bad publicity of testifying before committees of Congress.[3] In the meantime, Ford was embarrassed by further quality problems requiring recalls of its Focus and Escape models. The company accelerated quality efforts, including joint programs with suppliers.[4]

TYPES OF QUALITY CONTROL

quality control
An organization's efforts to prevent or correct defects in its goods or services or to improve them in some way

Because of the negative consequences of poor quality, organizations try to prevent and correct such problems through various approaches to quality control. Broadly speaking, **quality control** refers to an organization's efforts to prevent or correct defects in its goods or services or to improve them in some way. Some organizations use the term *quality control* to refer only to error detection, whereas *quality assurance* refers to both the prevention and the detection of quality problems. However, this chapter uses *quality control* in the broader sense because it is the more common term.

Whichever term is used, many organizations—especially large ones—have a department or employee devoted to identifying defects and promoting high quality. In these cases, the supervisor can benefit from the expertise of quality-control

FIGURE 2.2
Types of Quality
Control

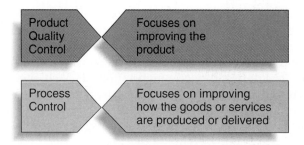

personnel. Ultimately, however, the organization expects its supervisors to take responsibility for the quality of work in their departments.

In general, when supervisors look for high-quality performance to reinforce or improvements to make, they can focus on two areas: the *product* itself or the *process* of making and delivering the product. Figure 2.2 illustrates these two orientations.

Product Quality Control

product quality control
Quality control that focuses on ways to improve the product itself

An organization that focuses on ways to improve the product itself is using **product quality control.** For example, employees in a print shop might examine a sample of newsletters or envelopes to look for smudges and other defects. A city's park district might consider ways to upgrade its playground equipment or improve the programs it offers senior citizens.

Computer technology can greatly improve product quality control. Morton Metalcraft Co., of Morton, Illinois, makes sheet-metal components for farm and industrial vehicles such as John Deere backhoes. Morton employees work with a computer system that uses digital photos, drawings, and key dimensions of products to create software routines for checking the quality of the entire product and its subsections. To cope with last-minute design changes by customers, Morton has programmed the system with customized routines that enable a change in as little as five minutes. The system has cut inspection time too. Inspecting the cab of a John Deere backhoe used to take two operators $4\frac{1}{2}$ hours; now one operator can do it in less than 45 minutes.[5]

Process Control

process control
Quality control that emphasizes how to do things in a way that leads to better quality

An organization might also consider how to do things in a way that leads to better quality. This focus is called **process control.** The print shop, for example, might conduct periodic checks to make sure its employees understand good techniques for setting up the presses. The park district might ask the maintenance crew to suggest ways to keep the parks cleaner and more attractive. In this way, the park district can improve the process by which the crew members do their job.

A broad approach to process control involves creating an organizational climate that encourages quality. From the day they are hired, employees at all levels should understand that quality is important and that they have a role in delivering high quality. In the city park district example, managers and employees might consider ways to be more responsive to citizens' input. The greater responsiveness, in turn, could enable park district employees to recognize ways to serve the community better.

Process control techniques can be very effective. At Accurate Gauge and Manufacturing, based in Rochester Hills, Michigan, process control is an important part of the company's efforts to plan for quality and correct the causes of defects in the precision parts it manufactures for heavy equipment and commercial and automotive vehicles. Quality teams meet weekly to prevent problems, but some process improvements are responses to problems. Even when a failure occurred in a product line the company was preparing to phase out, engineering manager Mark Tario led efforts to correct the process by setting up procedures for operators to check both pressure and position simultaneously as the parts were being produced. In addition to impressing the customer with this extreme commitment to quality, the effort established a process that became the standard procedure for making other defect-free parts.[6]

METHODS FOR IMPROVING QUALITY

Within this broad framework, managers, researchers, and consultants have identified several methods for ensuring and improving quality. Today most organizations apply some or all of these methods, including statistical quality control, the zero-defects approach, employee involvement teams, Six Sigma, and total quality management. Table 2.2 summarizes these techniques.

In choosing a method—or, more commonly, applying the methods selected by higher-level management—supervisors must remember that a technique alone does not guarantee high quality. Rather, quality-control processes work when the people who use them are well motivated, understand how to use them, and exercise creativity in solving problems. For example, Veronica T. Hychalk, a registered nurse and vice president of professional services for Northeastern Vermont Regional Hospital, says her profession should measure quality of care in terms of what patients want: "compassion, caring, time, skill, communication, education, listening, and good results from their caregivers."[7]

Statistical Quality Control

statistical quality control
Looking for defects in parts or finished products selected through a sampling technique

It rarely makes economic sense to examine every part, finished good, or service to ensure it meets quality standards. For one thing, that approach to quality control is expensive. In addition, examining some products, such as packages of cheese or boxes of tissues, can destroy them. As a result, unless the costs of poor quality are so great that every product must be examined, most organizations inspect only a sample. Looking for defects in parts, finished goods, or other outcomes selected through a sampling technique is known as **statistical quality control.**

The most accurate way to apply statistical quality control is to use a random sample. This means selecting outcomes (such as parts or customer contacts) in a

TABLE 2.2
Quality Improvement Methods

Statistical quality control	Looking for defects in outcomes selected through a sampling technique
Statistical process control	Using statistics to monitor production quality during the production process
Zero-defects approach	All employees delivering such high quality that goods and services are free of problems
Employee involvement teams	Setting up teams of employees to identify and solve quality-related problems
Six Sigma	Using a formal process in which teams study processes and correct problems to limit defects to 3.4 per million operations
Total quality management	Focusing the whole organization on continuously improving every business process so it satisfies customers

FIGURE 2.3
Chart Used for Statistical Process Control

Source: From John A. Lawrence Jr. and Barry A. Pasternack, *Applied Management Science: A Computer-Integrated Approach for Decision Making*. Copyright © 1998 John Wiley & Sons, Inc. This material is used by permission of John Wiley & Sons, Inc.

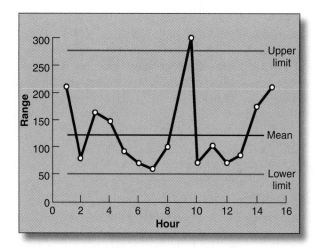

statistical process control (SPC)
A quality-control technique using statistics to monitor production quality on an ongoing basis and making corrections whenever the results show the process is out of control

way that each has an equal chance of being selected. The assumption is that the quality of the sample describes the quality of the entire lot. Thus, if 2 percent of the salad dressing bottles in a sample have leaks, presumably 2 percent of all the bottles coming off the assembly line have leaks. Or if 65 percent of customers surveyed report they were treated courteously, presumably about 65 percent of all customers feel that way.

Rather than wait until a process is complete to take a random sample, the operators of a process can use statistics to monitor production quality on an ongoing basis. This quality-control technique is known as **statistical process control (SPC).** The operator periodically measures some aspect of what he or she is producing—say, the diameter of a hole drilled or the correctness of an account number entered into a computer—then plots the results on a control chart such as the simplified one shown in Figure 2.3. The middle line in the chart shows the value that represents the standard—in this case, the mean (average). Above and below the mean value are lines representing the acceptable upper and lower limits. When a measured value falls between these limits, the operator may assume the process is working normally. When a value falls outside these limits, the operator is supposed to correct the process.

Thus, if a machine operator is supposed to make a part 0.0375 inch in diameter (the mean value in this case), the lower and upper limits might be 0.0370 and 0.0380 inch, respectively. If the operator measures a part and finds that its diameter is 0.0383 inch, the operator adjusts the machine or modify his or her actions to keep such errors from recurring. The measurements in Figure 2.3 indicate that the operator made some needed adjustments after one measurement exceeded the upper limit. After that point, the measurements are clustered much closer to the mean; the process is again under control. Clearly, SPC gives the operator great control over maintaining quality, so quality control does not need to be assigned to specialized personnel. That is one reason SPC is popular today, especially in manufacturing firms.

The idea of using SPC or other statistical methods makes some supervisors nervous about whether employees will be able to handle the statistics. However, the process requires only a basic knowledge of statistics, coupled with an understanding of what level of quality is desirable and achievable. The supervisor should see that employees get the training they need in using the SPC technique and adjusting the processes for which they are responsible. (Chapter 16 describes the supervisor's role in employee training.)

Zero-Defects Approach

zero-defects approach
A quality-control technique based on the view that everyone in the organization should work toward the goal of delivering such high quality that all aspects of the organization's goods and services are free of problems

A broad view of process quality control is that everyone in the organization should work toward the goal of delivering such high quality that all aspects of the organization's goods and services are free of problems. The quality-control technique based on this view is known as the **zero-defects approach.** An organization that uses the zero-defects approach provides products of excellent quality not only because the people who produce them are seeking ways to avoid defects but also because the purchasing department is ensuring a timely supply of well-crafted parts or supplies, the accounting department is seeing that bills get paid on time, the human resources department is helping find and train highly qualified personnel, and so on.

Thus, in implementing a zero-defects approach, managers and employees at all levels seek to build quality into every aspect of their work. Employees work with supervisors and other managers to set goals for quality and identify areas where improvement is needed. Management is responsible for communicating the importance of quality to the whole organization and rewarding high-quality performance.

Employee Involvement Teams

employee involvement teams
Teams of employees who plan ways to improve quality in their areas of organization

Recognizing that the people who perform a process have knowledge based on their experiences, many organizations directly involve employees in planning how to improve quality. Many companies set up **employee involvement teams** such as quality circles, problem-solving teams, process improvement teams, or self-managed work groups. The typical employee involvement team consists of up to 10 employees and their supervisor, who serves as the team leader. In this role, the supervisor schedules meetings, prepares agendas, and promotes the participation and cooperation of team members. (The next chapter describes general principles of teams, including the role of the team leader.)

The team meets periodically, usually at least once or twice a month for an hour or two during the workday. At these meetings, participants examine areas where quality needs improvement, and they develop solutions. The problems discussed may be identified by management or operative employees. In either case, the problems should be related to the employees' everyday work, because this is where they have the greatest expertise. In a typical process, the members of the team might take the following steps (see Figure 2.4):

1. Identify quality problems related to the employees' areas of responsibility.
2. Select the problems to focus on first. A newly formed group may find it helpful to focus on simple problems so the group can build on its successes.
3. Analyze the problem to identify its causes.
4. Identify possible solutions and select one to recommend to management.

Depending on the organization's policies, one or more managers usually must approve the recommendations of the employee involvement team. Once a recommendation is approved, the appropriate people in the organization must implement it. The team should follow up on the implementation to ensure that the problem actually was solved.

Quality and productivity have steadily improved at General Cable Corporation's factory in Moose Jaw, Saskatchewan, Canada, through the efforts of

FIGURE 2.4
**Typical Procedure
for an Employee
Involvement Team**

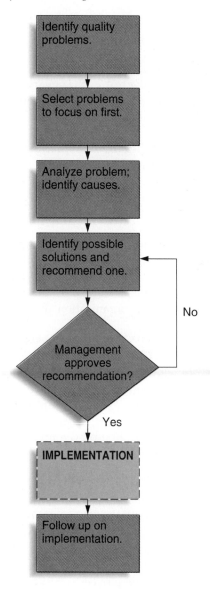

employee teams. Production teams seek improvements in costs and quality, saving the company hundreds of thousands of dollars a year. On the basis of their firsthand experience, production workers can identify solutions as simple as adjusting the running speeds for machinery. For example, slowing the speed of the factory's triple extrusion process cut scrap costs in half. Ray Funke, the facility's production manager and a former production worker, credits employee participation and the free flow of information with the company's successes. All of General Cable's employees receive data about production and financial performance so that they can identify problems and see the impact of solutions. Says Funke, "People leave here [at the end of the day] thinking there's something we can improve on."[8]

As at General Cable, employee involvement teams are most likely to succeed if supervisors apply the principles of problem solving (described in Chapter 9) and the guidelines for supervising groups (discussed in Chapter 3). In addition, successful teams typically have the characteristics shown in Figure 2.5. Employee involvement teams must have support from supervisors and higher-level managers, and the participants should have the skills necessary to contribute. To get the group off to a good start, the organization should provide training at the first meeting or meetings. Skills to teach might include problem-solving techniques, approaches to quality improvement, and methods for leading a group discussion and encouraging participation. Finally, employee involvement teams are most successful when all group members are eager to participate. For that reason, it is a good idea to make membership in the team voluntary.

Six Sigma

Six Sigma
A process-oriented quality-control method designed to improve the product or service output to 99.97 percent perfect

Applying the terminology and methods of statistical quality control and the strong commitment of the zero-defects approach, manufacturers and other companies have used a quality-control method they call **Six Sigma.** This is a process-oriented quality-control method designed to reduce errors to 3.4 defects per 1 million *operations*, which can be defined as any unit of work, such as an hour of labor, completion of a circuit board, a sales transaction, or a keystroke. (*Sigma* is a statistical term defining how much variation there is in a product. In the context of quality control, to achieve a level of six sigma, the output of operations would be 99.9997 percent perfect.) Along with the basic goal of reducing variation from the standard to almost nothing, Six Sigma programs typically include a

FIGURE 2.5
Characteristics
of Successful
Employee
Involvement
Teams

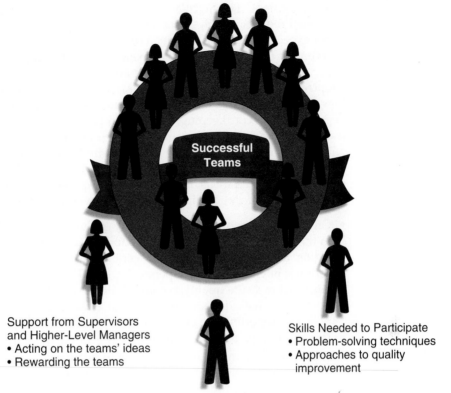

Successful
Teams

Support from Supervisors
and Higher-Level Managers
• Acting on the teams' ideas
• Rewarding the teams

Skills Needed to Participate
• Problem-solving techniques
• Approaches to quality
  improvement

Desire to Participate

rigorous analytical process for anticipating and solving problems to reduce defects, improve the yield of acceptable products, increase customer satisfaction, and deliver best-in-class organizational performance. These improvements, in turn, boost profits.[9]

In the mid-1980s Motorola became the first U.S. company to institute a large-scale Six Sigma program, and the firm now teaches Six Sigma concepts and courses to other organizations. General Electric also offers its customers high-level instruction in Six Sigma methods. GE's first effort, undertaken by GE Medical Systems, brought the quality program to a handful of health care customers and resulted in more than $94 million in benefits.[10] Bank of America has used Six Sigma to cut errors in mortgage applications and credit card services.[11]

Six Sigma is highly structured and emphasizes costs and profits. An organization forms process improvement teams and trains employees to become Black Belts, who act as liaisons with upper management. The Black Belts, who are usually well-regarded and technically competent product or line personnel, help the teams define problems, measure defects, use statistics to analyze the reasons for defects, set priorities, develop and test a plan to solve each problem, and institute ongoing control measures to keep the problem from coming back.

total quality management (TQM)
An organization-wide focus on satisfying customers by continuously improving every business process for delivering goods or services

Total Quality Management

Bringing together aspects of other quality-control techniques, many organizations have embraced the practice of **total quality management (TQM),** an organization-wide focus on satisfying customers by continuously improving every business process for delivering goods or services. Some of the leading users of TQM are

Federal Express, Hewlett-Packard, Motorola, 3M, Westinghouse, and Xerox Business Products and Systems. The objective of TQM is to meet or exceed customer expectations. Thus, it is not a final outcome but an ongoing commitment by everyone in the organization. For example, Weyerhaeuser Company's insurance department, which serves other departments within the forest products firm, adopted TQM principles. In weekly classes, the department's 12 members learned how to work in small teams to evaluate risk management software, improve departmental recordkeeping, and accomplish other departmental goals. The teams plan and evaluate their quality efforts and run brainstorming sessions with outside vendors and internal customers to find ways to improve their services.[12]

Today most companies accept the basic idea of TQM—that everyone in the organization should focus on quality. Three experts who played important roles in spreading this idea are Philip B. Crosby, W. Edwards Deming, and Joseph M. Juran.

- Crosby, known worldwide as a quality expert, pioneered the quality movement in the United States. To achieve product quality, Crosby maintains, the organization must be "injected" with certain ingredients, much as a vaccination serum is intended to keep a person healthy. These ingredients are integrity, systems that measure quality, communications about progress and achievements, operations that educate suppliers and employees in delivering quality, and policies supporting the organization's commitment to quality.
- Deming taught statistical quality control in Japan shortly after World War II and became an important contributor to quality-improvement efforts there for decades before his emphasis on total quality became widely discussed in the United States. Deming emphasizes that to achieve product quality, the organization must continually improve not only the product's design but also the process of producing it.
- Like Deming, Juran taught quality concepts to the Japanese. He emphasizes the view that management should seek to maintain and improve quality through efforts on two levels: the organization as a whole and individual departments in the organization.

A basic strategy for implementing TQM is to use groups, such as employee involvement teams, to identify and solve problems. Another is to review criteria for improving quality (such as the categories for the Baldrige Award, described subsequently) and then seek to meet those criteria. Typically, these efforts address the processes used for delivering goods and services, not just the products themselves.

Because TQM strategies call for the involvement of employees at all levels, the organization needs to educate employees about why quality improvement is needed and how the TQM process will work. Supervisors can help a TQM effort succeed by behaving as if quality is important. Among TQM users, this commonly is called "walking the talk." For example, if everyone is to receive training in quality improvement, supervisors who walk the talk will participate fully in the training sessions, even if they have other urgent matters to which to attend.

Total quality management requires that employees at all levels focus on meeting or exceeding the expectations of their customers. This principle assumes that everyone has a customer to serve. A salesclerk and a nurse can easily identify their "customers," but even the back-office personnel at a manufacturer are delivering services to someone. Satisfying customers requires knowing who they are. They may be the people who buy the company's products; the taxpayers who support the government agency; or the other employees in the organization who use the reports, advice, or other support prepared in a given department. Ritz-Carlton Hotel Co., well known for its focus on quality, sets quality standards based on detailed knowledge of what the customer wants. Customers' expectations are always changing, so Ritz-Carlton's quality process includes performance improvements and daily coaching of employees, including supervisors.[13]

QUALITY STANDARDS

Malcolm Baldrige National Quality Award
An annual award administered by the U.S. Department of Commerce and given to the company that shows the highest quality performance in seven categories

How can supervisors and others in the organization know whether they are satisfying their internal or external customers? How can they tell whether they are using practices likely to foster high quality? To answer such questions, supervisors and other managers set standards using the guidelines for the Baldrige Award, ISO 9000 standards, benchmarking, and a focus on customer value.

The **Malcolm Baldrige National Quality Award** is an annual award administered by the U.S. Commerce Department's National Institute of Standards and Technology (NIST) and given to the organization that shows the highest quality performance as measured by seven categories:[14]

1. Leadership
2. Strategic planning
3. Customer and market focus
4. Information and analysis
5. Human resource focus
6. Process management
7. Business results

All competitors for the award receive feedback that recommends areas for further improvement. Many organizations, whether or not they apply for the award, use the Baldrige evaluation categories as a basis for assessing their own performance. Pat Mene, Ritz-Carlton's vice president of quality, calls the Baldrige Award "the road map for business excellence."[15] The Baldrige programs also have served as the basis for almost 60 international and more than 50 state-sponsored quality awards.

Participation in the Baldrige and other award programs is increasing. Since 1998, more than 850 applications have been submitted for the Baldrige Award, and attendance at the related Quest for Excellence conference is growing. One reason for participating is the effort to improve business performance. Since the mid-1990s, the NIST has compared stock performance of the winners of the Baldrige Award and Standard & Poor's index of 500 U.S. businesses. In most years, the Baldrige winners have outperformed the S&P 500 by as much as 6 to 1.[16]

ISO 9000
A series of standards adopted by the International Organization for Standardization to spell out acceptable criteria for quality systems

Another measure of success in quality management is ISO 9000 certification. **ISO 9000** is a series of standards adopted by the International Organization for Standardization to spell out acceptable criteria for quality systems. To be certified, an organization is visited by independent audit teams; if the auditors determine that the key elements of the standards are in place, they issue a certification of compliance. (Note that they are evaluating quality processes, not product quality.) Organizations seek ISO 9000 certification for a number of reasons. A customer may require it as a condition of doing business, or a nation's government may require it of organizations selling in that nation. As more businesses become certified, those that want to remain competitive will have to be certified as well.

Managers at all levels can evaluate their success in improving quality by comparing their processes and results with those at other departments and organizations. This practice is known popularly as **benchmarking**: identifying, learning, and carrying out the practices of top performers. The term first referred to the practice of comparing the products and processes at one's own company with those that are the best in the world. For example, General Mills observed a NASCAR pit crew to get ideas for speeding up changes in Betty Crocker production lines.[17] Although this might seem like an activity for higher-level managers, supervisors can apply the technique to their own department's operations or even to their own career and management style.

These quality-improvement practices can make the organization effective at whatever it does, yet they may not assess whether employees are doing what customers *want*. For example, an accounting department might use the zero-defects approach so well that it produces a year's worth of reports without a single error. But if the reports do not contain information useful to the recipients, has the department done high-quality work? Recognizing this principle, an increasing number of organizations have concluded that they need to provide a context for their efforts at quality improvement. In other words, quality improvement should be directed at a larger goal: to deliver greater customer value. In this sense, **value** refers to the worth the customer places on what he or she gets (the total package of goods and services) relative to the cost of acquiring it.

Quality improvement directed toward value begins when the organization's employees communicate with customers to determine their needs and wants. Customers may be evaluating a lot more than whether a product adheres to specifications; value may include timely delivery, helpful customer service, low need for maintenance, and information that helps them fully benefit from using the company's services.[18] The information about what customers want defines what the organization should focus on doing.

GUIDELINES FOR QUALITY CONTROL

As with the other responsibilities of supervisors, success in quality control requires more than just picking the right technique. The supervisor needs a general approach that leads everyone involved to support the effort to improve quality. To develop such an approach, the supervisor can start by following the guidelines illustrated in Figure 2.6.

Prevention versus Detection

It is almost always cheaper to prevent problems from occurring than it is to solve them after they happen; designing and building quality into a product is more efficient than trying to improve the product later. Therefore, quality-control programs should not be limited to the detection of defects. Quality control also should include a prevention program to keep defects from occurring. One way to prevent problems is to pay special attention to the production of new goods and services. In a manufacturing setting, the supervisor should see that the first piece of a new product is tested with special care, rather than wait for problems to occur down the line. Also, when prevention efforts show that employees are doing good work, the supervisor should praise their performance. Employees who are confident and satisfied are less likely to allow defects in goods or services.

FIGURE 2.6
Guidelines for
Quality Control

Standard Setting and Enforcement

If employees and others are to support the quality-control effort, they must know exactly what is expected of them. This calls for quality standards. In many cases, the supervisor is responsible for setting quality standards as well as for communicating and enforcing them. These standards should have the characteristics of effective objectives detailed in Chapter 6: They should be written, measurable, clear, specific, and challenging but achievable. Furthermore, those standards should reflect what is important to the client.

Baptist Hospital Inc. (BHI), located in Florida, has clear and specific goals for quality service. They begin with BHI's Standards of Performance, which all employees must read and agree to follow. The standards govern employee attitudes, appearance, service to patients, commitment to co-workers, and other aspects of a hospital worker's job. Employees also are taught what to say in different situations to convey an attitude of helpfulness. For example, if an employee sees a hospital visitor who appears lost, the employee is supposed to say, "May I take you to where you are going?" And BHI tracks a variety of performance measures, including quality of clinical care, medication errors, patient satisfaction, employee morale, and percentage of revenue devoted to caring for poor patients. BHI's performance on these measures exceeds community and national norms.[19]

In communicating standards, a supervisor should make sure employees know why quality is important. Employees should receive specific information about the costs of poor quality and the benefits of excellent quality. For example, if employees know how much it costs to make a component or win a new customer, they can understand the costs of remaking a defective component or alienating a customer. In addition, employees must understand the difference between poor quality and excellent quality. One way to do this is to use examples. In teaching a new employee how to manufacture a part, a supervisor could show a sample of a part that meets specifications and one that does not.

To enforce the standards, a supervisor must participate in inspecting the quality of goods and services that employees produce. This process may entail examining a random sample of parts, accompanying a salesperson on sales calls, or visiting the workplace where employees interact with customers. Quality inspections are a central part of the work of field supervisors in the home construction industry, as described in the "Supervision Across Industries" box. The timing of

SUPERVISION ACROSS INDUSTRIES

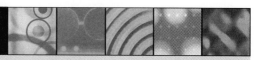

THE CONSTRUCTION INDUSTRY

GRAYSON HOMES

Building a new home requires so many tasks, workers, and materials that field supervisors practically have to be a walking encyclopedia and calendar rolled into one. Most days, the field supervisors for Grayson Homes spend hours at job sites, where they investigate whether each home is on schedule and each task completed according to tough standards. Whenever they see a problem, they have to follow up with the responsible supplier or contractor.

In the past, field supervisors jotted notes about problems on a pad of yellow paper. Later, they returned to their office with their notes and either called each contractor on the phone or two-way radio or sent a fax detailing the problems. Finally, they settled down at a desktop computer to enter the pertinent facts into spreadsheets. Employees had to type reports of the inspections and problem resolutions into a computer database; all that typing meant that the database tended to be weeks out of date. When the supervisors determined that the problems on a list had been resolved, they tore that page from their legal pad and threw it away.

Grayson's management knew that supervisors needed up-to-date information and a simpler way to track all the details. So, the company invested in a system giving every supervisor a BlackBerry handheld computer with software for quality management, e-mail, calendar, and Internet searches. The device also makes phone calls. Supervisors now leave their legal pads and binders in the office and travel to job sites with just the BlackBerry. When they spot a defect, they select the relevant information from lists and menus and enter the details into the BlackBerry, which sends updates to the database in a central computer. At the end of the day, the supervisor prints a report of houses under construction and unresolved problems. During the next workday, the supervisor investigates whether each problem on the report has been resolved.

The system also sorts the problems by contractor and sends each contractor a list of problems that are outstanding. The database matches information from a job site with details such as lot numbers, product numbers, and even architectural drawings to be sent to the relevant contractor. Supervisors also can generate reports that tell them which types of defects are most frequent, which phases of construction experience the most problems, and what experience Grayson has had with each of its contractors. The reports help them prevent and resolve issues without relying on memory and anecdotes.

This information technology, coupled with training and rewards, has helped Grayson Homes deliver an extremely high level of customer satisfaction. According to customer surveys, 96 percent of Grayson's customers say they would choose Grayson again when buying a home or would refer Grayson to a friend shopping for a home. The company also recently won the industry's coveted National Housing Quality Gold Award.

Sources: Grayson Homes Web site, www.graysonhomes .com/news/, accessed July 3, 2006; ATSG, "Case Study: Wireless Technology Drives Superior Quality Control for U.S. Homebuilder," ATSG Web site, www.atsgi.com, accessed June 14, 2006; Mark Ward Sr., "Technology on the Job Site," Steve Zurier, "Berry Happy," *Builder,* September 1, 2005, www.builderonline.com; NAHB Research Center, "Local Home Builder Receives National Recognition for Quality Achievements," news release, September 23, 2004, www.nahbrc.org.

these inspections should be unpredictable enough that employees cannot adjust their performance because the supervisor will be checking up on them that day. When an inspection uncovers a quality problem, the supervisor should inform the responsible employees immediately. Then they should begin solving the problem. The appropriate response may include apologizing to customers as well as fixing a problem within the organization. Demanding a quick response demonstrates the importance of quality. For the enforcement of standards to be effective, the employees must know that management is serious about quality. A catchy slogan posted on bulletin boards, inscribed on buttons, or taped to cash registers is meaningless unless supervisors and other managers pay attention to these principles, reward employees for following them, and live up to them themselves.

THE PRODUCTIVITY CHALLENGE

Stiff competition from around the world is forcing U.S. businesses to pay attention to productivity. In addition, citizens' opposition to paying higher taxes is forcing governments to make their operations more productive. To help improve productivity, supervisors must understand why it is important and what limits an organization's productivity.

Trends in Productivity in the United States

When the productivity of organizations in a country is improving, people benefit. They can get goods and services at lower prices or with lower taxes than they otherwise could. Employers tend to pay higher wages and salaries to workers who are more productive. People also have access to more and better goods and services. Because of these benefits, statisticians track productivity trends in various countries.

The amount of goods and services produced by the average U.S. worker remains higher than that for most other industrialized nations. In 2000, the average output per hour in the manufacturing sector, measured against the index year 1992, was 142.8 percent for the United States and 134.1 percent for Japan. Hourly manufacturing output closely trailed that of the United States in France (141.1) and exceeded it in Sweden (150.4). As Figure 2.7 shows, manufacturing output per hour in the United States has been rising over the last two decades. The earnings of manufacturing workers have grown along with their output. Businesses pay more for more productive workers, so unit labor costs (compensation divided by output) have stayed near the index year throughout most of the period.[20]

Constraints on Productivity

When you read about ways to improve productivity, keep in mind that several constraints limit the impact of a supervisor or even a higher-level manager.

FIGURE 2.7

Productivity in the United States: Manufacturing Workers

Source: Data from U.S. Department of Labor, Bureau of Labor Statistics, "Major Sector Productivity and Costs Index," accessed July 3, 2006, http://data.bls.gov.

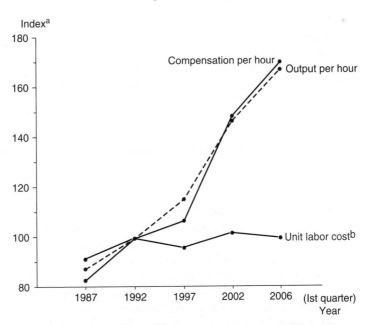

[a]To track productivity, the Bureau of Labor Statistics measures percentage changes in output and compensation from one quarter to the next. The index compares the current quarter with 1992 (which is an index of 100). For example, an index of 50 would be half the 1992 level, and an index of 200 would be twice the 1992 level.
[b]Compensation per hour divided by output per hour.

Supervisors and other managers should be aware of these constraints so that they can either plan ways to overcome them or set realistic goals within them. Some of the most important constraints on productivity are management limitations, employee attitudes and skills, government regulations, and union rules.

Management Limitations

Operative employees will contribute to improve productivity only if they believe management is truly committed to this objective. Too often, however, employees believe management is more interested in the next quarter's profits than in producing high-quality goods or services as efficiently as possible. Employees become frustrated, especially when managers seem to ignore their ideas.

The most important way supervisors can overcome this constraint is to set a good example. Supervisors should demonstrate by their actions and words that they are interested in the department's productivity. This behavior includes seeing that the job is done right the first time, as well as using resources wisely, which, on a personal level, includes being well organized. Supervisors also must communicate instructions clearly and plan carefully so that employees are able to live up to managers' expectations. Furthermore, supervisors should listen to employees' concerns and ideas about improving productivity. If the organization has a formal program for submitting ideas, supervisors can offer to help employees write down or explain their suggestions. In organizations that allow or expect employee participation in planning and decision making, supervisors should encourage this participation.

Employee Attitudes and Skills

Improving productivity requires changes. People have a natural tendency to resist change because it is challenging and often frightening (see Chapter 14). Employees who fear or resent productivity improvements will not be motivated to make the changes work. Part of a supervisor's job is to identify employee attitudes and, when necessary, help employees take a more positive view. (The last section of this chapter addresses this issue in greater detail.)

Employees' skills also influence how effective productivity-building efforts will be. When an organization wants each member to contribute more, each member must either work faster or do the job differently. Some employees can perform new tasks or do their jobs in a new way with little or no training. Other employees understand only one way of working. When employees want to change but don't know how, supervisors can overcome this constraint by providing more training. When employees are unwilling or unable to learn, this constraint is more difficult to overcome.

Attitudes and skills may require improvement when productivity suffers as a result of *culture shock*—the set of physical and emotional discomforts people tend to experience when they move from one cultural environment to another. Until they adapt, people undergoing culture shock may swing among high enthusiasm, hostility, and confusion.[21] Immigrant employees, supervisors of people from another culture, and employees whose cultures differ from that of most of their co-workers find that others do not respond to their behaviors in an expected manner. In addition, employees in a strange culture do not know how they are expected to behave and do not receive the credit they expect for their achievements, skills, and ideas. Common responses include depression, loneliness, aggression, short attention span, frustration, passivity, and quickness to fatigue. To help prevent or correct the consequences of culture shock, the basic solution is more exposure to a variety of people. The more that people are exposed to diversity and the more they learn about it, the more comfortable they will be. Supervisors and their employees may benefit from formal training in this area. It is also helpful to be open and honest about the problem. Discussing feelings helps diffuse culture shock and leads people to a better understanding of one another.

Government Regulations

Businesses and other organizations in the United States are regulated in many areas, including payment of overtime wages, disability compensation, environmental pollution, building codes, minimum safety standards, and child labor. Following these regulations costs money, but the laws reflect the values of the majority in our society. For example, it might be cheaper to hire children to assemble electronic components, but few people want to return to the days of children laboring long hours within factory walls. Likewise, scrubbers on power-company smokestacks cost money, but clean air to breathe is essential. Even when government regulations seem illogical or unreasonable, an organization can face serious penalties for ignoring or disobeying them. Thus, the proper role of supervisors and other managers is to know these regulations and seek ways to improve productivity without violating the law.

Union Rules

Union contracts typically specify rules for what tasks particular employees may do, what hours they may work, and how organizations may use them. Sometimes an organization's managers see a way to improve productivity that violates one of these rules. For example, it might be more efficient to have two employees learn each other's jobs so that they can get the work done even when one of them is away or busy. However, the union contract might contain a rule against this.

When employers and unions collaborate on a solution, they can overcome such constraints, although the process usually takes time. If an organization explains how everyone will benefit from the changes, the union may agree to revise the contract, especially if the alternative is employee layoffs. Even though a supervisor can propose changes, it is not part of a supervisor's job to remove these constraints. Supervisors must do their best to get work done as efficiently as possible under the existing work rules.

MEASURING PRODUCTIVITY

The basic way to measure productivity is to divide outputs by inputs (see Figure 2.1). In other words, productivity is the amount of output produced with the inputs used. Table 2.3 provides examples of inputs and outputs for several types of organizations. The productivity equation can compare the output and input for an individual, a department, an organization, or even an entire country's paid workforce. The remaining discussion focuses on the direct concern of supervisors with the productivity of their department and their individual employees.

By applying basic arithmetic to the formula for productivity, the supervisor can see what has to change for productivity to increase. The right side of the equation is a fraction. Remember that when the top (numerator) of a fraction gets bigger, the number becomes greater. When the bottom (denominator) of a fraction gets bigger, the number becomes smaller. For example, $3/2$ is greater than $1/2$, and $1/5$ is less than $1/3$. To increase productivity, a supervisor needs to increase outputs, reduce

TABLE 2.3
Examples of Inputs and Outputs

Source: Adapted from Samuel C. Certo, *Modern Management*, 6th ed., Allyn & Bacon, 1994.

Organization	Inputs	Outputs
Bus line	Buses; gas, oil, and other supplies; terminals; drivers; ticket sellers; managers; tickets; schedules; funds; data	Transportation services to passengers
Manufacturing firm	Trucks; plants; oil, rags, and other supplies; raw materials; purchased parts; production workers; supervisors; engineers; storekeepers; bills of material; inventory records; production schedules; time records; funds; data	Goods for use by customers
Hospital	Ambulances; hospital rooms; beds, wheelchairs, X-rays; receptionists; administrators; nurses; doctors; medicines; drugs; splints, bandages, food, and other supplies; medical charts; funds; data	Health care services to patients
Police force	Cars and vans; offices; police officers; forms; handcuffs, radios, guns, office supplies, and other supplies; office furniture; equipment for forensic research; uniforms; funds; data	Protection of public safety

inputs, or both. Consider an employee who processes 96 driver's license applications in an eight-hour day at the secretary of state's office. One way to measure this employee's productivity is 96/8, or 12 applications per hour (see Figure 2.8). A supervisor might note that a more experienced employee can process 20 applications per hour, so by this measure, the first employee is less desirable and might require more training, better motivation, or just more experience.

FIGURE 2.8   **Productivity Measurement**

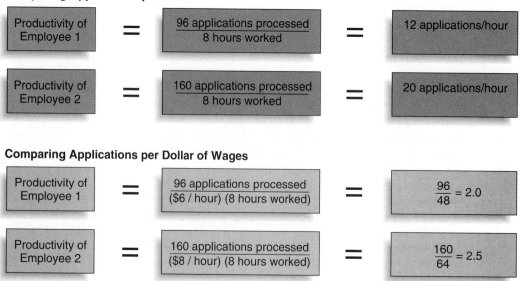

Comparing Applications per Hour

| Productivity of Employee 1 | = | 96 applications processed / 8 hours worked | = | 12 applications/hour |

| Productivity of Employee 2 | = | 160 applications processed / 8 hours worked | = | 20 applications/hour |

Comparing Applications per Dollar of Wages

Productivity of Employee 1 $= \dfrac{96 \text{ applications processed}}{(\$6\,/\,\text{hour})\,(8\text{ hours worked})} = \dfrac{96}{48} = 2.0$

Productivity of Employee 2 $= \dfrac{160 \text{ applications processed}}{(\$8\,/\,\text{hour})\,(8\text{ hours worked})} = \dfrac{160}{64} = 2.5$

But the organization is also interested in the cost of the employee. So the supervisor might measure the input as the employee's cost per day (hourly wage times number of hours). If the employee earned $6 per hour, the productivity measure would be 96/($6 × 8), or 2 (see Figure 2.8). If the employee who processes 20 applications per hour earns $8 per hour, that employee's productivity would be 160/($8 × 8), or 2.5. Thus, the more experienced employee is more productive, even considering the higher wage rate.

In this example, high productivity offsets the high cost of labor, but in practice, some companies have difficulty competing because productivity gains lag behind rising compensation. General Motors has struggled to compete with other automakers because its compensation is relatively high, especially when including the cost of employee benefits. At GM's facility in Arlington, Texas, workers earn hourly wages ranging between $26.50 and $30.50; benefits bring the total compensation above $80 an hour. In San Antonio, Texas, Toyota operates a facility where workers earn between $15.50 and $25.00 per hour, with benefits bringing the total hourly compensation to $35. (GM's costs include large payouts for benefits to retirees.) GM's Arlington employees have made great strides in productivity; among factories assembling large SUVs, Arlington assembles each vehicle with the fewest labor hours. However, the labor cost is so much higher than Toyota's that even working faster, GM's employees cost about $1,800 per vehicle, compared with $800 per vehicle at Toyota's San Antonio facility.[22] Cost differences such as these help explain why some U.S. manufacturers have lost sales to foreign-owned companies.

The output measured in the productivity formula is only goods and services of acceptable quality. A rude salesclerk and a production worker making defective components are not really productive. In these cases, the productivity formula would include only the number of correctly made components or the amount of sales made courteously and accurately. The production worker in the cartoon shown in Figure 2.9 has evidently missed this point.

FIGURE 2.9
Quantity without Quality Does Not Boost Productivity

Source: From *Front Line Supervisor's Bulletin,* July 10, 1992. Reprinted with permission of Bureau of Business Practice, 125 Eugene O'Neill Drive, Suite 103, New London, CT 06320.

"I don't get it! I turn out a record 370 units, and I don't even get a lousy 'thank you!'"

IMPROVING PRODUCTIVITY

When supervisors and other managers look for ways to boost productivity, they often start by looking at their costs per unit of output. Productivity improves when the department or organization can do as much work at a lower cost and when output rises without a cost increase. Another way to improve productivity is to improve process quality so that employees work more efficiently and do not have to spend time correcting mistakes or defects. Mistakes, errors, and rework are a drag on productivity. Poor quality can slow the output of both individuals and the firm as a whole. For that reason, one of the supervisor's most important tasks is to think of and implement ways to get the job done right the first time.

Many of the quality-control strategies introduced in this chapter, such as Six Sigma, zero defects, and employee involvement, apply to productivity improvement. For example, 3M Corporation uses Six Sigma as its primary method for improving process and product quality. Beginning with processes in its factories and then turning to the efficiency of other processes, such as finance and customer service, 3M has been using Six Sigma and other programs to cut about $300 million from its costs each year.[23]

Because of their direct contact with employees, supervisors play an important part in most of these initiatives. Supervisors can increase their own and their team's or group's productivity by understanding the goals of quality programs and their own role in achieving those goals. Through leadership and motivation, they can help employees contribute to quality goals. Finally, they can use their specific knowledge of the tasks and processes their teams perform to find unique ways to contribute to productivity.

To lower costs, supervisors can use a number of strategies. (See the basic alternatives summarized in Figure 2.10.) These strategies are not mutually exclusive. Supervisors can get the greatest productivity by using as many of these strategies as will work. In deciding which strategies to use, supervisors should consider which will appeal to higher-level management, which will be acceptable to employees, and which involve areas within their control.

An important part of many of these strategies is encouraging and using employees' ideas for saving money. Operating the machines, preparing the reports, and serving clients or customers gives employees a close-up view of how things are done, enabling them to see the shortcomings of the organization's way of doing things. For instance, Bic Corporation, the maker of pens, razors, and

FIGURE 2.10 Cost-Control Strategies

Use budgets.
Increase output.
Improve methods.
Reduce overhead.
Minimize waste.
Regulate or level work flow.
Install modern equipment.
Train and motivate employees.
Minimize tardiness, absenteeism, turnover.

cigarette lighters, has a standing team of 15 production-line employees who meet once a week to review suggestions from the plant's suggestion boxes. Supervisors have 10 days to implement suggestions that the group approves, and Bic credits the program with increasing morale, productivity, and ultimately profits.[24]

Use Budgets

Not surprisingly, before a supervisor can make intelligent decisions about how to trim costs, he or she has to know where the money is going. The most important source of such information is budget reports, described in Chapter 6. By reviewing budget reports regularly, a supervisor can see which categories of expenses are largest and identify where the department is spending more than it budgeted. Then a supervisor should spend time with workers, observing how they use the department's resources, including their time. The process of gathering information about costs and working with employees to identify needed improvements is part of a supervisor's control function.

Increase Output

Remember that the numerator in the productivity equation (output/input) represents what the department or organization is producing. The greater the output at a given cost, the greater the productivity. Thus, a logical way to increase productivity is to increase output without boosting costs.

Sometimes, by applying themselves, people can work faster or harder. Servers in a restaurant may find they can cover more tables, and factory production workers may find they can assemble more components. Of course, it is not always possible to increase output without sacrificing quality. Also, this method of improving productivity often makes employees unhappy. A supervisor who wants to boost productivity by increasing output must first ensure that the new output goals are reasonable, perhaps by including employees in the decision-making process. A supervisor must also communicate the new goals carefully, emphasizing any positive aspects of the change. For example, a supervisor might mention that if employees are more productive, the organization has a chance to remain competitive without layoffs. In the end, improving productivity by increasing output works only when employees are motivated to do more (see Chapter 11).

Some companies use technology to ensure productivity. Software programs that monitor e-mail and Internet usage have many uses, including applications that identify computer use that is not work related or that violates company rules. Electronic monitoring can also provide basic productivity measures such as how long order takers spend processing each customer order. The American Management Association reports that 76 percent of employers use some form of electronic monitoring, and one-fourth of companies have fired an employee for misuse of the Internet.[25] (See "Supervision and Ethics" for a discussion of issues related to electronic monitoring.)

Improve Methods

There are only limited ways of doing the same thing better or faster. Reviewing and revamping the way things are done is the basic principle of *reengineering*. Process control techniques for improving quality also can improve productivity. Kato Engineering, located in Mankato, Minnesota, used a process called *kaizen*, in which teams map the details of each work process, looking for ways to eliminate waste. The manufacturing company improved productivity in office procedures as well as factory operations. Now Kato answers requests for quotes in one-sixth the original time and processes order changes in 2 hours instead of 24.[26]

SUPERVISION AND ETHICS

DOES ELECTRONIC MONITORING INVADE EMPLOYEES' PRIVACY?

A midsize manufacturing company recently decided to begin monitoring employees' use of the Internet, with the goal of making sure employees visit only Web sites that are related to their work. Employees complained to their supervisor that the monitoring amounted to spying or treating them like children. The supervisor was at a loss as to how to raise employees' morale. Some logical arguments might be that monitoring makes the workplace fairer to conscientious employees. Knowing which employees are planning vacations or chatting with friends online helps the company reward employees who refrain from goofing off. Likewise, monitoring extends the same controls to salespeople and office workers that companies tend to exert on employees who are easier to monitor—notably, the production workers.

Companies justify electronic monitoring on the grounds that it helps them catch behavior that reduces productivity and even may expose the company to liability for misdeeds. In a survey by *Sales & Marketing Management* magazine, over half the companies that checked on salespeople's electronic behavior said they found some sales reps were wasting significant amounts of time on personal matters. An Internet business once used monitoring to discover that a disloyal sales employee was leaking information to a friend at a competing company. And when Dow Chemical used electronic monitoring to investigate an employee complaint, it learned that hundreds of employees were using their computers to store and send material with sexual and violent content.

Electronic monitoring also can capture good performance. For example, software can analyze phone calls to customer service, searching for particular words or tones of voice. Such software can identify which salespeople were able to defuse anger fastest or how many callers said, "Cancel my order." This information provides companies with information about the customer experience as well as employees' performance.

The ethical and practical downside of electronic monitoring is that employees may feel insulted by it, and they may believe the company is invading their privacy. But given the increasing usefulness of this technology, today's supervisors must be able to sell its advantages.

Sources: "Ask Annie: Does Big Brother Software Treat Staff Like Kids?" *Fortune,* March 8, 2004, downloaded from Infotrac, http://web3.infotrac.galegroup.com; Erin Strout, "Spy Games," *Sales & Marketing Management,* February 2002, downloaded from Infotrac, http://web3.infotrac.galegroup.com; Chuck Salter, "'This Call Is Being Recorded for . . . ' More than You Think," *Fast Company,* January 2004, downloaded from Infotrac, http://web7.infotrac.galegroup.com.

A potentially powerful approach to improving methods is to give employees more control over the way they work. Much of the growth in productivity in the 1990s came from efforts such as getting production ideas from nonmanagement employees and linking rewards to high performance.[27] Similarly, designing jobs to include variety and responsibility makes the jobs more interesting, which should motivate employees to deliver higher quality as well as work harder.

Like managers at all levels, supervisors should be constantly on the lookout for ways to improve methods. Some ideas will come from supervisors themselves. (Chapter 9 provides suggestions for creative thinking.) Employees often have excellent ideas for doing the work better because they see the problems and pitfalls of their jobs. Supervisors should keep communication channels open and actively ask for ideas.

overhead

Expenses not related directly to producing goods and services; examples are rent, utilities, and staff support

Reduce Overhead

Many departments spend more than is necessary for **overhead,** which includes rent, utilities, staff support, company cafeteria, janitorial services, and other expenses not related directly to producing goods and services. Typically, an organization allocates a share of the total overhead to each department based on the department's size. This means that a supervisor has limited control over a department's overhead expenses. However, a supervisor can periodically look for sources of needless expenses, such as lights left on in unoccupied areas or messy work areas that mean extra work for the janitorial staff. By reducing these costs to the company, a supervisor ultimately reduces the amount of overhead charged to his or her department.

Staff departments in particular can be guilty of contributing too much to the cost of overhead by generating unnecessary paperwork. Supervisors and their employees who produce or handle reports and forms should evaluate this paperwork, whether hard copy or electronic, to make sure it is needed. Another way to reduce the amount of paper is to make sure that when a procedure calls for a form with several parts, all the parts are actually used.

Minimize Waste

Waste occurs in all kinds of operations. A medical office may order too many supplies and wind up throwing some away or taking up unnecessary storage space. A factory may handle materials in a way that produces a lot of scrap. A sales office may make unnecessary photocopies of needlessly long proposals, contributing more to landfills than to the company's profits.

idle time, or downtime
Time during which employees or machines are not producing goods or services

A costly form of waste is **idle time,** or **downtime**—time during which employees or machines are not producing goods or services. This term is used most often in manufacturing operations, but it applies to other situations as well. In a factory, idle time occurs while a machine is shut down for repairs or workers are waiting for parts. In an office, idle time occurs when employees are waiting for instructions, supplies, a computer printout, or a response to a question they asked the supervisor. In both settings, idle time may occur because jobs and work processes are poorly designed. Productivity consultant Edgar Burnett visited a factory that assigned six operators to six machines. Their work involved periodically monitoring the machine's output and feeding in materials about every 40 minutes. Burnett quickly determined that one operator could run two machines without difficulty. Similarly, Burnett observed a receptionist who spent less than three hours a day on tasks related to receiving visitors. The company solved the problem of the receptionist's idle time by training her to perform clerical tasks as well.[28]

detour behavior
Tactics for postponing or avoiding work

Another form of wasted time results from **detour behavior,** which is a tactic for postponing or avoiding work. Employees and their supervisors use a wide variety of detour behavior: A supervisor enjoys a cup of coffee and the newspaper before turning to the day's responsibilities or an employee stops by a colleague's desk to chat. Detour behavior may be especially tempting when a person's energy is low or a person is facing a particularly challenging or unpleasant assignment. (The opposite of detour behavior is effective time management, discussed in Chapter 13.)

Wasted time may be an even more important measure of lost productivity than wasted costs. For office employees, a major cause of wasted time is spam—messages that are unrelated to work, unwanted, and often distasteful or fraudulent. Organizations are countering the problem with filtering software that searches messages and attachments for viruses and worms, inappropriate content, and other signals that a message is likely to be spam. They also are training employees to be more wary about opening e-mail attachments from unknown senders.

Supervisors should be on the alert for wasted time and other resources in their department. They can set a good example for effective time management and make detecting waste part of the control process (see Chapter 6). Often, employees are good sources of information on how to minimize waste. The supervisor might consider holding a contest to find the best ideas.

FIGURE 2.11
The Costs of
Uneven Work Flow

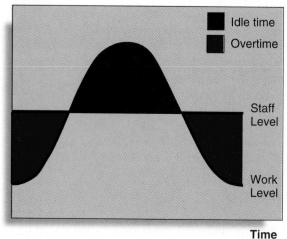

Dollars

- Idle time
- Overtime

Staff Level

Work Level

Time

Regulate or Level the Work Flow

An uneven flow of work can be costly (see Figure 2.11). When work levels are low, the result is idle time. When the department faces a surge in demand for its work, employees have to work extra hours to keep up. As a result, the department may have to pay workers overtime rates—one and a half or two times normal wages—during peak periods. In addition, people get tired, so they are rarely as efficient during overtime hours as they are during a normal workday. If a supervisor can arrange to have a more even work flow, the department can be staffed appropriately to get the job done during normal working hours, and fewer employees will be idle during slow periods.

A supervisor can take several steps to regulate departmental work flow:

1. A supervisor should first make sure that adequate planning has been done for the work required.

2. A supervisor may also find it helpful to work with his or her manager and peers or form teams of employees to examine and solve work-flow problems. Cooperation can help make the work flow more evenly or at least more predictably. For example, a manager who travels extensively may assign a great deal of work upon her return, not realizing that she is clustering deadlines instead of spreading them out for an even work flow. The sales department may be submitting orders in batches to the production department instead of submitting them as soon as they are received.

3. If the work flow must remain uneven, a supervisor may find that the best course is to use temporary employees during peak periods, an approach that can work if the temporary employees have the right skills.

Install Modern Equipment

Work may be slowed because employees are using worn or outdated equipment. If that is the case, a supervisor may find it worthwhile to obtain modern equipment. Although the value of installing modern equipment is obvious for manufacturing departments, many other workplaces can benefit from using modern equipment, including up-to-date computer technology. Today, automated teller machines (ATMs) do work once performed by tellers, and kiosks in airports process routine tasks of ticket agents such as printing out tickets and handling seat assignments.

FIGURE 2.12
Basic Formulas for Evaluating an Investment

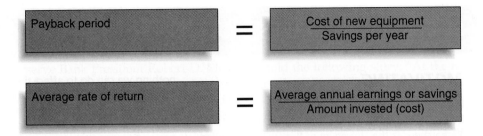

$$\text{Payback period} = \frac{\text{Cost of new equipment}}{\text{Savings per year}}$$

$$\text{Average rate of return} = \frac{\text{Average annual earnings or savings}}{\text{Amount invested (cost)}}$$

Dozens of McDonald's restaurants have installed computer terminals where customers can place orders and pay by credit card. This equipment automates work performed by humans, but it does not necessarily replace human workers. Banks, for example, have actually hired more tellers in the years since ATMs became popular; the tellers now handle nonroutine problems. McDonald's franchisees that installed kiosks were surprised to find that they needed to increase their staff. Customers liked being able to control the ordering process, and they liked skipping the usual lines at lunchtime, so outlets with kiosks began selling more than they could handle with their existing staff.[29]

In deciding to buy new equipment or recommending its purchase, a supervisor needs to determine whether the expense will be worthwhile. One way to do this is to figure out how much money per year the new equipment will save in terms of, for example, lower repair costs, less downtime, and more goods produced. Then compute the number of years before the savings will offset the cost of buying the equipment, a time known as the **payback period.** A payback period is computed according to the first formula shown in Figure 2.12. Thus, if a computer system will cost $120,000 and is expected to save the office $40,000 per year, the payback period is three years ($120,000/$40,000 per year). Higher-level management or the finance department usually has an opinion on what payback period is acceptable for the organization.

Another way to evaluate whether an investment is worthwhile is to find its **average rate of return (ARR).** The ARR is a percentage that represents the organization's average annual earnings for each dollar of a given investment. An ARR of 15 percent means that each dollar invested yields income (or savings) of 15 cents a year. A basic formula for ARR is the second equation in Figure 2.12. For the computer system in the previous example, the ARR would be the $40,000 annual savings divided by the $120,000 cost, or 0.33—a 33 percent return. To determine whether this return is acceptable, a supervisor compares it with what the money spent could earn in another form of investment. Again, higher-level management or the finance department usually has established standards for this measure.

Payback period and ARR, as described here, are only two simple ways to evaluate investments. Other, more complex methods consider factors such as the timing of payments and earnings. Software is available to compute payback periods, ARR, and other analyses of the financial worthiness of an investment.

payback period
The length of time it will take for the benefits generated by an investment (such as cost savings from machinery) to offset the cost of the investment

average rate of return (ARR)
A percentage that represents the average annual earnings for each dollar of a given investment

Train and Motivate Employees

To work efficiently, employees need a good understanding of how to do their jobs. Thus, a basic way to improve productivity is to train employees. As you will see in Chapter 11, training alone does not lead to superior performance; employees also must be motivated to do good work. In other words, employees must want to do a good job. Motivation is a key tactic for improving productivity because employees carry out most changes and are often in the best position to think of ways to achieve their objectives more efficiently (see "Supervisory Skills: Motivating").

SKILLS MODULE

PART ONE: CONCEPTS

Summary

2.1 Describe the consequences suffered by organizations as a result of poor quality work.

Poor quality work gives an organization a negative image, which drives away customers and makes it harder to recruit superior employees and borrow money. Poor quality work also can lead to higher costs associated with attracting customers, inspecting for and correcting defects, replacing defective products, and defending against lawsuits.

2.2 Compare product quality control and process control.

Both types of quality control involve preventing and detecting quality-related problems. Product quality control focuses on ways to improve the product. Process control focuses on how to do things in a way that results in higher quality.

2.3 Summarize techniques for quality control.

Statistical quality control involves looking for defects in parts or finished products selected through a sampling technique. In statistical process control, the operator takes samples during the process, plots the results on a chart, and makes corrections when the chart indicates the process is out of control. The zero-defects approach holds that everyone in the organization should work toward the goal of delivering such high quality that all aspects of the organization's goods and services are free of problems. Employee involvement teams plan ways to improve quality in their areas of the organization. In periodic meetings, team members examine needs for improvement and develop solutions. Six Sigma is a structured approach in which teams define problems in work processes and identify solutions that bring defects down to 3.4 per million. Total quality management is an organization-wide focus on satisfying customers by continuously improving every business process involved in delivering goods or services. Thus, TQM is a continuous process that unfolds gradually and focuses on satisfying customers.

2.4 Identify ways organizations measure their success in continuous quality improvement.

Organizations compare their practices and performance with various sets of guidelines. They may compete for the Malcolm Baldrige National Quality Award or assess their performance using its evaluation categories. They may seek certification for meeting the standards of ISO 9000. Also, they may compare their performance with that of organizations that excel in particular areas—a practice known as benchmarking. To ensure that any of these methods are focused on the right measures, the organization can set performance standards in terms of customer value. Focusing on preventing quality problems is cheaper than detecting them. Supervisors and other managers should set, communicate, and enforce standards for quality control. The organization should insist on high quality from its suppliers inside and outside the organization. Supervisors and higher-level managers should provide valued rewards for high-quality work.

2.5 Identify constraints on productivity.

Productivity is the amount of results (output) an organization gets for a given amount of inputs such as labor and machinery. Management limits productivity when it does not seem truly committed to improving it. Employee attitudes and skills limit productivity when employees are unable or unwilling to meet standards for performance. Government regulations impose responsibilities on organizations that limit their productivity to achieve other objectives. A union contract may contain work rules that limit productivity.

2.6 Describe how productivity and productivity improvements are measured.
To measure productivity, divide the amount of outputs by the amount of inputs. Outputs are the amount of work done or goods and services produced, assuming that these are of acceptable quality. Inputs may be measured as dollars, hours, or both. Productivity increases when output increases, input decreases, or both.

2.7 Identify ways productivity may be improved.
Two ways to improve productivity are to control quality and to control costs. Controlling quality involves minimizing defects or errors. Controlling costs involves producing the same amount of goods or services at a lower cost or producing more at the same cost. A supervisor may increase output by having people or machines work faster or harder. A more effective approach may be to improve methods, that is, to get things done more efficiently. The supervisor may identify ways to reduce overhead and minimize waste, including idle time and wasted physical resources. Regulating or leveling the work flow can make staffing more efficient. Installing modern equipment reduces costs when the new equipment is more efficient. To cut costs related to personnel, a supervisor should see that workers receive adequate training and motivation, and he or she should take steps to minimize tardiness, absenteeism, and turnover.

2.8 Explain why employees have fears about productivity improvement and how supervisors can address those fears.
Many employees are fearful of productivity improvements because many organizations make such changes through layoffs and extra work for the remaining employees. Supervisors can respond by keeping employees informed about the organization's plans, emphasizing the benefits, and listening to employees.

Key Terms

productivity, *p.* 31
quality control, *p.* 33
product quality control, *p.* 34
process control, *p.* 34
statistical quality control, *p.* 35
statistical process control (SPC), *p.* 36
zero-defects approach, *p.* 37

employee involvement teams, *p.* 37
Six Sigma, *p.* 38
total quality management (TQM), *p.* 39
Malcolm Baldrige National Quality Award, *p.* 41
ISO 9000, *p.* 41
benchmarking, *p.* 42

value, *p.* 42
overhead, *p.* 52
idle time/ downtime, *p.* 53
detour behavior, *p.* 53
payback period, *p.* 55
average rate of return (ARR), *p.* 55
turnover, *p.* 56

Review and Discussion Questions

1. Brand X Corporation seeks to be the lowest-cost maker of lawn chairs and toboggans. To keep costs down, management tells the production department, "Keep that assembly line moving. We have an inspector on staff to catch the mistakes later." What are the consequences Brand X Corporation is likely to experience as a result of this approach to manufacturing?

2. What is the difference between product quality control and process control? Give an example of each. (If possible, use examples from a job you have held.)

3. Define the zero-defects approach to quality control. Do you think zero defects is attainable? Why or why not?

4. Michelle LeVerrier supervises a group of tellers at a bank located in a city. The bank manager has asked her to lead an employee involvement team designed to

improve the processes of serving individual customers at the teller windows. The four steps the team must take are to (*a*) identify quality problems in the specific area of responsibility, (*b*) select one problem to focus on, (*c*) analyze the problem, and (*d*) identify solutions and select one to present to management. How might Michelle use this four-step procedure to conduct her first team meeting?

5. What is total quality management (TQM)?

6. Imagine that you are the supervisor responsible for a pharmacy. You have received a few complaints about mistakes in customers' prescriptions. To improve the quality of service delivered by the pharmacists, you can concentrate on (*a*) doing a better job of catching errors in the future or (*b*) doing a better job of avoiding errors. Which approach would you choose? Explain.

7. Frank Ouellette works at a government agency in which neither managers nor employees seem to worry about how long it takes to complete an assignment. Should Frank's co-workers be concerned about productivity? Why or why not?

8. Anna Holt, a supervisor in a boot manufacturing plant, just received a memo from her manager informing her that productivity on her shift must increase by 10 percent during the next fiscal quarter. However, when she recently approached her manager about upgrading two of the machines, she was turned down. In addition, she knows that her employees' union will balk at an increase in the number of boots her group must produce in a given shift. What constraints on productivity does Anna face? How might she attempt to resolve them?

9. At the claims-processing office for All-Folks Insurance, 25 employees process 2,500 claims a day. The claims-processing office for Purple Cross Insurance uses a state-of-the-art computer system, and its 15 employees process 3,000 claims a day.

   a. Which office is more productive?

   b. At which office would you expect employees to be paid more? Why?

   c. Suppose that half the claims processed by the employees at Purple Cross contain errors and all of the claims processed at All-Folks are done correctly. Which office would you say is more productive? Why?

10. Where can supervisors get information to help them determine costs?

11. How would you expect employees to respond to each of these efforts to cut costs?

    a. A plan to increase output by scheduling fewer rest breaks.

    b. A plan to increase output by hiring someone to bring supplies to laboratory workers, rather than having them get their own supplies.

12. Rachel Roth supervises a shift of workers who manufacture ski clothing. Because of its seasonal nature, the work flow tends to be uneven, and Rachel feels that this hurts productivity. What steps might Rachel take to try to regulate the work flow in her department?

13. A maintenance supervisor learned that installing a type of high-efficiency light bulb in the building can save the organization $1,000 a year. Replacing the current system with the new one would cost about $2,500.

    a. What is the payback period for this system?

    b. What is the average rate of return?

    c. Do you think this is a worthwhile investment? Why or why not?

14. How does high turnover hurt productivity? What can a supervisor do to minimize turnover?

15. Why do employees sometimes resist productivity improvements? How can supervisors prepare for and respond to employee attitudes?

PART TWO: SKILL-BUILDING

YOU SOLVE THE PROBLEM

Reflecting back on page 31, discuss how it might have felt to be a supervisor at Hayward's Nashville facility when management set up teams to improve quality and productivity. If you were a supervisor, would you have resented or welcomed the emphasis on getting ideas from employees? Why? Then, working as a group, summarize three ways in which a Hayward supervisor could have supported the company's efforts to improve the productivity and quality of its work processes. For ideas, review the management functions and skills introduced in Chapter 1.

Problem-Solving Case: *Fast Food Is All about Service*

David Drickhamer, editorial research director for *Industry Week* magazine, tells about a recent stop he made to buy lunch for his hungry child. They were running errands, so Drickhamer pulled into the drive-through lane of a fast-food restaurant.

The customer experience began when Drickhamer pulled up to the ordering station and heard a recorded message urging him to try the chain's new chicken sandwich. He ordered a child's meal featuring chicken pieces and a dipping sauce.

Drickhamer drove up to the cashier's window. Jon, the cashier, asked him to please wait while he left to get new batteries for the headset through which he received orders. Jon returned a minute later and requested payment—but for the wrong total amount. While he had been away getting the batteries, two more orders had come in, so Jon tried to figure out how to make his computer return to Drickhamer's order. Jon apologized and called for a supervisor to help. The supervisor walked over and wordlessly corrected the order on the computer. Jon took the payment and made change as he entered the next customer's order.

Drickhamer pulled up to the next window to receive his food. There, a woman named Mary asked his choice of dipping sauce. He replied "None" as he looked inside the bag. Seeing that no napkins were included (even though this was a child's meal that usually comes with a sauce), he requested napkins—twice. She, like Jon, was wearing a headset and didn't reply.

Drickhamer remained at the pickup window, waiting for napkins. A few seconds later, the window opened again. A third employee

was there, ready with the next customer's order. Drickhamer repeated his request for napkins. The third employee handed over the napkins, and Drickhamer drove away with a contented passenger in the backseat.

1. What forms does quality take in a fast-food restaurant? That is, what aspects of the food, service, atmosphere, and so on do you consider to be acceptable in terms of quality, and what would exceed your expectations?

2. Productivity efforts in a fast-food restaurant often involve behind-the-scenes work in the kitchen. But in describing his experience, Drickhamer emphasizes that in a service business, production includes interactions with the customer. Identify one or two places in this case study where productivity could have been better.

3. Working alone or in a group, draw a diagram of the work process described in this case study. In your diagram, show what materials each employee needed, as well as what each employee provided to the customer. Evaluate where the process could be improved, based on the information given and any experiences you have with fast-food restaurants. Finally, prepare a list of actions to improve the quality and productivity of this work process. As directed by your instructor, submit the diagram and list as a written report or present your findings to the class.

Source: Based on David Drickhamer, "Fine-Tuning the Fast Food Lane," *Industry Week*, June 2004, downloaded from InfoTrac, http://web4.infotrac.galegroup.com.

Knowing Yourself

Test Your Personal Productivity

Place a check mark next to each of the activities you do or habits you have formed. The more check marks, the more productive you can be.

_____ 1. I complete tasks right away, without procrastinating.

_____ 2. I take notes during meetings and conversations to avoid misunder-standing and omissions.

_____ 3. I plan tomorrow's work today by writing a few notes before quitting time.

_____ 4. I prioritize my tasks, tackling the most important or most difficult ones first every day.

_____ 5. I keep a follow-up file.

_____ 6. I plan realistic deadlines, allowing time for delays.

_____ 7. I keep my workspace or desk neat and uncluttered.

_____ 8. I delegate wherever possible and reasonable to my assistant and/or my subordinates.

_____ 9. I limit the number and length of phone calls and monitor my own use of the Internet.

_____ 10. I am not afraid to say no in order to protect the time I have available for the job.

Pause and Reflect

1. Do supervisors need to be even more productive than people they supervise? Why or why not?

2. How can I use my time better in the future?

Source: Quiz from Ted Pollock, "Increasing Personal Productivity," *Supervision*, March 2001. Reprinted by permission of © National Research Bureau, 320 Valley Street, Burlington, IA 52601.

Class Exercise

Defining and Measuring Quality of Service

Because nearly 8 out of every 10 jobs in this country are in the service sector, it is important to understand the significance of providing quality customer service. This exercise is designed to help you apply what you learned in this chapter to a service-sector job.

Instructions

1. Form groups of two or three people. Identify a work setting where customer service is critical. The place should be one with which all of you are famil-iar. It might be a workplace where one of you has worked or at least been a customer (e.g., retail store, post office, bank, hospital, university, resort, restaurant).

2. Identify a specific job title for the work setting (e.g., waiter/waitress, nurse, clerk at the university bookstore, shoe salesperson at a store).

3. Review some of the principles covered in this chapter (see Figure A). Select those that are appropriate to the job you have identified, and develop specific customer service guidelines for the employees.

4. Now select principles appropriate for a supervisor of employees in the job you have identified, and develop some supervisory guidelines that focus on customer service. For example, how should the supervisor monitor performance

FIGURE A
Quality Principles from Chapter 2

- Process control
- Zero-defects approach
- Employee involvement teams
- Philip Crosby's five ingredients for quality (integrity, systems, communications, operations, and policies)
- Benchmarking
- Prevention versus detection
- Standard setting and enforcement
- The role of suppliers
- Rewards for quality
- Dimensions of quality (performance, features, reliability, conformance, durability, serviceability, aesthetics, and perceived quality from Table 2.1)

to determine that employees are practicing the quality service standards you have established?

5. Share your group's efforts with the class by presenting a written statement that includes work setting, job title, principles from Figure A and how your group applied them to the job, and principles from Figure A and how your group applied them to the supervisor.

Source: This team-building exercise was prepared by Corinne Livesay, Belhaven College, Jackson, Mississippi.

Building Supervision Skills

Improving Performance

Divide the class into groups of four to six people. Each group receives the following materials: 20 index cards, a roll of tape, a pair of scissors, and a felt-tipped pen. To complete the exercise, the groups may use these supplies and no others.

The instructor specifies how much time the groups will have to complete the project (10 or 15 minutes). When the instructor gives the signal to begin, each group is to use the materials provided to construct a house. The teams may use the materials in any way they see fit, but they may not use additional materials of their own.

When time is up, someone from each group brings the group's house to a table or other designated location in the classroom. The instructor appoints five class members to serve on a panel of judges. They rate each house on a scale of 1 to 5 (with 5 representing the highest quality). The judges' scores are totaled, and the house with the highest score is deemed the winner of this quality contest. Finally, the class discusses the following questions:

- On what basis did the judges rate the quality of the houses? How many of the criteria in Table 2.1 did they use?
- How did your group decide on a way to make its house? How well did your group work together to produce the house?
- Given your group's experience and the information about how the judges arrived at their scores, how would you want to improve the quality of your house if you could repeat the exercise? Are your changes process improvements or product improvements?
- Which team was most productive? Why? Did it use methods that could have helped the other groups? How could you have improved the productivity of your team?

Chapter **Three**

Teamwork: Emphasizing Powerful Meetings

Learning Objectives

After you have studied this chapter, you should be able to:

3.1 Explain why people join groups.

3.2 Distinguish types of groups that exist in the workplace.

3.3 Discuss how supervisors can get groups to cooperate with them.

3.4 Describe characteristics of groups in the workplace.

3.5 Identify the stages in the development of groups.

3.6 Explain why teamwork is important.

3.7 Describe how the supervisor can lead a team so that it is productive.

3.8 Discuss how to plan for effective meetings.

3.9 Provide guidelines for conducting effective meetings.

To succeed as a team is to hold all of the members accountable for their expertise.

—*Mitchell Caplan, CEO, E-Trade Group*

When some work teams go out to a restaurant together, it's a routine occasion in which most of the discussion might center around whether to try the special of the day. For Judy Duplisea and her team from CheckFree, however, lunch or dinner together is a real, and rare, event that calls for a reservation in the back room so the loud talk and laughter doesn't disturb other diners.

Duplisea, a regional vice president for the Atlanta firm, lives in Canton, Ohio, while the rest of her sales and client relationship staff live in Connecticut, Maryland, Michigan, New Hampshire, and New York. Their meetings are more like reunions.

CheckFree is a provider of electronic financial services that lets consumers receive and pay their bills online or electronically. Duplisea's team members, like some 23 million other employees in the United States today, work out of their homes and use computers, fax machines, and conference calls to create their "virtual" office. When Duplisea started at CheckFree in 1997, she had some doubts about whether working virtually was effective. "I didn't know if I could deal with the lack of socialization and control over my salespeople," she

says. But her experiences with her team, which began with a good foundation of personal relationships built through regular conference calls and face-to-face meetings as frequently as possible, has changed her mind. "My group is probably tighter now than any of the groups that I was working with in regular offices," says Duplisea. "We go out of our way to stay in contact with each other," using instant messaging throughout the day to ask quick questions or just have a little fun.

What makes a virtual team really work? Duplisea advises hiring "good people who you are certain you don't have to see every day. You must be able to trust them."

Not every supervisor is as willing as Duplisea to trust people who work in another state. As you read this chapter, think about what makes a team strong and why long-distance team leadership might be especially challenging.

Source: Michael Rosenwald, "Long-Distance Teamwork as 'Virtual Offices' Spread, Managers and Their Staffs Are Learning to Adapt to New Realities," *Boston Globe,* April 29, 2001, p. J1.

Judy Duplisea appreciates that her success in supervising CheckFree's sales force depends on building a strong team. Aisha Mootry also appreciates the importance of working with others at her organization, a media agency called Tapestry. When Mootry was promoted from media planner to media supervisor, she realized she would have to manage a complex set of working relationships, including those with the pair of media planners she supervises, her own manager, and her colleagues handling other functions and client groups at Tapestry. Mootry sums up every supervisor's challenge this way: "There are many layers of relationships that need to be managed."[1] A central fact of life for supervisors is that much of their work and almost all of their goals involve getting work done in groups.

group
Two or more people who interact with one another, are aware of one another, and think of themselves as a unit

To define that term formally, a **group** is two or more people who interact with one another, are aware of one another, and think of themselves as a group. The supervisor must see that groups of employees work together to accomplish objectives. An increasing number of organizations are expanding group efforts by forming teams. As leaders or members of a team, supervisors help plan and carry out a variety of activities. Many group and team efforts take place in meetings.

This chapter covers how the supervisor can work effectively as a leader and member of a team or other group. Some general characteristics of groups—why people join them, what kinds of groups operate in the workplace, how groups can be described, and how they develop—are described. Then efforts to build employee participation through the use of teamwork are discussed, and the basic benefits of teamwork and ways supervisors can lead teams effectively are outlined. Finally, the chapter provides guidelines for holding meetings.

REASONS FOR JOINING GROUPS

The opening of Colors restaurant in New York City came as a sign of rebuilding after a national tragedy. About half of the restaurant's 50 workers had been employees of Windows on the World, the famed restaurant near the top of the World Trade Center. After the bombing of the center in 2001, Windows employees who survived the attack confronted the grief of losing dozens of co-workers as well as their workplace and their own jobs. A group of former Windows employees joined other investors to start Colors, an establishment whose name reflects the ethnic diversity of the cuisine and the staff, which includes immigrants from over 20 nations. Executive chef Raymond Mohan not only runs the kitchen but also coaches the employee–owners in their role as restaurant investors. Mohan says, "Everyone has an opinion about how [Colors] should be run. . . . I try to make sure that they're doing things in a safe, healthy, and efficient way." An obvious reason to invest in and work for Colors is to pursue a career in the restaurant business. But for some employees, the relationships mean more. Bartender Patricio Valencia calls his co-workers from Windows "my second family."[2]

This example suggests that people belong to groups for many reasons. Sometimes group membership simply goes along with being an employee. In particular, all employees are members of the organization that employs them, most are part of a division or department, and some also join a union when they go to work for a particular company. At other times, employees join a group because their supervisor or some other manager asks them to do so. In such cases, an employee may join the group to advance his or her career or simply to avoid going against the manager's wishes. Finally, an employee may join a group because being a member satisfies his or her personal needs. The most common personal reasons for joining a group include the following (see Figure 3.1):

- *Closeness*—Being members of the same group builds ties among people. Friendships generally result from the shared experiences that come from membership in some kind of group, such as a class at school or a bowling team.

- *Strength in numbers*—Having ties to others gives people confidence they may lack when they act alone. Their sense of confidence is well founded. In an organization, a group of people tends to be more influential than one person acting alone.

- *Common goals*—When people have a goal to meet, they can get moral and practical support by working with or alongside others who have similar goals.

- *Achievement of personal objectives*—Membership in a group can help people achieve personal objectives in a variety of ways. The time spent with group

FIGURE 3.1
What Draws People to Groups?

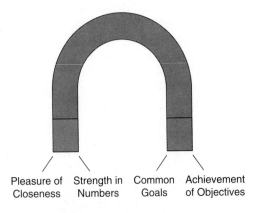

Pleasure of Closeness   Strength in Numbers   Common Goals   Achievement of Objectives

members can be enjoyable. Membership in certain groups can enhance a person's prestige. In a related vein, group membership can satisfy people's desire to feel important.

GROUPS IN THE WORKPLACE

As mentioned previously, all the employees of an organization form a group. On a practical level however, most organizations are too large for all their members to interact with one another. Therefore, except at very small organizations, most employees cluster into smaller groups. Some examples are departments, task forces, and groups that meet for lunch to play cards, do needlework, or talk about baseball. References to groups in this chapter generally mean these small groups, that is, groups small enough that all members interact with one another.

To fully benefit from the various groups in an organization, the supervisor needs to be able to identify them. The first step is to recognize the various categories of an organization's groups. Then the supervisor can apply several principles for building cooperation on the part of the groups.

Functional and Task Groups

functional groups
Groups that fulfill ongoing needs in the organization by carrying out a particular function

task groups
Groups that are set up to carry out a specific activity and then disband when the activity is completed

Some groups fulfill ongoing needs in the organization by carrying out a particular function, such as producing goods, selling products, or investing funds. These are called **functional groups.** For example, a hospital's accounting department has the ongoing responsibility for keeping accurate records of the flow of money into and out of the organization. In most cases, a functional group is one that appears on a company's organization chart.

Other groups, called **task groups,** are set up to carry out a specific activity, and they disband when that activity has been completed. A task group also may be formed for a task that is ongoing. For example, Piedmont Medical Center in Rock Hill, South Carolina, set up a Rapid Response Team to respond to cardiac arrests (heart attacks) among patients. Whenever a nurse senses that a person has conditions associated with a heart attack, he or she pages for the team to respond. The team—which includes a critical-care nurse, respiratory therapist, critical-care doctor, and nursing supervisor—evaluates the patient and intervenes according to the symptoms observed. One team member, Dr. Bill Alleyne, says the team reduces the need for intensive care, shortens hospital stays, and improves the chances that patients will survive.[3] Like many task groups, the Rapid Response Team may operate for years with no definite end date, because the hospital will probably always have patients at risk for heart attacks.

Formal and Informal Groups

formal groups
Groups set up by management to meet organizational objectives

informal groups
Groups that form when individuals in the organization develop relationships to meet personal needs

The examples of functional and task groups are also types of **formal groups.** These are groups set up by management to meet organizational objectives. Thus, these groups result from the management function of organizing (introduced in Chapter 1). A customer service department and a committee charged with planning the company picnic are formal groups.

Other groups result when individuals in the organization develop relationships to meet personal needs. These are **informal groups.** Figure 3.2 shows two informal groups in a small store. Perhaps the china department manager and four clerks like to jog after work; they might find themselves jogging together. Eventually they could build friendships around this shared activity. Most employees

FIGURE 3.2 Informal Group Structures

Source: From Samuel C. Certo, *Human Relations Today: Concepts and Skills* (New York: McGraw-Hill, 1995), p. 259.

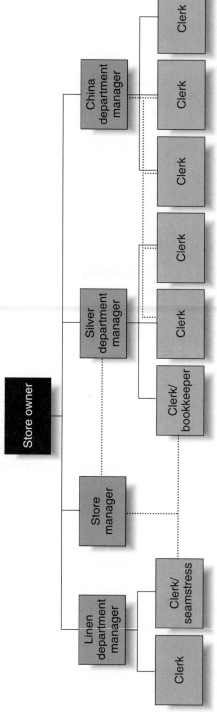

----- Informal links.

welcome the opportunity to be part of informal groups because these groups help satisfy social needs. The friendships established within the group can make work more enjoyable.

Informal subgroups can develop among members of a formal group when the formal group fails to meet some personal needs. For example, when some group members feel angry at the group's leader or uncertain about whether they really belong, they may form a subgroup. Subgroups may also form when some group members feel uncomfortable with the way they are expected to behave; for example, they might be expected not to express their feelings. In such a situation, the people who form a subgroup may feel more comfortable with the other members of the subgroup.

Getting the Group to Work with You

Groups have a lot to offer with regard to decision making and problem solving. A group can generate a creative solution that a single person might not think of, and the group process can build support by letting people make decisions about what affects them. To make the most of the potential benefits of working with groups, supervisors can use several tactics.

An important step is for the supervisor to make sure all members of a formal group know what they can and should be doing. This includes setting effective group objectives (described in Chapter 6) and clearly communicating those objectives. Group members also need to understand their authority, including the limits on what they can do. For example, a group assembled to solve a problem should know whether it is to implement the solution or simply to suggest solutions, leaving to the supervisor the task of choosing an alternative and implementing it.

In addition to communicating expectations, the supervisor should keep groups informed about what is happening in the organization and what changes are planned for the future. Making the effort to communicate with groups is a way of demonstrating that they are important to the organization. It also tends to create a climate in which group members readily let the supervisor know what is happening in the group.

The supervisor should support the group when it wants to bring legitimate concerns to higher management. For example, if some problem is keeping employees from getting their work done on time or up to standards, the supervisor should do what is possible to get the problem corrected. However, this does not mean adopting an "us versus them" attitude toward management. The supervisor is a part of management and must act accordingly.

A supervisor who is responsible for setting up a group can help it function well by making good choices about whom to assign to the group. In many cases, the group can benefit from a combination of people with a variety of strengths or backgrounds. At the same time, the supervisor needs to be careful about splitting up informal groups when creating a formal one; doing so could hurt morale within the formal group. In addition, the number of group members can be important. Although including all employees is sometimes important, for many tasks a group will work best with only 5 to 10 members.

Some of the guidelines for supervision discussed in other chapters also will help get the group's cooperation. Supervisors should treat all employees fairly and impartially, respect the position of the group's informal leader, and find ways to give rewards to the group as a whole, rather than to individual employees only. Finally, supervisors should encourage the group to participate in solving problems. As a result of following these practices, the supervisor can benefit by receiving the group's support.

FIGURE 3.3
Ways to Describe
Groups

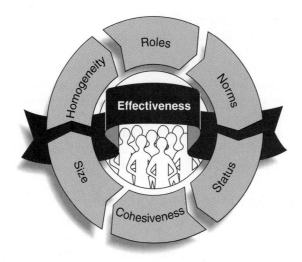

CHARACTERISTICS OF GROUPS

You can readily conclude from this discussion and from personal experience that working with a group is not like working alone. Social scientists have summarized a number of group characteristics, including ways to describe them, how effective they are, and what pressures they place on individuals. Supervisors who are aware of this theoretical information can use it to understand what is happening in a group situation. They can decide whether the group is effectively supporting the achievement of organizational objectives or if supervisors need to step in and make changes.

When looking at how groups are the same or different, it helps to consider some basic ways of describing them. Some of the most useful characteristics include roles, norms, status, cohesiveness, size, homogeneity, and effectiveness (see Figure 3.3).

Roles

roles
Patterns of behavior related to employees' positions in a group

The character taken on by each actor in a play is the actor's role. In an organization's groups, the various group members also take on **roles,** or patterns of behavior related to their position in the group. Some common roles that you may have encountered or even held include the (formal or informal) leader of a group, the scapegoat, the class clown, and the person to whom others take their problems.

What leads a person to take on a role? Sometimes a person's formal position in an organization dictates a certain role. For example, as described in Chapter 1, certain kinds of behavior are expected of a supervisor. Another source of a person's role is a combination of the person's beliefs about how he or she ought to behave and other people's expectations about how that person will act. For example, if Anne displays empathy toward a colleague who is going through a divorce, she may eventually find that many people in the department come to her for advice when a problem arises. If she continues to respond with sympathy and concern, she may take on a role in which she hears other people's troubles but is expected not to complain herself. Similarly, if Stuart makes wisecracks during a couple of meetings, group members may start expecting to hear jokes and funny remarks from him on a regular basis.

The kinds of roles people select serve different purposes. People may take on a role, such as leader or organizer, that helps the group get its work done. Or they may take on a role that holds the group together—the person who can be counted on to smooth ruffled feathers whenever conflicts arise among group members. Finally, group members may take on roles that help them meet personal needs. Thus, Stuart may be making jokes to cover up his own discomfort with being a group participant.

Awareness of roles is important because recognizing them can help the supervisor encourage desirable behavior or bring about a change in undesirable behavior. The supervisor would probably want to include an informal group's leader in planning how to carry out a change in policy. A supervisor who finds an employee's wisecracks to be a distraction during meetings needs to understand that other people may be encouraging this employee's behavior. Thus, to get the employee to stop, the supervisor will have to end the encouragement of the wisecracks as well as the wisecracks themselves.

role conflicts
Situations in which a person has two different roles that call for conflicting types of behavior

Sometimes supervisors also have to resolve problems involving **role conflicts,** situations in which a person has two different roles that call for conflicting types of behavior. Suppose, for example, that several employees have been members of a volleyball team for a number of years. At work, one of them is promoted to be supervisor of the others, with the expectation that he will end the goofing off that has been common in the department. The supervisor's role as teammate conflicts with his role as strict supervisor. The way the supervisor resolves this conflict— which role he chooses—will influence his performance as a supervisor as well as his relationship with the employees.

Norms

norms
Group standards for appropriate or acceptable behavior

Groups typically have standards for appropriate or acceptable behavior, called the group's **norms.** For instance, in some work settings, the employees have a norm of doing only what is expected of them and no more. They may fear that if they do an exceptional amount of work, management will expect that much from them every day. A new employee eager to develop a strong work record could anger the others if he or she violates the norm by doing "too much." Other norms may be stated rather than implied; for example, an organization expects everyone to arrive at work on time. For another example of norms and other group characteristics, see "Supervisory Skills: Team Building."

When a member of the group violates a norm, the group responds by pressuring the person to conform. Formal groups have procedures for handling violations of norms that are group policies, such as arriving at work on time. With unofficial norms, a typical first step would be for someone to point out to the violator how he or she is expected to behave. If that does not work, the group may resort to shutting the person out, ridiculing the person, or even threatening him or her with physical harm.

Employees whose norm is doing no more than is required have a norm that hurts the organization. When a supervisor finds that a group of employees seems to be behaving in a way that works against the achievement of organizational objectives, the supervisor could investigate whether these employees are following some norm of an informal group. This might be the case if half a dozen employees in the department regularly leave work 15 minutes early. One way to change this kind of norm is to look at the way the organization treats the behavior. Perhaps the organization or supervisor does not properly reward those who do follow the rules. In trying to persuade employees to change or ignore an informal group's norm, the supervisor must remember that violating norms carries negative consequences for group members.

SUPERVISORY SKILLS

TEAM BUILDING

GROUP CHARACTERISTICS IN THE U.S. ANTARCTIC PROGRAM

At the U.S. Antarctic Program's three research stations, every group must learn to be effective. The work is hard, the conditions primitive, the hours long—and there is nowhere else to go. Employees routinely put in more than 50-hour workweeks, outside temperatures fall well below zero, and there is no transportation off the continent between February and August.

So why do some employees sign up year after year? Six out of 10 people who work a full season return the following year. A major reason is the close-knit work groups. Dennis Hoffman, a network administrator who has signed up for 11 winters at the McMurdo Station, says he keeps coming back because of the friendships he has developed. Describing the many people who repeatedly return, recruiting manager Tamesha Johnson says, "When they go home, they hold retreats back in the States."

The Antarctic groups become so cohesive because they work so hard, depend on one another, and live close together. Maintaining the power plant and conserving water are life-and-death concerns. Norms develop over such matters as not looking "too clean" (only two 2-minute showers are allowed per week at the South Pole Station). The program's medical director, Dr. Ron Shemenski, explains, "There's very little hierarchy on 'The Ice.' We all do whatever is needed." He adds that group roles are peculiar to the situation: "The power plant manager is probably more important than the doctor, and the cook is the most important of all!"

Building such a cohesive group requires more than luck. Developing the groups in the Antarctic Program requires careful selection, training, and leadership. Job applicants must pass a strict psychological assessment and drug and alcohol screenings. Candidates also receive information about the challenges to expect in terms of jobs and working conditions. Those selected for the program participate in team-building activities in the Rocky Mountains and are reevaluated by psychologists several weeks after they start their new jobs. A few days after arriving in the Antarctic, they meet with their supervisors to discuss their expectations.

Rewards and communications also help keep groups functioning smoothly. Station managers hold weekly lunches with small groups of employees, during which they answer questions, respond to concerns, and quell rumors. Employees complete self-reviews, which help describe their accomplishments to their supervisors. A recognition system encourages employees to submit congratulations to employees "caught doing something right."

Systems to reward positive behavior are essential in the research stations, because there are few alternatives for handling negative behavior. Once, an employee at the McMurdo base was caught with illegal drugs. As at many organizations, this was grounds for dismissal, but the employee couldn't leave until a plane arrived. He agreed to continue working until then, and he was paid for the time. More common are employees who exceed typical job requirements. Scientists and others pitch in to wash dishes, clean facilities, bring in the mail, and handle chores that on any other continent would be left to lower-paid support staff.

Source: Ann Pomeroy, "HR on 'The Ice,'" *HRMagazine*, June 2004, downloaded from InfoTrac, http://web4 .infotrac.galegroup.com.

Status

status
A group member's position in relation to others in the group

A group member's **status** is his or her position relative to others in the group. Status depends on a variety of factors, including the person's role in the group, title, pay, education level, age, race, and sex. Thus, in one group, the person with the highest status might be a man who is the tallest and owns a cottage by a lake. The others find this person's presence impressive and hope for invitations to the cottage, so his status is high.

Status is important to supervisors because group members with the highest status have the most effect on the development of group norms. Group members with lower status tend to pattern their behaviors after those of high-status members. A supervisor who wants to reinforce or change group norms will have the greatest success by focusing on the high-status members of the group.

Cohesiveness

cohesiveness
The degree to which group members stick together

The degree to which group members stick together is known as **cohesiveness.** A cohesive group has members who want to stay with the group even during periods of stress. They abide by group norms even when under pressure to follow other norms.

Groups that are cohesive work harder than others and are more likely to accomplish their objectives. Thus, when a group's objectives support those of the organization, the supervisor will want the group to be cohesive. The supervisor can foster cohesiveness in several ways:

- By emphasizing to group members their common characteristics and goals. A supervisor of a research department might point out proudly that this is a select group of talented individuals working on an important project.
- By emphasizing areas in which the group has succeeded in achieving its goals. A history of successes, such as accomplishing tasks or increasing the status of members, tends to improve cohesiveness.
- By keeping the group sufficiently small—ideally no more than eight members—so that everyone feels comfortable participating. When a larger number of employees report to a single supervisor, he or she might want to support the formation of more than one group.
- By encouraging competition with other groups. In contrast, cohesiveness diminishes when group members are competing with one another.
- By encouraging less active members to participate in group activities. Groups tend to be more cohesive when everyone participates equally.

Figure 3.4 summarizes what makes groups cohesive.

Size

An organization's groups may vary widely in size. As few as two people can form a group. Up to 15 or 16 group members can get to know and communicate well with one another. Beyond 20 members, however, informal subgroups tend to form.

Big groups typically operate differently from small ones. Small groups tend to reach decisions faster and rely less on formal rules and procedures. Also, quiet group members are more likely to participate in a small group. If group processes seem overly cumbersome—for example, if the group tends to take too long to reach decisions—the supervisor might consider dividing the group into subgroups of about 8–12 members. A bigger group might make sense when a lot of work needs to get done and the individual group members can work independently most of the time.

FIGURE 3.4
Situations in Which Groups Stick Together

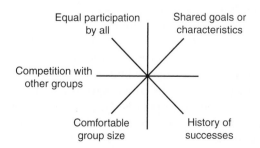

Homogeneity

The degree to which the members of a group are the same is known as **homogeneity.** Thus, a *homogeneous* group is one in which group members have a lot in common. When group members have many differences, the group is said to be *heterogeneous.* Group members can be alike or different according to age, sex, race, work experience, education level, social class, personality, interests, and other characteristics.

The members of a homogeneous group enjoy a number of benefits. Perhaps the most significant is that people feel most comfortable around others who are like themselves. This may be the reason that homogeneous groups offer better cooperation among members, greater satisfaction, and higher productivity, at least for simple tasks.

At the same time, the U.S. workforce is becoming more diverse. For complex, creative tasks, a heterogeneous group can perform better than a homogeneous one because group members offer a variety of skills, experience, and viewpoints. The heterogeneous group as a whole has broader skills and knowledge, and it can examine problems from different points of view.

Effectiveness

The preceding characteristics of groups can affect whether a particular group is effective—that is, whether it achieves what it has set out to do. To the supervisor, a group's effectiveness is one of its most important characteristics. In general, the organization's formal groups should be as effective as possible. The supervisor wants informal groups to be effective only to the extent that they support organizational goals. For example, a company softball team that builds morale and improves working relations is properly effective. A clique that hurts morale among the employees who feel left out is not supporting organizational objectives.

DEVELOPMENT OF GROUPS

In a sense, groups are living organisms with life stages. They grow, are subjected to stresses, and either mature or die as a result. Figure 3.5 shows one view of group development, that of groups passing through the following stages:[4]

- *Orientation*—When a group first forms, its members tend to be highly committed to the group, but they do not have the experience and skills to work together efficiently. Group members tend to be concerned about what the group is supposed to do and how they fit in. The supervisor's role is primarily to clarify objectives and provide direction.

- *Dissatisfaction*—If group members are able to learn their roles and the group's objectives, the group moves to the dissatisfaction stage. Although group members are more competent at working together, their initial enthusiasm has given way to disappointment with the day-to-day reality of being part of the group. While continuing to help group members develop competence, the supervisor must focus more on encouraging and motivating them.

- *Resolution*—If group members are able to reconcile the differences between their initial expectations and the realities they experience, the group moves to the resolution stage. During this stage, group members continue to be more productive and their morale improves. The supervisor should focus on helping resolve conflicts and encourage group members to participate in planning and decision making.

FIGURE 3.5
Stages of Group
Development

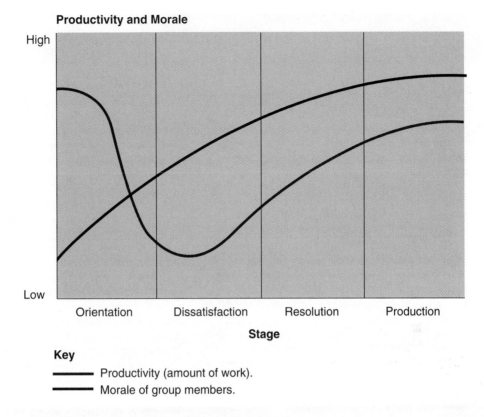

Productivity and Morale

Key

───── Productivity (amount of work).
───── Morale of group members.

- *Production*—If group members continue to resolve conflicts and develop a workable structure for the group, their output and morale will continue to increase. The group is effectively working as a team. When the group structure must change or other issues arise, the group resolves them quickly. The supervisor should give group members as much autonomy as possible.

- *Termination*—At some point, many groups must come to an end. If the group had reached the production stage, group members may be sad. If the group ends before that stage, members are more likely to be relieved.

Getting a group to the resolution and production stages is challenging for supervisors who are most comfortable telling employees what to do. Instead, this process requires skill in resolving conflicts and fostering employee development (topics of Chapters 14 and 16).

TEAMWORK

team

A small group whose members share goals, commitment, and accountability for results

Organizations today are increasingly looking for ways to involve employees in decision making and problem solving. For a growing number of organizations, teamwork is the means to employee involvement. A **team** is a small group whose members share goals, commitment, and accountability for results. When most organizations form a team, someone is appointed to be team leader. Often the team leader is a supervisor, and the team consists of operative employees.

Being an effective team leader draws on many of the same skills required of an effective supervisor. The team leader needs excellent communication skills, patience, fairness, and good rapport with team members. In addition, because the purpose of the team is to draw on the expertise of all team members, the team

SUPERVISION ACROSS INDUSTRIES

RETAILING

TEAMS RULE AT WHOLE FOODS MARKET

What can teams do in an organization? At Whole Foods Market, a chain of more than 150 supermarkets selling organic and natural foods, the answer is everything.

The employees in each Whole Foods store are assigned to one of eight functional teams, such as bakery, produce, or cashier/front-end team. And the team gets to decide whether they stay. Each new hire is provisional; after four weeks, the team votes whether to keep the employee on the team. To be hired permanently, the new employee needs a two-thirds favorable vote. Functional and store-level teams also make many of the decisions about what items the store carries.

The company's headquarters also assigns employees to additional teams. For example, there is a national information technology team and a national leadership team. The same hiring rules apply. Decisions, even on the level of the national leadership team, are team decisions.

The company's pay system encourages teams to select the best people. In addition to a wage, team members earn bonuses based on team performance. Every four weeks, the company calculates team performance and compares it to team goals. Teams that meet goals get a share of the profits as a bonus.

The team structure poses some challenges. In particular, the company has been so successful that it has grown rapidly, resulting in very large teams in stores. Even so, chief executive John Mackey remains faithful to the idea that the teams can handle decisions and problems. When a reporter asked the CEO how 140 cashiers in a store can function as one team, he replied, "That does sound like a problem. . . . But . . . I don't have the faintest idea how they've solved that problem. That's not my job anymore." The reporter investigated and learned that the team operates with 13 supervisors and one subteam, and the entire large team meets monthly.

The practice of letting employees make decisions about matters that affect them extends to other areas as well. For instance, the company determined that frontline employees care particularly about health insurance. Therefore, rather than having a specialist team in headquarters choose the policy, Whole Foods had its frontline employees vote on a plan.

Some people might think it would be difficult to coordinate activities in a company with so much teamwork, but the business results at Whole Foods are evidence that teams succeed. In contrast to most supermarkets, Whole Foods is profitable and growing much faster than its competitors.

Source: Charles Fishman, "The Anarchist's Cookbook," *Fast Company,* July 2004, downloaded from InfoTrac, http://web4.infotrac.galegroup.com.

leader will need to rely most on a leadership style that encourages involvement. (For more on this type of leadership, see Chapter 8.)

In the 1970s, it became popular to form teams in which employees suggested ways to improve the quality of their work. More recently, organizations have expanded their use of teams by creating **self-managing work teams.** These are groups of 5–15 members who work together to produce an entire product. The team members rotate jobs, schedule work and vacations, and make other decisions affecting their area of responsibility. Companies using self-managing work teams include Toyota, General Electric, and Xerox.

self-managing work teams
Groups of 5 to 15 members who work together to produce an entire product

Benefits of Teamwork

A basic benefit of using work teams is that they enable the organization to increase its usage of the insights and expertise of all its employees. (For an example, see "Supervision across Industries: Retailing.") In the marketing area, some companies are setting up sales teams that combine technical and sales experts to better address the needs of their major customers. For example, many high-tech and Internet firms combine experts in hardware, software, and technical support to help customers fully use the hardware and software they buy. IBM is encouraging its brilliant scientists to join sales experts in teams that call on potential clients. Sometimes the scientists on these teams need guidance in learning how to communicate effectively with business executives. IBM computer scientist Baruch Schieber, for example, says, "I used to believe that you could solve everything using math." Eventually, he recognized that equations were not the most persuasive way to show managers how IBM could solve their problems. When he joined a team working with Boston Coach, Schieber saw that math could solve the problem of scheduling the company's limousines. But he took his time listening to Boston Coach's headquarters employees before he explained that he could use the company's data to build a computer system that would allow drivers to pick up more customers each day.[5]

Teams can also serve as motivators. Employees who participate in planning and decision making are more likely to take responsibility for the quality of what they do. They also tend to be more enthusiastic about their work. Responsible, enthusiastic employees are more likely to work hard and deliver high quality.

Ultimately, motivating employees and drawing on their strengths should enhance the performance of the organizations that use self-managing work teams. One company that has enjoyed these benefits of teamwork is Rowe Furniture, based in Virginia. The upholstered-furniture maker wanted to avoid sending jobs overseas, as most of its competitors were doing. The company's management determined that the way to compete efficiently was to figure out how to build sofas in just 10 days, instead of the typical four to six weeks. The answer was to use teams. Teamwork began when employees were assigned to work with engineers to figure out how to rearrange production activities to save time. They set up work centers, called *focus factories*, in which cutters, sewers, framers, and upholsterers work in the same area. Most of them have been cross-trained so they can pitch in where they are needed most. Each week, within these groups, supervisor Fred Stanley gives a team member a pad of paper with the assignment to list "five things we're doing right and five things we're doing wrong." Production worker Rhonda Melton felt motivated by the chance to provide feedback, seeing it as a signal managers think she is "important to this company." The efforts are paying off, as the workers not only can make a couch in 10 days but also can produce at a higher rate and with fewer errors.[6]

Leading the Team

Whether an organization's teams achieve the benefits of teamwork depends in part on the teams' leaders. Broadly speaking, the goal of a team leader is to develop a productive team. Experts in teamwork have linked team productivity to the team characteristics described in Table 3.1. In general, these characteristics describe a team whose members want to participate, share ideas freely, and know what they are supposed to accomplish. Some ways to develop this kind of team include communicating often to be sure everyone understands the goals and reviews what is working well and what needs to change. Team leaders need to be good role models—trustworthy, cooperative, and team oriented. When the supervisor's role involves team leadership, he or she may want to get training in coaching, conflict management, and other skills to help team members work together effectively.[7]

Coaching the Team

The team leader who can stimulate high-quality performance is one who focuses on enabling team members to do their best. *Enabling* in this context means providing employees with the resources they need to do their job and removing

TABLE 3.1
Team Characteristics Associated with Team Productivity

Sources: Adapted from Edward Glassman, "Self-Directed Team Building without a Consultant," *Supervisory Management*, March 1992, p. 6; Louis V. Imundo, "Blueprint for a Successful Team," *Supervisory Management*, May 1992, pp. 2–3.

Characteristic	Description and Significance
Openness and honesty	These are signs that group members trust one another. Tact and timing also are important.
Leadership that does not dominate	The leader is flexible, changing with conditions and circumstances.
Decisions made by consensus	The leader will sometimes have to make a decision alone or reject suggestions, but all team members should have a voice in making many decisions, not simply a vote without the full opportunity to be heard.
Acceptance of assignments	Team members should willingly take on the tasks that must be done, then do them correctly and on time. Team members should view work as a cooperative effort, helping each other out as needed.
Goals that are understood and accepted	Goals give the team purpose and direction Team members should view accomplishing them as the team's primary purpose.
Assessment of progress and results	Team members should focus on results.
Comfortable atmosphere	Some conflict can stimulate desirable action and change, but there should be a basic level of cooperation.
Involvement and participation	Team members should be involved in the work of the group. When a team member is reluctant to speak up at meetings, the leader should seek his or her input during or outside the meeting.
Debate and discussion	If everyone agrees all the time, it may signify that team members are unable or unwilling to contribute.
Atmosphere of listening	Team members should listen to one another, even when they disagree.
Access to information	All team members need to know what is happening.
Win–win approach to conflict	Team members should work to resolve conflicts in ways that let everyone be a winner.
Relatively low turnover	Members of a team must have close relationships, which is impossible when the team's membership keeps changing.

obstacles that interfere with their work (e.g., procedures that slow employees down without adding value from the customer's perspective). Providing resources includes making sure employees have the training they need to be effective team members. Typically, employees are not used to working on a team and can benefit from training in decision making, conflict resolution, meeting management, interpersonal skills, problem solving, negotiation, and dealing with customers. Other ways the team leader can enable the team to do its best include expressing a vision for the team—that is, describing what the team can and should accomplish—and setting performance standards to help team members understand their goals. Team leaders also should be sure teams recognize their boundaries, such as limits set by management or union rules.[8]

By enabling teams to excel and empowering them to make decisions, team leaders are coaching employees. For example, instead of simply telling employees what to do, a coach asks questions that help them decide how to handle a situation.

The team leader encourages team members by expressing understanding and appreciation of their ideas and feelings. In place of criticism, the coach initiates discussions about "how we can do it better next time." The coach also pays attention to how team members interact, recognizing when it is time to wrap up a discussion and when to promote balanced participation from team members.

This style of leading may seem to leave a supervisor with less power than one who gives directions and checks up on performance. However, coaching enables the supervisor to build on the strengths and expertise of the whole group. The likely result is a stronger position for everyone, including the supervisor.

Selection of Team Members

A team leader may be charged with selecting either candidates for jobs that involve teamwork or existing employees to participate in a team devoted to a particular task. In either case, the supervisor should look for people who work well with others. If the team is to include people from several departments, the team leader should talk to other supervisors and employees to learn which employees would do best on the team.

Team Building

team building
Developing the ability of team members to work together to achieve common objectives

Once the team leader knows who will be on the team, he or she must develop the group's ability to work together to achieve common objectives. This process is known as **team building.** Team building includes several activities: setting goals, analyzing what needs to be done and allocating work, examining how well the group is working, and examining the relationships among the team members.

At some organizations, a consultant with expertise in team building carries out this process. However, hiring someone often is too expensive, especially for small organizations. When the supervisor is responsible for team building, he or she can carry out that responsibility at regular team meetings. At the end of a meeting, the supervisor can devote some time to asking team members how well they thought the meeting worked and whether they think they developed a creative solution. Participants can rate how well the meeting went in terms of whether everyone participated, whether they felt the others heard them, and whether the meeting's outcome was successful. Whole Foods Market CEO John Mackey ends team meetings with what he calls "appreciations"; each participant says something positive about each of the others.[9]

Consultant Jim Jenkins points out that team building need not take the expensive forms that are so widely reported, such as outdoor obstacle courses, well-known motivational speakers, or even late-night parties. Rather, effective ways to build strong working relationships may be as simple as 15-minute weekly sessions that focus on respectful dialogue.[10]

Communication in Teams

The way the team leader communicates with other team members will influence the success of the team. In general, the team leader should create a climate of trust and openness and encourage team members to collaborate. The team leader also should acknowledge disagreement, not squelch it. To determine whether you already have a communication style that would make you an effective team leader or if you need to make some changes to fill that role, complete the Knowing Yourself exercise at the end of this chapter.

Team leaders need this kind of communication style because successful teamwork requires open and positive communication among team members. Feeling able to express one's viewpoint and knowing how to do so constructively are essential for reaping the benefits of diverse viewpoints.

Dick Gorelick, a consultant and trainer specializing in graphic arts, sees positive communications as an important feature of successful production teams at printing and graphic arts companies. In observing hundreds of meetings, Gorelick has noted that participants from production and sales interact best when they focus on customer needs and express appreciation for one another's efforts. Team members from production can help salespeople serve customers by offering information about job status. Team members from sales can help production people deliver quality by educating them about customers' wants and needs.[11]

Rewards

For teams to remain productive, members must be rewarded appropriately. The organization should reward the entire team for its accomplishments instead of emphasizing individual rewards. At Rowe Furniture, where the company goals emphasize productivity, the rewards emphasize team productivity. Each morning, the assembly team receives a daily goal for the number of pieces of furniture to complete. Whenever the team is finished, it is allowed to leave. If it finishes early, team members go home early with a full day's pay. As the team improves efficiency, if the company finds it can meet goals with fewer employees, the savings will be distributed to the team members.[12] (For more on group incentives, see Chapter 11.)

Team members also are likely to value different rewards; therefore, the rewards should be varied enough that everyone feels motivated. For example, the typical salesperson is motivated by money, whereas technical people might be more interested in recognition and promotion. Thus, one approach might be to use the company's basic incentive plan and ask the team members to reach a consensus on what additional reward they would enjoy receiving for a specific accomplishment.

Labor Law and Teamwork

In the early 1990s, when self-managed work teams were a new and popular idea, some observers raised the concern that teamwork might violate federal labor law. Specifically, the National Labor Relations Act of 1935 forbids employers to dominate or interfere with the formation of any "labor organization" (i.e., a group such as a union that represents employees in dealings with management). The purpose of this part of the law was to prevent employers from setting up "fake unions" to interfere with employees' attempts to organize. Some people worried that empowering employees to make decisions about matters such as employment and work hours could be considered domination of a labor organization.

The National Labor Relations Board (NLRB) in 2001 issued a ruling that appears to lay these concerns to rest. The ruling accepted the use of employee teams at Crown Cork & Seal Company's aluminum-can manufacturing plant in Texas. Those teams made decisions about issues such as production and safety. According to the NLRB, the teams were not considered labor organizations because their authority to plan and implement decisions meant they had "supervisory" authority. Also, the teams were set up to solve problems, not for members to represent employees in bargaining with management. Employers today are less worried about the legality of teamwork when it involves problem solving but not employee representation. However, supervisors who are setting up or working with teams should verify that the company's human resource and legal experts are involved in making sure the details of the arrangement are legal.[13]

MEETINGS

Much of the work of teams and other groups occurs in meetings. When groups plan, solve problems, and reward successes, they usually do so in a meeting. Although the supervisor's role may be that of either participant in or leader of the meeting, this chapter emphasizes the latter. The principles described here apply to other situations as well, but supervisors will have less ability to make improvements when someone else is conducting the meeting.

Reasons for Meetings

Meetings should take place when they serve a purpose. As obvious as this sounds, many supervisors and other managers hold meetings at a regularly scheduled time, whether or not they have something particular to accomplish. A supervisor who is thinking of calling a meeting should consider specifically what the meeting is intended to accomplish. The group should be able to achieve that purpose by the end of the meeting. For keeping team members up-to-date on progress, a daily five-minute standup meeting may be most efficient. To analyze and solve a particular problem, the group may need a conference room for a few hours or more. Mixing the two kinds of issues into one meeting will just feel confusing.[14] And, of course, don't call a meeting at all for an illogical purpose such as making small matters seem important, proving you are being democratic, or rescuing a lost cause (e.g., building a groundswell of support for an idea the boss has vetoed).

There are several valid reasons for holding a meeting. One is to convey news to a group of people when their feedback is important. Conveying information in a meeting gives the supervisor a chance to see and respond to people's reactions to the news. A meeting is also appropriate when the supervisor wants the group to participate in decision making. (Chapter 9 describes the pros and cons of decision making in a group.) The supervisor may use meetings to prepare group members for a change and build support for that change. (Chapter 15 describes this process.) Meetings are especially important when some or all members of a group work in different locations—for example, when some employees telecommute, or work from home via computer connections. Meetings are essential to prevent the kinds of misunderstandings that can occur when people lack face-to-face contact.[15] Likewise, when meetings bring together people in different functions to discuss a common issue, the participants can see how each function contributes to the solution in a different way.

Google, for example, regularly holds meetings that bring together salespeople, product managers, engineers, and employees serving particular industries to see how they can meet newly defined needs. In the words of Google vice president Sheryl Sandberg, "We are in a constant mode of change, so we are in a constant mode of collaboration. . . . And when I think collaboration works best is when someone on the engineering side makes a customer point, and someone on the sales side makes a systems point." Then, Sandberg knows, the collaboration is helping everyone see the big picture.[16]

Preparing for a Meeting

To prepare for a meeting, the supervisor should decide who is to attend and when and where to meet. When the purpose of a meeting is to convey information to the whole department, naturally the whole department should be invited. In many cases, however, the participants are to provide or evaluate information. In these cases, the supervisor should invite only those who have the needed information or expertise.

As much as possible, a meeting should be scheduled at a time that is convenient for all participants. Times that tend to cause problems are peak working hours and the last few hours before a weekend or holiday. However, if a meeting is supposed to be brief, it makes sense to schedule the meeting for a half-hour before lunch or quitting time.

The location of the meeting usually depends on the available facilities. For a very small meeting, the participants might be able to meet in the supervisor's office. Larger meetings can take place in a conference room. When the whole department is called, finding a big enough space can be a challenge. In general, it is more comfortable to meet casually in the work area than to squeeze a big group into a stuffy conference room.

agenda
A list of the topics to be covered at a meeting

One of the most basic preparation tasks is to draw up an **agenda,** a list of the topics to be covered at the meeting. A practical approach is to put the most

FIGURE 3.6
Sample Agenda

Team for *Supervision* Text

Sheraton O'Hare

June 24, 2007

8:30 a.m.–3:00 p.m.

1. Workbook (8:30–10:00)
   a. Components and process
   b. Possible sources of material
   c. Tentative schedule
2. Remaining manuscript work (10:00–12:00)
   a. Examples in text
   b. Opening vignettes
   c. End-of-chapter material
   d. Changes based upon reviewer feedback
3. Working lunch (12:00–1:00)
4. Videos (1:00–2:00)
5. Ancillaries (2:00–3:00)
   a. Components
   b. Process

important topics first, to be sure they will be covered before time runs out. Putting the most important items first also encourages people to show up on time, so they won't miss the agenda items they care about most.[17] To keep the focus on important topics, it is helpful to recall the purpose of the meeting. Figure 3.6 is an agenda that was used at a meeting called by an editor to discuss the progress on this book. Notice that in addition to the topics to be covered, the agenda states the name of the group that is meeting, the location, the date, and the starting and ending times of the meeting.

A well-crafted agenda can make the difference between a meeting that merely accomplishes basic objectives and one that is motivational and inspirational as well. In *Manager of Choice*, consultant Nancy Ahlrichs compares two examples. A good meeting might follow an agenda in which the supervisor reports the group's recent financial and work performance and then offers some training material. After that, employees ask questions and practice the "skill of the week." An excellent meeting might require more thoughtful planning and involvement of employees. The supervisor opens with financial and performance information, but after that, employees get involved. One employee leads a discussion about a topic he or she has researched or an article everyone has read. Then each employee shares something learned during the past week, and everyone learns two more phrases of a foreign language agreed on by the group. The group ends by voting for the winner of the "idea of the week" prize.[18]

The agenda should be distributed to all participants in time for participants to review it before the meeting and make any necessary preparations. In addition, the person calling the meeting should make sure that participants have received any other documents they might need so they are prepared to contribute. At the regular staff meetings of a Midwest computer manufacturer, participants receive a statement of each meeting's topic ahead of time so that they can research the issue. For example, a topic might be "What actions should we take to reduce scrap rates by 10 percent?" This topic requires research to make the meeting worthwhile. In some situations, each participant takes responsibility for a particular item on the agenda.[19]

For further guidance on meeting preparation, see "Tips from the Firing Line."

Conducting a Meeting

Meetings should begin promptly at the scheduled starting time. This practice demonstrates respect for all participants' schedules, and it encourages people to be on time. It helps to announce an ending time and end the meeting promptly at that time. When critical issues come up near the end of a meeting, the group can reach an agreement to extend the meeting or continue the discussion at another time.

To make sure meetings are as fruitful as possible, the supervisor can facilitate the discussion in several ways. One is to rephrase ideas that participants express. For example, if an employee on a printing company's health and safety committee says, "We've got to do something about the fumes in the shop," the supervisor might comment, "You're recommending that we improve ventilation." This type of response helps ensure that the supervisor and other participants understand what has been said. Of course, the supervisor has to use this technique with care; participants might become annoyed if the supervisor sounds like their echo. Also, the supervisor should summarize key points often enough to make sure everyone is following the discussion. Times to summarize include at the conclusion of each agenda item, at the end of the meeting, and at times when people have trouble following the discussion.

TIPS FROM THE FIRING LINE

GETTING READY FOR A MEETING

People hate wasting time, especially when they have challenging jobs with important goals to meet. So it's no wonder that effective meetings are a big force behind employees' satisfaction with their jobs. The following tips for meeting preparation will help you make all of your meetings productive:

- *Pinpoint your purpose.* Then make sure that a meeting is the best way to accomplish your purpose. A meeting is a great way for a group to generate ideas or solve a problem, but if you're just going to make announcements, it might be more efficient to send an e-mail. An exception would be if the person making the announcement is also interested in getting feedback or if the people receiving the announcement might have questions that should be addressed within the group.

- *Target your invitations.* Some meetings are de-signed to bring the whole work group together. But if you're tackling a specific problem, be selective about who gets an invitation. Consider who offers expertise on the subject and who has the power to make and implement decisions. If some parts of your agenda will interest only part of the group, consider scheduling two meetings with two agendas, so as not to waste anyone's time. Chemical manufacturer Chemtura started holding smaller but more frequent sales meetings, inviting participants with an interest in particular regions and products. Although managers attend more meetings, they find that these meetings are more productive than the larger assemblies used in the past.

- *Write it down.* Prepare an agenda, and be sure it stays focused on the meeting's purpose. Give all participants a copy of the agenda in plenty of time for them to be prepared to participate. Assign someone to take notes during the meeting so that you'll have an accurate report of what happened.

Sources: Rebecca Aronauer, "Cure the Meeting Blahs: Tips to Make Your Meetings More Efficient and Productive," *Sales & Marketing Management*, June 2006; T. L. Stanley, "Make Your Meetings Effective," *Supervision*, April 2006, both downloaded from InfoTrac, http://web4.infotrac.galegroup.com.

The supervisor should be careful not to dominate the discussion; instead, he or she should make sure that everyone has a chance to participate. Having everyone sit around a table or in a circle makes people feel more involved. Some people find it easier than others to speak up during a meeting. The person leading the meeting is responsible for encouraging everyone to contribute, a task that can be as simple as saying, "Mary, what do you think about the suggestions that have been proposed so far?" Another way to encourage participation is to appoint different employees to take turns as discussion leaders. This is a way to offer leadership training and demonstrate trust in employees.[20]

Quieting participants who are monopolizing a discussion can be a more delicate matter. One approach is to begin with someone other than the talkative person, then go around the table and hear each person's views on some topic. Also, the supervisor could have a one-on-one talk with the person monopolizing discussions, letting the person know his or her contributions are important but that the lengthy discourse is unnecessary.

Throughout the meeting, the supervisor should take notes on what is being decided. This helps the supervisor summarize key points for participants. In addition, it helps the supervisor recall what actions are to be taken later and by whom.

When it is time for the meeting to end, the supervisor should help bring it to a close. A direct way to do this is to summarize what has been covered, state what needs to happen next, and thank everyone for coming. For example, at the end of a meeting called to decide how to make the company's purchasing decisions more efficient, the supervisor might say, "We've selected three interesting possibilities

FIGURE 3.7
Guidelines for
Conducting a
Meeting

to explore. Max will research the costs of each, then we'll meet back here in two weeks to select one." Then the supervisor's job becomes one of following up to make sure that plans are carried out. As in the example, following up may include planning another meeting.

Figure 3.7 summarizes these guidelines for conducting a meeting.

Overcoming Problems with Meetings

A frequent complaint about meetings is that they waste time because participants stray from the main topic and go off on tangents. Thus, an important job for the supervisor is to keep the discussion linked to the agenda items. When a participant begins discussing an unrelated topic, the supervisor can restate the purpose of the meeting and suggest that if the topic seems important, it could be covered in another meeting.

In steering the discussion back on course, it is important to avoid ridiculing the participants and to respect their efforts to contribute. The supervisor can do this by focusing on the effects of particular kinds of behavior instead of on the personalities of the participants. For example, if a participant tends to interrupt when others are speaking, the supervisor should not say, "Don't be so inconsiderate." A more helpful comment might be, "It's important that everyone in our group have a chance to state his or her ideas completely. Interruptions discourage people from participating."

Other problems arise because the meeting leader and participants have failed to prepare for the meeting. If there is no agenda, the discussion may ramble aimlessly. If someone failed to bring necessary background information, the participants may be unable to make plans or reach decisions, and the meeting will be unproductive. These kinds of problems lead to frustration and anger among participants who feel they are wasting precious time. The solution is to follow the guidelines described previously, including the creation and distribution of an agenda well before the meeting. When the supervisor is prepared to lead the meeting but others are unprepared to participate, the supervisor should probably consider rescheduling the meeting.

SKILLS MODULE

PART ONE: CONCEPTS

Summary

3.1 Explain why people join groups.

People may join a group because membership in that group goes along with being an employee. (All employees are members of the organization that employs them.) Employers may ask employees to join particular groups such as committees or task forces. An employee also may join a group because doing so satisfies personal needs such as closeness, common goals, and achievement of personal objectives.

3.2 Distinguish types of groups that exist in the workplace.

Functional groups fulfill ongoing needs in the organization by carrying out a particular function. Task groups are set up to carry out a specific activity and disband when the activity is completed. Formal groups are set up by management to meet organizational objectives. Informal groups result when individuals in the organization develop relationships to meet personal needs.

3.3 Discuss how supervisors can get groups to cooperate with them.

The supervisor should make sure all members of a formal group know what they can and should be doing. The supervisor also should keep groups informed about what is happening in the organization and what changes are planned. The supervisor should support the group when members want to bring legitimate concerns to higher management. When the supervisor is responsible for setting up a group, he or she should combine people with a variety of strengths and backgrounds but avoid separating members of informal groups. Finally, general principles of effective supervision apply to supervising groups as well as individuals.

3.4 Describe characteristics of groups in the workplace.

Group members have various roles, or patterns of behavior related to their position in the group. Group members are expected to follow norms, or the group's standards, for appropriate or acceptable behavior. The status of each group member depends on a variety of factors, which may include his or her role in the group, title, pay, education level, age, race, and sex. Some groups are more cohesive than others; that is, the members of some groups are more likely to stick together in the face of problems. Groups may vary widely in terms of size, with subgroups likely to form in groups of more than 20 members. Homogeneity refers to the extent to which group members are the same. All these characteristics can influence the effectiveness of a group. In general, a supervisor wants a group to be effective when its goals support the achievement of organizational goals.

3.5 Identify the stages in the development of groups.

In the orientation stage, the group forms, and its members are highly committed to the group but lack the experience and skills to work together efficiently. In the dissatisfaction stage, group members are more competent at working together but their initial enthusiasm has given way to disappointment with the day-to-day reality of being in the group. During the resolution phase, group members become more productive and their morale improves as group members begin to resolve their conflicts. By the production phase, the group is working effectively as a team with still higher morale and productivity. At some point, many groups pass through a termination phase, during which group activity ends.

3.6 Explain why teamwork is important.

Teams bring employees together to collaborate on solving problems and making decisions. By using teams, the organization can draw more fully on the insights and expertise of all its employees. Teams also can motivate employees by giving them a say in how things are done. As a result, organizations that use teams can benefit from improved performance, which is measured by higher quality and greater productivity and profits.

3.7 Describe how the supervisor can lead a team so that it is productive.

If building the team includes selecting team members, the supervisor should include people who work well with others. The supervisor should adopt a coaching role, enabling employees by providing them with the resources they need and removing any obstacles in their way. Then the supervisor builds the team by helping it set goals, analyzing what needs to be done and allocating the work, examining how well the group is working, and examining the relationships among team members. The supervisor can increase the success of the team through effective communication that creates a climate of trust and encourages collaboration. The supervisor should see that teams receive group rewards valued by team members.

3.8 Discuss how to plan for effective meetings.

The supervisor should hold a meeting only when there is a valid reason for doing so. He or she should schedule the meeting at a convenient time and plan who is to attend and where the meeting will take place. The supervisor should create an agenda, which lists the topics to be covered at the meeting. The agenda should be distributed to all participants far enough in advance that they can be prepared to contribute at the meeting.

3.9 Provide guidelines for conducting effective meetings.

Meetings should start and end promptly. The supervisor should facilitate the discussion through such means as rephrasing what participants say and summarizing key points without dominating the discussion. The supervisor should make sure that everyone participates in the discussion, take notes of what is being decided, and keep the discussion on track by reminding participants of the topic under consideration. After the meeting, the supervisor should follow up to make sure plans are carried out.

Key Terms

group, *p. 65*
functional groups, *p. 67*
task groups, *p. 67*
formal groups, *p. 67*
informal groups, *p. 67*
roles, *p. 70*

role conflicts, *p. 71*
norms, *p. 71*
status, *p. 72*
cohesiveness, *p. 73*
homogeneity, *p. 74*
team, *p. 75*

self-managing work
teams, *p. 76*
team building, *p. 79*
agenda, *p. 82*

Review and Discussion Questions

1. Think of your current job or the most recent job you held. (If you have never been employed, consider your role as a student.)

   a. Of what groups are you a member? For example, what organization employs you? In which division or department do you work? Are you a member of any informal groups?

   b. Why did you join each of these groups?

2. State whether each of the following groups is formal or informal. Then state whether it is a functional group or a task group.

   a. Six employees who have decided on their own to research the possibility of establishing an onsite day care facility.

   b. The board of directors of a major corporation.

   c. Three employees who decide to plan a birthday celebration for a co-worker.

   d. Software developers at an educational publisher.

3. Joseph Dittrick is a supervisor in the marketing department of a toy manufacturer. He is responsible for leading a group of employees in finding ways to improve a problematic product. In what ways can Joseph encourage the group to be as effective as possible?

4. Why do supervisors need to know about each of the following characteristics of groups?

   a. Roles of group members.

   b. Status of group members.

5. Yolanda Gibbs supervises employees in the reference department of a public library. Her team meets once a month to discuss ways to improve the quality of services delivered at the library. Yolanda wants the team to be cohesive so that its members will work hard. How can she encourage the cohesiveness of this group?

6. A supervisor observes that the members of a committee are not as enthusiastic about their work as they initially were. How can the supervisor help the committee move into the resolution stage of group development?

7. Peter Wilson is a supervisor who also leads a team that has been working on revamping an old product—snow saucers—to make them seem new and more attractive to a new generation of customers. The team includes both design and salespeople. What type or types of rewards might Peter consider for his team members if the project is successful?

8. How can a supervisor at an organization with self-managing work teams help the organization avoid violations of federal labor law?

9. Bonnie First supervises respiratory therapists at a large community hospital. One day her manager said, "Your department used too much overtime again last week. I want you to propose a solution to this problem, and I think you need to involve the employees in finding the solution. Get back to me in a week with your ideas." To prepare for the next meeting with her manager, Bonnie decided she needed to hold a department meeting at 1:00 the next afternoon. She asked two therapists to spread the word about this meeting.

   At the meeting, Bonnie described the problem. To her disappointment, no one seemed to have any suggestions. She said, "Unless someone has a better idea, you're just going to have to help each other out more when someone is having trouble keeping up. And don't hesitate to ask me to pitch in, too."

   How could the supervisor have better planned this meeting?

10. As a supervisor, you have done everything you can to prepare for a meeting, including writing up and distributing an agenda. At the meeting, you have problems with two of the participants. Ken dominates the conversation, drifting off to subjects that are not on the agenda. Sheryl refuses to talk at all, even though you know she has read the agenda and probably has something insightful to contribute. What steps might you take to elicit more positive participation from Ken and Sheryl?

PART TWO: SKILL-BUILDING

YOU SOLVE THE PROBLEM

Reflecting back on page 65 and Table 3.1 on page 78, discuss whether all of the characteristics listed in the table can be present in a "virtual" team, such as the sales team at CheckFree. See if your group can come up with ways for Judy Duplisea to develop all of those characteristics in her sales team. Try to identify one method to increase each characteristic listed in the table. (If you have difficulty with some team characteristics, keep in mind that most of these topics will be covered in later chapters. If time permits, repeat this exercise at the end of your course, and see whether your group has more and better ideas.)

Problem-Solving Case: *Peer Groups Help Eastman Kodak Employees Resolve Disputes*

When employees have difficult disagreements at Eastman Kodak Company, they can get help from a team of their peers. Kodak offers a peer/management dispute-resolution process. Frontline and management employees volunteer to serve as panelists who hear complaints and recommend solutions. Generally, they offer to serve because they are attracted to this approach to problem solving and they want to help; many think of themselves as eligible because they consider themselves good leaders, listeners, or problem solvers.

The peer/management dispute-resolution process brings together a panel of employees and managers, with the employees being in the majority. The panel cannot change company policies or work rules. Rather, they address whether the people in the situation they are reviewing were correctly applying company policies and rules. Kodak agrees that it will abide by the panel's decision; the employee who brings the complaint need not abide by the decision and may pursue other remedies.

Peer/management review is part of a larger conflict-resolution system at Kodak. The system's director, Mary Harris, says the ability to choose peer/management review adds to employees' satisfaction.

Some managers, however, were nervous when Kodak introduced peer/management review. The company had to reassure them that they would not be punished if a review panel overruled decisions they had made. Rather, the company explained that the process was a resource available to managers and employees alike. Experience with the process convinced Don Franks, an operations manager at the Kodak Park manufacturing facility. An employee used the process to challenge a decision Franks had made. Franks explains that he initially "wasn't too thrilled" to have one of his decisions publicly questioned, but he felt "ready for help" in resolving the problem with the employee. In the end, the panel upheld Franks's decision, and the employee was satisfied. Franks believes the employee would have continued to question the decision if the procedure had not been in place to give the issue an airing.

Harvey Caras, whose consulting firm helped Kodak set up the peer review system, says only a small percentage of supervisors need to be convinced that the system will benefit them. And in Caras's experience, they see the benefits after they understand how the system will work. He tells about the manager of a manufacturing plant who told him the dispute-resolution process has been a positive learning experience. According to Caras, the manager said, "Every time we get overruled [by a panel], we learn something that helps us make this a better place to work."

At Kodak, supervisor Patrick Teora has participated in several panels. He has found that employees from the shop floor contribute a valuable firsthand perspective, and the managers who participate contribute to gaining a grasp of required documents and procedures. He believes the two kinds of participants work well as a team because all the team members take their role seriously. Teora also has discovered that serving on a panel makes him a better supervisor. Because he's "not crazy about someone picking apart my decision," he now is more careful about how he uses his authority.

1. What challenges could arise from bringing together employees and managers to work as a group on a dispute-resolution panel? How can Kodak address these challenges?

2. To staff its peer/management review panels, Kodak requests volunteers. What are some advantages and disadvantages of using volunteers instead of another approach, such as hiring people for the job or requiring employees to participate?

3. Imagine you are the leader of a peer/management panel such as the one described in this case. Your panel is being asked to hear an employee's complaint that her supervisor unreasonably turned down her request to participate in a training program. Prepare an agenda for the panel's meeting to hear the complaint. Whose viewpoints will you need to hear? How will you ensure that all those viewpoints are heard? How will you set up the meeting to ensure that the whole panel participates in the decision?

Source: Margaret M. Clark, "A Jury of Their Peers," *HRMagazine*, January 2004, downloaded from InfoTrac, http://web4.infotrac.galegroup.com.

Knowing Yourself

How Do You Communicate as a Team Leader?

In response to each item, circle the answer that reflects what you think you always do (SA), often do (A), rarely do (D), and never do (SD). Your answer should reflect your own perceptions of the way you communicate. Be honest with yourself; you are the only one who will see the results.

1. When people talk, I listen attentively; that is, I do not think of other things, such as my response or a deadline, or read while someone is talking to me. SA A D SD
2. I provide the information the group needs, even if someone else is its source. SA A D SD
3. I get impatient when people disagree with me. SA A D SD
4. I ask for and carefully consider advice from other people. SA A D SD
5. I cut off other people when they are talking. SA A D SD
6. I tell people what I want, speaking rapidly in short, clipped sentences. SA A D SD
7. When people disagree with me, I listen to what they have to say and do not respond immediately. SA A D SD
8. I speak candidly and openly, identifying when I am expressing opinions or feelings rather than reporting facts. SA A D SD
9. I finish other people's sentences. SA A D SD
10. I find it difficult to express my feelings, except when stresses build up and I become angry. SA A D SD
11. I am conscious of how I express myself: facial expressions, body language, tone of voice, and gestures. SA A D SD
12. When people disagree with me, I avoid arguments by not responding. SA A D SD
13. During meetings, I prefer to listen rather than to talk. SA A D SD
14. When I talk, I am concise and to the point. SA A D SD
15. I prevent arguments during team meetings. SA A D SD

Agreeing (SA or A) with items 1, 4, 8, 11, and 14 and disagreeing (D or SD) with the rest suggests that you encourage openness and candor; you create a climate of trust by involving the team in important decisions that affect their lives. You communicate clearly and concisely and balance task and process dynamics.

Agreeing with items 2, 3, 5, 6, and 9 suggests you tend to be task oriented and dominate the team. You are frequently intolerant of disagreement and may squelch involvement and discussion. Disagreeing with these items does not necessarily indicate that you encourage collaboration; it could be blocked by passive communication.

Agreeing with items 7, 10, 12, 13, and 15 suggests you squelch disagreement by avoiding it and therefore undermine the team's task and process dynamics. A lack of leadership will more likely destroy a team than tyrannical leadership. At least people know what to expect from a tyrant.

Source: From *Supervisory Management,* May 1992. Copyright ©1992 by American Management Association. Reproduced with permission of American Management Association via Copyright Clearance Center.

Pause and Reflect

1. When is it helpful to be task oriented? When is it better to focus on getting contributions from the whole team?
2. Why can disagreement be beneficial in teams?
3. How can I encourage people to express their thoughts when we disagree? How can I express my own disagreements in a constructive way?

Class Exercise

Meeting Participation Skills
A key characteristic of any effective meeting is participants who know how to listen. Write a list of dos and don'ts for being a good listener in a meeting, and share your ideas with the class. Here are a few to get you started: *Do:* Be alert, concentrate on the speaker, and avoid making hasty judgments about what is said. *Don't:* Interrupt, talk to others in the room, or let your feelings about the speaker get in the way.

Building Supervision Skills

Evaluating Team Performance
In working with teams, most managers believe in the following axiom: "None of us is as smart as all of us." Let's see if this axiom holds true for this exercise.

Instructions

1. Perform this part of the exercise on your own. When your instructor starts the clock, you will have two minutes to fill in the U.S. state names on Chart 1. The first letter of each of the 50 states is provided. Write the state name out in full; do not use abbreviations. Do not talk among yourselves during this step.
2. Form teams of three to five students to work on Chart 2. Your team should select someone to record your group's list. Without looking back at the first chart you completed, your group will have two minutes to fill in the second chart. Speak quietly among yourselves so that other teams will not overhear your answers.
3. Your instructor will read the 50 state names so that you may check your answers. Then fill in the information about your team's performance.

Chart 1: Working alone
Number of correct answers for each team member: _____ _____ _____ _____
What is the average of these scores? _____

Chart 2: Working in teams

Number of correct answers your team completed: _____

How many members of your team got the same or a better score on Chart 1 than the group got on Chart 2? _____

Questions for Discussion

1. How many individual students, working alone, did as well or better than students working in one of the teams?
2. Benefiting from the collective knowledge of a group to help solve a problem is but one advantage to working in groups. Name some other advantages of working in an effective group or team that normally cannot be realized when individuals work alone.

Source: Prepared by Corinne Livesay, Belhaven College, Jackson, Mississippi.

CHART 1
Working Alone

1. A	26. M
2. A	27. N
3. A	28. N
4. A	29. N
5. C	30. N
6. C	31. N
7. C	32. N
8. D	33. N
9. F	34. N
10. G	35. O
11. H	36. O
12. I	37. O
13. I	38. P
14. I	39. R
15. I	40. S
16. K	41. S
17. K	42. T
18. L	43. T
19. M	44. U
20. M	45. V
21. M	46. V
22. M	47. W
23. M	48. W
24. M	49. W
25. M	50. W

(continued)

CHART 2
Working in Teams

1. A	26. M
2. A	27. N
3. A	28. N
4. A	29. N
5. C	30. N
6. C	31. N
7. C	32. N
8. D	33. N
9. F	34. N
10. G	35. O
11. H	36. O
12. I	37. O
13. I	38. P
14. I	39. R
15. I	40. S
16. K	41. S
17. K	42. T
18. L	43. T
19. M	44. U
20. M	45. V
21. M	46. V
22. M	47. W
23. M	48. W
24. M	49. W
25. M	50. W

Chapter **Four**

Meeting High Ethical Standards

Learning Objectives

After you have studied this chapter, you should be able to:

4.1 Define ethics and explain how organizations specify standards for ethical behavior.

4.2 Identify benefits of ethical behavior and challenges that make ethical behavior more difficult in the modern workplace.

4.3 Discuss the impact of cultural differences on ethical issues.

4.4 Describe major types of ethical behavior that supervisors should practice.

4.5 Outline ways to make ethical decisions.

4.6 Provide guidelines for supervising unethical employees.

4.7 Define whistle-blowers and describe how the supervisor should treat such employees.

You treat people the way you want to be treated. If you treat everyone with respect, somehow it comes back to you. If you are honest and aboveboard, somehow it comes back to you.

—*Dick Parsons, CEO, Time Warner*

A Supervisor's Problem: Choosing the Right Salesperson

The Small Business Administration's Web site offers business owners and managers advice on a variety of topics. The SBA's advice about business ethics includes an example that, with modifications, applies equally well to supervisors.

Imagine that Sally supervises a sales force of three people for a small software business. The company is prospering, and the sales force is having difficulty keeping up with its workload. Sally obtains approval to hire a fourth salesperson. She interviews several candidates and decides that Mary is the best of the group. On Monday, Sally calls Mary to say she is the best candidate and that Sally will ask the company's human resource department (that is, a specialist named Paul) to draft a letter offering her the job. They agree that Mary will start in two weeks, and in the meantime, Mary will make an appointment with Paul to fill out the necessary paperwork.

The next day, a friend of Sally's calls her to say she found the "perfect person" for the salesperson's job. Sally tells her friend that she just offered the job to someone else. The friend insists, "Just meet this guy. Who knows, maybe you'll want to hire him in the future." Sally feels uncomfortable, but her friend persists, and Sally eventually says, "Well, if he can come in tomorrow, I'll talk to him, but I won't make any promises." Sally's friend says, "You won't be sorry. Gene is perfect for that job. I'll have him e-mail you his résumé."

On Wednesday afternoon, Gene arrives in Sally's office for an interview. Sally realizes, with some dismay, that her friend was right. Gene's experience and attitude are exactly what she was looking for. He is a better fit for the job than Mary is. He even has a list of new prospects for the company. It appears that whereas Mary could enable the company to meet its sales goals, Gene could exceed its goals.

Sally considers her options. It had been difficult to get the company to authorize hiring one additional salesperson, so she feels sure it would be impossible to hire both candidates. She concludes that she must either honor her promise to Mary or withdraw her offer in order to hire the best person for the job. Either way, it seems, she would be doing a good thing (keeping a promise or hiring well). And either way, she would be doing something wrong (breaking a promise or hiring the second best). What would you advise Sally to do?

Sources: Case adapted from Small Business Administration, "Business Ethics: The Foundation of Effective Leadership," leadership pages of Managing Your Business, SBA Web site, www.sba.gov, July 19, 2004; "You Solve the Problem" question on page 109 based on Barbara Ley Toffler, "Five Ways to Jump-Start Your Company's Ethics," *Fast Company,* October 2003, downloaded from InfoTrac, http://web7.infotrac.galegroup.com.

As the case about Sally indicates, many decisions that supervisors make are more complicated than a choice between right and wrong. In business, as in our daily lives, we make choices that affect other people in complex ways. To help you make choices that consider the impact on others, this chapter covers the role of ethics in the workplace. The chapter begins by distinguishing ethical behavior from unethical behavior. Next, guidelines describe how supervisors should behave ethically. The chapter also explains how to handle the challenges of supervising unethical employees and employees who report unethical or illegal behavior in the organization.

ETHICS IN THE WORKPLACE

ethics
The principles by which people distinguish what is morally right

In general, **ethics** refers to the principles people use to distinguish what is morally right. For example, most people would agree that cheating is wrong, or at least they would agree that it is unethical to cheat an elderly widow out of her life savings. Many decisions about ethics are more difficult. For example, is it cheating or just clever to pad an expense report or take advantage of a supplier's mistake in totaling a bill? The Knowing Yourself quiz on pages 110–111 is a chance for you to examine your own standards of ethical behavior. To get an accurate score, be honest with yourself!

Some people say that "business ethics" is an oxymoron—that is, a contradiction in terms. Can businesspeople behave ethically, and if so, should they? One view is that profitability should be the overriding concern of business. This view makes it easy to behave ethically unless an ethical choice is also costly to the organization. Another view is that organizations and their employees have an obligation to behave ethically, even if doing so cuts into short-term economic advantages. The implication is that we are all better off if organizations and individuals consider the common good.

As a supervisor, you will be looking for ethical behavior in your employees and also making sure you contribute to an environment that encourages ethical actions. Research suggests that such efforts do make a difference. A recent survey by the Ethics Resource Center found that over the past several years, employees have reported feeling less pressure to make ethical compromises and see fewer unethical actions by others. At the same time, the percentage of employees who have reported misconduct by co-workers has risen. This trend does not necessarily mean that more misdeeds are occurring but rather that employees trust their employer to act on their complaints.[1] Figure 4.1 summarizes some trends in this survey between 2000 and 2003.

Benefits of Ethical Behavior

In addition to being morally right, ethical behavior offers potential advantages to the organization. To be known as an ethical individual or organization is a satisfying way of maintaining a reputation for high standards. In a study of hundreds of salespeople, those who perceived that their organization maintained high ethical standards were more likely to trust their supervisor and be satisfied with their job, and salespeople who trusted their supervisor were more likely to plan to stay with the company.[2] Achieving this type of ethical climate is mostly a matter of day-to-day practices. For example, employees expect their supervisor to be fair. One way to demonstrate fairness involves performance reviews. Supervisors can give fair performance appraisals by setting clear, measurable standards, making sure employees know and understand these standards, and scoring performance objectively according to the standards.[3]

Ethical behavior is part of a range of behaviors that ensure an organization's long-term health and success. For a business, that success shows up in the performance of the company's stock. Some investors go out of their way to select companies with a good track record of ethical behavior. Jim Huguet built a

FIGURE 4.1

Highlights of the National Business Ethics Survey

Source: Ethics Resource Center, "2003 National Business Ethics Survey: Executive Summary," www.ethics.org, July 19, 2004; Ethics Resource Center, "Major Survey of America's Workers Finds Substantial Improvements in Ethics," news release, May 21, 2003, www.ethics.org.

Employees Who . . .

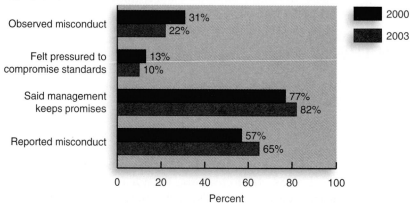

high-performing portfolio of stocks by looking at various performance measures including the companies' "corporate governance"—systems for ensuring that the leaders put the company's success ahead of enriching themselves.[4] A number of investment firms, including Calvert Funds, Domini Social Investments, and Pax World Funds, list ethical behavior as one of their criteria for choosing stocks. Analysts at such firms are likely to steer away from companies that have been fined by government regulators, have been audited by supposedly independent firms that are also earning fees for consulting, or pay executives more than $10 million per year.[5]

Ethical behavior can also improve the organization's relations with the community, which tends to attract customers and top-notch employees. Children's clothing company Hanna Andersson is well known for its concern for the community. That concern is expressed through charitable giving of a portion of its profits and the Hannadowns program for donating its clothing, which is durable as well as beautiful. The company also pays employees for working up to 16 hours a year as volunteers in their communities. Co-founder Gun Denhart says, "Businesses, like people, don't live in a vacuum. You can't have a healthy company in an unhealthy community."[6] As well as earning approval, ethical behavior tends to reduce public pressure for government regulation—a situation that most managers would view as beneficial.

In contrast, the costs of unethical behavior can be high. Organizations whose employees are unethical may lose respect, customers, and qualified employees who are uncomfortable working in an environment that compromises their moral standards. Unethical and illegal behavior caused the downfall of many companies in recent years, including Enron and Tyco. Others, among them Boeing and Martha Stewart Living Omnimedia, have struggled to recover from scandals.

Unethical behavior has personal consequences as well. Federal employees who accept gifts that fall outside federal government regulations can be suspended, demoted, or even fired. The restrictions require that the gifts not be given as a result of the recipient's position or office and not come from a "prohibited source," such as a person or organization that does business with the employee's agency. Sometimes gifts must be accepted in order not to offend the giver. These must be publicly reported and are considered gifts to the department rather than the individual employee. Examples include recent donations to CIA employees: Pakistani rugs valued at $500 each, an antique rifle valued at $750, and a "Middle Eastern filigree silver and partial gilt palm tree form night-light," valued at $500.[7] Some unethical acts that are also illegal may result in jail sentences. MBA students at the University of Maryland travel to the Federal Correction Institute in Cumberland, Maryland, where they meet white-collar executives and professionals serving time for fraud or embezzlement.[8]

Challenges to Ethical Behavior

Despite these implications, the restructurings, cutbacks, and layoffs of recent years have made ethical behavior harder to encourage. With greater responsibilities, supervisors and other managers in restructured or downsized organizations cannot monitor employees' day-to-day behavior. At the same time, the uncertainty of the work environment has made many employees afraid of being ethical when doing so conflicts with other goals. Fudging numbers on performance records or producing shoddy merchandise to keep costs down is tempting, if the alternative is to be laid off for failing to meet cost or performance goals. Hard-pressed employees need flexibility, authority, and ethical leadership to

SUPERVISION AND ETHICS

CAR RENTAL EMPLOYEES NEED AUTHORITY TO BE ETHICAL

In Slidell, Louisiana, along the Gulf Coast, the Perez family was among those receiving orders to evacuate on a Saturday morning in 2005 as Hurricane Katrina approached the coastline. For the Perezes, evacuating posed an additional challenge: Their car was in the shop for repairs. The family had obtained a rental car for that weekend, so they loaded it with their belongings and headed to Alabama for what they anticipated would be a short stay at the home of some friends.

The next day, the hurricane passed directly over Slidell, and floodwaters rose to 20 feet in some parts of town. In the days following the hurricane, returning to the devastated area was impossible. Still, that Tuesday, the car was due back at the flooded rental office.

Unsure what to do, the Perezes called the company's main customer service office. The representative had no ideas either and asked them to call back "in a couple of days." When asked how this would affect the terms of the contract, the representative could offer no information. Two days later, the family called again, and a representative said they should return it to the local Alabama facility and that they would not be charged for the two extra days.

However, when the Perezes returned the car, they received a bill for a full six-day rental—and at more than four times the rate per day charged in their original contract. Instead of about $150, the

family was asked to pay more than $1,500 for the car. When the Perezes objected, the agent at the counter insisted that the rules are the rules, and the family had not adhered to their original contract. The company could not waver from the contract, the agent maintained, because it was "just a business."

No one at the office was willing to call the central customer service office and verify the original promise, so the Perezes called on their cell phone and negotiated a total of $332. A week later, they managed to reach the person who had made the original promise, and after an hour's discussion, they obtained a refund of the difference.

Should employees bend contract terms to assist victims of a disaster? Do businesses as well as individuals have an ethical duty to help people in need? Apparently, one customer service representative was paralyzed by these questions. The second thought a discount was the right thing to do and perhaps that it was the best way to fulfill the agency's advertising promise to "try harder." The third agent focused only on the contract. (Of course, if the Perezes had followed the contract strictly and returned the car to Slidell, that car would have been underwater with all the other vehicles in the facility's parking lot.) All three agents' actions were influenced by their sense of what the company would allow them to do.

Source: Based on Herbert Jack Rotfeld, "It's Just Business," *Journal of Consumer Affairs,* Summer 2006, downloaded from Business & Company Resource Center, http://galenet.galegroup.com.

create an environment in which to make principled decisions. For an example of circumstances in which ethical decision making was difficult, see "Supervision and Ethics."

Other challenges arise from the supervisor's environment. According to Ethics Resource Center President Stuart Gilman, companies that single-mindedly focus on sales or profits can create an environment in which employees feel as if they have to bend the rules. According to Gilman, employees need training and guidance, as well as a readily available source of advice about ethical behavior.[9] Along with high-pressure goals, some organizations create a climate in which employees fear they need to be unethical to save the company's future or be treated as a team player. Figure 4.2 summarizes the most common reasons people feel pressured to compromise their ethical standards, according to a recent survey.

On a more mundane level, a supervisor may simply find that tolerating lapses of ethics leads employees to behave in increasingly unacceptable ways. For example,

FIGURE 4.2
Top Five Sources of Pressure to Compromise Ethical Standards

Source: "How to Help Reinvigorate Your Organization's Ethics Program," *HR Focus*, June 2003, downloaded from InfoTrac, http://web3 .infotrac.galegroup.com.

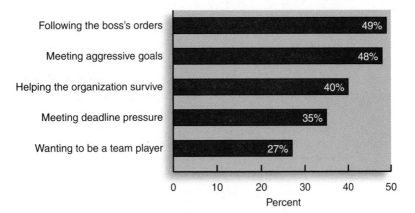

Following the boss's orders — 49%
Meeting aggressive goals — 48%
Helping the organization survive — 40%
Meeting deadline pressure — 35%
Wanting to be a team player — 27%

Percent

if the supervisor looks the other way when employees take home small items like pencils or screws, employees may eventually start "borrowing" bigger items.

Differing Measures of Ethical Behavior

code of ethics
An organization's written statement of its values and rules for ethical behavior

How can supervisors meet these challenges to ethical behavior? A good starting point is to seek guidance from the organization's **code of ethics,** if it has adopted one. This is an organization's written statement of its values and rules for ethical behavior. For instance, Figure 4.3 shows the credo (statement of beliefs) for

FIGURE 4.3
The Johnson & Johnson Credo (Statement of Beliefs)

Source: Johnson & Johnson, "Our Company: Our Credo," corporate Web site, www.jnj .com, November 14, 2005.

We believe our first responsibility is to the doctors, nurses and patients, to mothers and fathers and all others who use our products and services.
In meeting their needs everything we do must be of high quality.
We must constantly strive to reduce our costs in order to maintain reasonable prices.
Customers' orders must be serviced promptly and accurately.
Our suppliers and distributors must have an opportunity to make a fair profit.

We are responsible to our employees, the men and women who work with us throughout the world.
Everyone must be considered as an individual. We must respect their dignity and recognize their merit. They must have a sense of security in their jobs.
Compensation must be fair and adequate, and working conditions clean, orderly and safe.
Employees must feel free to make suggestions and complaints.
There must be equal opportunity for employment, development and advancement for those qualified.
We must provide competent management, and their actions must be just and ethical.

We are responsible to the communities in which we live and work and to the world community as well.
We must be good citizens—support good works and charities and bear our fair share of taxes.
We must encourage civic improvements and better health and education.
We must maintain in good order the property we are privileged to use, protecting the environment and natural resources.

Our final responsibility is to our stockholders. Business must make a sound profit. We must experiment with new ideas.
Research must be carried on, innovative programs developed and mistakes paid for. New equipment must be purchased, new facilities provided and new products launched.
Reserves must be created to provide for adverse times.
When we operate according to these principles, the stockholder should realize a fair return.

Johnson & Johnson Corporation, which serves as a code of ethics for that company. The Carnegie Council of the United States and Uehiro Foundation of Japan have established a code of ethics based on the common world heritage of Plato, Aristotle, and Confucius.[10]

Meeting high ethical standards is especially challenging for those who work with people from more than one culture, because ethical standards can vary from culture to culture. In a study comparing values of professionals in the United States, Canada, and Mexico, respondents from all the countries agreed that honesty is one of the most important qualities for representing ethical standards in business. However, only Canadian professionals included loyalty among the top three values, and only Mexican professionals put compromise in the top three.[11] Even when ideals match, people in different parts of the world may accept different standards of behavior from businesspeople. Transparency International tracks perceived levels of corruption, such as bribery of public officials, and finds a wide variation in the amount of corrupt practices people observe from country to country. As shown in Figure 4.4, people in Finland, Denmark, and New Zealand observe very little corruption. In contrast, corruption is common in Haiti, Nigeria, and Bangladesh.[12]

FIGURE 4.4   **A Sampling of Countries' Perceived Corruption Levels**

Source: From "Transparency International Corruption Perception Index 2003." Reprinted with permission.

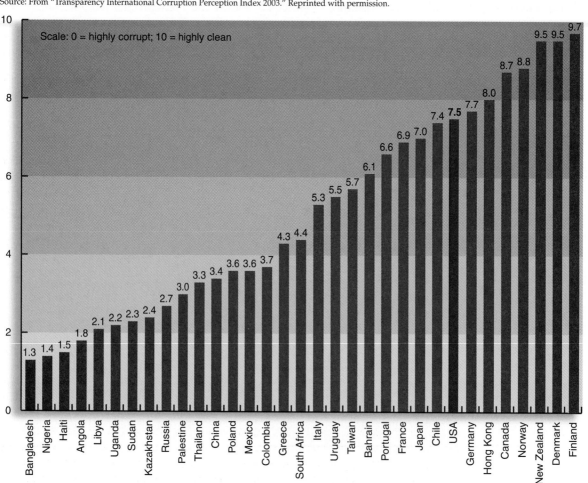

If an organization does business in a country where corruption is expected, employees can have more difficulty meeting high standards. Coca-Cola sells beverages in almost every country in the world, with two-thirds of its sales coming from outside the United States. To serve the 9 million stores selling Coke, the company has contracts with hundreds of bottlers, which add water to the company's trademark concentrate and distribute the soft drinks in cans and bottles. To gain entrance into some countries, the company found that it was expected to use politically connected individuals as its bottlers. In Iran, that person was a relative of the country's president; in Uzbekistan, it was a son-in-law of the president, who brought in his brother to help run the company. For oil companies, entering a foreign market to drill for oil generally involves negotiating huge contracts with the government, however unsavory that government might be. ExxonMobil's payments to Angola's President, Jose Eduardo dos Santos, in the 1990s helped to fund that country's civil war. The company's chairman, Lee Raymond, defends such arrangements on the grounds that an oil company cannot choose where to operate: "You kinda have to go where the oil is."[13]

One reason for perceived differences in corruption levels is that gift giving in the workplace can have different meanings from one culture to another. In the United States, the giving of gifts often is interpreted as bribery, an attempt to buy influence. However, in many parts of the world, giving a gift is the proper way to indicate one's gratitude toward and respect for the receiver. Cross-cultural gift giving and receiving can present sensitive issues, and it can be difficult for the supervisor to apply accepted U.S. standards to situations in international business or with employees and managers from different cultures. Here are a few guidelines for successful gift giving in a multinational environment:

- Avoid gifts and cards of a religious nature or that would be offensive to certain religions (e.g., ham for a Jewish or Muslim recipient, liquor for a Muslim recipient).
- Make it clear that you intend the gift as a gift and not a bribe. Sometimes this will mean giving a group gift rather than an individual one.
- Know the meanings of everyday objects and their quantity. Leather goods are not acceptable among Hindus; the Chinese consider watches and clocks reminders of death. Flowers have special meanings in many cultures. The numbers four and nine are unlucky in Japan, whereas gifts in sets of eight are welcomed.
- Know how to give and receive. The U.S. custom of gleefully tearing the package open is not universal.
- To avoid confusion that gifts are intended as bribes, establish a policy that all gifts are to be of a value that signals respect but not enough to influence the receiver. The company might arrange to have its brand printed or embroidered on a set of gifts that meet these criteria.[14]

What can a supervisor do if refusing a gift might insult the giver? Most important, the supervisor must follow company policy, and in many cases, that means turning down the gift. At the same time, however, the supervisor should explain carefully and politely the reason for not accepting the gift. If a supervisor has immigrant employees who might not understand U.S. views about gift giving, this might be an area about which to educate all employees before such a problem arises. Find out if there are any company policies or codes of ethics covering the situation. Following these policies is essential for all employees, including supervisors, and provides a way to show that turning down a gift is not meant as an insult to the giver. Some companies have helped individuals make ethical choices in an international context by signing the voluntary United Nations Global Compact. The compact includes principles of global citizenship, such as working against extortion and bribery. So far, 1,700 organizations have signed the compact; of these, 61 are U.S. organizations, including Nike and Goldman Sachs.[15]

ETHICAL BEHAVIOR OF SUPERVISORS

If supervisors wish to see a high standard of ethical behavior in the workplace, they must behave ethically themselves. Supervisors in particular must exhibit important dimensions of ethical behavior including loyalty, fairness, and honesty (see Figure 4.5).

As a leader, a supervisor is expected to be loyal to the organization, to his or her manager, and to his or her subordinates (see Chapter 8). When these loyalties conflict, ethical dilemmas result. These loyalties also may come into conflict with the supervisor's self-interests. If supervisors are seen by others in the organization to put their own interests first, they will have difficulty earning the loyalty, trust, and respect of others.

Fairness is another important trait of a supervisor. Employees expect to be treated evenhandedly. They resent it if the supervisor plays favorites or passes the blame for mistakes on to them. In some cases, their resentment can breed unethical responses that make the situation even worse. Consider the case of the consultant who worked with a lumber company that suffered falling profits despite strong sales. The consultant observed that employees were treated harshly, and he asked an employee why absenteeism was low and quality was high, considering that these measures often suffer when employees are unhappy. The employee had a ready answer: Whenever employees were upset, they would "feed the hog," a large wood chipper. The chipper was there to grind up scrap for chips to make particleboard; angry employees would "feed" it finished lumber, and management

FIGURE 4.5
Important Dimensions of Ethical Behavior by Supervisors

would never know the difference. Employees didn't want to miss work, because they had "hog quotas"—if they didn't feed the hog, they put $20 into a fund that was used for parties every few months.[16] In this situation, employees felt they were treated unfairly, so they tried to even the score by cheating their employer. Ironically, no one is really benefiting; rather, fair treatment of employees and profitability would go hand in hand.

Supervisors may find it harder to be fair—or to convince others that they are fair—when they supervise their own relatives. Therefore, supervisors may find it wise to avoid **nepotism,** the hiring of one's own relatives. A related problem can arise when supervisors accept a gift from a supplier or someone else who may wish to influence their judgment. Even if a supervisor is sure about remaining objective in the acceptance of cash, lavish entertainment, or other gifts, other people may question whether the supervisor can be fair. When supervisors place themselves in such a position, management tends to doubt their ability to exercise good judgment.

nepotism
The hiring of one's relatives

Honesty includes several types of behavior by the supervisor. First, when employees make a suggestion or accomplish impressive results, the supervisor should be sure that the employees get the credit. Pretending that other people's accomplishments are your own is a type of dishonesty. So is using the company's resources for personal matters. For example, a supervisor who spends work time chatting with friends on the phone or who takes supplies home for personal use in effect is stealing what belongs to the organization. Furthermore, the supervisor is demonstrating that such behavior will be overlooked, thus encouraging employees to be equally dishonest. Finally, supervisors should be honest about what the organization can offer employees.

Making Ethical Decisions

Assuming that it is desirable to choose ethical behavior and to help employees do so, the challenge is to decide what action is ethical in a particular situation and then determine how to carry it out. There are no hard-and-fast rules for making ethical decisions. In some cases, two possibilities might seem equally ethical or unethical. Perhaps someone will get hurt no matter what the supervisor decides. In addition, as discussed previously, people from different cultures may have different measures of ethical or unethical behavior. "Tips from the Firing Line" offers recommendations for making decisions when faced with this kind of dilemma.

Sometimes the supervisor can promote ethical decision making by involving others in the process. When the group discusses the issue, group members can offer their perspectives on the situation and the underlying values. Discussing the ethical implications of the decision can help the supervisor see consequences and options that he or she might not have thought of alone. (Chapter 9 provides further guidelines for group decision making.)

Deciding what behavior is ethical does not always end an ethical dilemma. Employees are sometimes afraid that doing what is morally right will cause their performance to suffer and may even cost them their jobs. The National Business Ethics Survey, mentioned at the beginning of this chapter, found that such fears are most common among younger employees and those who have been with an organization for less than three years.[17] However, supervisors can help alleviate these concerns. Employees respond when supervisors and higher-level managers model ethical behavior and include ethical standards in performance discussions and rewards (even as simple as praising ethical actions).

TIPS FROM THE FIRING LINE

MAKING ETHICAL CHOICES

In some situations, the ethical course of action is obvious. But how can supervisors decide what to do when the alternatives are a mixture of benefits and harm, greed and good? On its Web site, Loyola Marymount University's Center for Ethics and Business offers a three-step strategy for resolving ethical dilemmas. This strategy combines two ways that people usually think about ethics: by weighing an action's consequences and by evaluating the action itself.

Consequences are usually easier to compare, so first think about the consequences of each alternative. List who will be helped by each alternative, then list who will be harmed. For each person or group on the list, consider the kind of benefit and harm that will result. Will the benefit or harm be great or minor? Consider both the short-term and long-term consequences. Look for the alternative that offers the best mix of great benefits and minor harm.

Next, shift from the consequences and consider the action itself. Does each alternative action involve behaviors that meet high moral standards, such as fairness, honesty, and respect for people's dignity? Do any of the actions violate moral principles? Try to find an alternative that meets the highest standards of behavior.

Finally, compare the choices that result from each way of thinking about ethics. If the first two steps lead to the same alternative, your decision is complete. If not, you will have to make a difficult decision, considering which way of thinking about ethics best reflects your own values.

Source: Center for Ethics and Business, "Resolving an Ethical Dilemma," www.ethicsandbusiness.org/strategy.htm, July 19, 2004.

Supervising Unethical Employees

It is tempting to ignore the unethical behavior of others, hoping they will change on their own. However, the problem usually gets worse as the unethical employee sees that he or she can get away with the behavior. Consequently, when the supervisor suspects that an employee is behaving unethically, the supervisor needs to take prompt action. Figure 4.6 summarizes the steps to take.

The first step is to gather and record evidence. The supervisor needs to be sure that unethical behavior is actually occurring. For example, if the supervisor suspects that one or more employees are padding their expense accounts, the supervisor regularly should review expense reports. As soon as the supervisor sees something that looks odd, he or she should ask the employee about it. After confronting the employee with the evidence, the supervisor should follow the organization's disciplinary procedure. (Discipline is discussed in Chapter 12.)

After dealing with the specific problem, the supervisor should try to understand what conditions contributed to this problem. That effort can help the supervisor avoid similar ethical lapses in the future. In analyzing why an employee has behaved unethically, consider whether you have created a climate for ethical

FIGURE 4.6   Steps to Take When an Employee Is Suspected of Unethical Behavior

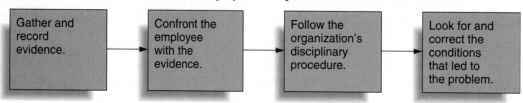

behavior in the department. Have you set a good example through your own ethical behavior? Are the rewards for productivity so great that they tempt employees to cut ethical corners? Do the employees hear messages that say the organization cares only about achievements, such as, "I don't care how you get it done, just do it"? Ethics consultant Frank Bucaro says a salesperson who believes his or her job depends on meeting a sales target can risk the company's reputation. One overeager salesperson can give customers the impression that the whole organization puts ethics and customer satisfaction on the back burner.[18]

TREATMENT OF WHISTLE-BLOWERS

whistle-blower
Someone who exposes a violation of ethics or law

Someone who exposes a violation of ethics or law is known as a **whistle-blower.** Typically, a whistle-blower brings the problem first to a manager in the organization. If management seems unresponsive, he or she then contacts a government agency, the media, or a private organization. The whistle-blower's hope is that the negative publicity will spur the organization to do the right thing. Of course, the negative publicity also can damage the organization. As described in "Supervisory Skills," strong ethical leadership is essential at that point.

A whistle-blower's report may be embarrassing as well as costly to the organization. Nevertheless, whistle-blowers are protected by federal laws, the laws of several states, and some recent court decisions. For example, federal laws protect employees who make complaints pertaining to violations of antidiscrimination laws, environmental laws, and occupational health and safety standards. Most recently, the Sarbanes-Oxley Act forbids employers from retaliating against an employee who reports possible accounting, auditing, or reporting misdeeds that deceive investors. Thus, in general, employers may not retaliate against someone for reporting a violation. Suppose an employee files a complaint of sexual harassment; the organization may not react by firing the employee who complained.

In addition, under a Civil War–era law that was little used until the late 1980s, whistle-blowers who report on companies that are cheating the government stand to receive up to 30 percent of whatever money the company ultimately pays as a penalty for the fraud. The number of cases filed by whistle-blowers under the False Claims Act jumped from 66 in 1987 to 533 in 1997, and the cases filed each year continues to be high (394 in 2005). Recoveries under the False Claims Act since 1987 have totaled more than $17 billion, with an average of almost 17 percent awarded to the whistle-blowers.[19] In a dramatic recent case, paralegal R. C. Taylor filed a whistle-blower lawsuit claiming that the law firm he formerly worked for had engaged in fraud, attempting to deceive the Federal Communications Commission. In a settlement, the firm agreed to pay $130 million to the Justice Department; Taylor (and his attorneys) will receive more than $30 million of that amount.[20]

Despite these protections, whistle-blowers often suffer for going public with their complaints. Typically, the whistle-blower is resented and rejected by co-workers and may be demoted or terminated. Even when the courts agree that the whistle-blower was treated unlawfully, it can take years for that person to be compensated by the organization or even appreciated by the public. Even when a whistle-blower keeps his or her job, there are consequences. Daniel Thobe blew the whistle at DPL Inc., a utility company. Thobe informed DPL's audit committee that he had concerns about the company's financial reporting and corporate governance. The committee hired an independent law firm to investigate, and the lawyers agreed with some of Thobe's concerns. Three top executives

SUPERVISORY SKILLS

LEADING AT BOEING

In recent years, aircraft powerhouse Boeing has been weakened by scandals, lawsuits, and negative publicity. The bad publicity hurt the bottom line as well as Boeing's image. Boeing's chief financial officer was found to have discussed job opportunities with an Air Force procurement officer. This was a conflict of interest because the Air Force officer, Darleen Druyun, had been involved in negotiating a contract to lease and buy aerial tankers from Boeing. Boeing eventually hired Druyun. Another accusation was that two Boeing employees used documents stolen from Lockheed Martin to compete with Lockheed for a contract to launch rockets for the Air Force. According to the allegations, one of the employees took the documents from Lockheed when Boeing hired him away from that company. Boeing was further embarrassed by accusations that it repeatedly downplayed the situation to the government and Lockheed. The government put on hold a billion dollars' worth of work on rocket launching, as well as Boeing's bid for the aerial tankers, worth more than $20 billion.

In this tainted environment, Boeing's top executives had to make ethics a cornerstone of the company to rebuild its reputation. Each of the company's employees must sign a code of conduct. Boeing created a 100-person office to administer ethics policies. Its duties include staffing a hotline and training employees. Executives also repeatedly traveled to Washington, D.C., to meet with officials and lawmakers. Government officials cautiously waited for the company to clean house before continuing to do business with Boeing.

Recently, the Department of Justice announced a settlement with Boeing over the Lockheed investigation: The company agreed to pay a record $615 million penalty and accepted responsibility for its employees' actions. Boeing Chairman and CEO Jim McNerney said, "We have put in place an ethics and compliance program that is as rigorous as any that exist in industry today. . . . It is our goal to make Boeing as well known for ethics and compliance as it is for the quality of its products and technologies."

Sources: Associated Press, "Boeing Settlement Is a Record," *The Olympian*, July 1, 2006, www.theolympian.com; Jonathan R. Laing, "Taking Flight," *Barron's Online*, July 5, 2004, http://online.wsj.com/barrons/; J. Lynn Lunsford and Andy Pasztor, "New Boss Struggles to Lift Boeing above Military Scandals," *The Wall Street Journal*, July 14, 2004, http://online.wsj.com.

resigned, and DPL promised to strengthen its financial controls. Even though Thobe was protected by the Sarbanes-Oxley Act and kept his job, he faced the embarrassment of scathing criticism by DPL's executives during the investigation. And like other whistle-blowers who keep their jobs, Thobe is in the awkward position of working for a company he is known to have subjected to an investigation.[21] Because of these consequences—and out of fairness to one's employer—a would-be whistle-blower should try to resolve problems within the organization before blowing the whistle.

Today, many organizations are protecting ethics-minded employees and themselves with hotlines that make it easier to report and resolve ethical disputes within the organization. HCA, which runs hospitals and other health care facilities, uses a hotline that receives more than 1,000 calls a year. More than half of the calls involve personnel problems; the remainder include complaints about harassment, fraud, patient care, billing errors, and issues related to environmental protection. HCA's goal is to respond to every complaint within 24 hours, keep records of its response, and make the records available to the caller. (Anonymous complainers can look up the record by case number.) The procedure has uncovered a conspiracy that involved fraudulent billing of HCA by a temporary-help agency, as well as a situation in which a supervisor borrowed several thousand dollars from employees and then failed to pay back most of the money. The unethical supervisor was fired.[22]

A supervisor's general attitude toward whistle-blowing should be to discourage reports of wrongdoing when they are motivated simply by pettiness or a desire to get back at someone. Yet, when someone does complain, the supervisor should investigate the complaint quickly and report what will be done. This lets employees know that their complaints are taken seriously and that the supervisor wants to handle them fairly and appropriately. The supervisor should bear in mind that the typical whistle-blower is not simply a troublemaker but a person with high ideals and competence. Keeping communication flowing and responding to problems will allow the organization to find solutions without the costs and embarrassment of public disclosure. Finally, engaging in ethical behavior can eliminate the need for whistle-blowing—and the other negative fallout of misconduct—in the first place.

SKILLS MODULE

PART ONE: CONCEPTS

Summary

4.1 Define ethics and explain how organizations specify standards for ethical behavior.

Ethics refers to the principles by which people distinguish what is morally right. Organizations are particularly concerned about ethical behavior because modern technology has made the potential consequences of unethical behavior enormous. Recognizing the importance of preventing ethical lapses, many organizations have adopted a code of ethics. Codes of ethics provide guidelines for behavior and support top management's assertion that they care about ethical behavior.

4.2 Identify benefits of ethical behavior and challenges that make ethical behavior more difficult in the modern workplace.

To be known as an ethical organization is a satisfying way of maintaining a reputation for high standards. When customers, clients, and suppliers see that they are treated ethically, they are more likely to want to work cooperatively with the organization and do their best for it. Ethical behavior can also improve community relations, attracting customers and qualified employees. Unethical behavior, in contrast, can cause an organization to lose both respect and the best employees (who may be uncomfortable working for an unethical organization). Unethical behavior may even land employees and managers in jail if they break the law.

An uncertain work environment can make ethical behavior harder to encourage. Fear of losing one's job can lead employees to cooperate with unethical activities sponsored by others, so it is important for supervisors to foster a climate that encourages ethical behavior.

4.3 Discuss the impact of cultural differences on ethical issues.

In some cases, ethical standards and behavior vary among cultures. The biggest risk of operating in the most corrupt countries is potential shifts in the political winds. One reason for perceived differences in levels of corruption is that gift giving in the workplace is interpreted differently from country to country. The supervisor should always follow company policy but do so carefully and politely in order not to offend members of another culture.

4.4 Describe major types of ethical behavior that supervisors should practice.
Supervisors should be loyal to the organization, their manager, and their subordinates. Supervisors should treat others, especially employees, fairly. Ways to dispel any doubts about one's fairness are to avoid nepotism and decline gifts from suppliers and others seeking influence. Finally, supervisors should be honest, which includes giving subordinates credit for their accomplishments and avoiding personal use of the company's resources.

4.5 Outline ways to make ethical decisions.
There are no hard-and-fast rules for making ethical decisions, but asking some essential questions can help. The supervisor can promote ethical decision making by involving others in the thought process. Discussing the ethical implications of the decision can help the supervisor see consequences and options that he or she might not have thought of alone.

4.6 Provide guidelines for supervising unethical employees.
When the supervisor believes an employee is doing something unethical, he or she should take immediate action. The supervisor first should gather and record evidence. Then the supervisor should confront the employee with the evidence and follow the organization's disciplinary procedure. After dealing with a specific problem, the supervisor should try to understand what conditions contributed to the problem and then seek to correct those conditions.

4.7 Define whistle-blowers and describe how the supervisor should treat such employees.
Whistle-blowers are people who expose a violation of ethics or law. They are protected from retaliation by federal and state laws as well as recent court decisions. The supervisor should discourage reports of wrongdoing when they are motivated simply by pettiness or a desire for revenge. However, when someone does complain, the supervisor should quickly investigate the complaint and report what will be done. This lets employees know that their complaints are taken seriously. Keeping communication flowing and responding to problems ultimately allows the organization to find its own solutions.

Key Terms	ethics, *p.* 95	nepotism, *p.* 103
	code of ethics, *p.* 99	whistle-blower, *p.* 105

Review and Discussion Questions

1. What are some benefits of ethical behavior? What are some challenges to ethical behavior?
2. Gift giving in the workplace is interpreted differently from culture to culture. What can a supervisor do if his or her company prohibits accepting gifts but a customer from another culture insists on offering one?
3. In what ways can loyalty create conflict for a supervisor?
4. How should a supervisor practice honesty in the workplace?
5. In each of the following situations, what would have been the ethical thing for the employee or supervisor to do? What criteria did you use to decide? What would you have done in that situation? Why?
   a. Upon being hired, a new employee offers his supervisor confidential information about his former employer's marketing plan for a new product. The two companies have competing product lines.

b. The associate editor of a magazine learns that a particularly newsworthy individual wants to be paid to grant an interview with the magazine. The magazine's policy is never to pay for interviews, but the editor knows she could "bury" the expense elsewhere in her budget. She desperately wants the story; she knows it will be good for both the magazine and her career.

6. Devon Price supervises a crew of maintenance workers. One day a secretary at the company took him aside and asked, "Do you know that Pete [a member of the crew] has been taking home supplies like nails and tape to work on personal projects?" What should Devon do?

7. Assume that Pete, the maintenance worker in question 6, was discovered pilfering supplies and was disciplined. Upset, he decides to act on some safety problems he has observed and complained about, and he reports them to the local office of the Occupational Safety and Health Administration (OSHA). When Devon, Pete's supervisor, finds out that the department will be investigated by OSHA, he is furious. It seems as though Pete is nothing but a troublemaker. What should Devon do?

PART TWO: SKILL-BUILDING

YOU SOLVE THE PROBLEM

Reflecting back on page 95, compare Sally's alternatives (hiring Mary or hiring Gene) in terms of three questions:

- Is the alternative legal?
- Is it balanced (fair to everyone in the short and long term)?
- Is it right?

See if your group can arrive at a unanimous decision to hire Mary or Gene.

If the solution isn't obvious, try this suggestion from writer Barbara Ley Toffler: Discuss the problem in terms of a word that has a strong image. Instead of asking what would be the *ethical* choice for Sally, ask, "What would be the *responsible* thing to do? What would be the *decent* thing to do? What would be the *honorable* thing to do?" Now can your group arrive at a unanimous decision?

Summarize your decision and your basis for selecting it. What has this group discussion taught you about making ethical decisions?

Problem-Solving Case: *Lawyers, Ford, and Firestone: Who's to Blame?*

One of the country's top traffic-safety consulting firms, Strategic Safety, identified 30 cases of Firestone tire failures on Ford Explorers in 1996, after Texas lawyers bringing suits against Bridgestone and Firestone retained the company's services. Although a few of these cases had resulted in deaths, Strategic Safety and the lawyers passed on several opportunities to tell the National Highway Traffic Safety Administration (NHTSA) about them. Sean Kane, a partner in Strategic Safety, says lawyers were "very leery" of letting the government know, lest an investigation find nothing wrong and the firm's pending individual lawsuits be compromised. "You don't want to be tipping your hand to the defendants," Kane said, who later also claimed that he had tried to alert the media with information he had gotten from NHTSA's own database.

After 1996, however, more problems with Firestone tires surfaced, particularly in Texas where prolonged high-speed driving in hot weather contributed to deadly tread separation in the tires.

Kane disclosed in July 2000 that Ford was recalling Firestone tires in Venezuela, and the resulting pressure forced a similar recall in the United States. Firestone recalled 6.5 million tires in the fall of 2000, all of which had been sold to Ford Motor Company for its Ford Explorer sport utility vehicle, and it was revealed that accidents related to the Explorer were responsible for 203 deaths in the United States, all but 13 of them occurring after 1996.

Ford claims the tires were flawed and voluntarily recalled 13 million more of them, giving drivers free replacements. Firestone countered with data that it claimed showed the design of the Explorer to be fatally flawed. It said, for instance, that tread separations occurred 10 times as often on the Explorer as they did on the Ford Ranger pickup, which uses the same tires and the same chassis. The NHTSA fell behind in its investigation for lack of funding and has yet to investigate Firestone's claims about the Explorer's design. Meanwhile, victims' lawyers say that Ford and Firestone knew more than anyone else about the reasons for the accidents but kept everyone in the dark.

Although it seems clear that, as former NHTSA administrator Joan Claybrook says, "For some reason, a Firestone tire on a Ford Explorer is a deadly combination," it appears it will be a long time before the truth is finally known.

1. Do you think anyone involved in the Ford–Firestone case acted unethically? Why or why not?
2. If there had been a whistle-blower early on in the situation, do you think the problem would have grown as large as it did? Why or why not?
3. Imagine that you are part of a team preparing a new code of ethics for Ford or Firestone. Write one or more principles for the code of ethics that would help employees avoid the type of problem described in this case.

Sources: Joann Muller and Nicole St. Pierre, "Ford vs. Firestone: A Corporate Whodunit," *BusinessWeek,* June 11, 2001, pp. 46–47; Keith Bradsher, "Lawyers Hid Tire Failures from Agency Attorneys," *Denver Post,* June 24, 2001, p. A1; James Cox and Jayne O'Donnell, "Consultant Denies Withholding Ford/Firestone Accident Data," *USA Today,* June 25, 2001, p. B2.

Knowing Yourself

How Ethical Is Your Behavior?

The following list is taken from a recent survey of 1,300 workers who said they had engaged in unethical activities. Check the activities you would do or consider doing, and rate yourself using your own values (there is no score!). If you wish, you can compare your standards with those of the respondents at the end.

1. _____ Cut corners on quality control.
2. _____ Covered up incidents.
3. _____ Abused or lied about sick days.
4. _____ Lied to or deceived customers.
5. _____ Put inappropriate pressure on others.
6. _____ Falsified numbers or reports.
7. _____ Dismissed or promoted an employee unfairly.
8. _____ Lied to or deceived superiors on serious matters.
9. _____ Withheld important information.
10. _____ Misused or stole company property.
11. _____ Engaged in or overlooked environmental infractions.
12. _____ Took credit for someone's work or idea.
13. _____ Discriminated against a co-worker.
14. _____ Abused drugs or alcohol.
15. _____ Engaged in copyright or software infringement.
16. _____ Lied to or deceived subordinates on serious matters.

17. _____ Overlooked or paid or accepted bribes.

18. _____ Had extramarital affair with business associate.

19. _____ Abused an expense account.

20. _____ Abused or leaked proprietary information.

21. _____ Forged name without person's knowledge.

22. _____ Accepted inappropriate gifts or services.

23. _____ Filed false regulatory or government reports.

24. _____ Engaged in insider trading.

Percentage of original respondents who admitted to each infraction: (1) 16%, (2) 13%, (3) 11%, (4) 9%, (5) 7%, (6) 6%, (7) 6%, (8) 5%, (9) 5%, (10) 4%, (11) 4%, (12) 4%, (13) 4%, (14) 4%, (15) 3%, (16) 3%, (17) 3%, (18) 3%, (19) 2%, (20) 2%, (21) 2%, (22) 1%, (23) 1%, (24) 1%.

Source: From Henry Fountain, "Of White Lies and Yellow Pads," *The New York Times,* July 6, 1997. Copyright © 1997 The New York Times. Reprinted with permission.

Pause and Reflect

1. Are your answers a good measure of how ethical you are? Can you think of any other behaviors that should be on this list?

2. Should a supervisor be held to higher ethical standards than the supervisor's employees?

3. In what areas of conduct are you most ethical? In what areas do you think your standards should improve?

Class Exercise

Supervising Unethical Employees

Each student should complete the survey in Figure 4.7 anonymously, circling all the answers that apply. The instructor then tabulates the results and distributes them for discussion during the next class session.

For each item in the survey, discuss the following questions:

- Which answer or answers were selected by most students?
- What is the justification for the answers selected?
- If you were the supervisor of an employee who acted in this way, how would you respond (assuming that you observed the behavior)?
- If your supervisor learned that you had acted in the way indicated by the survey response, how do you think your career would be affected?

Source: This exercise is based on a suggestion submitted by James Mulvihill, Mankato, MN.

Building Supervision Skills

Decision Making

One way to make ethical decisions is to ensure that your decisions follow your organization's code of ethics. In this exercise, you will develop an example of such a decision.

As a team, agree on a code of ethics to study. You can choose an organization that interests you and visit its Web site to look for a code of ethics or a values statement. Or you can use the hyperlinks in "The Index of Codes," published online by the Illinois Institute of Technology's Center for the Study of Ethics in the Professions (http://ethics.iit.edu/codes/codes_index.html). Another option is to use Johnson & Johnson's credo in Figure 4.3.

Choose one of the principles in the code of ethics. Prepare a skit that illustrates that principle. Your skit should be about a workplace dilemma involving your chosen principle, showing how the people in the skit resolve the dilemma. If you

FIGURE 4.7
Survey for Class Exercise

Which of the following actions would you take?
Circle the letters of as many choices as apply to you.
1. Put false information in your résumé:
    a. If necessary to get a job.
    b. Only about minor details.
    c. If most people are doing it.
    d. Never.
2. Tell a competing company secrets about your employer's product or procedures:
    a. To land a job with the competitor.
    b. In exchange for $100.
    c. In exchange for $1 million.
    d. Never.
3. Cheat on a test used as the basis for promotion:
    a. If you have a family to support.
    b. If you think the test is unfair.
    c. If your co-workers are doing it.
    d. Never.
4. Use the office copier:
    a. To make a copy of your dentist's bill.
    b. To make six copies of a report that is related to charitable work you do.
    c. To make 50 copies of your résumé.
    d. Never for copies unrelated to work.
5. Pad your expense account for a business trip:
    a. If you believe you are underpaid.
    b. Only for small amounts that the employer won't miss.
    c. Only when you are experiencing financial problems.
    d. Never.
6. Call in sick when you aren't sick:
    a. If you're worn out from working on a big project.
    b. If your child is sick.
    c. If you need to recover from the weekend.
    d. Never.
7. Lie about your supervisor's whereabouts when he or she takes a long, liquid lunch:
    a. Only if specifically instructed to do so.
    b. If the supervisor gives you a generous raise in return.
    c. Only when the person asking is your supervisor's superior.
    d. Never.

can, base your skit on a work-related situation that at least one of your team members has experienced.

The teams will then take turns presenting their skits to the whole class. Have the class try to identify the ethical principle each skit illustrates. Finally, the class should vote on whether the solution presented in the skit actually follows the principle from the code of ethics.

Chapter **Five**

Managing Diversity

Learning Objectives

After you have studied this chapter, you should be able to:

5.1 Define diversity.

5.2 Discuss how the U.S. workforce is changing and its impact on the supervisor.

5.3 Differentiate among prejudice, discrimination, and stereotypes in the workplace.

5.4 Explain how sexism and ageism are barriers to diversity and how supervisors can be more aware of them.

5.5 Describe some ways to communicate more effectively in the diverse workplace.

5.6 Describe the goals of diversity training.

5.7 List the most important recent legislation affecting diversity and its provisions.

Diversity [is] the art of thinking independently together.

—*Malcolm Stevenson Forbes, publisher (1919–1990)*

A Supervisor's Problem: Diversification under Fire

New York City's Fire Department (FDNY) has a force 11,334 members strong that is nearly 94 percent white and almost entirely male. So it would seem that a program designed to attract minority and female recruits to its ranks would be an unqualified good thing. But the story of the FDNY's Cadet Program shows just how difficult it is to devise a diversity program that everyone will welcome.

The Cadet Program allows candidates who underwent long and intensive instruction and training as emergency medical technicians to enter the fire academy with lower written and physical scores than the firefighter's job usually requires. The department's December 2000 graduating class was the first to include participants from the program. Overall, the class was 2.9 percent Asian, 10.7 percent black, 14.3 percent Hispanic, and 1.4 percent female.

But because the Cadet Program is open to anyone, only 60 percent of entrants into the program have been women or minority group members. Some critics contend that the remaining 40 percent of white males is a high enough proportion to prevent the program from realizing its goal of making the fire department more diverse. Another possible flaw in the program, detractors say, is that those whites who have benefited from its admissions policy are sons and close relatives of high-ranking supervisors in the department and the firefighters' union.

The union, for its part, opposes the Cadet Program on the grounds that it relaxes standards and increases the dangers of the job. Says Uniformed Firefighters Association President Kevin Gallagher, "We have a hundred-year history of the merit system. This job is too dangerous a job to be lowering standards in order to address the diversity issue."

But the FDNY remains proud of the program. Says Commissioner Thomas Von Essen, "This is a terrific program which has helped provide us with the largest percentage of minorities we've ever had. If we could duplicate this once a year, we would go a long way towards bringing greater diversification to the ranks."

Obviously, both sides hold strong opinions about the merits of increased diversity in the fire department. Think about what you might do to resolve this issue as you read the chapter.

Source: Elissa Gootman, "Effort to Diversify Fire Department Bears Fruit, While Drawing Criticism," *The New York Times*, November 16, 2000, pp. B1, B6.

WHAT IS DIVERSITY?

The New York City Fire Department's diversity efforts may be controversial, but they reflect the growing awareness of diversity in the workplace. Dealing successfully with cultural, ethnic, age, gender, and racial diversity is a lifelong process for most of us. However, being ready to work successfully in a multicultural environment is a goal supervisors can set immediately and work toward in every business encounter.

Our understanding of cultural diversity has matured in recent decades. The old "melting pot" model, in which immigrants were expected to assimilate their language and culture into the mainstream, has long since been left behind. The view today is that our diversity is our strength. We define **diversity** as the characteristics of individuals that shape their identities and the experiences they have in society.[1] Visible reminders and celebrations of our diverse heritage, such as Martin Luther King Jr. Day and Gay Pride celebrations, enrich and renew our society and our culture. Ensuring diversity within an organization offers supervisors the opportunity to make the best fit between the employee and the job, allowing varied points of view to be aired and improving decision making. Many forms of discrimination, in hiring and elsewhere in business practices, are illegal in the United States. Yet even if they were not, ethical considerations would encourage the supervisor to seek many kinds of diversity within his or her department or team.

Businesses and governments also are striving to acknowledge diversity in their communications and interactions with citizens, employees, and customers.

diversity
Characteristics of individuals that shape their identities and the experiences they have in society

SUPERVISION AND DIVERSITY

DIVERSITY MEANS OPPORTUNITY AT BANK OF AMERICA

Given that more than 90 percent of non-Hispanic whites in the United States already have checking accounts, Bank of America (BofA) is looking to find new customers from other, less-served ethnic groups. BofA, the second-largest U.S. bank with 4,200 bank branches in 21 states, has enjoyed rising retail revenues because of its ability to meet the needs of underserved groups, including Hispanic, Asian, and black Americans.

Two-thirds of Hispanic Americans—a large, young, fast-growing group—are of Mexican origin. Recent immigrants in particular are likely to speak primarily Spanish and live in extended families. Many want to send financial help to relatives in Mexico, and some lack U.S. documentation for opening a bank account. To serve this group, BofA allows Mexican immigrants to open accounts using the Matricula Consular, a document issued by Mexican consulates. Other banks accept the Matricula too, but Bank of America lures customers with unique services such as SafeSend, which enables customers to transfer money from their BofA checking accounts to ATMs located throughout Mexico. Instead of traveling to a wire transfer service and paying a $35 fee, BofA customers can transfer funds using their phone, computer, or an ATM. Bank of America was the first U.S. bank to offer Spanish-language ATMs. The bank also has begun issuing home mortgages to extended families on the basis of the credit histories of up to four family members. These new credit standards may sound riskier, but the default rate on home mortgages is less than half that among non-Hispanic whites.

Of course, serving customers involves more than creating products. The bank needs employees who can interact effectively with its customers. Bank of America hires Spanish-speaking tellers, loan officers, and customer service personnel to handle the needs of its Spanish-speaking customers. The company knows that these employees are important to its strategy, so managers' incentive pay is partly based on how well they meet diversity-related hiring goals. Employees also serve on Diversity Advisory and Diversity Business Councils that identify issues and propose solutions to make the bank an environment in which diverse employees can all contribute.

Sources: Shawn Tully, "Bank of the Americas," *Fortune,* April 14, 2003, downloaded from InfoTrac, http://web7 .infotrac.galegroup.com; Brian Grow, *"Hola, Amigo!* You're Approved," *BusinessWeek,* April 12, 2004, downloaded from InfoTrac, http://web4.infotrac .galegroup.com; Cora Daniels, "50 Best Companies for Minorities," *Fortune,* June 28, 2004, downloaded from InfoTrac, http://web4.infotrac.galegroup.com; Bank of America, "Diversity," and "Diversity Fact Sheets," Careers page, Bank of America Web site, www.bankofamerica .com/careers/, August 9, 2004.

Boston Goodwill, for example, has found valuable potential in workers with disabilities. The organization hired a man named Paul and trained him to do maintenance work. Before then, Paul had received public assistance because a learning disability had made it difficult for him to communicate, complete school, and find jobs. However, at Goodwill, Paul soon mastered maintenance and janitorial tasks. Eventually, he was promoted to night shift supervisor at the Barnes Federal Building. He is a patient leader of his crew of seven, and his attitude helps him keep employee turnover low.[2] The "Supervision and Diversity" box details how Bank of America serves Hispanic consumers in the United States, an effort that requires talented Spanish-speaking bankers. The bank similarly has been a leader in providing banking services in other languages, including Mandarin, Cantonese, Taiwanese, and Vietnamese. Its services include the U.S.–Asia Banking Center, established to serve customers with needs in both the United States and Hong Kong, and a self-managed 30-member team of bankers called the Chinese Banking Team, which operates from offices in the state of Washington.[3]

This chapter explores the challenges and opportunities related to workforce diversity, emphasizing how they affect supervisors. The chapter begins by summarizing some measures of America's increasing diversity. It then focuses on diversity-related challenges, such as prejudices and stereotypes. Finally, the chapter describes how supervisors can help organizations realize the advantages of diversity through communication, training, and the fulfillment of legal requirements.

A LOOK AT OUR DIVERSITY

The face of the United States is changing. This process is not new; the country was built on the concept of diversity as waves of immigrants and homesteaders arrived on its shores. Today, however, we recognize both subtle and obvious differences among employees at every organizational level. These differences call on all of a supervisor's management skills.

As recently as 1980, white men accounted for half of U.S. workers. Today, the participation of women in the workforce has risen to above 50 percent, and a recent survey found that women held half of all management, professional, and related occupations.[4] Mothers of young children in particular have entered the workforce as a permanent contingent at a rate that shows no sign of slowing. The workforce also is expected to continue to age, as some older workers postpone retirement to continue working and the first wave of the large generation commonly called baby boomers (those born between 1946 and 1964) reaches their 50s and 60s. The proportions of African Americans, Asian Americans, and Hispanics in the U.S. population and workforce are rising gradually and expected to continue to do so (see Figure 5.1). Some of that increase is fueled by immigration. More than 1 in 10 workers in the United States was born in another country. Of these foreign-born workers, almost half are Hispanic, and nearly one-fourth are

FIGURE 5.1 **Composition of the American Workforce by Ethnic Group, Percentages, 1990–2030**

Source: Mitra Toossi, "A Century of Change: The U.S. Labor Force, 1950–2050," *Monthly Labor Review*, May 2002, pp. 15–28.

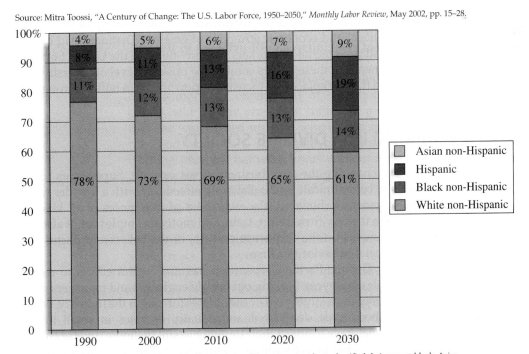

Note: Percentages total slightly more than 100% because some Hispanic respondents classified their race as black, Asian, or "other."

SUPERVISION AND ETHICS

ROMANCE FOR SOME MAY BE HARASSMENT FOR OTHERS

Considering that people give some of their liveliest and most creative hours to the workplace, it's no wonder that romances sometimes are kindled between co-workers. However, when one of those romantic partners is a supervisor, sticky ethical situations can arise.

It's easy to see the problems when the supervisor is interested in romance but the employee being supervised merely wants a working relationship. If the supervisor issues an invitation to dinner, can the employee truly respond in a way that will not affect their relations at work? A flat "no" will hurt the supervisor's feelings, and the employee may worry that the supervisor will retaliate at work, perhaps in subtle ways such as failing to provide opportunities for training and promotions. If the employee gives an ambiguous answer, the supervisor might keep issuing invitations, and the employee would become increasingly uncomfortable. Either way, the supervisor now has a problem too. If the employee's work is unsatisfactory in any way, the supervisor will need to correct the employee, and the employee might interpret the supervisor's action as retaliation for refusing to date the supervisor. Thus, it becomes impossible for the supervisor to provide proper discipline.

But what if the employee is attracted to the supervisor? Even that apparently happy situation is full of problems. Employees who inevitably find out about the romance will be weighing every workplace decision to see if it is fair. More problems occur if and when the affair comes to an end. The employee might bring charges of sexual harassment, claiming that the relationship was unwanted or that the supervisor is retaliating against the employee for ending the affair.

A particularly messy situation occurred at the Valley State Prison for Women in California. The chief deputy warden of one facility was known to be having affairs with three employees, including his secretary and the associate warden. The chief deputy warden was then promoted to the position of warden of another facility. There, a committee selecting a correctional counselor was asked to promote the new warden's secretary to the position. The woman was not selected, so the warden told the committee to "make it happen." The woman then bragged about her power over the warden. Next, the associate warden (the second lover) applied for and received a transfer to the new facility, where she reported directly to the warden instead of to her immediate supervisor. Finally, the warden's third lover was transferred to the warden's facility, where she also bragged about her relationship and her power over the warden. An employee named Miller competed with this third woman for a promotion, and though Miller had better qualifications, the other employee received the promotion. As if these decisions weren't unpleasant enough, the three women publicly fought about their relationships with the warden.

Eventually Miller complained, first to management and then to the federal Equal Employment Opportunity Commission (EEOC). The EEOC agreed that Miller had a legitimate case to claim sexual harassment because the circumstances could be seen as creating a "hostile work environment," even though Miller was never pressured for sexual favors.

Few workplaces have quite this level of drama, but the story reinforces how important it is for a supervisor to be fair, even if fairness limits some opportunities for romance.

Source: Based on Jonathan A. Segal, "Dangerous Liaisons," *HR Magazine*, December 2005, downloaded from Business & Company Resource Center, http://galenet.galegroup.com.

and minorities have experienced in rising through the corporate ranks is well-enough documented to be given a name. The "glass ceiling" refers to a certain level of responsibility to which many qualified applicants find themselves rising, and then no higher, despite their ability and willingness to contribute further to the goals of the firm. Changes for the better are occurring every day, but much progress remains to be made.

sexual harassment
Unwanted sexual attentions, including language, behavior, or the display of images

The most blatant form of sexism is **sexual harassment,** defined as unwanted sexual attentions, including language, behavior, or the display of images. Offenses have ranged from sexual jokes and displays of explicit pictures in the workplace to touching, sexual advances, and requests for sexual favors. In most cases of sexual harassment, women have been the victims and men the aggressors, but that need not be the case. No matter who is involved, sexual harassment is illegal, and experts advise supervisors to adopt a policy of "zero tolerance," take any complaints seriously, and investigate them at once. Some states, including Connecticut and California, require companies to train their supervisors in how to prevent sexual harassment. Even when not required by law, supervisors and their companies may request training to help them meet their ethical obligations and demonstrate that the supervisor and organization take the problem seriously.[16] Also, as described in the "Supervision and Ethics" box, supervisors must be extremely cautious about entering into romantic relationships with individuals who work at the same company. These relationships often create awkward situations that may be considered unethical or even amount to a hostile environment for other employees.

Ageism

Your chances of someday supervising older workers are fairly high. The number of people aged 65 years and older in the U.S. labor force is growing for at least two reasons: The share of the population that is 65 years and older is growing, and more people in that age bracket have decided to continue working at least part-time. Already, the share of older workers is greater than at any time since World War II, a trend that is expected to continue.[17]

Although older workers offer significant experience, they sometimes encounter discrimination. They generally must look for work longer than younger adults, and recent research found that older workers are more afraid of discrimination than of change.[18] Discrimination based on age is called **ageism.** Often, prejudices are at the root of ageism. Some people expect older workers to perform less effectively, but evidence shows such negative expectations are often unfounded. A survey by the Society for Human Resource Management found that older workers bring their employers a number of strengths, which are summarized in Figure 5.3.

ageism
Discrimination based on age

FIGURE 5.3
10 Reasons to Hire Older Workers

Source: J. Collison, *SHRM/NOWCC/CED Older Workers Survey* (Alexandria, VA: Society for Human Resource Management, June 2003), cited in Nancy R. Lockwood, "The Aging Workforce: The Reality of the Impact of Older Workers and Eldercare in the Workplace," *HR Magazine*, December 2003, downloaded from InfoTrac, http://web5.infotrac .galegroup.com.

1. They are flexible about working different schedules.
2. They can serve as mentors to younger co-workers.
3. They offer invaluable experience.
4. They have a strong work ethic.
5. They are more reliable than young workers.
6. They add diversity of thought and approach.
7. They are particularly loyal.
8. They take their work very seriously.
9. They have established networks.
10. They are less likely to quit.

Margit Gerow expressed the situation well while she was hunting for a job in the software industry: "It's a young person's industry," said Gerow of the software business in Seattle, where she is trying to find a new job since being laid off. "I stick out like a sore thumb because I'm over 60. But I'm a national resource, like iron. And I think I'm worth mining for a bit."[19]

As the baby-boomer generation ages, and as improvements in health care and nutrition allow for longer and healthier lives, older workers (both men and women) are sure to become a more common sight. The Age Discrimination in Employment Act (1967) makes it illegal to fail to hire, or fire, on the basis of age. When inexperienced younger workers are given preference over equally or better-qualified elders or when downsizing lets disproportionately more older (and often better-paid) workers go, ageism costs the organization the benefit of experience, perspective, and judgment that senior workers can bring. John Renner, a psychologist with Hagberg Consulting Group, says the firm's collected data on 4,000 executives shows that while willingness to take risks declines after about age 40, patience, a key management trait, doesn't blossom until after the age of 45 years, while open-mindedness and teamwork are abilities that actually increase with age.[20]

In a few rare cases, such as the Federal Aviation Agency's limit of 64 years of age for airline pilots or acting roles that call for persons of very young or very advanced age, age represents what is called a **bona fide occupational qualification (BFOQ),** an objective characteristic required for an individual to perform a job properly. In all other cases, experts suggest that supervisors should beware of making decisions based on assumptions about age, such as that older employees are less physically capable or have failing eyesight that prevents them from performing well on the job. Tests that measure proven job qualifications, such as a vision test, can ensure that age is not being used as a discriminator and that valuable workers are not being overlooked or lost.

There is no longer a mandatory age for retirement, and many workers find it economically necessary to continue their careers. The Census Bureau estimates that 20 percent of the population will be over 65 years of age by 2030 (see Figure 5.4), and it is likely that many of those citizens will remain on the job. They will be a potent force, and many firms are prepared to train retirees who decide to return to work.

bona fide occupational qualification (BFOQ)
An objective characteristic required for an individual to perform a job properly

FIGURE 5.4
Percentage of People over Age 65 in the United States, 2000 and 2030

Source: U.S. Census Bureau, "U.S. Interim Projections by Age, Sex, Race, and Hispanic Origin," March 18, 2004, U.S. Census Bureau Web site, www.census.gov.

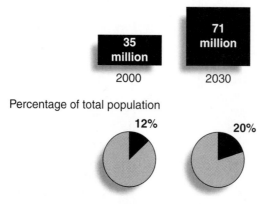

FIGURE 5.5
Sources of Diversity in the Workplace

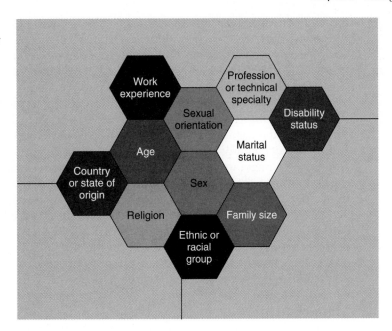

IMPLICATIONS FOR THE SUPERVISOR

Supervisors can expect that their employees will be diverse in at least some of the ways described in this chapter. Figure 5.5 illustrates some possible sources of diversity in a work group. The supervisor's challenge is to build on the advantages of this diversity. Doing so requires effective communication that bridges cultural differences. Supervisors also can benefit from training in diversity and working closely with the company's human resource staff to learn how they and their employees must behave to obey laws related to workforce diversity.

Advantages of Diversity

Overcoming the challenges to supervising a diverse workforce can require consistent effort and a willingness to learn from mistakes, particularly for the new supervisor. But there are rewards, among them the confidence that such behavior is both ethical and fair. Other advantages for the individual supervisor are more concrete and include the opportunity to learn from the varied perspectives of those unlike ourselves, a better motivated and more loyal team of employees, enhanced communication skills, improved management ability, and enhanced opportunities for career advancement.

The firm as a whole can also benefit from a supervisor's successful efforts. Some advantages of diversity for the business organization are greater ability to attract and retain the best employees for the job, increased productivity, higher morale and motivation throughout the company, a more resilient workforce, greater innovation, reduced turnover, and enhanced performance leading to greater market share. For example, immigrant workers overcame obstacles to travel to the United States and find a job despite language barriers. Individuals with such a high success drive, energy level, and motivation have the potential to inspire the entire work group. They also may bring valuable ideas from their experiences in their country of origin.[21] The research organization Catalyst recently studied the financial performance of major U.S. businesses and learned that companies with more women among their senior executives were more successful. It would be overly simple to say that women are better at running businesses, but a reasonable conclusion is that management skill includes attracting the best talent without regard to gender, race, and the like.[22]

Even the best and most necessary efforts to manage diversity must be handled with care. Among the many challenges supervisors face in the newly diverse workplace is the task of adjusting job schedules and workloads to religious and ethnic holidays, family needs such as a sick child or an elderly parent needing temporary or ongoing care, and unique arrangements such as job sharing and telecommuting. Special equipment and training are sometimes needed to ease the stress of a disability in a capable employee or to tailor a workstation to an employee's physical needs. Bilingual employee manuals and the creation of benefit programs that offer medical coverage to life partners of either sex are other examples. Adjustments like these, while beneficial to the firm, can occasionally create dissatisfaction among other employees. Supervisors need to be aware that these problems also can occur and be prepared to deal with them.

Communication

Our attitudes toward others are perhaps nowhere as evident as in our communication with them. Communication in the workplace therefore is one area in which supervisors can serve as particularly good role models of managing diversity constructively.

Nonverbal communication is just as powerful in many contexts as the actual words we say, and body language differs from one culture to another (and even between genders) as much as spoken language does. It's important to try not to rely too much on generalizations about culture, because even within cultures, there are variations in behavior among individuals. But to draw some basic conclusions about how supervisors might best shape their communications with others, both managers and subordinates, we need to rely on a few simple statements. Keeping in mind that they do not reflect the real complexity of any foreign culture or of any individual, here are a few examples:[23]

- The Japanese value the ability to be physically still.
- Whites in North America interpret eye contact as a sign of honesty, while in many other cultures, eyes are dropped as a sign of respect to one's superiors.
- Americans tend to smile at everyone, while in Germany smiles are reserved for friends. The Japanese smile not just to express gladness but also to cover embarrassment and even anger.
- In Bulgaria, people nod their heads to signal no and shake their heads to mean yes.
- Latin Americans stand closer to people of the same sex than North Americans do, but North Americans stand closer to those of the opposite sex.
- In Asia, the Middle East, and South America, friends of the same sex can hold hands or walk arm-in-arm in public, while opposite-sex couples who touch in public are seen as slightly shocking.
- In North America, the person sitting at the head of a table is generally assumed to be the leader of the group unless that person is a woman, in which case observers tend to assume the leader is one of the men.

Nonverbal communication or body language seldom occurs without some accompanying words. Verbal communication, both written and spoken, offers many opportunities for bridging the gaps between cultures—just as many chances for us to fail to convey our intended meaning. One of the many ways in which supervisors can improve their communication with others in the diverse workplace of the future is to choose words with extra care, particularly when giving directions.

Many English words have more than one meaning, and the English language is full of slang, idioms, and borrowed expressions, such as "in the red," "out of left field," and "get the nod." These have the potential to mislead, confuse, and frustrate nonnative speakers of English and should be used with care, if at all. Doris West-Walkin, a human resource consultant for Johns Hopkins Medical Institutions, observes the need to communicate carefully with the nurses her organization recruits from the Philippines. These employees speak English but not the dialect and slang of their American-born colleagues. Thus, says West-Walkin, supervisors need to avoid using idioms like "Hit the call button" when they mean "Answer the patient's call button now!"[24]

Supervisors should also be aware that every industry has its own particular jargon and that specialized terms can pose particular problems. Publishing, for example, has its own specific meanings for such terms as *widow, orphan, register,* and *river.* Since even native speakers of English will find jargon unfamiliar at first, explanations of terms should be a standard part of orientation and training. When employees have a native language different from English, careful communication is even more important. The "Supervisory Skills" box offers suggestions for improving communication with employees whose primary language is not English.

The point of all these examples is not that the supervisor must become an expert in other cultures. That would be an impossible and probably pointless goal. What these differences do suggest, however, is that it is most important not to make assumptions in communications with others, particularly regarding the way one's own words and actions are interpreted. Thinking before communicating, in order to understand the potential reaction to our words and gestures, is a good habit to foster. Checking for understanding is a simple but very effective way to ensure that we are conveying the meaning we intend.

Diversity Training

To reap the full benefits of having a diverse workforce, supervisors first need to ensure that cultural differences are perceived by everyone as a positive force within the firm. Sometimes formal diversity training, such as a two- or three-day workshop, is needed to raise employee awareness of multiculturalism and help reduce such barriers to success as prejudice and stereotypes. These programs are often credited with attracting minority recruits and raising sensitivity to differences among people. Improved communications skills are also a common goal of diversity training, along with improving interpersonal and technical skills, increasing English proficiency, and facilitating mentoring. Some firms, however, have experienced a backlash against diversity training; problems include the reinforcement of group stereotypes and even lawsuits based on offensive statements made during "awareness raising" sessions.[25] Appropriate controls and guidelines should accompany the training, which should be administered by professional trainers.

Jonathan Segal, a human resource specialist, has observed that training is especially important for supervisors, because they interact directly with employees, and sometimes good intentions are the worst protection. Segal has found that a supervisor who cares about employees may be quick to wade into situations

SUPERVISORY SKILLS

COMMUNICATING

SUPERVISING WORKERS WHO DON'T SPEAK THE SAME LANGUAGE

The history of the United States is a history of immigrants, and the U.S. workforce continues to include many people who primarily speak a language other than English. Today many workers in the United States speak Spanish, Tagalog, Polish, or Vietnamese as their primary language. Supervisors need to be able to motivate and lead these employees and help them work well with the rest of the organization's people.

Communicating with workers whose primary language is not English begins with an awareness of the challenges posed by the language barrier. The supervisor needs to make an extra effort to be sure they understand directions, questions, rules, warnings, expectations, customer feedback, and even small talk. The language difficulty may make these employees feel insecure and afraid. Supervisors can use the following measures to help employees overcome the language barrier:

- Identify and recruit bilingual and multilingual employees to act as interpreters.
- Have all printed information and instructions translated in employees' language(s).
- Post diagrams and pictures throughout the workplace. Good illustrations can help all workers, even those who read English.
- Continually learn about the cultures of immigrant employees. Other than language differences, do they have different customs related to eye contact, titles used to address people, or the distance they stand from other people?
- Show appreciation and respect for employees' cultures. Take advantage of opportunities to share the foods and musical styles of employees' cultures.
- If many employees need help with English, find out whether the company can offer English as a second language (ESL) classes or reimburse the cost of such classes at a community college.
- When employers establish English-only rules, supervisors should work with their human resource departments to be sure such rules are implemented in a way that meets federal requirements. For example, employers may require the use of English to promote safety or effective communication with customers. Such rules cannot be adopted as a means of discrimination (e.g., to make it hard for immigrants to get a job with the company).
- Clearly require that employees treat one another with dignity. Racism and discrimination poison the atmosphere of the entire work group and can put the employer at risk for legal action.

Sources: Based on Robert D. Ramsey, "Supervising Employees with Limited English Language Proficiency," *Supervision*, June 2004, downloaded from InfoTrac, http://web5.infotrac.galegroup.com; Equal Employment Opportunity Commission, *EEOC Compliance Manual*, Section 13(C), National Origin Discrimination: English-Only Rules, EEOC Web site, www.eeoc.gov, August 9, 2004.

that have legal implications of which the supervisor is unaware. For example, a supervisor might conclude that an employee's performance is suffering because of a mental or emotional condition. The supervisor might decide that the most helpful way to work with the employee is to identify the source of the problem. However, many legal requirements are designed to prevent discrimination against disabled employees; if the employee decides that he or she has a disability, the supervisor's well-intentioned efforts may place the company in a difficult situation.[26] Because diversity-related problems can become so complex, supervisors should seek out training and take it seriously when the organization provides it. When diversity is embraced by top management and built into policies and procedures that are fairly enforced, and when the goals of diversity training are continually reinforced within the corporate culture, it has the greatest chance of contributing to the company's goals. If such ideal support is lacking, supervisors

TABLE 5.1
Some Important Equal Employment Opportunity Legislation

Legislation	Result
Title VII of 1964 Civil Rights Act, as amended	Created the Equal Employment Opportunity Commission; bars discrimination based on race, color, religion, sex, or national origin.
Equal Pay Act of 1963	Requires equal pay for men and women performing similar work.
Age Discrimination in Employment Act of 1967	Bars discrimination against those 40 years old and older because of age.
Vocational Rehabilitation Act of 1973	For jobs connected with the federal government, requires affirmative action to employ qualified handicapped persons and prohibits discrimination against them.
Pregnancy Discrimination Act of 1978	Bars discrimination in employment against women based on pregnancy, childbirth, or related conditions.
Vietnam Era Veterans' Readjustment Assistance Act of 1974	Mandates affirmative action in employment for veterans of the Vietnam War era.
Americans with Disabilities Act of 1990	Prohibits discrimination against disabled employees in the private sector and encourages reasonable accommodations for them.
Civil Rights Act of 1991	Places the burden of proof on the employer and allows for compensatory and punitive damages in discrimination cases.

can still support diversity by consistently setting a good example in their dealings with others. Such seemingly innocent practices as hiring only people who appear to fit into the "corporate culture" can lead supervisors to staff a firm with workers from similar backgrounds; with identical religious, ethnic, or racial characteristics; or from the same age bracket. Even if no legal actions are brought against such firms, they still are losing one of their best potential resources—the creativity and vitality that come from bringing people into contact with others from whom they can learn.

Legal Issues

A review of all the relevant employment law is beyond the scope of this text. Table 5.1 summarizes some major legislation that governs the areas of workplace diversity and that supervisors should know. These rules govern hiring, pay, promotion, and evaluation, all within the scope of the supervisor's responsibilities.

The Equal Employment Opportunity Commission (EEOC) was instituted by Title VII of the 1964 Civil Rights Act as amended in 1972. The EEOC consists of five members appointed by the president to serve a five-year term. This agency acts as the federal government's major means of enforcing equal employment opportunity laws and has the power to investigate complaints, use conciliation to eliminate discrimination when found, and file discrimination charges on behalf of an individual if needed. Individual states have also passed their own laws to fill perceived gaps in federal law.[27]

SKILLS MODULE

PART ONE: CONCEPTS

Summary

5.1 Define diversity.

Diversity refers to the characteristics of individuals that shape their identities and the experiences they have in society. Racial, cultural, ethnic, age, gender, and other kinds of diversity are welcomed and considered a strength in business organizations today.

5.2 Discuss how the U.S. workforce is changing and its impact on the supervisor.

The number of women and minorities in the workforce is increasing. The workforce is aging as well, and new technologies are integrating the disabled into the workforce with valuable skills and insights. Technical workers from abroad are bringing their expertise to many U.S. firms. All these changes offer supervisors both a challenge to their management skills and an opportunity to build a strong and flexible team of workers.

5.3 Differentiate among prejudice, discrimination, and stereotypes in the workplace.

Prejudice is a preconceived judgment about an individual or group of people. Discrimination is unfair or inequitable treatment based on prejudice. Stereotypes are generalized, fixed images we hold of others.

5.4 Explain how sexism and ageism are barriers to diversity and how supervisors can be more aware of them.

Sexism and ageism refer to discrimination against others on the basis of sex or age. Supervisors should be aware that sexism can be either subtle, as in sexist language, or blatant, as in sexual harassment, defined as unwanted sexual attentions including language, behavior, or the display of images. Sexual harassment is illegal. Ageism can cost the organization the benefit of experience, perspective, and judgment that older workers bring. Discrimination based on age is illegal except in the (rare) case of a bona fide occupational qualification (BFOQ).

5.5 Describe some ways to communicate more effectively in the diverse workplace.

Supervisors can communicate more effectively by being aware that verbal and nonverbal communication varies in meaning across cultures. Avoiding slang and idioms, explaining technical jargon, and checking for meaning will help improve communication.

5.6 Describe the goals of diversity training.

Diversity training is intended to raise employee awareness of multiculturalism and help reduce such barriers to success as prejudice and stereotypes. Other goals include improved communications and interpersonal and technical skills.

5.7 List the most important recent legislation affecting diversity and its provisions.

Title VII of the 1964 Civil Rights Act, amended in 1972, created the Equal Employment Opportunity Commission (EEOC), which investigates and acts on complaints of discrimination. See Table 5.1 for a summary of recent legislation.

Key Terms

diversity, *p.* 115
corporate culture, *p.* 118
prejudice, *p.* 119
discrimination, *p.* 119

stereotypes, *p.* 120
sexism, *p.* 121
sexual harassment,
p. 122

ageism, *p.* 123
bona fide occupational
qualification (BFOQ),
p. 124

**Review and
Discussion
Questions**

1. What is diversity? How has its meaning changed?

2. Rasheen supervises the mail room for a large financial services firm. He has been told he will be attending a diversity training program next week. Rasheen believes that because he has recently hired three women from his native country, he does not need to know any more about diversity. As his supervisor, what would you say to Rasheen to prepare him for the training program?

3. Some research suggests that the increasing racial and cultural diversity in the United States is limited to the larger cities. How would you account for this trend? Does it suggest that only supervisors in these cities need be concerned about diversity?

4. Distinguish between prejudice and discrimination. How do stereotypes contribute to each?

5. Aaron, clerical supervisor for a health maintenance organization, wants to hire the best person for the receptionist job. Ramona, his manager, is doubtful that the candidate Aaron has selected will be capable because she uses a wheelchair. Ramona is concerned that other workers will have to spend a lot of time helping the receptionist get in and out of the office for lunch, breaks, and so on. How can Aaron ensure that his candidate will be an asset to the firm?

6. List as many English expressions as you can think of that might be confusing to a nonnative speaker of the language. Next to each, write a brief expression that conveys the same meaning with greater clarity.

7. Mariah's boss calls her "honey," although he refers to her co-workers as Jason, Rick, and Harrison. How can Mariah ask her boss to correct this situation?

8. Several members of your team are out ill, and you are falling behind your production schedule for the week. A new employee comes to you and asks for a half-day off for a religious holiday you have never heard of. What should you do?

9. What is the EEOC, and what are its responsibilities and powers?

PART TWO: SKILL-BUILDING

YOU SOLVE THE PROBLEM

Reflecting back on page 115, consider the issue of diversity in the New York City Fire Department. Begin by acknowledging that the members of your group may have diverse opinions on this subject. List the ways in which members of your group are diverse. Do you include several ethnic or racial groups and both sexes? Different ages? Different kinds of work experience? How else are you "diverse"? As you continue the discussion, consider whether group members' different life experiences will help them see the problem in different ways, and try to listen carefully, especially to perspectives that are different from your own. Ideally, this process will help you understand the situation more fully.

Discuss how well the FDNY's recruitment policies are achieving the goal of diversifying its workforce. Then discuss how well the policies are meeting the goal of getting the best people for the job. Agree on two changes the department can make so that it will better balance those two goals. Summarize those changes in a memo to the manager of human resources for the fire department.

Problem-Solving Case: *Wal-Mart Struggles with Diversity*

Wal-Mart Stores, with 1.3 million employees, is the biggest private (nongovernment) employer in the United States. In 2004, the company also became the defendant in the largest-ever class-action lawsuit charging sex discrimination. According to the original lawsuit, filed by six women in 2001, Wal-Mart systematically denied them the pay levels and promotion opportunities available to its male employees. A federal judge found that the company's practices raised the possibility that unfair treatment was a pattern, justifying a class-action lawsuit and meaning more than a million female employees could receive damages if Wal-Mart loses the case.

The complaint launching this lawsuit arose when a female assistant manager in a California Sam's Club discovered that a male assistant manager was earning $10,000 more per year than she was. The woman, Stephanie Odle, inquired and was told the reason for her male co-worker's higher pay: He had a wife and children to support. Odle received a raise but only after submitting a household budget, and even with the raise, her pay remained below that of her male colleague. Odle claims she later was fired for complaining, and she took her case to the Equal Employment Opportunity Commission. Eventually, her complaint was combined with that of other female Wal-Mart employees.

The plaintiffs in the lawsuit use numbers to make their case. They point out that two-thirds of Wal-Mart's hourly employees are women, yet slightly more than one-third of its managers are women. Among the top managers of Wal-Mart's stores, only 14 percent are women. In addition, according to the lawsuit, female Wal-Mart employees in hourly jobs earn 5 to 15 percent less than men holding the same jobs.

In its defense, Wal-Mart points out that most employment decisions are not made at its headquarters but within each store. As a result, the company cannot be engaged in a pattern of discrimination. Also, Wal-Mart says the pay gap does not exist in 90 percent of its stores. With regard to the low proportion of women in management ranks, the company says the cause is that a low proportion of women apply for promotions. The company also noted that it expects managers to move frequently; presumably, female employ-ees are less likely than men to accept this career requirement.

Some recent changes at Wal-Mart could make treatment of employees more evenhanded. The company hired a director of diversity, restructured pay scales, and contracted with consultants to rewrite its job descriptions. Executives' bonuses are partly based on meeting diversity-related goals. A new electronic system enables employees throughout the company to apply for management training. Until a few years ago, only hourly jobs—not management jobs—were posted within stores; most retailers post all job openings as a way to show the fairness of their promotion practices. Christine Kwapnoski, one of the parties to the lawsuit, complained that she wanted to become a supervisor, but the Sam's Club where she worked lacked an application process, so she had to rely on word of mouth. According to Kwapnoski, her male co-workers spent more time socializing with management, so they had better access to promotions. (She also said she was told that if she wanted a promotion, she should "doll up.")

If Wal-Mart works with the government to settle the case, it is likely to make further changes. Some companies that have settled similar lawsuits have agreed to accept a court-appointed monitor to supervise the company's employment practices. Another common result of discrimination settlements is for the employer to establish objective criteria for measuring employees' performance.

1. Wal-Mart's vision is to achieve superior customer service and low prices by applying three basic beliefs of founder Sam Walton: "respect for the individual, service to our customers, and strive for excellence." How might workforce diversity help a company fulfill this vision? How might diversity make this vision more challenging to achieve? Based on the information given in this case, how well do you think Wal-Mart has fulfilled its vision?

2. Defenders of Wal-Mart point out that a company with more than a million employees cannot be expected to ensure that every single person is treated fairly; it has to trust lower-level managers to do the right thing. What general

requirements does this viewpoint place on store managers and department supervisors?

3. Prepare an argument supporting either the female employees' charges or Wal-Mart's defense. (If your instructor directs, this exercise could be part of a class debate.) Look up recent news stories about the case, and see if they contain additional facts you can use to support your argument.

Sources: Based on Wal-Mart Stores, "3 Basic Beliefs," About Wal-Mart pages, Wal-Mart Web site, www.walmartstores.com, August 12, 2004; Wendy Zellner, "A Wal-Mart Settlement: What It Might Look Like," *BusinessWeek,* July 5, 2004, downloaded from InfoTrac, http://web4.infotrac.galegroup.com; Ann Zimmerman, "Wal-Mart Faces Class Action in Sex Discrimination Case," *The Wall Street Journal,* June 22, 2004, http://online.wsj.com; Cora Daniels, "Women vs. Wal-Mart," *Fortune,* July 21, 2003, downloaded from InfoTrac, http://web4.infotrac.galegroup.com.

Knowing Yourself

Avoiding Age Bias

Place a 0 next to any statements you believe are true; write 10 for those you think are false.

_____ 1. Worker productivity declines with age.

_____ 2. Older employees are more expensive.

_____ 3. Older employees are more difficult to get along with.

_____ 4. Older employees are coasting until they can retire.

_____ 5. Older employees are prone to accidents and absenteeism.

_____ 6. Older employees can retire because they are financially secure.

_____ 7. Retraining older employees is more expensive because their future with the company is shorter than average.

Scoring: The higher your score, the less likely you are to be biased about an employee's age. All the statements are false.

Source: Adapted from Margaret J. Cofer, "How to Avoid Age Bias," *Nursing Management,* November 1, 1998, p. 11.

Pause and Reflect

1. Can you think of any other common prejudices about older workers?

2. Who are some older workers you know? Pick one or two, and consider what qualities they bring to their job. How well do they fit the seven stereotypes listed here?

3. How can you learn from your older co-workers? How can they learn from you?

Class Exercise

Managing Diversity

Cultural Analysis Inventory

For each topic, there are two questions. Write brief responses to each. After you are finished, your instructor may wish to discuss your responses in class, or you may share them in small groups, or you may conduct a "culture hunt" by trying to find people in your class who answered the questions as you did.

1. Weddings
   a. What is the most important part of the wedding ceremony?
   b. What is the most important part of the reception?

2. Dinners
   a. Who carves the meat at large family dinners?
   b. Who clears the table at large family dinners?

3. Funerals

   a. What is the correct decision regarding "viewing" the remains?

   b. Where should a funeral be held?

4. Family

   a. What is the most important activity that your family does together?

   b. How far down the family tree does the obligation go to be responsible for a family member (e.g., lend money, take care of children, pay for food, let the person live with you temporarily)?

5. Ethnicity

   a. How does your family identify itself ethnically?

   b. What represents your family's cultural and ethnic identity? (For example, if you put "Hungarian," you might refer to a Hungarian lullaby or food that your family eats.)

Source: From Dan O'Haire and Gustav Friedrich, *Strategic Communication in Business and the Professions,* 2nd ed. Copyright © 1995 by Houghton Mifflin Company. Used with permission.

Building Supervision Skills

Providing Employee Orientation

Your work team is responsible for interviewing candidates for openings in the group and making hiring recommendations. For a current opening, you have interviewed several qualified people and decided which is the best. However, the candidate is quite young, and most of the members of your work group are in their 50s. Although they are impressed with the candidate's skills, you sense that they are reluctant to change the composition of the team so drastically. You are concerned that the workflow should continue without disruption and that the team spirit you have developed should remain high.

Assume the candidate is hired. Break into groups and brainstorm strategies for bringing the new person onto the team in such a way that the existing team members are accepting and welcoming.

Part Two Video Cases

MANAGER'S HOT SEAT VIDEO 1: "WORKING IN TEAMS: CROSS-FUNCTIONAL DYSFUNCTION"

Chapter 3 talks about how a supervisor can work successfully as a leader, bolstering employee participation and group effectiveness to accomplish a particular goal.

Read the following scenario describing the video selection "Working in Teams: Cross-Functional Dysfunction," and then watch the video selection. Afterward, answer the three questions that pertain to the specific challenges in this supervisor–employee situation.

SCENARIO

The executive director of operations at the architecture firm Wolinsky & Williams has assigned Joe Tanney (senior account manager) the role of team leader for a high-priority project. The task is to generate a proposal for streamlining the antiquated blueprint-generation process. Each office is at different stages of computerization, with different teams preferring different technologies for particular tasks. This makes everything more complex—from collaboration to revisions to cost and time management—and is having a serious impact on the company's bottom line. The team includes Rosa Denson, Cheng Jing, and Simon Mahoney.

QUESTIONS

1. Page 80 speaks of the importance of rewards in motivating and determining the success of a team. What kind of rewards could Joe have offered each of the members of the team, considering what you know of them?
2. Table 3.1 lists management activities related to quality assessment. Pick two characteristics, and show how Joe succeeded in effectively using them to better the group in the meeting. Alternatively, pick two other characteristics that Joe did not use to facilitate the best outcome from his group. What were the effects all the characteristics had on the significance of the team dynamics?
3. Simon has been with the company the longest amount of time. Knowing what you do about Simon's place in the company, how would you have tried to incorporate his input to have a successful meeting and accomplish the team's goals?

MANAGER'S HOT SEAT VIDEO 2: "DIVERSITY: MEDIATING MORALITY"

As we saw in the previous video, different types of people have different skill sets and work ethics within a company. Chapter 5 notes that as the workplace becomes more diversified, supervisors have new challenges to face when managing employees.

Read the following scenario describing the video selection "Diversity: Managing Morality," and then watch the video selection. Afterward, answer the three questions that pertain to the specific challenges in this supervisor-employee situation.

SCENARIO

At the conclusion of a previous meeting between Syl Tang and two employees, Daniel Simmons and Bob Franklin, Daniel asked Syl about the same-sex partner benefits that he had requested earlier, incidentally informing Bob Franklin that he was homosexual. Bob expressed both discomfort and disapproval and refused to continue to work with Daniel as a result of this revelation. Syl suggested meeting with each of them separately to discuss their concerns and then to regroup and discuss a solution. The individual meetings have occurred and now they are meeting together.

(continued)

QUESTIONS

1. Syl begins the meeting by setting forth the specific goals of (*a*) completing the project and (*b*) how to get that work done. By focusing on these things, is she ultimately ignoring the problem between the two men? How does this help or hurt the situation?

2. Chapter 5 talks about the implications for the supervisor in managing diversity, one of which is good communication and particularly nonverbal communication. What does Syl communicate by her body language? Does this work? Could she have done something differently to be successful and/or ease tensions during the meeting?

3. At the end of the meeting, Syl asks Daniel to come up with an alternative plan to what Bob has suggested be done. What would you have done to get Daniel more involved in the situation to feel more empowered?

Functions of the Supervisor

Successful Supervisors Lead to Reach Goals
Stockbyte/Punchstock Images

Chapter **Six**

Reaching Goals:
Plans and Controls

Learning Objectives

After you have studied this chapter, you should be able to:

6.1 Describe types of planning that take place in organizations.

6.2 Identify characteristics of effective objectives.

6.3 Define *management by objectives (MBO)* and discuss its use.

6.4 Discuss the supervisor's role in the planning process.

6.5 Explain the purpose of using controls.

6.6 Identify the steps in the control process.

6.7 Describe types of control and tools for controlling.

6.8 List characteristics of effective controls.

Today's smart supervisor relies on collaboration to get the job done. The more difficult or impossible the job or the time constraints, the more important it is to get your people involved in creating a plan to get it done.

—*Edward J. Felten, former president (retired), First Supply Group*

A Supervisor's Problem: Planning for Quality at Apache Stoneworks

As the owner of Apache Stoneworks in Denver, Romarico Nieto supervises a five-person crew that lays beautiful stone and tile floors. The company specializes in high-end jobs, so customers expect flawless work. Nieto and his crew deliver just that, thanks to careful planning and high standards.

Customers often expect Nieto's crew to start installing tiles soon after they arrive, but two days of preparation are typical. The effort is what Nieto calls "our most important work." Nieto begins by using his computer to plan installation procedures for each job. The software generates a model (a "critical path plan") of the process, including details such as colors. He prints out copies of the plan for every member of the crew. That way, each crew member knows exactly where to be at any stage of the process. Close teamwork is essential for the company to operate efficiently.

At the site, the crew uses tools such as levels and plumb bobs to measure how much the floors and walls vary from being perfectly flat or vertical. Surfaces are never quite flat, and corners are never quite square, so the layout has to be adjusted to hide the irregularities. Surfaces can be smoothed in various ways, and tiles can be laid out to minimize evidence of an imperfect angle. Nieto says, "We've spent hours laying out one room to maximize the use of full tiles and avoid sliver cuts on the outside. Forethought, patience, and attention to detail not only enhance quality but also increase productivity." The crew lays out a row of tiles and determines how the arrangement will look around the perimeter; the plan is then adjusted if necessary to avoid slivers of tile or stone around the edge.

Surprisingly, professional tilers have been known literally to work themselves into a corner, where they have to wait while the mortar dries. Nieto's detailed planning avoids this problem. His crew members know exactly what to do first, next, and last. They start with the walls, then do counters, then the center of the floor, and finally the perimeter.

Quality controls continue as the tilers carry out their work. For example, they use a "puck" to determine that all tiles are at the same, even level. The workers set one tile and level it. They cut a 1-by-2-inch rectangle of the same material (the puck), making sure it is the same height as the first tile. They attach the puck to one end of a level. By setting the level on the tile and moving the puck around, the workers make sure that all the tiles they install as far as the puck will lie along a flat plane. As they lay each tile, they check it with the level and the puck. "When we're done," says Nieto, "you can slide the puck across the floor and it'll slide like it's on ice because it won't hit any edges or drops."

Construction jobs, such as those Apache Stoneworks does, require precision to complete correctly. Romarico Nieto must make sure his employees complete work well, on time, and within budget—and please his customers.

QUESTIONS

1. Think about the levels of planning that go into an Apache Stoneworks job. What types of planning skills—for quality, time, and budget—does Nieto need to complete a job successfully?

2. What skills does Nieto need to use each day to handle problems on the job, such as measuring his employees' progress and quality of construction? What skills does he need in dealing with customer complaints and concerns?

Source: Romarico Nieto, "Tiler's Secrets: The Critical Path to Flawless Installation," *Tools of the Trade,* January–February 2003, downloaded from Business & Company Resource Center, http://galenet.galegroup.com.

Through careful planning, Romarico Nieto ensures that his crew reaches its goals and objectives. Doing so requires knowledge of what the crew is supposed to accomplish and whether the crew is actually accomplishing it. Supervisors acquire that important knowledge by carrying out the functions of planning and controlling.

This chapter describes how supervisors can and should carry out those functions. The chapter begins with a description of how planning occurs in organizations, including the types of objectives and planning that are common. Next, the chapter discusses the supervisor's role as planner: setting and updating objectives and including employees in these processes. The second half of the chapter addresses the management function of controlling. It describes the process supervisors follow and some of the tools they use in controlling, as well as the characteristics of effective controls.

SUPERVISORY SKILLS

GOAL SETTING

HINTS FOR SETTING GOALS

If you can think of goals as agreements between you and your employees, you will find that goal setting is as much an art as a science. Goals that are too high are discouraging to your employees; goals that are too low fail to motivate them. Many supervisors find that the best strategy for goal setting is to include employees in the process as much as possible.

Here are a few tips for goal setting:

1. Try to set individual goals for each employee, particularly if you can allow each to create his or her own goals.

2. Help people enhance their sense of their own worth by getting to know their individual strengths and abilities.

3. Use your employees' perspectives to determine what goals are realistic and what aren't.

4. Make goals concise and measurable, with target completion dates.

5. Think of yourself as a resource that supports employees in reaching their goals.

6. Look for ways to help others instead of criticizing them or giving them ultimatums.

7. Remain flexible and open-minded to new ideas and suggestions as your team works toward its goals.

8. Allow employees to take risks and make mistakes, recognizing that mistakes and minor setbacks are part of the growing process.

9. Celebrate progress. Also celebrate mistakes and learn from them.

10. Make sure that everyone keeps the company's mission or vision firmly in mind.

Sources: Jody Urquhart, "Manage by Mobilizing," *Journal of Property Management,* May–June 2001, p. 6; Ken Fracaro, "Optimism on a Rainy Day," *Supervision,* May 1, 2001, p. 5.

PLANNING IN ORGANIZATIONS

planning
Setting goals and determining how to meet them

As you learned in Chapter 1, **planning** is the management function of setting goals and determining how to meet them. For supervisors, this process includes figuring out what tasks the department needs to complete to achieve its goals, as well as how and when to perform those tasks. For action-oriented people, planning can seem time consuming and tedious. But the need for planning is obvious, especially if you consider what would happen in an organization in which no one plans. For example, if a store did not implement planning, customers would not know when the store would be open, and employees would not know what inventory to order or when to order it. The location of the store might be an accident, with no marketing research to determine where business would be sufficient to generate a profit. The managers would not know how many employees to hire, because they would have no idea how many customers they would be serving. Clearly, this business would fail in the mission of providing its customers with high-quality service and merchandise. See the "Supervisory Skills" box for ideas about goal setting.

Supervisors and other managers plan for several reasons. Knowing what the organization is trying to accomplish helps them set priorities and make decisions aimed at accomplishing their goals. Planning forces managers to spend time focusing on the future and establishes a fair way to evaluate performance. It helps managers use resources efficiently, thus minimizing wasted time and money. Time spent in planning a project can reduce the time required to carry it out. The total time for planning and execution can actually be shorter for a thoroughly planned project than for one started in haste.

Many inexpensive software packages can help supervisors plan projects efficiently. Templates that supervisors can customize for their own purposes lead the way through the various planning steps and help establish project phases and the order in which they need to be accomplished, project goals and deadlines, people and departments involved in the project, anticipated obstacles and action plans for overcoming them, and budgets and other resources.

Finally, the other functions that managers perform—organizing, staffing, leading, and controlling—all depend on good planning. Before supervisors and other managers can allocate resources and inspire employees to achieve their objectives, and before they can determine whether employees are meeting those objectives, they need to know what they are trying to accomplish.

Supervisors rarely have much input into the way an organization does its planning. Rather, they participate in whatever process already exists. To participate constructively, supervisors should understand the process.

Objectives

objectives
The desired accomplishments of the organization as a whole or of part of the organization

goals
Objectives, often those with a broad focus

Planning centers on the setting of goals and objectives. **Objectives** specify the desired accomplishments of the organization as a whole or of a part of it. According to one school of thought, **goals** are objectives with a broad focus. For example, an organization seeks to be the number one supplier of nursing home care by the end of next year. That would be considered a goal. In contrast, the accounting department seeks to have all invoices mailed within two weeks of a patient's departure; this is more specific and therefore an objective. This text uses the term *objectives* in most cases and treats the terms *objectives* and *goals* as synonyms.

No matter which term is used, an organization's goals identify what its people should be striving toward. At General Cable Corporation, management wanted to reduce an expensive problem: scrapped materials, which amounted to 4 percent of the company's cost of materials. After analyzing where most of the scrap was occurring. General Cable made sure that all employees saw and understood the charts pinpointing the problem areas. Then employees began looking for ways to reduce scrap by setting goals to fix problems in the costliest areas. Four years later, the scrap rate was down to 1.1 percent with a goal of 0.85 for the following year. Because General Cable makes sure equipment operators have information about where problems are occurring, these employees can contribute to meeting the scrap reduction goals.[1] For an example of how some banks are choosing their objectives, see the "Supervision across Industries" box.

Strategic Objectives

strategic planning
The creation of long-term goals for the organization as a whole

Planning should begin at the top, with a plan for the organization as a whole. **Strategic planning** is the creation of long-term goals for the organization. These goals typically include the type and quality of goods or services the organization is to provide and, for a business, the level of profits it is to earn.

General Electric (GE), for example, has a broad strategy of seeking ways to innovate so that the company can sell more profitable new products rather than competing just by keeping prices low. The company has granted funding to the GE Lighting business group to develop a new technology called organic light-emitting diodes (OLEDs). Scientists at GE Lighting hope the company will be able to produce OLEDs in rolls of flexible material such as plastic that can be used to make light-up ceiling tiles or curtains. As this technology has improved, it has shown the potential to replace traditional light bulbs in the future. Management has determined that OLED development fits its overall business strategy. However, getting the products to market may take another 15 years.[2]

SUPERVISION ACROSS INDUSTRIES

BANKING

DATABASE MARKETING AGENCY HELPS BANKS AIM FOR PROFITS

When banks set objectives, they want to achieve profits, but what makes a bank profitable? A lot of banks consider objectives for increasing the number of customers or the number of accounts. But according to Rich Weissman, chief executive of Database Marketing Agency, this focus on volume has important drawbacks.

Through his experience helping banks build profitability, Weissman has found that a small subset of a bank's customers bring in most of the profits. If these customers leave or even take just part of their business elsewhere, the bank's profits can all but disappear.

Sometimes banks counter that risk by setting volume objectives related to cross-selling, that is, selling more products to existing customers. But Weissman says this objective too can be unprofitable.

Weissman advises banks to look at what he calls "share of wallet" and "profit dynamics." His company helps banks break down their customer data to identify which customers are most profitable in terms of their total relationship with the bank. Then they look at dynamics: what branches and employees are doing to cultivate these successful relationships. Finally, the bank sets objectives related to doing more of what builds profitable relationships.

Source: Janet Bigham Bernstal, "The Profit Pursuit," *Bank Marketing*, April 2004, downloaded from InfoTrac, http://web6.infotrac.galegroup.com.

Usually it is top managers who engage in strategic planning; in other cases, a planning department prepares objectives for approval by top management. Either way, the managers at the top decide where the organization should be going.

Operational Objectives

operational planning
The development of objectives that specify how divisions, departments, and work groups will support organizational goals

The objectives for divisions, departments, and work groups support the goals developed in strategic planning. These objectives, developed through **operational planning,** specify how the group will help the organization achieve its goals. Operational planning is performed by middle managers and supervisors. Table 6.1 summarizes the characteristics of strategic and operational planning.

Middle managers set objectives that will enable their division or department to contribute to the goals set for the organization. Supervisors set objectives that will enable their department or work group to contribute to divisional or departmental goals. For example, if the organizational objective for a bank is to increase profits by 8 percent next year, the goal of a branch located in a high-growth area might be to increase its own profits by 9 percent. At this branch, the vice president (supervisor) in charge of lending operations might have the objective of increasing loans to businesses by 15 percent. The head teller might have the objective of keeping customer waits to five minutes or less. (The good service is designed to support organizational objectives by attracting new customers to the bank.)

TABLE 6.1
Characteristics of Strategic and Operational Planning

	Strategic Planning	Operational Planning
Planners	Top managers, possibly with a planning department	Middle managers and supervisors
Scope	Objectives for the organization as a whole	Objectives for a division, department, or work group
Time Frame	Long range (more than one year)	Short range (one year or less)

Operational objectives should get all employees focused on their role in supporting the company's strategy. At Cardinal Health, a Dublin, Ohio, company that produces health care products and services, operational objectives support company goals in four areas: growth, excellence in operations, development of leaders, and focus on customers. At the beginning of each year, employees establish objectives for themselves, which are supposed to include an objective that supports each of the company-level goals. Conway Transportation, a freight carrier based in Ann Arbor, Michigan, provides each driver with information about how his or her performance contributes to the company's profits. Drivers are expected to meet operational objectives related to productivity, safety, delivery times, absenteeism, costs, and damage to goods shipped.[3]

Notice in these examples that the objectives become more specific at lower levels of the organization, and planning tends to focus on shorter time spans. This is the usual pattern for planning in an organization. Thus, top managers spend a lot of their time thinking broadly over several years, whereas much of the supervisor's planning involves what actions to take in the current week or month.

Personal Objectives

In addition to planning for the department as a whole, each supervisor should apply good planning practices to his or her individual efforts. This includes determining how to help the department meet its objectives, as well as how to meet the supervisor's own career objectives. Another important application of planning is effectively managing the use of one's time. (Chapter 13 discusses time management.)

Characteristics of Effective Objectives

For objectives to be effective—that is, clearly understood and practical—they should have certain characteristics. They should be written, measurable or observable, clear, specific, and challenging but achievable (see Figure 6.1).

Putting objectives *in writing* might seem like a nuisance, but doing so gives them importance; employees can see they are something to which managers have devoted time and thought. The people required to carry out the objectives can then look them up as a reminder of what they are supposed to be accomplishing, and they can take time to make sure they understand them. Finally, writing down objectives forces the supervisor to think through what the objectives say.

FIGURE 6.1
Characteristics of Effective Objectives

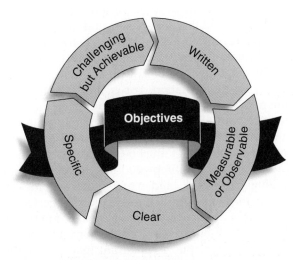

Making objectives *measurable* or at least observable provides the supervisor with a way to tell whether people are actually accomplishing them. Measurable objectives might specify a dollar amount, a time frame, or a quantity to be produced. Examples are the number of sales calls made, parts manufactured, or customers served. The words *maximize* and *minimize* are tip-offs that the objectives are not measurable. If the objective is to "maximize quality," how will anyone know whether maximum quality has been obtained? Instead, the objective might call for a defect rate of no more than 2 percent or for no customer complaints during the month. Other objectives that are difficult to measure are those that simply call for something to "improve" or "get better." The person writing the objective should specify a way to measure or observe the improvement.

When the supervisor needs other people to play a part in accomplishing objectives, those people must understand the objectives. Thus, it is easy to see why objectives should be *clear*. The supervisor can make sure the objectives are clear by spelling them out in simple language and asking employees whether they understand them.

Making objectives *specific* means indicating who is to do what and by what time to accomplish the objective. Specific objectives describe the actions people are to take and what is supposed to result from those actions. For example, instead of saying, "Computer files will be backed up regularly," a specific objective might say, "Each word-processing operator will back up his or her files at the end of each workday." Being specific simplifies the job of ensuring that the objectives are accomplished; the supervisor knows just what to look for. Also, specific objectives help employees understand what they are supposed to be doing.

Objectives that are *challenging* are more likely to stimulate employees to do their best than those that are not. However, the employees have to believe they are capable of achieving the objectives. Otherwise, they will become frustrated or angry at what seem to be unreasonable expectations. Most of us have had the experience of tackling a challenging job and enjoying the sense of pride and accomplishment that comes with finishing it. In setting goals, the supervisor should remember how stimulating and confidence building such experiences can be.

Policies, Procedures, and Rules

To meet his objective of staffing his information systems department with top-quality employees, Bruce Frazzoli hired some people he used to work with at his former job. He was later embarrassed to be called on the carpet for violating his employer's policy that managers must work with the personnel department in making all hiring decisions. Frazzoli learned that supervisors and other managers must consider the organization's policies, procedures, and rules when setting objectives. The content of the objectives and the way they are carried out must be consistent with all three.

policies
Broad guidelines for how to act

Policies are broad guidelines for how to act; they do not spell out the details of how to handle a specific situation. For example, a firm might have a policy of increasing the number of women and minorities in its workforce. Such a policy does not dictate whom to hire or when; it merely states a general expectation. Figure 6.2 summarizes a dress code policy for a Wisconsin bank.

procedures
The steps that must be completed to achieve a specific purpose

Procedures are the steps that must be completed to achieve a specific purpose. An organization might specify procedures for hiring employees, purchasing equipment, filing paperwork, and many other activities. Publishing company McGraw-Hill's management guidelines include suggested procedures for how to conduct performance appraisals and employment interviews. A supervisor may be responsible for developing the procedures for activities carried out in his or her own department. For example, a restaurant manager might spell out a cleanup

FIGURE 6.2
Dress Code Policy for a Wisconsin Bank

Source: Adapted from Mary Siegel, "Sample Dress Code Policy," *Teller Vision*, June 2003 (M&I Bank Dress Code, 124th Street Branch), downloaded from Business and Company Resource Center, http://galenet.galegroup.com.

Professional attire, neatness, cleanliness, and good personal health habits are important to the impression we make on our customers. Clothing should fit appropriately (i.e., not snugly). Hair, makeup, and jewelry styles should be suitable for business and not excessive or distracting.

Supervisors are responsible for the professional appearance and image of their areas.

For All Employees
- Visual body piercing other than the norm (i.e., the ears) is not allowed unless the jewelry is removed while at work.
- Tattoos must be covered at all times.
- Low-rise pants are not acceptable.

For Women
- Dresses, skirts, and coordinated pant outfits are acceptable.
- Shorts, golf skirts, miniskirts, sundresses, backless dresses, and dresses with low necklines are not allowed.
- Tube tops, halter tops, tank tops, and T-shirts are not allowed.
- Businesslike shoes are to be worn to work.

For Men
- Employees with public contact or supervisory or professional responsibilities are expected to wear a suit or sport coat, slacks, and tie. Apparel for employees in nonpublic areas should be clean, neat, and moderate in style.
- Jeans, sweatshirts, tank shirts, T-shirts, sandals, tennis shoes, and similar items of casual wear do not present a businesslike appearance.
- Hair length should not extend beyond the shirt collar.

procedure or a maintenance supervisor might detail the shutdown procedure for a piece of machinery. Procedures free managers and employees from making decisions about activities they carry out repeatedly.

rules
Specific statements of what to do or not do in a given situation

Rules are specific statements of what to do or not do in a given situation. Unlike policies, they are neither flexible nor open to interpretation. For example, one rule at Opto Technology is that employees must wear safety goggles whenever they handle chemicals and when they weld, solder, drill, or cut wires. Restaurants have rules stating that employees must wash their hands before working. Rules of this kind are often imposed by law.

Action Plans

action plan
The plan for how to achieve an objective

Objectives serve as the basis for action plans and contingency plans (see Figure 6.3). An **action plan** is a plan for how to achieve an objective. If you think of objectives as statements of where you want to go, then an action plan

FIGURE 6.3
Areas of Planning

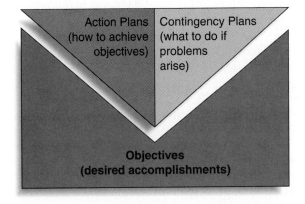

is a map that tells you how to get there. For a successful trip, you need both kinds of information.

The supervisor creates an action plan by answering the questions *what, who, when, where,* and *how:*

- *What* actions need to be taken? Do sales calls need to be made, customers served in a certain way, goods produced? The supervisor should outline the specific steps involved.
- *Who* will take the necessary steps? The supervisor may perform some tasks, but many activities will be assigned to specific employees or groups of employees.
- *When* must each step be completed? With many types of processes, certain steps will determine when the whole project is completed. The supervisor should be particularly careful in scheduling those activities.
- *Where* will the work take place? Sometimes this question is easy to answer, but a growing operation may require that the supervisor plan for additional space. Some activities may require that the supervisor consider the arrangement of work on the shop floor or the arrangement of items in a warehouse or supply room.
- *How* will the work be done? Are the usual procedures and equipment adequate, or does the supervisor need to innovate? Thinking about how the work will be done may alert the supervisor to a need for more training.

Contingency Planning

contingency planning
Planning what to do if the original plans don't work out

A lot of people believe in Murphy's law: "If anything can go wrong, it will." Even those who are less pessimistic recognize that things don't always go as planned. A delivery may be delayed by a strike or a blizzard, a key employee may take another job, a "foolproof" computer system may crash. The sign of a good supervisor is not so much that the supervisor never has experienced these nasty surprises but that he or she is prepared with ideas about how to respond.

Planning what to do if the original plans don't work out is known as **contingency planning.** The wise supervisor has contingency plans to go with every original plan. One useful technique for contingency planning is to review all objectives, looking for areas where something might go wrong. Then the supervisor determines how to respond if those problems do arise.

During the summer of 2003, a power company blackout cut off electricity to much of the northeastern United States, as well as parts of the Midwest and Canada. More than half the manufacturers in Ohio were affected, costing them an estimated $1.1 billion. Ford Motor Company was forced to shut down almost two dozen factories in Michigan, Ohio, and Ontario. However, the company was prepared. Teams of employees quickly switched the most important operations to batteries and generators to preserve data and maintain customer service. Others worked to repair damage. Ford was prepared for such a contingency, but many

management by objectives (MBO)
A formal system for planning in which managers and employees at all levels set objectives for what they are to accomplish; their performance is then measured against those objectives

companies are not. A survey by Robert Half Management Resources found that more than one-third of companies lacked a plan for continuing operations following a storm, fire, blackout, terrorist strike, or other catastrophe.[4]

Contingency planning is not always formal. It would be too time consuming to create a written contingency plan for every detail of operations. Instead, the supervisor simply has to keep in mind how to respond if some details of the operation do not go as planned.

Management by Objectives

Many organizations use a formal system for planning known as **management by objectives (MBO),** a process in which managers and employees at all levels set objectives for what they are to accomplish. Their performance then is measured against those objectives. Basically, MBO involves three steps:

1. All individuals in the organization work with their managers to set objectives, specifying what they are to do in the next operating period (such as a year).
2. Each individual's manager periodically reviews the individual's performance to see whether he or she is meeting the objectives. Typically, these reviews take place two to four times a year. The reviews help the individual and the manager decide what corrective actions are needed, and they provide information for setting future objectives.
3. The organization rewards individuals on the basis of how close they come to fulfilling the objectives.

Figure 6.4 shows examples of objectives for employees at several levels of an organization using MBO. Notice that the sample objective for the nonmanagement

FIGURE 6.4
Sample Objectives in an Organization Using MBO

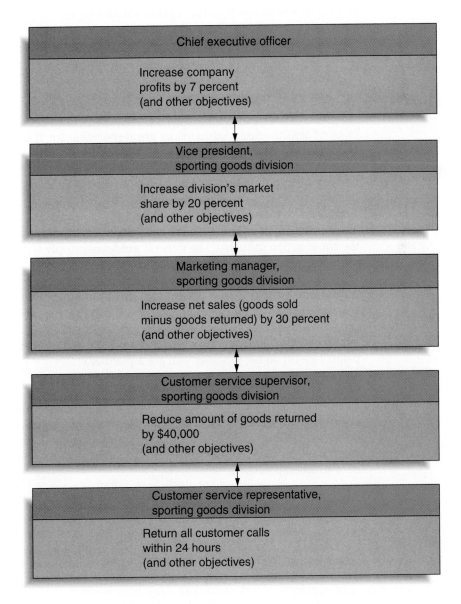

Chief executive officer

Increase company
profits by 7 percent
(and other objectives)

Vice president,
sporting goods division

Increase division's market
share by 20 percent
(and other objectives)

Marketing manager,
sporting goods division

Increase net sales (goods sold
minus goods returned) by 30 percent
(and other objectives)

Customer service supervisor,
sporting goods division

Reduce amount of goods returned
by $40,000
(and other objectives)

Customer service representative,
sporting goods division

Return all customer calls
within 24 hours
(and other objectives)

employee supports the achievement of the supervisor's objective, which in turn supports the achievement of his or her manager's objective, and so on up the hierarchy. (In practice, of course, each person in the organization would have several objectives to meet.)

For the effective use of MBO, managers at all levels (especially top management) must be committed to the system. Also, the objectives they set must meet the criteria for effective objectives described previously. For example, a salesperson would not be expected merely to "sell more" but to help develop specific objectives, such as "make 40 sales calls a month" and "sell 50 copiers by December 31." Finally, managers and employees must be able to cooperate in the objective-setting process.

Some people dislike MBO because setting and monitoring the achievement of objectives can be time consuming and requires a lot of paperwork. However, the organization can benefit from involving employees in setting goals, which may lead to greater commitment in achieving them. Also, the employees can benefit from a system of rewards that is rational and based on performance rather than personality. In light of these advantages, a supervisor may want to use the MBO principles with the employees in his or her own department even if the organization as a whole has not adopted a formal MBO system.

THE SUPERVISOR AS PLANNER

In most organizations, supervisors are responsible for the creation of plans that specify goals, tasks, resources, and responsibilities for the supervisor's own department. Thus, at the supervisor's level, objectives can range from the tasks he or she intends to accomplish on a certain day to the level of production the department is to achieve for the year. To be an effective planner, the supervisor should be familiar with how to set good objectives in these and other areas. The "Supervisory Skills" box describes the planning responsibilities of supervisors in the construction industry. The general guidelines apply to similar challenges met by supervisors in many different settings.

Although supervisors might resist doing the necessary paperwork, thoughtful planning is worth the investment of time and effort. In carrying out their planning responsibilities, supervisors may engage in a variety of activities, from providing information to allocating resources, involving employees, coaching a team's planning effort, and updating objectives. (Take the Knowing Yourself quiz on pages 168–169 to see whether you are a planner.)

Providing Information and Estimates

As the manager closest to day-to-day operations, the supervisor is in the best position to keep higher-level managers informed about the needs, abilities, and progress of his or her department or work group. For that reason, higher management relies on supervisors to provide estimates of the personnel and other resources they will need to accomplish their work.

Allocating Resources

The department for which the supervisor is responsible has a limited number of resources—people, equipment, and money. The supervisor's job includes deciding how to allocate resources to the jobs that will need to be done.

The process of allocating human resources includes determining how many and what kind of employees the department will need to meet its objectives. If the

SUPERVISORY SKILLS

PLANNING

SETTING PRIORITIES FOR PROJECTS

James Adrian, a consultant to companies in the construction industry, believes that the performance of the on-site supervisor is the most important ingredient in a construction company's profits. The supervisor's planning and decision making should help the company cope with the challenges of weather, suppliers, and labor unions. Careful planning guides the onsite supervisor as he or she makes up to 80 decisions a day related to project time, cost, quality, and safety.

To fulfill these demands, supervisors need to understand the importance of each project they are planning. Adrian recommends listing each of the day's construction tasks in a worksheet. Next to each task, indicate the cost per unit for completing it. Then rate each task in three areas: (1) whether completing the task on time is critical to meeting the overall schedule; (2) whether productivity risk—the chance that quality or efficiency will suffer if the supervisor is not involved—is high, low, or somewhere in between; and (3) whether the task is new or unfamiliar to the employees who will perform it. Finally, taking into account the costs and ratings, the supervisor ranks the tasks according to how much direct supervision will be needed. The supervisor should give the highest priority to tasks that have high costs, are critical to meeting the schedule, have high productivity risk, and are new or unfamiliar. High priority means the supervisor makes a point of observing the task and being available to help resolve problems.

Adrian has observed many workplace situations in which his planning worksheet could have improved the supervisor's skills. For example, in the construction of a concrete foundation wall, the tasks include building forms, placing rebar, and pouring concrete from the truck into the wall. Typically, the supervisor observes the pouring of concrete. However, schedule and cost problems more often occur during the stage of building the forms. In this case, the productivity risk is greater for building forms, suggesting that this stage requires more attention from the supervisor.

Similarly, Adrian has discovered that many construction supervisors are unfamiliar with costs of materials and equipment. He demonstrated the significance of this problem to a group of students in a course on productivity. He took the group to a construction site to observe the work and note productivity problems. Everyone criticized the fact that a group of workers (who were paid more than $40 an hour) were taking a 15-minute break. But no one commented on a piece of equipment that stood idle for four hours. The students didn't think about it because none of them realized the rental cost of that equipment was more than $120 per hour.

Most supervisors are familiar with planning that addresses spending and scheduling. In addition, busy supervisors would do well to try adapting Adrian's practical view of planning how to allocate time.

Source: Based on James Adrian, "Improving Your Supervisor's Work Day," *Pavement,* January 2006, downloaded from Business & Company Resource Center, http://galenet.galegroup.com.

department's workload is expanding, the supervisor may need to plan to hire new employees. He or she also must plan for employee vacations and other time off, as well as for employee turnover.

The process of allocating equipment resources includes determining how much equipment is needed to get the job done. For example, does every bookkeeper need a personal computer, or will calculators be enough? The supervisor may find that the department needs to acquire more equipment. In that case, the supervisor must justify the request to buy or rent it by showing how it will benefit the organization.

Developing a Budget

budget
A plan for spending money

The process of allocating money resources is called *budgeting.* A **budget** is a plan for spending money. Many households use budgets to decide how much of each paycheck should go for housing, car payments, food, savings, and so on. Businesses

TABLE 6.2
Sample Budget for a Machine Shop Project

Source: From *Industrial Supervision: In the Age of High Technology*, by David L. Goetsch. Copyright © 1992 Pearson Education, Inc. Reprinted by permission of Pearson Education, Inc., Upper Saddle River, NJ.

Budget Monitoring Report

Organizational unit <u>Machine shop</u>   Job number <u>1763</u>   Period <u>January–June</u>
Total parts needed <u>6,000</u>   Parts produced to date <u>2,700</u>   Remaining work <u>3,300</u>
Parts per month projection <u>1,000</u>   Current production per month 900   Difference <u>−100</u>

Actual Expenditures

Line Item	Budgeted Amount	January	February	March	April	May	June
Direct labor	$60,000	$10,000	$10,000	$10,000			
Indirect labor	5,400	900	900	900			
Material	13,200	2,195	3,156	1,032			
Operating supplies	3,000	1,200	0	296			
Equipment repair	5,400	0	0	3,600			
Total	**$87,000**	**$14,295**	**$14,056**	**$15,828**			

use budgets to break down how much to spend on items such as wages and salaries, rent, supplies, insurance, and so on. These items would be part of an *operating budget;* big-ticket items such as machinery or a new building would more likely be accounted for separately as part of a *capital budget.*

Some organizations expect their supervisors to prepare a budget showing what they think they will need to spend in the next year to meet departmental goals or carry out a specific project. Table 6.2 illustrates a sample budget for a machine shop project. The line items show different categories of expenses. The first column of figures contains the amounts budgeted for expenses in each category. The right-hand columns have the actual amounts spent each month in each category. The supervisor uses the actual amounts in controlling, which is described subsequently in this chapter.

In preparing a budget, the supervisor typically has rules and guidelines to follow. For example, one company may say that pay increases for the department as a whole must be no more than 5 percent of the previous year's budget for salaries. Another organization may specify a total amount that the department may spend, or it may give the supervisor a formula for computing the department's overhead expenses. On the basis of these guidelines, the supervisor then recommends how much to spend in each area. In most cases, the supervisor and his or her manager review the budget. The supervisor must be willing to modify it when higher-level managers require a change.

Scheduling

scheduling
Setting a precise timetable for the work to be completed

Gantt chart
Scheduling tool that lists the activities to be completed and uses horizontal bars to graph how long each activity will take, including its starting and ending dates

The supervisor continually needs to think about how much work the department needs to accomplish in a given time period and how it can meet its deadlines. Setting a precise timetable for the work to be done is known as **scheduling.** This process includes deciding which activities will take priority over others and deciding who will do what tasks and when.

Many organizations expect supervisors to use one or more of the techniques and tools that have been developed to help with scheduling. Two of the most widely used techniques are Gantt charts and PERT networks. A **Gantt chart** is a scheduling tool that lists the activities to be completed and uses horizontal bars to graph how long each activity will take, including its starting and ending dates. The sample Gantt chart in Figure 6.5 was created with software called QuickGantt, which automatically fills in the chart using activity and schedule information entered on a spreadsheet.

FIGURE 6.5 **Sample Gantt Chart for a Building Project**

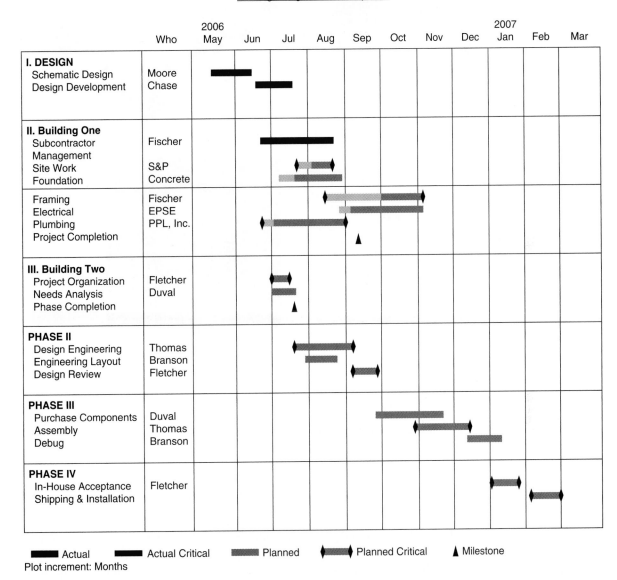

Project Schedule Chart
Architects & Contractors, Inc.
Building Design and Development

program evaluation and review technique (PERT) Scheduling tool that identifies the relationships among tasks as well as the amount of time each task will take

The **program evaluation and review technique (PERT)** is a scheduling tool that identifies the relationships among tasks and the amount of time each task will take. To use this tool, the planner creates a PERT network. For example, in Figure 6.6, the circles represent the events that must occur to produce a film. The arrows between the circles represent the sequence of activities. The letter on each arrow refers to the activity that results in the corresponding event. Many PERT charts also include information about how long each task is expected to take. An important piece of information in a PERT network is the *critical path*—the sequence of

FIGURE 6.6
PERT Scheduling Tool

Source: www.smartdraw.com/ resources/examples/ business/images/ coded_pert_full. gif.

FILM PRODUCTION

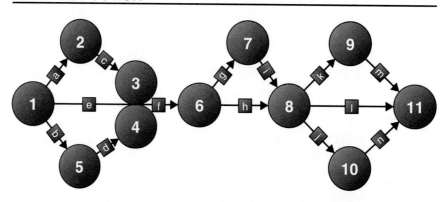

	ACTIVITIES	
CODE	**MEANING**
a	Obtain funds, loans, investors
b	Solicit director interest
c	Draw up staff contracts, agree on salaries
d	Pick and hire production staff
e	Advertise, contact agents
f	Scout locations
g	Build sets
h, i	Film scenes
j	Pick a conductor, choose songs
k	Edit film
l	Write press releases, buy ads, create preview
m	Prescreen with audiences
n	Create soundtrack CD

	EVENTS
CODE	**MEANING**
1	Obtain script
2	Budget acquired
3	Talent hired
4	Production staff hired
5	Director signed contract
6	Locations picked
7	All sets final
8	Filming completed
9	Film edited
10	Soundtrack complete
11	Film released

tasks that will require the greatest amount of time. A delay in the critical path will cause the entire project to fall behind.

In addition to these tools, supervisors may use a computer to help with scheduling. Many project management software packages have been developed for this application.

Involving Employees

To make sure that employees understand objectives and consider them achievable, supervisors may involve them in the goal-setting process. Employees who are involved in the process tend to feel more committed to the objectives, and they may be able to introduce ideas that the supervisor has not considered. In many cases, employees who help set objectives agree to take on greater challenges than the supervisor might have guessed.

One way to get employees involved in setting objectives is to have them write down what they think they can accomplish in the coming year (or month or appropriate time period). Then the supervisor discusses the ideas with each employee, modifying the objectives to meet the department's overall needs. Another approach is to hold a meeting of the entire work group at which the employees and supervisor develop objectives as a group. (Chapter 3 provides ideas for holding successful meetings.)

To set objectives for salespeople at Davis & Geck (a medical supply company), sales manager Dave Jacobs asks the salespeople and their regional supervisors to come up with sales levels they can guarantee. The supervisors are expected to discuss each salesperson's figures with him or her to assess how realistic they are. Jacobs then may modify those numbers in light of broad industry trends. The first year Jacobs used this bottom-up approach, some projections were overly optimistic. Since then, supervisors have begun asking salespeople to prepare action plans detailing how they expect to achieve their numbers. The result: more accurate numbers.[5]

Planning with a Team

In many applications of teamwork, teams, not individual managers, are charged with planning. In these cases, supervisors are expected not only to seek employee involvement in planning but also to coach their team in carrying out the planning function. This requires knowing and communicating a clear sense of what the plan should encompass and encouraging team members to cooperate and share ideas freely.

When teams draw on the many viewpoints and diverse experience of team members, they can come up with creative plans that dramatically exceed past performance. American Airlines recently turned to a team approach when it decided it could make its maintenance centers so efficient that the company could profitably sell maintenance services to other airlines. American formed teams of union and management employees to figure out how to raise the productivity of each maintenance center. At the center in Tulsa, one solution was to overhaul the basic approach to heavy maintenance. Under the traditional arrangement, an airplane would be parked in the hangar, and hundreds of workers would swarm over it, removing and replacing parts. The teams figured out it would be more efficient to set up three work areas and move each plane from one stage to the next. With suggestions from workers at all levels, the company redesigned the entire workplace, repositioning supervisors and rearranging parts and equipment to place them nearer to where they would be needed. With these and other changes, American expects the Tulsa facility to meet its overall goal: to reduce costs and increase revenue for a total gain of $500 million.[6] (Chapter 3 provides a more detailed discussion of managing teamwork.)

Updating Objectives

Once the supervisor has set objectives, he or she should monitor performance and compare it with the objectives. (The control process will be described subsequently in this chapter.) Sometimes the supervisor determines that objectives need to be modified.

When should supervisors update the objectives for their department or work group? They will need to do so whenever top management updates organizational objectives. Also, organizations with a regular procedure for planning will specify when supervisors must review and update their objectives.

THE SUPERVISOR AS CONTROLLER

controlling
The management function of ensuring that work goes according to plan

As you learned in Chapter 1, **controlling** is the management function of making sure that work goes according to plan. Supervisors carry out this process in many ways. Consider the following fictional examples:

- Bud Cavanaugh told his crew, "I expect the work area to be clean when you leave each day. That means the floors are swept and all the tools are put away."
- Once or twice each day, Maria Lopez took time to check the documents produced by the word-processing operators she supervised. Maria would look over a few pages each employee had produced that day. If one of the employees seemed to be having trouble with some task—for example, deciphering handwriting or preparing neat tables—Maria would discuss the problem with that employee.
- Sonja Friedman learned that citizens calling her housing department complained of spending an excessive amount of time on hold. She scheduled a meeting at which the employees discussed ways they could handle calls faster.

As shown in these examples, supervisors need to know what is going on in the area they supervise. Do employees understand what they are supposed to do, and can they do it? Is all machinery and equipment (whether a computer-operated milling machine or a cell phone) operating properly? Is work getting out correctly and on time?

To answer such questions, a supervisor could theoretically sit back and wait for disaster to strike. No disaster, no need for correction. More realistically, the supervisor has a responsibility to correct problems as soon as possible, which means that some way to *detect* problems quickly must be found. Detection of problems is at the heart of the control function.

By controlling, the supervisor can take steps to ensure quality and manage costs. Visiting the work area and checking up on performance, as Maria Lopez did, allows the supervisor to make sure that employees are producing satisfactory work. By setting standards for a clean workplace, Bud Cavanaugh reduced costs related to spending time looking for tools or to slipping on a messy floor. Sonja Friedman engaged her employees to improve work processes. In many such ways, supervisors can benefit the organization through the process of control.

The Process of Controlling

Although the specific ways in which supervisors control vary according to the type of organization and the employees being supervised, the basic process involves three steps. First, the supervisor establishes performance **standards**, which are measures of what is expected. Then the supervisor monitors actual performance and compares it with the standards. Finally, the supervisor responds, either by reinforcing success or by making some adjustment to bring performance and the standards into line. Figure 6.7 illustrates this process.

standards
Measures of what is expected

If the control system is working properly, the supervisor should be uncovering problems before customers and management discover them. This gives the supervisor the best opportunity to fix a problem in time to minimize damage.

Establish Performance Standards

Performance standards are a natural outgrowth of the planning process. Once the supervisor knows the objectives employees are to achieve, he or she can determine what employees must do to meet those objectives. Assume that the objective of an eight-person telephone sales (telemarketing) office is to make 320 calls an

FIGURE 6.7
The Control Process

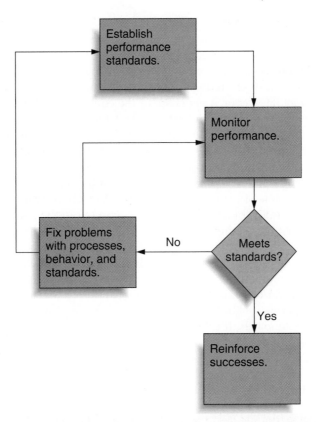

evening, resulting in 64 sales. To achieve this objective, each salesperson should average 10 calls an hour, with 2 in 10 calls resulting in a sale. Those numbers could be two of the office's performance standards.

Standards define the acceptable quantity and quality of work. (The measure of quantity in the example is the number of telephone calls made; the number of sales measures the quality of selling, that is, turning a telephone call into a sale.) Other standards can spell out expectations for level of service, amount of money spent, amount of inventory on hand, level of pollution in the workplace, and other concerns. Ultimately, all these standards measure how well the department contributes to meeting the organization's objectives to serve its customers and—for a business—earn a profit.

The way supervisors set standards depends on their experience, their employer's expectations, and the nature of the work being monitored. Often, supervisors use their technical expertise to estimate reasonable standards. Past performance also is a useful guide for what can be expected. However, the supervisor must avoid being a slave to the past. In creating a budget, some supervisors assume that because they have spent a given sum in a given category in the past, that expense will be appropriate in the future. Sometimes there are better alternatives. Supervisors may have additional sources of information in setting performance standards. Equipment manufacturers and systems designers can provide information about how fast a machine or computer system will perform. Some companies arrange for time-and-motion studies to analyze how quickly and efficiently employees can reasonably work.

To be effective, performance standards should meet the criteria of effective objectives; that is, they should be written, measurable, clear, specific, and challenging but achievable. Standards also should measure dimensions of the goods or services that customers care about and that support the company's strategy. A bank once based some marketing-related performance standards on the types of products it expected to be most profitable. The bank had determined that home equity lines of credit brought in a high return, so it had branches promote this product. However, a big share of the consumers who applied for the lines of credit were in southern Florida. Most of them were retired people who didn't really want the cash they could borrow against their home equity. Rather, they wanted the product as a kind of "insurance" that they could get cash if they ever needed it. The bank was going to the expense of approving the credit and setting up the accounts, but it wasn't earning much from consumers actually borrowing against their line of credit. An employee or branch that met objectives for opening the lines of credit contributed less than expected to the bank's profit.[7]

Not only should the supervisor have standards in mind, but the employees should also be aware of and understand those standards. In communicating performance standards, the supervisor should put them in writing so that employees can remember and refer to them as necessary. (Chapter 10 provides more detailed suggestions for communicating effectively.)

The supervisor should also be sure that the employees understand the rationale for the standards. It is human nature to resist when someone lays down restrictive rules, but the rules seem less a burden when they serve a purpose we can understand. Thus, if a law office's word-processing department has a standard to produce error-free documents, the department's supervisor can explain that it is part of the firm's plan to build a prestigious clientele by delivering an excellent product. With such an explanation, the word processors are less likely to feel overwhelmed by the stringent quality standard and more likely to feel proud that they are part of an excellent law firm.

Monitor Performance and Compare with Standards

Once performance standards are in place, the supervisor can begin the core of the control process: monitoring performance. In the example of the telephone sales force, the supervisor would want to keep track of how many calls each salesperson made and how many of those calls resulted in sales.

One way to monitor performance is simply to record information on paper or enter it into a computer, a task that can be done by the supervisor, the employees, or both. The telephone salespeople in the example might provide the supervisor with information to enter into a log such as the one shown in Table 6.3. Some types of machinery and equipment have electronic or mechanical counting systems that provide an unbiased way to measure performance. For instance, the electronic scanners at store checkout stations can track how fast cashiers are ringing up merchandise.

As described in the "Supervision and Ethics" box in Chapter 2, a growing number of firms use forms of electronic monitoring to keep tabs on employees' performance. Some use software that tracks employees' use of the Internet. Others record the phone calls of customer service representatives. Electronic monitoring can be important for supervising employees who "telecommute," working from home or other locations away from the supervisor. Supervisors often worry about how to control the work of someone they cannot watch, so they may welcome the detailed information about employees' activities. However, it is also important to consider other ways of supervising remote workers. Supervisors need to focus on results more than activities, asking "What did you accomplish today?" rather than "What did you do today?" Supervisors of telecommuters also need superior

TABLE 6.3
Sample
Performance Record

Week of <u>November 22, 2007</u>
Performance Standard: <u>40</u> calls, <u>8</u> sales

Name	Number of Calls Completed	Number of Sales Made	Action
Forrest	32	6	Discuss slow pace of work.
French	41	8	Praise performance.
Johnson	39	7	None.
Munoz	47	9	Praise performance.
Peterson	38	8	Praise performance.
Spagnoli	50	7	Praise hard work; discuss how to turn more calls into sales.
Steinmetz	29	5	Discuss poor performance; discipline if necessary.
Wang	43	9	Praise performance.
Total	**319**	**59**	

listening skills so they can become aware of employees' concerns and problems expressed over the telephone, between the lines in e-mail, or even indirectly in the quality and type of work delivered.[8]

Of course, the monitoring must be efficient and accurate. In addition to using electronic monitoring, supervisors can get accurate information by observing workers directly. The supervisor's physical presence signals that the supervisor is interested in employees and what they are doing, and it makes the supervisor available to answer questions and help solve problems. An active supervisor not only checks on workers and ensures that they are meeting goals but also takes on many other roles, including teacher, safety officer, and advocate for employees.[9]

From a quality perspective, monitoring performance should include assessing whether customers are satisfied. In the case of groups that provide services to other employees in the organization, supervisors should ask those "internal customers" whether they are getting what they need when they need it. At Bristol-Myers Squibb Company, regular surveys ask whether employees are satisfied with in-house services such as housekeeping, grounds crews, and employee dining. The giant pharmaceutical company recently set up a team to improve the surveys so that they would use measures that are "actionable," meaning the department providing the services can use the results to identify types of changes that are needed. For example, the survey about dining facilities used to ask for an overall rating, but an overall rating of "fair" or "excellent" doesn't suggest areas for improvement. The new surveys ask questions such as "Are the menu choices currently being offered meeting your dietary needs?"[10]

When monitoring performance, the supervisor should focus on how actual performance compares with the standards he or she has set. Are employees meeting standards, exceeding them, or falling short? Two concepts useful for maintaining this focus are variance and the exception principle.

variance
The size of the difference between actual performance and a performance standard

In a control system, **variance** refers to the size of the difference between actual performance and the standard to be met. When setting standards, the supervisor should decide how much variance is meaningful for control purposes. It can be helpful to think in terms of percentages. For example, if a hospital's performance standard is to register outpatients for lab tests in 10 minutes or fewer, the supervisor might decide to allow for a variance of 50 percent (5 minutes). (In a manufacturing setting, a variance of 5 to 10 percent might be more appropriate for most standards.) As described in Chapter 2, some organizations strive for a standard of accepting zero defects.

exception principle
The control principle stating that a supervisor should take action only when variance is meaningful

According to the **exception principle,** the supervisor should take action only when the variance is meaningful. Thus, when monitoring performance in the previous example, the supervisor would need to take action only if outpatients spent more than 15 or fewer than 5 minutes registering for lab tests.

The exception principle is beneficial when it helps the supervisor manage his or her time wisely and motivate employees. A supervisor who did not tolerate reasonable variances might try to solve the "problem" every time an employee made one component too few or went over the budget for office supplies by the cost of a box of paper clips. In such a case, employees might become frustrated by the control system, and morale would deteriorate. At the same time, the supervisor would be too busy with trifles to focus on more significant issues.

Reinforce Successes and Fix Problems

The information gained from the control process is beneficial only if the supervisor uses it as the basis for reinforcing or changing behavior. If performance is satisfactory or better, the supervisor needs to encourage it. If performance is unacceptable, the supervisor needs to make changes that either improve performance or adjust the standard. The right-hand column in Table 6.3 lists some ways the telemarketing supervisor plans to respond to performance data.

reinforcement
Encouragement of a behavior by associating it with a reward

When employees are doing excellent work, customers are happy, and costs are within budget, the supervisor needs to reinforce these successes. **Reinforcement** means encouraging the behavior by associating it with a reward. Praise from the supervisor for performance that meets standards not only gives the employee a good feeling but also clarifies what is expected. For exceptionally high performance, the supervisor also may reward the employee with a monetary bonus. The supervisor's actions will depend on company and union rules regarding superior performance.

problem
A factor in the organization that is a barrier to improvement

When performance significantly falls short of standards, the supervisor should investigate. Below-standard performance is the sign of a **problem**—some factor in the organization that is a barrier to improvement. The supervisor's task is to identify the underlying problem. For example, if the supervisor in the telephone sales company learns that the group is not meeting its sales objectives, the supervisor could find out who is falling short of the sales goals: everyone or only one or two employees. If everyone is performing below standard, the problem may be that the sales force needs better training or motivation. Or the problem may lie outside the supervisor's direct control; the product may be defective or customers may lack interest for some other reason, such as poor economic conditions. If only one employee is failing to make sales, the supervisor needs to search for the problem underlying that employee's poor performance. Does the employee understand how to close a sale? Does the employee have personal problems that affect performance?

symptom
An indication of an underlying problem

Poor performance itself is rarely a problem, but a **symptom**—an indication of an underlying problem. To use the information gained through controlling effectively, the supervisor needs to distinguish problems from symptoms. In the example of the Bristol-Myers Squibb survey described previously, the facilities department was surprised to learn that employees were dissatisfied with the menu variety offered in company cafeterias. The apparent problem was that menus had too few items. But before squeezing more offerings into the dining

FIGURE 6.8
Tools for Fixing Performance Problems

Adjust Processes

Make processes simpler, more efficient, or more flexible.

Improve Behavior

Offer new rewards, better training, or clearer directions.

Adapt Standards

Align standards with actual abilities, resources, and objectives.

facilities, Ann McNally, the team leader responsible for the surveys, assembled a group of employees to talk about the problem. The employees in these groups described their busy days. When they headed for the café to grab lunch, they didn't study all the menu choices but just grabbed whatever they usually bought. The team determined that the complaint about menu variety was really a symptom of a communication and time problem. Employees needed to be able to see their alternatives at a quick glance. The department worked with its supplier of dining services to display alternatives differently and post menus online for employees to check ahead of time at their convenience. Adding more choices to the menu would have increased the company's costs without solving the real problem.[11]

Sometimes a problem underlying significant variance is that the standard is too low or too high. For example, if no employees on the telephone sales force are achieving the desired number of sales, the standards may be too high, given current economic or market conditions. In other cases, what the manager learns about performance may indicate that a standard is not measuring the right thing.

Fixing the problem may entail adjusting a process, the behavior of an individual employee, or the standard itself (see Figure 6.8). For process and behavioral problems, supervisors can choose from among a number of possible actions:

- Develop new rewards for good performance.
- Train employees.
- Improve communications with employees.
- Counsel and/or discipline poor performers.
- Ask employees what barriers are interfering with their performance, then remove those barriers. (Common barriers include insufficient supplies or information, poorly maintained equipment, and inefficient work procedures.)

The best response to problems related to standards is to make the performance standard more appropriate. The supervisor may need to make the standard less stringent or more challenging.

Whatever actions the supervisor selects, it is important to give employees feedback soon after observing a deviation from the standard. This enables the employees to make changes before performance deteriorates further. A problem that has been allowed to continue is often harder to correct. For example, an employee may get into the habit of doing a task the wrong way or fall so far behind that it is impossible to catch up.

Modifying standards brings the control process full circle. With new standards in place, the supervisor is again ready to monitor performance.

Types of Control

From the description of the control process, it might sound as though controlling begins when employees' work is complete: The employees finish their jobs, then the supervisor checks whether a job was done well. However, this is only one type of controlling. There are three types of control in terms of when it occurs: feedback control, concurrent control, and precontrol.

feedback control
Control that focuses on past performance

Feedback control is the type just described, that is, control that focuses on past performance. A supervisor reviewing customer comments about service is practicing feedback control. The customers provide information about the quality of service; the supervisor reacts by reinforcing or trying to change employee behavior.

concurrent control
Control that occurs while the work takes place

The word *concurrent* describes things that are happening at the same time. Thus, **concurrent control** refers to controlling work while that work is being done. A restaurant manager who greets customers at their tables and visits the kitchen to see how work is progressing is practicing concurrent control. This supervisor is gathering information about what is going smoothly and what problems may be developing. The supervisor can act on any problems before customers or employees become upset. Another technique for concurrent control is statistical process control, described in Chapter 2.

precontrol
Efforts aimed at preventing behavior that may lead to undesirable results

Precontrol refers to efforts aimed at preventing behavior that may lead to undesirable results. Such efforts may include setting rules, policies, and procedures. A production supervisor might provide employees with guidelines about the detection of improperly functioning machinery. The employees can then request repairs before they waste time and materials on the machinery. Precontrol is one of the functions of the management philosophy known as total quality management (see Chapter 2).

Tools for Control

When considering how to monitor performance, the supervisor can start with some basic tools used by most managers. Budgets and reports are common in most organizations. In addition, supervisors can benefit from personally observing the work.

Budgets

Creating a budget—a plan for spending money—is part of the planning process. In controlling, a budget is useful as a kind of performance standard. The supervisor compares actual expenses with the amounts in the budget.

Table 6.4 is a sample budget report based on the example in Table 6.2. The first column shows each category of expenses for the machine shop project, which was scheduled to last for six months, from January through June. Thus, the six-month budget represents the total the supervisor expected to spend in each category for the project. This report was prepared on March 31 (halfway through the project), so the next column shows what would be budgeted for half of the project. The adjacent column shows the amounts that actually were spent during the first three months. In the right-hand column appears the variance between the actual and budgeted amounts. In this case, the machine shop has a negative total variance because the project is $679 over budget for the first three months.

TABLE 6.4
Budget Report for a Manufacturing Project

Source: From *Industrial Supervision: In The Age of Technology*, by David L. Goetsch. Copyright © 1992 Pearson Education, Inc. Reprinted by permission of Pearson Education, Inc., Upper Saddle River, NJ.

Line Item	Six-Month Budget	Budgeted Year to Date (Jan.–Mar.)	Actual Year to Date (Jan.–Mar.)	Variance
Direct labor	$60,000	$30,000	$30,000	$ 0
Indirect labor	5,400	2,700	2,700	0
Material	13,200	6,600	6,383	217
Operating supplies	3,000	1,500	1,496	4
Equipment repair	5,400	2,700	3,600	−900
Total	**$87,000**	**$43,500**	**$44,179**	**−$679**

Organizational Unit Machine Shop   Job Number 1763   Date March 31, 20xx

When using such a budget report for controlling purposes, the supervisor focuses on the variance column, looking for meaningful variances. In Table 6.4, the supervisor would note that the total unfavorable variance is due entirely to a large expense for equipment repair. The machine shop is otherwise under budget or exactly meeting the budget standards. Following the exception principle, the supervisor takes action when meaningful variance occurs. Typically, this involves looking for ways to cut costs when the department goes over budget. The supervisor in the example will want to focus on avoiding further equipment breakdowns. Sometimes the supervisor can change the budget when a variance indicates that the budgeted figures were unrealistic.

Performance Reports

performance report
A summary of performance and comparison with performance standards

A well-structured report can be an important source of information. A **performance report** summarizes performance and compares it with performance standards. These reports can simply summarize facts, such as the number of calls made by sales representatives or the number of deliveries completed by delivery personnel, or they can be analytical; that is, they may interpret the facts.

Most supervisors both prepare and request performance reports. Typically, the organization requires that the supervisor do a particular type of reporting of the department's performance. The supervisor's role is to prepare this report. Supervisors also may request that employees prepare reports for them. In that case, the supervisor can influence the type of reporting.

Consider the reporting needs for a customer service call center. The center's supervisor needs to provide management with regular reports that show the volume of work and the speed and effectiveness with which employees handle the calls. In most organizations, management will want to know the size of the workload, the costs and revenues (if employees take orders), and customer satisfaction, among other measures. The supervisor would identify the specific measurements available, given the company's measurement technology, and decide how to include them in the report. For example, the report might plot weekly or monthly call volume on a line graph, and it might compare actual and forecasted volume. Comparing actual performance with goals and forecasts is important for identifying problem areas. Whenever actual performance varies significantly from standards, the report should provide an explanation. If the service level fell and the average time to answer a call rose during a month, the explanation might be a power outage that led to higher call volumes. Such explanations help with planning and problem solving. Useful reports clarify rather than conceal problems. Hiding

FIGURE 6.9 Graph of Variances Determined from Table 6.3

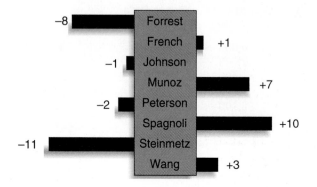

Calls Completed—Variances from a Standard of 40

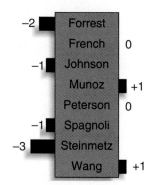

Sales Made—Variances from a Standard of 8

performance problems can make it difficult for supervisors to convince managers that the group needs more resources or training.[12]

As much as possible, supervisors should see that reports are simple and to the point. A table or log may be more useful than an essay-style report. Graphs can sometimes uncover a trend better than numbers in columns. Figure 6.9 shows how the data from Table 6.3 can be converted into a graph. In this case, variances were first computed for the difference between each employee's performance and the performance standards. Notice how easy it is to tell from the graph the wide variation in the number of calls made by each employee. Does this mean some employees are working harder than others? Maybe, but remember the process of searching for a problem. It is also possible that some employees are better at keeping calls short and to the point.

Perhaps even more important is the supervisor's role in creating a climate that fosters full and accurate reporting. Supervisors can shape a favorable climate by actively seeking ideas from employees and being willing to listen to reports that something may be wrong.

The supervisor also should determine whether every report he or she is receiving is still useful. Many reports continue to be generated long after they have lost their usefulness. In deciding whether to continue using a report, the supervisor can consider whether it has the characteristics of effective controls, described at the end of this chapter.

Personal Observation

A supervisor who spends the entire day behind a desk reading budgets and reports is out of touch. An important part of controlling involves spending time with employees and observing what is going on. Management consultant Tom Peters has popularized this approach, which he calls "management by walking around." While engaged in this approach, the supervisor can listen to employees, help them discover better ways of doing their jobs, and make the changes necessary to help employees carry them out. For example, a nursing supervisor might observe that the nurses frequently spend time debating which demands to respond to first. The supervisor could discuss this with the nurses and help them develop criteria for setting priorities.

Personal observation can help the supervisor understand the activities behind the numbers in reports. However, the supervisor must be careful in interpreting what he or she sees. Often the presence of a supervisor causes workers to alter their behavior. Also, the supervisor must visit work areas often enough to be sure of witnessing routine situations, not just an unusual crisis or break in the action. At the same time, the supervisor must not spend so much time among employees that they feel the visits interfere with their work. How much time is the right amount to spend in management by walking around? The supervisor probably will have to rely on trial and error, weighing employee reactions and the amount of information obtained.

The inability to control through personal observation is a challenge of supervising employees who work at home. This issue is growing in importance as communications technology makes telecommuting possible for people with disabilities, working parents, and others who simply prefer not to dress up. How can a supervisor make sure employees are not devoting their time to raiding the refrigerator and catching up on the latest soap operas?

Evidence suggests that employees who choose to work at home tend to be self-motivated. If anything, they have trouble taking a break. One telecommuter reportedly became so wrapped up in his computer programming that he gave himself headaches by working for hours without interruption. He eventually had to set a clock radio to go off every two hours, reminding him to take a break. Dramatic examples aside, supervisors and employees alike can benefit from training in handling the long-distance relationship. For instance, supervisors can learn ways to keep in touch with these employees. Without the extra effort to communicate, telecommuters tend to get left out of the loop. Keith Binder, who supervises two telecommuters, makes weekly phone calls to each of these employees so they can hear and comment on workplace decisions.[13]

CHARACTERISTICS OF EFFECTIVE CONTROLS

No supervisor can keep track of every detail of every employee's work. An effective control system is one that helps the supervisor direct his or her efforts toward spotting significant problems. Normally, a supervisor has to use whatever control system higher-level managers have established. However, when making recommendations about controls or setting up controls to use within the department, the supervisor can strive for the following characteristics of effective controls.

Timeliness

The controls should be *timely,* enabling the supervisor to correct problems in time to improve results. For example, an annual budget report does not let the supervisor adjust spending in time to meet the budget's goals. In contrast, monthly budget reports give the supervisor time to identify spending patterns that will pose a problem. If the supervisor's annual budget includes $500 to spend on overnight couriers but the department has already spent $200 by the end of February, the supervisor knows that work must be planned far enough ahead that materials can be sent by other, less expensive means.

Cost Effectiveness

The controls should be *economical.* In general, this means that the cost of using the controls should be less than the benefit derived from using them. In a supermarket, for example, an elaborate system designed to ensure that not a single item of inventory gets lost or stolen may not save the store enough money to justify the cost of the system.

Acceptability

The controls should be *acceptable to supervisors and employees.* Supervisors want controls that give them enough information about performance that they can understand what is going on in the workplace. Employees want controls that do not unduly infringe on their privacy. One area of controversy has been electronic monitoring of employee performance. For example, computers can track how many telephone calls operators handle and how much time they spend on each call. Electronic monitoring gives the supervisor a lot of information, including how much time operators spend going to the bathroom. Does this scrutiny enhance performance by encouraging employees to work hard, or does it merely lower morale and remove the incentive to take time to greet customers in a friendly way? The answer lies partly in the way supervisors use this information.

Employees also appreciate controls that focus on areas over which they themselves have some control. For example, a control that measures the number of units produced by an employee would be acceptable only if the employee always has the parts needed to produce those units. An employee whose performance looks poor because of an inventory shortage would feel frustrated by the control.

Flexibility

Finally, the controls should be *flexible.* This means the supervisor should be able to ignore variance if doing so is in the best interests of the organization. For example, in comparing expenditures to a budget, a supervisor should be aware of occasions when spending a little more than was budgeted actually will benefit the company. That might be the case when employees have to put in overtime to fill an order for an important customer. In the future, better planning might make it possible to avoid the overtime, but the immediate goal is to satisfy the customer.

One reason flexibility is important is that performance measures might be incompatible. For instance, employees may find it impossible to cut costs and improve quality at the same time. In that case, the supervisor may have to set priorities or adjust the control measures. Such actions are a type of planning, an example of how controlling and planning work together to help the organization reach its goals.

SKILLS MODULE

PART ONE: CONCEPTS

Summary

6.1 Describe types of planning that take place in organizations.
At the top level of an organization, managers engage in strategic planning, which is the creation of long-term goals for the organization. The plans for divisions, departments, and work groups are known as operational plans and are set by middle managers and supervisors. Operational plans support the strategic plan; they are more specific and focus on a shorter time frame. Supervisors also must apply good planning practices to their individual efforts.

6.2 Identify characteristics of effective objectives.
Effective objectives are written, measurable or observable, clear, specific, and challenging but achievable.

6.3 Define *management by objectives (MBO)* and discuss its use.

Management by objectives is a process in which managers and employees at all levels set objectives for what they are to accomplish, after which their performance is measured against those objectives. In MBO, all individuals in the organization work to set objectives, each employee's manager periodically reviews the employee's performance against the objectives, and the organization rewards individuals on the basis of how close they come to fulfilling the objectives. To use MBO effectively, managers at all levels of an organization must be committed to the system.

6.4 Discuss the supervisor's role in the planning process.

Supervisors are responsible for the creation of plans that specify goals, tasks, resources, and responsibilities for their own departments. Supervisors keep higher-level managers informed about the needs, abilities, and progress of their groups. They decide how to allocate resources to the jobs that need to be done, including creating budgets. Supervisors also engage in scheduling. When possible, they should involve employees in the planning process.

6.5 Explain the purpose of using controls.

By identifying problems in time for them to be corrected, controlling enables supervisors to ensure high-quality work and keep costs under control.

6.6 Identify the steps in the control process.

First, the supervisor sets and communicates performance standards in writing. The supervisor then monitors performance and compares it with the standards. Depending on whether performance is above, at, or below the standards, the supervisor reinforces successes or fixes problems. Fixing a problem may entail adjusting a process, the behavior of an employee, or the standard itself.

6.7 Describe types of control and tools for controlling.

Feedback control focuses on past performance. Concurrent control occurs while the work is taking place. Precontrol is aimed at preventing behavior that may lead to undesirable results. Budgets, performance reports, and personal observation are all tools for controlling.

6.8 List characteristics of effective controls.

Effective controls are timely, economical, acceptable to both supervisor and employee, and flexible.

Key Terms

planning, *p.* 140
objectives, *p.* 141
goals, *p.* 141
strategic planning, *p.* 141
operational
planning, *p.* 142
policies, *p.* 144
procedures, *p.* 144
rules, *p.* 145
action plan, *p.* 145
contingency
planning, *p.* 146

management
by objectives
(MBO), *p.* 146
budget, *p.* 149
scheduling, *p.* 150
Gantt chart, *p.* 150
program evaluation
and review technique
(PERT), *p.* 151
controlling, *p.* 154
standards, *p.* 154
variance, *p.* 157

exception
principle, *p.* 158
reinforcement, *p.* 158
problem, *p.* 158
symptom, *p.* 158
feedback control, *p.* 160
concurrent control, *p.* 160
precontrol, *p.* 160
performance
report, *p.* 161

Review and Discussion Questions

1. Why is it important for supervisors and other managers to plan?

2. Define policies, procedures, and goals. How does each relate to an organization's objectives?

3. Jill Donahue is the supervisor of the telephone operators who handle emergency calls from citizens and dispatch police, firefighters, and ambulances. One of her objectives for the coming year is to reduce the average time it takes for calls to be answered from 1 minute to 30 seconds. How can Jill create an action plan to achieve this objective? What questions must she answer? Suggest a possible answer for each question.

4. Assume you are the supervisor of the machine shop whose budget appears in Table 6.2.

   a. Modify the budgeted amounts to create a budget for a new project of the same size and type. Use the following assumptions and guidelines:
   - The organization says that direct labor costs may increase by no more than 6 percent.
   - You have been instructed to cut expenses for equipment repair by 10 percent.
   - You expect that materials costs will increase about 5 percent.

   b. What additional assumptions did you make to create the budget?

5. What is wrong with each of the following objectives? Rewrite each so that it has the characteristics of an effective objective.

   a. Improve the procedure for responding to customer complaints.

   b. Meet or exceed last year's sales quotas.

   c. Minimize the number of parts that are defective.

   d. Communicate clearly with patients.

6. What are some advantages of involving employees in the process of developing objectives? How can supervisors do this?

7. Your best friend just got promoted to a position as a supervisor and feels uncomfortable about "checking up on people." How can you explain to your friend why controlling plays an important role in helping the organization meet its goals?

8. What are the steps in the process of controlling?

9. How is the control process related to the management function of planning?

10. Bonnie Goode supervises telephone operators in the customer service department of a software company. The operators are expected to handle 50 phone calls per day (250 in a five-day workweek). Every Monday, Goode receives a report of each operator's weekly performance relative to this standard. Her most recent report contained the following information

Operator	Mon.	Tues.	Wed.	Thurs.	Fri.	Total	Variance
Brown	10	28	39	42	16	135	−115
Lee	48	51	58	43	49	249	−1
Mendoza	65	72	56	83	61	337	87
Smith	53	48	47	40	45	233	−17

   a As supervisor, how should Goode respond to each operator's performance?

   b. Is this control system an effective one for ensuring quality performance? Explain.

11. If failure to meet a performance standard indicates some type of underlying problem, how might the supervisor attempt to solve the problem?

12. Mildred Pirelli supervises salespeople in a department store. One day she walked around her department to observe the salespeople in action. She saw a salesperson approve a charge card purchase without following the company's policy of verifying the signature on the card.

    a. How should Pirelli respond to this variance from company policy?

    b. Should the way Pirelli obtained the information (personal observation) influence her choice of how to act? Explain.

13. Why do controls need to be timely and economical?

PART TWO: SKILL-BUILDING

YOU SOLVE THE PROBLEM

Reflecting back on page 139, discuss how Apache Stoneworks' emphasis on thorough planning and strict quality standards might affect Romarico Nieto's job as supervisor.

Assign one person in your group the role of Nieto and one person the role of a customer. Imagine that the crew is arriving for a second day of work, and the customer wonders why no tiles have yet been laid. The customer wants to talk to the supervisor to find out why the work is "taking so long." Nieto wants his crew to do excellent work and satisfy this customer. Role-play how Nieto should handle the situation. Perhaps additional members of your group will need to play the roles of crew members as Nieto handles this situation.

After the role-play, discuss whether the customer was satisfied, and suggest other ways for the supervisor to meet this challenge. Try the role-play again with different group members.

Problem-Solving Case: *MBO Clarifies Objectives at Edward Don & Company*

At Edward Don & Company, a distributor of supplies and equipment for the food service industry, employees in the credit department know what they are supposed to achieve. The reason is that the company's corporate credit manager, Jeff Ingalls, set up a management by objectives (MBO) program.

Ingalls meets with each staff member once a year to evaluate how well he or she met the previous year's objectives and set objectives for the coming year. He and the employee set five to seven objectives for the year. They may change the next year's goals based on past performance or new technology that will affect performance. Every three to six months, Ingalls meets again with employees to discuss whether they are making progress toward their goals. Even when employees can meet their objectives without Ingalls's help, meeting with them reminds the department that the objectives are important.

Objectives for credit department employees include quality, efficiency, and professional development. For example, the objectives for a credit analyst might involve keeping bad debt low relative to total loans made, approving at least a minimum number of new accounts, and learning computer skills. For collectors, objectives might include achieving a given increase in the percentage of accounts that are current (payments up-to-date), reducing the percentage for which payments are 90 days past due, and learning a new skill.

When an employee is failing to meet an objective, Ingalls and the employee discuss the problem and look for a way to resolve it. For example, an accounts receivable supervisor was having trouble with a goal that involved the accuracy with which the supervisor's employees recorded information. In an average month, the supervisor's employees made 40 to 50 errors for a transaction known as cash applications. The supervisor's objective called for a much lower error rate.

Ingalls and the supervisor set up a form on which the supervisor would record every cash application error. The supervisor recorded errors and identified the cause of each error. Most errors involved the employee receiving incorrect information or the employee receiving correct information but recording it incorrectly. To fix these basic problems, the supervisor met with each employee who made an error, discussed the source of the problem, and asked the employee to be more careful. This process demonstrated to the employees that their errors mattered. They responded by recording entries more carefully. Before long, cash application errors dropped to the range of 7 to 10 a month. As the department spent less time correcting errors, productivity improved, helping Ingalls meet his own objectives.

Ingalls says he prefers working for organizations that use MBO. He says MBO makes managing employees easier. Employees know what they are supposed to achieve, so Ingalls can let them focus on how to reach those objectives while he focuses on broader issues facing the credit department.

1. Without MBO, would it have been harder for Ingalls to detect and correct the problem the supervisor was having with cash application errors? Why or why not?

2. The examples of objectives for credit analysts and collectors include objectives for personal development through training. Why do you think Ingalls includes this category of goals? How, if at all, might they help Ingalls achieve his objectives for the credit department or contribute to the company's overall performance?

3. Write a personal development objective for yourself. Make sure it meets the criteria for effective objectives shown in Figure 6.1. Show your objective to a friend or classmate, and discuss with that person how you plan to achieve your objective.

Source: "MBO Improves Credit Department Performance," *Credit & Collection Manager's Letter,* April 1, 2003, downloaded from Business & Company Resource Center, http://galenet.galegroup.com.

Knowing Yourself

Are You a Planner?
Answer each of the following questions with a Yes or No.

1. Do you decide the night before what to wear each day? _____
2. Do you buy birthday gifts at the last minute? _____
3. Do you divide up household chores with your roommates or family members? _____
4. When you receive a paycheck, do you designate certain portions of it for specific expenses? _____
5. At the beginning of the workday or school day, do you make a list of what you must accomplish? _____
6. Do you buy a big-ticket item because a friend has the same item and raves about it? _____
7. Do you start studying for final exams before the last week of classes? _____
8. When you purchase a new piece of electronic equipment, such as a computer or DVD player, do you read the instructions about how to use it? _____
9. Before taking a trip, do you study a map? _____

10. When you have several projects to handle at once, do you first tackle the one that appeals to you most? _____

Scoring: Answering Yes to questions 1, 3, 4, 5, 7, 8, and 9 and No to questions 2, 6, and 10 indicates that you are a planner.

Pause and Reflect

1. Before you took this quiz, did you think of yourself as a careful planner? Did this quiz change your opinion?
2. Is planning more important for a supervisor than for an employee who is not in management? Why or why not?
3. Think of one or two planning tools you would like to try. When will you try them? How will you decide whether they are helping you?

Class Exercise

Setting Goals

This exercise provides you with an opportunity to practice what you learned in this chapter. You will practice setting personal goals (objectives) that are written, measurable, specific, clear, and challenging.

Instructions

1. In the space provided on the next page, write four goals that are important for you to achieve during the remainder of this semester.
2. Some of the goals should be short term (maybe something you need to finish by the end of this week); others should have a longer time frame (maybe by the end of the semester).
3. Write your goal statement so you can check all four boxes (measurable, specific, clear, and challenging) as being represented. Provided here is a brief summary of each term:
   - *Measurable*—Provide a tangible way (dollar amount, time frame, or quantity) to determine whether you have reached your goal; avoid *maximize, improve,* and other terms that cannot be measured.
   - *Specific*—Describe the actions you will need to take to achieve your goal.
   - *Clear*—Use simple language.
   - *Challenging* (yet realistic and obtainable)—Choose motivating and stimulating goals that when achieved will give you a sense of pride and build your confidence.
4. Your four goals should represent several different areas; for example, academic, job, career, spiritual, family, financial, social, or physical goals. An example of a financial goal that meets all four criteria is "I will save 20 percent of every paycheck starting this Friday so I'll have enough to pay for my auto insurance when it comes due the last week of the semester." If you are having trouble meeting any of the four criteria in your personal goals, discuss your goal with a classmate or your professor to see if one of them can help you define that goal more clearly.
5. After successfully achieving each goal, write the date in the "Follow-up" column next to the goal.

Source: This class exercise was written by Corinne Livesay, Belhaven College, Jackson, Mississippi.

Goal:	Follow-up
	(When you've achieved this goal, write the date here.)
✓ if statement is: Measurable ☐ Specific ☐ Clear ☐ Challenging ☐	

Goal:	Follow-up
	(When you've achieved this goal, write the date here.)
✓ if statement is: Measurable ☐ Specific ☐ Clear ☐ Challenging ☐	

Goal:	Follow-up
	(When you've achieved this goal, write the date here.)
✓ if statement is: Measurable ☐ Specific ☐ Clear ☐ Challenging ☐	

Goal:	Follow-up
	(When you've achieved this goal, write the date here.)
✓ if statement is: Measurable ☐ Specific ☐ Clear ☐ Challenging ☐	

Building Supervision Skills

Controlling a Yacht-Making Operation

Divide the class into groups of five or six members. One member of each group will act as the supervisor; the rest are employees. Because few real-life work groups get to choose their supervisor, the instructor might arbitrarily designate the supervisor in each group. The instructor provides each group with square sheets of paper; $5 \frac{7}{8} \times 5 \frac{7}{8}$ inches is a good size.

1. Each person reviews instructions for making origami yachts (see Figure 6.10).
2. The supervisor in each group sets performance standards for making the yachts in 10 minutes. These should include quality as well as quantity standards. In setting the standards, the supervisor may use whatever information he or she can obtain; it is up to the supervisor whether to seek input from the group.

   At the same time, each employee estimates how many yachts he or she can make correctly in 10 minutes. The employee writes down this estimate but does not reveal it to the supervisor at this time.

FIGURE 6.10   Instructions for Origami Yachts

Source: Corinne Livesay of Belhaven College, Jackson, Mississippi, supplied the origami instructions.

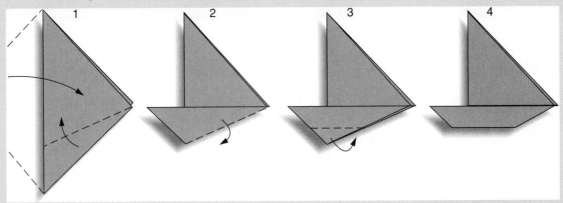

3. For 10 minutes, the employees make as many yachts as they can according to the instructions. During that time, the supervisor tries to monitor their performance in whatever way seems helpful. If employees seem to be falling short of the performance standard, the supervisor should try to find ways to improve performance. (This may include simply waiting patiently for skills to improve, if that seems most beneficial.)

4. After the 10 minutes have ended, determine how many yachts each group made and assess the quality of the work. As a class, discuss the groups' performance. Did each group meet its supervisor's performance standards? If not, was any variance significant? Based on their own estimates of how much they could do, do employees think their supervisor's standards were reasonable?

5. The class should also consider supervisors' efforts to take corrective action. Did supervisors intervene too much, or not enough? How did supervisors' attempts help or hurt employees' efforts? What does this experience reveal about the way supervisors should behave in the workplace?

Chapter **Seven**

Organizing and Authority

Learning Objectives

After you have studied this chapter, you should be able to

7.1 Describe organization charts.

7.2 Identify basic ways in which organizations are structured.

7.3 Distinguish between line and staff authority and between centralized and decentralized authority.

7.4 Compare and contrast *authority, power, responsibility,* and *accountability.*

7.5 Identify the steps in the process of organizing.

7.6 Describe four principles of organizing.

7.7 Discuss why and how supervisors delegate.

7.8 Identify causes of reluctance to delegate.

You have to make sure you have created an organization that is able to operate with or without you.

—*Carley Roney, Co-founder and Editor-in-Chief,* The Knot *(wedding planning publication and Web site)*

Raytheon is a huge defense contractor, earning more than $18 billion a year. Every year the company spends hundreds of millions of dollars to develop new products. Its tens of thousands of employees work in seven lines of business, including missile systems, intelligence systems, aircraft, and space systems.

In a corporation of that size, people with truly innovative ideas can have difficulty finding an audience. Yet Raytheon depends on the ideas of its talented scientists and engineers. So the company set up a structure in which people can try out ideas away from the structure of a corporate giant.

The independent group works in what Raytheon calls the Bike Shop, referring to the bicycle shop where the Wright brothers developed their airplane. Only 15 scientists and engineers work at the Bike Shop, located in Tucson, Arizona. The atmosphere is intentionally designed to foster creativity. The usual work attire is blue jeans, and the facility is in the back of a commercial development, not in a sleek high-tech corridor. Models are built with whatever parts the employees can pick up at the local Home Depot. The team's leader, physicist James Small, explains, "We have more fun than is generally allowed on company time."

Small staffed the Bike Shop team by recruiting the most creative and bored experts he could find within Raytheon. He lures them with top-of-the-line equipment and authorization to charge up to $250,000 on corporate credit cards. The credit-card privilege frees the team members to buy items as needed, without moving through the company's formal purchasing process.

A recent project at the Bike Shop is called the Whirl, a prototype for an unmanned aircraft that can hover in one spot for several days. The project began when Small was talking to a military official about ideas for aircraft with such capabilities. Small promised to return in a week with an idea. He brought together three members of the Bike Shop team to brainstorm ideas. Then a physicist ran analyses of aerodynamics while another team member searched his garage for model airplane components and a third got the machine shop ready to build the first prototype of the concept, which looks something like a ceiling fan. A week later, Small was reporting back to the military with the idea and received approval to continue testing and development.

Small says the Whirl is not as advanced as other projects at the Bike Shop. However, most of the projects are secret.

Maintaining a creative spark in a large organization can be difficult. Raytheon's idea was to set up the Bike Shop as a smaller group in which staff members can experiment and produce new products, rather than work on pieces of a larger, scheduled project.

QUESTIONS

1. Think about the roles of each Bike Shop team member. What skills did James Small need as a supervisor when he organized the team? How did he ensure creativity in team processes?

2. What skills can Small use to be sure that each employee accomplishes crucial tasks for the overall project and that each can justify his or her work to Small and Raytheon?

Sources: Jonathan Karp, "At the 'Bike Shop,' Secretive Defense Work Starts at Home Depot," *The Wall Street Journal*, September 8, 2004, http://online.wsj.com; Raytheon Company, "Backgrounder," May 2004, "About Us" page, www.raytheon.com.

organizing

Setting up the group, allocating resources, and assigning work to achieve goals

In the opening story, the physical organization of a firm has evolved to meet the company's needs. As you read in Chapter 1, **organizing** is the management function of setting up the group, allocating resources, and assigning work to achieve goals. By organizing, supervisors and other managers put their plans into action. When done well, organizing helps ensure that the organization uses its resources—especially human resources—efficiently. For this reason, a business that is well organized is in a better position to be profitable.

Managers in even the simplest organizations need to organize. If you were to set up a softball team, you would have to collect equipment, arrange for a place to play, find players, decide what position each is to play, and create a batting lineup. If you were operating a one-person business, you would have to decide where you would work, what activities you would need to accomplish, and whether you should contract with vendors to provide some services.

This chapter describes the ways organizations are structured and how supervisors organize. The process of organizing includes sharing authority and responsibility. The chapter explains how supervisors share both of these functions with the people who report to them.

THE STRUCTURE OF THE ORGANIZATION

Some of the most fundamental and far-reaching organizational decisions involve the structure of the organization as a whole. For example, top management could assign a manager authority for a particular product, a particular geographic region served by the organization, or a particular specialty such as sales or finance. Supervisors have little, if any, input into this type of decision. However, supervisors need to understand how they and their departments fit into the big picture, and that includes understanding the structure of the organization.

Organization Charts

Businesspeople have come up with a standard way to draw the structure of an organization: the organization chart. These charts use boxes to represent the various positions or departments in an organization (usually just at management levels). Lines connecting the boxes indicate who reports to whom. Figure 7.1 is an organization chart showing the structure of an international company. Note, for example, that someone is in charge of all North American operations, and someone is in charge of all international operations. These two managers report to the person who serves as president and chief operating officer of the entire company.

FIGURE 7.1   Organization Chart: An International Company

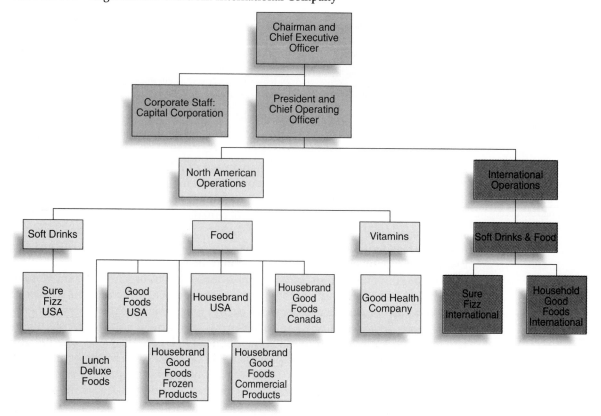

The positions at the top of an organization chart are those with the most authority and responsibility. Logically, the people in these positions are referred to as the top managers. By following the lines from the top managers down the chart to the lower levels, you can see which middle managers report to these top managers. In other words, the top managers are authorized to direct the work of the middle managers who report to them and are responsible for the performance of those middle managers. The bottom of the chart may show the first-level managers (or sometimes operative employees). Supervisors are not shown on the chart in Figure 7.1.

Organization charts sometimes show only a portion of an organization. Like Figure 7.1, a chart may show only the top levels of management, or it may show a single division in a large company. Reading the titles of the people associated with each box gives an indication of the scope of a particular organization chart.

Being able to understand organization charts enables supervisors to figure out where they fit in the organization and where opportunities for future promotions might lie. Supervisors can see the variety of responsibilities held by others at their level in the organization. Knowing where they fit in helps supervisors determine how their department or group contributes to achieving the goals of the organization.

Types of Structures

department
A unique group of resources that management has assigned to carry out a particular task

departmentalization
Setting up departments in an organization

An organization with more than a handful of people works most efficiently when it is grouped into departments. A **department** refers to a unique group of resources that management has assigned to carry out a particular task, such as selling the company's products to customers in the Midwest, treating patients with cancer, or teaching mathematics. The way management sets up the departments—an activity called **departmentalization**—determines the type of structure the organization has.

Over the years, organizations have been structured in a limited number of ways. Traditionally, organization charts have indicated structures that fall into four categories: functional structure, product structure, geographic structure, and customer structure. More recently, organizations have sought other structures that achieve greater flexibility and responsiveness to customer needs.

In deciding which types of structure to use and how to combine them, managers look for the organizational arrangement that will best achieve the company's goals. As top managers learn from their experiences or as the company and its environment change, the structure may require minor adjustments or major overhauls. Thus, the "restructuring" that has occurred at many organizations in recent years consists of changes in the structure designed to respond to stiffer competition, tougher economic conditions, or the desire to benefit from new practices such as decision making by teams of employees.

Functional Structure

A functional structure groups personnel and other resources according to the types of work they carry out. For example, a business might have vice presidents of finance, production, sales, and human resources. Assigned to each vice president is the staff needed to carry out these activities. Figure 7.2 provides an example of a company with a functional structure. Wiss, Janney, Elstner Associates is an architectural firm in which one vice president is responsible for operations (that is, the work of all the architects and engineers who provide services to customers), and another is responsible for administration (that is, support services). Under the

FIGURE 7.2 Functional Structure
Partial organization chart for Wiss, Janney, Elstner Associates

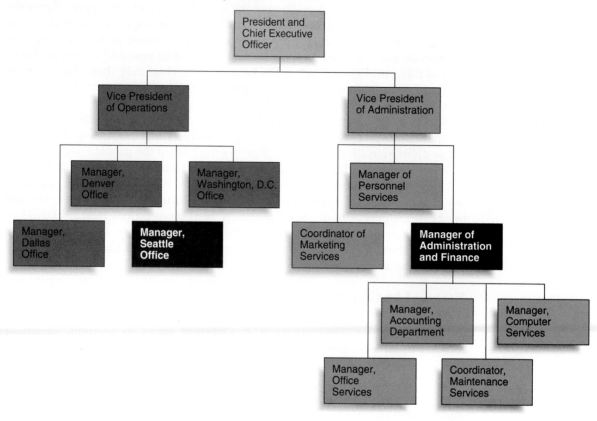

vice president of administration, the organization is divided into such functions as marketing and personnel.

Product Structure

In an organization with a product structure, work and resources are assigned to departments responsible for all the activities related to producing and delivering a particular product (good or service). In an automobile business, there might be one department for each make of automobile. Colleges and universities are often departmentalized according to the subject matter taught. At the company shown in Figure 7.1, North American operations are departmentalized according to three product categories: soft drinks, food, and vitamins. Figure 7.3 illustrates a product structure in the consumer and commercial banking division of a bank. Although a large bank's offerings are more widespread than would fit on the page, this partial organization chart shows that the division is structured according to the type of product, such as loans to consumers, commercial loans, various bank accounts, and so on.

Geographic Structure

A geographic structure results when an organization is departmentalized according to the location of the customers served or the goods or services produced. A manufacturing company might have a department for each of its factories scattered around the world. An insurance company might have a department for

FIGURE 7.3   **Product Structure**
Partial organization chart for a bank division

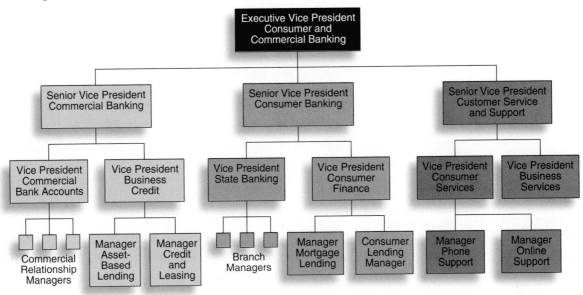

each of its 12 sales territories. The manager of each department would be responsible for producing and/or selling all the company's goods or services in that geographic region. At the architectural firm in Figure 7.2, operations are departmentalized on the basis of the cities where the offices are located: Dallas, Denver, Seattle, Washington, DC, and other cities not shown.

Customer Structure

A customer structure departmentalizes the organization according to the type of customer served. For example, an aerospace company might have different departments serving businesses, the military, and the space program. Rackspace, a Web-hosting company based in San Antonio, Texas, has a customer structure aimed at achieving its goal of giving customers "fanatical support." Various businesses, such as retailers and game sites, use Rackspace to handle the nuts and bolts of operating on the Internet. The company's customer service employees are grouped into teams, which include a leader, two or three account managers, and specialists in billing and technical support. Each team serves a set of customers of a particular size and complexity. When a customer calls with a problem requiring a specialist, that employee is seated near the one taking the phone call.[1]

Combinations

As you can see from the figures, organizations often combine the basic types of structures. Thus, Figure 7.1 combines geographic and product structures, whereas Figure 7.2 combines functional and geographic structures. A typical arrangement would be a large corporation with divisions for each of its product lines. Within each division, managers are assigned responsibility for carrying out a particular function, including sales and operations (that is, making goods or delivering services). Each sales department in turn is structured geographically.

Various combinations of structures occur when the organization forms teams of employees to meet objectives such as improving quality, developing products, or applying new technology. These teams may require diverse kinds of expertise, so the organization brings together people who perform different functions or work in different geographic areas. Often these teams of employees are grouped according to product or customer. For example, a team formed to develop a new type of speaker for a sound system might combine employees from the sales, engineering, and production functions under the umbrella of that new product. For a more in-depth discussion of forming and leading teams, see Chapter 3.

New Organizational Structures

organic structure
Organizational structure in which the boundaries between jobs continually shift and people pitch in wherever their contributions are needed

The managers of many organizations consider the basic forms of departmentalization too rigid for a turbulent, highly competitive environment. Grouping people according to function or geographic area can create barriers that interfere with coordinating activities and sharing ideas. A rigid structure is rarely suitable for a very small organization. Such organizations typically have a highly **organic structure,** one in which the boundaries between jobs continually shift and people pitch in wherever their contributions are needed.

Larger organizations, too, are seeking the flexibility of organic structures. They may do so by organizing around teams and *processes* (series of activities that deliver value to customers) or *projects* (groups of tasks with defined scope and ending points). Large-volume clinical laboratories sometimes use a process organization. Technicians specialize in performing certain categories of tests, especially those requiring extra training (e.g., genetic testing). But the specialized work can become boring, and it limits employees' chances to develop new skills and fill in for one another. Therefore, many other clinical labs rotate employees among workstations or assign employees to core groups that work wherever they are needed most.[2]

Research into the experiences of managers at seven large corporations found that a top challenge of this approach is that employees may become confused about the details of their roles and responsibilities.[3] As a result, managers at all levels, including supervisors, must take the time to be sure that all employees involved in a project or process have clear directions and a job description for their work on the particular project or process. If a supervisor is leading the team, the supervisor must be sure that all necessary roles have been assigned. Along with the usual roles, such as designing a product or setting up a production line, some teams may have unique goals requiring specially created roles.

network organizations
Organizations that maintain flexibility by staying small and contracting with other individuals and organizations as needed to complete projects

A growing number of organizations are trying to stay flexible by staying small. Rather than adding employees to meet customer demands, these organizations, called **network organizations,** contract with other individuals and organizations as needed to complete specific projects.[4] In practice, this structure may involve *outsourcing,* or paying another organization to carry out a function. Insurance companies typically outsource the defense of lawsuits, after-hours call centers for loss reporting, and management of their investments.[5] More recently, the news has featured a form of outsourcing called *offshoring,* in which companies move departments from headquarters to cheaper overseas locations. Popular offshoring locations include India, China, and Eastern Europe, which have large numbers of engineers and scientists. Delphi Corporation, for example, has more than 20 manufacturing sites in Poland, the Czech Republic, and other Eastern European countries. These facilities are conveniently located near the European factories of the automobile companies that buy parts from Delphi.[6] Other organizations arrange *alliances,* or relationships based on partnership, including joint ventures, minority investments linked to contractual agreements, agreements to jointly fund research,

SUPERVISION ACROSS INDUSTRIES

MANUFACTURING

BUILDING JEEPS IN A VIRTUAL ORGANIZATION

To reduce manufacturing costs (and save U.S. jobs), DaimlerChrysler and the United Auto Workers recently agreed on an innovative plan for building Jeep Wranglers in Ohio. Under the plan, DaimlerChrysler is outsourcing more than half of the production activity to its suppliers. These companies invest in the plants and machinery, and they pay workers to produce the Wrangler components. The hope is that each company will be able to design and operate in its specialty more efficiently than the Chrysler plant did when it was handling more of the manufacturing itself.

Together, DaimlerChrysler and its suppliers are investing $900 million to replace an aging factory in Toledo, Ohio. Three suppliers are bearing about one-third of the cost and will operate on the same site. Kuka Group, a German corporation, will assemble vehicle bodies. Durr Industries, also based in Germany, will build and operate the facility's paint shop. Hyundai Mobis, a South Korean company, will build chassis. Chrysler will handle the final trim and assembly, including attachment of the body to the chassis. The companies will operate in separate buildings linked by conveyor belts.

The total number of employees will remain about the same (4,000) as when Chrysler handled all these activities. One-fourth of the jobs will shift to the suppliers. The pay for workers at Kuka and Durr will remain the same, and the chassis workers will receive lower pay. Chrysler also will outsource jobs in materials handling and janitorial work. The union accepted the plan because it expected that the old factory would have simply been closed otherwise.

DaimlerChrysler predicts that savings from this arrangement will enable the company to invest in the development and production of new models. If the expected savings materialize, the company is likely to seek virtual organizations for some of its other 13 North American assembly plants.

Sources: Joann Muller, "Saving Chrysler," *Forbes,* August 16, 2004, downloaded from Business & Company Resource Center, http://galenet.galegroup.com; "DaimlerChrysler, Suppliers Team Up," *Detroit News,* August 4, 2004, www.detnews.com.

and other, less formal arrangements. At the extreme is a *virtual organization,* in which a small core organization (maybe a single person) arranges alliances as needed to carry out particular projects. Hardinge Inc. used a virtual organization when it purchased Bridgeport Machines and moved Bridgeport's manufacturing line from Connecticut to Elmira, New York. Hardinge brought together key employees from Bridgeport Machine and Hardinge as well as experts from other companies. People from the JCIT Training Institute helped lay out the manufacturing flow. Participating suppliers included Zeller Electric and Skico (which makes component parts). This virtual team achieved the goal of moving the entire manufacturing process intact and setting it up in a way that improved quality and efficiency.[7] The "Supervision across Industries" box describes another example of a virtual organization.

A growing number of firms are creating "intrapreneurships," in which a small team or group within the company is given the resources to develop new ideas and new ventures without leaving the parent organization. One such intrapreneurship is described in the opening case on page 173. At Elite Information Systems in Los Angeles, Mark Goldin, who had been the company's chief technical officer, launched an Internet venture called Elite.com with funding, office space, and resources from within Elite. One of the best things about the decision, according to CEO Chris Poole, was that Goldin can work without the "that's how we've always done it" constraints.[8]

Like the organizations themselves, supervisors in these new structures must be flexible. They have to contribute wherever the organization currently needs their talents—a requirement that calls for continually knowing, updating, and communicating one's skills. They may have to identify how they can contribute to a particular project and then be ready to move to a new assignment when they no longer add value to the current one. In addition, supervisors in the new structures must rely more on human relations skills than on technical skills. Coaching a team or project group requires the ability to motivate, lead, and communicate as the team handles many project- or process-related decisions. This ability is especially needed for coaching teams that bring together people from a variety of functions.

AUTHORITY

authority
The right to perform a task or give orders to someone else

When a supervisor assigns duties, he or she gives employees the authority to carry them out. **Authority** is the right to perform a task or give orders to someone else (see Table 7.1). The supervisor in turn has authority in certain areas, and his or her manager has even broader authority.

Line, Staff, and Functional Authority

line authority
The right to carry out tasks and give orders related to the organization's primary purpose

The basic type of authority in organizations is **line authority,** or the right to carry out tasks and give orders related to the organization's primary purpose. Line authority gives a production supervisor at Deere & Company the right to direct a worker to operate a machine; it gives the head chef in a restaurant the right to direct the salad chef to prepare a spinach salad using certain ingredients. At the architectural firm represented in Figure 7.2, the manager of the Seattle office has line authority.

staff authority
The right to advise or assist those with line authority

In contrast, **staff authority** is the right to advise or assist those with line authority. For example, the employees in the human resource department help other departments by ensuring that they have qualified workers. The quality-control manager at a manufacturing company helps the production manager see that the goods produced are of acceptable quality. In Figure 7.2, the manager of administration and finance has staff authority.

An amusing story from the Shark Tank column of *Computerworld* magazine illustrates the need for staff authority. According to this story, a technical support employee went to a company's payroll department in response to a complaint that the printer had jammed while printing payroll checks. As the tech support person

TABLE 7.1
Everyday Meaning of Terms Related to Organizing

Source: Adapted from Brad Lee Thompson, *The New Manager's Handbook* (Burr Ridge, IL: Richard D. Irwin, Inc., 1995), p. 49.

Term	Everyday Meaning
Departmentalization	"Let's divide up the work."
Authority	"I (or you) get to decide how this is going to get done."
Responsibility	"I (or you) own this job; you can hold me accountable for it."
Accountability	"The buck stops here."
Unity of command	"No matter who else you work with, you are accountable to only one person."
Span of control	"There are limits to how many people a manager can effectively manage."
Delegation	"You have the responsibility and authority to accomplish this assignment."
Empowerment	"I trust you to perform these functions and accomplish these results; this means much more than just delegating a task to you."

approached the printer, the payroll clerk jumped in front of it, exclaiming that the tech person was not permitted to look at the checks. The tech employee wondered how it would be possible to fix the printer without approaching it. The payroll clerk replied, "You'll have to keep your eyes closed."[9] Obviously, this company's technical support employees need broad enough staff authority to work with their eyes open.

Conflicts often arise between line and staff personnel. Line personnel may feel that staff workers are meddling and don't understand their work or how important it is. Staff personnel may conclude that line personnel are resisting new ideas and don't appreciate the valuable assistance they are getting. Whether the supervisor has line or staff authority, he or she can benefit from being aware that these kinds of conflicts are common and trying to appreciate the other person's point of view.

functional authority
The right given by higher management to specific staff personnel to give orders concerning an area in which the staff personnel have expertise

Supervisors and other personnel with staff authority may also have **functional authority.** This is the right given by higher management to specific staff personnel to give orders concerning an area in which the staff personnel have expertise. For example, members of the accounting department might have authority to request the information they need to prepare reports. Or the human resource manager might have authority to ensure that all departments are complying with the laws pertaining to fair employment practices.

Centralized and Decentralized Authority

In some organizations, the managers at the top retain a great deal of authority; in others, management grants much authority to middle managers, supervisors, and operative employees. Organizations that share relatively little authority are said to be centralized; organizations that share a lot of authority are said to be decentralized.

These terms are relative. In other words, no organization is completely centralized or decentralized, but organizations fall along a range of possibilities from one extreme to another. An organization can even make changes in the degree to which it centralizes authority, depending on its strategic plan and goals. Even individual functions within an organization may make this type of change. Many corporations, including Agilent Technologies, AutoNation, and Cisco Systems, have made their finance operations more centralized and more decentralized at the same time. How can this be? The basic strategy is to identify which finance tasks, such as handling sales and payments, are routine. These repetitive tasks are centralized into one operation with one set of procedures, to make them as efficient as possible. Other finance tasks, such as planning what to spend to achieve long-range goals, are carried out by finance experts assigned to particular business units. These employees then can become experts in the particular businesses, helping their unit make better decisions.[10]

Supervisors who know whether their employer has a centralized or decentralized structure understand how much authority they can expect to have. Suppose a supervisor wants to expand the authority of her position so that she can make improvements in the department. This ambition probably will be viewed less favorably in a centralized organization than in a decentralized one.

Power, Responsibility, and Accountability

power
The ability to get others to act in a certain way

It is easy to confuse authority with power, accountability, or responsibility. However, when used precisely, these terms do not mean the same thing. **Power** is the ability (as opposed to the right) to get others to act in a certain way. The supervisor's authority usually confers a degree of power; employees usually do what their supervisor asks them to do. However, some people have power that comes from sources other than their positions in the organization. Also, some people with authority have trouble getting others to act in the desired way. (Chapter 14 discusses power in greater detail.)

responsibility
The obligation to perform assigned activities

Responsibility is the obligation to perform assigned activities. People who accept responsibility commit themselves to completing an assignment to the best of their ability. Of course, doing a good job is easier when you have the authority to control the necessary resources, including personnel. An important aspect of the supervisor's job therefore is to ensure that people have accepted responsibility for each of the tasks that the work group must complete—and that they clearly understand what those responsibilities are. The supervisor also must ensure that people have enough authority to carry out their responsibilities.

Employees who accept responsibility may be rewarded for doing a good job, and those who do not may be punished. This practice is called *accountability* (see Chapter 1). Assume an organization makes a supervisor responsible for communicating policies to his or her employees. Accountability means the supervisor can expect consequences related to whether that responsibility is met. Thus, accountability is a way of encouraging people to fulfill their responsibilities.

The authority to transfer (delegate) responsibility to employees and hold them accountable adds to a supervisor's power. At the same time, even when a supervisor delegates, the supervisor remains accountable for employees' performance. Carley Roney, who founded the Web site The Knot, aimed at couples planning weddings, learned this lesson when she had to balance leadership of her company with the demands of a second child in her family. Roney could no longer put the company first all the time, and she discovered that she could trust her staff members to do their work. In a far sadder situation, a supervisor at Advanced Tent Rental learned about accountability after two workers were injured while taking down the support pole of a tent. The pole hit a live power cable, and both workers were injured; one eventually died. A court held the supervisor liable for failing to ensure there were no live power lines near the tent and failing to let the workers know about the danger. The supervisor might have thought it was acceptable to delegate the responsibility to be safe, but in fact, the supervisor was still accountable for their safety.[11]

THE PROCESS OF ORGANIZING

For a supervisor, organizing efforts are generally focused on allocating responsibilities and resources in a way that makes the department or work group operate effectively and efficiently. In addition, supervisors may want or need to set up teams (see Chapter 3). Whether the organizing job involves setting up a new company, restructuring an existing one, or deciding how to organize a department or team, the process should be basically the same. The supervisor or other manager should define the objective, determine what resources are needed, and then group activities and assign duties. This three-step approach leads to a structure that supports the goals of the organization (see Figure 7.4).

Define the Objective

Management activities should support the objectives developed during the planning process. In the case of organizing, the supervisor or other manager should begin by defining what objective the department or work group is supposed to be

FIGURE 7.4
The Process of Organizing

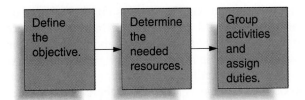

achieving. If the supervisor does not know, then he or she has not finished planning and should complete that job before trying to organize work. Recently, Dow Jones and Company decided to change from a product structure to a customer structure to meet the objective of operating more efficiently. The new structure includes three major divisions: the Consumer Media Group (activities related to the print and online *Wall Street Journal* and other products aimed at consumers), the Enterprise Media Group (which provides newswires, financial information, and other products and services for companies), and the Community Media Group (which publishes community newspapers). The company's top management determined that this structure would enable the company to operate effectively with fewer employees.[12]

Determine the Needed Resources

The planning process also should give the supervisor an idea of what resources—including personnel, equipment, and money—are needed to achieve goals. The supervisor should review the plans and identify which resources are needed for the particular areas being organized.

To achieve Ritz-Carlton's lofty goals that all of its customers be satisfied and return again, its managers have determined that they need employees committed to ensuring high quality. They also realize that every employee must be empowered to contribute to customer satisfaction. This responsibility in turn requires that employees have access to information about what customers want and how well the company's processes are working. Modern information systems help fulfill that need.

Group Activities and Assign Duties

The final step in the process is what most people think about when they consider organizing. The supervisor groups the necessary activities and assigns work to the appropriate employees. To ensure that all the necessary responsibilities are assigned, the supervisor also can involve employees in this step of the organizing process. Employees are deeply involved in these decisions at Harley-Davidson's motorcycle plant in Kansas City, Missouri. Representatives from management and the union established an overall structure based on teamwork. Most of the work takes place in what the company calls *natural work groups* (NWGs), teams of up to 15 workers who handle all the tasks for specialized functions (painting, fabrication) or for assembling particular motorcycle models. Each NWG decides how to meet its goals—for example, deciding how to arrange the machinery and equipment and solving quality problems. Workers in the NWG rotate through the group's various jobs so that they can fill in for one another as needed. The groups have authority for solving problems. For example, when a machine on the production line for welding frames broke down, the groups affected by the breakdown worked together to fix the machine and called in the next shift early to get caught up.[13]

At the Ritz-Carlton in New York, this step has included creating the position of director of quality. Paul Roa, who holds that job, says technology and training help keep the hotel's staff knowledgeable about what customers want. The hotel's employees receive training in how to notice guest preferences (for example, feather rather than polyester pillows, more oranges than apples in fruit baskets). Employee observations are entered into the company's national database. Each day, the hotel prints a report highlighting the preferences of the guests scheduled to arrive the next day. A full-time guest history coordinator analyzes the report so that the hotel can cater to those preferences. Furthermore, all employees are empowered to resolve guest complaints and rebate up to $2,000 a day per guest without management approval. They also are expected to analyze the problem and prepare an action plan for solving it. If defects recur, the company forms a team to engage in a formal problem-solving process to eliminate future occurrences.[14] In sum, staffing decisions and highly decentralized authority contribute to achieving Ritz-Carlton's quality objectives.

The remainder of this chapter discusses how to carry out the third step of the organizing process.

PRINCIPLES OF ORGANIZING

Supervisors, especially those who are new to the job, may be unsure how to group activities and assign duties. The task seems so abstract. Fortunately, management experts have developed some principles that can guide the supervisor: the parity principle, unity of command, chain of command, and span of control.

Parity Principle

parity principle
The principle that personnel who are given responsibility must also be given enough authority to carry out that responsibility

Parity is the quality of being equal or equivalent. Thus, according to the **parity principle,** personnel must have equal amounts of authority and responsibility. In other words, when someone accepts a responsibility, he or she also needs enough authority to be able to carry out that responsibility. If a head teller at a Citibank branch is responsible for providing high-quality customer service but does not have the authority to fire a surly teller, the head teller will find it difficult or impossible to carry out this responsibility.

Unity of Command

Meredith Buckle handled the maintenance jobs for a small office building. When building occupants experienced a problem, such as a leaky faucet or a cold office, they would call Buckle. Often, to get a faster response, they would call her repeatedly, complaining about how the problem was interfering with work. As a result, Buckle felt she could never keep everyone satisfied, and she had trouble deciding which jobs to do first.

unity of command
The principle that each employee should have only one supervisor

According to the principle of **unity of command,** each employee should have only one supervisor. Employees who receive orders from several people tend to get confused and aggravated. As a result, they tend to do poor work. It would have helped Buckle if the building manager had collected messages from the occupants and assigned the jobs to her along with a schedule for completing them.

Sometimes a supervisor's manager violates this principle by directing the employees who report to the supervisor. This puts the employees in the awkward position of receiving directions from two people, and it puts the supervisor in the awkward position of needing to correct his or her manager's behavior. In this kind of situation, the supervisor might want to approach his or her boss with a tactful way to restore unity of command. The supervisor might say, for instance, "I've noticed that my team gets confused when you and I both give directions. I'd like to suggest that you let me know what you want, and I'll relay it to the team." Of course, the supervisor also should refrain from directing employees who report to someone else.

Chain of Command

chain of command
The flow of authority in an organization from one level of management to the next

In a chain, each link is connected to no more than two links, one on either side. In an organization, authority progresses like the links on a chain. Along this **chain of command,** authority flows from one level of management to the next, from the top of the organization to the bottom.

When someone skips a level, the principle of the chain of command is violated. For example, suppose that Fred Paretsky wants to take Friday off, but he suspects that the division manager will be more sympathetic to his request than his supervisor. So Paretsky goes directly to the division manager, who grants permission. Unfortunately, though the division manager does not know it, Paretsky's group will be understaffed on Friday because two other workers also will be absent. By violating the chain of command, Paretsky and the division manager have created a staffing problem that the supervisor could have avoided with a little planning. Similarly, in the preceding example of a supervisor's manager directing the supervisor's employees, the boss is violating both the principles of chain of command and unity of command.

Taking every decision through every level of the organization can be time consuming and difficult, especially in an organization with many layers of management. The solution is to use common sense. For example, a request for information probably does not have to travel through every layer of management. In contrast, a decision that will affect the group's operations should probably pass through the chain of command. For more advice on the chain of command, see "Tips from the Firing Line."

Span of Control

span of control
The number of people a manager supervises

Clearly, keeping track of and developing the talents of one employee is easier than supervising 100 employees, but hiring a supervisor for every employee would be tremendously expensive. The number of people a manager supervises is known as the manager's **span of control.** The more people the manager supervises, the greater the span of control. Today, spans of control have increased as organizations try to save money by eliminating management positions and empowering employees to make more decisions. As shown in Figure 7.5, large companies typically have a span of control as great as one manager to nine employees; the span of control tends to be lower in smaller companies. In the federal government, downsizing during the 1990s has resulted in even larger spans of control—for example, one manager to 15 employees in the Social Security Administration.[15] This trend makes the supervisor's job more challenging than ever. Modern supervisors need top-notch skills in communicating, motivating, and monitoring the performance of larger teams of workers.

In organizing, managers must be aware of how many people they can supervise effectively. Ideally, managers supervise as many people as they can effectively guide toward meeting their goals. That number depends in part on several factors that describe the work situation:[16]

- *Similarity of functions*—The more similar the functions performed by employees, the greater the span of control can be.

TIPS FROM THE FIRING LINE

DON'T BREAK THE CHAIN

Is it ever wise to go over your boss's head? Adrian DeVore has done it, and she says there's a cost.

DeVore held retail and hotel jobs where she believed her boss was treating her unfairly. When DeVore thought she was underpaid, she complained to her boss's superiors. She did the same when she believed she had been discriminated against. Her reasoning was that she lacked confidence in her supervisors and doubted they could help her. DeVore believes she did what was necessary, but she acknowledges that she will never get a positive reference from those bosses to help her pursue a career elsewhere.

Experts say skipping a link in the chain of command usually hurts the employee more than the boss. The boss is likely to feel betrayed, and repairing the trust in that relationship will be difficult.

In most situations, a more effective approach is to bring problems to one's immediate supervisor and do so professionally. That means you prepare supporting evidence for your problem. Discuss actions, behaviors, or other measures that you and your boss can measure directly. Speak as calmly and objectively as possible.

Only if this well-planned effort fails should you go to the next link in the chain of command. Before you do, check your ideas with a trusted friend or mentor to make sure your view of the situation is reasonable and worth risking your relationship with your immediate boss.

There are, however, times when you might need to bypass a link in the chain of command. If you have seen or experienced illegal behavior or harassment, or if someone is being endangered, you should take your complaints as high as you need to go to get a helpful response.

Source: Mike Drummond, "Consultants Caution to Think Twice before Bypassing the Boss," *Knight Ridder/Tribune Business News*, August 16, 2004, downloaded from Business & Company Resource Center, http://galenet .galegroup.com.

- *Geographic closeness*—The closer subordinates are physically, the greater the span of control can be.
- *Complexity and change*—The simpler and more familiar the functions performed by subordinates, the greater the span of control can be. Frequent or rapid changes can make jobs seem more difficult, so a smaller span of control is necessary.
- *Coordination*—Managers need a smaller span of control when they must spend a great deal of time coordinating the work of their subordinates with one another and with other groups. The less time they need to spend on coordination,

FIGURE 7.5 **Typical Spans of Control**

Source: Barbara Davison, "Management Span of Control: How Wide Is Too Wide?" *Journal of Business Strategy*, July–August 2003, downloaded from Business & Company Resource Center, http://galenet.galegroup.com.

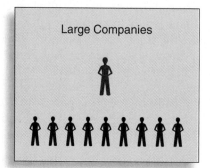

the greater the span of control can be. In many organizations, information technology is making larger spans of control possible because employees easily can obtain the information they need and share information throughout the company.

- *Planning*—The less time a manager needs to spend on planning, the greater the span of control can be.
- *Availability of staff support*—The more staff specialists available to provide support in a variety of areas, the larger the span of control can be.
- *Performance standards*—If there are clear, objective standards for performance and employees are familiar with them, the span of control can be larger than in a situation where the supervisor continually must clarify what is expected of employees.

Characteristics of the managers and employees also are important. Managers may find that, as their experience grows, so does the number of people they can supervise effectively. Managers with strong skills in time management and decision making also are likely to be able to supervise more employees. As for employees, the better able they are to work independently, the greater their supervisor's span of control can be.

DELEGATING AUTHORITY AND RESPONSIBILITY

A recent nationwide survey of U.S. employees found that more than half believed they were overworked, were overwhelmed by their workload, and lacked the time needed to complete their tasks.[17] The concept of organizing implies that one person cannot do all the work of an organization. Even a one-person business usually contracts with outside people to provide some services. For example, Lars Hundley runs a one-person business from a corner of his living room. His firm, CleanAirGardening.com, is the largest online dealer in the United States of Brill push-reel lawn mowers, a top German brand. Hundley now outsources his incoming telephone orders to a professional call service so he can spend more time testing and selecting new products and fielding customer service calls.[18] Giving someone else the authority and responsibility to carry out a task is known as **delegating.** You can explore your delegation effectiveness by taking the Knowing Yourself quiz on page 196.

delegating
Giving another person the authority and responsibility to carry out a task

Benefits of Delegating

Whereas the performance of most nonmanagement employees is evaluated in terms of their individual accomplishments, a supervisor's performance is evaluated according to the achievements of the whole department. Thus, the department's output will be of the highest quality and the supervisor will look best when he or she draws on the expertise of employees. W. H. Weiss, a writer and consultant in industrial management, says a supervisor's effectiveness and success "depend greatly on your ability to delegate responsibility and authority to others and to hold those so delegated accountable for results. . . . The best way to expand your personal authority is to delegate as much responsibility as you can. Hoarding authority serves to diminish your own status and importance."[19]

For example, a production supervisor might establish a team of employees to devise ways to make the workplace safer. Those employees are likely to come up with more ideas than the supervisor could identify alone. Some employees might have backgrounds or areas of expertise that lead them to notice where improvements are needed—improvements that the supervisor might never have considered.

A supervisor who delegates also has more time for the jobs only a supervisor can do, such as planning and counseling. Kelly Hancock, who supervises the order takers for classified ads at the *Toronto Sun,* says, "Delegating gives me more opportunity to do tasks of a more pressing, creative nature. I can work on special projects . . . such as sales contests for the staff." One way to think of this benefit of delegating is that it is an important tool for time management (discussed in Chapter 14). If the production supervisor in the example handled all aspects of safety, it could take weeks simply to identify and describe safety problems and solutions. That time might be better spent scheduling and arranging for employees to receive various types of training.

Likewise, a supervisor of a financial services company caused problems by failing to delegate. The company had placed a technical expert in charge of its information technology (IT). This manager knew a tremendous amount about computer hardware and put in long hours keeping the company's systems running smoothly. When the firm decided it should add a wider variety of systems to handle its business needs, the manager worked harder and harder to keep up with the mushrooming demands. He continued to try applying his own expertise, rather than delegating to the IT staffers. But he simply could not keep up with all the company's needs alone. Eventually, the company had to move the manager to a job without anyone to supervise, and a new manager was hired to delegate and focus on developing the knowledge of the people in the IT group.[20]

Delegating also has a beneficial effect on employees. Delegation of work gives employees a chance to develop their skills and their value to the organization. Depending on the kinds of tasks delegated, this additional responsibility can enhance their careers and their earning potential. It also can make employees' work more interesting. It is reasonable to expect that employees who are more interested in their work and more involved in meeting the organization's objectives are likely to do higher-quality work and remain with the organization longer. (This topic will be discussed in Chapter 9.) Thus, the production employees who serve on the safety team might find that this added responsibility leads them to care more about the quality of their day-to-day work.

Executive Petty Officer Rodney Randall heads the Coast Guard rescue mission at Eaton's Neck on Long Island Sound (New York). He sees delegating as a major way for the crew members under his supervision to gain the experience they need, and he frequently avoids going out on calls with them. "If you've got somebody there who you think has the answers," he says, "it's easier [for them] to ask the question than to think it out. They ask me, 'What do you think? What do you think?'" Instead of giving answers, Chief Randall trains the men and women he supervises to think on their feet by giving them the authority to make decisions, right or wrong.[21]

Empowerment

These benefits of delegating explain why many organizations use employee involvement to improve the quality of their goods and services (see Chapter 2). In other words, they delegate decision-making authority and responsibility in a variety of areas to employees. This practice—called **empowerment**—is based on the expectation that employees will provide more insight and expertise than managers can provide alone and that this participation will make employees more committed to doing their best.

empowerment
Delegation of broad decision-making authority and responsibility

FIGURE 7.6
The Process of Delegating

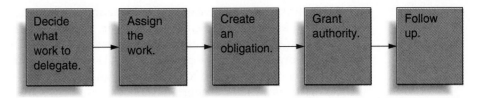

An empowered employee on a commercial banking team devised a new way to organize the team's work. She suggested team members consider specializing in particular types of clients, rather than tackling whichever assignment came in next. The team decided to try her idea temporarily. They found that with some adjustments, the plan made their work more interesting, and they were more committed to their tasks.[22]

The Process of Delegating

When delegating effectively, the supervisor is not merely handing out jobs at random but should be following a logical process: deciding what work to delegate, assigning the work, creating an obligation, granting authority, and following up (see Figure 7.6).

Decide What Work to Delegate

There are several ways to select which tasks to delegate. When an employee knows how to do a particular task better than the supervisor, delegation makes sense. Another approach is to delegate simple tasks that employees clearly can handle. For example, Kelly Hancock of the *Toronto Sun* has her employees handle administrative duties such as counting the lines for birth and death notices. The supervisor also can delegate the tasks that he or she finds most boring. This approach can backfire, however, if employees perceive they always are chosen to do the dirty work. Tasks performed regularly are good candidates for delegation because it may be worth the effort to train employees to do them.

Of course, a supervisor should *not* delegate some tasks, including personnel matters and activities assigned specifically to the supervisor. Thus, the supervisor should not assign duties such as appraising performance and resolving conflicts. Likewise, if a sales supervisor's boss has asked her to fly to Vancouver to resolve a customer complaint, it would be inappropriate for the supervisor to delegate this assignment to someone else.

Assign the Work

The supervisor continues the delegation process by selecting employees to carry out the work. In delegating a particular task, the supervisor considers who is available and then determines which of them to assign. The decision may be based on who is best qualified or most efficient, or the supervisor may make assignments to provide training and development for employees who have shown potential. The supervisor also weighs the personalities involved, safety considerations, and any company policies or union rules that may apply. Supervisors can be most effective in carrying out this step when they know their employees well. Matching assignments to employee desires and skills can help the organization reap the full potential of its human resources. Based on her experience as a teller supervisor for WestStar Credit Union, Geraldine Albores (now a branch manager) advises, "Get to know each employee, know their strengths and weaknesses, then you can delegate."[23]

When two jobs must be done at the same time and the same person is best qualified to do both, the process of selecting an employee to do the work becomes complex. In such cases, the supervisor must set priorities. The supervisor must consider how important the particular task is to achieving the department's goals and serving customers. If priorities among jobs are unclear, the supervisor should check with his or her manager.

To finish the step of assigning work, the supervisor tells the designated employees what they are supposed to do. The supervisor must be sure that the employees understand what they are supposed to be doing and have the necessary knowledge and skills. Clear directions are specific, but they should give employees some room to apply their knowledge and skills creatively. Denise O'Berry, president of The Small Business Edge Corporation, advises that supervisors detail the *results* they want, not the procedure to follow.[24] This approach gives employees freedom to improve upon processes. The supervisor would then monitor results to be sure the employee does not need clearer or more detailed direction. To be sure employees understand an assignment, the supervisor can ask them to restate the assignment in their own words. (Chapter 10 provides more information about how to communicate clearly.) For more advice about delegating fairly and effectively, see the "Supervisory Skills" box.

Create an Obligation

When the supervisor makes an assignment, he or she needs to be sure the employee accepts responsibility for carrying it out. A supervisor can encourage employees to accept responsibility by involving them in making decisions and by listening to their ideas. Workers who feel involved are more apt to feel responsible. Supervisors cannot force employees to feel responsible, but fortunately, many employees willingly take on responsibility as a matter of course. In addition, by making employees accountable for their actions, supervisors lead them to accept responsibility.

Although the employee should accept responsibility for carrying out a task, this does not mean the supervisor gives up the responsibility for its proper completion. The organization still holds the supervisor accountable. Therefore, following delegation, both parties have responsibility for the work. The supervisor's job becomes one of ensuring that the employee has the necessary resources and that the task is completed and meets quality standards. The supervisor does so through the management function of controlling, described in the previous chapter.

Grant Authority

Along with responsibility, supervisors must give employees the authority they need to carry out their jobs. This is how supervisors follow the parity principle, discussed previously in this chapter. Thus, if a supervisor at Abbott Laboratories gives a researcher responsibility to carry out a particular procedure, the researcher must also be given the authority to obtain the materials and equipment needed to do the job.

Follow Up

After assigning duties and the authority to carry them out, the supervisor needs to give the employees some freedom to act independently and creatively. This does not mean the supervisor should abandon employees to succeed or fail on their own; after all, the supervisor is equally responsible for the success of the work. Therefore, it should be made clear to employees that the supervisor is available for guidance. The supervisor also should set forth a plan for periodically checking on the progress of the work. The supervisor may find that employees

SUPERVISORY SKILLS

DELEGATING

KNOW WHEN TO BACK OFF

For many supervisors, the great challenge of delegation is the feeling that the supervisor can do the job faster or better than the employees. Supervisors who feel this way are tempted to hover so much that employees never really learn to make decisions independently. Or at the other extreme, some supervisors aren't sure how to lead and motivate, so they just assign duties and leave the results up to the employees. Of course, these employees aren't really being supervised at all, and they may fall short of goals because they don't know how to succeed or they doubt that their efforts will be noticed and rewarded.

Thus, the art of delegating involves knowing when to back off and when to become more involved. On the basis of his experience in the finance industry, Mark Roberts suggests that the solution is to distinguish the results (what needs to be accomplished) from the methods (how to achieve the desired results). Roberts says, "Delegation involves telling your staff what needs to be achieved but not forcing on them your chosen method of achieving it." However, depending on the employee's skills, the supervisor may need to discuss what the employee will be doing and be sure that the employee has ideas for achieving his or her goals. The supervisor also needs to be aware of whether the goals are being met, so that it is clear when the supervisor needs to get involved in coaching, training, or disciplining employees.

For Orest Protch, who once supervised employees in a steel mill, the art of delegating is a kind of balancing act that requires the supervisor to tread a path between getting overly involved and ignoring what is happening. To keep the balance, Protch stresses, it is essential to be fair and treat employees with dignity and respect. Part of fairness is for the supervisor to investigate the cause of any mistake and accept the blame when the supervisor is part of the cause (e.g., by communicating unclearly). In particular, the supervisor must consider how much authority was delegated. If the supervisor did not delegate authority to make decisions in an emergency, the employee cannot be held responsible for what happened in an emergency.

How much authority should the supervisor delegate? Protch recommends delegating the least amount required for getting the employee's job done correctly but also giving the employee some latitude for emergencies. If the employee is capable, the supervisor should let him or her do the job. In the steel mill where Protch was a supervisor, he once came into work just in time to learn that all shipments had stopped because the union to which the trucking firm's employees belonged had gone on strike. Nothing was leaving the facility. Protch headed for the shipping office and settled down at a desk near the shipping clerk. He let the clerk tackle the problem. Two hours later, the shipping clerk had lined up plenty of independent truckers to get the products to the customers. Protch was available to help, but he didn't jump in where he wasn't needed. The problem was solved, and an employee had risen to the challenge.

Sources: Based on ideas in Mark Roberts, "Supervision: The Delegation Game," *Money Marketing*, September 15, 2005; Orest Protch, "Delegation of Authority," *Supervision*, April 2006, both downloaded from Business & Company Resource Center, http://galenet.galegroup.com.

need additional information or help removing obstacles to success, or perhaps they simply need praise for the work they have done so far.

If an employee's performance of an unfamiliar task is less than perfect, the supervisor should not be discouraged from delegating in the future. Everyone needs time to learn, and disappointing performances may offer a chance for the supervisor to learn what is needed to strengthen an employee's skills. In addition, poor performance may have resulted from the way the work was delegated, not from a problem with the employee.

Reluctance to Delegate

Ruby Singh works late every night, reviewing all her employees' work and preparing detailed instructions for them to carry out the next day. Her own manager has suggested that she give the workers more freedom, which would save her a lot of time and probably increase their job satisfaction. However, Singh is afraid that if she does not keep close tabs on her employees, the department's performance will suffer.

Many supervisors are convinced that they are able to do a better job than their employees. They might even say, "If you want something done right, you have to do it yourself." Often they may be correct, particularly if their own promotion to a supervisory post resulted from high performance. Observing an employee making mistakes can be difficult, especially if the supervisor will look bad for allowing the mistake to occur.

These risks cause many supervisors to fear delegation. Psychologist Donna Genett speculates that this fear arises because "so many people move up to management on the basis of their own successes. When they get into management, a shift has to happen where their success comes from letting other people shine."[25] In other words, the organization needs supervisors to develop and coach employees so the employees can be more valuable to the organization. This requires delegation, even though learning may involve some mistakes.

In some cases, employees may really be unable to carry out jobs that they have been delegated. If so, the supervisor must consider ways to bring the workforce's talents into line with the department's needs. Perhaps employees need training or the department's hiring practices need improvement. (For more on selecting and training employees, see Chapters 15 and 16.)

As mentioned previously, delegating frees supervisors to concentrate on the tasks that they do best or that only they can do. Sometimes a supervisor is more comfortable being an expert at the employees' work than struggling with supervisory responsibilities such as motivating employees and resolving conflicts. However, the supervisor must overcome any discomfort or fear, because the organization needs supervisors who supervise.

SKILLS MODULE

PART ONE: CONCEPTS

Summary

7.1 Describe organization charts.

Organization charts are a standard way to draw the structure of an organization. Boxes represent the departments or positions, and connecting lines indicate reporting relationships. The positions at the top of the organization chart have the most authority and responsibility.

7.2 Identify basic ways in which organizations are structured.

Unless they are very small, organizations are grouped into departments. An organization with a functional structure groups personnel and other resources according to the types of work they carry out. A product structure groups work and resources according to the product produced and delivered. In a geographic structure, the departments are set up according to the location of the customers served or the goods or services produced. A customer structure departmentalizes the organization according to the category of customer served.

Organizations now often combine the basic types of structures, particularly when teams of employees are formed to meet objectives such as improving quality or applying new technology. Those seeking flexibility often favor an organic structure—one in which boundaries between jobs continually shift and people pitch in wherever their contributions are needed. They may form network organizations, which contract with other individuals and organizations to complete specific projects (instead of adding permanent employees).

7.3 Distinguish between line and staff authority and between centralized and decentralized authority.
Authority is the right to perform a task or give orders to someone else. Line authority is the right to carry out tasks and give orders related to the organization's primary purpose. Staff authority is the right to advise or assist those with line authority. When authority is centralized, it is shared by a few top managers; when authority is decentralized, it is spread among a greater number of people.

7.4 Compare and contrast *authority, power, responsibility,* and *accountability.*
Authority is the right to perform a task or give orders. Power is the ability (as opposed to the right) to get others to act in a certain way. Responsibility is the obligation to perform certain tasks. Accountability is the practice of imposing penalties for failure to adequately carry out responsibilities and giving rewards for success in meeting responsibilities. The authority to transfer responsibility to employees and hold them accountable adds to a supervisor's power. (However, a supervisor always is held accountable for his or her employees' performance.)

7.5 Identify the steps in the process of organizing.
To organize a department or work group, the supervisor should first define the objective of the department or work group, then determine what resources are needed. Finally, the supervisor groups activities and assigns duties to appropriate employees.

7.6 Describe four principles of organizing.
According to the parity principle, personnel with responsibility must also be given enough authority to carry out that responsibility. The principle of unity of command states that each employee should have only one supervisor. A chain of command is the flow of authority from one level of the organization to the next; most decisions and information should flow along the chain of command. Finally, supervisors and other managers should have an appropriate span of control; the best number of employees for a specific situation depends on a variety of factors.

7.7 Discuss why and how supervisors delegate.
Supervisors delegate to enhance the quality of the department's and supervisor's performance by drawing on the expertise of employees. Delegation also frees time for supervisory tasks. It may improve employee morale and performance by empowering them to make decisions in a variety of areas. To delegate, supervisors follow a five-step process: Decide what work to delegate, assign the work, create an obligation, grant authority, and follow up. When delegating, supervisors must make sure employees understand and are able to do the work, and they retain the responsibility to see that the work is done properly.

7.8 Identify causes of reluctance to delegate.
Many supervisors are reluctant to delegate because they believe no one else can do the job as well. They may not want to give up activities they enjoy. Some supervisors are more comfortable doing what their employees should be doing than carrying out supervisory responsibilities.

Key Terms

organizing, *p.* 173
department, *p.* 175
departmentalization, *p.* 175
organic structure, *p.* 178
network organizations, *p.* 178
authority, *p.* 180

line authority, *p.* 180
staff authority, *p.* 180
functional authority, *p.* 181
power, *p.* 181
responsibility, *p.* 182
parity principle, *p.* 184

unity of command, *p.* 184
chain of command, *p.* 185
span of control, *p.* 185
delegating, *p.* 187
empowerment, *p.* 188

Review and Discussion Questions

1. Emily Sanford has just been promoted to supervisor of the salespeople in the gift department at a department store. Which of the following organizing activities is she likely to carry out?
   a. Scheduling her employees' work hours.
   b. Forming a team of her employees to work on a promotional event within the department.
   c. Helping decide the best location for a new branch of the department store.
   d. Assigning an employee to sit at the bridal registry desk.
   e. Determining whether the department store should launch its own line of products.

2. What might be the best structure for each of the following organizations?
   a. A three-person company that sells complete, prepackaged gourmet dinners to specialty grocery stores.
   b. A small organization that supplies antique cars to movie studios.
   c. A manufacturer of windows, with offices in Toronto, Seattle, Miami, and Chicago.

3. What special attributes must supervisors have to be successful in some of the new types of organizational structures?

4. Which of the following supervisors have primarily line authority? Which have staff authority?
   a. The production supervisor at a publishing company, who is responsible for getting books typeset and printed.
   b. The housekeeping supervisor at a hospital.
   c. The word-processing supervisor at a law firm.
   d. The payroll department supervisor for a fire department.

5. In recent years, many organizations have become more decentralized. Typically this change involves eliminating middle-management jobs and sharing more control with those at lower levels of the organization. How do you think this affects the role of supervisors in those organizations?

6. Does someone with authority always have power? Does a person who accepts responsibility necessarily have authority? Explain.

7. What are the steps in the process of organizing? How would they apply to the manager of an Olive Garden restaurant who needs to schedule employees? Explain in general how this supervisor could follow each step.

8. Describe each of the following principles of organizing:
   a. Parity principle.
   b. Unity of command.
   c. Chain of command.
   d. Span of control.

9. A production supervisor at a company that makes furniture learns about the factors that should influence the span of control. The supervisor believes that his own span of control is too large for him to supervise effectively. Is there anything a person in his position can do? If not, explain why. If so, suggest what he can try.

10. Harry Jamison, CPA, is planning to set up a business to prepare tax returns. Harry is the only person in the business, at least for now. Can he delegate any work? Should he? Explain.

11. What steps do you think a supervisor who is reluctant to delegate could take to overcome this discomfort?

PART TWO: SKILL-BUILDING

YOU SOLVE THE PROBLEM

Reflecting back on page 173, what challenges do you see for James Small as a supervisor who works apart from the rest of Raytheon's organization? As a group, list three ways in which planning the work of employees in Raytheon's Bike Shop would be different from planning the work of production employees making a standard part. List three ways in which controlling the work would be different.

As a supervisor, James Small also serves as a kind of "linking pin" between the expert scientists in his group and Raytheon's overall business needs. Assign three members of your group to the roles of James Small, Small's manager, and a Bike Shop employee who has been working on the Whirl. Have them role-play a conversation in which the manager is seeking an update on the status of the Whirl. What will be the manager's goals, and what will be the employee's? How can Small contribute to business needs while also giving his employees enough leeway to experiment?

Problem-Solving Case: *Is Thor Industries Organized for Growth?*

Thor Industries is the largest maker of recreational vehicles in the world. If you have never heard of this company, that fact may have something to do with the way it is organized. The company's headquarters consists of a three-room office on the sixth floor of a building in midtown Manhattan. Here, chief executive Wade Thompson and his assistant oversee the activities of a company that recently enjoyed more than $150 million in sales.

The rest of the work occurs throughout North America at the company's 20 recreational vehicle (RV) and three bus factories. Thor makes RVs sold under many brand names, including Airstream, Keystone, Dutchmen, Outback, Four Winds, and General Coach.

Thompson built Thor by purchasing RV and bus manufacturers and letting them operate independently. In effect, the 10 RV companies that Thor has acquired continue to compete with one another under the corporate umbrella. And brands within a division operate independently. At Keystone, for example, there are 14 brands, and they have separate factories, each with its own manager in charge of that brand. Keystone Executive Vice President William Fenech says, "I tell the guys, 'If you want to make pink units go ahead. But then you'll have to sell pink units.'" Within a facility, there are different functional groups, such as cabinetmaking, plumbing, electrical, and finishing. Each group has a floor leader. The leader and the group together have the responsibility to improve efficiency, including the authority to eliminate unproductive workers.

In addition to operating independently, the divisions are rewarded independently. The president of each division receives 15 percent of that division's pretax profits, and some of them earn more than the corporation's chief executive. The financial rewards at lower levels also are linked to performance. Factory workers in some cases are paid a rate based on the amount of production, rather than their hours worked. Also, the entire workforce at a facility earns a percentage of its sales. Each functional group within the facility—for example, plumbing or electrical—receives a given share of that amount.

According to Thompson, this structure encourages innovation and customer service. The basic parts for any RV are essentially the same. Brands distinguish themselves by style, service, and special features. Thompson believes that when each division handles its own sales, manufacturing, and research and development, they will have more incentive to outdo the other brands. Also, the smaller divisions can more readily hear and respond to customer feedback than a centralized corporation could. A Michigan dealer explains, "They don't have to go up this giant chain of command to get something done." In effect, this is the structure that General Motors (GM) once had, with different organizations for each of its makes. However, GM eventually became more centralized because it couldn't afford to continue duplicating so many functions.

What does this leave for the chief executive to do? Primarily, Thompson keeps track of the major financial measures. When a division is slipping, he gets involved. More recently, he has required division presidents to share some information about improving quality and efficiency.

1. Does this description of Thor Industries sound more like a functional, product, geographic, or customer structure, or some combination of these? Explain. Is Thor Industries highly centralized or decentralized? Explain.

2. Is Wade Thompson a good example of a manager delegating authority? Why or why not?

3. Imagine you are a production supervisor in one of Thor's factories. Suggest how you would handle each of the following challenges within this company's organizational structure:

   a. You want to improve the quality of cabinet installation, and you would like to get ideas from supervisors at a division where the quality is very high.

   b. You want to cut the cost of electrical work by operating more efficiently—building the same number of RVs with fewer workers. You want the electrical team to accept responsibility for this challenge.

   c. You like to camp, and based on an idea you heard from some campers in a park you visited, you want to try building RVs with a new feature: computer workstations.

Sources: Jonathan Fahey, "Lord of the Rigs," *Forbes,* March 29, 2004, downloaded from Business & Company Resource Center, http://galenet.galegroup.com; Thor Industries, Annual Report 2003, www.thorindustries.com.

Knowing Yourself

Do You Delegate?

To test your delegating skills, answer the following questions with Yes or No.

1. Do you regularly work a lot of overtime? _____
2. Are you usually busier than the people you work with? _____
3. Must you often rush to meet deadlines? _____
4. Are you ever unable to complete important projects? _____
5. Are you too busy to plan or prioritize your work? _____
6. Do you return from vacation to find piles of unfinished business waiting for you? _____
7. Have you neglected training someone to take over your job on short notice? _____
8. Do you feel other people are taking breaks or leaving on time while you do their work for them? _____
9. Do you feel you are the only one who can do the job right? _____
10. Do you have difficulty expressing yourself? _____

The more Yes answers you give, the more likely it is that you have trouble delegating.

Source: Janet Mahoney, "Delegating Effectively," *Nursing Management,* June 1997, p. 62. Reprinted with permission of Lippincott Williams & Wilkins.

Pause and Reflect

1. When is it hardest for you to delegate?
2. When do you want others to delegate more to you?

Class Exercise

Networking

Six Degrees of Separation

Some experts feel that no matter how an organization is designed, the key to efficiency is the creation of shortcuts between different levels of the firm. Studies have shown that it takes only a few such connections between well-connected individuals to make a very small world out of a large one. This is the idea that underlies the concept of "six degrees of separation," which originated in the work of Harvard social psychologist Stanley Milgram in the 1960s.

Milgram gave randomly selected people in Kansas and Nebraska each a letter addressed to someone they did not know in Massachusetts. He asked them to mail the letter to an acquaintance who would bring it closer to the target addressee. Each participant needed an average of only five intermediaries to make the connection.

Break into small groups and re-create Milgram's experiment as a thought exercise. Let one person in the group name a friend at a different school or university than the one you attend. Go around your group to see whether each person can mention someone who can lead you closer to your target friend. See whether you can at least reach the right campus, if not the person named, and compare notes with the other groups in your class to see how many "degrees of separation" were needed in the smallest and the largest chains.

Building Supervision Skills

Delegating

Organizing a Fund-Raising Team

Divide the class into teams of four to six members. Appoint a leader to act as supervisor for each team. Each team will hold the initial meeting to organize a fund-raising event for a cause of their choice. The teams should define their objectives, determine the needed resources, group activities, and assign duties. The supervisor should delegate whatever responsibilities he or she can, including asking for a volunteer to take notes at the meeting itself.

Before the end of class, a spokesperson for each team may report to the class on the effectiveness of the meeting: How quickly were objectives defined? How evenly were duties assigned? What was each member's responsibility? How efficient was the supervisor at delegating? Did some members seem to have more power than others?

Chapter **Eight**

The Supervisor as Leader

Learning Objectives

After you have studied this chapter, you should be able to:

8.1 Discuss the possible link between personal traits and leadership ability.

8.2 Compare leadership styles that a supervisor might adopt.

8.3 Explain contingency theories of leadership.

8.4 Identify criteria for choosing a leadership style.

8.5 Describe guidelines for giving directions to employees.

8.6 Indicate why supervisors need to understand and improve their views of themselves.

8.7 Explain how supervisors can develop and maintain good relations with their employees, managers, and peers.

If people see you looking out only for your own best interests, they won't follow you.

—*Carlos M. Gutierrez, U.S. Secretary of Commerce and former CEO, Kellogg*

From the beginning of his career, Frederick W. Hill has been learning to be a successful leader. These lessons have propelled him to an executive position with JP Morgan Chase.

Hill's career started when he took an entry-level job at the Mellon Bank, on the evening shift. Hill worked hard and after six months earned a promotion to shift supervisor. The entire group that the young black man supervised was white, female, and at least 20 years older than he. As Hill learned to lead this group, he determined that he was most effective when he was pleasant but did not confuse his supervisory role with friendship. He would be "friendly, but not friends."

Next, Hill's career took a major turn: He worked as a police officer for the State of Pennsylvania. The job taught him to observe carefully and pay attention to details. A colleague was seriously injured in an undercover operation with an unprepared backup team. Hill learned the importance of ensuring that every detail of a plan is in place.

While working as a police officer, Hill earned his undergraduate and law degrees, then took a position as a litigator with a large law firm. There he learned to question everyone, including the experts hired by the opposition to present sophisticated-sounding arguments. This lesson has since helped Hill be courageous as a leader facing doubt or criticism in difficult situations.

Hill's next career move brought him back to the management ranks. He worked for Westinghouse as a lawyer, then a lobbyist, and finally as head of the company's marketing and communications department. At the same time, he taught at the University of Pittsburgh. As a teacher, Hill improved his ability to coach and motivate others. He learned that praising is easy, and criticizing is difficult; criticism must be constructive to be effective.

From Westinghouse, Hill moved to McDonnell Douglas, again to head marketing and communications. The job was challenging. The company had been suffering both financially and in terms of its reputation, and the communications group suffered low status in an organization led by former fighter pilots. Now Hill's leadership skills would be critical to his group's success. Hill started by inspiring his team, encouraging them to take risks and do great work within the sphere they controlled. He also drew on lessons he had learned from his father and grandfather, who responded to the racial discrimination of their times by acting "as if they really did belong," thereby forcing others to treat them fairly. Hill encouraged his staffers to act as if they should participate in management decision making. His team created an inspiring corporate ad campaign that helped reestablish McDonnell Douglas's good name and earned his group respect within the company.

Following McDonnell Douglas's merger with Boeing, Hill moved to JP Morgan Chase, where he is executive vice president of marketing and communications. From that position, Hill sums up his leadership lessons: "Leadership is about raising the hopes, calming the fears, firing the imagination, and strengthening the resolve of real people." By that measure, Hill is a real leader.

Building effective leadership skills can take time, as Frederick W. Hill learned throughout his career. Today's organizations need supervisors who can motivate and oversee employees in a variety of situations.

QUESTIONS

1. Think about the different leadership roles Hill has assumed during his career. Do you think Hill is a "natural leader," whose personal characteristics made him bound to succeed, or could his skills be taught to others?

2. What skills did Hill learn in each of his supervisory positions? Make a list, including each of his different jobs and the ways they contributed to his success.

Source: Frederick W. Hill, "Leadership: A Personal Journey," *Executive Speeches,* February–March 2004 (presentation at Sixth Annual Conference of the Harvard Business School African-American Alumni Association, Boston, October 10, 2003), downloaded from Business & Company Resource Center, http://galenet.galegroup.com.

When the supervisor knows what employees should be doing and who should be doing what, the job becomes one of creating the circumstances in which employees will do what is required of them. In other words, supervisors must be leaders. As you learned in Chapter 1, **leading** is the management function of influencing people to act or not act in a certain way.

This chapter explores what makes leadership work. The chapter describes a variety of leadership styles and provides criteria for matching a style to a situation.

leading
Influencing people to act or not act in a certain way

SUPERVISORY SKILLS

LEADING

BEING A "SERVANT LEADER"

Author Robert Ramsey says his favorite way to explain leadership is simply "removing obstacles." He assumes employees will do what they should if their path is clear and easy to follow. Surprisingly, this means that the supervisor's role looks more like someone who is serving employees (by clearing the path) than one who merely looks on from a high position and calls out directions.

Ramsey experienced this role of "servant leader" firsthand when he was assigned to supervise a company's human resource department. When he arrived on the job, most employees in the company distrusted his department—sometimes they were even hostile toward it. Why? The department had seen itself as mainly an enforcer of rules, dishing out penalties whenever an employee or department failed to meet a deadline or follow a procedure. Ramsey's staff felt demoralized by their negative role in the company.

Ramsey's solution was to change the way the department viewed itself. He started calling the human resource department the "People Office," defining new goals that focused on service to the company. The ultimate objective would be to make employees' work lives simpler and more rewarding. To meet these goals, Ramsey and his staff began reorganizing procedures and systems to make them easier for employees to use. They rewrote the employee handbook to focus on how the department would help employees meet requirements, raise their income, and obtain all the employee benefits to which they were entitled. Employees in the department began sending out suggestions and updates, focusing on building positive relationships. Eventually, Ramsey's service-oriented approach gave the company's employees a positive opinion of his department—and made the employees in the department enthusiastic about doing better and better work.

How else can supervisors apply servant leadership? Ramsey suggests coaching, teaching, and modeling the desired behaviors. He urges supervisors to learn about their employees and spend plenty of time walking around the workplace to reinforce positive behaviors and learn about what employees need. Servant leadership also includes giving employees the freedom to make decisions and the resources they need to do their job. In a nutshell, Ramsey advises "showing employees the desired direction, setting them up for success, and then getting out of the way."

Source: Robert D. Ramsey, "The New Buzz Word," *Supervision,* October 2005, downloaded from InfoTrac, http://web2.infotrac.galegroup.com.

It also discusses how to carry out an important activity related to leadership: giving directions. Because leading mainly requires human relations skills, the chapter concludes with a discussion of how supervisors can relate effectively to the various people in an organization.

CHARACTERISTICS OF A SUCCESSFUL LEADER

What is the difference between a manager and a leader? According to consultant and author Paul Taffinder, "Managers seek and follow direction. Leaders inspire achievement." Trainer and consultant Deborah Gavello uses an analogy: "Managing is 'running a tight ship'; leadership is 'inspiring the crew.'" And the Small Business Administration emphasizes the leader's role in envisioning new ideas and inspiring others with that vision—typically building commitment to a fresh approach to solving a stubborn problem.[1] A leader provides that inspiration by instilling in employees a sense of common purpose, a belief that together they can achieve something worthwhile. For one former supervisor's perspective on how to accomplish this goal, see the "Supervisory Skills" box.

To find out whether people are natural leaders, social scientists have studied the personalities of effective leaders, looking for traits they hold in common. Presumably, such traits would be predictors of good leadership. Some traits that might be considered significant are the following:

- *Sense of responsibility*—A person who is promoted to a supervisory position is given responsibility for the work of others as well as for his or her own performance. Supervisors must be willing to take this responsibility seriously.
- *Self-confidence*—A supervisor who believes in his or her ability to get the job done will convey confidence to employees.
- *High energy level*—Many organizations expect supervisors to put in long hours willingly to handle the variety of duties that come with the job. Some supervisory positions also are physically challenging, requiring that the supervisor actively observe and participate in what is happening in the workplace.
- *Empathy*—In settling disputes, answering questions, and understanding needs, supervisors should be sensitive to the feelings of employees and higher management. Supervisors who have difficulty understanding what makes people tick will be at a disadvantage.

internal locus of control
The belief that you are the primary cause of what happens to yourself

- *Internal locus of control*—An **internal locus of control** is the belief that you are the primary cause of what happens to yourself. People with an external locus of control tend to blame others or events beyond their control when something goes wrong. Those with an internal locus of control are thought to be better leaders because they try harder to take charge of events.
- *Sense of humor*—People with a good sense of humor are more fun to work with and work for (assuming they use appropriate humor—not racist or sexist anecdotes—and do not overuse rehearsed jokes that are unrelated to work).

Focusing on traits such as these, ask yourself whether you have leadership qualities. Also, determine whether you are CEO material by taking the Knowing Yourself quiz on page 221.

Although these traits sound plausible as the characteristics of a successful leader, results of various studies about leadership traits have been inconsistent. Some studies have found one set of traits to be significant, while others have identified a completely different set of traits. As a result, research has not established a clear link between personality traits and leadership success. Thus, if you have most of the traits described here, you may be a successful leader, but your success is not guaranteed. Also, if you have only a few of these traits, you need not be discouraged; you can still develop the skills that effective leaders use.

LEADERSHIP STYLES

Anita O'Donnell runs a tight ship; she lays down the rules and tolerates no deviation from them. Greg Petersen focuses on what he perceives to be the needs of his employees; they in turn do good work out of loyalty to him. George Liang is an easygoing supervisor when the work is routine, but when a big order comes in, he turns tough.

If you have worked for more than one boss, chances are you have experienced more than one leadership style. O'Donnell, Petersen, and Liang illustrate only some of the possibilities. Some supervisors instinctively lead in a way they are comfortable with; others adopt their leadership style consciously. However, a supervisor who is aware of the basic types of leadership styles is probably in the best position to use the style (or styles) that will get the desired results.

Degree of Authority Retained

One way to describe leadership styles is in terms of how much authority the leader retains. Do employees get to make choices and control their own work? Or does the supervisor make all the decisions? To describe the possibilities, management theorists refer to authoritarian, democratic, and laissez-faire leadership.

authoritarian leadership
A leadership style in which the leader retains a great deal of authority

With **authoritarian leadership,** the leader retains a great deal of authority, making decisions and dictating instructions to employees. An example would be a military commander who expects unquestioning obedience.

democratic leadership
A leadership style in which the leader allows subordinates to participate in decision making and problem solving

Some supervisors share more authority than authoritarian supervisors do. With **democratic leadership,** the supervisor allows employees to participate in decision making and problem solving. A supervisor with a democratic style of leadership might have the staff meet weekly to discuss how to improve client relations. When a conflict arises, this supervisor asks the group to discuss possible solutions and select one.

laissez-faire leadership
A leadership style in which the leader is uninvolved and lets subordinates direct themselves

At the opposite extreme from authoritarian leadership is **laissez-faire leadership.** A laissez-faire manager is uninvolved and lets employees do what they want. Supervisors are rarely, if ever, able to practice this style of leadership because the nature of the supervisor's job requires close involvement with employees.

Nor are many supervisors totally authoritarian or totally democratic. Most supervisors give employees some degree of freedom to do their jobs, but they still make some of the decisions for the department. Years ago, Robert Tannenbaum and Warren H. Schmidt drew a graph showing the continuum, or range of possibilities, for the degree of authority a manager can retain. This continuum is still popular today as a way to picture the possibilities (see Figure 8.1).

Task Oriented versus People Oriented

Another way to look at differences in leadership styles is to consider what supervisors focus on in making decisions and evaluating accomplishments. In general terms, leaders may be task oriented or people oriented. A task-oriented leader is

FIGURE 8.1 **Possibilities for Retaining Authority**

Source: Adapted from Robert Tannenbaum and Warren Schmidt, "How to Choose a Leadership Pattern," *Harvard Business Review*, May–June 1973.

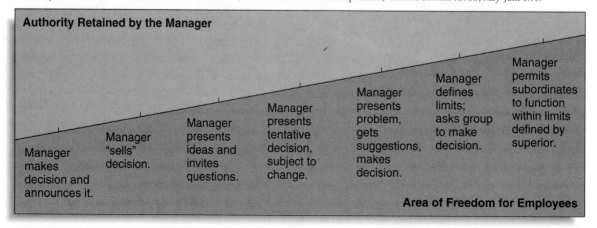

one who focuses on the jobs to be done and the goals to be accomplished. When the work gets done correctly and on time, a task-oriented leader is satisfied. On the other hand, a people-oriented leader is concerned primarily with the well-being of the people he or she manages. This type of leader emphasizes issues such as morale, job satisfaction, and relationships among employees.

Of course, the organization expects that its supervisors and other managers will care about meeting organizational objectives. Consider an unfortunate (for Boston) decision made by Grady Little during a baseball game played in the waning days of the 2003 season. Little, then manager of the Boston Red Sox, had to decide whether to leave in star pitcher Pedro Martinez against the New York Yankees. Little believed a relief pitcher could help the team defeat New York, but Martinez told Little he wanted to stay in the game. A win by Martinez would thrill the crowd and satisfy Martinez's desires, so Little granted the superstar's wish. But the Red Sox lost the game and the team's chances to play in the World Series. In hindsight, it appears that a people-oriented decision conflicted with the team's major objective.[2]

Most organizations expect that their supervisors can combine some degree of task orientation with some degree of people orientation. A supervisor who tends to focus on getting out the work should remember to check sometimes how employees are feeling and getting along. A supervisor who regularly sticks up for employees' welfare should make sure that he or she also remembers to promote the organization's goals.

Researchers Robert R. Blake and Jane S. Mouton recommend that supervisors and other managers be strong in both leadership orientations. They developed a Managerial Grid® (see Figure 8.2) that identifies seven styles of leadership by managers. Along one axis is the manager's concern for people, and along the other is the manager's concern for production. Blake and Mouton's research led them to conclude that productivity, job satisfaction, and creativity are highest with a (9, 9), or team management, style of leadership. To apply this model of leadership, supervisors identify where their current style of leadership falls on the managerial grid, then determine the kinds of changes they must make to adopt the (9, 9) style, which is high in concern for both people and production.

Leader Attitudes

Theory X
A set of management attitudes based on the view that people dislike work and must be coerced to perform

Theory Y
A set of management attitudes based on the view that work is a natural activity and that people will work hard and creatively to achieve objectives to which they are committed

In observing the behavior of managers, Douglas McGregor noted that many tend to have a group of attitudes that reflect their beliefs about workers and the workplace. He termed this set of attitudes **Theory X.** To summarize, a Theory X manager assumes that people dislike work and try to avoid it, that they therefore must be coerced to perform, that they wish to avoid responsibility and would prefer to be directed, and that their primary need is for security. Not surprisingly, these beliefs influence how supervisors and other managers behave. A Theory X supervisor would adopt an autocratic role, keeping a close eye on employees and looking for occasions when they need to be disciplined to keep them performing adequately.[3]

McGregor advises that managers can benefit from adopting a much different set of attitudes, which he terms **Theory Y.** According to Theory Y, working is as natural an activity as resting or playing, and people will work hard to achieve objectives to which they are committed. They can learn to seek responsibility and to be creative in solving organizational problems. Supervisors and other managers who adhere to Theory Y focus on developing the potential of their employees.

FIGURE 8.2 The Managerial Grid

Source: The Leadership Grid® figure from *Leadership Dilemmas—Grid Solutions*, by Robert R. Blake and Ann Adams McCanse (formerly the Managerial Grid® figure by Robert R. Black and Jane S. Mouton) (Houston: Gulf Publishing Company), p. 29. Copyright © 1991 by Scientific Methods, Inc. Reproduced by permission of the owners.

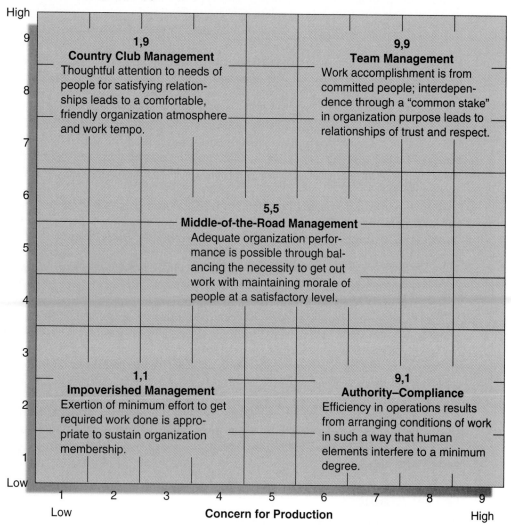

Their style of leadership tends to be democratic. Table 8.1 summarizes these two sets of assumptions.

Today a common view among people studying management is that Theory Y is appropriate for many situations. To see what a Theory Y manager looks like, consider Don T. Davis, who manages the Beverly Hills, California, branch of Smith Barney, a brokerage division of Citigroup. Davis focuses on providing the office's 85 financial consultants with the resources they need to serve their clients. Explains Davis, "I've been around here a long time. I'm able to call someone [at Citigroup] and say, 'I need you to help me out here.'" Every day, Davis takes several walks around the brokerage offices, making himself available to the financial consultants in case they have problems or need encouragement. He often accompanies them on calls to prospects so he can better coach them in sales and teamwork.

TABLE 8.1
Contrasting Leader Attitudes

Source: Based on Douglas McGregor, *The Human Side of Enterprise* (New York: McGraw-Hill, 1960).

Theory X	Theory Y
People dislike work and try to avoid it.	Working is as natural an activity as resting or playing.
People must be coerced to perform.	People will work hard to achieve objectives to which they are committed.
People wish to avoid responsibility.	People can learn to seek responsibility and prefer to be directed.
People's primary need is for security.	Many people are able to be creative in solving organizational problems.

He also identifies situations in which he can help employees by pairing them with those who have expertise in products the client needs. In one situation, a financial consultant was having difficulty getting a new client set up, so Davis arranged for this major prospect to travel to New York and meet experts at Citicorp. The trip smoothed the process for the financial consultant, who has since been able to set up services for that client.[4]

In the last decade, management experts extended their view of managing and leading to include **Theory Z.** Theory Z supervisors seek to involve employees in making decisions, consider long-term goals when making plans, and give employees relatively great freedom in carrying out their duties. This theory is based on comparisons of management styles in the United States and Japan. It assumes that whereas Japanese workers are more productive than their U.S. counterparts, the difference stems in part from different management styles. Thus, Theory Z was developed in an attempt to adapt some Japanese management practices to the U.S. workplace. The Japanese practices include employee involvement and lifetime employment.

Theory Z
A set of management attitudes that emphasizes employee participation in all aspects of decision making

Contingency Theories of Leadership

With all these possibilities, is there one best approach to leading employees? Should the supervisor consciously cultivate one leadership style? A common view is that the best style of leadership depends on the circumstances.

Fiedler's Contingency Model

One of the first researchers to develop such a theory—called a *contingency theory*—was Fred Fiedler. According to Fiedler, each leader has a preferred leadership style, which may be relationship oriented (i.e., people oriented) or task oriented. Whether relationship-oriented or task-oriented leaders perform better depends on three characteristics of the situation: leader–member relations, task structure, and the position power of the leader (see Figure 8.3). Leader–member relations refers to the extent to which the leader has the support and loyalty of group members. Task structure describes any specified procedures that employees should follow in carrying out the task. Position power refers to the formal authority granted to the leader by the organization.

Fiedler recommends that a leader determine whether his or her preferred leadership style fits the situation. For instance, if a situation involves good leader–member relations, a structured task, and strong position power, the situation calls for a leader who is task oriented. If the leader's preferred style does not fit, Fiedler says, the leader should try to change the characteristics of the situation.

FIGURE 8.3 **Fiedler's Contingency Model of Leadership**

Source: Adapted from Fred E. Fiedler, "Engineer the Job to Fit the Manager," *Harvard Business Review*, September–October 1965.

Leader–Member Relations	Good	Good	Good	Good	Poor	Poor	Poor	Poor
Task Structure	Structured	Structured	Unstructured	Unstructured	Structured	Structured	Unstructured	Unstructured
Leader Position Power	Strong	Weak	Strong	Weak	Strong	Weak	Strong	Weak
Which Leader Performs Better?	Task-Oriented Leader	Task-Oriented Leader	Task-Oriented Leader	Relationship-Oriented Leader	Relationship-Oriented Leader	Relationship-Oriented Leader	Task- or Relationship-Oriented Leader	Task-Oriented Leader

 Characteristics of the situation   Optimal leadership style for situation

In the preceding example, a relationship-oriented leader might try to make the task less structured; the result would be a situation in which the leader is likely to be more effective.

Hersey-Blanchard Theory

Fiedler's work led others to develop their own contingency theories of leadership. For example, Paul Hersey and Ken Blanchard developed a model called the *life cycle theory*.

This model, like Fiedler's, considers the degrees to which managers focus on relationships and tasks. Unlike Fiedler's model, however, the Hersey-Blanchard theory assumes that the leader's behavior should adapt to the situation. Specifically, the leadership style should reflect the maturity of the followers, as measured by traits such as ability to work independently.

According to the Hersey-Blanchard life cycle theory, leaders should adjust their degree of task and relationship behavior in response to the growing maturity of their followers. As followers mature, leaders should move through the following combinations of task and relationship behavior:

1. High task and low relationship behavior.
2. High task and high relationship behavior.
3. Low task and high relationship behavior.
4. Low task and low relationship behavior.

In special conditions, such as short-term deadlines, the leader may have to adjust the leadership style temporarily. However, Hersey and Blanchard maintain that this pattern of choosing a leadership style will bring about the most effective long-term working relationship between a leader and followers.

Choosing a Leadership Style

Viewing contingency theories as a whole provides some general guidelines for choosing a leadership style. To identify the most effective style, the supervisor

FIGURE 8.4   Characteristics Affecting Choice of Leadership Style

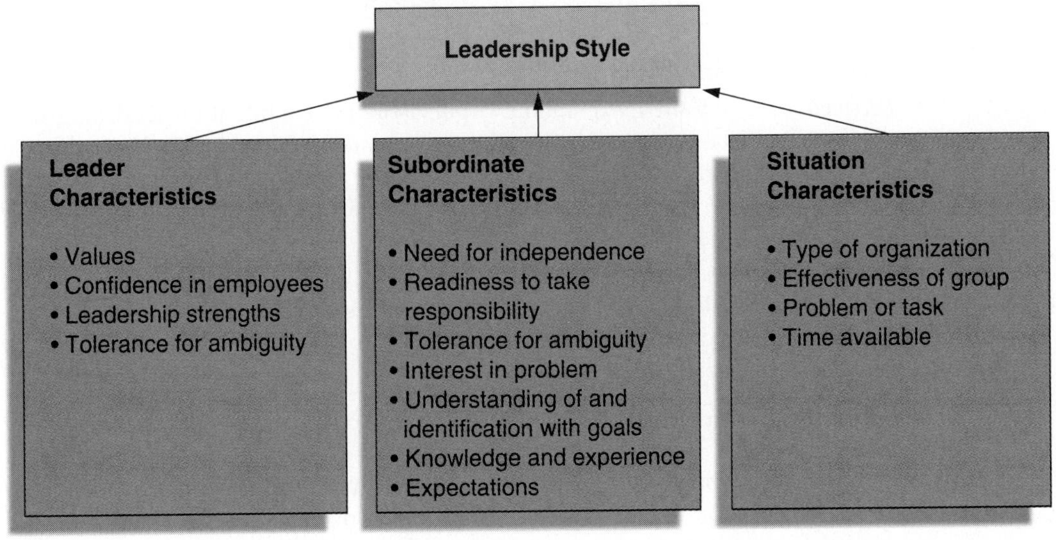

Leadership Style

Leader Characteristics

- Values
- Confidence in employees
- Leadership strengths
- Tolerance for ambiguity

Subordinate Characteristics

- Need for independence
- Readiness to take responsibility
- Tolerance for ambiguity
- Interest in problem
- Understanding of and identification with goals
- Knowledge and experience
- Expectations

Situation Characteristics

- Type of organization
- Effectiveness of group
- Problem or task
- Time available

should consider the characteristics of the leader, the subordinates, and the situation itself. Figure 8.4 shows some key characteristics to weigh.

Characteristics of the Leader

Thanks to sources of variation such as personality type and cultural values, different leaders prefer different styles of leading. Whereas one supervisor might feel more comfortable backed up by a clear system of rules, regulations, and schedules, another might prefer to come up with creative approaches on the spur of the moment. One supervisor may like the results of involving employees in decision making, whereas another cannot get used to the time and effort this requires.

One common characteristic of good leaders is the ability to act as a good role model. One writer suggests that this is largely a matter of how the supervisor does the "little things" in relating to employees: arriving for meetings on time, calling employees by name, returning e-mail and phone calls promptly, listening carefully, giving employees full credit for their accomplishments, avoiding waste (e.g., turning off the lights when leaving a room), and demonstrating respect by using good manners.[5] Together, these small acts add up to behavior that employees can and will respect.

To some extent at least, a supervisor gets the best results using the leadership style with which he or she feels comfortable. That comfort level depends on characteristics such as the following:

- *The manager's values*—What is most important to the supervisor in carrying out his or her job? Is it the department's contribution to company profits? The employees' or the manager's own growth and development? A manager concerned about developing employees is most likely to involve them in making decisions.
- *Level of confidence in employees*—The more confidence the supervisor has in employees, the more he or she will involve them in planning and decision making. Marty Schottenheimer, coach of the NFL's San Diego Chargers, once had a rule that no player would be allowed to play on any Sunday if he had not been at practice by the preceding Friday. However, as the coach developed

confidence in an executive committee of players, he began to respect concerns, such as the idea that a player might need a full week to recover from an injury. As his confidence in the committee increased, he more often relaxed the rule based on the committee's input.[6]

- *Personal leadership strengths*—Some supervisors have a talent for leading group discussions; others are better at quietly analyzing information and reaching a decision. Some are good at detecting employee wants and needs; others excel at keeping their focus on the numbers. Effective leaders capitalize on their strengths.

- *Tolerance for ambiguity*—When the supervisor involves employees in solving problems or making decisions, he or she cannot always be sure of the outcomes. Supervisors differ in their level of comfort with this uncertainty, which is called *ambiguity*.

Logically, greater diversity in the workplace would generate greater diversity in some of these characteristics, such as values and leadership strengths. Particularly noteworthy is the possibility that women bring a different set of values and experiences to the workplace than men do, a theory that has received wide attention in the business press. UCLA professor Helen Astin, who conducted a study of well-known female leaders, believes there is a "feminine way of leadership." She claims that women tend to focus on interpersonal issues and emphasize collective leadership, which involves empowering followers. The female leaders Astin studied tended to describe accomplishments as the accomplishments of the whole group, not just the leader.

Similarly, Alice H. Eagly, a social psychology professor at Purdue University, reviewed more than 360 studies on gender and leadership. She found that the only significant difference between men and women in these studies was that women tended to be more democratic in their leadership style. In many cases, this leadership style is supported by a view that the people in an organization are interdependent. A leader with this belief is more likely to respond to a problem by saying to employees, "Let's work out a solution together." To learn how leadership practices might also vary across cultures, see the "Supervision and Diversity" box.

Characteristics of Subordinates

In selecting a leadership style, smart supervisors consider their employees as well as themselves. Employees who are at their most creative and productive when they have a lot of freedom will dig in their heels if their supervisor is autocratic with them, even if that is the supervisor's natural leadership style. At the other extreme, employees who expect and rely on structure and direction will tend to drift and even become paralyzed if their leader has a laissez-faire or democratic style.

What should the supervisor look for in deciding the kind of supervision employees want? Here are some characteristics that should influence the choice:

- *Need for independence*—People who want a lot of direction will welcome autocratic leadership.

- *Readiness to assume responsibility*—Employees who are eager to assume responsibility will appreciate a democratic or laissez-faire style of leadership.

- *Tolerance for ambiguity*—Employees who are tolerant of ambiguity will accept a leadership style that gives them more say in solving problems.

- *Interest in the problem to be solved*—Employees who are interested in a problem and think it is important will want to help solve it.

SUPERVISION AND DIVERSITY

LEADING ACROSS CULTURES

Supervisors can most effectively lead their employees when they are aware of cultural values that shape the way people respond to leaders. Awareness of those values can signal leaders when they need to adapt their words or deeds.

Cultures vary in terms of showing respect to a person in authority. In some cultures, questioning a leader would be disrespectful, so leaders do not expect to hear fresh ideas from their followers. U.S. organizations tend to emphasize employee empowerment and seek employees' ideas, so U.S. leaders in foreign countries have to persistently communicate their desire for employees to offer questions and suggestions. When Johnson & Johnson entered Russia, managers had to persevere in conveying to Russian marketing staffers that they should speak up when they had more effective ideas for launching products in their own country.

Some cultures and organizations want employees to take risks in order to innovate; others are quick to punish failure. In an organization that promotes innovation and risk taking, leaders may have to actively promote this value in their goals and rewards. A multinational manufacturing company overcame this hurdle in Eastern Europe by telling new employees that for a two-year period, they could make reasonable mistakes and learn from those mistakes without suffering consequences. Communication and productivity improved as the employees felt more relaxed about trying new ideas.

Some cultures place great importance on a person's status and reputation within the group. In China, Wal-Mart consciously assigns importance to each individual's role. This effort gives Wal-Mart an advantage in China, because the company's strategy depends on having highly motivated workers.

Many cultures, including Latin cultures, value communication that is relationship oriented. Other cultures value privacy more highly, so work communication focuses more on getting the job done. A non-Hispanic supervisor of Hispanic employees might lead more effectively by adopting a greater relationship orientation.

Sources: Keith S. Collins, "Penetrating Barriers: Communicating Clearly in the International Organization," *Communication World*, June–July 2003; Arturo Castro, "Effective Leadership of Latin Employees," *Club Management*, April 2003, both downloaded from Business & Company Resource Center, http://galenet.galegroup.com.

- *Understanding of and identification with goals*—Employees who understand and identify with organizational or departmental goals will want to play an active role in deciding how to meet those goals. Furthermore, the supervisor will find that such employees are reliable in carrying out their responsibilities. Employees who don't identify with goals may need more active direction and control from the supervisor.

- *Knowledge and experience*—Employees with the knowledge necessary to solve a problem are more apt to want to help find a solution. Furthermore, their input will be more valuable to the supervisor. Thus, someone who is new on the job will probably need a supervisor who engages in both task-oriented and relationship-oriented behavior, but the supervisor can become less involved as the employee gains experience.

- *Expectations*—Some employees expect to participate in making decisions and solving problems. Others think that a supervisor who does not tell them what to do is not doing a good job.

Organizations that use self-managing work teams (see Chapter 3) generally encourage a variety of employee characteristics that are associated with the successful use of democratic leadership and a low degree of task-oriented behavior. They tend to train employees to assume extensive responsibility (or select such employees). They generally provide the team with information about issues to be handled and the performance of the organization and the team. This information should produce knowledgeable employees with an understanding of the problems faced by the team. Finally, the members of a self-managing work team expect to be involved in making a wide variety of decisions. What is left for a leader to do? Much of importance: communicating a vision of the team's mission and fostering a climate in which team members contribute to and care about the success of the team and the organization.

Characteristics of the Situation

In addition to the personalities and preferences of the supervisor and subordinates, the situation itself helps determine what leadership style will be most effective. Several characteristics are important:

- *Type of organization*—Organizations often lend themselves to one leadership style or another. If the organization expects supervisors to manage large numbers of employees, a democratic leadership style may be time consuming and relatively challenging. If higher-level managers clearly value one style of leadership, the supervisor may find it difficult to use a different style and still be considered effective. Lee Cockerell, who recently retired from his post as executive vice president of operations for Walt Disney World, got his start in business as a waiter at the Hilton Hotel in the Washington, DC. A supervisor took a chance on hiring Cockerell, who had never been in such an upscale establishment, and then directed his every move to meet the hotel's exacting standards. Cockerell recalls that this supervisor's autocratic but respectful leadership style was a necessary education in the standards of the company. Cockerell took a similar commitment to quality with him when he continued his career at Disney, where the attitudes and actions of frontline employees are what make each customer's experience memorable.[7]

- *Effectiveness of the group*—Regardless of the characteristics of individual employees, some groups are more successful in handling decisions than others. If a department, team, or other work group has little experience in making its own decisions, the supervisor may find that an authoritarian approach is easier to use. Supervisors should delegate decisions to groups that can handle the responsibility.

- *The problem or task*—The work group or individual employees can easily reach a solution to relatively simple problems, but the supervisor should retain greater control of complex or difficult problems. In addition to its difficulty, the supervisor should consider how structured a task is. A structured task—that is, one with a set procedure to follow—is best managed by an autocratic leader. However, some tasks, such as generating ideas to improve customer service or planning the department picnic, are relatively unstructured. These tasks benefit from the employee involvement sought by a democratic, people-oriented leader.

- *Time available*—An autocratic leader is in a position to make decisions quickly. Group decision making usually requires more time for discussion and the sharing of ideas. Thus, the manager should use a relatively democratic leadership style only when time allows for it.

One study reported in the *Harvard Business Review* found that the most effective leaders choose from six distinctive styles, depending on their goals and the situation. The styles can be briefly summarized as follows:

1. Coercive, which demands compliance. (The leader says, "Do what I tell you!")
2. Pace-setting, which sets extremely high performance standards. ("Do as I do, now!")

3. Coaching, which focuses on developing people. ("Try this.")

4. Democratic, which seeks consensus through participation. ("What do you think?")

5. Affiliative, which creates harmony and emotional bonds. ("People come first.")

6. Authoritative, which mobilizes employees with enthusiasm and vision. ("Come with me.")[8]

When employees and managers work in teams, a democratic leadership style based on Theory Y, which emphasizes people, is appropriate. Some management experts think that a coach is a good analogy for this leadership style. Coaches delegate responsibility to carry out operations, and they are willing to share authority. They focus on picking qualified people, helping them learn to do their jobs well, and inspiring peak performance. Joseph Lipsey, who manages training and development for a major insurance company, credits this leadership style with transforming his department from one with little impact to one that works effectively:

> By driving out fear, hiring top-notch people . . . implementing a team structure, making decisions by consensus, and unleashing the tremendous creativity and desire to contribute and to find meaning in work that is innate to everyone, we have created a real "force" within this organization.[9]

GIVING DIRECTIONS

Supervisors can practice leadership by giving directions. In the workplace, giving directions can range from issuing detailed formal procedures for a particular task to inspiring the work group with a mission that unites them in a common cause. The supervisor can give directions simply by stating what an employee is to do in a particular situation. Or, if the supervisor leads a group that is expected to make many of its own decisions, the supervisor's directions may emphasize broad principles: "In our group, we don't waste time blaming; we figure out how to convert this angry customer into a happy one." In all cases, the way the supervisor gives directions can influence how willingly and how well employees respond. (See Figure 8.5.)

The supervisor should make sure that the employee understands the directions. If the supervisor says, "I need those figures today," can the employee leave a note on the supervisor's desk at 6:00 p.m., half an hour after the supervisor has left? Or does the supervisor need time to review the numbers, so that he actually needs

FIGURE 8.5
Checklist for Giving Directions

☑	Wording is appropriately specific for the task
☑	Wording is clear and unambiguous
☑	Employee can restate directions
☑	Supervisor verifies progress toward completion
☑	Directions do not change after project is assigned
☑	Employees know reasons for the directions
☑	Supervisor's tone is confident and polite, not apologetic

them by a specific time, say, 3:00 p.m.? Thus, the supervisor should state directions in specific, clear terms. Another way to make sure employees understand is to ask them to restate what they are supposed to do and to check on their progress before they are finished. (Chapter 10 provides further guidelines for effective communication.)

Supervisors may benefit from regularly asking their employees for feedback about their ability to give directions. The most useful feedback comes from specific questions: "Are my directions usually clear, or do you depend on co-workers to help you figure out what I want?" and "Do I often change my mind about what you should do after you've already started an assignment?" When the supervisor emphasizes conveying broad goals and letting employees work out the details, the supervisor will need to seek evidence that employees know what those broad goals are.

The supervisor should make sure employees also see the reason for the directions. In a crisis, people are willing to pitch in; they easily can see a need. Thus, if a hospital patient has a cardiac arrest, the staff members do not object to someone barking orders in an effort to revive the patient. But sometimes the supervisor has to identify the crisis or explain the need. The supervisor on a loading dock could say, "This order is for our biggest customer, who's getting fed up with late shipments. If we don't get the order on the truck today, we'll be in deep trouble." That approach is more likely to get results than giving no reason and shouting, "Get moving!"

The most effective way to give instructions is to do so confidently and politely, but without apologies. If a supervisor says, "I'm sorry—I know you're busy, but I'd appreciate seeing those lab results by noon," the employee may think that he or she has been given an option, not instructions. The employee also may be unclear about who is in charge of the department. Instead, the supervisor can say, "Please have those lab results ready by noon." Of course, it is never appropriate to be rude.

If employees are not complying with a supervisor's directions, the supervisor can examine whether the directions follow these guidelines. Perhaps employees do not understand what is expected of them, or perhaps they do not realize that the supervisor is giving them directions, not a suggestion.

HUMAN RELATIONS

Leading is clearly an application of human relations skills and is perhaps the most important measure of whether the supervisor excels at relations with his or her employees. Of course, supervisors need good human relations skills for other relationships as well. They need to work effectively with their manager and peers and be positive about themselves.

Most books about business focus on the technical skills of managing. How can a supervisor develop human relations skills? Ways to get along with almost anyone include projecting a positive attitude, taking an interest in other people, and helping out. In addition, the supervisor can take steps to work on each of the categories of relationships that are important to his or her success.

Supervisors' Self-Images

Order-processing supervisor Eleanor Chakonas thinks of herself as a risk taker and a person who makes things happen. When she was asked to plan the expansion of her department, she attacked the job with a gusto that inspired her employees to contribute to the effort. The result was a plan that called for extra efforts by employees but would result in the department performing beyond management expectations. A supervisor who considers him- or herself more cautious or prone to error than Eleanor would have approached the planning job differently.

self-concept
A person's self-image

The self-image a supervisor has—that is, the supervisor's **self-concept**—influences the supervisor's behavior. Someone who believes that he or she has power will act powerfully; someone who thinks of him- or herself as intelligent is apt to make careful decisions. It is worthwhile for supervisors to be aware of the thoughts they have of themselves. Business consultant Susan Surplus has observed that supervisors typically are people who were experts and high performers at jobs they now supervise. Their self-concept often involves thinking of themselves as people who individually could get the job done. Success as a supervisor requires shifting that self-concept. As leaders, supervisors must think in terms of how to create a positive team environment, in which the team members can get the job done.[10]

Awareness of their self-concepts can also help supervisors cultivate positive thoughts, which will help them act in positive ways. When you find yourself thinking "I'm so stupid" or "I wouldn't lose my cool the way he did," notice what you are thinking, and consider what it says about your self-concept. Take time to consider what your strengths and goals are. When you do something well, give yourself credit. When someone compliments you, smile and say thank you. Making the effort to behave this way will allow you not only to understand yourself better but also to discover that your beliefs about yourself are more positive.

Supervisors' Relationships with Their Employees

A supervisor who is liked and respected by employees will inspire them to work harder and better. But this does not mean the supervisor should be friends with employees. Instead, the supervisor should consistently treat them in a way that reflects his or her role as a part of management. Today's supervisor empowers rather than commands employees, seeking consensus and spending time with employees to learn what they need for job success and career development.

Some of the most inspiring stories of leadership describe leaders who genuinely care about employees and value their ability to contribute to the organization. Basketball coach Phil Jackson is a familiar example of a leader who takes an interest in his team's players. For example, he determined that Shaquille O'Neal responded well to a fatherly kind of mentoring. Jackson encouraged O'Neal to finish earning his college degree and gave the star player time off during the 2000–2001 season to attend his graduation at Louisiana State University. At the Pacific Gas and Electric Company (PG&E), division manager Gayle Hamilton showed her dedication to her employees by her physical presence, even in difficult circumstances. During an earthquake, her division's office building in Santa Cruz, California, was seriously damaged. PG&E offered to let her work from an office farther north, but Hamilton opted to stay with her crew, even though she had to work in a trailer parked next to railroad tracks. She made her choice out of a commitment to be "a part of what is going on, rather than apart from [it]."[11]

Supervisors as Role Models

For employees, the supervisor is the person who most directly represents management and the organization. Thus, when employees evaluate the organization,

SUPERVISION AND ETHICS

HOW TO BE A GOOD ROLE MODEL

A role model is someone who shows us how to behave properly. Organizations depend on supervisors to act as role models for ethical behavior. Supervisors should think about the kinds of behavior they expect from their employees, and then be sure to engage in the same kind of behavior themselves.

Here are some suggestions for being a good role model:

- Give employees a respectful hearing. If an employee's performance is poor, listen to the employee's side of the story before taking action.
- Give rewards based on objective measures. This shows that you are fair.
- Make time for worthy causes. Volunteer for charitable work during your personal time.
- Call daily meetings before work gets started. Give employees a chance to communicate their questions and concerns. Listen respectfully, and make positive changes when you can.
- Assign reasonable amounts of work to each employee. Give all qualified employees a chance at the tasks they enjoy, and spread unpopular tasks around fairly, too.
- Promote opportunities for employees to learn new skills or advance in the organization.
- In terms of priorities, put your employees ahead of your ego. When employees are successful or creative, make sure they get the credit. Trust that when they look good, you will look good too.
- Apply ethical standards to all decisions. Never lie, cheat, or steal, even on small matters.

Sources: T. L. Stanley, "Be a Good Role Model for Your Employees," *Supervision*, January 2004, downloaded from InfoTrac, http://web5.infotrac.galegroup.com; Edward E. Lawler III, *Treat People Right: How Organizations and Individuals Can Propel Each Other into a Virtuous Spiral of Success* (San Francisco: Jossey-Bass, 2003), pp. 205–209.

they look at the supervisor's behavior. They also use the supervisor's behavior as a guide for how they should act. If a supervisor takes long lunch breaks, employees will either think that the use of the supervisor's time is unimportant or believe that the company unfairly lets managers get away with violating rules.

To set a good example for employees, the supervisor should follow all the rules and regulations that cover employees. The supervisor should be impartial in the treatment of employees—for example, assigning unpopular tasks to everyone, not just to certain employees. Supervisors also should be ethical, that is, honest and fair. (Chapter 4 discusses ethics in greater detail.) For more ideas on being a positive role model, see the "Supervision and Ethics" box.

Developing Trust

In leading employees, a supervisor is asking them to go somewhere new, to strive for a more challenging goal. Employees will be reluctant to take a chance on pursuing the supervisor's vision unless they feel they can trust the supervisor. Therefore, building trust is an essential part of leadership.

Trust comes from being trustworthy. Employees are most likely to trust a leader who has what human relations expert Ed Lisoski calls "the three *c*'s" of courage, character, and conviction.[12] *Courage* is necessary for speaking the truth, taking a chance on a new idea, and taking responsibility for one's mistakes. *Character* involves behaving ethically, as described in Chapter 4. *Conviction* means standing firm, remaining faithful to one's carefully chosen values and goals. Paul Taffinder, quoted on leadership at the beginning of this chapter, emphasizes that conviction is important because it energizes other people when they see it in their leader. Taffinder notes that people who have had to overcome difficult experiences in their past often make good leaders because the hard times inspired them to reflect on what they believe in and where they are headed. This process develops the leaders' conviction about great ideas, so when these leaders express their conviction, others believe in and trust them.[13] Even if you have been fortunate not to have experienced great suffering, you can develop your ability to lead by thinking about your values and objectives and practicing how to express them with conviction.

Building trust takes time and effort, yet the supervisor can lose it with a single unreasonable act. The most important way to build trust is to engage in fair, predictable behavior. The supervisor should fulfill promises and give employees credit when they do something well. Keeping the lines of communication open also builds trust. When the supervisor listens carefully and shares information, employees will not think that he or she is hiding something from them. Training and education consultant Jim Kouzes keeps his firm's computer printer next to his desk. He considers the resulting interruptions worthwhile because of what he learns from his employees when they stop by to pick up their documents.

Supervisors' Relationships with Their Managers

No matter how good you are at planning, organizing, and leading, your ability to get along with your manager can determine the course of your career at a particular organization. That may not always seem fair, but your manager is the person who usually decides whether you will be promoted, get a juicy assignment or a raise, or even have a job next week. A manager who likes to work with you is more likely to take a favorable (or at least tolerant) view of your performance.

Expectations

Although every manager is different, most expect certain kinds of behavior from the people they manage. As summarized in Figure 8.6, a supervisor can reasonably assume that the manager expects loyalty, cooperation, communication, and results.

FIGURE 8.6
What Managers Expect of Supervisors

- *Loyalty* means the supervisor says only positive things about company policies and about his or her manager. If the supervisor cannot think of anything positive to say, silence is better than criticism.
- *Cooperation* means the supervisor works with others in the organization to achieve organizational goals. If the manager offers criticism, the supervisor should listen and try to make improvements. If the criticism seems unreasonable, the supervisor should first make sure that there was no misunderstanding and then try to find constructive aspects of the criticism.
- *Communication* means the manager expects the supervisor to keep him or her informed about the department's performance.
- *Results* means the supervisor should see that the department meets or exceeds its objectives. The best way to look good to the manager is to have a high-performing department.

Learning about Your Manager

You can better meet your manager's expectations if you understand him or her as an individual. Observe how your manager handles various situations, try to determine his or her leadership style, and notice what issues are of most importance to your manager. As much as possible, adapt your own style to match your manager's when you are with this person. Also, ask what your manager's expectations are for you and how your performance will be measured.

If You Are Dissatisfied

Despite your best efforts, you may find that you are dissatisfied with your manager. It happens to many people at some point in their career. If you are unhappy, begin by considering the source of the problem. Most interpersonal problems arise from the behavior and attitudes of two people, so determine what changes you can make to improve the situation.

If you cannot improve the situation enough by changing your own behavior, talk to your manager, stating the types of actions you are dissatisfied with and how those actions are affecting you. If you cannot resolve the problem, your best bet is probably to hunt for another job. But try to keep your present job while you look for a new one. Prospective employers look more favorably on job candidates who are already employed.

Supervisors' Relationships with Their Peers

If you get along well with your peers in the same and other departments, they will help you look good and get your job done. Their resentment or dislike for you can cause an endless stream of problems. Therefore, supervisors need to cultivate good relations with their peers.

Competition

Sometimes your peers will be competing with you for raises, bonuses, or promotions. Remember that the more you can cooperate, the better you will all look. This means that your competition should be fair and as friendly as possible. If you try to sabotage a co-worker, you probably will be the one who ultimately ends up looking bad.

Criticism

Because you are trying to maintain a positive attitude, you should not go looking for things to criticize about your peers or anyone else. However, if you know that a co-worker has done something that works against the organization's best interests, you should go directly to that person and point out the problem. It usually helps to be polite and diplomatic and to assume that the problem was unintended—an error or an oversight.

If the co-worker resists listening to your criticism and the problem will harm the company, its employees, or its customers, then you should go to your manager to discuss the problem. Focus on the problem and its consequences to the organization, not on the personalities involved. Gossip is not the behavior of a leader; overcoming problems is.

SKILLS MODULE

PART ONE: CONCEPTS

Summary

8.1 Discuss the possible link between personal traits and leadership ability.
To find which people will succeed as leaders, researchers have looked for traits that successful leaders hold in common. Traits that may be significant include a sense of responsibility, self-confidence, high energy level, empathy, an internal locus of control, and a sense of humor. However, research results have been inconsistent, leading to the conclusion that traits alone do not predict success as a leader.

8.2 Compare leadership styles that a supervisor might adopt.
Depending on how much authority they retain, supervisors can be authoritarian (retaining much authority), democratic (sharing authority), or laissez faire (giving up most authority). Supervisors may also be task oriented, people oriented, or both. They may build their leadership style on Theory X assumptions that employees must be coerced to work, on Theory Y assumptions that employees can be motivated to seek responsibility and achieve objectives creatively, or on Theory Z values such as employee involvement and a focus on long-term goals.

8.3 Explain contingency theories of leadership.
These theories hold that leaders can be most effective by matching different leadership styles to varying circumstances. For example, Fiedler's contingency model says that whether people- or task-oriented leaders perform better depends on leader–member relations, task structure, and the leader's position power. Fiedler recommends that if the leader's preferred leadership style does not fit the situation, the characteristics of the situation should be changed. In contrast, Hersey and Blanchard's life cycle theory maintains that the leader should modify his or her behavior to fit the situation. As followers mature, leaders should use varying levels of task and relationship behavior.

8.4 Identify criteria for choosing a leadership style.
The supervisor should select a leadership style that suits his or her own characteristics, as well as those of the employees and the situation. Criteria for evaluating the characteristics of the leader are his or her values, level of confidence in employees, leadership strengths, and tolerance for ambiguity. Criteria for evaluating the characteristics of employees include their need for independence, readiness to assume responsibility, tolerance for ambiguity, interest in the problem, expectations, understanding of and identification with

goals, and knowledge and experience. Criteria for evaluating the characteristics of the situation include the type of organization, effectiveness of the group, the nature of the problem or task, and the time available.

8.5 Describe guidelines for giving directions to employees.
The supervisor should make sure that employees understand the directions and the reasons behind them. The supervisor should give the instructions confidently and politely, but without being apologetic.

8.6 Indicate why supervisors need to understand and improve their views of themselves.
The supervisor's self-concept influences how he or she behaves. People who believe they are capable tend to act capably. The supervisor needs to cultivate the self-concept of an effective leader.

8.7 Explain how supervisors can develop and maintain good relations with their employees, managers, and peers.
The supervisor should project a positive attitude, take an interest in others, and help out as needed. With employees, the supervisor should set a good example, be ethical, and develop trust. The supervisor should give his or her manager loyalty, cooperation, communication, and results and adapt to the manager's style. The supervisor should keep competition with peers as fair and friendly as possible and offer any necessary criticism in a constructive way.

Key Terms

leading, *p.* 199
internal locus of control, *p.* 201
authoritarian leadership, *p.* 202

democratic leadership, *p.* 202
laissez-faire leadership, *p.* 202

Theory X, *p.* 203
Theory Y, *p.* 203
Theory Z, *p.* 205
self-concept, *p.* 213

Review and Discussion Questions

1. Describe the six traits that researchers believe may indicate a good leader. However, research has *not* established a clear link between personality traits and leadership success. What other factors do you think might contribute to success or failure?

2. Claire Callahan supervises the camping department of a large outdoor equipment store. The store manager (Callahan's boss) has given her the objective of increasing sales by 10 percent during the next quarter. Choose one of the three leadership styles (authoritarian, democratic, or laissez faire). Then state three or more steps that Callahan might take to influence her employees to meet the new sales objective.

3. Ann Wong is the accounts payable supervisor at an insurance company. During a time of layoffs, she decides to adopt a more people-oriented leadership style than the style she normally uses. What does this change mean?

4. Pete Polito supervises a cross-functional team whose task is to evaluate whether the in-line skates his company manufactures are safe and up-to-date in design and style. Using Theory Y, what steps might Polito take to lead his team to its goal?

5. Do you think it is more realistic to expect supervisors to adjust the situation to meet their preferred leadership style, as suggested by Fiedler's contingency model of leadership, or to adjust their leadership style to fit the situation, as suggested by Hersey and Blanchard? Explain your reasoning.

6. In which of the following situations would you recommend that the supervisor use an authoritarian style of leadership? In which situations would you recommend a democratic style? Explain your choices.

   a. The supervisor's manager says, "Top management wants us to start getting employees to suggest ways to improve quality in all areas of operations." Each department is given wide latitude in how to accomplish this.

   b. A supervisor is uncomfortable in meetings and likes to be left alone to figure out solutions to problems. The supervisor's employees believe that a good supervisor is able to tell them exactly what to do.

   c. A shipment of hazardous materials is on its way to a warehouse. The supervisor is responsible for instructing employees how to handle the materials when they arrive later that day.

7. Prakash Singh prefers a very democratic style of leadership and is uncomfortable telling someone what to do. His solution is to make his instructions as general as possible so that employees will feel they have more control. He also tends to apologize for being authoritarian. Do you think this method of giving directions is effective? Why or why not?

8. Why should supervisors have a positive view of themselves? What are some ways a supervisor can be aware of and improve his or her self-concept?

9. Identify the human relations error in each of the following situations. Suggest a better way to handle each.

   a. Carole Fields's boss compliments her on the report she submitted yesterday. She says, "It was no big deal."

   b. When Rich Peaslee was promoted to supervisor, he told the other employees, "Now, remember, I was one of the gang before this promotion, and I'll still be one of the gang."

   c. The second-shift supervisor observes that the first-shift employees have not left their work areas clean for the last three days. He complains to his manager about the lax supervision on the first shift.

10. Carla Santos doesn't get along with her new manager; the two have disliked each other since the day they met. Santos was transferred to a new department when the previous supervisor left the company, so neither she nor her manager actually chose to work together. Santos doesn't want her job as a supervisor to be jeopardized by an unpleasant relationship. What steps might she take to improve the situation?

PART TWO: SKILL-BUILDING

YOU SOLVE THE PROBLEM

Reflecting back on page 199, what characteristics of an effective leader does Frederick Hill exhibit? Hill learned much about leading by listening to advice, as well as observing and responding to challenging situations over the course of many years. As a group, discuss whether Hill's lessons could be taught to a new supervisor over a shorter period of time.

List the lessons that Hill has learned about leading, and develop a one-week training plan for teaching those lessons to new supervisors. Consider any reasonable training idea, including lectures (and who would conduct them), trips, movies, role-playing, and any other learning methods you have used in this or other courses.

Do you think your group's training program will be as effective for new supervisors as Hill's life lessons were for him? Why or why not?

Problem-Solving Case: *Top-Down and Bottom-Up Style at US Airways*

Rakesh Gangwal was chief executive of US Airways Group (formerly USAir) until 2001. He planned to expand US Airways' route network, increase its fleet, improve profitability, and enhance several key aspects of service, such as on-time performance. His management style is an active one that matches his ambitious goals, but what many observers have noticed about Gangwal is that he manages in two ways—from the top down and from the bottom up.

The top-down part of his method was apparent in the way he reviewed decisions made deep within the organization. At the same time, the dozens of task forces he established asked employees to look into and report on everything from in-flight safety to corporate competitive advantages, and that is where the bottom-up style comes in. As he says, "I love it when frontline employees come up with ideas, because I know they are the things that generally work."

Although Gangwal is happiest working in two different directions at once, some of his division heads had to adjust to the flow of information and input from below. Far from allowing them to relinquish their authority, however, Gangwal demanded that his managers also develop and implement their own ideas. Known for his candor, he admitted that his expectations were high—about three-quarters of the firm's vice presidents were replaced after he came on board. "I do impose my views in setting directions and in what we are trying to attain, but then I let the process take over. It's a very fine line," he says.

Another characteristic of Gangwal's style is that he pays attention to details. He personally reviewed training videos for the airline's flight attendants and worried about awkward body language in the films. He also reviewed menu changes, edited the script that flight attendants use for their preflight and in-flight announcements, and adjusted the duties of maintenance supervisors. He hoped at some point to step back from the details, but he first wanted to put his "imprint" on US Airways. He put in 12-hour days at the office and worked several more hours at home each night.

Gangwal resigned from US Airways in November 2001 to take a position as president of a travel reservation system. In an unusual move, the Transport Workers Union (TWU) in 2003 nominated Gangwal for a seat on US Airways' board of directors. (The TWU and the Association of Flight Attendants share a seat on the board of directors. They received this position in exchange for making wage concessions in 2002.) At the time of the nomination, Bill Gray, a TWU official, described Gangwal as "tough but fair," adding, "He has our respect." However, Gangwal declined the nomination.

1. Would you characterize Rakesh Gangwal as an authoritarian, a democratic, or a laissez-faire leader? Why?

2. Do you think Gangwal has a Theory X, Theory Y, or Theory Z attitude? Explain your answer.

3. US Airways recently declared bankruptcy and announced plans to restructure itself as a discount airline similar to JetBlue or America West. This was US Airways' second declaration of bankruptcy since the airline industry suffered a drop in business following the terrorist attacks of September 2001. How do you think this change in the business environment affects the role of leading US Airways? Does the bankruptcy require a different kind of leadership? Imagine you were a supervisor of baggage handlers for US Airways. How do you think the bankruptcy filing and restructuring would affect the way you should lead your group?

Sources: Adam Bryant, "Like His Mentor at US Airways, the Chief Has an Eye for Details," *The New York Times,* November 29, 1998, sec. 3, p. 2; Ted Reed, "Unions Proposed Former Chief for US Airways Board," *Knight Ridder/Tribune Business News,* April 8, 2003, downloaded from Business & Company Resource Center, http://galenet.galegroup.com; Susan Carey, "US Airways Files for Chapter 11 a Second Time," *The Wall Street Journal,* September 13, 2004, http://online.wsj.com.

Knowing Yourself

Could You Be a CEO?

Every year *Inc.* magazine surveys the 500 fastest growing firms in the country and reports on their success. In 1998, *Inc.*'s editors also examined the personal and professional characteristics of the 500 company CEOs. The following quiz will tell you how you stack up, with scoring based on the game of baseball.

1. *Marriage*—More than 80 percent of the CEOs in *Inc.*'s survey were married with a stable home life. You get two hits for being married and staying that way. Anything else is a strikeout.

2. *Education*—Education matters more than family income among this elite group; nearly half the CEOs are graduates of four-year colleges. Give yourself two hits if you plan a graduate degree, one for a college degree, and a strikeout for anything less.

3. *Age*—More than three-quarters of the CEOs were 40 or younger. Two hits are awarded for being under 41, and one hit for being between 41 and 50. Outside that range, you've struck out.

4. *Business sector*—The service sector has grown at the expense of manufacturing and selling and distribution. You get one hit if you run a service company; otherwise, you strike out.

5. *Industry*—The percentages of computer-related and telecommunications businesses among the top 500 have grown dramatically, and almost all other kinds of firms have lost ground. Add two hits if you're in computers or telecommunications and one if you're in business services. Everything else earns a strikeout.

6. *Capital*—One of five of the top firms started with less than $5,000 in capital, and most of the company founders on the list never borrowed their start-up costs. If you have enough cash right now to get under way, you score one hit. Otherwise, you strike out.

7. *Advantage*—Technology skills or the rights to some intellectual property drove the success of most of the top firms. If you control valuable intellectual property you get two hits, one if you know more about your field than anyone else, and a strikeout if neither of the above.

8. *Revenues*—"Meat and potatoes" selling by an in-house sales staff compensated with traditional salary-plus-bonus structures has produced an average growth rate of about 75 percent a year for the *Inc.* 500. You get one hit for doing things the old-fashioned way and keeping your firm growing 25 percent a year. Otherwise, you strike out.

Here's how to score. You've had 34 turns at bat, so divide your total number of hits by 34. If your "batting average" is above .300, you're doing well. Above .350 and you're doing extraordinarily well. Keep up the good work.

Source: *Inc. 500* by Eric Kriss. Copyright © 1998 by Business Innovator Group Resources/*Inc.* Reproduced with permission of Business Innovator Group Resources/*Inc.* via Copyright Clearance Center.

Pause and Reflect

1. Some of the characteristics identified in this quiz do not describe leadership ability. Why do you think marital status, education level, and age are related to CEO status?

2. Do you aim to lead as a CEO someday, or would you prefer to exercise leadership in another capacity?

FIGURE 8.7   Human Relations Competencies Checklist

Source: From *Your Attitude Is Sharing,* by Elwood N. Chapman. Copyright © 1995 Pearson Education, Inc. Reprinted by permission of Pearson Education, Inc. Upper Saddle River, NJ.

1. Consistently communicate the following attitudes to co-workers, superiors, customers, or patients:

❑ Send out positive verbal and nonverbal signals in all contacts, including telephone.
❑ Remain positive while working with those who are negative.
❑ Be positive and sensitive when those you are dealing with are not.
❑ Deal with all people in an honest, ethical, and moral way.
❑ Avoid ethnic or sexual remarks that could be misinterpreted.
❑ Maintain a sense of humor.
❑ Recognize when you begin to become negative, and start an attitude renewal project.
❑ Develop and maintain a good service attitude.

2. Demonstrate the following human relations skills in dealing with co-workers:

❑ Build and maintain equally effective horizontal working relationships with everyone in your department. Refuse to play favorites.
❑ Build a productive, no-conflict relationship with those who may have a different set of personal values.
❑ Build relationships based on mutual rewards.
❑ Develop productive, healthy relationships with those who may be substantially older or younger.
❑ Maintain a productive relationship even with individuals who irritate you at times.
❑ Treat everyone, regardless of ethnic or socioeconomic differences, with respect.
❑ Work effectively with others regardless of their sexual orientation.
❑ Do not take human relations slights or mistakes from others personally; do not become defensive or attempt to retaliate in kind.
❑ Repair an injured relationship as soon as possible.
❑ Even if you are not responsible for the damage to a working relationship, protect your career by taking the initiative to restore it.
❑ Permit others to restore a relationship with you.
❑ Release your frustrations harmlessly without damaging relationships.
❑ Handle teasing and testing without becoming upset.

3. Demonstrate the following human relations skills in dealing with your superiors:

❑ Build a strong vertical relationship with your supervisor without alienating co-workers.
❑ Be a high producer yourself and contribute to the productivity of co-workers.
❑ Survive, with a positive attitude, under a difficult supervisor until changes occur.
❑ Establish relationships that are mutually rewarding.
❑ Show you can live up to your productivity potential without alienating co-workers who do not live up to theirs.
❑ Live close to your productivity potential without extreme highs or lows regardless of difficult changes in the work environment.
❑ Do not underestimate or overestimate a superior.
❑ Report mistakes or misjudgments rather than trying to hide them.
❑ Show that you can turn any change into an opportunity, including accepting a new supervisor with a different style.
❑ Refuse to nurse small gripes into major upsets.

4. Demonstrate the following professional attitudes and human relations skills:

❑ Be an excellent listener.
❑ Establish a good attendance record.
❑ Keep a good balance between home and career so neither suffers.
❑ Demonstrate that you are self-motivated.
❑ Communicate freely and thoroughly.
❑ Prepare yourself for a promotion in such a manner that others will be happy when you succeed.
❑ Share only positive, nonconfidential data about your organization with outsiders.
❑ Pass only reliable data on to others.
❑ Keep your business and personal relationships sufficiently separated.
❑ Concentrate on the positive aspects of your job while trying to improve the negative.
❑ Make only positive comments about a third party not present.
❑ Leave a job or company in a positive manner; train your replacement so that productivity is not disturbed.
❑ If you prefer to be a stabilizer, develop patience; if you prefer to be a zigzagger, don't stomp on other people's feet, hands, or heads while climbing the success ladder.
❑ Always have a Plan B (a contingency plan for your career).
❑ Avoid self-victimization.

Class Exercise

Practicing Human Relations Principles

Divide the class into groups of four or five students. Each group is assigned one of the four sections in Figure 8.7, which is a checklist of ways that employees, including supervisors, can demonstrate competence in human relations.

Each group discusses the principles in its section of the checklist. Based on jobs they have held or situations they have observed, group members describe good or bad human relations practices. In particular, consider how you have seen supervisors practice or fail to practice these principles.

After the groups have discussed these principles among themselves, they take turns making presentations. Each group selects one principle to present to the class. One representative (or more) from the group gives a brief illustration of that principle.

Source: This exercise was suggested by Corinne R. Livesay, Belhaven College, Jackson, Mississippi.

Building Supervision Skills

Leading a Team

Divide the class into teams of four to six. Either appoint a supervisor for each team, or ask for volunteers. The teams have the following objective: to determine whether the campus library is as user-friendly as it could be and to come up with suggestions for improvement if necessary.

Each supervisor should privately choose a leadership style (task oriented or people oriented) and an attitude (Theory X or Theory Y) and practice these during the exercise. Team members should decide on their own characteristics, such as a need for independence, readiness to assume responsibility, and so forth.

At the end of the exercise, each team should discuss with the rest of the class how effective its leader and team members were. Also, they should present their results: Did they come up with some good suggestions for the library?

those who know what issues to focus on and respond to problems in a positive way. By solving the right problems—the ones that can improve the quality of work—effective supervisors improve their department's activities and the service they deliver to their customers.

decision
A choice from among available alternatives

A **decision** is a choice from among available alternatives. Solving problems involves making a series of decisions: deciding that something is wrong, deciding what the problem is, deciding how to solve it. Successful problem solving depends on good decisions. This chapter describes how supervisors make decisions and offers some guidelines for doing so effectively. The chapter includes a discussion of decision making in groups and suggestions for thinking creatively.

THE PROCESS OF DECISION MAKING

Much of a supervisor's job consists of making decisions that cover all the functions of management. What should the supervisor or the department accomplish today or this week? Who should handle a particular project or machine? What should a supervisor tell his or her manager about the customer who complained yesterday? Do employees need better training or just more inspiration? How can a supervisor end the ongoing dispute between two staff members? These are only a few of the issues on which a typical supervisor must act.

In many cases, supervisors make decisions like these without giving any thought to the process of deciding. A supervisor automatically does something because it feels right or because he or she always has handled that problem that way. When a decision seems more complex, a supervisor is more likely to give thought to the decision-making process. For example, in deciding whether to purchase an expensive piece of machinery or fire an employee, a supervisor might make a careful list of pluses and minuses, trying to include all the relevant economic, practical, or ethical concerns. (Making ethical decisions is discussed in Chapter 4.) Even though making many decisions seems automatic, supervisors can improve the way they make them by understanding how the decision-making process works in theory and in practice.

The Rational Model

If you could know everything, you could make perfect decisions. How would an all-knowing person make a decision? This person would probably follow the rational model of decision making, illustrated in Figure 9.1.

Identify the Problem

According to this model, a decision maker first identifies the problem. Recall from Chapter 6 that it is important to distinguish the symptoms of a problem from the problem itself. Usually a supervisor notices the symptoms first, so he or she has to look for the underlying problem.

FIGURE 9.1 The Rational Model of Decision Making

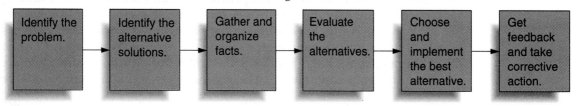

For example, Dave Frantz finds that he has to work 60 hours a week to do his job as the supervisor of a group of janitorial service workers. Frantz works hard and spends little time socializing, so his effort is not the problem. He observes that he spends approximately half his time doing paperwork required by higher-level management. He decides that the major problem is that too much of his time is spent on paperwork. (Along the way, Frantz also may find and resolve minor problems.)

Identify Alternative Solutions

The next step is to identify the alternative solutions. In our example, Frantz thinks of several possibilities. He might delegate the paperwork to other employees, hire a secretary, buy software that will automate some of the work, or persuade management to eliminate the required paperwork.

Gather and Organize Facts

Next, a decision maker gathers and organizes facts. Frantz asks his manager if he really has to do all the paperwork; the manager says yes. From the human resources office, Frantz gets information about pay scales for secretaries. He evaluates which aspects of his work could be delegated, and he collects advertisements and magazine articles about various personal computers and software.

Evaluate Alternatives

A supervisor then evaluates the alternatives from the information gathered. This process should be as objective as possible. For a supervisor, relevant criteria include the time required, the money involved, the ethical and legal acceptability of each alternative, and human considerations, such as the likely impact on employees and customers. Ideally, the alternative chosen should have a positive impact in these areas—for instance, lower costs, higher sales, better quality, and more satisfied customers and employees.[2] In the example of Dave Frantz, he determines that he cannot eliminate or delegate the paperwork. He knows that software will cost much less than a secretary, though a secretary would save more of his time. He predicts that his manager will be more open to buying the software than to hiring a secretary.

Choose and Implement the Best Alternative

A supervisor next chooses and implements the best alternative. In our example, Frantz decides he wants to buy the software and prepares a report showing the costs and benefits of doing so. He emphasizes how the company will benefit when he is more efficient and can devote more time to leading and controlling. He selects the program he thinks will best meet his needs at a reasonable cost.

When evaluating and selecting alternatives, how can a supervisor decide which is best? Sometimes the choice is obvious, but at other times, a supervisor needs formal criteria for making decisions, such as these:

- The alternative chosen should actually solve the problem. Ignoring the paperwork might enable Frantz to leave work on time, but it would not solve the problem of how to get the job done.
- An acceptable alternative must be feasible. In other words, a supervisor should be able to implement it. For example, Frantz learned that requesting less paperwork was not a feasible solution.
- The cost of the alternative should be reasonable in light of the benefits it will deliver. Frantz's employer might consider a software program to be a reasonable

expense but believe the cost of a full-time secretary is high compared with the benefits of making his job easier.

Get Feedback

The last step is to get feedback and take corrective action. In the example, Frantz takes his proposal to his manager, who suggests some additions and changes, perhaps including helping others in the company to work with the new kind of reports Frantz will be generating. Frantz orders the software, and when it arrives, he automates some of his work, using his experiences to improve on his original ideas.

When a decision will affect the course of someone's career or the expenditure of a lot of money, a supervisor will want to make the best decision possible. One way of doing so is to try to complete each of the steps in the rational model. In general, supervisors can benefit from using this model when they are making complex, formal decisions or when the consequences of a decision are great.

Human Compromises

The example of the rational model of decision making may appear far removed from the daily experiences of most supervisors. Often supervisors have neither the time nor the desire to follow all these steps to a decision. Even when supervisors try to follow these steps, they often have trouble thinking of all the alternatives or gathering all the facts they need. Sometimes no alternative emerges as clearly the best.

Given these human and organizational limitations, supervisors—like all decision makers—make compromises most of the time (see Figure 9.2). The resulting decision may be less than perfect, but it is typically one with which the decision maker is willing to live. A supervisor who is aware of the kinds of compromises people make is more apt to be aware of when he or she is using them. In addition, a supervisor may find that though some kinds of compromises are useful in some situations, others are to be avoided as much as possible.

Simplicity

Although we often think we have approached a problem with a fresh perspective and analyzed all the options, most people take a simpler approach. Usually we

FIGURE 9.2
Human
Compromises in
Decision Making

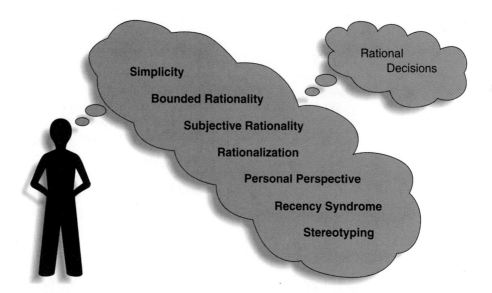

Simplicity

Bounded Rationality

Subjective Rationality

Rationalization

Personal Perspective

Recency Syndrome

Stereotyping

Rational Decisions

FIGURE 9.3
The Process of Bounded Rationality

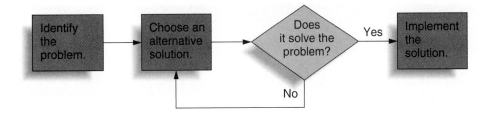

simply mull over our experiences and consider ways we have handled similar problems in the past. If we consider a few possibilities, we conclude we have covered them all. People tend to select an alternative that they have tried before and that has delivered acceptable results. The downside of this attempt at simplicity is that it tends to bypass innovative solutions, even though they sometimes deliver the best results.

Bounded Rationality

bounded rationality
Choosing an alternative that meets minimum standards of acceptability

When time, cost, or other limitations, such as the tendency to simplify, make finding the best alternative impossible or unreasonable, decision makers settle for an alternative they consider good enough. Choosing an alternative that meets minimum standards of acceptability is a form of **bounded rationality;** that is, a decision maker places limits, or *bounds,* on the *rational* model of decision making. (Figure 9.3 shows how bounded rationality works.) The decision maker considers alternatives only until one is found that meets his or her minimum criteria for acceptability.

For example, a supervisor who is fed up with tardiness might first be inclined to fire everyone who was late in a particular week. But she knows that choice will be demoralizing, create a sudden and large need for hiring and training, and probably not impress her manager. She therefore rejects that alternative. Then she remembers that she gave "timeliness awards" last year, but that did not stop tardiness, so she rejects that alternative. Finally, she remembers reading an article that recommends spelling out the consequences of the undesirable behavior and then letting the employee experience those consequences. She decides to try that approach. There probably are other ways to solve the problem—maybe even better ways—but the supervisor does not spend any more time trying to think of them.

Subjective Rationality

When people analyze alternatives, they tend to rely on their intuition and gut instincts instead of collecting impartial data. For example, a sales supervisor might estimate, "I think orders will be up next year, but just slightly, say, 2 percent." The sales supervisor did not arrive at that figure through marketing research or an analysis of industry data; instead he relied on his experience with trends in demand for the product. Thus, even when the process for arriving at the decision is otherwise rational, the numbers used in the process may be subjective and thus not completely accurate.

Rationalization

People tend to favor solutions that they believe they can justify to others. For example, production supervisor Renata King knows that her manager focuses on containing costs. When King is considering alternative ways to approach a problem, she tends to favor the low-cost alternative. Another alternative might be more

SUPERVISION AND ETHICS

WHAT DECISIONS CAN YOU JUSTIFY?

To illustrate a trap in ethical decision making, business professors Ian Ayres and Barry Nalebuff offer the example of a rider on the Metro-North commuter train from New Haven, Connecticut (where they teach), to Grand Central Station in New York City. The train is crowded, and the conductor never punches the rider's ticket. If you are that rider, you might want to keep that ticket, because it is valid for three months, and no one can see that you already used it.

Ayres and Nalebuff say their students usually reply that they would reuse the ticket, and they are ready with justifications. For example, some say the conductor is at fault for not punching the ticket. Why should the customer have to hunt for a conductor? They might squirm at the idea of simply ripping up a ticket to be honest. Others suggest giving it to a homeless person, though they object to other forms of stealing from Metro-North to aid the poor.

Other justifications are more complex and quantitative. Some students have told Ayres and Nalebuff that reusing a ticket makes up for a past late arrival or a previously lost ticket, as if ethical decisions are a means of making life fairer. Students have offered the rationale that Metro-North can raise prices to account for unpunched and reused tickets, though they are less comfortable with the comparable scenario of shoplifting occasionally because stores raise prices to cover that loss. Eventually, these discussions lead most students to conclude that they should not reuse the ticket.

From carrying on such conversations, Ayres and Nalebuff have concluded that people often seek to rationalize unethical behavior instead of admitting they might have made a mistake. The professors write, "The reasoning goes as follows: 'I am an ethical person. Hence, if I did something, it must be ethical. Let me find the ethical justification for it.'"

This is a precarious means of decision making for supervisors, who must meet high standards not only for themselves but also as role models for their employees. Before supervisors try to explain away ethical concerns, they should consider the risk that their thinking is merely rationalizing.

Source: Ian Ayres and Barry Nalebuff, "Throwaway Tickets," *Forbes,* August 16, 2004, downloaded from InfoTrac, http://web7.infotrac.galegroup.com.

---

successful, but King believes that whatever the outcome, her manager is likely to appreciate her effort to keep costs down.

Rationalization also interferes with good decisions when the decision maker focuses more on justifying an alternative than on weighing alternatives against previously defined criteria. For example, in considering how to spend the organization's money, a supervisor or manager should think about the impact on customers, employees, and company goals. But in recent scandals, some chief executives have spent great sums for purposes that seem only to enrich those executives personally. For example, when Dennis Kozlowski was CEO of Tyco International, the company bought him a $6,000 shower curtain and a $2,200 gold-plated wastebasket, among many other extraordinary expenses. Kozlowski claimed such decisions were acceptable because the Tyco board of directors authorized the spending.[3] The "Supervision and Ethics" box describes problems that rationalization causes when applied to ethical matters.

To combat problems related to rationalization, supervisors should set clear goals, communicate them to employees, and focus on meeting them. When supervisors focus on what is most important, their employees are likely to do the same.

Personal Perspective

In supervising computer programmers, Abraham Wassad has to review their documentation and the instructions they write for using their programs. Wassad pointed out to one programmer that some portions of his instructions needed clarification. "It's OK the way it is," insisted the programmer. "*I* understand it."

People often make this programmer's mistake: assuming everyone sees things the way they do. The programmer thinks the instructions must be clear to any (reasonable) person. Such assumptions can lead to incorrect decisions in many areas, including how much information to convey, what working conditions are most important to employees, or what product characteristics customers want. To avoid this problem, decision makers must find out what other people are thinking and then consider those views.

At a company that manufactures coated steel, operators were careless about measuring the coating thickness, although it was an important aspect of product quality. When the thickness was uneven or improper, customers would experience problems with their products. However, the problems might take years to become apparent, and the operators were more focused on what they could see each day, such as the amount of material leaving the plant. The company decided that the solution was to address workers' limited point of view. The workers participated in discussions with product designers, salespeople, and customers. They visited the testing facility where problems were uncovered and installations where the faulty product was in use. This effort helped workers envision why coating thickness was important, and they quickly began improving quality.[4]

Recency Syndrome

recency syndrome
The tendency to remember more easily those events that have occurred recently

People more readily remember events that have occurred recently than those that took place sometime in the past. This tendency is known as the **recency syndrome.** For example, a supervisor might remember that the last time she gave a negative performance appraisal, the employee became hostile but will not recall that a negative appraisal two years earlier led an employee to improve his performance. Clearly, in most situations, an event should not carry more weight simply because it is more recent. This is one reason decision makers need to consider alternatives as fully as is reasonable.

Stereotyping

stereotypes
Rigid opinions about categories of people

Rigid opinions about categories of people are called **stereotypes.** Stereotyping interferes with rational decision making because it limits a decision maker's understanding of the people involved. Stereotypes distort the truth that people offer a rich variety of individual strengths and viewpoints. For example, the stereotype that African-American people are athletic may seem flattering at face value but is insulting and misleading when applied to a particular African-American employee whose strengths are reliability and a gift for public speaking. No doubt, this employee would prefer to be recognized on the basis of his or her unique talents rather than on some stereotypical ones, and a supervisor who can do that will be best able to lead this employee.

The cure for stereotyping is to *not* assume that everyone is alike. Not only does this assumption oversimplify the situation, but it is also, in effect, an insult to other people. It ignores the strengths and values people receive from their culture. Rather, a supervisor should make a conscious, ongoing effort to learn about the various groups of people represented in the workplace. The purpose is to acquire information that serves as a starting point for understanding others while recognizing that individuals within any group are unique.

In addition, a supervisor needs to be aware of his or her own stereotypes about people and situations. In making a decision, a supervisor should consider whether those stereotypes truly describe the situation at hand.

SUPERVISORY SKILLS

MAKING DECISIONS AND SOLVING PROBLEMS

AUTOMATION THAT DECIDES WHO ANSWERS THE PHONE

Most people who have called a customer service phone number for help can report a mixture of good and bad experiences. Some callers stay on hold for three-quarters of an hour; others have experienced the joy of a call picked up after a ring or two. Some customer service agents seem entirely familiar with a problem's solution; others need to consult a supervisor for help.

For supervisors, the problem is ensuring that agents work efficiently and keep customers satisfied. Behind the scenes, this process involves a series of decisions about which agents should answer calls, how they can handle each call efficiently, and whose call to answer next. Fortunately, modern technology offers a variety of tools that can automate most of these decisions, freeing supervisors to concentrate on helping employees develop their skills.

To help employees work efficiently, call centers may decide to adopt performance management software. These programs are best known for collecting data on how well employees meet certain targets, such as completing calls in a given amount of time. Advanced performance management software can also automate employees' decisions. For example, on the basis of information provided by callers, the software may display scripts for employees to follow, including solutions to customers' problems, as well as related products that tend to interest customers with similar needs. In addition, performance data can help employees and their supervisors identify areas in which they need to improve so that they can make decisions about training and coaching.

Computer software can also make sophisticated decisions about routing phone calls to help the call center meet its overall goals. You might think that when you call a center, each call would be answered in order as the call center's agents become available. In fact, many call centers use software to direct the calls according to a variety of goals. A relatively simple way to do this is to assign priority levels to customers. Using the customer's phone number or another ID, the software determines the customer's value to the company (e.g., heavy spenders have high priority). So that lower-value customers don't stay on hold beyond the limits of their patience, their priority level rises gradually as they wait for a turn.

More sophisticated software also takes into account the skills of the agents answering the calls. The agents are rated on the basis of data gathered about such measures as their training and history of resolving complaints without needing help from others. When customers call, the system collects information about the type of problem, and then the call is routed to the agent best positioned to help with that type of call most efficiently.

Of course, software will not be perfect at handling out-of-the-ordinary decisions. But considering the huge volume of calls to be routed and answered by call centers, automation saves a tremendous amount of decision-making power and time.

Sources: Keith Dawson, "Turn Measurement into Action and Change," *Call Center,* August 1, 2006; Eli Borodow and Kevin Hayden, "IP Contact Center Technology: Eliminating the Risks (Part VII)," *Customer Interaction Solutions,* August 2005, both downloaded from Business & Company Resource Center, http://galenet.galegroup.com.

GUIDELINES FOR DECISION MAKING

Should a supervisor always avoid human compromises in making decisions? Not necessarily. In some situations, seeking to match the rational model would be too costly and time consuming. Sometimes supervisors minimize human compromises by using computer technology to automate part of the decision-making process. For an example, see the "Supervisory Skills" box. With or without modern technology, a supervisor has a variety of ways to make decisions more rationally. The following paragraphs provide further guidelines for making decisions in the workplace.

Consider the Consequences

A supervisor should be aware of the possible consequences of a decision. For example, hiring and firing decisions can have great consequences for the performance of the department. Purchases of inexpensive items are less critical than purchases of major equipment and computer systems. Some decisions affect the safety of workers, while others make only a slight difference in their comfort.

When the consequences of a decision are great, a supervisor should spend more time on the decision, following the rational model of decision making and seeking to include as many alternatives as possible. When the consequences of the decision are slight, a supervisor should limit the time and money spent in identifying and evaluating alternatives. A supervisor may choose to accept some of the human compromises described previously.

Respond Quickly in a Crisis

When a nuclear reactor is overheating, the supervisor has no time to weigh each employee's qualifications and select the best employee for each task in handling the crisis. When a store's customer is shouting about poor service, the supervisor has no time to list all the possible responses. Both cases require fast action.

In a crisis, a supervisor should quickly select the course of action that seems best. This is an appropriate application of bounded rationality. Instead of waiting to evaluate other alternatives, the supervisor should begin implementing the solution and interpreting feedback to see whether it is working. On the basis of the feedback, the supervisor may modify his or her choice of a solution.

Reflecting on his career, Jackson Tai, now chief executive of the financial services company DBS Group Holdings, is most proud of a decision in which he acted quickly to meet high ethical standards. A few years ago, a Hong Kong branch was being renovated, and dozens of safe deposit boxes were destroyed in an accident. The company immediately assumed full responsibility, apologized publicly, and offered compensation to the customers whose items were damaged or destroyed. Tai says the company was admired "for the fact that we were decisive and took seriously our accountability to customers."[5]

Inform the Manager

A supervisor's manager does not want to hear about every minor decision the supervisor makes each day. However, the manager does need to know what is happening in the department, so the supervisor should inform the manager about major decisions, including those that affect meeting departmental objectives, responses to a crisis, and any controversial decision.

When the manager needs to know about a decision, it is usually smart for a supervisor to discuss the problem before reaching and announcing the decision. The manager may see an aspect of the problem that has escaped the supervisor's attention or have different priorities that lead to a veto or modification of the supervisor's solution. For example, when a supervisor wanted to create a new position for a valued employee, her director gave approval on the condition that the supervisor would not increase her total budget. Knowing and adjusting for such information while weighing the alternatives is less embarrassing to the supervisor and avoids annoying the manager. Of course, in a crisis, the supervisor may not have time to consult with the manager and will have to settle for discussing the decision as soon as possible afterward.

Be Decisive yet Flexible

Sometimes it is difficult to say which alternative solution is most likely to succeed or will bring the best results. Two alternatives may look equally good, or perhaps none of the choices look good enough. In such cases, a supervisor may find it hard to move beyond studying the alternatives to selecting and implementing one of them. However, avoiding a decision is merely another way of deciding to do nothing, and doing nothing is usually not the best choice. Furthermore, employees and peers find it frustrating to work with someone who never seems to make up his or her mind or get back to them with answers to their questions. Therefore, supervisors need to be decisive.

Being decisive means reaching a decision within a reasonable amount of time. What is reasonable depends on the nature of the decision. For example, a supervisor should not spend hours deciding what assignments to give technicians each morning, but he or she would probably spend several days selecting a candidate to fill a job opening because this decision is more complex and its consequences are greater. The supervisor should pick the alternative that looks best (or at least acceptable) within the appropriate timeframe for the decision, and then focus on implementing it.

Certain kinds of behavior are typical of a decisive supervisor. A decisive supervisor quickly clears his or her desk of routine matters, promptly referring them to the proper people, and keeps work moving. A decisive supervisor assumes complete responsibility for getting the facts needed when he or she must solve a problem. Finally, a decisive supervisor keeps his or her employees informed of what they are expected to do and how they are progressing relative to their objectives.

Being decisive does not mean a supervisor is blind to signs that he or she has made a mistake. When implementing a solution, a supervisor needs to seek feedback that indicates whether the solution is working. If the first attempt at solving a problem fails, a supervisor must be flexible and try another approach. After the supervisor in a Carmel, California, post office removed posters by a popular local cartoonist to comply with a U.S. Postal Service policy to standardize the appearance of its offices, he had to contend with protesters who gathered more than 1,000 signatures on petitions objecting to the action. The protesters even involved their congressman, Sam Farr, who persuaded postal authorities to bend the regulations in favor of local tastes. With its supervisor freed to give his patrons what they wanted, the Carmel post office planned a celebration ceremony to accompany the rehanging of the cartoons.[6]

Avoid Decision-Making Traps

Some supervisors seem to delight in emergency deadlines and crises, and they act as though each decision is a life-or-death issue (see Figure 9.4). But good planning can avert many crises; life-or-death issues are not the usual stuff of a supervisor's job. Making a major issue out of each decision does not make the supervisor more important, but it does interfere with clear thinking. A supervisor must be able to put each issue into perspective so that he or she can calmly evaluate the alternatives and devote an appropriate amount of time to finding a solution.

Another trap for decision makers is responding inappropriately to failure. When a supervisor makes a wrong decision, the supervisor will look best if he or she acknowledges the mistake. Finding someone to blame only makes the supervisor seem irresponsible. At the same time, supervisors need not agonize over their mistakes. The constructive approach is to learn whatever lesson the mistake can teach and then move on.

FIGURE 9.4
Decision-Making
Traps

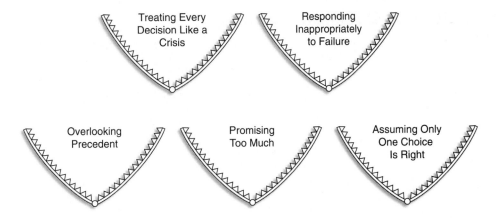

By trying to save time or work independently, some supervisors fail to draw on easily available information. One important source of information is precedent. Have some of the alternatives been tried before? If so, what was the outcome? Answering these questions can help a supervisor evaluate alternatives more realistically. For problems and decisions that are likely to recur, supervisors can set up a system for collecting information to use in future decisions. By consulting with other members of the organization or outside experts, a supervisor often can find readily available data that will improve his or her decision. The supervisor may need to ensure that employees are sharing information effectively. It might be easier to assume all the employees know what they need to know, but that assumption must be tested occasionally. For example, a manufacturer was trying to solve a problem involving a power generator it had been using for more than five years. Because the machinery had been around so long, management doubted that employees needed technical training to solve the problem. However, a group of operators, electricians, engineers, and others scheduled a few hours to review how the generator worked. A few minutes into the presentation, it became apparent that members of each group used different terms for the parts and had different views about the generator's processes. Before they could communicate well enough to solve the original problem, the group members had to establish a common understanding.[7]

Sometimes supervisors are tempted to promise too much. This mistake traps many supervisors because the promises keep people happy—at least until they are broken. For example, a supervisor may promise an angry employee a raise before being sure the budget can handle it. This promise may solve the immediate problem of the employee's anger, but it will backfire if the supervisor cannot deliver the raise. Similarly, a supervisor may tell her manager that she can continue meeting existing deadlines even while a new computer system is being installed. She is not sure of this, but making the promise is a way of avoiding a confrontation with her manager (until the department misses a deadline). Ultimately, everyone will be more pleased if supervisors make realistic promises. Then it is possible to arrive at solutions that will work as expected.

Another trap is to assume there is one "right" decision. In his popular book about creative thinking, *A Whack on the Side of the Head*, Roger Von Oech says we need to move past the first, most commonly used idea—the "one right answer"—to come up with new and possibly better ideas. Von Oech says, "It's the second, third or tenth right answer that solves the problem in an innovative way."[8]

TOOLS FOR DECISION MAKING

In preparing a budget for next year, LaTanya Jones, manager of a store's appliance department, needed to determine how many sales associates should work each day of the week. At a factory that produces air conditioners, production supervisor Pete Yakimoto had to determine why the rate of defects was rising and what to do to correct the problem. Yakimoto's employees complained that they were making mistakes because they had to work too fast, and he wondered if hiring more workers could be justified economically.

Problems such as these are difficult to solve mentally. Usually a supervisor facing such complex decisions needs tools and techniques for analyzing the alternatives. Some widely used tools include probability theory, decision trees, and computer software.

Probability Theory

Sometimes a supervisor needs to choose which action will have the greatest benefit (or least cost), but a supervisor cannot completely control the outcome. Therefore, a supervisor cannot be 100 percent sure what the outcome will be. For example, a sales supervisor can tell salespeople whom to call on but cannot control the behavior of the customers. Pete Yakimoto in the previous example can recommend that new workers be hired, but he has only limited control over how the workers will perform. In statistical terms, situations with uncertain outcomes involve risk.

probability theory
A body of techniques for comparing the consequences of possible decisions in a risk situation

To make decisions about risk situations, a supervisor can compare the consequences of several decisions by using **probability theory.** To use this theory, a supervisor needs to know or be able to estimate the value of each possible outcome and the likelihood (probability) that this outcome will occur. For example, a production supervisor is comparing two stamping presses. The supervisor wants to use a press to produce $1 million in parts per year. Press A costs $900,000, and Press B costs $800,000. Based on the suppliers' claims and track record, the supervisor believes there is a 90 percent chance that Press A will last 10 years (thus producing $10 million in parts) and only a 10 percent chance that it will fail after 5 years (thus producing $5 million in parts). The supervisor believes there is a 30 percent chance that Press B will fail after five years.

To use probability theory to make decisions about risk situations, the supervisor can begin by putting the possible outcomes into table format. Table 9.1 shows the possible outcomes for the stamping presses. In this case, the supervisor subtracted the cost of the press from the value of what the press could produce in 5 or 10 years. Notice that because Press B is cheaper, the possible outcomes for that press are greater. Remember, however, that Press B is also more likely to fail after five years. To find the *expected value* (EV) of each possible outcome, multiply the possible outcome (O) by the probability of that outcome (P). Stated as a formula, $EV = O \times P$. Table 9.2 shows the results of this computation. The supervisor should select the press with the highest expected value, which in this case is Press A.

TABLE 9.1
Possible Outcomes for a Risk Situation

	Five Years of Production	Ten Years of Production
Press A	$5 million – $900,000 = $4.1 million	$10 million – $900,000 = $9.1 million
Press B	$5 million – $800,000 = $4.2 million	$10 million – $800,000 = $9.2 million

Note: Outcomes are computed as the value of production minus the cost of the press.

TABLE 9.2
Expected Value of Possibilities

	Five Years of Production	Ten Years of Production
Press A	$4.1 million × .10 = $410,000	$9.1 million × .90 = $8.2 million
Press B	$4.2 million × .30 = $1.3 million	$9.2 million × .70 = $6.4 million

Note: Values are computed as possible outcomes (from Table 9.1) times the probability of those outcomes.

Decision Trees

In the real world, most decisions involving probability are at least as complex as the preceding example of purchasing machinery. Sorting out the relative value of the choices can be easier with the use of a graph. Thus, a supervisor may find it helpful to use a decision tree for making decisions in risk situations. A **decision tree** is a graph that helps decision making by showing the expected values of decisions in varying circumstances.

decision tree
A graph that helps decision makers use probability theory by showing the expected values of decisions in varying circumstances

As depicted in Figure 9.5, a decision tree shows the available alternatives, which stem from decision points. For each alternative, one of several chance events may occur. As before, the decision maker estimates the probability of each chance event occurring. To find the expected value of each outcome, the decision maker multiplies the probability by the value of the outcome ($EV = O \times P$). The decision maker should select the alternative for which the expected value is greatest.

For example (see Figure 9.5), a sales supervisor is trying to decide whether to hire a new salesperson at a salary of $40,000. The supervisor estimates that with the

FIGURE 9.5   **A Simple Decision Tree**

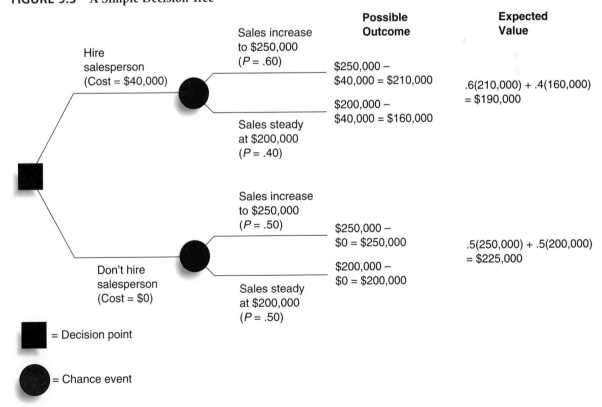

new salesperson on board, there is a 60 percent chance that the department's sales will increase from $200,000 to $250,000. Without the new salesperson, the chance for the sales increase is only 50 percent. The supervisor assumes that, at worst, the department will hold steady in either case. The dollar value of each possible outcome is the amount of sales minus the cost of the choice (hiring or not hiring). To find the expected value of each choice, the supervisor multiplies the probability of each outcome by the value of that outcome. Assuming there is a 60 percent chance of sales increasing if the supervisor hires a salesperson (and a 40 percent chance of sales remaining steady), the expected value of hiring is .60($210,000) + .40($160,000), or $190,000. The expected value of not hiring is $225,000. According to the greater expected value for not hiring, the supervisor should decide that it makes more economic sense not to hire a salesperson at this time.

Computer Software

decision-making software
A computer program that leads the user through the steps of the formal decision-making process

Some computer programs have been developed to help people make decisions. This **decision-making software** leads the user through the steps of the formal decision-making process (see Figure 9.1). In addition to having the user identify alternatives, the programs ask the user about his or her values and priorities.

For help in sorting out information, a supervisor might also use spreadsheet or database management software. Spreadsheet software, such as Excel, helps the user organize numbers into rows and columns; it can automatically perform computations such as adding a column of numbers. A database management program, such as Access, IBM DB2, or Oracle Database, systematically stores large amounts of data and makes it easy for the user to request and retrieve specific categories of data. A computerized index of periodicals at your library is an example of this kind of software.

Commerce Bank turned to database management software when it found that some administrators were spending more than two-thirds of their time answering employees' questions. Sometimes branch employees had to wait weeks to receive the information they needed to make decisions. Commerce Bank set up a computer system it named the Wow Answer Guide, which contains details about all the processes involved in bank transactions. When customers have questions or want an employee to help them with an unfamiliar transaction, the employee can find the necessary information in this database.[9]

These kinds of computer software do not make decisions for supervisors, but they can make it easier for supervisors to organize their thoughts and gather information. A supervisor still must creatively identify alternatives and use his or her judgment to select the best solution.

GROUP DECISION MAKING

Some organizations allow or expect supervisors to work with a team or other group to arrive at a decision. For example, a supervisor might seek input from a team of employees to decide how to meet production targets or encourage them to come up with a solution among themselves. The supervisor also might call on peers in other departments to share their expertise.

Advantages and Disadvantages

Group decision making has some advantages over going it alone. Group members can contribute more ideas for alternatives than an individual could think of alone.

SUPERVISION ACROSS INDUSTRIES

THE TRUCKING INDUSTRY

GROUP DECISION MAKING HELPS POLICY BECOME REALITY

A family-owned trucking business was in a difficult situation. Facing external pressures such as rising oil prices and insurance costs, as well as internal factors like high employee turnover and difficulty recruiting new drivers, the firm was also trying to double in size during a recent calendar year. But its efforts to grow were hampered by ongoing disagreements within the company about how to enforce safety standards for existing drivers.

The safety department supervisor knew which drivers had poor safety records. But the operations department supervisor wanted to keep them on their jobs because they were productive and difficult to replace. So the firm's safety policies were never fully implemented, because to do so would have cost the company these drivers.

However, several highly publicized traffic accidents convinced the owner that the entire fleet was in danger of losing a great deal of its business.

He convened a company-wide meeting to develop a set of minimum criteria for drivers, including maximum numbers of moving violations, preventable accidents, and off-the-job violations in the preceding 12-, 24-, and 36-month periods. These standards, once enforced, easily identified six drivers who should be let go. One of them had been with the company since its founding and had a reputation for on-time delivery and excellent customer service.

It was a difficult decision, and the group debated for some time. But in the end, the supervisors decided that making exceptions to the rule was not in the fleet's best interest, and all six drivers with poor safety records were let go.

Without that decision, the new policies would have suffered the same fate as the old ones—being ignored when they were inconvenient. Supervisors in all fields may face similarly difficult decisions. In this case, willingness to turn policy into action led the way to improving both safety and the bottom line.

Source: Jim York, "Safety Scorecard," *Fleet Owner,* March 2001, pp. 34–35.

Because people tend to draw on their own experiences when generating and evaluating alternatives, a group will look at a problem from a broader perspective.

Also, people who are involved in coming up with a solution are more likely to support the implementation of that solution. They will better understand why the solution was selected and how it is supposed to work, and they will tend to think of it as *their* solution. Chapter 3 elaborates on ways organizations are enjoying these benefits by establishing self-managing work teams and transforming the supervisor's role from commander to coach. For an example of a company that built support for an implementation by using group decision making, see the "Supervision across Industries" box.

Of course, group decision making also has disadvantages. First, an individual usually can settle on a decision faster than a group can. Second, there is a cost to the organization when employees spend their time in meetings instead of producing or selling. Third, the group can reach an inferior decision by letting one person or a small subgroup dominate the process. Fourth, groups sometimes fall victim to **groupthink,** or the failure to think independently and realistically that results when group members prefer to enjoy consensus and closeness.[10] Here are some symptoms of groupthink:

groupthink
The failure to think independently and realistically as a group because of the desire to enjoy consensus and closeness

- An illusion of being invulnerable.
- Defending the group's position against any objections.
- A view that the group is clearly moral, "the good guys."
- Stereotyped views of opponents.
- Pressure against group members who disagree.

- Self-censorship, that is, not allowing oneself to disagree.
- An illusion that everyone agrees (because no one states an opposing view).
- Self-appointed "mindguards," or people who urge other group members to go along with the group.

In the experience of Johanna Rothman, a consultant specializing in software and information technology (IT) projects, IT experts tend to be eager to reach decisions. When many such people are on a team, that team is vulnerable to groupthink because the group readily latches on to the first idea without searching for different views. Successful IT project managers try to put together teams with more diverse outlooks, including people who are known for questioning ideas and arguing unpopular viewpoints.[11]

When a supervisor notices that his or her group is showing the symptoms of groupthink, it is time to question whether the group is really looking for solutions. A supervisor who also is the group leader should draw forth a variety of viewpoints by inviting suggestions and encouraging group members to listen with an open mind. Another way to overcome groupthink is to appoint one group member to act as devil's advocate, challenging the position of the majority. When the group has reached a decision, the leader also can suggest that everyone sleep on it and settle on a final decision at a follow-up meeting.

Using Group Decision Making

Given the advantages and disadvantages of group decision making, a supervisor would be wise to involve employees in some but not all decisions. When a decision must be made quickly, as in an emergency, a supervisor should make it alone. Individual decisions also are appropriate when the potential benefit of a decision is so small that the cost of working as a group to make the decision is not justified. But when a supervisor needs to build support for a solution, such as measures to cut costs or improve productivity, the group process is useful. Group decision making also can be beneficial when the consequences of a poor decision are great; the benefits of a group's collective wisdom are worth the time and expense of gathering the input.

A supervisor can have a group actually make the decision, or a group may simply provide input, leaving more decision-making responsibility to the supervisor. For example, a supervisor might ask a group only to generate alternatives. If a group is to make the decision, a supervisor may let group members select any alternative, or a supervisor may give the group a few alternatives from which to choose. Whenever supervisors ask for input, they should be sure they intend to use the information. Employees are quickly wise to—and offended by—a supervisor who only pretends to be interested in their ideas.

Encouraging Participation

Because a main benefit of making decisions as a group is the variety of opinions and expertise available, a supervisor leading a decision-making meeting should be sure that everyone participates. One basic way of encouraging participation is for a supervisor to avoid monopolizing the discussion. The supervisor should focus on hearing participants' opinions. Also, some group members will find it easier than others to speak up. The supervisor should notice which participants are quiet and ask their opinions about specific topics being discussed. Finally, a supervisor can encourage participation by reacting positively when people contribute ideas. A barrage of criticism or ridicule will quickly discourage group members from speaking.

Learning to listen takes commitment and practice. Brax Wright runs the family business, Associated Supply Company. He wanted to be seen as involved in the day-to-day operations, so he overwhelmed employees with directions and criticism. When he and his family members learned that this kind of "micromanaging" was hurting the company's performance, they decided to give employees more control. In one situation, Wright learned that employees can outperform management at problem solving. After a problem surfaced involving errors in an inventory count, Wright complained and called a meeting. The employees resisted the owners' focus on assigning blame and successfully turned the discussion to planning improvements in the company's inventory process.[12]

Another barrier to participation is an "us–them" mentality that can pit team members against one another instead of letting them work together to solve a problem. Mark Turner, vice president of corporate risk at Ford Motor Credit Co., tells the following story:

> We were meeting with a group of managers from Ford Motor. On the first day, one of the Ford Motor guys piped up, "If you guys in credit would just do this." Don [Winkler, chairman and CEO of Ford Motor Credit] said, "Hang on. I'm an officer of Ford Motor Co. We're all part of Ford. If you're going to sit in this room and work on this team, you've got to drop this 'we' and 'they.'. . . I'm just trying to make the point that this is a collective effort."[13]

Brainstorming

brainstorming
An idea-generating process in which group members state their ideas, a member of the group records them, and no one may comment on the ideas until the process is complete

Another way to generate ideas in a group is to use brainstorming. **Brainstorming** is an idea-generating process (see Figure 9.6) in which group members state their ideas, no matter how far-fetched they may seem. A member of the group records all the ideas, and no one may criticize or even comment on them until the end of the process.

Donald Winkler, chairman and CEO of Ford Motor Credit Co., has a unique method for keeping brainstorming on a positive track: He won't allow the word "but" to be spoken in his presence. Greg Smith, one of the company's vice presidents, reports that Winkler's feeling about this rule is so strong that at meetings in the office in Colorado Springs, "There is a jar sitting on a table. Every time someone says 'but,' that person puts a dollar in the jar."[14]

Hearing other people's ideas often stimulates the thinking of group members. The supervisor can further open people's thought processes through such mind-expanding tactics as meeting in the work area rather than the usual conference room, asking people outside the group to identify problems, or requesting employees prepare for the meeting by individually listing problems to name at the meeting. Once all the ideas have been listed, the group can evaluate those that hold the most promise.

FIGURE 9.6
The Brainstorming Process

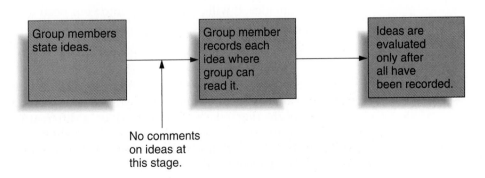

CREATIVITY

Rebecca Liss, a branch operations manager with Kemper Securities, had to be creative when she hired Gail as a new employee. With Gail on board, Liss's group was larger than it ever had been, but there was no money in the budget for additional office space or a computer terminal for Gail. That meant two employees would somehow have to share a terminal. Working with her staff, Liss developed the idea to arrange the desks into an island formation with a computer terminal between the two employees who were to share it.

This example shows how creative thinking can lead to excellent solutions. **Creativity** is the ability to bring about something imaginative or new. With decision making, it means being able to generate innovative or different alternatives from those used in the past. When a problem seems unsolvable, the supervisor especially needs creativity to find a fresh approach.

A common notion is that some people are creative, whereas the rest of us are stuck with following routine and ordinary courses of action. Taking the Knowing Yourself quiz on page 248 will provide you with a measure of the state of your own creative skills. If you do not score as high as you would like, take heart—the evidence suggests that people can develop their ability to be creative.

creativity
The ability to bring about something imaginative or new

Thinking More Creatively

A fundamental way to become more creative is to be open to your own ideas. When trying to solve a problem, think of as many alternatives as you can. Jot them all down without rejecting any; evaluate them only when you are done. This is like the group process of brainstorming. When you can, brainstorming with a group can help stimulate the creativity of the other participants as well as your own. Whether you are alone or in a group, practice should help your ideas flow more easily.

Years ago, advertising executive James Webb Young described a five-step technique for generating creative ideas:[15]

1. Gather the raw materials by learning about the problem and developing your general knowledge. Young says, "Constantly expanding your experience, both personally and vicariously, [matters] tremendously in an idea-producing job."[16]
2. Work over those materials in your mind. As you think of partial ideas, jot them down so you can refer to them later.
3. Incubate; let your unconscious mind do the work. Instead of thinking about the problem, do whatever stimulates your imagination and emotions, such as listening to music.
4. Identify an idea. It will probably pop into your head unexpectedly.
5. Shape and develop the idea to make it practical. Seek out constructive criticism.

Three decades after Young developed this technique, it still remains practical.

Young points out that creative thinking is not always a conscious process. Sometimes creative ideas come from dreaming or daydreaming or come to you while you are doing something else. If you are stuck on a problem, leave it for a while. Walk the dog, take a shower, work on a different task. Above all, do not neglect time for resting and daydreaming. If you are trying to solve the problem as a group, and the discussion is not going anywhere, adjourn or at least take a break, and then continue the discussion later.

Ray Kurzweil, an entrepreneur who invented a music synthesizer and a machine that converts printed words to speech for the vision impaired, uses dreams to develop his ideas. Before retiring for the night, Kurzweil chooses an issue and some criteria for a solution, and then he ponders the problem as he falls asleep. Often, he dreams about aspects of the solution. By reflecting on his dreams as he awakens, Kurzweil sometimes can unite the imaginative ideas of his dreams with the practicalities of the real-world problem, thus arriving at a creative solution.[17]

Of course, supervisors may not be able to take a nap or a shower before every major decision, but they can find other ways to take a break and allow time for creativity. Here are just a few suggestions.[18] Keep an open mind. Don't act so busy that your colleagues and employees hesitate to share their ideas and concerns with you. Employees who tend to be quiet and shy may have great ideas that you'll never hear unless you take the time to encourage them. When someone makes a suggestion, think about it carefully before you respond. Sometimes an idea that sounds faulty contains the seeds of an improvement. Keep a file of ideas that you can review later with a fresh mind. Include ideas that pop up in your reading, conversations, and daydreaming. Try making little changes to your daily routine to keep your creative juices flowing. React to new ideas as if they are something to try out and play around with rather than as challenges to the routine. When coming up with ideas, try out different questions:

- "What could we do if we had all the money in the world?"
- "What if we had no deadline for solving the problem?"
- "How might a child solve this problem?"
- "What would the ideal solution look like?"

Establishing and Maintaining a Creative Work Climate

A supervisor can benefit from the entire work group's creativity by establishing a work climate that encourages creative thinking. The most important step a supervisor can take in this regard is to show that he or she values creativity. When employees offer suggestions, a supervisor should listen attentively and look for the positive aspects of the suggestions. A supervisor also should attempt to implement employees' ideas and should give them credit.

When ideas fail, a supervisor should acknowledge that failure is a sign that people are trying. A supervisor should help employees see what can be learned from the failure. The aim is to avoid discouraging employees from making more suggestions in the future. As management trainer Rayona Sharpnack observed, "The only way to learn is through failure . . . the only way to grow is through experimentation, practice, and risk."[19]

Overcoming Barriers to Creativity

Often supervisors and employees have difficulty being creative because they are afraid their ideas will fail. A supervisor can overcome this barrier by accepting that failures by employees will occur. Overcoming your own fear of failure is more challenging; indeed, the organization may not always reward creativity. The best the supervisor can do is to keep in mind that a lack of creativity will probably prevent big successes as well as big failures.

If an idea does fail, the supervisor should acknowledge the problem and not try to pass the blame on to someone else. The emphasis should be on finding a solution, not on placing blame. Most managers admire supervisors who try ideas after careful thought and who focus on learning from mistakes rather than passing blame. A supervisor who prepares contingency plans (see Chapter 6) and is prepared to focus on solutions is likely to impress his or her superiors, even when the specific idea does not work out as hoped.

Another barrier to creativity is being overly busy. As described previously, creative thinking requires time for quiet and rest. If a supervisor cannot get these breaks at the workplace, he or she needs to allow time for thinking elsewhere—at home, while walking in the woods, while driving. For example, the supervisor can turn off the television for a while each evening. In addition to reflection, another good substitute for television watching is reading. The imagination required to read a book actually helps people develop their ability to think, but the average U.S. adult reads only minutes a day.

Isolation also interferes with creativity. Supervisors need to talk to co-workers in other departments of the organization. They need to talk and listen to their employees. Colleagues in other organizations can be a good source of ideas, as can friends and family members. However, the supervisor must be careful about spending a great deal of time with the same few people. They are less likely to be sources of fresh ideas than are new or less familiar acquaintances.

SKILLS MODULE

PART ONE: CONCEPTS

Summary

9.1 Identify the steps in the rational model of decision making.

According to the rational model, the decision maker first identifies the problem and then identifies the alternative solutions. Next, he or she gathers and organizes facts. The decision maker evaluates alternatives and then chooses and implements the best alternative. Finally, he or she gets feedback and takes corrective action.

9.2 Discuss ways people make compromises in following the decision-making model.

People usually simplify the rational approach to decision making, selecting an alternative that they have tried before and that has delivered acceptable results. Choosing an alternative that meets minimum standards of acceptability is a form of bounded rationality. People tend to analyze alternatives subjectively, relying on intuition and instinct, and favor solutions they can justify. People's analyses also tend to be clouded by the adoption of a personal perspective, the tendency to remember recent events best, and the use of stereotypes.

9.3 Describe guidelines for making decisions.

Supervisors should be aware of the possible consequences of their decisions. In a crisis, a supervisor should respond quickly. With regard to crises and other situations that influence the department's performance, a supervisor should inform his or her manager about the decision, if possible, before making it. Supervisors should be decisive but flexible. They should avoid decision-making traps such as treating all problems as crises, responding inappropriately to failure, failing to draw on available information, and promising too much.

9.4 Explain how probability theory, decision trees, and computer software can help in making decisions.

Probability theory defines the expected value of an outcome in a risk situation as the value of the possible outcome times the probability of that outcome. A decision maker using this theory selects the outcome with the greatest expected value. A decision tree is a graph that shows the expected values of decisions in varying circumstances. Thus, it helps the decision maker use probability theory. Decision-making software leads the user through the rational decision-making process, and spreadsheet and database management software helps users organize their information. The software does not make the decision, but it helps the user think through the problem more logically.

9.5 Discuss advantages and disadvantages of making decisions in groups.

Group members can contribute more ideas for alternatives than an individual could alone. Also, people who are involved in coming up with a solution are more likely to support its implementation. Disadvantages include that groups make decisions more slowly than individuals, the process is more costly, and groups may fall victim to groupthink, actually suppressing different viewpoints.

9.6 Describe guidelines for group decision making.

A supervisor can benefit from group decision making when time permits and when the consequences of a poor decision justify the cost of group decision making. Group decision making is also useful when a supervisor needs to build support for the alternative selected. The group may actually make the decision, or it may provide input such as suggested alternatives, letting the supervisor make the final decision. A supervisor leading a decision-making meeting should make sure that everyone is participating and should react positively when they do so. Brainstorming, in which members state their ideas no matter how far-fetched they may seem, often helps stimulate the thinking of group members.

9.7 Describe guidelines for thinking creatively.

A fundamental way to become more creative is to be open to your own ideas. When trying to solve a problem, think of as many alternatives as you can, without rejecting any. Some people use the five-step technique: gathering raw materials, thinking about the materials, incubating, identifying an idea, and shaping and developing the idea. Creative thinking is not always conscious; dreaming, daydreaming, and engaging in distracting activities actually can help generate ideas.

9.8 Discuss how supervisors can establish and maintain a creative work climate.

Supervisors should show that they value creativity. They should listen to and encourage suggestions. When ideas fail, supervisors should acknowledge that failure is a sign that people are trying. Instead of focusing on blame, the supervisor should see what lessons can be learned from the failure.

9.9 Identify ways to overcome barriers to creativity.

Some barriers to creativity are fear of failure, excessive busyness, and isolation. To overcome these barriers, supervisors need to remember that failing inevitably accompanies trying, to set aside time for thinking and resting, and to communicate with co-workers and peers in other organizations.

Key Terms

decision, *p.* 226
bounded
rationality, *p.* 229
recency syndrome, *p.* 231
stereotypes, *p.* 231

probability
theory, *p.* 236
decision trees, *p.* 237
decision-making
software, *p.* 238

groupthink, *p.* 239
brainstorming, *p.* 241
creativity, *p.* 242

Review and Discussion Questions

1. Andrea is in charge of scheduling the work for the service department of a car dealership. Lately, people in the sales department have been taking telephone calls from customers and promising that service work can be completed on a certain day or by a certain time. Consequently, everyone is unhappy—mechanics, salespeople, customers, and Andrea—because the work schedule is disrupted and the service department can't keep up with the promises made to customers. Using the rational model of decision making, what steps might Andrea take to correct the situation?

2. Define *bounded rationality*. Describe a situation in which you resorted to bounded rationality as a method of decision making. What were the results of your decision? Do you think this was the best way to make a decision under the circumstances? Why or why not?

3. Franklin Jones, a supervisor in the buying department for a department store, says, "I think these men's jackets are going to be hot this fall. Let's place a big order." What kind of compromises to rational decision making is he using in making his decision? Using the decision-making model, what would be a more rational approach?

4. In each of the following situations, what is interfering with the supervisor's ability to make the best decision? Suggest how the supervisors can improve their decision making.

   a. "I think this new answering machine model should be blue," said the design supervisor. "I like blue."

   b. "Let's conduct training at three o'clock on Fridays," said the customer service supervisor. "After all, it's been slow the last couple of Friday afternoons."

   c. "I'll bet we could boost sales by attracting more women," said the sales manager at an auto dealership. "To generate some traffic, we could hold a little fashion show or a makeup demonstration or something like that every week or so."

5. This chapter presents several guidelines for decision making: Consider the consequences, respond quickly in a crisis, inform the manager, be decisive but not inflexible, and avoid decision-making traps. How would such guidelines influence the way a nursing supervisor handles the following two situations?

   a. The supervisor is scheduling nurses for the next month.

   b. One of the nurses calls on Friday afternoon to say her father just died, so she will be out next week.

6. Philip is a supervisor who likes to work independently. Whenever he faces a new situation, he prefers to analyze it and make his decision without consulting other sources. How might this method of decision making impact the results of his decision? What might be a better way for Philip to proceed?

7. Rita McCormick is the supervisor of the state office that processes sales tax payments. She has noticed that workers are falling behind and wants to get authorization either to hire two more employees or to schedule overtime until the work gets caught up. McCormick estimates there is an 80 percent chance the workload will continue to be this high and a 20 percent chance that work

will fall back to previous levels, which the current employees can handle during regular working hours. (She assumes there is no chance of less work in the future.) Because she will have to pay time and a half for overtime, she assumes that the annual cost of overtime will be $150,000, whereas a workforce with two more employees will cost only $140,000.

   a. Construct a decision tree for this problem.

   b. Which alternative should the supervisor choose?

8. What are some advantages of making decisions as a group? What are some disadvantages?

9. What are the symptoms of groupthink? What can a supervisor do to overcome groupthink in a team meeting?

10. Roberto Gonzalez wants to make his solutions more creative. When he has a problem to solve, he sits down at his desk and tries to generate as many alternative solutions as he can. Unfortunately, he usually gets frustrated before he comes up with an alternative that satisfies him, so he just picks an acceptable solution and tries to implement it. How can Gonzalez modify his decision-making process to come up with more creative ideas?

11. How can supervisors foster creativity in their department or work group?

PART TWO: SKILL-BUILDING

YOU SOLVE THE PROBLEM

Reflecting back on page 225, discuss the staffing problem faced by supervisors at emergency-call centers. Is the number of vacant positions a problem or a symptom of the problem? Working as a group, come up with a sentence or two that defines the problem.

Next, brainstorm some ideas for solving the problem. Finally, when everyone has had a chance to suggest solutions, have each person rate each idea as either 2 (likely to help), 1 (might help), or 0 (unlikely to help). Find the average rating for each idea.

Did any of your group's ideas receive an average rating near a 2 (likely to help)? If you were a call center supervisor, where would you turn for ideas to solve this problem? Would getting ideas from actual dispatchers improve the quality of the ideas?

Problem-Solving Case: *Improvement Ideas from a Costco Cashier*

Steve Heller, an assistant manager at Costco Wholesale Corp.'s store in Carlsbad, California, had a problem to solve. The store's cashiers were not productive enough. Specifically, they were processing customers through checkout stations more slowly than Costco's standards. Heller wanted to find ways to help the cashiers work more efficiently.

To solve this problem, Heller called a meeting with the other store managers. Together, he and the other managers listed possible solutions and discussed the merits of each.

As Heller left the meeting, he passed a bulletin board featuring the store's top-performing employees. He noticed that a cashier named Pam LaBlanc had earned a spot on the board for the first time since she had been hired. Heller walked over to the register where LaBlanc was working and thanked her for her contribution to the store's performance. Then he asked how she had done so well.

Heller learned more than he had expected from such a simple question. LaBlanc explained that she needed to work as a team with the assistants, so she made it a habit to ask them for suggestions. She also gave assistants suggestions for how to help her. From day to day, she worked with different people, so the process became a kind of network of idea sharing.

Heller asked LaBlanc for specific examples, and she offered many. Heller discovered more ideas for productivity improvement from this quarter-hour conversation than he and his management colleagues had thought of in their hours of brainstorming and discussion.

Heller decided the best way to improve productivity would be to have LaBlanc teach what she had learned. She passed her ideas on to the other cashiers. After that, more than half the cashiers in the Carlsbad store were surpassing the company's productivity standards. Heller believes that listening to and acting on a cashier's ideas has also improved the attitudes and work relationships of his employees.

1. How did Steve Heller define the problem described in this case? How did Pam LaBlanc define the problem? How did the problem definition affect the way these two people initially solved the problem?

2. What advantages and disadvantages of group decision making does this case illustrate?

3. Working alone or in groups of three or four students, list ways that Heller can apply what he learned from this experience to continue improving cashier performance. In other words, how can Heller continue enabling employees to improve productivity and quality of service? How might he continue to include them in problem solving?

Source: Bob Nelson, "Good Listeners Make Good Leaders," *Bank Marketing,* March 2004, downloaded from Business & Company Resource Center, http://galenet.galegroup.com.

Knowing Yourself

How Creative Are You?

How many of the following statements apply to you? The more that apply to you, the more likely it is that you can think creatively.

1. I ask a lot of questions.
2. I enjoy word games and puzzles.
3. I write down all my ideas.
4. I know what time of day I am most likely to think of something new.
5. I read and listen to ideas that are contrary to my own beliefs.
6. I often wonder, "What if . . . ?"
7. I enjoy finding out how things work.
8. I make time every day to be alone in a quiet place.
9. I don't make assumptions about people or situations.
10. I read about my own field of work.
11. I read about areas outside my field of work.
12. I can think of more than one way to do most everyday activities.
13. I can laugh at my own mistakes.
14. I speak (or would enjoy learning) a second language.
15. I am willing to take risks.

Pause and Reflect

1. Did more than half the statements apply to you? If a statement does *not* apply to you, does it describe something you can change about yourself?
2. Before you read this chapter and took this quiz, did you think of yourself as a creative thinker? How did the chapter and quiz affect your opinion?

Class Exercise

Making Decisions

This exercise will test your ability to think creatively about a problem to help someone else come to a decision. Divide into teams of two and decide which of you is to represent the employee and which the supervisor. The employee wishes to persuade the supervisor, who is reluctant, to agree to a brief telecommuting trial.

Take a few minutes for the "employee" to prepare. The "employee" should decide how to address the problem and then present a solution designed to overcome the "supervisor's" skepticism. The "supervisor" gets a few minutes to make his or her decision, and then presents the steps in the process and the reasoning behind the answer. If both of you are satisfied with your performance, volunteer to role-play your problem-solving and decision-making scenario to the class.

Building Supervision Skills

Learning from Mistakes

Everyone who makes decisions makes some mistakes; the trick is to learn from them. Divide the class into teams and let each team member present one mistake he or she has made at work or in school, such as missing a deadline or appointment or misunderstanding some instructions. Discuss what the team can learn from each mistake, and choose the one mistake about which every member agrees he or she learned the most. Let each team present the winning mistake and list the lessons they drew from it.

Part Three Video Cases

In business, supervisors must constantly be aware of potential problems that may surface, realizing they may be held responsible by their own managers for any errors in judgment. Therefore, it is vital for supervisors to show their managers they can successfully deal with problems and make wise decisions. The video "Project Management: Steering the Committee" shows a supervisor who is being watched closely by superiors who are worried about a potential problem. Read the following scenario, and watch the video selection. Then, answer the three questions that pertain to the specific challenges in this supervisor–employee situation.

SCENARIO

Three months ago, Patrick was given the goal of implementing a computerized tracking system on the factory floor with the expectation that it would raise quality control and workflow by a significant percentage. The team spends an enormous amount of time revising/fixing chips after they fail quality-control testing—mostly due to lack of information. A serious review of the project will be conducted now that the first phase is complete.

Patrick is called to a meeting with three top executives. The tracking system project is very costly and has not been proven, though the company was gung ho for it, because competitors were using computerized systems in their production facilities. Patrick has spent little time writing a report but is feeling generally confident.

QUESTIONS

1. A supervisor can play many roles while he or she oversees employees. To ensure work goes according to plan, a supervisor must assert control over situations that arise. Which control do you believe would have made Patrick's project more successful? Why?

2. Chapter 6 details several things a supervisor can do to help him or her monitor performance. What are four tools Patrick could have implemented to avoid the problems his project was heading toward?

3. In the second meeting, even though Patrick assures the executives that the project will be under budget and completed in time, they still "strongly suggest" Patrick accept help to keep him on track. Why do you think the executives do this?

MANAGER'S HOT SEAT VIDEO 2: "PRIVACY: BURNED BY THE FIREWALL?"

In any organization, supervisors must deal with other supervisors in different departments, such as human resources. In dealings between supervisors, each person must recognize his or her own leadership style to achieve positive interaction. In the second video, both participants are supervisors in separate areas of the company; keep this in mind when you view the segment.

Read the following scenario describing "Privacy: Burned by the Firewall?" and then watch the video. Afterward, answer the three questions that pertain to the specific challenges in this supervisor–employee situation.

SCENARIO

An employee, Willy Kushing, has been put on administrative leave by the HR department for misuse of company property (Internet service and telephone). His manager is just returning from vacation and had no prior notice that Willy would be put on leave. The manager meets with HR to find out what has happened.

QUESTIONS

1. Lynn and Janet are in different departments, and neither person reports to the other or is technically higher up on the organization's scale. Even so, the meeting the women have seems led by one person—Janet. Look at the section "Characteristics of the Leader" in Chapter 8. On what values did Janet base her decision to put Willy on administrative leave? In not informing Lynn of her decision? What were her values in her meeting with Lynn? Likewise, what were Lynn's values coming into the meeting with Janet?

2. Chapter 8 speaks of leadership styles that are task oriented or people oriented but points out that a leader often is expected to be both. How are Lynn and Janet both task-oriented and people-oriented leaders?

3. The meeting between the supervisors was not a success. Choose to be in either Lynn's or Janet's shoes and explain how you would have changed your approach during the meeting to enable a favorable outcome.

Part Four

Skills of the Supervisor

Successful Supervisors Communicate, Motivate, and Counsel Employees
Eric Audras/Photoalto/PictureQuest

Chapter Ten

Communication

Learning Objectives

After you have studied this chapter, you should be able to:

10.1 Describe the process of communication.

10.2 Distinguish between hearing and listening.

10.3 Describe techniques for communicating effectively.

10.4 Identify barriers to communication and suggest ways to avoid them.

10.5 Distinguish between verbal and nonverbal messages, and name types of verbal messages.

10.6 Identify the directions in which communication can flow in an organization.

10.7 Distinguish between formal and informal communication in an organization.

10.8 Discuss the role of the grapevine in organizations.

Visibility is incredibly important. It's very hard to lead through e-mails.

—*Bill Zollars, CEO, Yellow Roadway*

A Supervisor's Problem: Getting Xerox Workers to Share Ideas

In today's fast-changing, high-tech workplace, employees' value to the organization comes not so much from their strength and agility as from what they know. Experienced employees build up personal sets of tools and techniques for solving problems, sometimes in ways that have never occurred to their supervisors and that deliver superior results or save time and money. If the employees teach one another these tricks of the trade, the whole organization will be better off. But the challenge for supervisors is that employees often keep their ideas and methods to themselves.

At Xerox, this became a problem among the technicians who serviced the company's photocopiers. Xerox gave each technician a printed manual detailing how to make repairs, but more often than they consulted the manuals, the technicians swapped tips on how to diagnose and fix problems. Often, they gathered informally at the company's warehouse to share stories about their work. Management saw something other than loafing; the conversations were an important means of sharing knowledge. So Xerox issued every technician a two-way radio. Technicians could chat over the radio whenever they were looking for ideas.

Radio consultations were handy, but the communication was too limited. Generally, a technician would talk only to individuals he or she already knew. Information sharing traveled only among acquaintances, potentially bypassing technicians who knew a great deal more but had fewer friendships with colleagues.

Xerox's next step was to set up Eureka, a computer database containing repair ideas. However, this innovation ran into a roadblock: Technicians rarely bothered to submit ideas. It felt strange to sit down at a computer and try to type in everything they knew about fixing a copier. Idea sharing became a management challenge. Some supervisors offered rewards, including cash, to employees who provided suggestions. They also collected suggestions from engineers to get some valuable ideas into the system, making its value more apparent. Contributors' names were included with suggestions, so contributors started receiving thank-you messages from people who benefited. Today, thousands of service technicians contribute ideas to Eureka, in part for the emotional reward of being considered a "thought leader," someone who can solve the company's tough problems.

In Xerox and other companies, supervisors need to encourage their employees to share knowledge so that the whole organization can benefit from what they know. The sharing of knowledge may take place through all kinds of communications, from formally created systems to brief conversations.

QUESTIONS

1. Why might the Xerox employees have been reluctant to share what they know?
2. How can supervisors encourage more of this type of communication?

Sources: Scott Thurm, "Companies Struggle to Pass On Knowledge that Workers Acquire," *The Wall Street Journal,* January 23, 2006, http://online.wsj.com; Rochelle Garner, "The Digital Storyteller," *Computer Reseller News,* December 13, 2004, downloaded from Business & Company Resource Center, http://galenet.galegroup.com; Pamela Babcock, "Shedding Light on Knowledge Management," *HRMagazine,* May 2004, downloaded from Business & Company Resource Center, http://galenet.galegroup.com.

---

communication
The process by which people send and receive information

High-quality work requires effective communication by supervisors and their employees. **Communication** is the process by which people send and receive information. The information may be about opinions, facts, or feelings. Even hard-nosed businesspeople need information about feelings; for example, a supervisor should know when his or her boss is angry or when employees are discouraged.

Communication is at the heart of the supervisor's job. To work with their managers, their employees, and supervisors in other departments, supervisors send and receive ideas, instructions, progress reports, and many other kinds of information. These and other communications can occupy three-quarters of a supervisor's workday. Thus, supervisors need to know how to communicate and how to do so effectively. This chapter describes basic communication skills and the types of communication that commonly occur in organizations.

HOW COMMUNICATION WORKS

On March 13, 2001, Neil L. Patterson, chief executive of software developer Cerner Corp., sent an e-mail message to about 400 of his company's managers. In the memo, Patterson demanded increased productivity and insisted that the managers put employees on time clocks, charge unapproved absences to vacations, reduce staff by 5 percent, and hold staff meetings at 7:00 a.m. and 6:00 p.m., as well as on Saturday mornings. Two things made this communication unusual: It was extremely angry and rancorous, and it quickly found its way to other employees of the Kansas City firm and even onto a public Yahoo! message board where investors could see it.

The memo—which included phrases such as "Hell will freeze over before this CEO implements another employee benefit in this culture" and "You have a problem and you will fix it or I will replace you"—was never intended to be released to the public. Patterson quickly apologized for it with a follow-up e-mail to employees and an interview with the *Kansas City Star*. According to company spokesperson Stan Sword, the original e-mail was "an overstatement" that arose from Patterson's passion for work, and the employees understood it as such.

Still, the company's stock dropped 22 percent over the next three days, and *Fortune* magazine jokingly apologized for having recently chosen Cerner as one of the 100 best firms in the country for which to work. While the stock price recovered within a few weeks, most observers say that Patterson's e-mail broke several rules of good communication. Among those rules are the following: Don't communicate in anger; remain open to feedback; and model effective leadership. Two additional rules Patterson violated apply to electronic communication: Don't try to hold large-group discussions via e-mail, and never forget that e-mail isn't private.[1]

At times all of us, like Neil Patterson, have found that simply talking or writing does not guarantee effective communication. Rather, our intended audience should be receiving and understanding the message.

The Communication Process

To describe and explain issues such as these, social scientists have attempted to diagram the communication process. As a result, we have a widely accepted model of how communication works. Figure 10.1 illustrates one version of this model.

Communication begins when the sender of a message encodes the message. This means the sender translates his or her thoughts and feelings into words, gestures, facial expressions, and so on. The sender then transmits the encoded message by writing, speaking, or other personal contact. If communication works properly, the intended audience receives the message and is able to decode, or interpret, it correctly. Of course, mistakes do occur. Communication breakdowns may occur because of **noise,** that is, anything that can distort a message by interfering with the communication process. Examples of noise are distractions, ambiguous words, and incompatible electronic equipment used to transmit the message.

The sender of the message can recognize and resolve communication problems by paying attention to feedback. **Feedback,** in this sense, is the way the receiver responds—or fails to respond—to the message. Feedback may take the form of words or behavior. For example, an electronic Internet monitoring program detected four page views of Web pornography within 10 minutes at one Colorado firm with only four employees, and at another larger firm in Denver, there were

noise
Anything that can distort a message by interfering with the communication process

feedback
The way the receiver of a message responds or fails to respond to the message

FIGURE 10.1
The Communication
Process

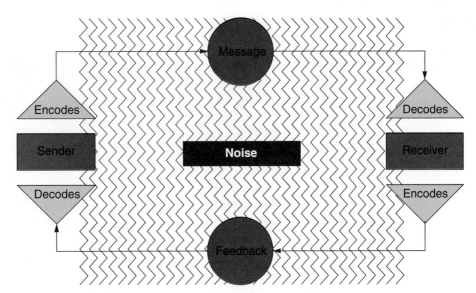

3,000 online shopping transactions, 4,000 day-trading hits, and 500 pornography views within five days.[2] Whatever one may think about the merits of such surveillance, results like these tell supervisors that employees are not paying enough attention to their tasks. For Neil Patterson of Cerner, such results might have been feedback indicating that he hadn't communicated clearly enough about how employees should use the Internet during work hours.

Hearing versus Listening

Notice in Figure 10.1 that the receiver must decode the message, meaning that the receiver as well as the sender has an active role to play in communication. If the receiver is not playing that role, communication is not occurring.

In many cases, this means the receiver of a message must *listen* to it rather than just *hear* it. Hearing means the brain is registering sounds. Most of us have at some point heard a parent nagging us to clean our rooms or a co-worker complaining about working conditions, but we may not be listening. Listening means paying attention to what is being said and trying to understand the full message. This is the meaning of "decoding" a message. When parents nag or co-workers complain, we often choose not to listen to them.

Thus, as the model of the communication process shows, when we want communication to work, we need to make sure that people are decoding messages as well as sending them. Because communication is an essential part of a supervisor's job, a supervisor must practice good listening skills as well as good writing and speaking skills. The next section discusses listening in greater detail.

COMMUNICATING EFFECTIVELY

Supervisors need to understand the requests that cross their desks and the questions that employees raise. They need to know when the boss is angry or impressed. They need to ensure that employees understand their instructions. When supervisors succeed in these responsibilities, they are communicating effectively. Figure 10.2 demonstrates that effective communication is most likely to occur when the parties communicate from the receiver's viewpoint, learn from feedback, use strategies for effective listening, and overcome barriers to communication.

FIGURE 10.2
Techniques
for Effective
Communication

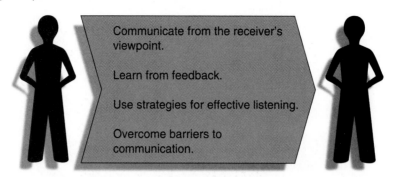

- Communicate from the receiver's viewpoint.
- Learn from feedback.
- Use strategies for effective listening.
- Overcome barriers to communication.

Communicate from the Receiver's Viewpoint

Even though we know that other people do not share all our experiences, views, priorities, and interests, we find it is easy to forget this when we are communicating. But such differences make the intended audience more likely to ignore or misunderstand the messages we send. For example, a business owner may find it fascinating and noteworthy that the company has been in the family for four generations. Skilled sales personnel, on the other hand, know that customers would rather hear how the company's services will benefit them. The salespeople therefore communicate with the audience's viewpoint in mind; they focus on what the company can offer customers.

This sales principle applies to all kinds of communication. Simply put, if you want the receiver's attention, interest, and understanding, you must communicate from his or her viewpoint. Applying this principle includes tactics such as using understandable vocabulary, referring to shared experiences, and addressing the receiver's interests. Thus, in explaining to employees that the department will be reorganized, a supervisor should focus on topics such as job security and job design, not on how the changes will make the company more profitable or more like its nearest competitor. After all, employees naturally are most concerned about their own jobs. For more advice on communicating from the receiver's viewpoint, see "Tips from the Firing Line."

Learn from Feedback

Feedback can help supervisors communicate effectively. When a supervisor sends a message, he or she generally expects a certain kind of response. Suppose a supervisor explains a policy requiring that all employees take their lunch breaks at some time between 11:00 a.m. and 1:00 p.m. One type of feedback would be the expressions on employees' faces—do they seem to understand, or do they look confused? Employees also might respond verbally; one might ask whether employees are to take a two-hour lunch break. Another type of response comes from the employees' subsequent behavior. If the employees understood the message, no one will be having lunch after 1:00 p.m. By evaluating the words, facial expressions, and behavior of the people who received the message, the supervisor can determine whether they understood it.

When feedback indicates that a message was not received fully and correctly, the supervisor can try modifying it so that it is better adapted to the receiver. The supervisor may have to eliminate sources of noise, for example, by talking in a location with fewer distractions or choosing clearer words.

A supervisor also can use feedback when he or she is receiving a message. In particular, when a supervisor is uncertain about the meaning of a message, he or she can ask the sender to clarify it. Asking questions is usually a smarter tactic than guessing.

TIPS FROM THE FIRING LINE

COMMUNICATING WITH A "YOU" ATTITUDE

Occasionally supervisors feel that their employees or managers are tuning them out—not hearing an important message they want to convey. The cause is often that the supervisor has failed to communicate from the readers' or listeners' point of view. The cure is to adopt a "you" attitude, which means thinking about the audience's interests, knowledge, and concerns. Here are some ideas for writing and speaking with a "you" attitude:

- Watch your pronouns. If you are saying, "I want" and "My goals," the focus is not on the audience. Find out what your audience wants. Address your message to *their* goals.

- Remember how it feels to be overwhelmed with too much information. Instead of trying to impress people with everything you know, select the most important piece of information to convey. Highlight your main point, and let people digest it. Make the details available in background materials for those who want to know more.

- Choose examples that are meaningful to your audience. If you want to use stories from sports or popular culture, make sure your audience follows the same sports and watches the same TV shows. Managers once assumed everyone watched football and played golf. Your group might be more familiar with soccer—or piano recitals.

- Choose words that are meaningful to your audience. Avoid technical terms and abbreviations unless you are certain everyone knows them. Skip fancy-sounding words such as *paradigm* and *parameters* unless you are speaking in a technical sense to technically savvy people.

- Pay attention. You want your audience's attention, and your audience wants yours. If you are talking to someone, the e-mail can wait. It really is not possible to give someone your full attention while multitasking.

Source: From *Management World,* June 2004, Institute of Certified Professional Managers. Copyright © 2004 by the AMS Foundation. Reproduced with permission of AMS Foundation via Copyright Clearance Center.

One company that appreciates the importance of feedback is C. R. Bard, which makes products for diagnosing and treating a variety of medical problems. To meet its goals for product innovation and cost reduction, the company needs a flow of ideas from employees at all levels. Bard has communicated this need by posting on its Web site an invitation for suggestions. At some companies, ideas from employees seem to disappear; employees make a suggestion but receive no response. At Bard, however, teams are in place to review each idea and give employees timely feedback. Within a month, each employee who submits a suggestion receives a report of whether the idea has passed the company's screening process. If the idea has value, the employee also receives a reward with this feedback. The quick responses and rewards send employees a message that the company really does care about the ideas submitted. Consequently, in the first 20 months of the idea-generation program, Bard had received more than 1,000 ideas.[3]

Use Strategies for Effective Listening

"Things just aren't done like they used to be," grumbled Tom Wiggins to Allen Pincham, his supervisor at the construction site. "Oh, boy," thought Pincham, "here we go again with the complaining." Pincham began studying some blueprints, ignoring Wiggins until he had blown off some steam and returned to work. Later that week, the general contractor confronted Pincham with a report he had received from Wiggins that some work was not being done according to code. Wiggins had complained that he had tried to inform Pincham but that his attempts were ignored.

FIGURE 10.3
10 Rules for
Good Listening

1. Remove distractions and give the speaker your full attention.
2. Look at the speaker most of the time.
3. When the speaker hesitates, give a sign of encouragement such as a smile or nod.
4. Try to hear the main point and supporting points.
5. Distinguish between opinions and facts.
6. Control your emotions.
7. Be patient; do not interrupt.
8. Take notes.
9. At appropriate times, ask questions to clarify your understanding.
10. Restate what you think the speaker's point is, and ask whether you heard correctly.

Better listening could have saved the construction project much expense and saved Allen Pincham considerable embarrassment. Listening is a key part of communication, and most supervisors could be better listeners. (Test your own listening skills by taking the Knowing Yourself quiz on pages 283–284.) Figure 10.3 lists 10 rules for being a good listener.

Effective listening begins with a commitment to listen carefully. A supervisor should not assume that a message will be boring or irrelevant and should instead decide to listen carefully and try to identify important information. For example, when an employee complains frequently about seemingly petty matters, the complaints may hide a broader concern that the employee is not stating directly. Sometimes a supervisor does not have time to listen when someone wants to talk. When that happens, the supervisor should schedule another time to continue the conversation. Supervisors also should keep in mind that some employees are by nature more vocal than others. Quiet employees may have excellent ideas but need encouragement to share them. Employees should not only look for ideas in meetings but also encourage one-on-one conversations to give quieter employees a chance to offer ideas.[4]

A supervisor should also concentrate on the message and tune out distractions. A major type of distraction is planning one's own responses; another is assuming that the listener has nothing interesting to say. When tuning out distractions proves difficult, it may help to take brief notes of what the person is saying, focusing on the key points.

If the speaker uses words or phrases that evoke an emotional reaction, a supervisor must try to control those emotions so that they do not interfere with understanding. One way to respond is to consider whether the speaker is merely trying to vent emotions. In that case, the best response is to listen and acknowledge the emotions without agreeing or disagreeing. Wait until the employee is calm before trying to solve a problem. Then ask questions that seek out the facts underlying an emotional statement: "Stan, you say you are treated unfairly. Would you give me some examples?"

active listening
Hearing what the speaker is saying, seeking to understand the facts and feelings the speaker is trying to convey, and stating what you understand that message to be

In many situations, a supervisor can benefit from using a technique called active listening, pioneered by psychologist Carl R. Rogers. **Active listening** is not only hearing what the speaker is saying but also seeking to understand the facts and feelings the speaker is trying to convey and then stating what you understand the message to be. The sample dialogues in Table 10.1 illustrate two types of listening. In Example 1, the supervisor is simply hearing the employee's words; in Example 2, the supervisor is using active listening. According to Rogers, active listening is a way that supervisors can help employees understand their situation,

TABLE 10.1
Hearing versus Active Listening

Source: Based on "Active Listening" by Carl R. Rogers and Richard E. Farson.

Example 1: Hearing	**Word-Processing Operator:** Hey, Wanda, is Finchburg kidding? He wants the whole report ready by the end of the day? That's impossible! **Supervisor:** But that's the job. You'll have to work as fast as you can. We're under tremendous pressure this week. **Operator:** Doesn't he realize we're behind schedule already because of the quarterly reports? **Supervisor:** Look, Don, I don't decide what the managers want. I just have to see that the work gets done, and that's what I'm trying to do. **Operator:** How can I tell my wife I'll be working late *again?* **Supervisor:** You'll have to handle that with her, not me.
Example 2: Active Listening	**Word-Processing Operator:** Hey, Wanda, is Finchburg kidding? He wants the whole report ready by the end of the day? That's impossible! **Supervisor:** Sounds like you're pretty upset about it, Phyllis. **Operator:** I sure am. I was just about caught up after doing all these quarterly reports. And now this! **Supervisor:** As if you didn't have enough work to do, huh? **Operator:** Yeah. I don't know how I'm gonna meet this deadline. **Supervisor:** Hate to work late again, is that it? **Operator:** That's for sure. I made other plans two weeks ago. Seems like everything we do around here is a big rush. **Supervisor:** I guess you feel like your work cuts into your personal time. **Operator:** Well, yeah. I know Finchburg needs this report to land a big customer. I guess that means that this job really *is* important. Maybe if Joel will help me by doing the tables, I can get out of here at a reasonable hour.

take responsibility, and cooperate. However, active listening is used effectively only when a supervisor demonstrates a genuine respect for employees and a belief in their ability to direct their own activities.[5]

Be Prepared for Cultural Differences

Supervisors today, more often than in the past, encounter employees or customers from cultures other than their own. Preparation for cultural differences can help supervisors communicate clearly with these people. To be prepared, supervisors can acquaint themselves with basic guidelines for cross-cultural communication.[6]

Stick to simple, basic words: "use" not "utilize," and "before" not "prior to." Use the literal meanings of words. Every culture has its own slang and idioms, such as "over the hill" and "in the ballpark." People from other cultures, especially those who speak another language, may be unfamiliar with these terms. In addition, avoid using the jargon of your industry. For example, supervisors at the Johns Hopkins Medical Institutions have had to learn to use literal expressions—"Answer the call button now," not "Hit the call button!" Many Hopkins nurses are from the Philippines, where they spoke English but not always with the same idioms as a U.S.-born speaker. When communicating goals and expectations, the supervisor should be literal about what behaviors are desired.

When speaking, talk slowly and pronounce words carefully. You do not need to speak loudly; a common error is to assume that a loud tone of voice is the only way to get the message across. Limited knowledge of English does *not* mean a person is hard of hearing, slow to learn, or even uninterested in learning English. Rather, the person may simply need time to learn the language. Supplement your words with gestures, illustrations, and facial expressions. The first employee of David Hodges's gourmet-food business was a Mexican immigrant who spoke mostly Spanish. Hodges said that at first, "There was a lot of hand gesturing, with me demonstrating what I needed him to do." But he and his employee were open to learning each other's languages, and Hodges considers the effort worthwhile: He was rewarded with a loyal and innovative employee.

With written information, the same guidelines about simple rules apply. Also, you may be able to provide a translated version of the information. However, employees may wish to receive an English version as well. ShawCor Pipe Protection has mainly Hispanic employees, and they often take home English versions of work-related information as a way to practice their English skills. In some situations, supervisors cannot assume that employees can read even in their native language. Illustrations are especially important when reading skills are in doubt.

Seek feedback by asking your listener what he or she has heard, but do not ask, "Do you understand?" Many people are too embarrassed to respond that they do not understand the message. Instead, they might remain silent or try to change the subject. In general, yes-or-no questions stimulate too little feedback. For example, instead of asking, "Do you work tomorrow?" (the answer will not guarantee that the person understood), ask, "When are you off this week?" (the person must have some understanding to give a reasonable answer).

Make sure you understand what the other person is saying. Ask for clarification when you need it. Help the speaker relax, and invite him or her to speak more slowly. If you are having trouble understanding a word pronounced by a non-native speaker of English, try asking the person to spell it or show you what he or she means. Most important, assume you can understand, and then try.

Learn about the communication styles used by people from different cultures, and try to match them when appropriate. For example, Asian Americans tend to have a less assertive conversational style than other Americans. Some have complained that they are frequently interrupted. Employees from some Hispanic cultures consider it inappropriate to talk about their accomplishments, so a careless supervisor may underestimate what they have contributed. Also, Hispanic workers may assume that the boss's role is to tell them what to do, so they may consider it wrong to bring up ideas and suggestions. Immigrants from some countries may even have experiences that cause them to distrust people in authority, so they will be unlikely to speak up about safety concerns or other problems at work. Of course, these are only general patterns; a wise supervisor will avoid jumping to conclusions about an individual's character on the basis of cultural preferences. A supervisor can also signal respect for the employees and their culture by learning some statements of praise in the employees' native language.

Supervisors also can help their employees communicate by stressing the importance of keeping communication simple. Share what you learn about communication styles. Compliment employees as they make progress in cross-cultural communication. Thomas Chen, founder of Crystal Window & Door Systems Ltd. in Flushing, New York, offers free English classes to his 200 employees, about three-quarters of whom are Chinese Americans. Bilingual staff members conduct the classes on evenings and weekends and use multimedia and personal instruction to cover everything from conversational English to the technical vocabulary of the industry. On "English-only Fridays," everyone, including the company's growing population of Hispanic workers, gets to practice what has been learned in class. And since everyone is doing it, no one feels uncomfortable.[7]

BARRIERS TO COMMUNICATION

The model of the communication process suggests where barriers to communication can arise. In general, the sender may fail to encode the message clearly, the message may be lost in transmission, or the receiver may misinterpret the message. In practice, these categories of problems often overlap. The resulting barriers may take the form of information overload, misunderstandings, and biases related to perception.

Information Overload

Today's world is often called the information age. People are bombarded with information daily (see Figure 10.4). On the way to work, radio ads and billboards suggest which brand of automobile or soft drink to buy. At the workplace, memos, magazines, and managers report on trends, policies, and responsibilities. During the course of a day, many employees get information from colleagues, computer screens, printed pages, and telephone calls. In the evening, family members and television announcers recount the day's news. People cope with this barrage of information by tuning out a lot of what they see and hear.

How can a supervisor respond to this barrier to communication? An important way is to give employees only information that will be useful to them. For example, when employees need instructions, a supervisor should think the instructions through carefully, so that new instructions don't have to be provided later. Also, a supervisor should be sure that employees are paying attention. The way to do this is to observe the people receiving the information and look for feedback. A supervisor can say to an employee, "Do you understand what I want you to do? Try putting it in your own words." To his or her manager, a supervisor might say, "Do you think this idea supports your goals for the department?"

FIGURE 10.4
A Tidal Wave: Information Created in One Year

Source: School of Information and Management Systems, University of California at Berkeley, "How Much Information? 2003," executive summary, October 27, 2003, www.sims.berkeley.edu/ research/projects/how-much-info-2003.

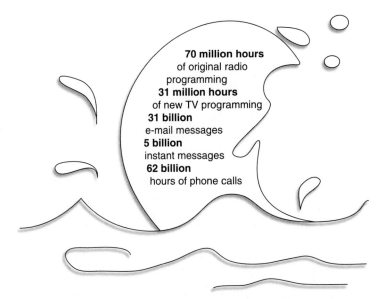

70 million hours of original radio programming
31 million hours of new TV programming
31 billion e-mail messages
5 billion instant messages
62 billion hours of phone calls

Misunderstandings

In decoding a message, the receiver of a message may make errors that lead to misunderstandings. This barrier can arise when a message is needlessly complicated. Imagine a supervisor's memo that reads, "The deterioration of maintenance practices will inevitably lead to conditions that will be injurious to our hitherto admirable safety record." The person who receives this memo is likely to misunderstand it because so much effort is required to figure out what the words mean. Instead, the supervisor could write, "Because the maintenance workers are no longer tuning up the machines each month, the machines are going to wear out and cause injuries."

When the supervisor is the receiver of a message, he or she needs to be careful to understand its true meaning. The supervisor should not hesitate to ask questions about unclear points. It is also helpful to check on the meaning with such responses as, "So you'd like me to . . . " or "Are you saying that . . . ?" A supervisor also needs to recognize when people are intentionally vague or misleading. On those occasions, the supervisor should interpret messages with particular care.

Likewise, supervisors should be aware that vulgar language is counterproductive at best and offensive at worst. In a case currently pending, a customer service representative for Verizon Communications Inc. says she was fired for uttering a crude expletive during a disciplinary review. While the reaction may seem extreme, some companies including Verizon and General Motors do prohibit profanity. Experts disagree about whether supervisors can reasonably be expected to "listen to every word workers utter."[8]

Word Choices

To avoid misunderstandings, a supervisor should be careful to make appropriate word choices when encoding the message. In addition to choosing simple words, this means avoiding ambiguous words. If an employee asks, "Should I use the solvent in the bottle on the left?" the supervisor should not say, "Right."

Problems also can arise from using words that attribute characteristics to another person. Saying "You're so irresponsible!" leads an employee to tune out a message. Instead, a supervisor could describe specific behaviors and his or her own feelings: "That's the second time this week you've made that mistake. I get annoyed when I have to explain the same procedure more than once or twice." This approach is called using "I statements" instead of "you statements." Table 10.2 gives examples of the differences between the two types.

Choosing words carefully is especially important in addressing others. A careful supervisor uses the name of a co-worker or customer instead of "dear" or "honey" unless the supervisor is certain that the receiver in a business setting likes being called by such endearments.

Word choice is also an important element of clarity. Supervisors should avoid using language that obscures their meaning, such as this sentence from a prospectus sent to clients of Federated Investors: "Redemptions will be processed in a manner intended to maximize the amount of redemption which will not be subject to a contingent deferred sales charge."[9] One good way to check your written communication for clarity is to read it out loud before sending it.

Cultural Differences

Another concern involves misunderstandings that result from cultural differences. For example, the mainstream culture in the United States places relatively great emphasis on expressing one's personal opinion. A supervisor from this

TABLE 10.2
Two Ways to Address Comments to Others

	You Statements	I Statements
Examples	"You're so irresponsible!"	"I'm upset that you've missed the deadline for the third time. When someone in the department misses a deadline, the whole department looks bad. What can we do?"
	"At the next department meeting, you'd better be prepared and be on time, or you're going to be sorry when we review your salary."	"I was not pleased that you were late to the meeting and unprepared. I expect a higher standard of performance."
	"You're bugging the women with those dirty jokes, so just knock it off before we get in trouble."	"I have received complaints from two of the employees in the department that you are embarrassing them by telling dirty jokes. Our company policy and the law both forbid that type of behavior."
Likely response	Defensiveness, ignoring speaker.	Listening, collaborating on a solution.

culture thus could expect that employees would feel free to share ideas and express disagreements. In contrast, people from a culture that places a high value on harmony (for example, Japan) might agree with the speaker out of politeness rather than a shared opinion. People from a culture that values demonstrating respect according to one's place in the hierarchy (for example, Mexico, the Middle East) might be reluctant to express disagreement to a manager or other high-ranking person. A U.S. manager who was unfamiliar with such values might assume mistakenly that employees from these cultures were unable or unwilling to contribute their ideas.

To avoid misinterpreting the words and behavior of others, a supervisor must be familiar with the communication styles of the various cultures of people with whom he or she works. Table 10.3 identifies some aspects of communication affected by culture and provides examples of cultural differences. Information about the values and customs of different cultures, of course, does not apply to every member of any culture, but it can sensitize a supervisor to areas in which extra care may be needed to promote understanding.

Inferences versus Facts

inference
A conclusion drawn from the facts available

Misunderstandings also can arise when the listener confuses inferences with facts. An **inference** is a conclusion drawn from the facts available. A supervisor may observe that an employee is not meeting performance standards. That would be a fact. If a supervisor says, "You're lazy!" he or she is making an inference based on the fact of the below-par performance. The inference may or may not be true.

Statements using the words *never* and *always* are inferences. A supervisor may claim, "You're always late"—knowing for certain that the employee has been late to work six days straight. However, the supervisor cannot know for certain what the employee *always* does.

One business writer tells the story of a manager who berated a supervisor and crew of maintenance workers as they stood by a piece of machine that was to be dismantled. The manager had concluded that the workers were "goofing off" and

TABLE 10.3
Cultural Differences in Communication

Sources: Roger E. Axtell, *Gestures: The Do's and Taboos of Body Language around the World* (New York: Wiley, 1991); Philip R. Harris and Robert T. Moran, *Managing Cultural Differences*, 3rd ed. (Houston: Gulf Publishing, 1991); Deborah Tannen, *Talking from 9 to 5* (New York: William Morrow, 1994); Sondra Thiederman, *Bridging Cultural Barriers for Corporate Success: How to Manage the Multicultural Work Force* (New York: Lexington Books, 1991); Chanthika Pornpitakpan, "Trade in Thailand: A Three-Way Cultural Comparison," *Business Horizons* 43, no. 2 (March–April 2000), pp. 61–70.

Aspect of Communication	Example
Language	Even within the United States, employees may speak many different languages.
Word choices	In the United States, a direct refusal is considered clear and honest; in Japan, it is considered rude and immature.
Gestures	In the United States, nodding means *yes* and shaking the head means *no;* the reverse is true in Bulgaria, parts of Greece, Turkey, and Iran.
Facial expressions	In mainstream American culture, people smile relatively often and view smiling as a way to convey goodwill. Someone from the Middle East might smile as a way to avoid conflict, and someone from Asia might smile to cover up anger or embarrassment.
Eye contact	Arabs often look intently into the other person's eyes as a way to know and work well with the other person; in England, blinking one's eyes is a sign that the other person was heard and understood.
Distance between speaker and listener	Middle Easterners may interpret standing a foot apart as an indication of involvement in a conversation; an American may interpret standing that close as a sign of aggression.
Context (situation in which message is sent and received)	Holding a business conversation during the evening meal is acceptable in the United States but rude in France.
Conversational rituals (phrases and behaviors that are customs, not meant to be interpreted literally)	In the United States, people often greet one another with "How are you?" not expecting an answer; in the Philippines, they ask, "Where are you going?" Men make more use of jokes and friendly putdowns; women more often use equalizers such as saying, "I'm sorry," and make requests indirectly.

shouted at them to begin immediately. The supervisor explained that they were waiting for a required written work permit, which would outline the safety precautions they were to take. At this, the manager apologized for jumping to a conclusion without knowing the facts.[10]

To overcome mistakes caused by treating inferences as facts, a supervisor should be aware of them. When sending a message, a supervisor should avoid statements that phrase inferences as facts. When listening to a message, a supervisor should be explicit with his or her inferences. For example, a supervisor in a bakery could say, "When you tell me the test of the recipe was a failure, I assume you mean the quality of the bread is poor. Is that correct?"

Biases in Perception

On the basis of their experiences and values, the sender and receiver of a message make assumptions about each other and the message. The ways people see and interpret reality are known as **perceptions.** Look at the picture in Figure 10.5. What do you see? You may perceive either an old woman or a young woman.

When perceptions about others are false, messages might get distorted. Imagine that supervisor Al Trejo has decided his employees would like him to pay more attention to their day-to-day problems and successes. So Al stops by the

perceptions
The ways people see and interpret reality

FIGURE 10.5
A Drawing That
May Be Perceived
in More Than
One Way

Source: Edwin G. Boring, "A New Ambiguous Figure," *American Journal of Psychology*, July 1930, p. 444. See also Robert Leeper, "A Study of the Neglected Portion of the Field of Learning—The Development of Sensory Organization," *Journal of Genetic Psychology*, March 1935, p. 62. Originally drawn by cartoonist W. E. Hill and published in *Puck*, November 8, 1915.

desk of one of his employees, Kim Coleman, and asks, "What are you doing?" Based on her experiences, Coleman believes that supervisors are quick to criticize, so she perceives that Trejo's question is intended to determine whether she is goofing off. Feeling defensive, Coleman snaps, "My work, of course." Trejo then perceives that Coleman does not want to discuss her work with him.

Prejudices

prejudices
Negative conclusions about a category of people based on stereotypes

Broad generalizations about a category of people—stereotypes—can lead to negative conclusions about them. These negative conclusions are called **prejudices,** and they can distort perceptions. In U.S. culture, it is common to attribute certain characteristics to women, African Americans, Asian Americans, blue-collar workers, and many other groups. Of course, these characteristics often do not apply to a particular person. Imagine that a male manager assumes women are irrational and highly emotional and that a female supervisor who reports to him discusses her desire for a raise. Even if she outlines a series of logical points supporting her request, he may perceive her request as irrational and may respond by telling her to "take it easy, things will work out OK." If such poor communication continues, the supervisor might eventually quit in frustration.

The way to overcome communication barriers resulting from prejudices is to be aware of the assumptions we make. Are we responding to what a person is saying or to what he or she is wearing? Are we responding to the message or to the speaker's accent? To the words or to our beliefs about the person's race? Awareness enables the sender and the receiver of a message to focus on understanding rather than assuming.

Biases in Paying Attention

Perception begins when people pay attention to a message or other stimulus. However, biases occur even at this early stage of the perception process. People tend to pay more attention to a message that seems to serve their own self-interests. They also are more apt to hear messages that fit their existing viewpoints and discount messages that contradict those viewpoints. Imagine that an employee suggests a new procedure, to which the supervisor responds, "Your idea will never work." The employee is more likely to think the supervisor is opposed to change than that the idea is unworkable.

The supervisor can combat biases in attention by phrasing messages carefully to appeal to the receiver. In the case of the new idea from an employee, the supervisor might say, "Thank you for your suggestion. I estimate that it will save us about $50 a month. Can you think of a way we can modify it so that implementing it will cost less than $1,500?" This response shows the supervisor was paying attention to the suggestion and recognized at least some of its merit.

TYPES OF MESSAGES

When Sandy walked into her cubicle at the insurance company where she worked, a note signed by her supervisor was on her desk: "See me," it read. "Uh-oh," thought Sandy nervously, "what did I do?"

Sandy walked into her supervisor's office and saw that he was smiling. "Congratulations," he said, "you got the raise we requested."

In this example, Sandy's supervisor communicated with her through a note, a facial expression, and spoken words. Two of the messages were **verbal messages;** that is, they consisted of words. The third—the smiling face—was a **nonverbal message;** that is, it was conveyed without words.

verbal message
A message that consists of words

nonverbal message
A message conveyed without using words

Nonverbal Messages

How can anyone get a point across without using words? Although the idea of nonverbal messages might seem surprising or unimportant at first, we continuously send and receive messages through our facial expressions, posture, and other nonverbal cues. In the example of Sandy, the message conveyed by the supervisor's facial expression was as important as the verbal message, "See me." The smile, unlike the note, conveyed to Sandy that her supervisor had good news.

Major types of nonverbal messages are gestures, posture, tone of voice, facial expression, and even silence. We learn the meaning of many such messages simply by participating in our culture. From experience, we can recognize a friendly handshake, a cool silence in response to something we say, and the "proper" distance to stand from the person with whom we are talking, part of a concept known as personal space (see Figure 10.6). Imagine that a supervisor and an employee are discussing a problem concerning the employee's work. The employee drops her eyes, looking away from the supervisor. Based on the usual assumptions in American culture, a supervisor is apt to conclude that the employee is dishonest, uninterested, or guilty of something.

Because we learn the meaning of nonverbal messages from our culture, people from different cultures have different nonverbal vocabularies. In the previous example, if the employee is a Cambodian woman, she may be trying to communicate respect; according to Cambodian custom, looking her supervisor in the eye would be rude. The meanings of nonverbal cues may vary even among different groups of people born in the United States. Failure to recognize different interpretations of nonverbal signals can be misleading, as in the case of a European-American speaker who concludes, on the basis of eye contact, that an African-American listener is not interested in what he or she is saying.

FIGURE 10.6
The Etiquette of Proper Distance: Some Cross-Cultural Examples

Source: Based on Sondra Thiederman, *Bridging Cultural Barriers for Corporate Success: How to Manage the Multicultural Work Force* (New York: Lexington Books, 1991), p. 132.

- Americans, on average, stand 2 feet apart when conducting business.
- Middle Eastern males typically stand up to 18 inches apart.
- Asians and many African cultures leave a space of 3 feet or more.

When a person is sending both verbal and nonverbal messages, the nonverbal message may have more influence on the receiver. This point was clearly understood by a group of protestors who opposed Citigroup's planned purchase of Associates First Capital, a firm that was under investigation at the time. The activists rallied before a courthouse in Durham, North Carolina, carrying red umbrellas, the symbol of Citigroup, with holes cut in them.[11] Figure 10.7 shows the weight that different components of a message may carry. If the relative importance of nonverbal communication seems surprising, imagine that someone is saying, "You're in trouble!" in an angry tone of voice. Now imagine the same person saying that while laughing. Are the messages identical?

Given the significance of nonverbal messages, supervisors need to be aware of the messages they send. For example, supervisors' nonverbal messages, such as conservative clothing and a firm handshake, should communicate a professional, businesslike attitude. In addition, employees often consider the physical presence of the supervisor as a nonverbal message that the supervisor is interested in what the employees are doing. Employees at an aerospace manufacturer told a consultant that they wanted workplace visits from managers as a sign that the managers cared enough to listen to the employees. This nonverbal message is especially powerful if the supervisor makes eye contact, listens to employees, and asks employees what *they* want to discuss.[12] The nonverbal message of caring sent by

FIGURE 10.7
Relative Contributions of Several Factors to Total Impact of a Message

Source: Data from Albert Mehrabian, "Communication without Words," *Psychology Today*, September 1968, pp. 53–55.

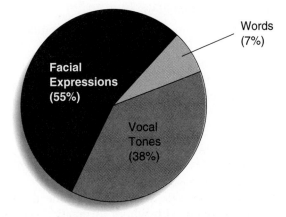

When a message is both verbal and nonverbal, the nonverbal message may have more impact on the receiver than the words themselves. This pie chart shows the relative impact, expressed as a percentage, of words, vocal tones (tone of voice), and facial expressions.

the supervisor's physical presence is what Bill Zollars is referring to in the quotation at the beginning of this chapter. Zollars, chief executive of the trucking firm Yellow Roadway, took on that job when the company was experiencing problems, so his top priority as a leader was to visit and talk with employees.[13]

Verbal Messages

Most nonverbal communication supplements verbal messages. People send verbal messages by speaking (oral communication) or writing (written communication).

Oral Communication

To communicate with employees, supervisors usually depend on oral communication. Every day they talk to employees to explain work duties, answer questions, assign tasks, check progress, and solve problems. This type of communication gives the supervisor an opportunity to send and receive many nonverbal cues along with the verbal ones. Thus, a supervisor can benefit from applying nonverbal communication skills when talking to employees. For example, the supervisor should use a well-modulated tone of voice and allow plenty of time for questions.

Most oral communication occurs face to face—in conversations, interviews, meetings, and formal presentations. (Meetings were discussed in Chapter 3.) Technology offers an increasing selection of oral communication channels for people in different locations. We take telephone calls for granted; newer technologies include voice mail, teleconferencing, and videoconferencing.

Speaking before a group makes many supervisors nervous, but nervousness can be positive if it inspires supervisors to be well prepared. Following these steps can help you give a successful presentation:[14]

1. Prepare a timeline of the steps you need to take, and mark the approximate date for each on your calendar to avoid procrastinating.

2. Find out something about your audience, as individuals if possible or as a group. Assess what they already know and what they need to find out from you. What do they feel, and how can you motivate them?

3. Outline your presentation, including an effective opening. Begin with a brief story or an intriguing question. Try not to open with a joke.

4. Limit your main points—three is a reasonable number—and state them clearly as a preview of your presentation.

5. Use explicit transitions from each of your main points to the next, and sum up as you go along.

6. Move around the room (but don't pace), use natural gestures, and make eye contact with every part of the room. Vary your inflection and keep the audience involved. For instance, instead of saying, "The cashiers must wait for the stock workers to close," say, "Juan and Janet must wait for Cho and Mark before they close."

7. Use an effective closing that either refers back to your opening, summarizes your main points, or calls for action. Be considerate of your audience and end on time.

8. Still nervous? Remember that you can overcome most jitters by preparing, rehearsing (enlist a friend with whom to practice), checking and rechecking visual aids and audiovisual technology before you begin, and striking up a friendly conversation with someone who arrives early.

SUPERVISION ACROSS INDUSTRIES

FRAGRANCES

FABERGE SUPERVISOR WRITES HIS WAY TO SUCCESS

According to Raymond Dreyfack, what powered his career was writing ability. Beginning as a supervisor at Faberge Perfumes (now part of Unilever and headquartered in Europe), Dreyfack learned to present managers with useful ideas that helped him advance in the company.

As a supervisor of data-entry employees, Dreyfack observed that his organization encountered a variety of problems. Although these problems were not earthshaking, customers complained, and billing statements occasionally contained errors. Employees had misunderstandings, and procedures slowed people down. Such problems are common in most organizations. Dreyfack decided that his role at Faberge would be to look for answers and offer them to the people who were in positions to act.

Dreyfack considered that busy managers would dislike interruptions from a supervisor continually sticking his head in the door to announce a new idea. The better alternative was to write his ideas briefly and persuasively. That way, his boss could read the ideas at a convenient time, when the boss had time to consider the ideas' advantages. Learning to confine ideas to concise memos taught Dreyfack to focus on key points and logical argument.

Eventually, Dreyfack acquired a reputation at Faberge as someone the company could turn to for clear communications and logical thinking. Management called on him to compose responses to unhappy customers and to clarify ambiguous corporate procedures. Over the course of several years, Dreyfack's responsibilities grew, and his salary nearly tripled.

Dreyfack concluded that he enjoyed writing so much he would make a career of it. Few supervisors are likely to follow his path of leaving the corporate world to become professional writers. However, any supervisor can benefit from writing skills.

Source: Raymond Dreyfack, "The Write Way to Jump-Start Your Career," *Supervision*, April 2004, downloaded from InfoTrac, http://web2.infotrac.galegroup.com.

If you want more formal, in-depth help with speaking before a group, your organization may be willing to send you to one of the many training seminars available or to a speech class at a community college. Many people have benefited from participating in meetings of the Toastmasters organization. Practice not only can improve your public speaking skills but also diminish your anxiety.

The ability to speak confidently in any public setting is an important attribute for a supervisory or management career. William Converse relied on his communications skills to save his firm when the television show *Inside Edition* claimed that Alpine Industries' air purifiers actually polluted the air instead of cleaning it. With sales plummeting and a state investigation launched, Converse went on radio talk shows to counter the story.[15]

Written Communication

Many situations call for a record of what people tell one another. Therefore, much of the verbal communication that occurs in organizations is in writing. The "Supervision across Industries" box offers an example of a supervisor who used written communication to advance his career and benefit his company. Common forms of written communication include memos, letters, reports, electronic messages, bulletin board notices, and posters.

Memos (short for *memoranda*) are an informal way to send a written message. At the top of the page, the sender types the date, receiver's name, sender's name, and subject matter. Because of their informality, memos lend themselves to communication within an organization.

People writing to someone outside the organization usually send a letter, which is more formal than a memo but has basically the same advantages and disadvantages. Both provide a written document for the receiver to review, and both take a relatively long time to prepare and deliver.

An analysis of how to meet a need or solve a problem takes the form of a report. A report describes the need or problem, then proposes a solution. Many reports contain charts and graphs to make the message easy to understand. Another helpful technique for a long report (more than two pages) is to start with a paragraph that summarizes the contents. Busy managers can review what the report is about, even if they cannot read the full report right away.

Written messages also can be sent electronically by fax machine or e-mail. In recent years, e-mail has become a popular channel as computer use has spread into almost every organization. The Bureau of Labor Statistics recently determined that more than half of employees use a computer at work. The most common computer activity at work is accessing e-mail and the Internet, performed by about two out of five employees.[16]

E-mail makes communication easier in many ways, but it has its complications, as we saw in the story about Neil Patterson of Cerner Corp. on page 256. As Patterson discovered, the complications often arise precisely because of how easy it is to send an e-mail. Whereas preparing a letter or report takes time, offering a chance for reflection and change, an e-mail message is informal. Writers may dash off a message and click "Send" before considering whether it will be misunderstood. The situation is even riskier with the ease of the "Reply to All" feature, which sends the message to anyone who was copied on the original message, not just the original sender. A comment meant for one colleague's eyes suddenly becomes public information for several people, perhaps including one's boss, customers, or vendors. Most common today is the unthinking use of "Reply to All" to send a message that is irrelevant to most of the recipients. When Ben Swett's company, Windowbox.com, lets some employees of a customer know that a product is out of stock, Swett often gets meaningless feedback in the form of politically motivated comments along the lines of "Someone's got to do something about this," copying everyone so the co-workers can see how dedicated the sender is. Likewise, a big customer of Windowbox periodically sends out messages to Windowbox and other suppliers, and one or two suppliers will reply to all with messages such as, "We enjoyed your recent visit to our facility."[17] Rather than becoming a nuisance, e-mail users should send messages only to those who will be interested in the contents.

To communicate a single message to many people, the organization may use posters and electronic or printed bulletin board notices. These are efficient but impersonal ways to send messages, so they usually supplement more personal types of communication. For example, if a factory's managers want to promote quality, they can use posters that say "Quality First." For the message to be effective, however, managers and supervisors also should praise individuals for doing quality work, discuss quality when evaluating performance, and set an example in the quality of their own work.

Technology and Message Types

Developments in technology have provided an increasing number of ways to deliver messages. Among the more recent developments are e-mail, instant messaging, teleconferencing, cellular phones, and videoconferencing.

These message types provide exciting options but make selecting a communications channel more difficult. Furthermore, the ability to send and receive

FIGURE 10.8
Put It in Writing?

Use written communication when . . .

. . . you can wait for the receiver to read it.

. . . you can't afford to bring people together.

. . . the message is complex.

. . . the information is more factual than sensitive.

. . . you won't be embarrassed for others to read the message.

. . . you need a record of the communication.

. . . the receiver is able to read your language and use your technology (print, e-mail, electronic file, etc.).

Use oral communication when . . .

. . . the message is sensitive.

. . . you need immediate feedback.

. . . the receiver might have difficulty reading.

. . . you want to build a relationship or see reactions.

information not only in the workplace but also in one's home, car, and airplane seat can contribute to the information overload described earlier in this chapter. Some employees may feel as if they are never able to leave their workplaces fully because they can be reached by fax or cellular phone wherever they are.

Choosing the Most Effective Message Type

With so many ways to send a message, which medium is the best for a supervisor to use? Although face-to-face communication conveys the most information (words *plus* tone of voice *plus* body language *plus* immediate feedback), the most effective and efficient method for a message depends on the situation. Figure 10.8 gives criteria for choosing written or oral communication. When deciding whether to call, meet with, or e-mail or fax a message to someone, the supervisor should consider time and cost limits, the complexity and sensitivity of the issue, the need for a record of the communication, the need for feedback, and the capabilities of the audience.

Time and Cost Limits

When the supervisor needs to reach someone in a hurry, a letter or memo may be too time consuming. An employee might be easy to find at his or her desk or on the shop floor. Often, the fastest way to reach someone in the organization is to make a telephone call.

Modern technology shortens the time required to send messages. Fax transmissions, e-mail, and voice mail allow a supervisor to contact people who are away from the telephone much of the day or who are taking other calls. However, these technologies do not ensure that messages will be *received* quickly, because it is the receiver who decides when to pick up the fax or retrieve messages from voice mail or e-mail.

Like time, costs place some limits on the choice of communications media. When people who need to discuss an issue are located far apart, the costs of a videoconference may be less than the costs of bringing everyone together. Midway Games, for example, has its headquarters in Chicago and operates studios in Austin, Texas; Los Angeles; San Diego; Seattle; and Newcastle, England, as well as a sales office in Europe. Videoconferencing is a practical way for the video game company to arrange for employees share information. In fact, Midway uses its videoconferencing system almost daily.[18]

Complexity and Sensitivity of the Issue

A complex message is clearer if written. For example, the results of a survey or the analysis of a work group's performance are easier to understand in a written report. In a meeting, an oral report will be clearer if supplemented with written handouts, PowerPoint slides, posters, or overhead transparencies. When speed is critical in communicating complex information to someone outside the organization, it may be cost effective to use a fax machine or computer modem.

For emotionally charged issues or when the state of mind of employees is at issue, communicators need the information that comes from tone of voice, gestures, and facial expressions. Such information is also essential for assessing how well employees (especially new ones) are doing. Written communications such as e-mail are thus best suited for objective messages. Sarcasm, humor, and emotion-laden messages are likely to be misinterpreted by receivers of e-mail. Max Messmer, chairman of Accountemps, advises, "Face-to-face meetings reduce the potential for miscommunications." However, a survey commissioned by his company found that most managers preferred to send e-mail because it is so convenient.[19]

The more sensitive a message or situation, the more opportunity there should be for nonverbal communication. Telephone calls, voice mail, and audio e-mail messages provide information through vocal tones. Most information, of course, comes from communicating face to face. Holding a one-on-one or group meeting allows the message sender to defuse anger and dispel misconceptions. It gives the receivers a chance to air their feelings and ask questions. For example, a supervisor who needs to discipline an employee must ensure that the employee understands the problem and has a chance to present his or her point of view. Similarly, an announcement of layoffs or restructuring should be made in person.

Need for a Record

As you will learn in Chapter 13, disciplinary action calls for a written record as well as a face-to-face meeting. A supervisor needs to combine a written message with oral communication. Other actions that call for written records include placing an order and establishing goals for an employee or department.

Need for Feedback

The easiest way to get feedback is to send an oral message. The listeners at the meeting or on the telephone can respond immediately with comments and questions. If feedback is critical, face-to-face communication is more effective than a telephone conversation because the person delivering the message can watch facial expressions as well as hear reactions. Do people look confused, excited, angry, satisfied? If a supervisor explaining a new procedure says, "Do you understand?" and the employee responds with a doubtful "I guess so," the supervisor knows that an example or some other clarification is needed.

Capabilities of the Receiver

People will receive a message only if it comes through a channel they feel comfortable using. In many settings, for example, some employees lack reading skills. If a supervisor believes that an employee cannot read the message, he or she will need to find ways to deliver it through the spoken word, pictures, gestures, or some other means of communication. This situation arises when an employee cannot read at all or reads too poorly to understand a particular message. Some employees may read well in other languages but not in English; in such a case, the supervisor may want to make written messages available in other languages.

The issue of illiteracy is a sensitive one. Supervisors must be tactful and look carefully for signs that employees have trouble reading. Employees with reading difficulties are typically embarrassed about this problem and try to hide it. At ShawCor Pipe Protection, located in Pearland, Texas, Angela Molis handles this sensitive issue by communicating through more than one channel to ensure understanding. Molis, who is ShawCor's health, safety, and environmental coordinator, prepares training materials that are written in both Spanish and English and contain many diagrams. In addition, during training sessions, she takes time to read the materials out loud. Furthermore, Molis trains employees to serve as "zone leaders." These employees share safety lessons with co-workers, who tend to respond better to training from a peer than from a supervisor.[20]

A potentially more widespread concern is people's comfort and skill in using modern technology. Some people feel frustrated or angry when a voice mail system answers the telephone. Supervisors can help by recording an answering message that offers information such as when to expect a return call and how to reach an operator or secretary. Likewise, information offered online will seem convenient to some and inaccessible to others.

COMMUNICATING IN ORGANIZATIONS

In business, government, and other organizations, communication tends to follow certain patterns. Understanding these patterns can help the supervisor make the best use of them.

Direction of Communication

downward communication
Organizational communication in which a message is sent to someone at a lower level

Think back to the organization charts in Chapter 7. When someone sends a message to a person at a lower level, **downward communication** is occurring. A supervisor is receiving a downward communication when listening to instructions or an evaluation from his or her manager or when reading a memo from top management describing a new company policy. The supervisor is sending a downward communication when he or she discusses a problem with an employee or tells an employee how to perform a task. Employees expect to receive enough downward communication to understand how to do their jobs, and they typically like to know enough so that they understand what is going on. For an important application of downward communication, see the "Supervisory Skills" box.

upward communication
Organizational communication in which a message is sent to someone at a higher level

When someone sends a message to a person at a higher level, **upward communication** is occurring. A supervisor is receiving an upward communication when an employee asks a question or reports a problem. A supervisor is sending an upward communication when he or she tells the manager how work is progressing or asks for a raise. Managers especially want to receive upward communications about controversial matters or matters affecting their own performance.

To be well informed and benefit from employees' creativity, a supervisor should encourage upward communication. Nick Visconti, field sales supervisor for ESP Pharma, says open communication is part of the culture at his company. He says ESP management welcomes his efforts to communicate while on business trips or in the office. ESP Pharma's vice president of human resources makes it a

SUPERVISORY SKILLS

COMMUNICATING VISUALLY

GRAPHS KEEP EMPLOYEES ON TARGET

Supervisors help employees meet high standards by setting challenging goals and then building employee commitment to meet those goals. In various departments, supervisors may help their employees meet goals for scrap rates, sales volume, inventory levels, reduction of product defects, absenteeism, injuries, on-time shipments, completion of steps in a project, or other measures. Employees need to know what the goals are, and they will be more motivated if they can also see their progress toward meeting each goal.

To communicate this information dramatically, many supervisors prepare graphs. On well-designed graphs, employees can easily see what they are striving toward and how far they have come. The following suggestions will help supervisors make their graphs more effective:

- Choose one to three measures that define your group's success. Create one graph for each of these measures.

- Show performance improvement in a consistent and obvious way. For example, a line trending upward generally looks like an improvement. Color schemes should be consistent from one graph to the next.

- Keep graphs simple, using just a few bars or lines per graph. Depending on the type of performance measure, you might show progress toward a goal or the current period's performance versus last period's. In some cases, you might show a longer-term trend, such as falling costs or rising sales.

- Update the graphs regularly, perhaps once a week or once a month. Do not wait several months to update a graph; employees will lose interest in an unchanging graph.

- Post the graph where it is easy for employees to notice. Make it large enough and the colors bold enough that it can be read easily wherever it is posted.

- In some settings today, much of the communication about performance takes place on computers. If you lack skills in preparing computer graphics, many community colleges offer courses that can bring you up to speed. Popular programs like Excel and PowerPoint offer tools for making easy-to-read graphs.

- Explain the graphs you are using, and seek feedback to make sure the employees understand what each graph means. Many organizations, including manufacturing facilities, expect their employees to use graphs so that they can monitor their own performance. Seek training resources for employees who would benefit from extra help in that skill.

- When you discuss performance with employees informally and in meetings, mention the results shown in the graphs. The emphasis you place on those results sends a message that the information in the graphs is important.

Sources: Ed Lisoski, "Checking Your Business Gauges," *Supervision,* January 2005; Ed Lisoski, "Rising from the Ranks to Management: How to Thrive versus Survive," *Supervision,* July 2006; Bob Trebilcock, "Manufacturing Goes Back to School," *Modern Materials Handling,* July 1, 2006, all downloaded from Business & Company Resource Center, http://galenet.galegroup.com.

daily practice to walk through the company's offices, so employees can easily stop her to ask questions.[21]

A supervisor can enhance upward communication by applying the strategies for effective listening. A supervisor should respond to employees so they know their messages have been received. Another means of encouraging upward communication is to establish a formal way, such as a suggestion box, for employees to provide comments and suggestions. When a Midwestern telecommunications company redesigned its suggestion program, it learned what kinds of programs are most successful. Supervisors can apply some of the lessons this company learned. For example, the supervisor should require that each suggestion be related to company goals. The supervisor might specifically ask for suggestions that decrease scrap or error rates or shorten response times. Some of the best suggestions come from asking employees to identify improvements to their own jobs. Finally, supervisors can request that the people making the suggestion support their ideas with facts and evidence showing the idea's benefits. When the supervisor states the requirement positively, employees become more involved in and excited about their ideas. Of course, the supervisor should implement the well-supported, goal-related ideas—and give credit to those whose ideas help the company.[22]

lateral communication
Organizational communication in which a message is sent to a person at the same level

A message sent to a person at the same level is **lateral communication.** Supervisors send and receive lateral communications when they discuss their needs with co-workers in other departments, coordinate their group's work with that of other supervisors, and socialize with their peers at the company.

Why should a supervisor need to know about the directions of communication? One way a supervisor can use this information is to be sure that he or she is communicating in all directions: enough downward communication so that employees know what is expected of them and the supervisor understands what is happening in the organization; enough upward communication so that his or her manager is aware of the supervisor's accomplishments and employees feel encouraged to offer ideas; and enough lateral communication so that the work of the supervisor's department is well coordinated with the work of other departments.

Formal and Informal Communication

formal communication
Organizational communication that is work related and follows the lines of the organization chart

The communication that follows the lines of the organization chart is known as **formal communication,** which is directed toward accomplishing the goals of the organization. For example, when a supervisor discusses an employee's performance with that employee, the supervisor is helping the employee perform high-quality work. When a supervisor gives the manager a report of the department's weekly activities, the supervisor is helping the manager perform his or her responsibilities for controlling.

However, much of the communication that occurs in an organization is directed toward meeting people's individual needs. For example, managers and employees alike may spend time discussing the performance of their favorite sports teams, the behavior of their children, and good places to eat lunch. This type of communication is called **informal communication.**

informal communication
Organizational communication that is directed toward individual needs and interests and does not necessarily follow formal lines of communication

Gossip and Rumors

Much informal communication takes the form of gossip and rumors. Gossip is like small talk but centers around people. People use gossip to indicate what behavior is acceptable. Thus, employees gossiping about who got promoted or who is dating the new supervisor in the payroll department are typically airing and refining their views about promotion policies and love affairs between co-workers.

Rumors are explanations, sometimes unfounded, for what is going on around us. For example, if a factory gets a visit from the company's board of directors, employees at the factory may spread rumors that the factory is to be sold or the operations moved to South Korea. When people are afraid, they spread rumors to ease their fear while trying to get at the facts. Thus, rumors tend to circulate chiefly during crises and conflicts—and they are often false.

Although rumors and gossip are a fact of life in the workplace, it does not look good for a supervisor to participate in spreading either. As a member of management, a supervisor is expected to know and report the facts about company business. When a supervisor spreads gossip or rumors, word eventually will get around that he or she is responsible for the message.

Although supervisors should distance themselves from rumors and gossip, a supervisor may occasionally hear a story that requires action. For example, team members may be unable to cooperate, or an employee may have violated a work rule. If the story suggests there is a problem requiring the supervisor's involvement, the supervisor must start by trying to learn the facts. Rumors and gossip rarely tell a complete or unbiased version of the truth. People tend to embellish the stories to make them more interesting, and even well-intentioned people perceive situations in a distorted way. For example, we recall the aspects of a situation that are most unusual and interpret them according to our own way of thinking. Therefore, the supervisor needs an open mind and should get the facts from those who are directly involved, not those spreading the rumor. Questions about the situation should focus on the main work-related issue that concerns the supervisor, and the supervisor should avoid words that imply a judgment. The supervisor should ask about observable actions, not opinions and hunches.[23] If the situation is complicated or involves legal issues, the supervisor should seek help from the company's human resource personnel. (Appendix B explores a number of legal areas involving supervisors.)

The Grapevine

grapevine
The path along which informal communication travels

The path along which informal communication travels is known as the **grapevine.** The grapevine is important to supervisors because employees use it as a source of information. Thus, a supervisor must expect that employees sometimes have information before the supervisor has delivered it. Supervisors also must realize that employees may be getting incorrect information through the grapevine, especially in times of crisis or conflict.

When supervisors and employees work different hours, maintaining good communication can be particularly difficult. According to a recent survey by Coleman Consulting Group, which focuses on 24-hour businesses that employ shift workers, nearly 70 percent of such firms reported major communication breakdowns between management and shift workers. The poll surveyed more than 22,000 employees and found that their communication with management had declined to the status of grapevine information in nearly 90 percent of the cases. Just 11 percent reported receiving information directly from their supervisors, and 59 percent inferred that management did not really care about them.[24]

The grapevine springs up on its own, and managers are generally unable to control it. However, knowing about the grapevine can help the supervisor seek out and correct misinformation. The supervisor also can take some steps to see that at least some of the messages in the grapevine are positive and in line with the organization's objectives:[25]

- Regularly use the tools of formal communication to inform employees of the organization's version of events.
- Be open to discussion; be someone employees will turn to when they want a rumor confirmed or denied.
- Use performance appraisal interviews as a way to listen to employees as well as to give them information.
- Have a trusted employee act as a source of information about the messages traveling the grapevine.
- When it is necessary to clear the air, issue a formal response to a rumor.

Furthermore, if supervisors and other managers are exercising their leadership skills to create an environment in which employees can and want to make positive contributions, both formal and informal communication are important. Supervisors will want to encourage communication among employees so they can improve the ways they work together.

At Southern Company, an electric utility based in Atlanta, Chris Womack says effective communication is an essential part of leadership. According to Womack, Southern's managers are expected to ensure that frontline employees know and understand the company's objectives. He considers open communication a necessary ingredient for retaining and motivating employees. Says Womack, "Honesty fosters a positive work relationship and makes people want to actually work [harder] for a company."[26]

SKILLS MODULE

PART ONE: CONCEPTS

Summary

10.1 Describe the process of communication.

The communication process occurs when people send and receive information. It begins when someone encodes a message by putting it into words or nonverbal cues. The sender of the message transmits it by speaking or writing. Then the receiver of the message decodes, or interprets, it. Usually the receiver gives the sender feedback.

10.2 Distinguish between hearing and listening.

Hearing occurs when the brain registers sounds. Listening occurs when the person who hears sounds also pays attention and tries to understand the message.

10.3 Describe techniques for communicating effectively.

Effective communication is most likely to occur when the parties communicate from the receiver's viewpoint, learn from feedback, use strategies for effective listening, and overcome barriers to communication. To listen effectively, the listener should make a commitment to listen, set aside time for listening, and then concentrate on the message. The listener also should try to control his or her emotions, not letting an emotional reaction interfere with understanding. Active listening involves hearing what the speaker is saying, seeking to understand the facts and feelings the speaker is trying to convey, and stating what one understands the message to be. Supervisors also should be prepared for cultural differences in order to communicate effectively. They should stick to simple words, avoid jargon, speak slowly, give the listener time to ask questions, ask for clarification, and learn about the communication styles of different cultures.

10.4 Identify barriers to communication and suggest ways to avoid them.

Barriers to communication include information overload, misunderstandings, perceptions and prejudices, and biases related to perception. Ways to avoid these barriers include giving employees only the information they need, encoding messages carefully and simply, observing feedback, avoiding name-calling, being aware of inferences and prejudices, and phrasing messages to appeal to the receiver.

10.5 Distinguish between verbal and nonverbal messages, and name types of verbal messages.

Verbal messages consist of words. Nonverbal messages are messages encoded without words, such as facial expressions, gestures, or tone of voice. Types of verbal messages include face-to-face discussions, telephone calls, memos, letters, reports, e-mail messages, faxes, and videoconferences.

10.6 Identify the directions in which communication can flow in an organization.

Organizational communication may flow upward, downward, or laterally. Upward communication travels to the sender's superior. Downward communication travels from managers to employees. Lateral communication flows between people at the same level.

10.7 Distinguish between formal and informal communication in an organization.

Formal communication travels along the lines of the organizational chart and is related to accomplishing the goals of the organization. Informal communication may travel in any direction among any members of the organization. It tends to be aimed at achieving personal, rather than organizational, objectives.

10.8 Describe the role of the grapevine in organizations.

The grapevine is the path of much of the organization's informal communications. Much of the information that travels through the grapevine is gossip and rumors. The supervisor generally cannot control this flow of information but should be aware that it exists and that he or she may have to correct misinformation. In addition, by encouraging communication with his or her employees, a supervisor may be able to ensure that some of the messages in the grapevine are positive.

Key Terms			
	communication, *p.* 255	verbal messages, *p.* 268	lateral
	noise, *p.* 256	nonverbal	communication, *p.* 277
	feedback, *p.* 256	messages, *p.* 268	formal
	active listening, *p.* 260	downward	communication, *p.* 277
	inference, *p.* 265	communication, *p.* 275	informal
	perceptions, *p.* 266	upward	communication, *p.* 277
	prejudices, *p.* 267	communication, *p.* 275	grapevine, *p.* 278

Review and Discussion Questions

1. Phyllis Priestley, a supervisor, wants to tell her boss what she plans to accomplish at a leadership seminar she will be attending next week. She decides to do so in the form of a memo. Briefly describe how this communication will follow the model shown in Figure 10.1.

2. Can a person be hearing but not listening well? Can a person be listening but not hearing well? Explain.

3. Every Monday morning, Ron Yamamoto, a supervisor, must attend a divisional meeting to discuss progress and make plans. Yamamoto finds that most people at the meetings are long-winded and that the meetings as a whole are boring. However, he needs to know what is going on in the division. How can he listen effectively, even though he is bored?

4. Sheila James owns a catering business employing four workers. She just got a contract to cater a wedding reception for a Chinese couple who speak very little English. What steps can James take to make sure her communication with the couple is successful? As a supervisor, what steps might she take with her employees to make sure they understand the couple's wishes as well?

5. In a staff meeting held to introduce new software that will provide office employees with information about the company's financial status, sales figures, and marketing plans, you notice that one of your employees is alternately staring out the window and doodling in his notebook. You are certain he is not paying attention. What barrier to communication might be occurring here? What steps might you take as a supervisor to overcome it?

6. The following examples describe some ways to send messages. Indicate whether each is verbal or nonverbal. For each verbal message, indicate whether it is oral or written.
   a. A long silence accompanied by an icy stare.
   b. A letter delivered by fax machine.
   c. Voice mail.
   d. Laughter.

7. As mail room supervisor, you need to report to your manager that a sack of mail has been misplaced (you are not sure how it happened). Would you want to send this message through written or oral communication? Would you want to deliver it face-to-face? Describe the form of communication you would choose and why you would choose it.

8. Nina Goldberg has been asked by her manager to give a presentation to employees about changes the company is going to make in health care benefits. Using the five steps described in this chapter, how should Goldberg prepare her presentation?

9. Face-to-face communication conveys the most information because the people communicating can learn from each other's body language and tone of voice as well as from the words themselves. However, why shouldn't a supervisor always choose face-to-face communication over other ways?

10. Lee Hamel is a busy supervisor. He rarely hears from his employees except when there is a production snag or scheduling problem. Hamel figures that as long as things run smoothly, his employees are happy. Why might his attitude be counterproductive in the long run? What steps could he take to improve upward communication from his employees?

11. Which of the following organizational communications are formal? Informal?
    a. A memo providing information about the company picnic.
    b. A meeting at which employees discuss the department's goals for the month.
    c. A rumor about a new vacation policy.
    d. A discussion between a supervisor and an employee about who will win the World Series.

12. Should a supervisor participate in informal communication? If so, when? If not, why not?

PART TWO: SKILL-BUILDING

YOU SOLVE THE PROBLEM

Reflecting back on page 255, why do you think it was a challenge to persuade Xerox technicians to share information by using the Eureka system? As a group, list all the barriers you can think of that would discourage this kind of communication. Once you have your list, formulate plans on how a supervisor of the technicians could overcome each of these barriers.

Problem-Solving Case: *Helping Retailers Improve Their E-Mail*

By some measures, the average employee devotes an hour or two each day to e-mail—reading it, replying to it, and deleting unwanted messages. At large organizations, almost half of the data stored in computers are e-mail messages and their attachments, nearly equaling company financial, production, and customer files. At home, too, consumers often feel as if they can barely find any messages of interest amid a flood of spam. Both at home and at work, people frantically scroll through lists of incoming messages, trying to weed out the junk.

In this context, the way a writer composes an e-mail message determines whether anyone will actually read it. The writer has to assume the message will appear in a long list and the recipient will be trying to eliminate irrelevant messages from that list. According to Web usability expert Jakob Nielsen, readers are most likely to pay attention to messages that appear to have a trusted source and that use subject lines expressing a message of interest.

Nielsen researched how readers process e-mail about purchase transactions. These messages related to various aspects of shopping, such as notifying customers that a purchase was completed, a package was shipped, or a refund was issued. In addition, the messages replied to requests for information or provided other customer service.

As Nielsen and his colleagues observed people reading their e-mail, many readers expressed stress and frustration. They complained that they were too busy for messages and wanted to avoid wasting time. They quickly deleted messages that seemed irrelevant.

On the basis of his observations, Nielsen advises writers to use care in wording the "from" and "subject" lines. The message should be from a recogniz-able name (such as the store, brand, or company) and indicate a recognizable function within the company (such as tickets @airlinename.com or ship-confirm@storename.com). The subject line should refer to a transaction that the customer initiated. According to Nielsen, the best subject line in his study was "Order was shipped." The phrase is both short and meaningful. In contrast, a message such as "Important information" is meaningless; it could be about anything the sender considers important.

Within the message, Nielsen advises putting the most significant information first. For an order that was shipped, customers want a list of what is in the package and a tracking number. Information about where to get further help also is important. The information's significance should be based on what the *reader* thinks is most important. Generally, customers are less interested in receiving marketing messages.

Consider how well these principles apply in the case of an actual order confirmation. UNICEF sells cards and gifts online at www.unicefusa .com. When it receives an order, the organization sends the following message:

Subj:	Your UNICEF order
Date:	9/16/2004 9:10:27 AM
From:	products@unicefusa.org
To:	janecustomer@isp.com

Thank you for placing an order with the U.S. Fund for UNICEF.

For regular delivery within the continental United States, you can expect delivery within 10 business days. For express delivery, you can expect delivery within two business days.

If you have any questions about your order, please contact a Customer Service Representative Monday through Friday at 1-888-238-8096 from 8 A.M. to 4:30 P.M. CST, or Email: products@unicefusa.org

The U.S. Fund for UNICEF wishes to take this opportunity to express our gratitude to you for helping UNICEF help the world's children.

Please tell your friends, family, and colleagues about the cards and gifts at unicefusa.org, because 75 cents of every dollar they spend goes to help support UNICEF's lifesaving programs. Click here: http://www.unicefusa.org/cards/friends.html

If you made a donation to the U.S. Fund for UNICEF in addition to your purchase, we thank you. A record of your tax-deductible contribution will be included in your receipt for this transaction.

Your Confirmation Number is: 30000

1. What principles of effective communication does the message from UNICEF use?
2. Suggest at least three changes to make the message from UNICEF more effective.
3. Consider the following situations in which a supervisor might want to send an e-mail. For each situation, pretend that you are the supervisor and compose a message that conveys what you need to say and respects the likelihood that the receiver is struggling with a high volume of messages. Be sure to write a brief subject line for each message.

a. The supervisor wants all the employees in the group to submit vacation requests. The supervisor's boss wants a vacation schedule in two weeks, so the supervisor needs everyone to reply a few days before then.

b. The supervisor is reminding two members of the work group that they are scheduled to attend a training session on Tuesday and Wednesday next week. (Decide whether this message will go to the whole group or just to the two employees.)

c. The supervisor is away from the workplace and visiting a major prospect as part of a team negotiating a sale. The supervisor needs to notify his or her group that the team's efforts succeeded. The group will likely have to work long hours for a few weeks so they can fill the large order the team has negotiated.

Sources: Jakob Nielsen, "Automated Customer Service Email and Transactional Messages," *Alertbox,* December 2003, www. useit.com; Jakob Nielsen, "Ten Steps for Cleaning Up Information Pollution," *Alertbox,* January 2004, www.useit.com; Stewart Alsop, "There's a Killer App on the Loose—but I'm on the Case," *Fortune,* March 17, 2003, downloaded from InfoTrac, http://web2.infotrac.galegroup.com; UNICEF, e-mail correspondence, September 16, 2004.

Knowing Yourself

Are You an Effective Listener?
On the line before each statement, score yourself on a scale of 1 (seldom) to 10 (usually) to indicate how often that statement is true about you. Be as truthful as you can in light of your behavior in the last few meetings or gatherings you have attended.

_____ 1. I listen to one conversation at a time.
_____ 2. I like to hear people's impressions and feelings, as well as the facts of a situation.
_____ 3. I really pay attention to people; I don't just pretend.
_____ 4. I consider myself a good judge of nonverbal communications.
_____ 5. I don't assume I know what another person is going to say before he or she says it.
_____ 6. I look for what is important in a person's message, rather than assuming it is uninteresting and ending the conversation.

_____   7. I frequently nod, make eye contact, or whatever to let the speaker know I am listening.

_____   8. When someone has finished talking, I consider the meaning of his or her message before responding.

_____   9. I let the other person finish before reaching conclusions about the message.

_____   10. I wait to formulate a response until the other person has finished talking.

_____   11. I listen for content, regardless of the speaker's "delivery" style.

_____   12. I usually ask people to clarify what they have said, rather than guess at the meaning.

_____   13. I make a concerted effort to understand other people's points of view.

_____   14. I listen for what the person really is saying, not what I expect to hear.

_____   15. When I disagree with someone, the person feels that I have understood his or her point of view.

Total Score

Add your total points. According to communication theory, if you scored 131–150 points, you strongly approve of your own listening habits, and you are on the right track to becoming an effective listener. If you scored 111–130, you have uncovered some doubts about your listening effectiveness, and your knowledge of how to listen has some gaps. If you scored 110 or less, you probably are not satisfied with the way you listen, and your friends and co-workers may not feel you are a good listener either. Work on improving your listening skills.

Pause and Reflect

1. Think of a situation in which you believe someone listened to you carefully and a situation in which you believe someone was not paying close attention to what you wanted to say. What was different about the way in which you were treated in those two situations?

2. Identify something you can and will do now to improve the way you listen to others. (If you need ideas, consider the behaviors listed in this quiz.)

Source: From *Management Solutions*, January 1989. Copyright © 1989 by American Management Association. Reproduced with permission of American Management Association via Copyright Clearance Center.

Class Exercise

Communicating Effectively

You learned many principles in this chapter to help you improve your communication skills. This exercise reviews six of those principles and gives you a chance to see how you can use them to improve supervisory communications.

Instructions

1. Review the following list of communication principles:
   a. Use feedback to verify that your message has been received accurately.
   b. Practice active listening.
   c. Select an appropriate method for sending your message.
   d. Be tuned in to nonverbal messages.
   e. Be well prepared when speaking before a group.
   f. Understand the important role of informal communication in the workplace, particularly rumors, gossip, and the grapevine.

2. Read the scenarios and determine which of the communication principles the supervisor violated. In each blank provided, write the letter of that principle from the list in Step 1. The principle you choose should indicate the one that the supervisor could have used to achieve a more positive outcome. (*Hint:* Each principle will be used only once; there is one *most* correct answer for each.)

Scenario

Principle

1. _____

On Tuesday afternoon, the plant manager gave each of the 12 supervisors throughout the plant a five-page document that spelled out some changes in the employee handbook that would be effective the following month. The plant manager instructed the supervisors to call departmental meetings sometime within the next three days to present the changes to their own staff. Jeff sent out a notice to his employees to be at a 45-minute meeting on Thursday afternoon. Several unexpected events occurred that demanded most of Jeff's time during the next two days. Jeff did manage to make it to the meeting; however, he had only a few minutes beforehand to skim the document. He ended up mostly reading aloud from the document at the meeting.

2. _____

Pete went to talk to his supervisor about a personal problem. He left the meeting feeling that he hadn't gotten through to his supervisor, who seemed preoccupied and distracted throughout their entire conversation.

3. _____

Sid was on his way out the door to meet a customer for a business lunch at a local restaurant. He stopped long enough to give about 90 seconds of hurried instructions about a task he needed one of his employees to do for an afternoon deadline that same day. Sid finished his instructions by glancing at his watch and saying, "I'm going to be late for my luncheon appointment. You got everything OK, didn't you?" The employee mumbled, "Yeah, I guess so," and Sid was out the door.

4. _____

Krista overheard one of the employees in her department telling someone on the phone that he had heard from a reliable source that the company was going to pink-slip 10 percent of the employees on Friday. Krista shook her head in disgust and thought to herself, "Another ridiculous rumor. With all the rumors floating around this place, I could spend all my time dispelling rumors. I'll let this one die a natural death on Friday; I don't have time to deal with it right now."

5. _____

Shannon had a long "to do" list for the day and decided to dispense with as many items as she could first thing in the morning by using the e-mail system. She had gotten rid of six tasks by sending messages to the appropriate people. She sent a seventh message that contained confidential information about one of her employees. The next day Shannon's manager spoke with her about a negative situation that had arisen as a result of her seventh message being accessed by some people who should not have seen it. He told her to consider more carefully the messages she chose to send via e-mail.

Michael had decided to delegate an important project to Susan, his most capable employee. He called Susan to go over some of the specifics of the project—one that he saw as a great opportunity for her to show higher management what she was capable of doing. Susan, however, did not share Michael's enthusiasm about her new work assignment. Michael ignored her expressionless face and chose to respond to her verbal responses. For example, when he asked her whether she agreed this was an exciting project, she responded after a few seconds of silence with a mere "yes."

6. _____

Source: This class exercise was prepared by Corinne Livesay, Belhaven College, Jackson, Mississippi.

Building Supervision Skills

Interpreting Communications

Divide the class into groups of at least three people. In each group, decide on a scenario that includes three sentences as follows:

1. The words, "I don't think that's right."
2. The sentence that came before it.
3. The sentence that came after it.

Also determine the physical setting and situation in which the sentences were spoken.

Let each group act out its scenario for the class. When all the scenarios have been presented, discuss the following:

- How did the context or situation change the meaning of "I don't think that's right?"
- How did the nonverbal behavior and setting differ in each scene?
- How could each group's "I don't think that's right" be paraphrased into a different sentence?
- Which component communicated the most information about the meaning of the scene—the words, the nonverbal behavior, or the situation?

Source: Adapted from Isa N. Engelberg and Dianna R. Wyann, *Working in Groups: Communication Strategies and Principles* (Boston: Houghton Mifflin, 1997).

Chapter **Eleven**

Motivating Employees

Learning Objectives

After you have studied this chapter, you should be able to:

11.1 Identify the relationship between motivation and performance.

11.2 Describe content theories of motivation.

11.3 Describe process theories of motivation.

11.4 Explain when financial incentives are likely to motivate employees.

11.5 Describe pay plans using financial incentives.

11.6 Discuss the pros and cons of keeping pay information secret.

11.7 Identify ways supervisors can motivate their employees.

This may sound soft and mushy, but happy people are better for business. They are more creative and productive, they build environments where success is more likely, and you have a much better chance of keeping your best players.

—*Shelly Lazarus, CEO, Ogilvy & Mather Worldwide*

A Supervisor's Problem: Keeping Connextions Employees Happy

When you call a company for help in installing your new printer, to get answers about your insurance plan, or to order some shirts from a catalog, you often wind up speaking to an employee of a company like Connextions. The company, based in Orlando, Florida, provides its clients with the services required to handle customer inquiries, sales, returns, and questions. Its operations include call centers staffed with employees who take calls on behalf of Connextions's clients.

In a sales call center, one of the biggest management challenges is keeping employees motivated to handle one call after another, each as politely and helpfully as they did at the beginning of the shift. In fact, it is sometimes difficult just to keep good employees on the job at all. A typical center has to fill jobs again and again as employees become frustrated with the fast pace, difficult customers, and relatively low-paid work, often with little opportunity for advancement.

Connextions maintains an edge in this industry by looking for ways to keep employees excited about their jobs. The company holds sales contests each week; employees who sell the most receive gift certificates or other prizes. Employees and their supervisors can nominate their co-workers for an Employee of the Month award, based on their high performance or extra efforts. Winners of this monthly prize receive certificates, cash bonuses, and group lunches with company executives. The top winner of the Employee of the Month contest receives a conveniently located special parking spot—a strange top prize, unless you consider that the parking lot is so huge that the walk into work can be a quarter mile.

Rewards for performance may not be the biggest reason employees stick around at Connextions. Unlike many of the company's competitors, Connextions has developed career paths in which employees can earn promotions as they develop their skills. For example, Todd Harris started out as an agent in a contact center, where he became one of the best salespeople. He received training to help him develop management skills and then was promoted to program supervisor in the Web sales group devoted to serving one of Connextions's clients, Blue Cross and Blue Shield of Florida. Harris, who supervises 19 agents, uses his own experience to inspire his employees to do their best, noting that his operation "is a stepping stone to building a career."

In addition to sharing this experience, Harris keeps his employees around for years by "knowing each agent, knowing what motivates them and what brings them up or down." In this way, Harris is following the lead of Connextions vice president of contact center operations, Mike Tripp, who says motivation is "about making sure [employees] don't turn into just a number." Instead, they need to hear thank-yous and feel appreciated on a day-to-day basis.

Keeping employees on board in an industry where turnover may be as high as 100 percent a year (as many people quit as hold a job) is a tough challenge for supervisors. Todd Harris has the advantage of working for a company that is committed to keeping its employees satisfied and productive.

QUESTIONS

1. What company policies and practices can help Harris keep employees motivated?

2. What can Harris do as an individual supervisor to keep employees satisfied and productive on the job?

Sources: Julia Chang, "Rules of Engagement," *Sales & Marketing Management*, April 2006, downloaded from InfoTrac, http://web2.infotrac.galegroup.com; Connextions, "What We Do," www.connextions.net, accessed August 24, 2006.

---

motivation
Giving people incentives that cause them to act in desired ways

Giving people incentives that cause them to act in desired ways is known as **motivation.** Among other things, supervisors must motivate their employees to do good work, complete assignments on time, and have good attendance. At Connextions, the contests, bonuses, special parking spaces, and career paths combine practical and fun methods of motivating employees.

When employees are motivated and also have the ability—the necessary skills, equipment, supplies, and time—they are able to perform well (see Figure 11.1). Thus, the objective of motivating employees is to lead them to perform in ways that meet the goals of the department and the organization. Because supervisors are evaluated largely on the basis of how well their group performs, motivation is an important skill for supervisors to acquire.

FIGURE 11.1   The Effect of Motivation on Performance

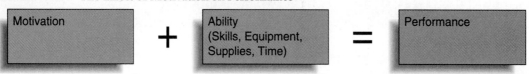

How the supervisor can make good use of the link between employees' objectives and their performance is discussed in this chapter. Theories of what motivates employees and how the motivation process works are described, legal issues are identified, and the role of money as a motivator is discussed. Finally, practical ways that supervisors can motivate employees are suggested.

HOW DOES MOTIVATION WORK?

"What's wrong with these people?" exclaimed Martha Wong about the sales clerks she supervises in the shoe department. "We pay them good wages, but when we hit a busy season like this, nobody's willing to put forth the extra effort we need—giving up a break once in a while or even just moving a little faster." Wong needs to figure out what to do so that employees will *want* to keep customers happy during busy periods. Perhaps they expect more money, or perhaps they want something else, such as a feeling of being part of a team.

Imagine that supervisors such as Wong could know exactly what motivates employees. For example, imagine that all salespeople were motivated solely by the money they earn and that social scientists have devised an accurate formula to determine how much money the company must pay to get a given amount of selling. Suppose all secretaries were motivated by flexible work hours and all production workers were motivated by recognition from the plant manager. A company that knew this would be in a position to devise the kinds of rewards that employees want. The supervisor could hand out the rewards and know that if employees had the necessary skills, they would do good work.

Of course, no such simple knowledge about motivation exists. Instead, supervisors have to rely on a variety of theories that social scientists have developed. None of the theories are perfect, proven explanations of how to get employees to behave in a certain way, but all give supervisors some guidance. Familiarity with the best-known theories can help supervisors think of ways to motivate their employees.

Content Theories

Some theories of motivation have focused on what things motivate workers. These are called *content theories* because they focus on the content of the motivators. Although money is the motivator that comes most readily to mind, some people respond more to other sources of satisfaction. To help you think about what motivates *you*, try the Knowing Yourself quiz on page 311 at the end of this chapter.

Three researchers whose content theories of motivation are widely used are Abraham Maslow, David McClelland, and Frederick Herzberg.

Maslow's Hierarchy of Needs

Psychologist Abraham Maslow assumed that people are motivated by unmet needs. When a person's need for something is not met, the person feels driven, or motivated, to meet that need. To give a basic example, a person who needs food feels hungry and therefore eats something.

According to Maslow's theory, the needs that motivate people fall into five basic categories:

1. Physiological needs are required for survival: food, water, sex, and shelter.
2. Security needs keep you free from harm. In modern society, these might include insurance, medical checkups, and a home in a safe neighborhood.
3. Social needs include the desire for love, friendship, and companionship. People seek to satisfy these needs through the time they spend with family, friends, and co-workers.
4. Esteem needs are the needs for self-esteem and the respect of others. Acceptance and praise are two ways these needs are met.
5. Self-actualization needs describe the desire to live up to your full potential. People on the path to meeting these needs will not only be doing their best at work and at home but also be developing mentally, spiritually, and physically.

Maslow argues that these needs are organized into a hierarchy (see Figure 11.2). The most basic needs are at the bottom of the hierarchy. People try to satisfy these needs first. At the top of the hierarchy are the needs people try to satisfy only when they have met most of their other needs. However, people may be seeking to meet more than one category of needs at a time.

According to this view, people tend to rely on their jobs to meet most of their physiological and security needs through paychecks and benefits such as health insurance. Needs higher on the hierarchy can be satisfied in many places. For example, people satisfy some of their social needs through their relationships with family and friends outside work, and they may seek to meet their self-actualization needs through volunteer work or membership in a religious organization. Nevertheless, people can also satisfy higher-level needs in the workplace. An employee who is applauded for solving a difficult problem or who takes pride in skillfully performing a craft such as carpentry is meeting some higher-level needs at work.

The rise of corporate social responsibility efforts combined with increasing needs for volunteerism in many communities is allowing some firms to meet employees' higher-level needs with organized opportunities to do good. For instance, nonprofit groups in California's Orange County benefited from the

FIGURE 11.2
Maslow's Hierarchy of Needs

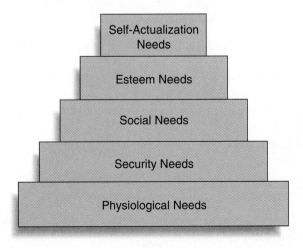

efforts of more than 30,000 local employees who tackled more than 100 projects in the Volunteer Center's 2001 annual Volunteer Connection Day. Home Depot workers by the hundreds repaired homes for the needy, and a group of hotel workers at Brea Embassy Suites collected diapers for needy mothers. Other employees of firms around the country work in soup kitchens, package and ship donated food, give time to counsel teens and seniors, raise funds for causes, and clean beaches and community parks. Said Monica Warthen, community relationships manager for Experian, an international computer services firm whose employees are active volunteers, "We believe that giving employees the opportunity to do things beyond their day-to-day work makes them more well-rounded, and therefore they feel better about their jobs and they're happier employees."[1]

Maslow's hierarchy is a widely cited view of motivation, but it has shortcomings. Critics (including Maslow himself) have noted that the theory is based on clinical work with neurotic patients and was not tested much for relevance to the work setting.[2] Are the needs identified by Maslow really all-inclusive? Do they describe people of many cultures, or just the majority of U.S. workers? The lack of studies investigating the hierarchy of needs makes it impossible to answer such questions with certainty. However, the popularity of Maslow's theory implies that it can be helpful in offering suggestions about what motivates people.

Applied to a work situation, Maslow's theory means the supervisor must be aware of the current needs of particular employees. During a serious recession, a factory supervisor may find that many employees are highly motivated just to keep their jobs so they can pay their bills. In contrast, employees who are less worried about keeping a job may respond well to efforts to meet social needs. At Wyndham International, when David Mussa became vice president, employees rarely stayed long, so he took the time to discuss work with small groups of employees. Mussa had thought that the problem would be money to meet physiological needs. Instead, he learned that the problem was esteem needs. Many of the employees felt the company did not value them, mainly because they rarely received feedback or coaching to help them do their job better. They wanted their supervisors to be more involved and show that they cared. So Mussa hired more supervisors, giving each one more time to spend coaching employees—in fact, supervisors were required to do so.[3]

In this era of increasing numbers of single parents and two-income families in the workforce, a practical concern of many employees is their need for flexibility in their work hours to balance the demands of home and work. Some organizations have responded with "family-friendly" policies, which typically include flexible work arrangements such as the following:

flextime
A policy that grants employees some leeway in choosing which 8 hours a day or which 40 hours a week to work

job sharing
An arrangement in which two part-time employees share the duties of one full-time job

- **Flextime**—This policy grants employees some leeway in choosing which 8 hours a day or which 40 hours a week to work.
- *Part-time work*—For employees who can afford to work less than full time, this option frees them to spend more time meeting other needs. It is economically appealing to organizations because few offer a full range of benefits to part-time employees.
- **Job sharing**—To create part-time jobs, two employees share the duties of a single position.
- *Telecommuting*—Some employees can and want to work from home, keeping in touch by means of computer and telephone lines.

Figure 11.3 shows estimates of the percentage of 945 U.S. companies offering various flexible work arrangements.

FIGURE 11.3

Share of 945 U.S. Companies Offering Flexible Work Options

Source: Hewitt Associates, "Hewitt Study Shows Work/Life Benefits Hold Steady Despite Recession," news release, May 13, 2003, http://was4.hewlitt.com/ hewitt/resource/newsroom/ pressrel/2002/05-13-02.htm.

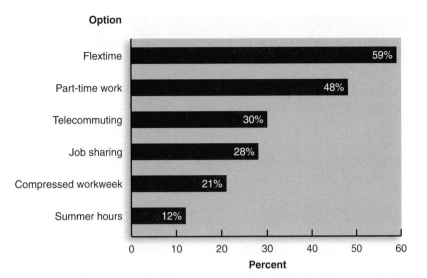

At IBS, which distributes tools, supplies, and components for manufacturers, managers believe the company's small size allows them to be flexible in meeting employees' needs. Michelle St. John, IBS's operations manager, says, "We allow employees to take time for what they need and make it up later."[4] St. John, like many human resources experts, sees family-friendly policies as an important way to get and keep the best workers.

Recent surveys have found flexible work arrangements at almost three-fourths of companies, with flextime available at more than half. (See Figure 11.3.) Other family-friendly benefits include referral services to help workers find day care for their children or elder care for aging parents.[5] However, some employees have seen these policies as benefiting certain employees at the expense of others. To learn how some firms are responding to this concern, see the "Supervision and Ethics" box.

McClelland's Achievement-Power-Affiliation Theory

In the 1960s, David McClelland developed a theory of motivation based on the assumption that through their life experiences, people develop various needs. His theory focuses on three such needs:

1. *The need for achievement*—the desire to do something better than it has been done before.
2. *The need for power*—the desire to control, influence, or be responsible for other people.
3. *The need for affiliation*—the desire to maintain close and friendly personal relationships.

According to McClelland, people have all these needs to some extent. However, the intensity of the needs varies from one individual to the next. The nature of a person's early life experiences may cause one of these needs to be particularly strong.

The relative strength of the needs influences what will motivate a person. A person with a strong need for achievement is more motivated by success than by money. This person tends to set challenging but achievable goals and to assess risk carefully. Someone with a strong need for power tries to influence others and seeks out advancement and responsibility. A person with a strong need for affiliation gives ambition a back seat in exchange for approval and acceptance.

SUPERVISION AND ETHICS

RETHINKING THE EQUITY OF "FAMILY FRIENDLINESS"

In the 1980s, more and more companies began offering flextime and other family-friendly work arrangements as a way to help employees balance the demands of work and home. Eventually, though, some employees began to complain that this effort to address the needs of particular workers was not being applied in a way that was completely fair to everyone. Sometimes one person's scheduling demands were favored in a way that made the job harder for co-workers. In other situations, an employee's part-time work hours might pose difficulties for customers. If productivity suffered, the benefits to one employee could hurt the company's owners and anyone else who received pay linked to overall company performance.

Realizing these shortcomings of family-friendly arrangements, companies have begun looking at ways to make their policies fairer to everyone and bring them more in line with business needs. For example, at the accounting firm RSM McGladrey, employees are expected to prepare a written report justifying how a flexible work schedule would help clients and co-workers, not just themselves. By forcing employees to rethink their needs, the firm actually helped some of them come up with better plans. Michelle Krapfl, a manager in RSM's office in Cedar Rapids, Iowa, had arranged to work 30 hours a week, but she consistently had to stay longer, and "flexibility" at her office was looking like something more rigid. When Krapfl and other colleagues with flexible arrangements submitted their reports, it became evident that Krapfl was not in the best position at her company for someone who wanted to work part-time. She transferred to another unit, where she now works with other employees and a supervisor who have part-time positions and support one another to complete assignments on time.

Another solution is to put employees themselves in charge of how they will get the work done under a flexible arrangement. At the Phoenix office of Chubb Corporation, an insurance company, employees have some flexibility in what hours they work, but they are responsible for figuring out how the team will complete their work within those hours. Most employees chose to adjust work hours, selecting compressed workweeks and flexible lunch hours, as well as some flexibility in starting and ending times. This control motivated them to plan their work flow carefully each morning so that they could enjoy working the hours most convenient to them. As a result, Chubb teams have become far more efficient, benefiting the company as well as themselves.

Source: Sue Shellenbarger, "Fairer Flextime: Employers Try New Policies for Alternative Schedules," *The Wall Street Journal*, November 17, 2005, http://online.wsj.com.

This theory offers a way to understand the behavior of the salespeople at a Westinghouse sales office. The manager in charge of that office told his 16 employees that he would buy and cook lunch for them if they met their sales goals. In the following 19 months, they exceeded their quotas 18 times. That exceptional performance made such an impression on headquarters that the company offered to pay for the meals. The manager declined reimbursement, however. Despite the widespread assumption that salespeople are motivated by money, the manager saw a need for affiliation: The staff members enjoyed their boss's personal attention as he bought and grilled steaks for them to share. Changing this interaction into a corporate reward program would remove its motivational power. Similarly, Pfizer inspired its older, more experienced sales reps by bringing them together into peer groups that competed with one another and coached the pharmaceutical company's younger representatives. The veteran salespeople, whose performance had declined as they increasingly felt isolated, improved when they began to enjoy stronger relationships with one another and a clearer role with respect to their younger colleagues.[6]

McClelland's theory differs from Maslow's in that it assumes different people have different patterns of needs, whereas Maslow's theory assumes the same

TABLE 11.1
Two-Factor Theory:
Hygiene Factors and
Motivating Factors

Hygiene Factors	Motivating Factors
Company policy and administration	Opportunity for achievement
Supervision	Opportunity for recognition
Relationship with supervisor	Work itself
Relationship with peers	Responsibility
Working conditions	Advancement
Salary and benefits	Personal growth
Relationship with subordinates	

pattern of needs for all people. Thus, McClelland considers individual differences. Both theories, however, imply that supervisors must remember that employees are motivated by a variety of possibilities.

Herzberg's Two-Factor Theory

Frederick Herzberg's research led to the conclusion that employee satisfaction and dissatisfaction stem from different sources. According to this two-factor theory, dissatisfaction results from the absence of what Herzberg calls *hygiene factors*, which include salary and relationships with others. For example, someone whose pay is poor (e.g., a physical therapist earning $5,000 less than the average pay for the position) is going to be dissatisfied with the job. In contrast, satisfaction results from the presence of what Herzberg calls *motivating factors*, which include opportunities offered by the job. Thus, an employee who sees a chance for promotion is likely to be more satisfied with the current job than one who does not. Table 11.1 lists the items that make up hygiene and motivating factors.

Herzberg found that employees are most productive when the organization provides a combination of desirable hygiene factors and motivating factors. According to this theory, an organization cannot ensure that its employees will be satisfied and productive simply by giving them a big pay raise every year. Employees also need motivating factors such as the ability to learn new skills and assume responsibility. Like the other content theories, Herzberg's theory tells supervisors that they need to consider a variety of ways to motivate employees.

Process Theories

Another way to explain how motivation works is to look at the process of motivation instead of specific motivators. Theories that pertain to the motivation process are known as process theories. Two major process theories are Vroom's expectancy-valence theory and Skinner's reinforcement theory.

Vroom's Expectancy-Valence Theory

Assuming that people act as they do to satisfy their needs, Victor Vroom set out to explain what determines the intensity of motivation. He decided that the degree to which people are motivated to act in a certain way depends on two things:

1. *Valence*—the value a person places on the outcome of a particular behavior. For example, a person may highly value the prestige and the bonus that result from submitting a winning suggestion in a contest for improving quality.
2. *Expectancy*—the perceived probability that the behavior will lead to the outcome. A person in the example may believe that his or her idea has a 50–50 chance of winning the quality improvement contest.

Vroom's expectancy–valence theory says that the strength of motivation equals the perceived value of the outcome times the perceived probability that the behavior

FIGURE 11.4 Vroom's Expectancy-Valence Theory

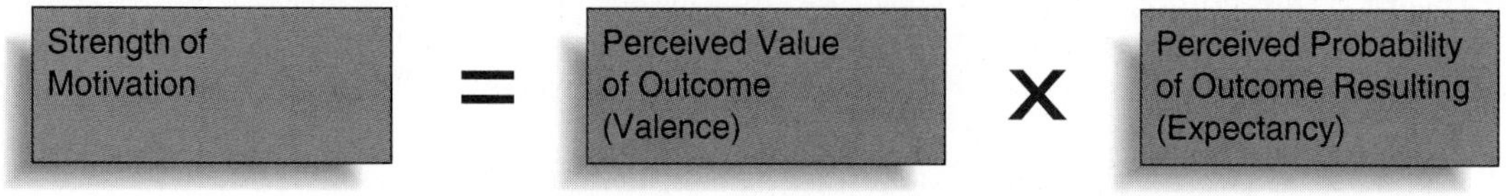

Strength of Motivation = Perceived Value of Outcome (Valence) X Perceived Probability of Outcome Resulting (Expectancy)

will result in the outcome (see Figure 11.4). In other words, people are most motivated to seek results they value highly and think they can achieve.

This theory is based on employees' *perceptions* of rewards and whether they are able to achieve them. Employees may place different values on rewards than a supervisor, and they may have different opinions about their abilities. If a supervisor believes that a good system of rewards is in place but that employees are not motivated, the supervisor might investigate whether employees think they are expected to do the impossible. To learn this, supervisors must be able to communicate well (see Chapter 10).

At Lee County Fleet Management, located in Fort Myers, Florida, fleet manager Marilyn Rawlings applied these principles by repeatedly showing employees they could meet high standards. She works with each employee to prepare a plan for personal growth, including goal setting. Rawlings encourages each employee to set one goal that is a stretch, and then she helps that employee achieve those goals. Rawlings says, "I want people to see that they can accomplish things that they don't think they can do." That experience may change their perceptions so that they will see themselves as able to accomplish more. When Rawlings wanted her organization to obtain the Automotive Service Excellence (ASE) Blue Seal of Excellence, she needed to have two additional technicians become certified by the ASE. The only two who were not yet certified had chosen not to try because they didn't believe they could pass the test. Rawlings raised the value of the outcome by telling each employee that obtaining the certification would make them a hero to the group—and that she would hold a celebration for everyone when the group won the award. The two technicians both tried the exam, and both passed.[7]

Skinner's Reinforcement Theory

From the field of psychology comes reinforcement theory, pioneered by B. F. Skinner. Reinforcement theory maintains that people's behavior is influenced largely by the consequences of their past behavior. Generally, people keep doing things that have led to consequences they like, and people avoid doing things that have had undesirable consequences. For example, praise feels good to receive, so people tend to do things that, in their experience, result in praise.

Reinforcement theory implies that supervisors can encourage or discourage a particular kind of behavior by the way they respond to the behavior. They can administer **reinforcement,** which can involve either giving a desired consequence or ending a negative consequence in response to behavior the supervisor wants. Or the supervisor can administer **punishment,** which is an unpleasant consequence of the behavior the supervisor wants to end. As described in the story at the beginning of this chapter, when salespeople performed well, they earned bonuses or won contests—a form of reinforcement. Using reinforcement theory to motivate people to behave in a certain way is known as **behavior modification.** In everyday language, we call it "using the carrot and the stick."

For long-term results, reinforcement is more effective than punishment. Psychologists have found that repeated punishment (or failure) can lead to an

reinforcement
A desired consequence or the ending of a negative consequence, either of which is given in response to a desirable behavior

punishment
An unpleasant consequence given in response to undesirable behavior

behavior modification
The use of reinforcement theory to motivate people to behave in a certain way

unhappy consequence called "learned helplessness." This means that if employees are punished repeatedly for failing in some aspect of their work, these employees will eventually believe that they are unable to succeed at the job. These employees begin to approach the job passively, believing that they will fail no matter what.

Together, Vroom's and Skinner's process theories support the idea that supervisors motivate most effectively when they place less emphasis on punishing infractions and more on giving employees a desirable goal and the resources that enable them to achieve that goal. These theories are consistent with the new management style adopted by Andy Pearson, who ran PepsiCo Inc. for nearly 15 years with a successful but abrasive style that earned him the reputation of being one of the 10 toughest bosses in the United States (according to *Fortune* magazine in 1980), partly for his track record of routinely firing the least productive 10 to 20 percent of the workforce. The former founding chairman of Yum! Brands, one of the largest restaurant chains in the world, Pearson changed his style. Instead of asking employees, "So what?" he asked himself, "If I could only unleash the power of everybody in the organization, instead of just a few people, what could we accomplish?" Of his change, Pearson told *Fast Company* magazine,

> A lot of people make the mistake of thinking that getting results is all there is to the job. They go after results without building a team or without building an organization that has the capacity to change. Your real job is to get results and to do it in a way that makes your organization a great place to work—a place where people enjoy coming to work, instead of just taking orders and hitting this month's numbers.[8]

Motivation Theories and the Law

Most of these motivation theories have one element in common: Supervisors must consider individual differences in designing rewards. What motivates one person may not motivate another, so supervisors need to offer a variety of rewards. At the same time, to avoid discrimination, employers must distribute benefits fairly.

The types of rewards a supervisor may use are not entirely under his or her control. Not only does a supervisor have to follow the organization's policies, but he or she must also obey a variety of laws requiring that employers provide certain types of benefits. For example, federal laws set requirements for overtime pay, rest breaks, health insurance for retirees, and many other areas. Most organizations have a human resources professional or department responsible for helping the organization comply with laws related to benefits. The details of these laws are beyond the scope of this book.

However, the requirements of the Family and Medical Leave Act of 1993 are worth noting because they affect the supervisor's role in scheduling work and staffing the department. Under this law, organizations with 50 or more employees within a 75-mile radius must give employees up to 12 weeks of unpaid leave to care for a newborn, adopted, or foster child within one year of the child's arrival. These employers also must offer this time off if employees need to care for a seriously ill child, parent, or spouse or if they themselves have medical conditions that prevent them from doing their jobs. During the time off, the employer must continue to pay the employee's health insurance premiums. The employer also must guarantee that the employee will be able to return to his or her job or an equivalent one. If the need for the leave is foreseeable, the employee must give the organization 30 days' notice.

In some organizations, the supervisor faces a significant challenge in planning and scheduling because of employees' leave. A recent survey by the Society for

Human Resource Management found that about one-third of the workforces of the surveyed companies had requested medical leave during the preceding year, and one-sixth had requested family leave. A leave can make it challenging to motivate the employees who shoulder the extra work. About one-third of the companies in the same survey reported employees had complained that co-workers took leave for reasons the complainers found questionable.[9]

MONEY AS A MOTIVATOR

Some supervisors and other managers assume that the main thing employees want out of a job is money. Most people work to earn at least enough to get by. Although money is only one of many available ways to motivate employees, it is an important one. In a study of low-wage, low-skill hospital workers, researchers found that workers were more likely to feel they were being treated with dignity when they had access to training, staffing levels were adequate, and their pay was relatively high for their type of job.[10] This finding suggests that money is important not only as a means to pay the bills but also as a signal of one's value to the organization.

When Money Motivates

The content theories of motivation imply that money motivates people when it meets their needs. Celia Talavera, a mother of four, takes a two-hour bus ride to reach her job as a housekeeper at Lowes Santa Monica (California) Beach Hotel. She favored a proposed "living wage" ordinance that would raise her pay from $9.88 to $10.50, because it would provide a small amount for savings and benefits. "I am fighting for a living wage because I want to work there for a long time," she says.[11] The opportunity to earn more can also be very important to a college student, considering the high cost of college tuition and the potentially great impact of a college degree on the student's future lifestyle. A retired person or a married person whose spouse earns a comfortable income might work primarily for nonfinancial rewards such as a sense of accomplishment or the satisfaction derived from performing a needed service.

If money is to work as a motivator, employees must believe they are able to achieve the financial rewards the organization offers. Thus, if a theater company offers its staff a bonus for selling a given number of season-ticket subscriptions over the telephone, the bonus will motivate the employees only if they believe they can sell that many tickets. Or, if an organization pays a bonus for employee suggestions that improve quality, the bonus will motivate employees only if they believe they are capable of coming up with ideas.

Pay Plans Using Financial Incentives

The way a pay plan is structured can influence the degree to which employees are motivated to perform well. Some pay plans offer bonuses, commissions, or other kinds of pay for meeting or exceeding objectives. For instance, a growing number of organizations tie raises and bonuses to success in retaining existing customers and meeting established quality goals (see Figure 11.5). Others pay employees a higher rate for learning additional skills, including how to operate lift trucks and computer-controlled machinery or how to develop computer applications to do

financial incentives
Payments for meeting or exceeding objectives

business globally. Such pay plans are said to use **financial incentives.** A recent survey found that more than 10 cents out of every payroll dollar went to some form of variable pay.[12]

FIGURE 11.5
Companies That Link Pay to Performance, 2000 and 2004

Source: WorldatWork annual "Salary Budget Survey," www.worldatwork.org.

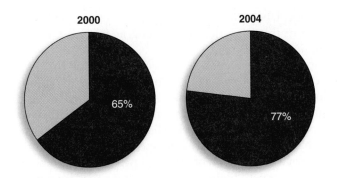

Supervisors rarely have much say in the type of pay plan an organization uses. However, they can motivate better if they understand the kinds of pay plans that offer a financial incentive. Knowing whether the organization's pay system is designed to motivate gives a supervisor clues about the needs of employees for nonfinancial incentives. If the organization's pay plan includes financial incentives but the employees remain unmotivated, a supervisor might look for other kinds of motivators. On the other hand, if the organization's pay plan contains no financial incentives, a supervisor might seek permission to include money for bonuses in the department's budget.

Piecework System

piecework system
Payment according to the quantity produced

The **piecework system** pays people according to how much they produce. This method is often used to pay independent contractors, that is, people who are self-employed and perform work for the organization. For example, a magazine might pay a writer a fixed rate for each word, or a clothing manufacturer might pay a seamster a set amount for each shirt sewed. Farm workers may be paid according to how much they harvest. Unlike independent contractors, however, few employees are paid under this system.

Production Bonus System

Production department employees may receive a basic wage or salary plus a bonus that consists of a payment for each unit produced. Thus, an employee might earn $8.50 or more an hour plus $0.20 for each unit produced. This is called a production bonus system. If employees do not appear to be motivated by a production bonus system, the bonus may not be large enough to be worth the extra effort. Employees who work faster earn more money under such a system, but the pay system does not necessarily encourage high-quality work.

There are other types of bonus as well. When a boom in business coincided with a shortage of qualified workers, Alan Hirsch, owner of Dilworth Mattress Co. in Charlotte, North Carolina, had to scramble to find the 10 workers he needed to keep his operation running. He hit upon the idea of giving a $50 biweekly bonus to workers with perfect attendance for the past two weeks.[13]

Saga Software, an enterprise software developer based in Reston, Virginia, gives out nearly $300,000 in on-the-spot performance bonuses. Nearly half the firm's 800 employees earned between $500 and $5,000 in one recent year; if they chose to defer all or part of the bonus, the firm marked the award up by 50 percent.[14]

Commissions

commissions
Payment linked to the amount of sales completed

In a sales department, employees may earn **commissions,** or payment linked to the amount of sales completed. For example, a real estate agent listed a house for a brokerage. Upon the sale of the house, the agent might receive a commission of 2 percent of the sale price. The selling agent and the brokerage also would get commissions.

Although commissions are most commonly paid to salespeople, companies have applied this type of pay to other positions where the company charges a client for the work the employee completes. At Pinard's Small Engine Repair, a shop located in Manchester, New Hampshire, service technicians receive a commission based on the amount billed for their work. The technicians keep track of the time they spend on billable work. Employees who spend at least half of their time doing billable repairs earn a commission of at least 4 percent of the amount billed for their work. Technicians can earn higher percentages for spending more of their time on billable work. A technician who spends at least 80 percent of his or her time on billable hours will earn a commission of 7 percent—a much larger commission, considering that the amount billed is also likely to be greater. Thus, the pay system encourages technicians at Pinard's to work more efficiently. The shop supports this arrangement by setting up work arrangements so that technicians are free to concentrate on repairs, rather than helping out in the store or answering phones.[15]

Most organizations that pay commissions also pay a basic wage or salary. Otherwise, the financial uncertainty can worry employees to the point that it interferes with motivation. Some people, however, like the unlimited earnings potential of a commission-only job.

Payments for Suggestions

To build employee participation and communication, many companies pay employees for making suggestions on how to cut costs or improve quality. Typically, the suggestion must be adopted or save some minimum amount of money before the employee receives payment. The size of the payment may be linked to the size of the benefit to the organization. In other words, an idea with a bigger impact results in a bigger payment.

Group Incentive Plans

group incentive plan
A financial incentive plan that rewards a team of workers for meeting or exceeding an objective

profit-sharing plan
A group incentive plan under which the company sets aside a share of its profits and divides it among employees

Organizations today are focusing increasingly on ways to get employees and their supervisors to work together as teams. A financial incentive to get people to work this way is the **group incentive plan,** which pays a bonus when the group as a whole exceeds some objective. An organization measures the performance of a work unit against its objectives, then pays a bonus if the group exceeds the objectives. At Continental Airlines, every employee receives at least $65 in cash for each month that the airline ranks among the top three in on-time performance as rated by the U.S. Transportation Department or completes at least 80 percent of its flights on schedule. For every month that Continental ranks first, the bonus rises to $100 each.[16]

A frequently used type of group incentive is the **profit-sharing plan.** Under this kind of plan, the company sets aside a share of its profits earned during a given period, such as a year, and divides these profits among the employees. The assumption is that the better the work done, the more the company will earn and, therefore, the bigger the bonuses. In the past, profit sharing was limited chiefly to executives, but more companies today are sharing profits among all employees. InterDyn Cargas, which sells business software and consulting services, uses a profit-sharing plan as a way to keep employees focused on team success rather than individual performance alone. One-fifth of InterDyn's profits are set aside and divided among employees every six months, with somewhat more allocated to employees who have been at the company longer.[17]

gainsharing
A group incentive plan in which the organization encourages employees to participate in making suggestions and decisions, then rewards the group with a share of improved earnings

An increasing number of companies are adopting a **gainsharing** program, under which the company encourages employees to participate in making suggestions and decisions about improving the way the company or work group operates. As performance improves, employees receive a share of the greater earnings. Thus, gainsharing seeks to motivate not only by giving financial rewards but also by making employees feel they have an important role as part of a team.

Secrecy of Wage and Salary Information

In our society, money is considered a private matter, and most people do not like to talk about what they earn. Thus, in private (nongovernment) organizations, employees generally do not know one another's earnings, though supervisors know what their subordinates earn. In contrast, government employees' earnings are public information, often published in local papers, because taxpayers ultimately pay their wages and salaries.

Does secrecy help or hurt the usefulness of money as a motivator? Certainly, it does not make sense to disclose information if it only embarrasses employees. Most employees overestimate what others earn. This overestimation can result in dissatisfaction because employees believe they are underpaid in comparison.

To motivate employees with the possibility of a raise and a belief that pay rates are fair, the organization must let them know what they can hope to earn. A typical compromise between maintaining privacy and sharing information is for the organization to publish pay ranges. These show the lowest and highest wage or salary the organization will pay an employee in a particular position. Employees do not know how much specific individuals earn, but the ranges show what they can expect to earn if they get a raise, promotion, or transfer to another position.

HOW SUPERVISORS CAN MOTIVATE

The first part of this chapter addressed the theories of motivating. These theories suggest some practical ways supervisors can motivate. Several possibilities are summarized in Figure 11.6.

FIGURE 11.6
Ways Supervisors Can Motivate Employees

Making Work Interesting
- Job rotation
- Job enlargement
- Job enrichment
- Customer contact

Having High Expectations

Providing Valued Rewards

Relating Rewards to Performance

Treating Employees as Individuals

Encouraging Participation

Providing Feedback

SUPERVISORY SKILLS

MOTIVATING EMPLOYEES

BANKS MAKE TELLERS' JOBS MORE INTERESTING

At many banks, the turnover among tellers is high. Customer service suffers, and the banks continually have to hire and train new employees. Other banks hang on to their tellers by motivating them with interesting work.

In Houston, Sterling Bancshares gave tellers greater authority in decisions such as when to credit checks deposited to a customer's account—immediately or after the check has cleared. Decision-making authority requires information, so the bank installed computer workstations for tellers to use. The company also set up a program to certify tellers at three levels. As the tellers successfully complete training for this program, they move up to higher pay levels.

In Rhode Island, Bank of Newport is teaching its tellers more about customer service and the banking business. The company instituted classroom training, so the tellers can better learn a variety of tasks as well as steer customers to financial products that may benefit them.

In Owosso, Michigan, Republic Bancorp broadened the scope of the teller's job. At Republic, tellers are called customer service representatives. Their responsibilities include calling customers during periods when traffic into the bank is light. During these calls, the tellers try to attract deposits and refer interested small businesses to the lending department. If they win business, they can earn incentive pay of up to 75 percent of their wages.

In Cleveland, Third Federal Savings and Loan trains employees, including tellers, to do various jobs. Third Federal employees are expected to fill in wherever they are qualified, so that the whole group meets its goals. Many of the bank's tellers can open savings accounts and originate loans. Officers, in turn, help tellers when their workload is heavy. Third Federal also includes tellers on various committees and task forces.

Source: Bill Stoneman, "To Reduce Turnover, Turn the Teller into a Team Player," *American Banker*, July 8, 2003, downloaded from Business & Company Resource Center, http://galenet.galegroup.com.

Making Work Interesting

job rotation
Moving employees from job to job to give them more variety

cross-training
Training in the skills required to perform more than one job

job enlargement
An effort to make a job more interesting by adding more duties to it

job enrichment
The incorporation of motivating factors into a job—in particular, giving the employee more responsibility and recognition

When employees find their work interesting, they are more likely to give it their full attention and enthusiasm. In general, work is interesting when it has variety and allows employees some control over what they do. Work can be made more interesting through job rotation, job enlargement, job enrichment, and increased customer contact. For examples, see the "Supervisory Skills" box.

Job rotation involves moving employees from job to job to give them more variety. For example, the employees in a production department may take turns operating all the machines in the factory. Job rotation requires that employees have relatively broad skills. As a result, the supervisor or company must provide for **cross-training**, or training in the skills required to perform more than one job. The opportunity to learn new skills through cross-training can in itself motivate employees.

Job enlargement is an effort to make a job more interesting by adding more duties to it. Thus, a machine operator might be responsible not only for running a particular machine but also for performing maintenance on the machine and inspecting the quality of the parts produced with the machine. As with job rotation, this approach assumes that variety in a job makes it more satisfying, with the result that employees are more motivated.

Job enrichment is the incorporation of motivating factors into a job. Herzberg called the factors that enrich a job "motivators." Generally, an enriched job gives employees more responsibility to make decisions and more recognition for good performance. Thus, enriched jobs are more challenging and, presumably, more rewarding. For example, instead of requiring salespeople in a department store to call a supervisor whenever a customer has a complaint, the store might authorize them to handle complaints as they see fit. They would have to call a supervisor only if solving the problem would cost the store more than some set amount, say, $500.

When modifying jobs to make them more interesting, the organization and supervisor must remember that not all employees are motivated by the same things at the same time. Thus, while some employees may eagerly accept the new variety in their jobs, others are likely to be less enthusiastic. Some workers may think jobs are being redesigned simply to get more work out of people for the same amount of money. A supervisor must be careful to emphasize the advantages of the new arrangement and listen to employee reactions.

Work also can be made more meaningful by giving employees some contact with the people who receive and use their products (goods or services). Nurses and salespeople are routinely in contact with the people they serve, but production workers and accounting personnel have less customer contact. Sometimes a supervisor can arrange to have workers visit the users of the products. For example, a group of production workers might be sent to visit a customer who is having trouble operating a machine the company manufactures. The workers not only would be able to help the customer but might also get some ideas for making the machine better. Accounting personnel might meet the people in the company who use their reports to make sure they understand and are satisfied with the reports.

Having High Expectations

Effective motivation can lead to performance beyond employees' own expectations of themselves. When someone expects a lot of us, we often find that we can do a lot. When little is expected, we tend to provide little. In either case, the expectations are self-fulfilling.

Pygmalion effect
The direct relationship between expectations and performance; high expectations lead to high performance

The direct relationship between expectations and performance is known as the **Pygmalion effect.** The name comes from the Greek myth of Pygmalion, a king of Cyprus who carved a statue of a beautiful maiden and then fell in love with her. He so wished she were real that she became real.

According to the Pygmalion effect, a supervisor who says to an employee, "You're so dense, you never get the procedures right," will not motivate effectively. Instead, the employee will decide that understanding procedures is beyond his or her capacity. Therefore, a supervisor who wishes employees to set high standards for themselves must think and speak with the assumption that the employees are capable of meeting high standards. A supervisor might say, "These procedures are complicated, but I'm sure that if you study them regularly and ask questions, you can learn to follow them."

An individual who recognizes the value of high expectations is minor-league baseball player Alex Gordon. When the Kansas City Royals selected him in 2005, he became the number two pick in that year's draft, and expectations for his baseball career soared. Gordon's reaction? As he prepared for the start of a game, playing with the Wichita Wranglers Class AA team, he told a reporter, "I actually liked the expectations. It gives me that little bit more motivation to do well."[18]

Providing Rewards That Are Valued

The content theories of motivation indicate that a variety of rewards may motivate but that not all employees will value the same rewards at the same time. The supervisor's challenge is to determine what rewards will work for particular

TIPS FROM THE FIRING LINE

EXPRESSING SINCERE APPRECIATION

Johanna Rothman helps project teams of information technology experts learn to work together effectively. As team leader and consultant, she has found that vague expressions of praise are much less effective than specific, personal statements. Rothman recommends that groups use a format she calls "appreciations." Here is Rothman's formula for an appreciation:

I appreciate you, [name], for [specific action]. [That action] [tell the action's effect on you or the group].

According to Rothman, the second part of an appreciation may feel awkward to say, but it is the part that really motivates people to continue the desired behavior.

Rothman illustrates her formula with several examples, including the following two (edited):

I appreciate you, Ron, for thinking about the project and testing intelligently. I've worked with testers who didn't know about our projects and didn't have the benefits I wanted from the testing. You found things I didn't know I'd put into the software code.

I appreciate you, Dawn, for reviewing my first draft of the project architecture so quickly. Because you reviewed it quickly, I had time to reorganize it, and our customers really like the way the product is organized now.

Source: Johanna Rothman, "Appreciations, Personalized Thank You's," *The Pragmatic Manager* 1, no. 2 (2003), Rothman Consulting Group Web site, www.jrothman.com.

employees at particular times. This means appreciating the needs people are trying to meet and the variety of ways a supervisor can provide rewards.

Sometimes an outrageously attractive award serves not only to recognize a valued employee but also to motivate others who can't help but notice the result of outstanding performance. Gordon M. Bethune, former chair of Continental Airlines, awarded a new Ford Explorer to Tampa, Florida, reservations agent Wendy Pignataro for a period of perfect attendance. Pignataro and six other winners received their prizes before a crowd of hundreds of fellow employees at the company's Houston headquarters.[19]

Of course, there are some limits to a supervisor's discretion in giving rewards. Company policy or a union contract may dictate the size of raises employees get and the degree to which raises are linked to performance as opposed to seniority or some other measure. However, supervisors can use the theories of motivation, coupled with their own experience, to identify the kinds of rewards over which they have some control. For example, a supervisor has great freedom in administering rewards such as praise and recognition. Many supervisors have some discretion in job assignments. Employees who have a high need for achievement (McClelland's theory) or are trying to meet esteem or self-actualization needs (Maslow's theory) may appreciate opportunities for additional training. Employees who have a high need for affiliation or are seeking to meet social needs may appreciate being assigned to jobs in which they work with other people.

Relating Rewards to Performance

The rewards a supervisor uses should be linked to employee performance. Unfortunately, employees seldom see a clear link between good job performance and higher pay. If there is a connection, employees should be aware of it and understand it. Another means of connecting rewards to performance is in the way supervisors express praise. "Tips from the Firing Line" suggests a way to offer performance-related praise. Linking rewards to the achievement of realistic objectives is a way to help employees believe they can attain desired rewards. As Vroom's expectancy–valence theory described, rewards are most likely to motivate employees when the employees view them as achievable.

At Great Scott Broadcasting, an independent broadcasting company in Pottstown, Pennsylvania, sales reps for the company's eight radio stations in Maryland and Delaware must be knowledgeable about audience demographics, marketing protocol, and other key information about selling radio spots. With a game called Trivia Feud, general manager Cathy Deighan ensures that the reps have the information they need to answer clients' questions quickly and accurately. The competitive 15-minute game is played at every weekly sales meeting— "It can get pretty crazy," says Deighan—and each person on the winning team gets a prize, such as a gift certificate for dinner, a free car wash, or cash.[20]

The use of objectives is a basic way to link rewards to performance (see Chapter 6). For example, the management by objectives (MBO) system provides rewards when employees meet or exceed the objectives they have helped set for themselves. Thus, if a museum's cafeteria workers are supposed to leave their work areas spotless at the end of each shift, they know whether they have done what is necessary to receive their rewards, such as regular pay raises or extra time off.

Using clear objectives to help motivate employees is an important way to make sure that when employees try hard, they are trying to do the right things. Rackspace, a Web-hosting service based in San Antonio, Texas, links rewards to its goal of delivering "fanatical" customer support. The company is divided into teams that bring together employees from various functions, including account management and tech support. Each team is responsible for meeting its own set of financial and service goals, including customer turnover, growth in existing customers' business with Rackspace, and number of referrals from customers. Each month, if teams meet their goals, team members receive bonuses in amounts up to 20 percent of their salaries. Customer praise gets posted on the walls, and individuals receive recognition through the monthly Straitjacket Award; employees grant this award by voting for the employee whose customer support was most fanatical.[21] (For a discussion of communicating goals and other information to employees, see Chapter 10.)

Treating Employees as Individuals

Most of the theories of motivation emphasize that different things motivate individuals to different degrees. A supervisor who wishes to succeed at motivating has to remember that employees will respond in varying ways. A supervisor cannot expect that everyone will be excited equally about cross-training or overtime pay. Some employees might prefer an easy job or short hours, so that they have time and energy for outside activities. *Business Week* editor Diane Brady, a working mother, was happy to find the privacy to pump breast milk for her infant son while on the job in her New York office.[22] "Pumping at work helps me feel close to my son while we're apart during the day," she says. Wolfgang Zwierner has waited tables at Brooklyn's famed Peter Luger Steak House for 38 years because, he says, "The job of a waiter is to like people. I make people comfortable. I spoil them if I can."[23] Figure 11.7 shows how U.S. workers rated job characteristics in a Gallup poll.

As much as possible, a supervisor should respond to individual differences. When a particular type of motivation does not seem to work with an employee, a

FIGURE 11.7   Job Characteristics Rated Important by U.S. Workers

Source: Data from Gallup poll cited in Patricia Braus, "What Workers Want," *American Demographics*, August 1992, pp. 30–31 ff.

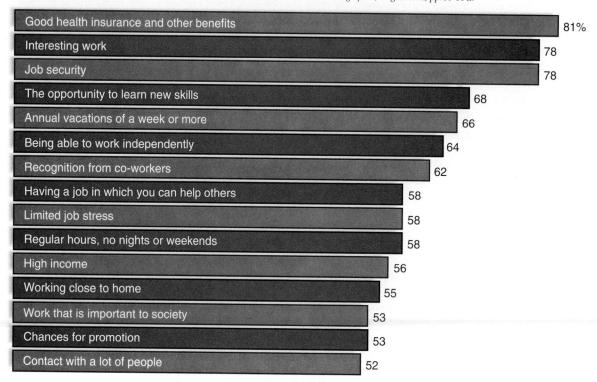

Good health insurance and other benefits	81%
Interesting work	78
Job security	78
The opportunity to learn new skills	68
Annual vacations of a week or more	66
Being able to work independently	64
Recognition from co-workers	62
Having a job in which you can help others	58
Limited job stress	58
Regular hours, no nights or weekends	58
High income	56
Working close to home	55
Work that is important to society	53
Chances for promotion	53
Contact with a lot of people	52

supervisor should try some other motivator to see if it better matches the employee's needs.

Encouraging Employee Participation

One way to learn about employees' needs and benefit from their ideas is to encourage employees to participate in planning and decision making. As you read in Chapter 9, employees tend to feel more committed when they can contribute to decisions and solutions. They also are likely to cooperate better when they feel like part of a team.

As described in the "Supervision across Industries" box in Chapter 3, Whole Foods Market gives teams of employees great decision-making authority. The supermarket chain extended this practice to a recent decision about health insurance benefits. The company had a self-insured plan, but claims overwhelmed the plan's funds, so Whole Foods developed a plan using medical savings accounts. The company deposits money into employee accounts, and the employees, who pay no premiums, pick up the first $500 of prescription costs and $1,000 of other medical bills. After that, bills are paid from the savings accounts. After a one-year trial, Whole Foods had its employees evaluate whether to continue the new savings account approach or opt for traditional insurance coverage. By an overwhelming margin, the employees voted to keep the medical savings accounts. Part of the appeal is likely that Whole Foods workers tend to be relatively young and healthy; in a recent year, only 10 percent of employees spent all the money in their accounts, and the remaining dollars rolled over into the next year's account.

Because the employees don't have to pay insurance premiums, more of them elect the insurance coverage as part of their benefits package. And Whole Foods is delighted, because the arrangement is helping it control health coverage expenses.[24]

Providing Feedback

People want and need to know how well they are doing. Part of a supervisor's job is to give employees feedback about their performance. When the supervisor tells employees that they are meeting or exceeding objectives, the employees know they are doing something right. When a supervisor tells employees that they are falling short of objectives, the employees know they need to improve. Most people will try to improve when given a chance to do so.

Praise is an important kind of feedback. In monitoring employees, a supervisor should look for signs of excellent performance and let the employees know, in specific terms, that the good work is appreciated and that it benefits the organization.

There are many ways to deliver praise. For example, a nursing supervisor might write a memo to a nurse, in which the supervisor comments on the nurse's courteous manner with patients and how it gives patients a good impression of the hospital. Or, a police force supervisor might remark to an officer that the officer's paperwork is always complete and legible. When Dave Marin was a bank manager, he invented a simple method of praise that surprised him with its impact. While preparing for a sales meeting, he bought a bag of stones and marked each one with a large U. The message: "You rock." Marin gave one out to each employee he praised at the meeting. Thinking the rocks were a little silly, Marin was surprised when employees started asking him if he would be giving them out at the next meeting. He was even more surprised when, years later, he began hearing that employees had kept their rewards as a valued possession.[25] Their value did not, of course, come from the worth of the rocks themselves, but from the treasure of public praise.

A supervisor does not have to use a dramatic approach to praising a behavior. Praise is so easy to give and its potential rewards are so great that the supervisor can and should use it routinely, as long as it is sincere.

SKILLS MODULE

PART ONE: CONCEPTS

Summary

11.1 Identify the relationship between motivation and performance.
To perform well, employees must be motivated. Motivation is giving people incentives to act in certain ways. For motivation to work, a supervisor needs to know what rewards employees value.

11.2 Describe content theories of motivation.
Content theories of motivation attempt to identify what motivates people. According to Maslow's theory, people are motivated by unmet needs. These needs fall into a hierarchy: physiological, security, social, esteem, and self-actualization. People attempt to satisfy lower-level needs before they focus on higher-level needs. According to McClelland, people have achievement, power, and affiliation needs. The intensity of each kind of need varies from person to person. Herzberg's two-factor theory says that employees are dissatisfied when hygiene factors are absent and satisfied when motivating factors are present.

11.3 Describe process theories of motivation.

Process theories explain how motivation works through its process. According to Vroom's expectancy-valence theory, the intensity of a person's motivation depends on the value the person places on the outcome of a behavior multiplied by the perceived probability that the behavior will actually lead to the outcome. People are most motivated to seek results they value highly and think they can achieve. Reinforcement theory, pioneered by B. F. Skinner, says people behave as they do because of the kind of consequences they experience as a result of their behavior. The supervisor can therefore influence behavior by administering the consequences (in the form of reinforcement or punishment).

11.4 Explain when financial incentives are likely to motivate employees.

Money motivates people when it meets their needs. The employees must believe they are able to achieve the financial rewards the organization offers.

11.5 Describe pay plans using financial incentives.

Under a piecework system, employees are paid according to how much they produce. A production bonus system pays a basic wage or salary plus a bonus based on performance; for example, an amount per unit assembled. Commissions are payments tied to the amount of sales completed. Some organizations pay employees for making useful suggestions about cutting costs or improving quality. Group incentive plans pay a bonus when the group as a whole exceeds an objective. Profit-sharing and gainsharing plans are types of group incentives.

11.6 Discuss the pros and cons of keeping pay information secret.

Keeping pay secret respects employees' desire for privacy. However, to be motivated by the possibility of greater earnings and a sense that pay rates are fair, employees must know what they can hope to earn. Typically, an organization balances these needs by publishing pay ranges that show the least and most the organization will pay an employee in a particular job.

11.7 Identify ways supervisors can motivate their employees.

Supervisors can motivate employees by making work interesting through job rotation, job enlargement, job enrichment, and contact with users of the product or service. Other ways to motivate include having high expectations of employees, providing rewards that are valued, relating rewards to performance, treating employees as individuals, encouraging employee participation, and providing feedback, including praise.

Key Terms

motivation, *p.* 289	financial	profit-sharing plan, *p.* 300
flextime, *p.* 292	incentives, *p.* 298	gainsharing, *p.* 301
job sharing, *p.* 292	piecework	job rotation, *p.* 302
reinforcement, *p.* 296	system, *p.* 299	cross-training, *p.* 302
punishment, *p.* 296	commissions, *p.* 299	job enlargement, *p.* 302
behavior	group incentive	job enrichment, *p.* 302
modification, *p.* 296	plan, *p.* 300	Pygmalion effect, *p.* 303

Review and Discussion Questions

1. Name and rank the five basic needs, from lowest to highest, that Maslow described in his hierarchy of needs. If a supervisor applies this hierarchy to his or her employees, what are some specific ways that employees' needs could be met?

2. What are some family-friendly policies that companies now have in place so that employees can balance home and work? What other family-friendly policies might help employees to meet the demands in their lives and thus motivate them at work?

3. What are the three categories of needs that McClelland identified in his theory? Which category of needs do you think is strongest for you?

4. What are the hygiene factors and motivating factors described by Herzberg? Consider your current job or one you held most recently. Which factors are (were) present at that job? How would you say they affect(ed) your level of satisfaction? Your level of motivation?

5. John Lightfoot believes he has a 75 percent chance of earning a bonus of $100. Mary Yu believes she has a 75 percent chance of qualifying for a raise of $1,000 a year. According to Vroom's expectancy–valence theory, is it correct to conclude that Mary will be more intensely motivated by her potential reward than John will be by his? Explain.

6. Andre Jones supervises computer programmers. He expects each programmer to turn in a progress report by quitting time each Friday.
   a. Name at least one way Jones can use reinforcement to motivate employees to turn in their reports on time.
   b. Name at least one way Jones can use punishment to motivate employees to turn in their reports on time.
   c. Which of these approaches do you think would be most successful? Why?

7. In which of the following situations do you think money would be an effective motivator? Explain.
   a. The economy is slow, and even though the salespeople think they are doing their best, sales are down. Sales supervisor Rita Blount tells the sales force that anyone whose weekly sales are up by 10 percent next week will receive a $5,000 bonus.
   b. A retailer such as Best Buy announces that the top performer in the store will be a prime candidate for a management job in a store the company is opening in another state. Whoever takes the job will receive a raise of at least 9 percent.
   c. A respiratory therapist who is the parent of two high school–aged children can earn an extra $500 this month by accepting a schedule that involves working on weekends.

8. Which type or types of pay plan (piecework, production bonus, commission, payment for suggestions, group incentive) would work best in each of the following situations? Why?
   a. A company wants to motivate employees in the manufacturing department to fulfill increased orders for wooden toys as the company tries to expand from a regional market to a national market.
   b. A car dealership wants to emphasize teamwork in its service department.

9. Antonio Delgado supervises the police officers of the Fourth Precinct. Name some ways in which he can make their work more interesting.

10. A supervisor at a mail-order catalog company reads a report stating that 15 percent of all orders subsequently are returned, but this figure is considered better than the industry average. How can she use the Pygmalion effect to motivate employees to reduce the number of returns even further?

11. What is wrong with each of the following attempts at motivation?

   a. A sales supervisor for an insurance company believes that employees appreciate an opportunity to broaden their experiences, so she rewards the top performer each year with an all expenses–paid leadership seminar. The seminar lasts a week and is conducted at a hotel in a city 200 miles away.

   b. The supervisor of a hospital cafeteria awards one employee a $50 bonus each month. To give everyone an equal chance at receiving the bonus, the supervisor draws names written on slips of paper from a jar.

   c. A maintenance supervisor in a pickle factory believes that qualified employees should be able to tell whether they are doing a good job. Therefore, the supervisor focuses motivation efforts on thinking up clever rewards to give out each year to the best performers.

PART TWO: SKILL-BUILDING

YOU SOLVE THE PROBLEM

Reflecting back on page 289, list the motivation techniques that Todd Harris uses at Connextions, according to the description. Then have one member of your group review each of the motivation theories described in this chapter. Each group member should then suggest one or two additional ideas for motivation, based on the theory he or she reviewed. Discuss each idea as a group. On the basis of your experience, how well will each idea motivate the employees in Harris's group?

Problem-Solving Case: *Motivating Employees at Nucor Corporation*

Today Nucor Corporation is the biggest steel company in the United States, so it's hard to believe it was once an underdog in a struggling industry. What has set the company apart is a focus on motivating and empowering employees. The employee focus is illustrated by the custom of printing each individual's name on the cover of Nucor's annual report. But the concern for employees is much more practical and goes far beyond symbols.

Nucor's pay system is remarkable. At all levels of the company, the largest share of employees' income is tied to their performance. Base pay for a Nucor steelworker is near $10 per hour, far below the industry range of $16 to $21. But on top of that, steelworkers can earn a bonus based on the amount of defect-free steel produced during their shift. Those bonuses can triple the workers' pay, taking it far above the industry average. Tying the bonus to the entire shift's performance also motivates employees to cooperate to get the job done. In addition, the company pays out profit sharing, encouraging employees to care about the entire company's performance. The company computes the bonus on every order of steel and pays it weekly, so employees have plenty of reinforcement. In 2005, a typical Nucor steelworker earned $79,000 plus $2,000 from a special bonus celebrating record earnings for the company plus nearly $18,000 in profit sharing. Managers receive similarly large amounts of their pay in the form of bonuses and profit sharing.

For employees new to Nucor, often used to relying on base pay, the compensation arrangement seems alarming at first. Once they get a taste of bonuses, however, they become highly motivated. When Nucor acquired a steel plant in Auburn, New York, workers wanted to keep their old pay system, so management simply continued paying them the old way but announcing what they would have made under Nucor's system. Eventually employees began to see that a new way of thinking could fill up their pocketbooks. David Hutchins, a Nucor supervisor in Auburn, says that before Nucor acquired his plant, workers in his group tended to relax whenever an earlier stage of operations slowed down. But with a bonus riding on their shift's output, the employees no longer think of themselves as separate groups: "Wherever the bottleneck is," explains Hutchins, "we go there, and everyone works on it." Before long, output in Auburn was up, and so were paycheck totals.

Motivation at Nucor is about more than pay, however. The company encourages employees to share ideas and empowers them to make decisions and solve problems. Supervisors, for example, make decisions more typical of a plant manager. Once, following the failure of an electrical grid at the Hickman, Arkansas, plant, a group of electricians at Nucor facilities in Decatur, Alabama, and Hertford County, North Carolina, traveled to Hickman to work on the problem. They didn't need to get a supervisor's approval; they just needed to do what they determined was most important.

Along with cooperation, Nucor fosters friendly competition in order to stimulate creative thinking. For example, plants often hold contests among the shifts to see which one can meet a goal related to output, safety, or efficiency.

1. How does performance-based pay motivate Nucor employees? Would this pay system be effective if Nucor did not also empower employees to make decisions? Why or why not?
2. Supervisors do not set up the pay system for a large company like Nucor. How can Nucor's supervisors contribute to employee motivation?
3. Does this description of Nucor sound like an organization in which you would feel motivated? Why or why not? Which theory of motivation would best explain your feelings?

Source: Nanette Byrnes, "The Art of Motivation," *BusinessWeek*, May 1, 2006, downloaded from InfoTrac, http://web2.infotrac.galegroup.com.

Knowing Yourself

What Motivates You?
What makes a job appealing to you? Rank the following job factors from 1 to 12. Assign 1 to the factor you consider most important and 12 to the factor you consider least important.

_____ 1. Work that is interesting and meaningful.
_____ 2. Good wages or salary.
_____ 3. Authority to make important decisions.
_____ 4. Comfortable work environment, such as a clean, modern laboratory, fancy store, or attractive office.
_____ 5. Likable co-workers.
_____ 6. Good relationship with supervisor.
_____ 7. Clear understanding of the department's and company's goals and performance requirements.
_____ 8. Appreciation and recognition for doing a good job.
_____ 9. Opportunities to learn new skills.
_____ 10. Prestigious title or occupation.
_____ 11. Chance for advancement.
_____ 12. Job security.

Pause and Reflect

1. Which of these motivators can you expect from working as a supervisor?
2. Can you modify your own job so that it includes more of these factors?
3. How can you as a supervisor make these motivators available to employees?

Class Exercise

Learning What Motivates Workers

If you have not already done so, answer the Knowing Yourself questions. Then, by a show of hands, determine how many class members selected each response as most important and how many as least important. The instructor might tally the responses on the chalkboard or overhead projector or fill in the table below:

	Number of Students Rating the Item	
Self-Quiz Item	Most Important	Least Important
1.	_____	_____
2.	_____	_____
3.	_____	_____
4.	_____	_____
5.	_____	_____
6.	_____	_____
7.	_____	_____
8.	_____	_____
9.	_____	_____
10.	_____	_____
11.	_____	_____
12.	_____	_____

Discuss the following questions:

- Which response or responses did most class members choose as most important?
- Which response or responses did most class members choose as least important?
- Do you think these choices are typical of most employees today? Why or why not?
- How could a supervisor use this information to motivate employees?

Building Supervision Skills

Developing Motivational Methods

This chapter deals with one of the most challenging areas for supervisors: motivating employees. This exercise will help you develop a comprehensive list of motivating methods on which to draw when faced with employees whom you feel are not performing to their full potential.

1. The figure on page 301 shows several motivational methods. Drawing on what you have learned about motivation in this class and elsewhere, list methods, techniques, and strategies that can serve as a source of ideas on how to motivate people.

2. For the purposes of this exercise, do not be concerned about the economic impact of your ideas or a plan for carrying them out. For example, if you suggest a bonus to reward your employees for good performance, there is no need to provide a formula for computing the bonus. At the same time, however, do not make ridiculous suggestions that would not make good business sense, such as suggesting that you reward all employees and their families with a two-week all expenses–paid vacation to Bermuda.

3. Divide the class into groups. Then develop a group list that can be copied for each group member. There will undoubtedly be many days in your management career when you will be able to use this list to help you generate some ideas about how to motivate an unmotivated employee. Also, the list can be improved over time as you develop greater expertise as a motivational leader.

Things I can do to be a motivational leader	Characteristics of a motivating work environment	Ways to reward my employees for good performance	Strategies I can use to improve the way work is done	Organizational policies or benefits
Help employees set challenging yet achievable goals	Goods and services employees believe in	Publish achievements in company newsletter	Communicate clear performance standards	Flexible work schedule to accommodate personal and family needs

Chapter **Twelve**

Problem Employees: Counseling and Discipline

Chapter Outline

Problems Requiring Special Action
Absenteeism and Tardiness
Insubordination and Uncooperativeness
Alcohol and Drug Abuse
Workplace Violence
Theft

Counseling
Benefits of Counseling
Appropriate Times to Counsel
Counseling Techniques

Discipline
Administering Discipline
Positive Discipline
Self-Discipline

Troubled Employees
Detection of the Troubled Employee
Confrontation of the Troubled Employee
Aid in and Evaluation of Recovery

Sources of Support

Learning Objectives

After you have studied this chapter, you should be able to:

12.1 Identify common types of problem behavior among employees.

12.2 Explain why and when supervisors should counsel employees.

12.3 Describe counseling techniques.

12.4 Discuss effective ways of administering discipline.

12.5 Describe the principles of positive discipline and self-discipline.

12.6 Explain how supervisors can detect and confront troubled employees.

12.7 Specify how supervisors can direct troubled employees in getting help and then follow up on the recovery efforts.

12.8 Discuss the role of the supervisor's manager and the human resources department in helping the supervisor with problem employees.

Starting and building a company is like going into battle—and I always prefer to go into battle with a team that is loyal to one another and to the cause.

—*Srivats Sampath, founder of McAfee.com and CEO of Mercora*

A Supervisor's Problem: Convincing Lab Workers to Follow the Rules

A laboratory that conducts medical testing recently hired someone for the position of lab manager, who is responsible for supervising the technicians. This new supervisor—let's call her Madison—has had difficulty persuading the technicians to follow basic safety rules and carry out their work without complaining. So Madison wrote to the "Management Q&A" column of a magazine called *Medical Laboratory Observer*, looking for leadership advice. She told the columnist, Christopher Frings, a management consultant, that her employees "gripe and complain when I give them instructions, and most simply will not do what I ask." According to Madison, the employees resist wearing their latex gloves, and they try to get away with eating and drinking while at work in the laboratory.

Madison told Frings that she has tried to address the problem with a strategy aimed at winning them over: "to be friendly and get them to like me." So far, however, she has seen no improvement in the technicians' behavior. She suspects that the problem may stem from her young age. She has the most difficulty with employees who have worked in the lab for 20 years or more. Younger employees tend to be more cooperative.

Although Frings called this supervisor's situation a "management disaster," he urged Madison to take command so that the lab, its employees, and management will not run into problems caused by the failure to follow basic precautions designed to keep them safe and ensure the accuracy of test results. Frings also drew on a panel of laboratory managers for some expert advice.

Marti Bailey, a work unit leader at Penn State's Milton S. Hershey Medical Center, advised Madison to "make your expectations clear to the staff and then hold them accountable." Bailey predicted that eventually at least one employee might have to be terminated before the staff would believe their supervisor was serious about the rules. She also suggested focusing on work rules during performance appraisals and giving pay increases only to employees who have been cooperating.

Lawrence Crolla, a chemist at several hospitals in the Chicago suburbs, pointed out that supervision is not about making friends with the staff: "The employees you supervise do not have to like you; they must, however, respect you and the job you do." Crolla added that an important way to gain respect is to treat employees fairly. He also suggested that the supervisor point out the purpose of each rule.

Alton Sturtevant, a manager with LabCorp in Birmingham, Alabama, advised spelling out each employee's responsibilities in writing and keeping track of performance. Sturtevant added that it is important for supervisors to work closely with the company's human resources department to be sure they are following all rules and policies for discipline. These measures help make a strong case for disciplinary actions and protect the supervisor from complaints that discipline is unfair.

As "Madison" discovered, leading employees who resist following the rules can be one of a supervisor's most difficult challenges.

QUESTIONS

1. How can this supervisor change from simply trying to please her employees and persuade them to improve their behavior?

2. Will the advice from these experts be enough to improve performance at Madison's medical laboratory?

Source: Christopher S. Frings, "Ensuring Staff Cooperation," *Medical Laboratory Observer,* July 2005, downloaded from Business & Company Resource Center, http://galenet.galegroup.com.

When a supervisor does a good job of leading, problem solving, communicating, and motivating, most employees will perform well. Even so, a supervisor occasionally faces the challenge of a "problem" employee, one who is persistently unwilling or unable to follow the rules or meet performance standards. In general, problem employees fall into two categories: (1) employees *causing* problems—for example, by starting fights or leaving early—and (2) employees *with* problems, such as an employee whose money worries are a distraction from work. By handling these troubled employees appropriately, a supervisor can help resolve the problem without hurting the morale or performance of other employees.

This chapter provides guidelines for supervising problem employees. It describes some common problems requiring special action on the part of a supervisor and explains two basic courses of action to take: counseling and discipline.

The chapter also discusses how to help a troubled employee. Finally, the chapter describes the kinds of support a supervisor can expect from superiors, the human resources department, and other experts.

PROBLEMS REQUIRING SPECIAL ACTION

For the third straight Monday, Peter Dunbar had called in sick. Other employees were grumbling about having to do extra work to make up for his absences, and rumors were flying about the nature of Dunbar's problem. His supervisor knew she would have to take action, beginning with some investigation into what the problem was.

When supervisors observe poor performance, they tend to blame the employee for lacking ability or effort. But when supervisors or employees need to explain their own poor performance, they may blame the organization or another person for not providing enough support. This inconsistency suggests that some digging is needed to uncover the true source of a performance problem. For example, the supervisor might consider the following questions:

- Has the employee performed better in the past?
- Has the employee received proper training?
- Does the employee know and understand the objectives he or she is to accomplish?
- Is the supervisor providing enough feedback and support?
- Has the supervisor encouraged and rewarded high performance?
- Are other employees with similar abilities performing well? Are they experiencing similar difficulties?

Although persistent failure to perform up to standards may result from many problems, the problems that supervisors most commonly encounter among employees are absenteeism and tardiness, insubordination and uncooperativeness, alcohol and drug abuse, workplace violence, and theft.

Absenteeism and Tardiness

An employee who misses work, even part of a day, is expensive for an employer. The company frequently must pay for those unproductive hours—for example, by providing sick pay to an employee who calls in sick. In addition, the other employees may be less productive when they have to cover for someone who is absent or tardy. A recent survey found that absenteeism cost employers an average of $645 per employee in 2003.[1]

Of course, employees who really are sick should take time off. The company provides sick days for good reasons: to allow employees to rest and recover and to prevent them from infecting the rest of the workforce. The problem arises with absences that are unexcused or recur with suspicious regularity. In addition, missing work is often a sign of a deeper problem, such as a family crisis, anger about something at work, or plans to leave the organization.

Effective action against tardiness and absenteeism targets the cause of this problem behavior. Unscheduled absences are more frequent at organizations where morale is poor. As shown in Figure 12.1, the most common reasons given for taking unscheduled time off are personal illness and family issues. Employers can help employees manage these needs through programs such as paid time-off banks, meaning employees are allowed a given number of paid days off, which

FIGURE 12.1
Why Employees Had Unscheduled Absences

Source: "2003 Unscheduled Absence Survey," *Medical Benefits*, December 15, 2003, downloaded from Business & Company Resource Center, http://galenet.group .com (data from CCH Inc.).

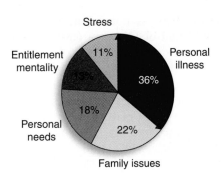

they can use when they are sick, have family needs, or want to take a vacation. If an employee takes days off for doctors' appointments or family crises, fewer days remain for vacationing. Wisco Industries offers positive reinforcement for good attendance: cash incentives to employees who work at least a minimum number of hours during each period.[2] In addition, supervisors can reduce absenteeism by creating a positive work environment in which morale is high.

Insubordination and Uncooperativeness

When poor performance results from not understanding how to do a job, the solution is relatively simple. A supervisor must make sure that instructions are communicated clearly and that the employee is receiving the proper training. But sometimes an employee performs poorly or breaks rules because he or she chooses to do so. Such an employee may simply be uncooperative, or the employee may engage in **insubordination,** the deliberate refusal to do what a supervisor or other superior asks.

insubordination
Deliberate refusal to do what the supervisor or other superior asks

Many kinds of negative behavior fall into these categories. An employee may have a generally poor attitude—criticizing, complaining, and showing a dislike for a supervisor and the organization. He or she might get into arguments over many kinds of issues. An employee may make an art form out of doing as little as possible. The employee might spend most of the day socializing, joking around, or just moving slowly. Another employee might regularly fail to follow rules— "forgetting" to wear safety equipment or sign out at lunchtime. Another kind of negative behavior—employee complaints of racism and retaliation—unfortunately have risen in recent years.[3]

Although these problems are serious, it is important for supervisors to see the difference between employees who don't do their work properly because they choose not to and employees who don't do their work because they need help. One manager who has this skill is Mike Speckman, vice president of sales for inSilica, a company that sells semiconductors. Speckman once had a salesperson who was disorganized and spent almost every minute on existing customers, rather than cultivating the new ones that could help the company grow. Where some supervisors might have seen a lost cause, Speckman saw an employee with a desire to learn. He decided to travel with the salesperson on calls to prospective customers. On the first call, Speckman led the conversation to show how the work was to be done. On the second call, he and the salesperson worked as a team. On the third call, the salesperson took the lead, and Speckman was there just to watch and provide support. The coaching gave the salesperson the necessary confidence to become successful.[4]

Alcohol and Drug Abuse

The abuse of alcohol and drugs by workers is costly in several ways. According to the National Institute on Drug Abuse, employees who use drugs are three times as likely to be tardy and more than three times as likely to be involved in an accident at work. Absences and medical costs also are much greater among drug abusers. And employees who abuse alcohol and drugs are far less productive than their co-workers who stay sober.[5]

Unfortunately, substance abuse is not uncommon at work. A study by the Department of Labor found that one-third of employees say drugs are illegally sold in their workplace, and one in five young employees say they have used marijuana while on the job. According to the federal government's Substance Abuse and Mental Health Services Administration, about 1 out of 10 full-time and part-time workers abuse or are dependent on alcohol or drugs. The problem is much greater at companies that are small or medium-sized (under 500 employees), perhaps because these companies are less likely to have formal procedures for maintaining a drug-free workplace. In a study of seven companies in various industries, the cost of substance abuse by employees came to more than $5,000 for extra health insurance benefits and lost productivity.[6]

The Americans with Disabilities Act (ADA), which prohibits discrimination on the basis of physical or mental disability, treats substance abuse arising from an addiction as a disability. Therefore, substance abuse may not be legal grounds for firing an employee. The supervisor should encourage the employee to get help, even if doing so requires adjusting the employee's work schedule or permitting the employee to take a disability leave to get treatment. In addition, actions taken with regard to the employee should focus on work performance, not on the substance abuse itself. For example, a supervisor might warn, "If I catch you picking fights with your co-workers again, I will have to suspend you." This warning addresses the employee's job-related behavior. (For more on the ADA and other laws against employment discrimination, see Chapter 15.)

Although a supervisor must treat each employee fairly and avoid discrimination, he or she also has a responsibility to help ensure that the workplace is safe for employees and others. If an employee's suspected substance abuse is creating a hazard, a supervisor must act. Again, the key is to address job-related behavior and job requirements, including safety. (The section on troubled employees, pages 330–333, provides guidelines for handling employees who abuse drugs or alcohol.) In addition to expecting supervisors to spot problem behavior, some companies for which safety is critical conduct random drug testing of employees. One of those companies is Ercole Electric, located in Fredericksburg, Maryland. Ercole's president, Greg Semuskie, said, "My employees thanked me for starting a drug [testing] program. They all knew who was taking drugs, and they didn't want to work with them. They told me they felt safer with this program."[7]

Workplace Violence

Security managers at *Fortune* 1000 companies recently responded to a Pinkerton survey by saying that workplace violence is their number one security threat. An estimated 2 million incidents of workplace violence occur each year, and according to the Bureau of Labor Statistics, since 1992, murder has been second only to highway accidents as the leading cause of death on the job. In 1999, 645 people were killed in the workplace.[8]

Kristin L. Bowl, spokesperson for the Society for Human Resource Management in Alexandria, Virginia, says about 15 percent of incidents of workplace violence result from substance abuse, and the Department of Labor found that 96 percent of nearly a million women who suffer domestic abuse from former or current domestic partners are also victims of workplace violence. Bowl agrees, "Domestic violence is a contributing factor to workplace violence." Her agency suggests that nearly 1 in 10 violent incidents is perpetrated by a spouse or ex-spouse or by a boyfriend, girlfriend, or relative, and Bowl offers this advice: "Employers can help to obtain protective orders and provide escorts to cars for those who have to work late hours, along with many security measures they provide to employees in general."[9]

Domestic violence is estimated to cost U.S. companies $3 billion to $5 billion a year in sick leave and reduced productivity.[10] For this and other reasons, some companies, such as Philip Morris Co. and Liz Claiborne Inc., offer information and help for employees who are victimized at work or at home. Rona Solomon, deputy director of the Center for Elimination of Violence in the Family Inc. (Brooklyn, New York), advises that employee assistance programs can be important referrals for victims of violence and that protecting the employee's privacy is a must.[11] "We don't know who goes in [counseling programs] and we don't keep records," says Philip Morris Management Corp.'s vice president of corporate affairs programs DeDe Thompson Bartlett.[12]

In the aftermath of workplace violence, employees often suffer psychological wounds that must be allowed to heal. The wise supervisor refrains from adopting the role of counselor but rather remains alert to those who may need special help, such as a referral for professional assistance or even reassignment or time off. After a shooting at Navistar in Melrose Park, Illinois, in February 2001, in which a former employee killed four workers, about 20 percent of the workforce took the next day off, and many spent the following day in counseling sessions to deal with complex feelings of grief, stress, and even guilt.[13]

Theft

The largest cause of missing goods and money for retailers today is not shoplifting, which accounts for 33 percent of losses, but employee theft, which makes up 44 percent of losses. (Paperwork errors and vendor fraud make up the remaining 18 and 5 percent, respectively.)[14]

When the manager of a Beall's Outlet store in the southeast began stealing small amounts of money from the cash register, she used various strategies to hide the thefts. Before long, she had taken $1,000, but even so, her misdeed might have gone undetected save for new software the company had installed to monitor cash register transactions. The computer program was able to monitor every sale, every voided sale, every "no sale," and every refund, and security personnel were able to set up surveillance within three weeks of the first theft and collect enough evidence in the following week to confront the manager and file charges.[15] Such monitoring software is being used more and more frequently.

Not all thefts involve money or tangible goods. Employees can also "steal time" by giving the employer less work than they are paid for, taking extra sick leave, or altering their time cards. Lost time is also more and more often spent surfing the Internet. Various new kinds of software programs can block particular Web sites from employees' view and monitor Internet activity. Some of these "activity monitors" capture keystrokes and mouse movements (by recording how long certain windows stay active and open), and they also create a complete record of the computer's use.[16] Privacy issues come into play when such tools are used, and some observers feel they imply a lack of trust on the employer's part that can be damaging to employee–employer relationships. Figure 12.2 summarizes average tangible losses per employee theft in various types of retail stores.

The theft of information also is a serious and growing problem, made even easier by new communications technology. Recently, an administrative assistant at the Coca-Cola Company was charged with offering to sell trade secrets to PepsiCo. Pepsi tipped off executives of its rival, who notified the FBI. In other cases, employees did not adequately protect data on computers, and the computers

SUPERVISION AND ETHICS

IDENTITY THEFT IN BANKS

Every company needs to protect its customer data, but the issue is particularly important for banks and other financial services firms. Most employees in these companies are honest, but a few dishonest people with access to financial records can drain customers' accounts or borrow in their name. Of the $3.4 billion that banks lost to fraud in 2004, more than half of the loss was caused by insiders.

Employee fraud includes using fake identities to borrow money and selling financial data to outsiders. Sometimes a member of an identity theft ring lands a job at an unsuspecting bank and then passes the information back to the theft ring. Or an outsider might bribe bank employees to pass on customer data.

Horror stories occur throughout the United States. In North Carolina, an employee of Centura Bank opened many accounts in fictitious names, deposited funds from company expense accounts, and then transferred the deposits to her personal account. Withdrawing amounts of less than $500 over the course of several years, the employee embezzled more than $2 million. In Wisconsin, a U.S. Bank employee stole from the accounts of several elderly customers. The employee forged documents to obtain funds and then deposited the money in her personal account. In North Dakota, an employee of U.S. Bank Service Center used customer data to make $28,000 in purchases charged to the customers.

An important step in preventing such crime is to screen employees carefully. In addition, supervisors should report suspicious activity immediately. A fraud or theft investigation can go on for years, so an early report can reduce losses significantly. Many financial institutions also use software that tracks employee behavior and issues reports identifying behavior patterns that raise suspicions. A classic example is an employee who declines to use vacation time; remaining at work is sometimes a way to prevent others from uncovering misdeeds.

Source: Karen Krebsbach, "The Enemy Within," *Banking Wire*, June 16, 2004, downloaded from Business & Company Resource Center, http://galenet.galegroup.com.

were stolen by outsiders. An employee of PSA HealthCare, based in Norcross, Georgia, downloaded data about patients into a laptop computer, which the employee then carried out of the office. Later the computer was stolen from the employee's car. This incident occurred even though PSA has policies forbidding employees from removing data from the company's offices.[17] Information theft is a particular concern at banks and other financial services companies, as described in the "Supervision and Ethics" box.

FIGURE 12.2
Average Amount Lost per Employee Theft

Source: From Jennifer S. Lee, "Tracking Sales at the Cashiers," *The New York Times*, July 11, 2001. Copyright © 2001, The New York Times. Reprinted with permission.

Average, all stores
$1,023

Supermarket and grocery stores
$183

Department stores
$746

Men's, women's, and children's apparel
$1,078

Discount stores
$1,123

Home centers, hardware, lumber, and garden supply stores
$1,146

The widespread nature of employee theft indicates that supervisors must be on guard against it. In addition to following the broad guidelines in this chapter for handling employee problems, supervisors should take measures to prevent and react to theft. Each organization has its own procedures, varying according to type of industry. In addition, supervisors should carefully check the background of anyone they plan to hire (part of the selection process described in Chapter 15).

To prevent information theft, the monitoring of employees may need to focus on access to and retrieval of data. For example, a financial services employee used his access to request credit reports for many customers. The employee then sold the data to companies that created fake identities for fraudulent purposes. Detecting exactly when and how employees are using data is extremely difficult, so employers are increasingly using high-tech tools. For example, access cards that employees swipe through a scanner provide a trail of electronic information about each employee's use of the company's information system.[18]

Supervisors should make sure that employees follow all procedures for record keeping. They should take advantage of ways to build employee morale and involvement; employees who feel like a part of the organization are less likely to steal from it. Supervisors also should make sure employees understand the costs and consequences of theft. Perhaps most important, supervisors should set a good example by demonstrating ethical behavior.

The Small Business Administration advises supervisors who suspect an employee is stealing not to investigate the crime themselves. Instead, they should report their suspicions to their manager and to the police or professional security consultants.

COUNSELING

If a supervisor responds to problem behavior immediately, he or she will sometimes be able to bring the problem to a quick end without complex proceedings. For example, a supervisor can respond to each complaint from an employee who constantly complains about the way things are done by calmly asking the employee to suggest some alternatives. Not only does this discourage complaining, but it also may uncover some good, new ways of operating. In many cases, however, the supervisor must take further steps to demonstrate the seriousness of the problem behavior.

counseling
The process of learning about an individual's personal problem and helping him or her resolve it

Often the most constructive way a supervisor can address problem behavior is through counseling. **Counseling** refers to the process of learning about an individual's personal problem and helping the employee resolve it. Employees themselves should be able to resolve a relatively simple problem, such as tardiness caused by staying up too late watching television, without the supervisor's help. For more complex problems, such as those stemming from financial difficulties or substance abuse, the solution will require getting help from an expert. Because counseling is a cooperative process between supervisor and employee, employees are likely to respond more positively to it than to a simple order that they "shape up or ship out."

Benefits of Counseling

Counseling benefits employees in several ways. It can ease their worries or help them solve their problems. Working cooperatively with a supervisor to resolve a problem gives employees a sense that the supervisor and organization are interested in their welfare. This belief in turn can improve job satisfaction and motivation. The resulting improvements in productivity benefit the employee through performance rewards.

The organization benefits too. Employees who receive needed counseling are well motivated and more likely to meet performance standards. The changes in an employee's attitudes also carry over to the work of other employees. When personal problems affect one employee's work, the others suffer consequences such as working harder to make up for the problem employee's lapses. Also, being around someone with a negative attitude tends to drag down the spirits of others in the group. After counseling improves the problem employee's performance and attitude, the whole group tends to do better.

Appropriate Times to Counsel

A supervisor should counsel employees when they need help determining how to resolve a problem that is affecting their work. Sometimes an employee will approach a supervisor with a problem, such as marriage worries or concern about doing a good job. At other times, a supervisor may observe that an employee seems to have a problem when, for example, the quality of the employee's work is declining.

It is essential for supervisors to remember that they lack training to help with many kinds of problems. They are not in a position to save a marriage, resolve an employee's financial difficulties, or handle an alcoholic family member. Only when qualified should a supervisor help an employee resolve the problem. In other cases, a supervisor should simply listen, express concern, and refer the employee to a trained professional. The human resources department may be able to suggest sources of help.

Counseling Techniques

Counseling involves one or more discussions between the supervisor and the employee. These sessions should take place where there will be privacy and freedom from interruptions. The sessions may be directive or nondirective (see Figure 12.3).

Directive versus Nondirective Counseling

directive counseling
An approach to counseling in which the supervisor asks the employee questions about the specific problem; when the supervisor understands the problem, he or she suggests ways to handle it

The most focused approach to counseling is **directive counseling,** in which a supervisor asks an employee questions about a specific problem. The supervisor listens until he or she understands the source of the problem. Then the supervisor suggests ways to handle the problem.

For example, assume that Bill Wisniewski, a computer programmer, has been absent a number of times during the past month. The supervisor might ask, "Why have you been missing so many days?" Wisniewski replies, "Because my wife has been sick, and someone needs to look after my kids." The supervisor would follow up with questions about the condition of Wisniewski's wife (for example, to learn whether the problem is likely to continue), the ages and needs of their children,

FIGURE 12.3
Directive versus Nondirective Counseling

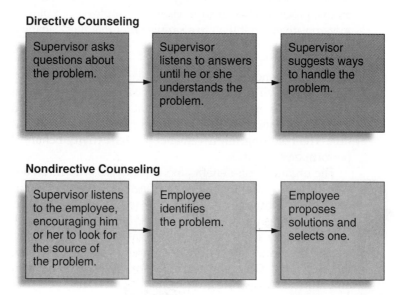

Directive Counseling

Supervisor asks questions about the problem. → Supervisor listens to answers until he or she understands the problem. → Supervisor suggests ways to handle the problem.

Nondirective Counseling

Supervisor listens to the employee, encouraging him or her to look for the source of the problem. → Employee identifies the problem. → Employee proposes solutions and selects one.

FIGURE 12.4   **The Counseling Interview**

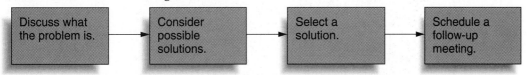

and so on. Then the supervisor might suggest finding alternative sources of care, perhaps referring Wisniewski to a company program designed to help with such problems.

In most cases, a supervisor and employee will receive the greatest benefit when the supervisor helps the employee develop and change instead of merely looking for a solution to a specific problem. To accomplish this, the supervisor can use **nondirective counseling.** With this approach, a supervisor should primarily listen, encouraging the employee to look for the source of the problem and propose possible solutions. In the preceding example, a supervisor would ask open-ended questions such as "Would you tell me more about that?" Ideally, by working out his own solution, Wisniewski would find that he has the ability to resolve many family problems without missing a lot of work.

nondirective counseling
An approach to counseling in which the supervisor primarily listens, encouraging the employee to look for the source of the problem and propose possible solutions

The Counseling Interview

The counseling interview starts with a discussion of what the problem is (see Figure 12.4). It then moves to a consideration of possible solutions and the selection of one solution to try. The interview ends with the supervisor scheduling a follow-up meeting.

The person who requested the counseling begins by describing the problem. If the employee requested help, the employee should begin. If the supervisor set up the interview because something seemed wrong, the supervisor should begin. The supervisor should focus on behavior and performance—what people do, not who they are—and encourage the employee to do the same. For example, if the employee says, "The other employees are prejudiced against me," the supervisor should ask the employee to describe what actions led to that conclusion. In addition, the supervisor should use the principles of active listening, described in Chapter 10.

Because counseling often occurs as a result of an employee's personal problems, the employee may be emotional during counseling sessions. The supervisor needs to be prepared for crying, angry outbursts, and other signs of emotion. He or she should be calm and reassure the employee that these signs of emotion are neither good nor bad. Of course, there are appropriate and inappropriate ways to express emotions. Suppose a salesperson in a hardware store has a 10-year-old son with behavior problems. It would not be appropriate for the salesperson to express his worry and frustration by snapping at customers.

Next, the supervisor and employee should consider ways to solve the problem. Instead of simply prescribing a solution, the supervisor usually can be more helpful by asking the employee questions that will help the employee come up with ideas. Employees are more likely to cooperate in a solution they helped develop. Asking an employee to suggest solutions can be an especially effective way to end constant whining and complaining by that employee. When the supervisor and employee agree on a particular solution, the supervisor should restate it to make sure the employee understands. (Chapter 9 provides more detailed guidelines for mutual problem solving.)

Finally, the supervisor should schedule a follow-up meeting, which should take place just after the employee begins to see some results. At the follow-up meeting, the employee and the supervisor review their plans and discuss whether the problem has been or is being resolved. For example, in the case of the salesperson in the hardware store, the supervisor might say, "I've noticed that we haven't received any more customer complaints about your service. In fact, one woman told me you went out of your way to help her." Notice that the supervisor is focusing on work performance, which the supervisor is qualified to discuss, rather than on the employee's family problems. If the employee replies, "Yes, I've been so much calmer ever since I started talking to that counselor about my son," the supervisor has a good indication that the employee is resolving the problem.

DISCIPLINE

discipline
Action taken by the supervisor to prevent employees from breaking rules

"I can't stand Marcia's surly attitude any longer!" fumed Don Koh, Marcia's supervisor. "If she doesn't cut it out, she's going to be sorry." This supervisor is eager for the employee to experience the consequences of her behavior. However, despite the anger and frustration that can be generated by supervising a problem employee, a supervisor needs to apply discipline in constructive ways. **Discipline** is action taken by a supervisor to prevent employees from breaking rules. In many cases, effective discipline can quickly bring about a change in an employee's behavior.

Administering Discipline

In administering discipline, a supervisor should distinguish between discipline and punishment. (See the Knowing Yourself quiz on pages 337–338 to help you determine the difference.) As described in Chapter 11, punishment is an unpleasant consequence given in response to undesirable behavior. Discipline, in contrast, is broader; it is a teaching process. The supervisor explains the significance and consequences of the employee's behavior and then, if necessary, lets the employee experience those consequences.

The specific ways in which a supervisor applies these steps may be dictated by company policies or the union contract, if any. Thus, a supervisor must be familiar with all applicable policies and rules. These should include respecting the rights of employees in the discipline process. Employees' rights include the following:[19]

- The right to know job expectations and the consequences of not fulfilling those expectations.
- The right to receive consistent and predictable management action in response to violations of the rules.
- The right to receive fair discipline based on facts.
- The right to question management's statement of the facts and to present a defense.
- The right to receive progressive discipline (described in the next section).
- The right to appeal a disciplinary action.

The Discipline Process

Before administering discipline in response to problem behavior, supervisors need to have a clear picture of the situation. They may observe the problem

FIGURE 12.5   **Possible Steps in the Discipline Process**

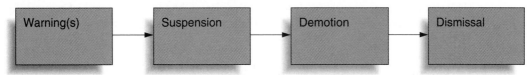

themselves, or someone may tell them about the problem. In either case, supervisors need to collect the facts before taking further action.

As soon as possible, a supervisor should meet with the employees involved and ask for each employee's version of what happened. For example, a supervisor who believes that one of his or her employees is using the office telephone for excessive personal calls should not make hasty accusations or issue a general memo stating company policy about phone use. Rather, the supervisor should ask the employee directly and in private what his or her telephone conversations were about. In getting the employee's version of a problem, a supervisor should use good listening practices and resist the temptation to get angry.

When a supervisor observes and understands the facts behind problem behavior, disciplining an employee occurs in as many as four steps: warnings, suspension, demotion, and dismissal (see Figure 12.5). This pattern of discipline is "progressive" in the sense that the steps progress from the least to the most severe action a supervisor can take. A warning is unpleasant to hear but fulfills the important purpose of informing employees about the consequences of their behavior before more punitive measures are taken. Suspension, demotion, and discharge are more upsetting to an employee because they hurt the employee in the pocketbook.

Warning

A warning may be either written or oral. Some organizations have a policy that calls for an oral warning followed by a written warning if performance does not improve. Both types of warning are designed to make sure that the employee understands the problem. A warning should contain the following information:

- What the problem behavior is.
- How the behavior affects the organization.
- How and when the employee's behavior is expected to change.
- What actions will be taken if the employee's behavior does not change.

Thus, a supervisor might say, "I have noticed that in the last two staff meetings, you have made hostile remarks. Not only have these disrupted the meetings, but they lead your co-workers to take you less seriously. I expect that you will refrain from such remarks in future meetings, or I will have to give you a suspension." As in this example, the warning should be brief and to the point.

In the case of a written warning, it is wise practice to ask the employee to sign the warning, which documents that the first step in the discipline process took place. If the employee refuses to sign the warning, even with minor changes, the supervisor should note the employee's refusal or call in someone (such as the supervisor's manager) to witness the refusal.

Suspension

A **suspension** is the requirement that an employee not come to work for a set period of time, during which the employee is not paid. The length of the suspension

suspension
Requirement that an employee not come to work for a set period of time; the employee is not paid for the time off

might run from one day to one month, depending on the seriousness of the problem. Suspensions are useful when the employee has been accused of something serious, such as stealing, and the supervisor needs time to investigate.

Demotion

demotion
Transfer of an employee to a job involving less responsibility and usually lower pay

A **demotion** is the transfer of an employee to a job with less responsibility and usually lower pay. Sometimes a demotion is actually a relief for an employee, especially if the employee has been goofing off or performing poorly because the job was more than he or she could handle. In such a case, the employee might welcome returning to a job where he or she is competent. More often, however, a demotion leads to negative feelings—a punishment that continues for as long as the employee holds the lower-level job.

Dismissal

dismissal
Relieving an employee of his or her job

The permanent removal of an employee from a job is called **dismissal,** or termination or discharge. The organization cannot really regard dismissal as a success because it then has to recruit, hire, and train a new employee. Nevertheless, a supervisor sometimes must dismiss an employee who commits a serious offense or who will not respond to other forms of discipline. Occasionally an employee or supervisor may decide that correcting a problem is impossible, or at least too difficult or expensive. In addition to continued failure to correct problem behavior, dismissal may occur because an employee deliberately damages the organization's property, fights on the job, or engages in dangerous practices (e.g., a railroad engineer who drinks on the job).

Dismissing an employee is never easy, but it is sometimes a necessary part of the job to ensure a positive work environment for the remaining employees. At Wire One Technologies, Ric Robbins had a sales representative who continuously sacrificed teamwork for personal gain. According to Robbins, a regional vice president, that employee would visit his colleagues' offices and glance around, looking for clues to sales leads. The employee's co-workers spent so much energy protecting themselves from the unethical employee that they couldn't work effectively. Robbins had to fire the sales rep to preserve the team's morale and performance.[20]

Many organizations have policies requiring a supervisor to involve higher-level management before dismissing an employee. Supervisors should be familiar with any such policy and follow it.

In following the steps in the discipline process, a supervisor should remember that the objective is to end the problem behavior. A supervisor takes only as many steps as are necessary to bring about a change in behavior: The ultimate goal is to solve the problem without dismissing the employee.

Guidelines for Effective Discipline

When an employee is causing a problem—from tardiness to theft to lack of cooperation—the supervisor needs to act immediately. That is not always easy to do. Pointing out poor behavior and administering negative consequences are unpleasant tasks. However, by ignoring the situation, a supervisor is signaling that the problem is not serious. As a result, the problem gets worse. Seeing that the problem behavior leads to no consequences, an employee may increase it, and other employees may follow this example.

In contrast, when Kathleen R. Tibbs was an in-flight supervisor with Eastern Airlines, she faced up to the unpleasant task of disciplining an employee with

TIPS FROM THE FIRING LINE

CRITICIZING CONSTRUCTIVELY

When employees engage in problem behavior, supervisors need to be able to discuss the situation in a way that leads to a solution. Generally, that includes some constructive criticism so the employee knows exactly what the supervisor is dissatisfied about. Here are some ideas for keeping your criticism constructive:

- Describe the behavior, not the person. Suppose an employee orders the wrong materials for a project. It won't help matters if you say, "How could you be so careless?" Better: "Ordering the wrong material is expensive. Please enter the item numbers more carefully next time."

- Be specific and accurate about the problem. A general comment like "Your work is sloppy" or "Your attitude is poor" is vague. What changes in behavior will correct these problems? Similarly, an exaggeration such as "You're always late" gives the employee an opening to offer examples to the contrary, rather than focusing on the problem.

- Give reasons for criticizing. Following orders feels easier when we know the purpose behind the orders.

- Use a neutral tone of voice. If you are too upset to speak calmly, wait until you calm down (except in an emergency, of course). Calming down is just as important for criticism that you put into writing. If you are making a written record of an incident, the principles described here matter more because the comments are more permanent.

- Keep it short. No matter how carefully you express yourself, criticism is painful to hear, so people resist it. The less you say, the more likely you will be heard.

- Criticize in private. Praise in public.

Source: Based on Jim Olsztynski, "How to Critique, Criticize Important for Supervisors," *Snips,* December 2005, downloaded from Business & Company Resource Center, http://galenet.galegroup.com.

unacceptable attendance. Tibbs had the employee suspended for seven days. Her action inspired the employee to address the personal problems that led to her poor attendance.

When discussing the problem with an employee, a supervisor should focus on learning about and resolving the issue at hand. This meeting is no time for name-calling or dredging up instances of past misbehavior. Nor is it generally useful for a supervisor to dwell on how patient or compassionate he or she has been. Instead, a supervisor should listen until he or she understands the problem and then begin discussing how to correct it in the future. Talking about behaviors instead of personalities helps the employee understand what is expected. For ideas on how to discuss problem behavior constructively, see the "Tips from the Firing Line" box.

A supervisor should keep emotions in check. Although it is appropriate to convey sincere concern about the problem, a supervisor's other feelings are largely irrelevant and can even stand in the way of a constructive discussion. When an employee breaks the rules or seems unwilling to do a good job, it is only natural for a supervisor to feel angry. The supervisor should get control over this anger before confronting the employee in order to be objective rather than hostile. Being calm and relaxed when administering discipline tells an employee that the supervisor is confident of what he or she is doing.

Discipline should be a private matter. The supervisor should not humiliate an employee by reprimanding the employee in front of other employees. Humiliation only breeds resentment and may actually increase problem behavior in the future.

A supervisor also should be consistent in administering discipline. One way to do this is to follow the four steps of the discipline process outlined previously.

FIGURE 12.6
Guidelines for
Effective Discipline

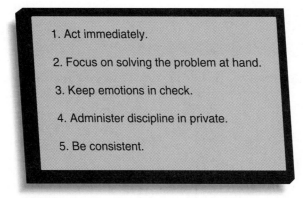

1. Act immediately.

2. Focus on solving the problem at hand.

3. Keep emotions in check.

4. Administer discipline in private.

5. Be consistent.

Also, a supervisor should respond to *all* instances of misbehavior rather than, for example, ignore a longstanding employee's misdeeds while punishing a newcomer. At the same time, the seriousness of the response should be related to the seriousness of the problem. The policy for workplace violence or drug use would likely be immediate dismissal because of the danger involved. Likewise, Stater Bros. Markets, a grocery store chain, has a policy of immediately dismissing any employee who engages in theft or sells liquor to a minor lacking proper identification.[21] The response to an occasion of tardiness would be less severe. The point is to have and follow a consistent policy for serious and minor problems. Even better, consistency should extend to praising and rewarding positive performance. The guidelines for effective discipline are summarized in Figure 12.6.

Documentation of Disciplinary Action

Employees who receive discipline sometimes respond by filing a grievance or suing the employer. To be able to justify his or her actions, a supervisor must have a record of the disciplinary actions taken and the basis for the discipline. These records may be needed to show that the actions were not discriminatory or against company policy. As noted previously, one type of disciplinary record is a signed copy of any written warning. In addition, other disciplinary actions should be recorded in the employee's personnel file, as directed by the human resources department.

Supervisors often use past performance appraisals as documentation of the need for disciplinary action. However, this approach often backfires because many supervisors are reluctant to give negative evaluations. A performance appraisal that has an employee's work recorded as average, adequate, or meeting only minimal standards does not support dismissal of that employee. This is why it is essential for the supervisor to give accurate performance appraisals (see Chapter 17).

Documentation is especially important when a supervisor must terminate an employee. Because the experience is so emotional, some former employees respond with a lawsuit. The employee's file should show the steps the supervisor took leading up to the termination and a record of the specific behaviors that led the supervisor to dismiss the employee.

Careful documentation also is essential for organizations, which have many disciplinary rules and policies aimed at protecting employees from arbitrary or politically based actions by supervisors. These rules may have the unintended consequence of protecting problem employees from well-deserved discipline, unless the supervisor can fully document the problem behavior, preferably with witnesses. An example of just how challenging this process can be involves alleged abuses of residents at the Communities of Oakwood, a state-run home for mentally disabled persons. Of 15 employees charged with abuse in recent years, about half had previously received reprimands or suspensions for various misdeeds as severe as being intoxicated at work and changing patients' prescriptions. Administrators at Oakwood must win the approval of a personnel board before they can dismiss such employees. This requirement protects the employees from being fired based on politics, but it also places a burden on supervisors to provide specific, supportable documentation of any problem behavior.[22]

Positive Discipline

positive discipline
Discipline designed to prevent problem behavior from beginning

Ideally, discipline should not only end problem behavior, it should also prevent problems from occurring. Discipline designed to prevent problem behavior from beginning is known as **positive discipline,** or preventive discipline. An important part of positive discipline is making sure employees know and understand the rules they must follow. A supervisor also should explain the consequences of violating rules. For example, a production supervisor might explain that company policy calls for the dismissal of any employee caught operating machinery while under the influence of drugs or alcohol.

A supervisor also can administer positive discipline by working to create the conditions under which employees are least likely to cause problems. Employees may engage in problem behavior when they feel frustrated. For example, if the organization sets a sales quota higher than salespeople think they can achieve, they may give up and goof off instead of trying their best. If computer operators complain that they need more frequent rest breaks to prevent health problems, and no changes are made, they may adopt a negative attitude toward the company's apparent lack of concern for their well-being. This reaction is related to another source of problem behavior: feeling as if one is not an important part of the organization. If employees conclude that they and management are at odds, some may turn their energy toward seeing what they can get away with.

To combat such problems, a supervisor needs to be aware of and responsive to employees' needs and ideas. A supervisor should encourage upward communication, promote teamwork, and encourage employees to participate in decision making and problem solving. The effective use of motivation techniques also helps prevent the frustration and alienation that can lead to problem behavior. Finally, through good hiring and training practices, a supervisor can help ensure that employee values, interests, and abilities are a good match with the job and the organization.

decision-making leave
A day off during which a problem employee is supposed to decide whether to return to work and meet standards or to stay away for good

At some companies, positive discipline includes a day off with pay for employees who fail to respond to efforts to educate them about following the rules and meeting performance standards. During this suspension, known as a **decision-making leave,** the employees are supposed to decide whether to return to work and meet standards or to stay away for good. If the employees choose to come back, they work with a supervisor to develop objectives and action plans for improvement.

Finally, a supervisor should not only punish problem behavior but also reward desirable kinds of behavior, such as contributing to the department's performance. For example, a supervisor should recognize those who make suggestions for improvements or resolve sticky problems. (See Chapter 11 for specific ideas.)

Self-Discipline

An effective program of positive discipline results in self-discipline, in which employees voluntarily follow the rules and try to meet performance standards. Most people get satisfaction from doing a job well, so self-discipline should result when employees understand what is expected. Supervisors can help encourage

SUPERVISORY SKILLS

LEADING

WHEN AN EMPLOYEE IS A BULLY

"Bully" is the label we place on people who routinely intimidate others. On the school playground, a bully was likely to beat up smaller children, especially those without a large circle of friends for support. In the workplace, a bully might establish control through sarcasm, threats, and verbal humiliation.

Supervisors cannot afford to tolerate bullying behavior. A bully makes the workplace uncomfortable for valued workers and shifts the focus from team goals to his or her own status. Organizations that allow bullying behavior are likely to experience high employee turnover and low productivity; they may even be sued by unhappy employees.

Management consultant Constance Dierickx recommends that a supervisor who wants to cope with a bully use the following actions:

- Define the problem behavior in a discussion with the bullying employee. Some supervisors might be tempted to analyze why the bully is behaving in negative ways or categorize behavior as "arrogant" or "mean." The supervisor's statements should, however, present only the observable, measurable facts, such as use of sarcasm or public criticism. When Dierickx had a co-worker who engaged in emotional outbursts, she calmly told that person she would not talk with him when he raised his voice, called her names, turned red in the face, and pounded his desk.

- Get help. If you are uncomfortable about discussing the problem with the employee, go to the human resources department. Make sure your boss also knows you are working on this problem. Keep written records of the behaviors you observe and the actions you have taken.

- If the employee will not abandon the bullying behavior, you may need to terminate the person's employment. Be sure all such actions are based on observable behaviors, and work with the human resources department to follow company procedures.

The supervisor's refusal to tolerate bullying sends a message to the entire work group about what behavior is acceptable. In this way, the supervisor helps create a positive work environment for everyone.

Source: From Constance Dierickx, "The Bully Employee: A Survival Guide for Supervisors," *Supervision,* March 2004. Reprinted by permission of National Research Bureau, 320 Valley Street, Boolington, IA 52601.

self-discipline by communicating not only the rules and performance standards but also the reasons for those rules and standards.

In addition, a supervisor who takes long lunch breaks or spends hours chatting with friends on the telephone or the Internet is in no position to insist that employees put in a full workday. If supervisors expect employees to follow the rules, they must set a good example by exercising self-discipline.

TROUBLED EMPLOYEES

So far, this chapter has emphasized problems that can be solved by giving employees more information or helping them change their behavior. However, some employees have problems that make them unable to respond to a simple process of discipline or counseling. That may be the case when one employee routinely bullies others, as described in the "Supervisory Skills" box. In addition to bullies, troubled employees may include people who are substance abusers or have psychological problems.

Detection of the Troubled Employee

The first signs that a supervisor has a troubled employee tend to be the kinds of discipline problems described previously in this chapter. A supervisor may notice that an employee is frequently late or that the quality of an employee's work has

TABLE 12.1
Possible Signs of Alcohol or Drug Use

Slurred speech.
Clumsy movements and increased accidents.
Personality changes.
Decreased ability to work as part of a team.
Smell of alcohol on the employee's breath.
Growing carelessness about personal appearance and the details of the job.
Increase in absenteeism or tardiness, along with unbelievable excuses.
Daydreaming.
Leaving the work area; making frequent visits to the restroom.
Violence in the workplace.

been slipping. If disciplinary action or counseling seem ineffective in resolving the problem, a supervisor may have a troubled employee.

In the case of substance abuse, the supervisor might notice signs that the employee has been using alcohol or drugs. The examples listed in Table 12.1 are among the most common behavioral signs. (Note that these are only hints that the employee might be using drugs or alcohol. There may be other explanations for these behaviors.) Perhaps a supervisor will even find the employee in possession of drugs or alcohol. When an employee is suspected of drug use, some organizations have a policy of confirming the suspicion through the use of drug testing.

Because there may be another explanation for symptoms that look like the effects of using alcohol or illicit drugs (e.g., taking prescription medications), a supervisor should avoid making accusations about what he or she believes is going on. For example, a supervisor should not say, "I see you've been drinking on the job." Instead, the supervisor should focus on job performance: "I see something is hurting the quality of your work this week. Let's talk about what the problem is and how to solve it."

Confrontation of the Troubled Employee

Ignoring a problem does not make it go away. Thus, hoping an alcoholic employee will seek help rarely works. It only helps the employee maintain the illusion that the substance abuse is not causing significant problems. After all, if the boss does not complain, how bad can the work be? Therefore, when a supervisor suspects a problem, he or she needs to confront the employee.

The first step is to document the problem. A supervisor should keep notes of instances in which an employee's performance is not acceptable. When collecting this information, a supervisor should be sure to keep notes on all employees whose performance is slipping, not just the one person targeted.

When a supervisor has gathered enough supporting evidence, he or she should confront the employee. The supervisor should go over the employee's performance, describing the evidence of a problem. Then the supervisor should refer the employee to a source of counseling or other help by saying something like, "I think something's troubling you, and I want you to see an employee assistance counselor." Finally, the supervisor should explain the consequences of not changing. In some cases, accepting help may be a requirement for keeping the job. Thus, the supervisor might say, "There's no shame in getting help, and we'll keep it private. But you are responsible for doing your job safely and up to standards. If you don't, I'll have to follow our disciplinary procedures for unacceptable performance." Experts agree that this type of warning from a supervisor can be one of the most effective ways to motivate a substance-abusing employee to get help.

During the confrontation, the employee may become angry or defensive. This reaction is common in such situations, so the supervisor should not take it personally or overreact. The employee also may come up with excuses that sound particularly sad and compelling. In any case, the supervisor must continue to focus on the employee's behavior on the job and the way the employee's behavior affects the organization. No matter how outraged the employee or how impressive or creative the excuse, the employee's behavior must improve.

Some caution is advisable, however. Supervisors should avoid taking on the role of doctor, counselor, or police officer. That means the supervisor must not try to diagnose what may be medical or psychological problems. Supervisors also should protect their employees' privacy and give employees a fair chance to respond to any complaints. Also, if the workplace is governed by a union contract, the supervisor must follow its requirements. By focusing on objective measures of job requirements and performance, the supervisor can avoid falling into traps such as pitying employees, covering up for them, or allowing the workplace to become unfair or unsafe because the supervisor is reluctant to confront problems.[23]

Aid in and Evaluation of Recovery

Most organizations have developed procedures for providing help to troubled employees. When a supervisor believes that problems are occurring because an employee is troubled, the organization's procedures need to be investigated. In most cases, the place to start is with the human resources department.

The type of treatment program tends to depend on the size of the organization. Many small organizations refer troubled employees to a counseling service. Another policy is simply to tell the employee to get help or lose the job. A supervisor should be careful in pursuing the latter approach. If possible, the ultimate objective should be the employee's rehabilitation, not dismissal. Not only is rehabilitation more compassionate, but it also tends to be less costly than hiring and training a new employee, and it is less likely to violate laws prohibiting employment discrimination.

employee assistance program (EAP)
A company-based program for providing counseling and related help to employees whose personal problems are affecting their performance

Other organizations, especially large ones, offer an **employee assistance program (EAP).** An EAP is a company-based program for providing counseling and related help to employees whose personal problems affect their performance. It may be simply a referral service, or it may be fully staffed with social workers, psychologists, nurses, career counselors, financial advisers, and other professionals. These programs are voluntary (employees do not have to participate unless they want to) and confidential (participation is a private matter). Services of EAPs include recovery from substance abuse, financial and career counseling, referrals for child care and elder care, AIDS education and counseling, and helping employees work with others of a different cultural background. Figure 12.7 identifies benefits that organizations have experienced as a result of using EAPs. A supervisor who is concerned about troubled employees might investigate such benefits and encourage the organization to consider offering an EAP. Some employees would be unlikely to seek out help without the push of a referral from their supervisor.[24]

The reason for providing EAPs and other sources of counseling is to improve the employee's performance. It is up to the supervisor to see that the treatment plan is producing the desired results at the workplace. Any signs of improvement not related to performance (for example, abstinence from alcohol) are irrelevant from the supervisor's point of view.

FIGURE 12.7 **Benefits of an Employee Assistance Program**

Source: U.S. Department of Health and Human Services and SAMHSA, "Employer Tip Sheet #8: Employee Assistance Programs,"
National Clearinghouse for Alcohol and Drug Information Publications, www.health.org, downloaded September 24, 2004.

- ☑ Through an EAP, employees can find treatment for problems affecting their performance.
- ☑ EAPs can help the organization develop policies, educate employees, and train supervisors.
- ☑ EAPs can relieve supervisors who feel pressured to help with employees' personal problems.
- ☑ By offering an alternative to firing troubled employees, EAPs save the cost of replacing them.
- ☑ Organizations with EAPs experience declines in accidents, absenteeism, and turnover.
- ☑ EAPs can help organizations maintain a drug-free workplace.

SOURCES OF SUPPORT

Supervising problem employees is a delicate matter. Supervisors must be careful to motivate and correct rather than to generate hostility and resentment. At the same time, supervisors must be careful to follow organizational procedures, union requirements, and laws regarding fair employment practices. Fortunately, supervisors can get support from their superiors, the organization's human resources department, and outside experts.

When an employee fails to respond to initial counseling attempts, a supervisor should try discussing the problem with his or her manager. The manager may be able to offer insights into how to handle the problem. In addition, some steps, such as suspension or dismissal, may require that the supervisor get authorization from a higher-level manager.

It is also wise to consult with the human resources department, which has information about company policies on discipline and how to document it. Human resources personnel can advise a supervisor on how to proceed without breaking laws, violating a contract with the union, or putting the organization at risk in case of a lawsuit. In addition, personnel specialists have expertise that can make them good sources of ideas on what to say or what corrective measures to propose. Sometimes just talking about a strategy helps a supervisor to think of new ways to approach the problem.

In small organizations with no human resource staff, a supervisor and his or her manager may agree that the problem requires the help of outside experts. They may contract with a consultant, a labor attorney, or a human relations specialist who provides services on a temporary basis. The fee paid to such an expert may seem high but can be far less than the cost of defending a wrongful-termination lawsuit. The local office of the Small Business Administration (SBA) also may be able to provide help. The SBA assistance may include a referral to an executive in one of its programs for providing small businesses with free advice.

In summary, when an employee's problems or problem behavior threatens to disrupt the workplace, a supervisor should not despair. The effective use of counseling and discipline can solve many of these problems. When they do not, a variety of people inside and outside the organization stand ready to help.

SKILLS MODULE

PART ONE: CONCEPTS

Summary

12.1 Identify common types of problem behavior among employees.

The problems that supervisors most often encounter are absenteeism and tardiness, insubordination and uncooperativeness, alcohol and drug abuse, workplace violence, and employee theft.

12.2 Explain why and when supervisors should counsel employees.

Counseling helps employees solve their problems, which enables them to perform better at work. It therefore improves productivity as well as the attitudes and job satisfaction of employees. Supervisors should counsel employees when they need help determining how to resolve a problem that is affecting their work. When an employee has a problem with which the supervisor is unqualified to help, the supervisor should refer the employee to a professional.

12.3 Describe counseling techniques.

Counseling consists of one or more discussions between the supervisor and the employee. These discussions may involve directive counseling, in which the supervisor asks the employee questions to identify the problem and then suggests solutions. Or the discussions may be nondirective, with the supervisor primarily listening and encouraging the employee to look for the source of the problem and identify possible solutions. At the beginning of the interview, the person who identified the problem describes it, focusing on behavior and performance. Next, the supervisor and employee consider ways to solve the problem. Finally, the supervisor schedules a follow-up meeting to review the planned solution and determine whether the problem is being resolved.

12.4 Discuss effective ways of administering discipline.

After collecting the facts of the situation, the supervisor should meet with the employee or employees involved and ask for their version of what has happened. The supervisor should use good listening techniques. Then the supervisor issues a warning. If necessary, the supervisor lets the employee experience the consequences of unsatisfactory behavior through suspension, demotion, and ultimately dismissal. The supervisor takes as many steps as are necessary to resolve the problem behavior. The supervisor should administer discipline promptly, privately, impartially, and unemotionally. The supervisor should document all disciplinary actions.

12.5 Describe the principles of positive discipline and self-discipline.

Positive discipline focuses on preventing problem behavior from ever beginning. It can include making sure employees know and understand the rules, creating conditions under which employees are least likely to cause problems, using decision-making leaves when problems occur, and rewarding desirable behavior. Effective positive discipline results in self-discipline among employees; that is, employees voluntarily follow the rules and try to meet performance standards. Supervisors who expect self-discipline from their employees must practice it themselves.

12.6 Explain how supervisors can detect and confront troubled employees.

The supervisor can look for discipline problems and investigate whether these are symptoms of personal problems. With substance abuse, the supervisor might notice signs that the employee is using alcohol or drugs. When the supervisor suspects that an employee is troubled, he or she should document the problem and then meet with the employee and describe the evidence of a problem, focusing on the employee's performance at work. The supervisor should refer the employee to a source of help and explain the consequences of not getting help. The supervisor should be careful not to overreact to an employee's emotional response or creative excuses.

12.7 Specify how supervisors can direct troubled employees in getting help and then follow up on the recovery efforts.

Supervisors should learn their organization's procedures for helping troubled employees and then follow those procedures. This may involve referring employees to help outside the organization or to the organization's employee assistance program. The supervisor is responsible for seeing that the employee's performance is improving, not for evaluating evidence of improvement unrelated to work.

12.8 Discuss the role of the supervisor's manager and the human resources department in helping the supervisor with problem employees.

The supervisor's manager and the human resources department can help the supervisor handle problem employees in ways that follow organizational guidelines, legal requirements, or union contracts. A supervisor should discuss the problem with his or her manager and the human resources department to get information about the organization's policies for handling problem employees and suggestions for addressing the specific problem. The organization may offer an employee assistance program whose ultimate goal is the employee's rehabilitation.

Key Terms	insubordination, *p.* 317	discipline, *p.* 324	decision-making
	counseling, *p.* 321	suspension, *p.* 325	leave, *p.* 329
	directive	demotion, *p.* 326	employee assistance
	counseling, *p.* 322	dismissal, *p.* 326	program (EAP), *p.* 332
	nondirective	positive	
	counseling, *p.* 323	discipline, *p.* 329	

Review and Discussion Questions

1. Dennis McCutcheon supervises the employees who work in the building supplies department of a large discount hardware store. One of his employees, Kelly Sims, has been late to work every Tuesday and Thursday for the last three weeks. Sometimes she disappears for more than an hour at lunch. Although Sims had a positive attitude when she started the job, recently McCutcheon has overheard her complaining to co-workers and being less than friendly to customers. Using the questions listed in the section "Problems Requiring Special Action" (pages 316–321), how might he uncover the true source of Sims's performance problem?

2. What is the difference between directive and nondirective counseling? Give an example of each in the form of a brief dialogue.

3. An employee explains to her supervisor that her performance has been slipping because she has been distracted and frightened by threats from her former husband.

   a. Should the supervisor counsel the employee about her job performance? Explain.

  b. Should the supervisor counsel the employee about the threats from her former husband? Explain.

4. While counseling an employee, a supervisor made the following statements. What is wrong with each statement? What would be a better alternative for each?

  a. "Your laziness is becoming a real problem."

  b. "Knock off the shouting! The way your performance has been lately, you have no right to be angry."

  c. "What you need to do is to take this job more seriously. Just focus on getting your work done, and then we won't have a problem."

5. What are the steps in the discipline process? In what kinds of situations would a supervisor take all these steps?

6. What additional type of information should be included in the following warning to an employee?

  "I noticed that you returned late from lunch yesterday and three days last week. This upsets the other employees because they get back promptly in order to give others a chance to take their breaks. Beginning tomorrow, I expect you to be back on time."

7. Describe four guidelines for disciplining employees effectively.

8. Jackie Weissman supervises a group of technicians in a laboratory that conducts medical tests. It is extremely important that the technicians follow lab procedures to obtain accurate test results. What steps can Weissman take to apply positive discipline with her group?

9. *a.* What are some signs that an employee has been abusing alcohol or drugs?

  b. Why should a supervisor avoid making a statement such as, "You've been coming to work high lately"?

10. What steps should a supervisor take in confronting an apparently troubled employee?

11. Rick Mayhew's nine-year-old son was recently diagnosed with a chronic illness that is difficult and expensive to treat. In addition, Mayhew's elderly mother-in-law is going to be moving in to live with his family. His supervisor has noticed that his performance has been suffering lately; he is often late to work, leaves early, and has trouble concentrating on his work. The supervisor does not want to lose Mayhew as an employee. Would an employee assistance program help Rick? Why or why not?

12. Tom Chandra has a problem with one of the production workers he supervises. The worker has been ignoring instructions about the new procedures for operating a lathe, preferring instead to follow the old procedures. What kind of help can Chandra get from his manager and the human resources department in handling this problem?

PART TWO: SKILL-BUILDING

YOU SOLVE THE PROBLEM

Reflecting back on page 315, what can this laboratory supervisor do to improve employees' behavior? As a group, role-play the following situations:

- The supervisor discovers an employee eating a sandwich at his or her work station during the lunch hour. (It is unsafe to eat food in a laboratory, because it may become contaminated or contaminate other materials.)

- The supervisor asks an employee to show a newly hired employee around the lab on the new person's first day. The first employee would prefer to stay with his or her usual projects.

- The supervisor notices that several employees are not wearing their gloves—again.

Discuss each role-play. Is the supervisor applying the advice from the experts and the principles described in this chapter? Which ideas do you think are most effective?

Problem-Solving Case: *Suspensions of Lexington, Kentucky, Police Officers*

A police officer in Lexington, Kentucky, was troubled by content some other officers had posted on the MySpace.com networking Web site. These officers discussed their work, including arrests they had made. Their postings included putdowns such as slurs about gays and mentally disabled people and comments that they worked for Lexington's "snobby people" and the "Lexington Fayette Urban Communist [instead of County] Government." Photos on these officers' MySpace pages showed them in uniform.

The officer who was disturbed by the content reported the sites to a supervisor. The supervisor pursued the complaints, and the police department sought guidance from Urban County's law department, so that the officers' First Amendment rights to free speech would be respected. A board of police and law officials met privately to review the officers' conduct and recommend appropriate discipline. The board recommended to Lexington's police chief, Anthony Beatty, that five officers be charged with conduct unbecoming an officer, be suspended for 80 hours without pay, and receive additional sensitivity training beyond the training routinely given to all Lexington's police officers. Police Chief Beatty accepted the recommendations and presented the plan for discipline to each of the officers.

The officers accepted their discipline. After completing their suspension, they were to return to full-duty status. Beatty told a reporter, "In my

discussions [with the officers] we certainly have talked about getting this behind us, moving on and making us an even better agency and enhancing our relationship with the community that we serve. And all of the officers are committed to doing just that and are very remorseful for what happened."

1. Was it appropriate for the police department to discipline the officers for behavior that took place outside their jobs? Why or why not?
2. If you had been the supervisor who received the complaint about the officers' MySpace postings, how would you have reacted? Whom would you talk to, and what would you ask?
3. Overall, as described here, does this case provide an example of effective discipline? Can you suggest a few ways a police department supervisor could add to the effectiveness of the discipline in this situation? (Keep in mind that government agencies, such as this police department, often have to follow strict procedures for documentation and decision making.)

Sources: Cassondra Kirby and Michelle Ku, "Two Officers Suspended for MySpace Postings: City Council Accepts Recommendation," *Lexington Herald-Leader*, June 23, 2006; Cassondra Kirby, "Three Police Officers Suspended for Web Postings," *Lexington Herald-Leader*, July 7, 2006, both downloaded from Business & Company Resource Center, http://galenet.galegroup.com.

Knowing Yourself

Can You Distinguish between Discipline and Punishment?
Write True or False on the line before each of the following statements.

_____ 1. If an employee failed to do something I requested, I would immediately dock his or her pay.

_____ 2. If I noticed that an employee was leaving work early on a regular basis, I would revoke his or her lunch privileges.

_____ 3. If I saw two employees arguing, I would ask each separately for his or her version of the story.

_____ 4. If I had to issue a warning to an employee, I would make certain that he or she understood exactly what behavior the warning referred to.

_____ 5. If an employee insults me personally, I will insult the employee in return, so that he or she understands how I feel.

_____ 6. No matter how angry I feel inside at an employee, I will not act hostilely.

_____ 7. If an employee is doing poorly, I will note that in the performance appraisal.

_____ 8. If an employee were late to work the day of the company picnic, I would force him or her to stay on the job rather than leave early with everyone else to attend the picnic.

_____ 9. If I smelled alcohol on the breath of an employee after lunch, I would immediately fire the person.

_____ 10. If I caught an employee violating a company policy, I would immediately discuss the behavior and its consequences with the person.

Scoring True responses to statements 1, 2, 5, 8, and 9 illustrate punishment; True responses to statements 3, 4, 6, 7, and 10 illustrate discipline.

Pause and Reflect

1. For statements 1, 2, 5, 8, and 9, try to think of a way to use positive discipline in place of punishment to prevent or correct the problem behavior.

2. Is punishment ever necessary or desirable in the workplace? If so, when might it be appropriate? If not, why not?

3. Can you think of a work situation in which you experienced punishment? If so, did it benefit you (for example, by teaching you a valuable lesson)?

Class Exercise

Evaluating Disciplinary Action

The postal service has adopted a disciplinary code that substitutes a letter of reprimand for the 7- to 14-day suspension without pay that repeated infractions once drew. As an extreme penalty, workers may be given one payless "day of reflection."

The post office feels the new policy treats "adults like adults." But the president of the National Rural Letter Carriers Association fears employees may see the new discipline as a mere "slap on the wrist."

Debate these two views.

Source: "World Week," *The Wall Street Journal,* November 3, 1998, p. 1.

Building Supervision Skills

Handling Performance Problems

This is a role-playing exercise. One class member volunteers to take on the role of supervisor. Another classmate volunteers to be the problem employee. The scenario:

Chris Johnson has been a teller in the main branch of a bank for five years. Lately, Chris has been making a lot of mistakes. Chris often counts out money wrong and has had to redo many receipts that contain errors. Customers have begun complaining about the mistakes Chris makes and the detached, distracted manner in which Chris provides service. But at Chris's most recent performance appraisal, just two months ago, Chris's overall rating was excellent, leading to a generous wage increase. Chris's supervisor, Pat Smith, must decide how to respond to the decline in Chris's performance.

Before the role-play begins, the class discusses what the supervisor should do. Based on the information given, should Pat use counseling, discipline, both, or neither? Once the class agrees on a general strategy, the two volunteers act it out. Then the class discusses what happened:

- Did the supervisor do a good job of applying the techniques selected? What did the supervisor do well? What could the supervisor have done better?
- Did the employee and supervisor arrive at a workable solution? Explain.
- How can the supervisor follow up to see whether the employee is improving?

Chapter **Thirteen**

Managing Time and Stress

Learning Objectives

After you have studied this chapter, you should be able to:

13.1 Discuss how supervisors can evaluate their use of time.

13.2 Describe ways to plan the use of time.

13.3 Identify some time wasters and how to control them.

13.4 List factors that contribute to stress among employees.

13.5 Summarize consequences of stress.

13.6 Explain how supervisors can manage their own stress.

13.7 Identify ways organizations, including supervisors, can help their employees manage stress.

Time is the coin of your life. It is the only coin you have, and only you can determine how it will be spent. Be careful lest you let other people spend it for you.

—Carl Sandburg, U.S. biographer and poet

A Supervisor's Problem: Mississippi Power Company's People under Stress

Experience could not have prepared the employees of Mississippi Power Company (MPC) for their task following Hurricane Katrina's onslaught. When the storm ended, the company had to repair damage on a scale it had never faced before. Every single one of MPC's 195,000 customers was without power. More than 300 transmission structures were destroyed, 119 out of 122 transmission lines were out of service, and many substations were flooded with saltwater. Technicians would have to replace more than 9,000 poles and 2,300 transformers. To even begin doing that, they had to work with tree-trimming crews, who cleared the area so the electricians could get near all this damaged equipment. Employees were under intense time pressure to work quickly to restore services essential to their community. Most crucially, fire departments and local government agencies needed power to carry out their rescue work. To add to the confusion, communication was difficult because phone systems also were knocked out of service.

Under any conditions, such difficult, dangerous, and significant work would be stressful. But other circumstances added to the challenge. The greatest strain was that most employees were struggling with personal losses caused by the same storm that had made their work so stressful. According to MPC's customer operations manager, Charlie Sentell, the homes of a majority of the company's employees had been significantly damaged, flooded, or completely destroyed. Workers were exhausted because they labored long hours with little rest. As the mud left behind by floodwaters dried up, it turned to dust, triggering sinus problems and breathing difficulty. Wearing masks for protection helped with that problem but added to the misery of working in high heat and humidity. The smell was oppressive, and crew members knew they might discover dead bodies when they went out to work. Supplies and materials ran out frequently. Yet the unprecedented size of the job, the number of contract workers, and the lack of easy communication meant that employees often had to stretch themselves to make decisions beyond the usual scope of their jobs.

How did employees cope under these circumstances? Some line workers said they drew on their training. Foreman Shawn Schmill said that even though he worked long hours with little rest, his training had prepared him well: "As you go through the apprentice program, you work in many different and difficult situations, and the journeymen teach you how to keep yourself going." In addition, the physically demanding nature of a line worker's job, although adding to fatigue, also helps these workers attain physical fitness, which helped them when the disaster required all their strength and stamina. Workers appreciated the efforts the company made to provide for their needs and the emphasis placed on safety, and some union electricians credited their union locals for supporting their efforts during emergency work. Workers also celebrated the acts of kindness directed toward them. For instance, a crew working in Pass Christian in the afternoon heat encountered two women, who walked half a mile to a first-aid station to obtain cases of bottled water for the crew members.

In addition, MPC had disaster plans and had anticipated many of the workers' needs, including the need to bring in thousands of workers from other states and Canada. The company had arranged for thousands of beds located in hotels, military facilities, college dormitories, mobile sleeper trailers, tents, and company facilities. Thirty staging sites had been stocked with tents, cots, bedding, meals, showers, Dumpsters, and portable toilets. Not only did MPC have to provide employees with the materials and equipment to do their jobs, but it also had to make sure that everyone had food, water, and gasoline for their vehicles—none of which was easy to obtain and deliver in the days following Katrina's landing.

Despite the host of challenges, MPC's employees in only 12 days restored electricity to all of the 169,000 customers who were able to receive it. The Edison Electric Institute granted the company its Emergency Response Award, but CEO Anthony Topazi gave full credit to the employees: "They put aside their own personal losses to lead a truly inspired restoration effort." And Johnny Atherton, MPC's vice president of external affairs, said, "Dozens of employees showed incredible leadership and adaptability as they became group supervisors, key decision makers, and area managers all burdened with responsibilities that far outweighed their normal job description."

Few workplaces have jobs as stressful as those involved in restoring services to the Gulf Coast during the days and weeks after Hurricane Katrina. In these circumstances, MPC's supervisors faced the challenge of helping their employees remain focused, safe, and committed to the tasks at hand.

QUESTIONS

1. How can supervisors recognize and prepare for sources of stress on the job?
2. What can a supervisor do to help employees cope with stressful work?

Sources: Steven M. Brown, "Power and Data Restored in Mississippi, but Rebuilding Continues," *Utility Automation & Engineering T&D,* June 2006; Terry Wildman, "Every Customer Lost," *Transmission & Distribution World,* Online Exclusive, July 1, 2006; Stuart M. Lewis, "Linemen Give It Their All," *Transmission & Distribution World,* February 1, 2006, all downloaded from Business & Company Resource Center, http://galenet.galegroup.com.

A supervisor who has a bad day may feel as though everything is out of control. Instead of working on what he or she wants, the supervisor attempts to solve unexpected problems and soothe upset employees and customers. Although workdays like this affect employees and managers at all levels, they are a particular problem for supervisors because a supervisor's people-oriented job means solving many needs and conflicts. To minimize and cope with these difficulties, supervisors must manage their time and stress.

This chapter describes basic techniques of time and stress management. It identifies ways supervisors can control how they use time. Then it defines stress and describes its consequences. Finally, the chapter suggests ways supervisors themselves can cope with stress and also help employees do so.

TIME MANAGEMENT

Sean Mulligan's typical day is hectic. Just when he gets on the telephone, someone is at the door with a problem; he almost never finds the time to sit down and ponder the problem. By the end of the day, Mulligan is exhausted, but he would be hard-pressed to say what he accomplished. Lisa Ng's days are also busy, but when someone interrupts her, she pulls out her calendar and makes an appointment for later. She starts out each day knowing what tasks are essential, and she always manages to complete them.

Which kind of supervisor would you rather have working for you? Which kind would you rather be? Time is the only resource we all have in equal shares: Everyone gets 24-hour days. To evaluate your own responses to time pressures, take the Knowing Yourself quiz on pages 367–368.

Supervisors who are in control of their time find that their jobs are easier and that they can get more done. Getting a lot done is a good way to impress higher-level management. The practice of controlling the way you use time is known as **time management.**

time management
The practice of controlling the way you use time

Time management techniques can be as simple as putting things away as soon as you are done with them, using an appointment calendar to keep track of your schedule, and getting all the information you need *before* you start on a project. Whereas this chapter provides broad guidelines for time management, each supervisor must work out the details. A look at the many different varieties of calendars, planners, and scheduling tools available in your nearest office supply store, whether in paper form or as software, will convince you that no two people get organized in quite the same way.

Understanding How You Use Time

Before you can take control over the way you use time, you have to understand what you already are doing. A practical way to learn about your use of time is to keep a **time log,** a record of what activities you are doing hour by hour throughout the workday. Figure 13.1 provides an example. Each half-hour during the day, write down what you did during the previous half-hour. Do not wait until the end of the day; this level of detail is too difficult to remember.

time log
A record of what activities a person is doing hour by hour throughout the day

After you have kept a time log for at least one typical week, review your log. Ask yourself the following questions:

- How much time did I spend on important activities?
- How much time did I spend on activities that did not need to get done?

FIGURE 13.1 Format for a Time Log

Date _____

Time	Activity	Others Involved	Location
7:30–8:00			
8:00–8:30			
8:30–9:00			
9:00–9:30			
9:30–10:00			
10:00–10:30			
10:30–11:00			
11:00–11:30			
11:30–12:00			
12:00–12:30			
12:30–1:00			
1:00–1:30			
1:30–2:00			
2:00–2:30			
2:30–3:00			
3:00–3:30			
3:30–4:00			
4:00–4:30			
4:30–5:00			
5:00–5:30			

- How much time did I spend on activities that someone else could have done (perhaps with some training)?
- What important jobs did I not get around to finishing?

From your review, you may see some patterns. Do you reserve a certain time of day for telephone calls or meetings? Do you frequently interrupt what you are doing to solve a problem or move on to something more interesting? Do you tackle the most important jobs first or the easiest ones? Do you get caught up in behaviors that waste time? One business writer describes common time wasters that plague supervisors: working without a plan, working with fuzzy goals or too many goals, oversupervising, worrying, excessive socializing, pursuing perfectionism, putting off delivering bad news, correcting your own mistakes or those of others, waiting, attending meaningless meetings, dealing with those who don't put in a full day's work, and getting angry.[1] Another waste of time is giving poor instructions. Poorly expressed or incomplete instructions create errors or send employees back to you for clarification.[2]

The answers to these and similar questions will help you see where you need to change. After you have tried applying the principles in this chapter for a while, you might want to try keeping a time log again to see how you have improved.

Keeping a time log is also helpful for people who feel out of control of their personal time. For example, if you are frustrated at how little time you spend with loved ones or if you cannot find the time for charitable work, keep a log of how you use your hours outside work. You may find that you are spending a lot of time on an unimportant activity that you can relinquish to free time for something else.

Planning Your Use of Time

On the basis of what you learned from keeping a time log, you can plan how to use your time better. You need to make sure that the most important things get done each day before you move on to less important activities. You must set priorities. Thus, your planning consists of deciding what you need to do and which activities are most important.

Planning your use of time begins with the planning process described in Chapter 6. If you follow the guidelines in that chapter, you will routinely establish objectives for the year, specifying when each must be completed. With these yearly objectives in mind, you can figure out what you need to accomplish in shorter time periods—each quarter, month, and week. Review your objectives regularly, and use them to plan what you will need to accomplish each week and day.

Making a "To Do" List

Many people find it helpful to spend a few minutes at the end of each week writing a list of things to do—what they must accomplish during the next week. When you have made your list, write an *A* next to all the activities that must be completed that week; they are your top priorities. Then write a *B* next to all the activities that are important but can be postponed if necessary. Label everything else *C*; these activities are your lowest priorities for the week. Schedule times for doing your A-level and B-level activities. If you have more time, work on your C-level activities. As you complete each activity on the "to do" list, check it off.

How do you know when is the best time to do the activities on your list? Here are some guidelines to follow for creating weekly and daily schedules:

- First, record all the activities that must occur at a set time. For example, you do not have any choice about when to schedule your regular Monday morning staff meeting or the appointment you made with your manager for 3:00 on Thursday.
- Next, find times for your remaining A-level activities. Try to avoid scheduling them at the end of the day (on a daily plan) or week (on a weekly plan). If a crisis comes up, you will need another chance to finish these activities. Schedule your B-level activities next.
- Schedule the most challenging and most important activities for the times of day when you are at your best. If you are sleepy after lunch or get off to a slow start in the morning, schedule top-priority activities for times when you are more alert.
- Learn to use the calendar or scheduling tools built into your computer operating system. For instance, Microsoft Works Calendar allows you to record upcoming events, meetings, appointments, and holidays, and it will also send you customized reminders of each (with audio signals, if you like). Other

programs, such as Lotus Notes, allow you to schedule a team meeting and post the day, time, and location on the calendars of all the team's members.

- Schedule time for thinking, not solely for doing. Remember that the creative process requires time for reflection (see Chapter 9).
- Do not fill up every hour of the day and week. Leave some time free to handle unexpected problems and questions from your employees and others. If problems do not occur, so much the better. You will have time for the C-level activities.

Be careful that your "to do" list serves its purpose and doesn't become a goal in itself. Some time-management consultants say writing lists can become a substitute for getting started on the list items. Certainly, list writing can become time consuming. Communications consultant Ilya Welfeld maintains lists of lists, including a priority list that supplements the "to do" list she keeps in Microsoft Outlook's Tasks. Deanna Brown, publisher of a magazine called *Breathe,* spends a half-hour each day composing a list of things to do. "Call mother" was on the list for a month, which Brown rationalized by saying that including the task was a sign "I'm thinking about her."[3]

Controlling Time Wasters

Many supervisors find that certain activities and attitudes are what most often lead them to waste time. Figure 13.2 identifies the most common time wasters: meetings, telephone calls, e-mail, paperwork, unscheduled visitors, procrastination, perfectionism, failure to delegate, and inability to say no. Some of the activities are necessary, but a supervisor does not always manage the time spent on them wisely.

Meetings

The main reason many supervisors hate meetings is that meetings often waste time. People slowly drift into the room, then devote time to chatting while waiting for latecomers. When the formal meeting finally gets under way, the discussion may drift off onto tangents, and the group may never complete the task that it gathered to address. Meetings like these are understandably a source of frustration.

When you attend a meeting chaired by someone else, it is hard to control wasted time. You can encourage careful use of time by being prompt. If meetings tend to start late, you might bring along some reading material or other work to do while you wait. If the discussion at the meeting seems irrelevant, you might try tactfully asking the speaker to explain how the current discussion will help in accomplishing the goal of the meeting.

FIGURE 13.2
Common Time Wasters

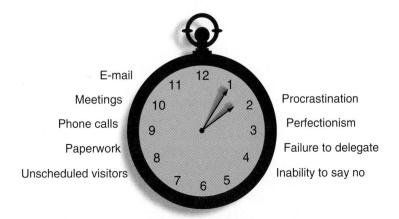

When you call a meeting, you can use time wisely by starting promptly. If the discussion veers off course, politely remind participants about the subject at hand. It is also smart to set an ending time for the meeting. If you cannot solve the problem in the time allotted, schedule a follow-up meeting. (Chapter 3 provides more ideas for holding effective meetings.)

Telephone Calls and E-Mail

When other people call you, they usually have no way of knowing whether the time is convenient. Consequently, most of us get telephone calls when we are busy with something else. When they interrupt the work flow, telephone calls are time wasters.

One way to take control of your time is to remember that you are not a slave to the telephone. If you are fortunate enough to have a secretary to screen your calls, have that person answer your telephone when you are working on top-priority jobs. If you answer the telephone while you are in a meeting or doing something important, explain to the caller that you cannot give the call the attention it deserves at that time, and schedule a convenient time to call back. Of course, you have to use this approach carefully. If the person calling is your manager or a customer, the telephone call may be your top priority.

When you are placing calls yourself, think ahead. Schedule time for making calls each day, bearing in mind different time zones when calling long distance. Before you call someone, make sure you have the information you need close at hand; it does not make sense to place a client on hold while you fetch the file containing the answers he or she wanted. Not only does that waste time, but it also annoys the person who has to wait. If the person you are calling is not available, ask when you can reach him or her instead of simply leaving a message. That way, you have control over when the call will be made.

For all its apparent convenience, e-mail can absorb another major block of supervisors' time. Some employees receive 100 or more messages a day. The time required to read and respond to the incoming messages challenges employees to come up with strategies for e-mail management. At the offices of *The Wall Street Journal*, one employee reads each message when it arrives, ignoring only the ones that are obviously spam, deletes about half as unimportant, and then saves the rest. Another employee periodically reviews her messages in the preview pane, deletes unimportant messages, reads the important ones, and then sorts the messages into folders so she can refer to them later. If a message requires further action later (for example, when she receives more information), this employee keeps it in her in box.[4]

In addition to the sheer volume of information, e-mail presents another challenge that is at least as serious: interruptions. According to studies of worker behavior, an interrupted worker takes 25 minutes to return the original task. The reason is that the worker usually detours into other activities after the interruption.[5] So every time you stop what you are working on to open a message, you can expect it will take a while before you return to your previous train of thought. Some highly productive people have figured out ways to minimize the impact of these interruptions. Some keep a word-processing page open for recording any ideas and reminders as they come to mind. These people can use the program's search feature to locate the ideas later. Others send themselves e-mail reminders because they have a habit of periodically checking their e-mail anyway. Still others follow the principle of fully handling an interruption only if it will take up to two minutes. Longer interruptions go straight to the person's "to do" list. Then the person tackles the next item on the list (the new item only if it's now the highest priority).[6]

To keep from being overwhelmed, supervisors should learn to prioritize their e-mail, delete junk mail unread, limit the number of messages sent and the number of recipients, and avoid forwarding or responding to chain letters or other kinds of nonbusiness correspondence. Business consultant and writer Jennifer White advises being ruthless about e-mail. One of her recommended strategies is to check your e-mail once and only once during each day, at a scheduled time. Checking it throughout the day destroys momentum and turns the task into a burden. Of course, this method is possible only if others are not depending on you to provide a quicker response to e-mail. Still, in the words of Merlin Mann, an expert on managing tech-induced information overload, "Unless you're working in a Korean missile silo, you don't need to check e-mail every two minutes."[7]

Paperwork and Reading Material

Supervisors spend a lot of time reading and writing. They receive mail, reports, and magazines to read, and they must prepare reports, letters, and memos to send to others. Reading and writing are not necessarily a waste of time, but many supervisors perform these activities inefficiently.

Most advice on how to manage paperwork is based on the principle of handling each item only once. Set aside specific time to read all the papers that cross your desk. At that time, decide whether each item is something you need to act on. If not, throw it away immediately. If you must act, determine the most efficient response. An efficient way to respond to a memo is to write a brief response across the top and return the memo to the sender. If you have a secretary, you can keep a tape recorder by your side and dictate responses to letters as you read them. Or consider whether you can respond to a letter with a telephone call. If you learn that you must set time aside to do research or prepare a report, schedule that time immediately.

Most supervisors have a multitude of magazines, newsletters, and newspapers from which to choose. Each supervisor will find that some of these are very helpful, others somewhat helpful, and still others not relevant at all. To cut the time spent poring over the unhelpful publications, a supervisor should decide which ones are useful and cancel subscriptions to the rest. It is wise to look at the table of contents in the somewhat helpful publications for relevant information rather than to turn every page. A supervisor who finds that an internal company report he or she receives provides little useful information might ask to be taken off the distribution list.

Unscheduled Visitors

Supervisors are interrupted at times by unscheduled visitors: customers, peers, employees, salespeople, or anyone else who turns up without an appointment. Because seeing these people is an unplanned use of time, the interruptions can interfere with getting the job done. Figure 13.3 shows some broad guidelines for handling this potential problem.

When a supervisor regularly spends time with unscheduled visitors on unimportant matters, a lot of time gets wasted. The key is to know which interruptions are important. For example, when an angry customer demands to see the manager and interrupts a supervisor in a store, an important part of the supervisor's job is to make that customer happy. When a supervisor's manager occasionally drops in to discuss an idea, the supervisor will probably have to work around the manager's schedule. But when a co-worker in another department stops in to report on his vacation or a salesperson shows up unannounced, the interruption does not carry a high priority.

FIGURE 13.3
Handling
Unscheduled
Visitors

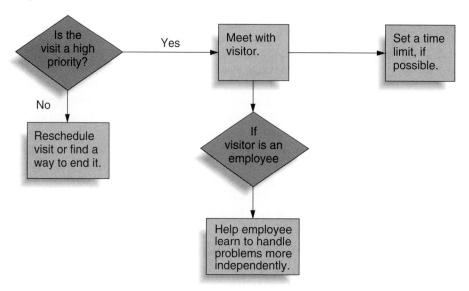

With low-priority interruptions, the supervisor needs to take control of his or her time diplomatically. The supervisor might say to the co-worker back from vacation, "It's great to hear you had fun last week. Let's have lunch together so you can tell me about it." When salespeople call without an appointment, a supervisor can ask them simply to leave some literature. Another response to unscheduled visitors is to set a time limit. For example, the supervisor might say, "I've got five minutes. What's on your mind?" If the problem is urgent or seems to deserve more time, the supervisor can arrange to meet the visitor later for a specified amount of time.[8]

Standing is a useful signal. If you see an unwanted visitor heading toward your office, stand and meet the visitor at your door, then talk to the visitor there. This sends a message that you expect the conversation to be brief. Meeting with someone else at his or her desk or in a conference room allows you to get up and leave when you have completed your business. If you meet with someone in your office, standing up when you finish sends a signal that the meeting is over.

Interruptions from employees can be tricky to handle because part of a supervisor's job is to listen to employees and help them with work-related problems. At the same time, a constant stream of interruptions could mean that employees have too little training or authority to handle their work. If an employee interrupts with a problem, one approach is to listen and then ask, "What do you suggest we do about that?" This shows that the supervisor expects the employee to participate in finding solutions. With practice, the employee may learn to handle problems more independently.

If the problem is not urgent—for example, if it does not hold up an employee's work—a supervisor may want to schedule a later time when supervisor and employee can meet to work on the problem. At that later time, of course, the supervisor should give priority to the meeting with the employee and discourage interruptions from others. Thus, employees will learn that a supervisor will listen and work with them, though not necessarily on a moment's notice.

Procrastination

Sometimes it is hard to start an activity. Maybe you have to write a proposal to buy a new computer system. You are not quite sure how to write that kind of proposal, so you are grateful when the telephone rings. You talk for a while, and that conversation reminds you to follow up on an order with a supplier. So you make another telephone call. You get up to stretch your legs and decide it is a good time to check on how your employees are doing. Bit by bit, you manage to get through the entire day without doing any work on the proposal. This process of putting off what needs to be done is called **procrastination.**

procrastination
Putting off what needs to be done

Procrastination is a time waster because it leads people to spend their time on low-priority activities while they avoid the higher priorities. The best cure for procrastination is to force yourself to jump in. To do that, focus on one step at a time. Decide what the first step is, then do that step. Then do the next step. You will find that you are building momentum and that the big job no longer seems so overwhelming.

If you need more incentive to get started, give yourself a reward for completing each step. For example, you might decide that as soon as you complete the first step, you will go for a walk in the sunshine, call a customer who loves your product, or take a break to open your mail. If the project seems thoroughly unpleasant, you can concentrate on the rewards. The ultimate reward of course is to finish the job.

Here are a few other tips for conquering procrastination:[9]

1. Pick one area at a time in which you tend to procrastinate and attack it. You might tend to put off starting new projects, for instance, or answering e-mail, or returning phone calls. Whatever the case, choose one task and start it.
2. Compartmentalize your work and force yourself to get through the task one step, one e-mail, or one phone call at a time. With each one you complete, begin the next one.
3. Try getting the biggest job done first, when you have the most energy. With that done, it's downhill the rest of the way.
4. Give yourself deadlines. Write them down where you can't miss them, and stick to them.
5. Don't pursue perfectionism.

Perfectionism

perfectionism
The attempt to do things perfectly

One reason people put off doing necessary work is that they are afraid what they do will not live up to their standards. Although high standards can inspire high performance, perfectionism can make people afraid to try at all. **Perfectionism** is the attempt to do things perfectly. It may sound like a noble goal, but human beings are imperfect. Expecting to be perfect therefore dooms a person to failure.

Instead of being a slave to perfectionism, determine the highest standard you realistically can achieve. You may be able to meet a higher standard by drawing on the expertise of employees and peers. When you find yourself avoiding a difficult task, remind yourself that your goals are realistic, and then give the job your best try.

Failure to Delegate

Perfectionism often underlies the failure to delegate work. Even when someone else can do a job more efficiently in terms of that person's cost and availability, supervisors may resist delegating because they believe only they can really do the job right. This attitude stands in the way of appropriate delegating. In terms of time management, the result is that the supervisor has taken on too much work. Instead, the supervisor should learn to delegate effectively. The "Tips from the Firing Line" box suggests ways that supervisors can put reasonable limits on what others expect from them—and what they expect of themselves.

TIPS FROM THE FIRING LINE

SETTING LIMITS

Many supervisors earned a promotion to their position from a job they enjoyed or at least felt confident handling. Perhaps the supervisory responsibilities feel less comfortable than nonmanagement responsibilities. Some supervisors discover they are working harder than they ever imagined, carrying out many of their former tasks along with their new duties. Many supervisors find that their job grows as companies try to operate with fewer employees and fewer layers of management. At some point, it becomes impossible to keep taking on new responsibilities without dropping any of the old ones.

Becoming overloaded and unable to complete your duties in the course of the workweek is a sign that you need to set some limits. A logical place to start is with a review of all your tasks. Some organizations have employees who devote time and energy to projects no one cares about—reports no one reads or products the company no longer supports. Are you performing any duties that once were important but no longer serve a purpose? If so, get permission to stop doing them.

Next, identify which of your activities can be delegated. If some of your employees have the necessary skills, those people might enjoy the added variety. If they lack necessary skills, this may be an opportunity to train and develop employees with potential. As they learn more, your group can deliver more value to your organization.

Evaluate what you can do in a week. If after delegation, you still have more responsibilities than you can reasonably handle, list them and discuss them with your boss. Some managers are surprised to learn how many tasks their employees are trying to handle. Ask your boss to help you define the top-priority tasks. You might feel uncomfortable bringing up this topic, but if you do it in a positive, problem-solving tone, you are likely to find that your boss would rather have the discussion than be surprised later when you are unable to complete a project.

Make sure your time away from work is really time off. When your workday is over, unless your job requires you to be on call, let your e-mail and voice mail wait until the next workday. Consider Diane Knorr's experience. The first time a manager called her late in the evening, Knorr was flattered by her apparent importance to the company. But eventually she had more and more difficulty keeping her work life separate from her family time. She began suffering from stress-related illness, which continued until she made a job change. Too late for her job with that employer, Knorr realized that to be successful for the long term, she had to take care of herself.

Sources: Johanna Rothman, "When Do You Say, 'No, That's Not My Job Any Longer'?" *Computerworld,* August 1, 2003, www.computerworld.com; John Schwartz, "Always on the Job, Employees Pay with Health," *The New York Times,* September 5, 2004, downloaded from Business & Company Resource Center, http://galenet.galegroup.com.

Inability to Say No

To control your use of time, you must be able to say no when appropriate. However, it is easy to let other people and their demands control how we use our time, so we end up overextending ourselves by taking on more tasks than we can possibly do well. How do you react when someone asks you to chair a committee, manage a new project, or take an active role in a local charity? Most people are uncomfortable saying no when the opportunity is for a worthwhile project or they do not want to hurt somebody's feelings. But when we take on too many things, we cannot do our best at any of them.

If someone comes to you with an opportunity that will require a significant commitment of time, learn to tell the person politely that you will consider the offer and reply later at some specific time. Then assess your present commitments and priorities. Decide whether you should take on this new task. You may decide that you have time for it, but in other instances you will have to decline, claiming that you do not have enough time to do justice to the task. If your life is already busy but the opportunity seems important, try asking yourself, "What activity am I willing to give up in order to make time for this new one?"

If your own supervisor asks you to take on an urgent new task, request help in deciding where the new task should fit into your current priorities or ask what should be given up to accomplish the new project.[10]

For those times when you can't say no, try these tips:

1. Ask the person making the request how the two of you can plan better for the next time.
2. Remind the person that he or she now owes you one and, for example, could cover your shift next time you need time off.
3. Suggest your own timetable. For instance, say, "I can do that by the end of the week."
4. Put a time limit on your participation. For instance, explain that you can only give an hour and no more.[11]

Whatever you decide, a thoughtful approach does both you and the other person a favor. If you do not have the time to complete a task well and on schedule, it is better to give the other person a chance to find somebody else. None of us like to find out that the person we have been counting on is overcommitted and doesn't have enough time to do the job well.

STRESS MANAGEMENT

Failure to manage time wisely is one reason supervisors find their jobs difficult. It is frustrating to leave the workplace knowing that you did not accomplish anything you really wanted to that day. Supervisors also have difficulty hearing a lot of complaints, working in a dangerous environment, and trying to live up to unrealistic expectations. To cope, supervisors can use the techniques of stress management.

stress
The body's response to coping with environmental demands

Stress refers to the body's response to coping with environmental demands such as change, frustration, uncertainty, danger, or discomfort. Usually when we think of stress, we think of the response to problems—for example, arguments, cold, or long hours of work. Stress also results from the challenges that stimulate us and from the happy changes in our lives. Thus, buying a car is stressful, and so is getting married or promoted. People experiencing stress typically undergo physiological changes such as faster heartbeat, faster breathing, higher blood pressure, greater perspiration, greater muscle strength, and decreased gastric (stomach) functioning, among other changes.

Causes of Stress

The environmental demands that cause stress may arise in the workplace, in people's personal lives, and in the conflicts that can arise between the two.

Work-Related Causes

Job factors linked to stress involve the organization's policies, structures, physical conditions, and processes (the way work gets done). Examples of each type are identified in Figure 13.4. Employees tend to experience the most stress if policies seem unfair and ambiguous, the structure makes jobs relatively unsatisfying, physical conditions are uncomfortable, and processes interfere with employee understanding of what is happening and how well they are doing.

David Stum, president of the Loyalty Institute at Aon Consulting, says employees feel increasingly stressed by "the new corporate expectation . . . to do everything

FIGURE 13.4
Job Factors Linked
to Stress

Source: From Samuel C.
Certo and Lee Graf, *Modern
Management: Diversity,
Quality, Ethics, & the Global
Environment*, 6th ed.
Copyright © 1994 Pearson
Education, Inc. Reprinted
by permission of Pearson
Education, Inc., Upper
Saddle River, NJ.

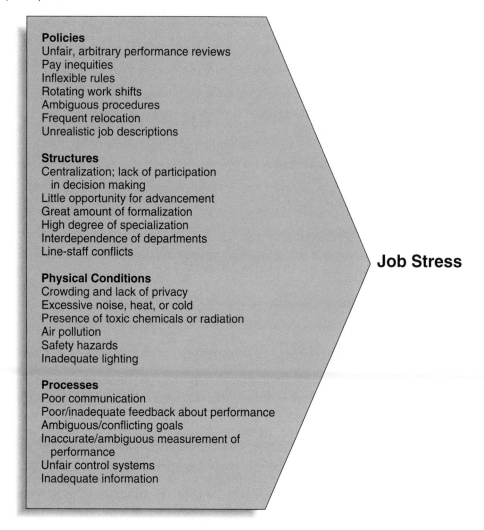

Policies
Unfair, arbitrary performance reviews
Pay inequities
Inflexible rules
Rotating work shifts
Ambiguous procedures
Frequent relocation
Unrealistic job descriptions

Structures
Centralization; lack of participation
  in decision making
Little opportunity for advancement
Great amount of formalization
High degree of specialization
Interdependence of departments
Line-staff conflicts

Physical Conditions
Crowding and lack of privacy
Excessive noise, heat, or cold
Presence of toxic chemicals or radiation
Air pollution
Safety hazards
Inadequate lighting

Processes
Poor communication
Poor/inadequate feedback about performance
Ambiguous/conflicting goals
Inaccurate/ambiguous measurement of
  performance
Unfair control systems
Inadequate information

Job Stress

better, faster and cheaper." He notes that days lost from work because of stress have increased in recent years, which Paul Rosch, president of the American Institute of Stress, tags with a cost to U.S. employers of $200 billion to $300 billion annually. That figure includes absenteeism, turnover, direct medical costs, workers' compensation and other legal costs, accidents, and diminished productivity.[12]

Studies of a representative sample of occupations done by the Bureau of Labor Statistics indicate that victims of occupational stress missed a median of 23 days of work in one year, compared with only 5 days for all injuries and illnesses. Workers in the financial, insurance, and real estate sectors account for 12 percent of all stress cases, while machine operators accounted for 15 percent and production supervisors 4 percent. Blue-collar workers accounted for most of the injuries and illnesses, while white-collar workers made up more than half the stress cases. Looking at the data by gender, the bureau found that men accounted for two-thirds of the injuries and ailments, while women accounted for two-thirds of the stress cases.[13]

Recurring efforts at downsizing have contributed to a great deal of employee stress. Many employees see job cuts as a long-term trend that prevails without regard to whether they do their best or the organization earns a profit. A case in point is Pam Cromer, who worked for Westinghouse Electric Corporation in

TABLE 13.1
Behavior Patterns Associated with Type A and Type B Personalities

Source: Adapted from Meyer Friedman and Ray H. Rosenman, *Type A Behavior and Your Heart* (New York: Fawcett Crest, 1974), pp. 100–101, summarized in Jane Whitney Gibson, *The Supervisory Challenge: Principles and Practices* (Columbus, OH: Merrill Publishing, 1990), p. 309.

Type A	Type B
Moving, walking, eating rapidly	Having varied interests
Feeling impatient with people who move slower than you	Taking a relaxed but active approach to life
Feeling impatient when others talk about something that is not of interest to you	
Doing two or three things at the same time	
Feeling unable to relax or stop working	
Trying to get more and more done in less and less time	

Pittsburgh. She worked up to 80 hours a week when the company was struggling during the early 1990s. One night part of her face went numb, which Cromer learned was caused from clenching her teeth too hard—the result of tension. Despite Cromer's willingness to sacrifice, she was laid off in cutbacks that occurred after she had been with Westinghouse 22 years. At a going-away party, her co-workers observed, "The winners get to leave, and the losers get to stay."[14]

A supervisor's own behavior also can be a source of stress for employees. A supervisor who communicates poorly, stirs up conflict, and metes out discipline arbitrarily is creating stressful working conditions. Other supervisory behaviors that can contribute to employee stress are demonstrating a lack of concern for employee well-being and checking up on every detail of an employee's work. If you've ever typed while someone peered over your shoulder, you know that you can almost feel your blood pressure rise. Supervisors also contribute to stress when they make the employees' job more difficult—for example, by giving vague directions or interrupting them with matters than can wait.

Michael Gelman is the executive producer of *Live with Regis,* a freewheeling morning television show filmed in New York. Over the 13 years he has held the job, Gelman has found his own way of coping with the particular stress of working with Regis Philbin. "There are absolutely no second chances on live television," comments Gelman. "When things go awry and Regis grumbles and complains, I don't take it personally. It's all part of his shtick. We just move on . . . there is that 5 percent of the time when my feelings are indeed hurt and I want to blurt out, 'Wait a minute.' But that would be out of character."[15]

Personal Factors

Even when faced with similar job factors and supervisory behavior, some employees will have a greater stress response than others. General feelings of negativism, helplessness, and low self-esteem can contribute to stress. In addition, some medical researchers have observed that the people who are more likely to have heart disease (presumably a sign of stress) tend to share a similar pattern of behavior, which the researchers have named the Type A personality. A **Type A personality** refers to the behavior pattern of constantly trying to get a lot done in a hurry. It includes the behaviors listed in Table 13.1. Research suggests that some Type A people seem to thrive on their approach to life, whereas others—those prone to heart disease—have an excess amount of hostility along with the basic Type A characteristics. To help those at risk, physicians often recommend adopting contrasting behaviors, known collectively as a **Type B personality** (see Table 13.1).

Another source of stress is the sheer inability to leave the job behind when it's appropriate to do so. According to a nationwide survey by Steelcase, which sells office furniture, more than 4 out of 10 workers say they spend some of their

Type A personality
A pattern of behavior that involves constantly trying to accomplish a lot in a hurry

Type B personality
A pattern of behavior that focuses on a relaxed but active approach to life

vacation time doing work. Technology makes it easy for employees to check e-mail, read messages on their cell phones or BlackBerries, or complete a report on their notebook computer. Although rest is necessary for people to refresh themselves so they can do their best, respondents to the survey most often justified working while on vacation as necessary for finishing an assignment or catching up on tasks.[16]

Work-Family Conflict

Stress also can be increased for people who experience conflict between the demands of work and home. Women have traditionally borne the primary responsibility for homemaking and the family's well-being, so as a group they are particularly vulnerable to this source of stress. A survey of 311 female nurses aged 50 to 70 years found that women who feel tension between demands from work and demands from home are at higher risk than other women of having serious heart disease. The risk was not associated with what the women achieved or how hard they worked but with the degree to which they felt a conflict between career and family. At greatest risk were the women who believed that having a family interfered with advancement in their careers.[17]

Consequences of Stress

Stress is a fact of life. Life would be boring without some sources of stress, and most people seek out some degree of stress. Some people even are attracted to jobs billed as challenging or exciting—those likely to be most stressful. On the job, employees tend to perform best when they are experiencing a moderate degree of stress (see Figure 13.5).

However, too much stress brings problems, especially when the sources of stress are negative (for example, a critical manager, unsafe working conditions). As Figure 13.5 indicates, performance falls when the amount of stress moves from moderate to high. In a highly stressful environment, people are more apt to come down with heart disease, high blood pressure, ulcers, and possibly other diseases. Because of illness and unhappiness, they take more time off from work. When employees are at work, the sources of stress may distract them from doing their best and make them prone to accidents.

In addition to hurting the organization through poor performance and attendance, excess stress can hurt employees as individuals. People experiencing stress tend to feel anxious, aggressive, frustrated, tense, and moody. They may be overly

FIGURE 13.5
Stress Levels and Performance

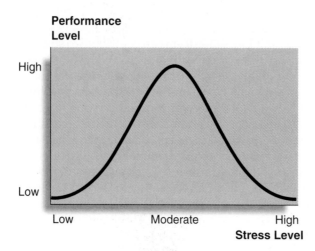

TABLE 13.2
Possible Signs of
Excess Stress

Decline in work performance.
Increase in use of sick days.
Increase in number of errors and accidents.
Moodiness and irritability.
Fatigue.
Loss of enthusiasm.
Aggressive behavior.
Difficulty making decisions.
Family problems.
Apparent loss of concern for others and their feelings.*
Feeling that it's impossible to help other people.*
Feeling of inability to get your job done fully or well.*

*Possible signs of burnout.

sensitive to criticism, have trouble making decisions, and be more likely to have trouble maintaining mutually satisfying relationships with loved ones. They may be unable to get enough sleep. People under stress are also at risk for abusing drugs and alcohol.

Because of these potential negative consequences of stress, supervisors should notice when employees seem to be experiencing more stress than they can handle effectively. Table 13.2 lists some signs that indicate when employees may be experiencing excess stress. If some of these signs exist, a supervisor should try to reduce the stress employees are experiencing and recommend some coping techniques. (Approaches to stress management are described in the next section.)

Burnout

burnout
The inability to
function effectively
as a result of ongoing
stress

A person who cannot cope with stress over an extended period of time may experience burnout. **Burnout** is the inability to function effectively as a result of ongoing stress. Employees who are burned out feel drained and lose interest in doing their jobs. Typically, burnout occurs in three stages:

1. The employee feels emotionally exhausted.
2. The employee's perceptions of others become calloused.
3. The employee views his or her effectiveness negatively.

Burnout is worse than just needing a vacation. Therefore, it is important to cope with stress before it leads to burnout.

Some signs of excess stress that may indicate burnout are indicated in Table 13.2. Supervisors who observe these signs in employees should not only seek to reduce stress but also be sure that employees are being rewarded for their efforts. Burnout is especially likely to occur when people feel they are giving of themselves all the time, with little or no return. For that reason, burnout is reported widely among employees in the so-called helping professions, such as health care and teaching.

Personal Stress Management

Because stress arises from both personal and job factors, a full effort at stress management includes actions at both levels. Personal stress management is especially important for people who hold jobs that are by nature highly stressful, such as the supervisor of nurses in a hospital's intensive care unit or the supervisor of a crew of firefighters.

SUPERVISORY SKILLS

MANAGING STRESS

COPING WITH THE DAILY COMMUTE

The amount of time people spend traveling to and from work has been growing. That's unfortunate, because a recent survey found that more than half of U.S. commuters experience stress on the way to their jobs. The response was even more likely among those taking public transportation than those who drive. Those who felt stressed placed the blame in several places, including traffic, starting late, annoyance with other commuters, and bad weather. And some stressed-out commuters express their tension as anger and impatience when they arrive at work.

Supervisors and other employees can take a number of actions to reduce the stress of their commute to work:

- Prepare to leave on time. Before going to bed at the end of the day, lay out your clothes and the items you need to take, such as your watch, keys, and wallet. Leave earlier so delays won't matter as much.

- If you can, travel during less busy times. Some employers allow flextime, so you may be able to travel before or after rush hour.

- Check traffic reports before leaving for work. If there is construction or an accident along your usual route, consider whether you can take an alternative route.

- Make your trip as pleasant as possible. Listen to calming music or an audio book; if you ride the train or bus, choose an interesting book or magazine to read.

- Share a ride with someone with whom you enjoy talking.

- Get plenty of rest and exercise. They help your body handle stress in all situations, including your commute.

Sources: "Morning Commuters Beware: The Toll on Your Heart Could Be Deadly," *PR Newswire,* September 21, 2004; Michael O'Connor, "Bad Drive to Work Can Override Drive to Succeed at the Office," *Knight Ridder/Tribune Business News,* August 17, 2003, both downloaded from Business & Company Resource Center, http://galenet.galegroup.com.

A variety of techniques are available for personal stress management: time management (discussed in the first part of this chapter), positive attitude, exercise, biofeedback, meditation, and well-rounded life activities. Supervisors can use these techniques to improve their own stress levels, and they also can encourage employees to use them. For examples of how these techniques apply to the stress of commuting to work, read the "Supervisory Skills" box.

Time Management

Making conscious, reasoned decisions about your use of time helps prevent the stress that can result from wasted time or unrealistic goals. Thus, a good start for handling the stress related to balancing work and family responsibilities is to set priorities. For example, different people will have different views about whether a promotion is worth the price of moving or working weekends. Then set aside time for the things you consider important, scheduling time for friends and family members as well as work-related commitments. As Rita Emmett says in *The Procrastinator's Handbook: Mastering the Art of Doing It Now,* the real point of finding ways to accomplish necessary tasks in an efficient and timely way is to make time to enjoy the rest of what life has to offer.[18]

Don't forget to include time for resting and recharging. Bolstered by research reports showing a link to improved safety and job performance, some managers are even putting naps on their schedules.

Time-management principles are also useful for managing the stress of balancing work and home responsibilities. If family activities are on your "to do" list, you have a built-in response when another request conflicts with family time: "I have other commitments at that time." Except in unusual circumstances, avoid taking work home with you. It signals to your family that work is more important to you than your time with them, and concentrating on work at home is difficult anyway. General Colin Powell understood this years ago when he took over a command in Frankfort, Germany. Powell told the officers under his command not to work on weekends unless it was absolutely necessary: "Anyone found logging Saturday or Sunday hours for himself or his troops had better have a good reason."[19]

Being realistic about time is ultimately less frustrating than expecting yourself to handle everything. Instead of criticizing yourself for what you did not do, make an effort to give yourself a pat on the back for all the times you strike a balance between home and work commitments.

Positive Attitude

As mentioned previously, people with a negative outlook tend to be more susceptible to stress. Thus, supervisors can reduce their stress response by cultivating a positive attitude. Ways to do this are to avoid making negative generalizations and look for the positives in any situation. Saying to oneself, "This company doesn't care about us; all it cares about is profits" or "I'll never get the hang of this job," contributes to a negative attitude. A supervisor can consciously replace such thoughts with more positive ones: "The competition is tough these days, but we each can contribute to helping this company please its customers" and "This job is difficult, but I will plan a way to learn how to do it better."

In the positive examples, a supervisor is focusing on the areas over which he or she has control. This helps to defuse the sense of helplessness that can increase stress and contributes to a positive outlook.[20]

Maintaining a sense of humor also is important to a positive attitude. Consultant Diane C. Decker explains, "If we can laugh at ourselves and see the humor in situations, then we don't feel it's the end of the world."[21] Decker recommends developing a list of things that bring you joy, then cultivating those areas of your life. She arrived at this idea through her own experiences as manager with a manufacturer that was experiencing production problems. She worried about her own future and that of her employees; to beat the stress, she signed up for a class in being a clown. Spending time getting others to laugh helped Decker to relax and put her problems into perspective.

Exercise

Experts on stress believe that the human body long ago developed a stress response to help people handle dangerous situations. Early peoples had to face storms or attacks by wild animals and human enemies. The basic responses are either to fight the danger or to run away. For this reason, the physical changes in response to stress are known as the "fight-or-flight syndrome."

Because the body's response to stress is to get ready for physical action, a logical way to respond to workplace stress is to look for an outlet through physical activity. Although it is never appropriate to punch your manager when he or she criticizes you or to run away when clients complain, other forms of exercise can provide a similar release without negative social consequences. Some people enjoy running, walking, or riding a bicycle before or after work—or as a way to get to work. Others prefer to work out at a health club, participate in sports, or dance. Besides letting off steam, exercising strengthens the body's organs so that they can better withstand stress.

Biofeedback

People who have devoted time to developing their awareness of such automatically controlled bodily functions as pulse rate, blood pressure, body temperature, and muscle tension have learned to control these functions. Developing an awareness of bodily functions in order to control them is known as **biofeedback.** People use biofeedback to will their bodies into a more relaxed state.

biofeedback
Developing an awareness of bodily functions in order to control them

Meditation

While meditation has religious overtones for many people, in its general form, it is simply a practice of focusing one's thoughts on something other than day-to-day concerns. The person meditating focuses on breathing, on a symbol, or on a word or phrase. People who practice regular meditation find that it relaxes them and that the benefits carry beyond the time spent meditating.

Well-Rounded Life Activities

For someone who gets all of his or her satisfaction and rewards from working, job-related stress is more likely to be overwhelming. No job is going to be rewarding all the time, so some of your satisfaction should come from other areas of life. For instance, if your manager is impatient and fails to praise you for completing an important project, you can offset your frustrations by enjoying the love of friends and family members or hearing the cheers of your softball teammates when you make a good play.

In other words, people who lead a well-rounded life are more likely to experience satisfaction in some area of life at any given time. This satisfaction can make stress a lot easier to cope with. Leading a well-rounded life means not only advancing your career but also devoting time to social, family, intellectual, spiritual, and physical pursuits. One person might choose to read biographies, join a volleyball team, and volunteer in a soup kitchen. Another person might take bicycle trips with the kids on weekends and be active in a religious congregation and a professional organization. These varied pursuits not only help people manage stress, but they also make life more enjoyable.

Organizational Stress Management

Although employees can take many actions to cope with stress, a significant reduction in stress requires attacking it at its source. Many sources of stress may arise from the policies and practices of the organization and its management. Therefore, any serious effort at stress management must include organizational interventions.

Organizational stress management can operate on several levels. Supervisors can adjust their behavior so that they do not contribute unnecessarily to employee stress. Also, many organizations have helped employees manage stress through job redesign, environmental changes, and wellness programs. Although a supervisor rarely can carry out all these measures single-handedly, he or she may be in a position to recommend them to higher-level managers. Also, a supervisor who knows about any stress-management measures offered by the organization is in a better position to take advantage of them and recommend them to employees.

Behavior of the Supervisor

Understanding sources of stress can help supervisors behave in a manner that minimizes unnecessary stress and enhances employee confidence. Supervisors should avoid behavior that contributes to raising employee stress levels. For instance, knowing that feelings of helplessness and uncertainty contribute to

TABLE 13.3
How Supervisors Can Minimize Organizational Stressors

Sources: Based on information in Samuel C. Certo, *Modern Management*, 6th ed. (Boston: Allyn and Bacon, 1994), pp. 308–10; Fred Luthans, *Organizational Behavior* (New York: McGraw-Hill, 1985), pp. 146–48.

Prepare employees to cope with change.	• Communicate thoroughly. • Provide adequate training to handle any new work demands. • Skip unnecessary changes during times of transition.
Foster a supportive organizational climate.	• Make policies and procedures flexible. • Establish fair policies and administer them fairly. • Investigate whether work can be done in more efficient ways that reduce work overload. • Make sure employees understand what is expected of them. • Praise individual and group successes.
Make work interesting.	• Give employees some control over decisions and work processes. • Match the challenge level to employees' abilities. • Assign a variety of tasks.
Encourage career development.	• Communicate with employees about their career prospects in the organization. • Encourage employees to take advantage of any career counseling programs available through the organization. • Make time to discuss career goals with employees.

stress, supervisors can minimize such feelings through clear communication and regular feedback. Where possible, supervisors also can empower employees to make decisions and solve problems, thereby giving them more control. Table 13.3 summarizes some basic approaches to reducing stress in the workplace.

Supervisors' behavior can help employees cope with stressful situations. For example, as described in the "Supervision and Ethics" box, employees cope with stressful situations better if they see their supervisor treating them ethically. Similarly, research shows that day care employees are more likely to feel satisfied and less likely to quit if their supervisor stresses that they are a valuable part of a team with a common mission and gives them a role in planning their work. Emergency medical services (EMS) workers cope better after traumatic incidents if their supervisors support them with encouraging words and give them some time to "calm down and decompress."[22] Employees understand that their supervisor cannot fix every cause of stress, but the supervisor *can* determine how he or she treats the employees.

As noted previously, employees with low self-esteem tend to be more susceptible to stress than those with high self-esteem. Therefore, supervisors should avoid behavior that can damage self-esteem, such as put-downs and criticism with no clue about how to improve. Better still, supervisors should behave in esteem-enhancing ways, including the generous use of praise (when it can be offered sincerely) and feedback to employees about how their efforts add value to the work group or the organization as a whole.

Changes in the Job

Recall from Figure 13.5 that many characteristics of a job can be sources of stress. Just a few of the job factors linked to stress include unfair policies, ambiguous procedures, lack of opportunities for advancement, and poor communication. A supervisor has at least some control over many of these matters. For example, supervisors can improve their ability to be fair and communicate instructions clearly and precisely.

SUPERVISION AND ETHICS

ETHICAL TREATMENT HELPS NURSES COPE

Most of us expect our pay to rise as we gain experience, but some companies have asked their employees to accept the unexpected: pay cuts to help the company stay competitive. Being told you are going to have to pay the bills with a smaller paycheck is a blow, so it's no wonder that employees have a stress response to this news. Researchers who studied nurses at four hospitals learned that when nurses were told their pay would be cut, they had difficulty sleeping at night. But they also found out that supervisors can help them cope by treating them ethically.

The study interviewed nurses at a group of four hospitals that phased in changes to a pay plan for nurses. Instead of paying them an hourly rate plus extra for overtime, the hospitals would start paying them a flat salary. Without overtime pay, the nurses' income would fall by about 10 percent. The company planned to change the pay at two hospitals first and then change the pay at the other two hospitals later. This arrangement gave the researchers a chance to follow nurses experiencing the stress of a pay cut and compare their situation with nurses whose pay didn't change.

The nurses whose pay was cut reported insomnia at higher rates than nurses whose pay was unchanged. Their reaction was even more significant considering that insomnia is associated with other problems, including accidents and reduced productivity.

But some of the nurses coped better than others. Most often, these nurses had supervisors who had received training in interactional justice—that is, treating employees in ways that they consider fair. The training covered ways to treat employees with dignity, politeness, and respect, to offer emotional support, and to avoid manipulating and degrading employees. These supervisors also reviewed how to explain decisions and discuss issues with their employees. Employees whose supervisors had received this training experienced a decline in insomnia during the weeks following the training. Nurses whose supervisors did not receive the training experienced less insomnia over time, but their improvement was much less.

Jerald Greenberg, who led the study, believes that most supervisors want to treat their employees fairly, but he thinks the training helped the supervisors keep that desire in mind during a stressful time in their employees' lives. When employees are under stress, fair and polite treatment becomes more important than ever. Greenberg said, "In a high-stress time like these nurses were experiencing, you really have to go over the top in convincing people that you care, and that you're there to support and help them."

Source: Based on "Pay Cuts Lead to Worker Insomnia, but Supervisor Training Helps," *Europe Intelligence Wire,* January 23, 2006, downloaded from Business & Company Resource Center, http://galenet.galegroup.com.

In general, an important part of stress management involves identifying job factors linked to stress and then modifying those factors when possible. Sometimes a supervisor cannot act alone to make a change; for example, he or she may not be powerful enough to resolve conflicts with another department. In such cases, a supervisor should be sure that higher-level managers know about the stress-related job factors and how they are affecting employees.

An example from the Hospice of Marion County Healthcare Alliance shows the importance of listening and responding to employee concerns. The hospice, located in Ocala, Florida, set up a program it calls Adopt a Senior Manager. Under the program, employees can arrange to "shadow" a senior manager or ask that person to shadow them (that is, accompany them as they carry out their work). When Sandy Parr was an admissions nurse at the hospice, she was concerned about the organization's efforts to increase each day's patient admissions. Parr was concerned that admitting so many patients would be stressful and impossible to do well, so she asked the hospice's chief executive, Alice Privett, to shadow her. Privett not only saw the need to reduce the workload but also increased her appreciation of the excellent work done by the admissions nurses.[23] A supervisor cannot act alone to establish a companywide program such as the one at the Hospice of Marion County. However, a supervisor is in the best position to ask for and investigate employee concerns, as Alice Privett did, and can bring them to the attention of higher-level managers.

When the sources of stress include boring or overly difficult jobs, the organization may be able to change the job requirements to make them less stressful. As described in Chapter 11, a routine job can be made more interesting through job enlargement or job enrichment. An overly difficult job can be made less so by giving employees further training or reassigning some responsibilities so that the work is divided more realistically.

Environmental Changes

As shown in Figure 13.5, some characteristics of the job environment can add to employee stress. For example, it is a strain on employees to cope with noise, poor lighting, uncomfortable chairs, and extremes of heat and cold. When possible, an organization should reduce stress by fixing some of these problems. A supervisor is frequently in an excellent position to identify needed environmental changes and report them to the managers who can make the changes. That is likely to be the case when employees complain about uncomfortable chairs or dark work areas.

Supervisors also can recognize environmental stressors that are beyond the organization's control. Recently, four hurricanes struck Florida during a six-week period. Employees throughout the state experienced stresses, sometimes dramatically. Some managers, including Dick Dobkin of Ernst & Young, helped employees cope by assuring them that family concerns took priority over job responsibilities. At some jobs, however, such assurances were impossible. Safety requirements demanded that air traffic controllers and airline dispatchers stay on the job. Hurricane Charley tore off part of the roof of AirTran Airways' headquarters in Orlando, sparing the area directly over the company's systems operations center. According to AirTran's public relations manager Judy Graham-Weaver, "Our dispatch people were actually in the building; they were literally hanging on, with air-conditioning units blowing off the roof and whatnot."[24] Such a crisis calls for leadership, dedication, and genuine appreciation for the employees who endure extraordinary environmental challenges.

Wellness Programs

wellness program
Organizational activities designed to help employees adopt healthy practices

Most organizations provide their employees with health insurance, and many also take an active role in helping employees stay well. The usual way to do this is to provide a **wellness program,** or organizational activities designed to help employees adopt healthful practices. These activities might include exercise classes, stop-smoking clinics, nutrition counseling, and health screening such as cholesterol and blood-pressure tests. Some organizations even have constructed exercise facilities for employees. In a recent survey, three-quarters of employers reported offering wellness programs. The most common services reported were flu shots at the workplace, communications about health and safety, weight management programs, onsite exercise facilities, health fairs, health-risk assessments, and smoking cessation programs.[25]

For example, in Bradenton, Florida, Tropicana operates a fitness center. About one-fifth of its 1,600 employees pay a small fee to participate. Jean Johnson, a customer logistics worker, says exercising there keeps her focused on health, reinforcing her efforts to stop smoking. The company also sponsored a "weight loss challenge," including personal assessments, workout plans, and weekly weigh-ins. The winner of the contest lost 54 pounds.[26]

Tropicana and other companies with wellness programs aren't just bringing down stress levels. They are also slashing costs related to unhealthy employees. Doctors Hospital in Sarasota, Florida, operates a fitness center, arranges discounts for employees who join the Sarasota YMCA, hosts Weight Watchers meetings, and offers 15-minute massages as stress breaks. These apparent luxuries are justified, says the hospital's director of human resources, Theresa Levering, because healthier employees tend to file lower health insurance claims.[27] After the city government of Chattanooga, Tennessee, set up in-house clinics and a fitness center for its employees, the city was able to negotiate a health insurance contract with no premium increase. Other nearby governments saw their insurance costs jump higher at the same time. At another Chattanooga employer, UnumProvident, employees can use onsite clinics for routine tests and shots. The arrangement improves productivity and reduces absenteeism because employees don't have to take time off to visit their doctor for these services.[28]

Given the benefits of wellness programs, it makes sense for supervisors to participate in and support them. When possible, supervisors can avoid scheduling activities that conflict with participation in the programs. They can encourage employees to participate, and they can set good examples by their own participation. However, supervisors should focus on encouraging all employees to participate in the program instead of singling out employees and encouraging them to make specific changes such as losing weight or cutting out cigarettes. After all, having a specialist conduct the wellness program frees the supervisor to concentrate on work-related behaviors—and avoid charges that the supervisor has discriminated against an employee with a disability such as obesity or addiction to nicotine.

A WORD ABOUT PERSONALITY

The guidelines given in this chapter for managing time and stress have worked for many people. However, the degree to which a person will succeed at using any particular technique depends in part on that person's personality. This text does not explore psychological theory, but a brief look at one approach to understanding personality types may be helpful. The Myers-Briggs Type Indicator is a test that classifies people into 16 personality types on the basis of the work of psychiatrist Carl Jung.[29] These 16 personality types describe the traits a person has along four dimensions (see Figure 13.6). For example, one individual might be an extrovert, an intuitive, a feeler, and a perceiver. Another person will have a different combination of the four traits. These traits are not considered good or bad; each has its own strengths and weaknesses.

Knowing your personality type can suggest suitable techniques for managing your own time and stress. Thus, an introvert may find that meditation is a pleasant way to relieve stress, whereas an extrovert may find meditation impossible but dancing with friends refreshing. Judgers have an easy time applying such time management aids as "to do" lists. Perceivers also make those lists, but they lose them and cannot seem to make time to find them. To manage their time, these personality types need heroic amounts of self-discipline—or maybe a job that requires flexibility more than structure.

When you discern that a particular behavior does not fit your personality type, you have a choice. You can make the effort to develop the contrasting trait. For

FIGURE 13.6
A Basis for Categorizing Personality Types

Source: Adapted from Otto Kroeger and Janet M. Thuesen, "It Takes All Types," *Newsweek*, Management Digest advertising section, September 7, 1992.

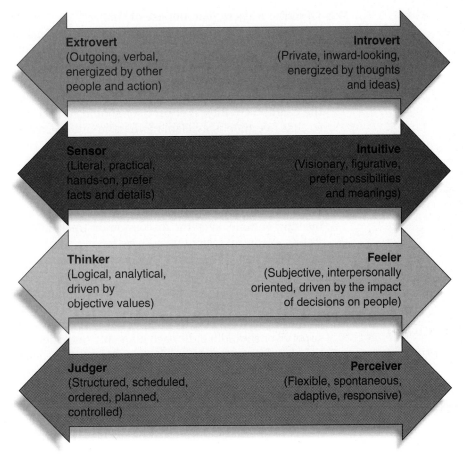

Extrovert
(Outgoing, verbal, energized by other people and action)

Introvert
(Private, inward-looking, energized by thoughts and ideas)

Sensor
(Literal, practical, hands-on, prefer facts and details)

Intuitive
(Visionary, figurative, prefer possibilities and meanings)

Thinker
(Logical, analytical, driven by objective values)

Feeler
(Subjective, interpersonally oriented, driven by the impact of decisions on people)

Judger
(Structured, scheduled, ordered, planned, controlled)

Perceiver
(Flexible, spontaneous, adaptive, responsive)

According to the Myers-Briggs Type Indicator, a person's personality traits fall somewhere along each of these four dimensions.

instance, a feeler might list logical criteria for making a decision that must be objective. Or you can avoid situations that require you to behave in ways unsuited to your personality. If the feeler in the previous example really hates making decisions objectively, this person might seek out a job or organization in which highly subjective decisions are valued.

In addition, recognizing different personality types can help you understand the behavior of other people. For example, if you think your manager's head is always in the clouds, perhaps he or she is an intuitive and you are a sensor. Such insights alone can ease a great deal of stress.

SKILLS MODULE

PART ONE: CONCEPTS

Summary

13.1 Discuss how supervisors can evaluate their use of time.

A practical way to evaluate time use is to keep a time log. A supervisor enters his or her activities for half-hour periods throughout the workday. After a week or two of keeping the time log, a supervisor reviews the information to see whether his or her time is being used efficiently.

13.2 Describe ways to plan the use of time.

A supervisor can plan his or her use of time by making a list of things to do for the day or week, then rating each item on the list as A (things that must be done), B (things that are important but can be postponed if necessary), or C (everything else). A supervisor then schedules specific times for completing the A- and B-level activities. When time permits, a supervisor works on the C-level activities. A supervisor should not fill up every hour of the day, so that free time is available to handle unexpected problems. A supervisor can plan his or her time with the help of a variety of computer software programs designed specifically for time management. A supervisor also can use programs called desktop organizers.

13.3 Identify some time wasters and how to control them.

Many meetings waste time. A supervisor who calls a meeting can start the meeting on time, keep the discussion on track, and end it on time. A supervisor can control telephone calls by having someone screen them, returning calls at the same time every day, preparing for calls to be made, and scheduling calls instead of leaving messages. Ways to manage e-mail include choosing times to read and answer messages, using e-mail software to keep messages organized in file folders, and adding time-consuming e-mail interruptions to a "to do" list. To handle paperwork and reading material, a supervisor should handle each item only once, decide which items are essential, dictate responses or make telephone calls when possible, and designate a time for reading. With unscheduled visitors, a supervisor can schedule a later meeting, stand to signal that a meeting is ending or will be short, or specify a time limit for the discussion.

The best way to handle procrastination is to tackle the project one step at a time, giving oneself rewards along the way. To combat perfectionism, a supervisor should set high but reasonable standards. Perfectionism is a cause of failure to delegate, so a supervisor must strive to delegate work effectively. Finally, supervisors sometimes find themselves taking on too many projects. The solution is to say no to projects they do not have time to complete properly.

13.4 List factors that contribute to stress among employees.

Certain job factors linked to stress involve the organization's policies, structures, physical conditions, and processes. Notably, when employees feel out of control and the workplace is unsafe or unpredictable, employees will suffer more from the effects of stress. Personal factors also can make a person more vulnerable to stress. Such factors include general feelings of negativism, helplessness, or low self-esteem, as well as a Type A personality—constantly trying to get a lot done in a hurry. Conflicts between work and personal life may be a further source of stress.

13.5 Summarize consequences of stress.

Stress is the body's response to coping with environmental demands. These demands can come from change, frustration, uncertainty, danger, or discomfort. Stress can be stimulating, but an excessive amount of it leads to illness and lowered performance. People under stress feel anxious, aggressive, frustrated, tense, and moody, and they may overreact to criticism. They are also at risk for abusing drugs and alcohol. When a person cannot cope with stress over an extended period of time, the person may experience burnout.

13.6 Explain how supervisors can manage their own stress.

Supervisors and others can manage stress by using time management, having a positive attitude, getting exercise, using biofeedback, meditating, and leading a well-rounded life. These actions do not reduce the amount of stress the person is under, but they do make a person better able to handle it.

13.7 Identify ways organizations, including supervisors, can help employees manage stress.

Supervisors and other managers can seek to eliminate or minimize the job factors linked to stress. They should communicate clearly, give regular feedback to employees, and empower workers to make decisions and solve problems. When working conditions are stressful, supervisors should make an extra effort to provide support and appreciation and treat employees ethically and with dignity. Supervisors also should behave in ways that enhance employees' self-esteem. In addition, they can make jobs more interesting through job enlargement or job enrichment and can ensure that the work environment is safe and comfortable. Organizations also can offer wellness programs that provide services such as health clinics, instruction in exercise and weight control, and stop-smoking programs.

Key Terms			
	time management, *p.* 342	stress, *p.* 351	burnout, *p.* 355
	time log, *p.* 342	Type A personality, *p.* 353	biofeedback, *p.* 358
	procrastination, *p.* 349	Type B personality, *p.* 353	wellness program, *p.* 361
	perfectionism, *p.* 349		

Review and Discussion Questions

1. For one week, keep a time log of your activities at work or at school. Follow the format of Figure 13.1. What does it tell you about your own time management habits?

2. Demetrius Jones prepared the following list of things to do:

Performance appraisal for Angela	A
Clean out files	C
Finish report due Wednesday	A
Prepare a plan for training employees	B
Find out why Kevin has been making more errors lately	B
Read professional journals	C

   a. Which activities should Demetrius consider most important? Least important?
   b. Which activities should Demetrius schedule for times when he is at his best?
   c. If Demetrius fits all these activities onto his weekly schedule and finds he has time left over, what should he do about the "free" time?

3. Assume you are the supervisor of social workers at a hospital. One of your co-workers, a nursing supervisor, asks you to meet with him in his office to discuss a mutual problem. When you arrive at the agreed-upon time, he says, "I'll be right back as soon as I deliver these instructions to one of the nurses and grab a cup of coffee." After you get started 10 minutes later, the supervisor takes several telephone calls, interrupting the meeting for 5 minutes at a time. "Sorry," he says after each call, "but that call was important." An

hour into the meeting, you have not made much progress toward solving your problem.

   a. How would you feel in a situation like this? How does your co-worker's behavior affect your performance? How does it affect his performance?

   b. How could you react in this situation to improve your use of time?

4. Imagine that you came to work an hour early so that you could get started on a large proposal that you have due in a week. Fifteen minutes into the project, a co-worker stops by to tell you about her recent vacation. After she leaves, your manager pokes his head into your office and asks if you can spare a minute. Finally, you settle into your proposal. Five minutes after the official start of the workday, one of your employees comes into your office and informs you that she is going to resign. What is the best way to handle each of these unscheduled visitors?

5. You know that you have an important assignment to complete by the end of the week, but you put off starting it on Monday because you want to get everything else out of the way first. In addition, you want a clean slate so that you can concentrate and do a perfect job. Suddenly on Thursday, you realize you can't possibly finish the assignment by the next day. You've procrastinated all week. What steps could you have taken to avoid procrastinating and thus complete the assignment on schedule?

6. Which of the following are sources of stress? Explain.

   a. A supervisor who gives you vague and confusing instructions and then criticizes your results.

   b. Buying a house.

   c. Working at a boring job.

   d. Getting a promotion to a supervisory position you have wanted for a year.

7. Sales supervisor Anita Feinstein does not understand all the fuss about stress. She feels stimulated by a job that is exciting and contains many challenges. Does her attitude show that stress is not harmful? Explain.

8. Describe the signs of burnout. Describe the three stages of burnout. What should a supervisor do when he or she observes burnout in an employee?

9. Name five job factors linked to stress over which a supervisor could have some control.

10. How do the following responses help a person cope with stress?

   a. Exercising.

   b. Using biofeedback.

   c. Meditating.

   d. Participating in a wellness program.

PART TWO: SKILL-BUILDING

YOU SOLVE THE PROBLEM

Reflecting back on page 341, imagine the role of supervisors at Mississippi Power Company in the weeks following Hurricane Katrina. Working as a group, list all of the job factors linked to stress under the circumstances. (For ideas, you can refer to Figure 13.4.) On your list, put a star next to each job factor that you think a supervisor can address. Discuss what actions the supervisor might take. For example, you might not be able to make uncomfortable working conditions go away, but you might be able to help your crew members cope.

Next, consider the personal factors that could have affected a supervisor's stress response while supervising workers restoring power. Thinking about the situation individually, consider your own qualities and behaviors. What strengths would you bring to this challenge? In what ways are you unprepared to handle this level of stress? Can you think of some areas in which you would like to manage your time more effectively so you can be stronger in the face of stress? Discuss your ideas with your group.

Problem-Solving Case: *Is It OK Not to Be Perfect?*

Debra Chatman Finely worked hard for 15 years to become vice president of marketing at Prudential Reinsurance Company/Everest Reinsurance Company in New Jersey. But instead of boosting her self-esteem, her success nearly cost Finely her health.

Concerned that being the highest-ranking African American in a mostly white company put extra performance pressure on her, Finely determined to outperform her co-workers and vowed she would never make a mistake on the job. When she hit the inevitable bumps in the road, she first became depressed, then forced herself to work even harder. She put in regular late nights and weekends in the office and studied hard for meetings. "My work was a large part of my identity. How well I performed determined how good I felt about myself," she says now.

Finally, however, Finely realized that the stress of trying to achieve the impossible—perfection—was becoming a serious problem. She quit her job, found professional counseling, and began working on a master's degree in psychology. Now she's changed her outlook on perfection: "I'm not afraid to make mistakes if I know I've done my best. Sometimes I can even find pleasure or humor in my shortcomings—it's such a relief."

1. What warning signs might have suggested to Finely that her goals for her own performance were unrealistically high?

2. How do you handle your mistakes? Do you think your strategy adds stress to your life, and if so, how can you improve it?

3. Imagine how it would feel to work with a perfectionist. Taking on each of the following roles, write a brief summary of the concerns you would have wanted to express to Finely while she worked for Prudential/Everest.

   a. Finely's supervisor.

   b. One of Finely's colleagues.

   c. An employee Finely supervised.

Source: Kellye M. Garrett, "Give Perfectionism the Boot," *Black Enterprise,* November 1998, p. 181.

Knowing Yourself	**How Well Do You Use Technology to Manage Time?**

How Well Do You Use Technology to Manage Time?
Complete this simple quiz to find out how well you use technology to save and manage time. Each of the following statements represents a simple yet tried-and-true method of time-saving technology. Rate yourself on each: If you practice the method regularly, give yourself a "3." Practice it sometimes, and give yourself a "2." Practice it rarely, you get a "1." And if you never practice it, you receive a "0." Now, take a moment to complete the quiz.

1. I skim professional journals via the Web.   3 2 1 0
2. I send agendas, meeting minutes, assignment summaries, and   3 2 1 0
   other notices to co-workers and employees using e-mail.

3. I maintain working files in a single, readily accessible directory, enabling me to work on current projects whenever I have spare moments.   3 2 1 0

4. Using planning or spreadsheet software, I list and monitor objectives, strategies, and tasks necessary for the completion of my goals.   3 2 1 0

5. I group tasks related to each software package together and complete each group of related tasks at the same time.   3 2 1 0

6. I organize documents with an intuitive file structure.   3 2 1 0

7. I maintain a perpetual "to do" list on a computerized task manager or in a special file, checking off items as they are completed.   3 2 1 0

8. Using numerical rankings in a spreadsheet, I analyze and identify priorities.   3 2 1 0

9. I maintain my calendar and other key information using portable digital technology.   3 2 1 0

10. I have software that maintains my key organizational resources, such as contacts, tasks, events, and crucial records.   3 2 1 0

11. I maintain "idea files" into which I post thoughts, jottings, and potential tasks.   3 2 1 0

12. I use e-mail to forward documents to co-workers.   3 2 1 0

13. I associate related files to each other with html links.   3 2 1 0

14. I consolidate Web searches into a specific time of the day or week.   3 2 1 0

15. I conduct "offline" Web searches to save time.   3 2 1 0

16. Through e-mail, discussion lists, and team software, I participate in virtual meetings.   3 2 1 0

17. Using shared directories, I post public files containing policies, forms, and other information regularly used by the people around me.   3 2 1 0

18. I transfer files from my office computer to my home or laptop, and vice versa.   3 2 1 0

19. I have begun using voice input to save keyboarding or personal dictating time.   3 2 1 0

20. I append the names of files with dates for easy retrieval.   3 2 1 0

21. I use my computer to send broadcast faxes and e-mails when appropriate.   3 2 1 0

22. I maintain a directory and bookmarks of commonly used reference materials.   3 2 1 0

23. I use shortcuts, such as templates and macros, to speed up my work.   3 2 1 0

24. I handle business transactions online.   3 2 1 0

25. I maintain financial data in a simple accounting program or, if appropriate, using spreadsheet or database software.   3 2 1 0

26. I maintain files for every person I work with, detailing meeting summaries, assignments, and other notes.   3 2 1 0

27. I automatically create multiple drafts of a document, noting relevant changes with each successive draft.   3 2 1 0

28. I automate correspondence and mailing functions using mail merge features.   3 2 1 0

29. I use spreadsheet software to prepare budgets, expense reports, statistical analyses, and other numerical data.   3 2 1 0

Now total your score and figure out where you stand. If you rated between 75 and 90, congratulations! You're developing some outstanding time-saving technology skills. A rating between 50 and 74 means that you've learned a number of practical skills, and you're probably aware of the many ways technology can help you master time. Maintain your commitment to learn more. A rating below 50 means that you may have some catching up to do. If you find yourself in this category (and even if you don't) review the principles noted in this time quiz. Read up on the latest technology. Take a course or seminar to learn how you can better use these remarkable tools in your daily life.

Pause and Reflect

1. Does technology help you manage your time? Why or why not?
2. Can some of these techniques, if misused, become time *wasters*?
3. Identify one of the technologies on this list that you haven't used but plan to try (or one you would like to use more, or differently).

Source: From Richard G. Ensman, "Technology and Time Management: How Do You Rate?" *Manage*, November 1, 2001. Reprinted with permission.

Class Exercise

Using Time Wisely

Each student, in turn, tells the class how he or she wastes time. The instructor lists the ways on the chalkboard or overhead projector. Then the class discusses the list.

- Which time wasters are most common?
- Are they really just time wasters, or are they also stress reducers?

Source: The idea for this exercise was provided by Sylvia Ong, Scottsdale Community College, Scottsdale, Arizona.

Building Supervision Skills

Managing Time and Stress

Divide the class into teams of four or five students. Assign each team an imaginary project with a completion date (or have the teams come up with one on their own). Suggested projects are cleaning up one of the common areas used by students at the school, recruiting classmates to participate in a fund-raising activity, or developing publicity for an upcoming arts event. Then have the teams (1) make a "to do" list outlining how they plan to set priorities for the project and use their time, (2) note how they plan to control time wasters, and (3) describe how they plan to manage any stress associated with trying to complete the project properly and on schedule.

At the end of the exercise, have students identify themselves as Type A or Type B personalities and discuss how this contributes to the way they approach getting things done as team members.

Chapter **Fourteen**

Managing Conflict and Change

Learning Objectives

After you have studied this chapter, you should be able to:

14.1 List the positive and negative aspects of conflict.

14.2 Define types of conflict.

14.3 Describe strategies for managing conflict.

14.4 Explain how supervisors can initiate conflict resolution, respond to a conflict, and mediate conflict resolution.

14.5 Identify sources of change and explain why employees and supervisors resist it.

14.6 Discuss how supervisors can overcome resistance and implement change.

14.7 Describe the types of power supervisors can have.

14.8 Identify common strategies for organizational politics.

Change should be a friend. It should happen by plan, not by accident.

—*Philip Crosby, quality advocate, author, and founder, Philip Crosby Associates*

A Supervisor's Problem: Accepting Change at Best Buy

Several years ago, morale was dropping at a division of Best Buy's retail group located in its Minneapolis headquarters. Cali Ressler, a human resource manager responsible for Best Buy's work–life balance programs, suggested to the group's manager that the division try making schedules more flexible. The employees would be able to adjust their hours as long as they achieved their work requirements. The 300 employees worked together to plan the new arrangement, which quickly began delivering results. Turnover among newly hired employees disappeared, job satisfaction scores rose, and, best of all for the manager, the division's performance improved as well.

Jody Thompson, in charge of organizational change at Best Buy, learned about the impact of this arrangement and saw something that could improve the whole company. Thompson convinced Best Buy's top management to permit the flexible work arrangement in every part of the company. No group is forced to adopt the plan, now called a results-oriented work environment (ROWE). But, when managers and employees decide they are ready to try "ROWE-ing," their entire team signs up for it. The arrangement has been spreading gradually to more groups, with over 2,000 of Best Buy's 100,000 employees ROWE-ing so far. With that change, productivity has increased, and claims for work-related stress conditions have fallen.

Although ROWE has delivered performance improvements and satisfaction to the teams that have adopted it, the change can be a struggle. For supervisors, the biggest problem can be learning to trust their employees. For experienced employees, the change can bring grief to those who for years sacrificed their personal goals to make a good impression by working long hours. Traci Tobias, who manages travel reimbursements for Best Buy employees, said employees in her group worried about whether people would be checking up on them. Human resource staff members help workers and their supervisors accept the new arrangement by using training sessions to give employees a chance to vent and uncover their old ways of thinking about work. When employees make snide remarks about co-workers' absences, they jokingly call the focus on other people's time "sludge" and eventually learn to see it as a bad habit. Focusing on who is not at their desk at 10:00 interferes with the new focus on results.

At first, everyone in Tobias's group used an online calendar to record where they would be during each workday. Eventually, as trust grew, employees stopped using the calendar. Now they use whiteboards outside their cubicles to note whether they are "in the office" or, say, "out of the office this afternoon, available by e-mail." E-mail also provides an easy way to send messages. Employees had to adjust to a new way of working. They are more likely to use their cell phones than to look for each other at their desks. They write more concise e-mail messages, because they are more focused on meeting their objectives. Meetings are much shorter and less frequent, because employees don't want to waste precious time.

Tom Blesener, a manager whose group adopted ROWE, found that one of the hardest parts of the change was accepting that his focus on face time (hours when the employee is visible at work) had been a big source of stress for his employees. He had to replace that old way of supervising with employee empowerment. When a client needed to have someone in Blesener's group be available on Saturdays, Blesener let the group decide how they would meet that need. The changes require him to plan more carefully, rather than springing extra work on employees at the end of the day or the week. He also finds that he needs to spend more time talking to his employees and getting to know them better.

Perhaps the biggest surprise is that some employees who are ROWE-ing find they work *too much*. Because their work is more flexible, they are less clear about when it is time to stop.

Adopting ROWE requires supervisors and their employees to make changes in the way they work and the way they think about work. Both kinds of change can be difficult, even when everyone involved is pleased with the results.

QUESTIONS

1. What skills does a supervisor need to sell employees on a major change like ROWE?

2. How can supervisors help employees carry out a change? When conflicts arise, as they often do during changes, what skills will help supervisors defuse them?

Sources: Jyoti Thottam, "Reworking Work," *Time*, July 25, 2006; Viv Groskop, "We Envy and Admire People Who Negotiate Shorter Hours—yet There's an Overwhelming Suspicion That They Are 'Skiving Off,'" *New Statesman*, March 13, 2006, both downloaded from Business & Company Resource Center, http://galenet.galegroup.com.

Best Buy made changes to help employees cope with conflicts between the demands of their families and their work. Conflicts and changes are bound to occur in any organization. Whether they are constructive or destructive depends significantly on the supervisor's ability to manage them.

This chapter addresses conflict management by examining the nature of conflict and ways to respond to conflict constructively. The chapter also discusses the role of change in the workplace and how supervisors can implement it. Finally, the chapter considers an aspect of organizational behavior that often affects the management of both conflict and change—organization politics—and describes how supervisors can use politics ethically and effectively.

CONFLICT

conflict
The struggle that results from incompatible or opposing needs, feelings, thoughts, or demands within a person or between two or more people

In the context of this book, **conflict** refers to the struggle that results from incompatible or opposing needs, feelings, thoughts, or demands within a person or between two or more people. If supervisor Janet Speers sees that an employee she likes is taking home office supplies, her feelings for the employee come in conflict with her belief that stealing is wrong. If her feelings and belief are both strong, she will have difficulty resolving the issue. Likewise, if two employees disagree over how to fill out time sheets for sick days, there is a conflict between the employees. In this case, the organization should have a clear procedure to make the conflict easy to resolve.

Positive and Negative Aspects of Conflict

Sometimes conflict is a positive force that can bring about necessary changes. Imagine that a business that develops computerized information systems has hired a new systems analyst, Jordan Walsh, the first African American in the company. Walsh gets all the boring and routine jobs—filing, running errands, proofreading documentation. If he acts cheerful, the other employees will assume there is no conflict (although he may feel one internally). Of course, this situation is not good for Walsh; he feels insulted, is bored every day, and is missing out on the experience he needs to develop his career. This arrangement is also bad for the employer, who is paying for a systems analyst but not benefiting from his talents. Furthermore, if Walsh quits, the company will have to bear the expense of repeating the hiring process. However, if Walsh complains to his supervisor about his limited role, the conflict will surface, and the resolution may leave everyone, including Walsh, better off. Thus, when conflict serves as a signal that a problem exists, it can stimulate a creative response.

Ongoing conflict also has negative consequences. People who are engaged in disputes are under stress, which takes a physical toll. In addition, people who are busy arguing and trying to persuade others to take their sides are not involved in more productive activities. Finally, depending on the source of the conflict, the people involved may be angry at management or the organization, so they may vent their anger in ways that are destructive to the organization, such as taking extra time off or sabotaging equipment.

The consequences of conflict may depend partly on the way that it is resolved. If people treat a conflict as an opportunity for constructive problem solving and change, the outcomes may well be positive. If people routinely see conflict as a need for someone to win at someone else's expense, or for a manager to impose control, the conflict is more likely to have negative consequences.

FIGURE 14.1   Types of Conflict

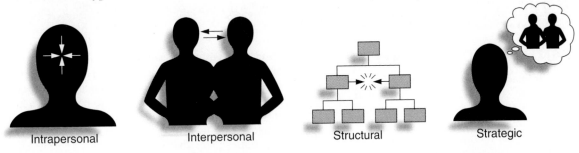

Intrapersonal   Interpersonal   Structural   Strategic

frustration
Defeat in the effort to
achieve desired goals

Most notably, when conflict is viewed as a win–lose proposition, the loser will experience **frustration;** that is, defeat in the effort to achieve desired goals. An employee who has her request for a flextime arrangement turned down experiences frustration. So does an employee who can't convince a prospective customer to return his phone calls. Most of us can handle a little frustration philosophically, with words such as, "Oh, well, I can't always have my own way" or "No one can have it all." However, repeated frustration tends to generate anger. A frustrated employee may engage in destructive behavior such as sabotage, aggression, insubordination, and absenteeism. (Chapter 12 covers the supervision of employees who engage in such behaviors.) To help supervisors head off problems arising from frustration, this chapter emphasizes forms of conflict resolution aimed at finding a solution that is satisfactory to all parties.

Types of Conflict

Before a supervisor can respond effectively to a conflict, he or she needs to understand the real nature of that conflict. Who is involved? What is the source of the conflict? A supervisor is likely to respond differently to a conflict that results from a clash of opinions than one stemming from frustration over limited resources.

As defined, conflict may arise within an individual (intrapersonal) or between individuals or groups. The basic types of conflict involving more than one person are called interpersonal, structural, and strategic (see Figure 14.1).

Intrapersonal Conflict

An intrapersonal conflict arises when a person has trouble selecting from among goals. Choosing one of two possible goals is easy if one is good and the other bad. For example, would you rather earn $1 a year as a drug dealer or $1 million a year as the microbiologist who discovered a cure for cancer? Of course, we rarely are faced with such unrealistically easy choices. Most choices fall into three categories:

1. A choice between two good possibilities (for example, having a child or taking an exciting job that requires travel year-round).
2. A choice between two mixed possibilities (for example, accepting a promotion that involves moving away from your family or keeping your current, but monotonous, job to be near your family).
3. A choice between two bad possibilities (for example, reorganizing your department in a way that requires either laying off two employees or eliminating your own position).

Because these choices are not obvious, they result in conflict.

Supervisors should consider whether they or their organization are contributing unnecessarily to intrapersonal conflicts. For example, do they reward unethical

SUPERVISION AND DIVERSITY

FAITH-FRIENDLY WORKPLACES

Just as many companies have helped employees cope with intrapersonal conflicts that involve balancing family and work, some companies have begun thinking about how they can help employees integrate their faith with their work. Faith and work do not necessarily have to be in conflict. Often, all that is needed to prevent conflicts is a combination of sensitivity to individuals' needs, some flexibility, and a commitment to ethical behavior.

In recent decades, many Americans have assumed that faith or religion is a topic one does not discuss at work. Even so, holding a religious belief and practicing that faith shape a person's values and may affect the demands on a person's time. Some employers today have decided that they can ease the burden on employees by being more open about how they accommodate these beliefs and practices. In the words of David Miller, executive director of the Center for Faith and Culture at Yale Divinity School and a professor of business ethics, faith-friendly workplaces "encourage employees to feel they no longer have to leave their spiritual identities, their souls, and their faith in the parking lot when they enter the workplace."

For some employees, a faith-friendly workplace means they can pull out their Bible at break time or their prayer rug at the times designated for Islamic prayers. For others, "faith friendly" means the organization helps them carry out values such as the just treatment of employees. Religions may call for special practices, such as particular clothing, dietary restrictions, or time away from work. Some employees live out their faith by expressing to others what they believe. In a faith-friendly workplace, such expressions would need to be done with mutual respect and without disrupting work. As people carry out these activities, whether speaking of their beliefs or advocating for justice, the law requires that they do so in ways that do not amount to harassment. In Fort Worth, Texas, Pulliam Aquatech Pools allows employees to leave early for special religious activities but requires that employees "not aggressively tout their religion in the workplace so as not to create controversy," which could disrupt work.

Miller says people are more satisfied and dedicated at organizations that honor "their whole self," including their spiritual lives. Faith-friendly policies also help organizations avoid problems that lead to charges of discrimination based on religion. These complaints most often tend to be brought by members of minority religions who feel their practices are misunderstood and not reasonably accommodated. Antidiscrimination laws require that the workplace be free of religious discrimination, that employers make accommodations that are reasonable (imposing no undue hardship), and that any religious activities be strictly voluntary (no one is punished or made uncomfortable for not participating). Thus, the operator of a gas station lost a discrimination case filed on behalf of an employee who was fired after declining the services of a company-sponsored chaplain and requesting she not receive company e-mails with religious messages. "Faith-friendly" policies are friendly only when they respect all faiths—and the absence of a faith.

Sources: David Miller, "Integrating Faith and Work," *Journal of Employee Assistance,* October 2005; Shabnam Mogharabi, "Keep the Faith," *Pool & Spa News,* September 26, 2005; Dudley Rochelle, "When Faith and Work Clash," *Security Management,* January 2005, all downloaded from Business & Company Resource Center, http://galenet.galegroup.com.

behavior or pressure employees to behave unethically? If so, they are setting up conflicts between employees' values and their desire to be rewarded. One way to avoid contributing to intrapersonal conflicts is to ensure that the job does not make it too difficult for people to practice their faith. For more on preventing this type of intrapersonal conflict, see the "Supervision and Diversity" box.

Listening to others with an open mind can help supervisors correct actions that add to conflict. Michael Feiner saw this principle when he was a PepsiCo executive. Feiner learned that one of his employees had bypassed the chain of command to ask higher-level management to increase salaries in the employee's group. Feiner was upset at what he perceived to be an action that undermined him as the supervisor, so he angrily confronted his employee. The employee explained that he went to higher-level managers because he had repeatedly brought his proposal to Feiner and Feiner had repeatedly rejected the salary increases without listening to the employee's arguments in favor of them. Feiner recognized that by neglecting to listen to the proposal, he had allowed the conflict to persist.[1] Listening to others and admitting one's mistakes can be difficult, requiring self-discipline and maturity. In Feiner's example, however, the effort made him a more effective manager.

Listening and talking to others can also help supervisors resolve their own intrapersonal conflicts. Sometimes conflicts persist because a person has not fully explored the alternatives. An example is conflict in balancing one's roles at work and at home. Management professor Stewart Friedman advises his students to look at work and family as aspects of one unified life and consider how to improve results overall, rather than trading off one area of life against the other. One of Friedman's assignments is for students to talk to their co-workers and family members about what is expected of them and then think creatively about how to meet those requirements. The students have found the assignment difficult at first but ultimately helpful in improving their work and family lives. For example, one married student discovered that his pregnant wife wanted him to go along on appointments with the doctor. He was surprised but negotiated an adjustment in his hours and discovered that he appreciated the morning family time. Speaking directly about the situation to his wife and boss helped him avoid the kind of conflict that might have arisen if he had arranged his time on the basis of his guesses about what they wanted from him.[2]

In many cases, a supervisor lacks the expertise to resolve an intrapersonal conflict. When supervisors notice that an employee is struggling with an intrapersonal conflict, they should consider who might be able to help. People with skills in handling various types of intrapersonal conflicts include psychologists, religious advisers, and career counselors.

Interpersonal Conflict

Conflict between individuals is called *interpersonal conflict*. Supervisors may be involved in interpersonal conflicts with their manager, an employee, a peer, or even a customer. In addition, they may have to manage conflicts between two or more of their employees. Interpersonal conflicts may arise from differing opinions, misunderstandings of a situation, or differences in values or beliefs. Sometimes two people just rub each other the wrong way. (Chapter 8 provides an in-depth discussion of leading employees, and a section later in this chapter describes some approaches to managing interpersonal conflict.)

One concept gaining in popularity is "emotional intelligence," or the ability to manage emotions and interpersonal relationships. Sometimes divided into the four components of self-awareness, self-management, social awareness, and social skills, emotional intelligence is being introduced in training programs at organizations as diverse as giant American Express, the U.S. Air Force, and Cooperative Printing, a 45-employee Minneapolis firm.[3] The hope is that by giving supervisors and managers a way to deal with their and others' emotions, such training will reduce conflict and improve performance.

Structural Conflict

Conflict that results from the way the organization is structured is called *structural conflict*. Conflict often arises between line and staff personnel, and production and marketing departments are often at odds. In the latter example, marketing wants to give customers whatever they ask for, and production wants to make what it can easily and well.

Structural conflict often arises when various groups in the organization share resources, such as the services of a word-processing or maintenance department.

Each group wants its jobs handled first, but the support department obviously cannot help everyone first. Some of the most unpleasant structural conflict occurs when the "shared resource" is one employee who reports to two different managers. Some organizations are structured so that employees report to a functional manager and a project manager, or perhaps a supervisor's manager ignores the chain of command and gives directions to the supervisor's employees. An extreme example made work impossible for Eric Knudsen. At the software company where he was selected to lead the development of a new product, he was expected to deliver results to a sales director and marketing director from one business group, as well as to a marketing director and a business operations manager from a different group. If that weren't hard enough, a vice president began directing Knudsen's efforts as well. Knudsen complained, "It was difficult to know who was holding the purse strings, who to support and who to ignore." Eventually, the structural conflict became unbearable, and Knudsen quit his job.[4]

When structural conflict arises between two groups of employees reporting to a supervisor or between a supervisor's group and another group, the supervisor may be able to help minimize or resolve it by providing opportunities for the two groups to communicate and get to know each others' viewpoints, having them collaborate on achieving a mutually desirable goal, and giving each group training or experience in what the other group does.

If some employees involved in a structural conflict report to another supervisor, managing the conflict requires the cooperation of the two supervisors. Engaging that cooperation may require the appropriate use of political tactics, discussed in the last section of this chapter.

Because supervisors do not establish an organization's structure, they have limited impact on the sources of structural conflict. However, they do need to be able to recognize it. Knowing that a conflict is structural frees a supervisor from taking the issue personally and alerts him or her to situations that require extra diplomacy. A supervisor also may be able to understand the other party's point of view and communicate it to his or her employees.

Strategic Conflict

Most of the conflicts described so far arise unintentionally when people and groups try to work together. However, sometimes management or an individual intentionally will bring about a conflict to achieve an objective. This is referred to as a strategic conflict. For instance, a sales department might hold a contest for the highest sales volume and the most impressive example of delighting a customer. Or a manager might tell two employees that they are both in the running for a retiring supervisor's job. In both examples, the intent is to use competition to motivate employees to do exceptional work.

MANAGING INTERPERSONAL CONFLICT

conflict management
Responding to problems stemming from conflict

Restaurant manager Phyllis Jensen schedules the hours each server will work during the upcoming week. She has noticed that one of the servers, Rich Yakima, scowls when he gets his assignments and does so for hours afterward. She asked Yakima about it, and he replied, "You know just what the problem is. You know I've been wanting an evening off every weekend so I can go out with my girlfriend, but every week you have me working Friday and Saturday nights. And I've noticed that Rita and Pat always get the hours they want." Responding to problems such as this is known as **conflict management**.

FIGURE 14.2
Strategies
for Conflict
Management

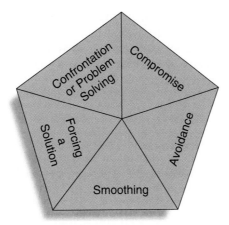

Strategies

How can Jensen manage the conflict involving Yakima? She can begin by recognizing the various strategies available for conflict management: compromise, avoidance, smoothing, forcing a solution, and confrontation or problem solving (see Figure 14.2). On the basis of her understanding of these strategies, Jensen can choose the most appropriate one for the circumstances. To see which conflict management strategy you tend to select most frequently, take the Knowing Yourself quiz on pages 397–398.

Compromise

compromise
Settling on a solution that gives each person part of what he or she wants; no one gets everything, and no one loses completely

One conflict management strategy is to reach a **compromise,** which means the parties to the conflict settle on a solution that gives both of them part of what they wanted. No party gets exactly what it wanted, but neither loses entirely either. Both parties presumably experience a degree of frustration—but at a level they are willing to live with.

People who choose to compromise are assuming they cannot reach a solution completely acceptable to everyone, but they would rather not force someone to accept a completely disagreeable choice. In that sense, compromise does not really solve the underlying problem; it works best when the problem is relatively minor and time is limited.

Avoidance and Smoothing

smoothing
Managing a conflict by pretending it does not exist

Conflict is unpleasant, so people sometimes try to manage conflict by avoiding it. For example, if sales supervisor Jeanette Delacroix finds the people in the human resources department stuffy and inflexible, she can avoid dealing with that department. When contact with human resources is absolutely necessary, she can delegate the responsibility to a member of the sales force. A related strategy is **smoothing,** or pretending that no conflict exists.

These strategies make sense if you assume that all conflict is bad. If you successfully avoid or smooth over all conflicts, life looks serene on the surface. However, people do disagree, and sometimes people with opposing viewpoints have important ideas to share. Avoiding those conflicts does not make them go away, nor does it make opposing points of view any less valid or significant. Therefore, it is important to be selective in avoiding or smoothing over conflicts. These strategies are most useful for conflicts that are not serious and for which a solution would be more difficult than the problem justifies.

This point is especially important with regard to today's diverse workforce. A person's point of view often seems puzzling, irritating, or downright incorrect to someone of another race, age, or sex. It takes extra work to understand people who are different from us. However, a supervisor must give equal attention to the views of all employees, not only those the supervisor understands best. Pretending that everyone is looking at a situation the same way does not make it so. It can even foster a belief among some employees that the supervisor is discriminating against them.

At the same time, people in many non-Western cultures believe it is best to avoid conflicts, placing a higher value on harmony than on "telling it like it is."[5]

People with these values are less likely than employees from Western cultures to complain to their supervisor or to deliver bad news. Thus, a supervisor may not realize there is a problem, such as a dispute between employees or a possibility that a task will be completed late. A supervisor must tactfully ensure that employees know that the supervisor wants to be aware of any problems in order to help resolve them.

Forcing a Solution

Because ignoring or avoiding a problem does not make it go away, a supervisor may want to try a more direct approach to ending a conflict. One possibility is to force a solution. This means that a person or group with power decides what the outcome will be. For example, if machinist Pete Desai complains to his supervisor that he never gets overtime assignments, the supervisor can respond, "I make the assignments, and your job is to do what you're told. This weekend it's going to be Sue and Chuck, so make the best of it." Or if two supervisors present conflicting proposals for allocating space among their departments, a committee of higher-level managers could select one proposal, allowing no room for discussion.

In an organization with self-managed work teams, another twist on forcing a solution is more likely. The team may decide that instead of reaching a consensus on some issue, it will simply vote on what to do. The majority makes the decision. Or the team leader may make the overall decision and let the group work out the details. During Timothy Riordan's management career in Ohio city governments, he once was trying to lead his employees in a project to reduce the time needed to process payments of citizens' taxes and water bills from three days to two days. The team was stuck on how to make employees work faster. Then Riordan forced a decision: The processing time would shrink from three days to completion on the day received. The forced decision shifted everyone's thinking. One supervisor exclaimed, "Well, we're going to have to do things differently around here." And the team began to restructure the whole process to make it more efficient.[6]

Forcing a solution is a relatively fast way to manage a conflict, and it may be the best approach in an emergency. Reaching consensus, for example, tends to be difficult and time consuming, whereas a team can vote on an issue quickly. However, forcing a solution can cause frustration. In organizations seeking teamwork and employee empowerment, forcing a solution works against those objectives by shutting off input from employees with a minority viewpoint. The bad feelings that accompany frustration and exclusion from decision making may lead to future conflict.

Confrontation or Problem Solving

conflict resolution
Managing a conflict by confronting the problem and solving it

The most direct—and sometimes the most difficult—way to manage conflict is to confront the problem and solve it. This is the conflict management strategy called **conflict resolution.** Confronting the problem requires listening to both sides and attempting to understand rather than to place blame. Next, the parties should identify the areas on which they agree and the ways they can both benefit from possible solutions. Both parties should examine their own feelings and take their time at reaching a solution. (Chapter 9 provides further guidelines for problem solving.)

Confronting and solving a problem makes a different assumption about the conflict than other strategies for conflict management, which tend to assume that the parties have a *win–lose conflict.* In other words, the outcome of the conflict will be that one person wins (that is, achieves the desired outcome), and the other person must lose. In contrast, conflict resolution assumes that many conflicts are *win–win conflicts,* in which the resolution can leave both parties better off. Frustration is avoided, and both sides feel like winners.

Initiating Conflict Resolution

When a supervisor has a conflict with another person, he or she needs to resolve that conflict constructively. Otherwise, the conflict is unlikely to go away on its own. When initiating conflict resolution, a supervisor should act as soon as he or she is aware of the problem. As the problem continues, a supervisor is likely to get increasingly emotional about it, which only makes resolution more difficult.

You cannot control the other person's response, so occasionally conflict resolution might not go much beyond your statement of the problem. Helene Dublisky once had reason to believe a colleague had given their supervisor false information that Dublisky had violated a policy of her employer, a utility company. Dublisky phoned her co-worker and described the situation as objectively as she could. According to Dublisky, the co-worker was silent for a moment, said, "I have to go now," and hung up the phone. Although the two employees did not discuss a solution, Dublisky had no further problems with backstabbing. Carl Robinson, a career coach, agrees that this kind of effort to resolve conflict is worthwhile, because it alerts the other employee that you will take action when conflicts arise. Similarly, management psychologist Nina Christopher suggests asking if there are any problems you should be aware of. If that does not generate a response, Christopher recommends adding, "I understand from others in the department that you have some issues you're unhappy about with me, and I'd like for us to discuss them directly."[7]

Prepare for conflict resolution by understanding what the conflict is (the first step in Figure 14.3). Focus on behavior, which people can change, not on personalities, which they cannot change. What is the action that is causing the problem, and how does that action affect you and others? For example, you might tell a supervisor in another department, "I haven't been getting the weekly sales figures until late Friday afternoon. That means I have to give up precious family time to

FIGURE 14.3   **Initiating Conflict Resolution**

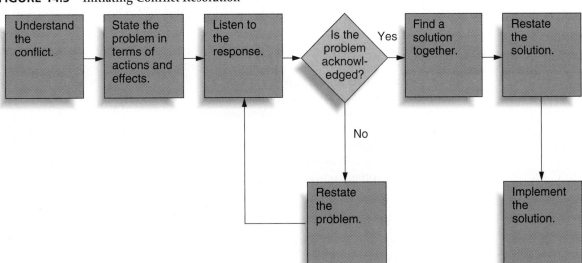

review them over the weekend, or else I embarrass myself by being unprepared at the Monday morning staff meetings."

When used politely, this type of approach even works with one's manager. You might say, "I haven't heard from you concerning the suggestions I made last week and three weeks ago. That worries me, because I think maybe I'm giving you too many ideas or not the right kind."

After you have stated the problem, listen to how the other person responds. If the other person does not acknowledge there is a problem, restate your concern until the other person understands or until it is clear that you cannot make any progress on your own. Often a conflict exists simply because the other person has not understood your point of view or your situation. When you have begun communicating about the problem, the two of you can work together to find a solution. Restate your solution to be sure that both of you agree on what you are going to do (the final steps in Figure 14.3).

Responding to a Conflict

Sometimes a supervisor is party to a conflict that is bothering someone else. When the other person makes the supervisor aware of the conflict, it is up to the supervisor to respond in a way that makes a solution possible. If an employee says, "You always give me the dirty assignments," it is not helpful to get angry or defensive.

Understand the Problem

The constructive way to respond to a conflict is first to listen to the other person and try to understand what the problem is really about. If the other person is emotional, let that person vent those feelings, then get down to discussing the problem. Try to interpret the problem in the terms you would use to express the problem yourself. Avoid statements of blame, and find out what specific actions the other person is referring to. For example, when an employee says, "You always give me the dirty assignments," you can ask the employee to give specific examples and then describe how he or she feels about the behavior.

Mark Preiser took this important first step when he was a partner with Walter F. Cameron Advertising in Hauppauge, New York. An account manager at his agency had committed to delivering a job by a particular deadline, but on the day of the deadline, the artist who was to prepare the visuals called in sick. The furious account manager was on the phone, shouting. He doubted that the artist was sick. Instead, he suspected the weather: The day was snowy, and the artist often missed work on snowy days. Preiser joined the conversation and learned that the artist was afraid. He had been in a serious car accident on a snowy day, and ever since, driving in the snow had terrified him. Preiser worked with the account manager and artist to arrange for the artist to be able to take work home whenever a snowstorm was in the weather forecast.[8]

Understanding the problem can be complicated if one of the people involved has a "hidden agenda"—a central concern that is left unstated. Typically, a person with a hidden agenda is angry or upset about something but directs those feelings toward some other issue. For example, a colleague in another department explodes, "What's wrong with you? The numbers in your report are off by a mile!" Your colleague is not really angry because you made a mistake. He is nervous because he has to make a presentation to the board of directors, and he wonders if the incorrect numbers are your way to mislead him so that he looks uninformed and you get the promotion he wants. Or maybe your colleague simply has had a frustrating day, and your mistake is the last straw.

FIGURE 14.4   **Responding to a Conflict**

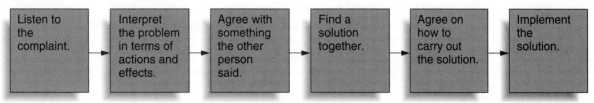

If another person's feelings seem to be out of proportion to the problem he or she is describing, look for a hidden agenda. Finding one can save you from trying to resolve the wrong conflict. In addition, when you are upset about something yourself, it is usually more constructive to describe the problem directly than to leave others guessing at your hidden agenda.

Work on a Solution

When you understand the problem, build an environment of working together on a solution. To do this, agree with some aspect of what the other person has said. In the previous example, you might say, "You've really disliked your last three assignments." Then you and the other person should be ready to begin identifying possible solutions. The final step is to agree on what the solution will be and how you will carry it out. Figure 14.4 summarizes this approach.

Mediating Conflict Resolution

Sometimes a supervisor is not personally involved in a conflict, but the parties ask the supervisor to help resolve it. If the parties to the conflict are peers of the supervisor, getting involved can be risky, and the supervisor might be wiser to tactfully refer the peers to a higher-level manager. If the parties to the conflict are the supervisor's employees, then mediating the conflict is part of the supervisor's job and an important way to keep the department functioning as it should.

To mediate a conflict, a supervisor should follow these steps:

1. Begin by establishing a constructive environment. If the employees are calling one another names, have them focus on the issue instead of such destructive behavior.
2. Ask each person to explain what the problem is. Get each person to be specific and to respond to the others' charges.
3. When all parties understand what the problem is, have them state individually what they want to accomplish or what will satisfy them.
4. Restate in your own words what each person's position is. Ask the employees if you have understood them correctly.
5. Have all participants suggest as many solutions as they can. Begin to focus on the future.
6. Encourage the employees to select a solution that benefits all of them. They may want to combine or modify some of the ideas suggested.
7. Summarize what has been discussed and agreed on. Make sure all participants know what they are supposed to do in carrying out the solution and ask for their cooperation.

Throughout this process, continue your efforts to maintain a constructive environment. Keep the emphasis off personalities and blame; keep it on your mutual desire to find a solution.

Other useful strategies include meeting with the parties separately first, to give each a chance to air his or her views. Then meet with everyone and explain your ground rule: "You're on safe ground so don't hold back, but everything you say must be in the best interest of the other person." Stop the discussion if anyone can't adhere to the rules, and finish by explaining that you expect them to continue to have more open conversations with one another as a result of the meeting.[9]

CHANGE IN THE WORKPLACE

Conflict is both a cause and a consequence of change. When people experience a conflict, they manage it by making changes to the situation or their attitudes. For instance, faced with conflicts between the demands of work and family, employees increasingly have tried to balance the two rather than choose one over the other. Their efforts have forced organizations to consider the adoption of policies and values that are more family friendly. When change occurs—in the workplace and elsewhere—conflict accompanies the need to let go of familiar behaviors and attitudes.

The greater desire to balance work and home life is only one of many sources of change in the workplace today.[10] External sources of change include higher expectations for quality and stiffer foreign competition. Modern technology has made communication faster and more flexible and has changed job requirements. Especially for workers in high-tech fields, training and retraining are essential for them to keep up with industry developments.

With stiff international competition, supervisors and higher-level managers endure continuing pressure to cut costs. As the price of health insurance rises year after year, some companies are trying to cut costs by persuading employees to make changes even outside of work. At Weyco, a medical-benefits company in Michigan, employees who smoke but don't participate in the company's stop-smoking program get fired, and employees who don't get a set of required medical tests and physical checkups must pay a higher share of their insurance premiums. And at Blue Cross/Blue Shield of North Carolina, employees who are obese must pay higher insurance premiums unless they participate in wellness programs. The plan's executive medical director, Dr. Don Bradley, explains that the wellness programs are offered as a way to pay the lower rate: "The secret here is to keep this as an incentive rather than a punishment."[11]

Because of these and many other changes, an organization's success (its profitability, in the case of a business) depends on how well it adapts to changes in its environment. For example, an organization must respond when a new competitor enters the marketplace or a new law limits how it may operate.

Change is a fact of organizational life, so supervisors do not decide *whether* organizations should change but *how* to make the changes work. They can do this better if they recognize the various factors that can affect the success of a change:

- *The change agent*—The person trying to bring about the change should have skills in implementing change and solving the related problems, as well as expertise in the area affected.
- *Determination of what to change*—Any changes should make the organization more effective in delivering high quality.
- *The kind of change to be made*—The change can involve process and equipment; policies, procedures, and job structure; and people-related variables such as attitudes and communication skills.

- *Individuals affected*—Some people are more open to change than others. Also, people will see some changes as beneficial to them but other changes as harmful.
- *Evaluation of change*—An evaluation can indicate whether it is necessary to modify the change process or make further changes.

Supervisors are the organization's primary link to operative employees, so they must understand how employees are likely to respond to changes, be able to communicate information about the changes to employees, and help employees respond positively.

Sources of Change

Changes can originate with management, employees, or external forces (see Figure 14.5). Organizations change when management sees an opportunity or a need to do things better. A need may arise because performance is inadequate. Examples of an opportunity are a new computer system that is more efficient or a new procedure that can lead to higher-quality service.

Sometimes even if the improvement is incremental, management will see a need for change. This was the case when Pitney Bowes Credit Corporation in Shelton, Connecticut, transformed itself from a big but bland division of Pitney Bowes Inc. to what Matthew Kissner, president and CEO, calls his "idea factory." The colorful new office space is full of unusual details that mark it as "a fun space that would embody our culture," he says. "This place wasn't broken. But we knew we could make it better."[12]

Even an organization's employees may bring about changes. Forming a union could lead to changes in the way management reaches agreements with employees and the conditions under which employees work. Many organizations actively respond to employee suggestions on how to improve quality and cut costs.

As the U.S. workforce becomes increasingly diverse in terms of age, race, and sex, the forces for change from employees are likely to strengthen. People of diverse backgrounds can offer a greater variety of creative solutions. In addition, the challenge of working harmoniously with different kinds of people can itself lead to a push for changes, such as provisions for different religious holidays or guidelines on how to treat people fairly.

Other changes are imposed from outside. New laws and regulations often lead to changes within organizations. A local government organization might have to make changes in response to voters' refusal to approve a tax increase. A series of lawsuits might cause an organization to reexamine how it makes a product. The size and composition of the workforce may affect whom the organization hires and how much training it provides.

Economic trends also are important. For example, businesses usually are able to seek growth more aggressively when the economy is expanding. But during downturns, change is also common and can be especially difficult. Many large

FIGURE 14.5
Sources of Change

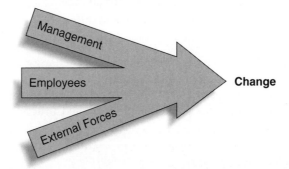

firms have experienced cutbacks. At the end of 2000, for instance, Gillette Co. announced the elimination of 8 percent of its workforce, or 2,700 jobs, and the closing of eight factories, a follow-up to a management shakeup on the heels of more than two years of disappointing financial performance. Gillette was eventually acquired by Procter & Gamble.[13]

Manufacturers are finding that selling the products they make is often less profitable than providing related services, such as repairs and maintenance of their products. This knowledge is a force for change in some companies' strategy. Some manufacturers are beginning to respond to the information by developing the staff, facilities, and know-how to add services to their product lines. For instance, Caterpillar set up systems to deliver spare parts anywhere within 24 hours, and Hyundai Motor Company offers extended warranties, delivering service to individual customers as needed. These changes affect a company's values, its staffing needs, and its focus on serving customers.[14]

Resistance to Change

Any change, such as the adoption of a new procedure in the workplace or the completion of a major training program, requires work. People are fearful because change carries the risk of making them worse off. For example, when a company announces a "restructuring," employees start worrying about layoffs and a dramatic increase in employee workloads.

People's resistance to change is greatest when they are not sure what to expect or why the change is necessary. Change stirs up fear of the unknown, another normal human response. Furthermore, when people do not understand the reasons for change, the effort to change does not seem worthwhile.

Sometimes even when change is positive, it meets resistance. At Xerox Corporation, employees complained that it took too long for them to receive reimbursements for expenses incurred in the course of business. Xerox undertook a benchmarking study of 26 other firms to try to find a solution to its problem and came up with a new system that entailed the use of more than one corporate credit card, new forms to fill out, and no cash advances. The advantage was that employees no longer had to worry about being reimbursed. But, said Warren D. Jeffries, manager of customer services benchmarking for Xerox, "everyone resisted the changes, even those that were unhappy with the old way."[15]

Implementing Change

To implement change, a supervisor must overcome resistance to it, ensure that the change is made, and create the conditions in which the change is likely to last. Noted behavioral scientist Kurt Lewin has set forth a model for this process (see Figure 14.6).[16] Lewin's model indicates that a successful change has three phases:

1. *Unfreezing*—People recognize a need for change.
2. *Changing*—People begin trying to behave differently.
3. *Refreezing*—The new behavior becomes part of employees' regular processes.

This model makes two assumptions about the change process. First, before a change can occur, employees must see the status quo as less than ideal. Second, when employees begin changing, the organization must provide a way for the new behavior to become established practice. As described in the

FIGURE 14.6
Lewin's Model of Change

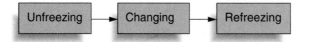

SUPERVISORY SKILLS

IMPLEMENTING CHANGE

PRODUCTION SUPERVISOR STIMULATES INNOVATION

Supervisors are in a position to make changes within their own work group. Even small changes can motivate employees and contribute to significant performance improvements. Supervisors can unfreeze this change process by encouraging their employees to think of themselves and their group as innovators. When the supervisor regularly asks, "How can we do our work better?" employees get in the habit of thinking about change as part of their responsibility.

One way to stimulate innovation is to make improvements part of the group's regular routine. At a Midwest computer manufacturer, a production supervisor calls a half-day meeting every three months. The group analyzes its work flow and recommends changes.

Ahead of this meeting, the supervisor announces the topic to be discussed. For example, at some of its meetings, the group has explored ways to reduce scrap rates by 10 percent, eliminate paperwork, and combine job functions to increase output. The employees know about the topic and the meeting time far enough ahead that they come prepared with suggestions. They also bring information about the costs and benefits of their ideas. Because the supervisor defines a topic, the meeting stays focused. Each employee has a chance to present his or her ideas. If someone presents a problem, the group should look for more than one possible solution; this ground rule stimulates creative thinking.

These meetings also present an opportunity to develop employees' leadership and teamwork skills. The supervisor can appoint one of the employees to be the discussion leader. Other employees can be assigned various topics on the meeting's agenda. Taking an active role gets employees more involved in the change process, increasing their commitment to the success of each innovation.

Change is a given in the modern workplace. Supervisors who develop their employees' ability to welcome and create change are building a valuable asset for their organization.

Source: David K. Lindo, "You Can Make It Better," *Supervision,* April 2004, downloaded from InfoTrac, http://web4.infotrac.galegroup.com.

"Supervisory Skills" box, supervisors can help create this kind of openness to change in their work groups.

Unfreezing

In the unfreezing phase, the supervisor or other person responsible for implementing the change must spell out clearly why a change is needed. When former NFL commissioner Paul Tagliabue wanted football team owners to agree to adopt free agency and a salary cap for players, most owners worried that they could not succeed under the new arrangement because the teams in the biggest markets would take all the best players. Tagliabue focused on showing owners why the change was actually in their best interests. Eventually, he convinced enough of them that a majority voted to accept the change.[17] In essence, then, unfreezing means overcoming resistance to change.

Many changes require not only performing new tasks but also adopting new attitudes, such as a willingness to assume decision-making responsibility and a strong commitment to customer value. Employees may have difficulty changing their attitudes, especially if they are unsure about management's sincerity.[18] Also, management needs to address employee resistance arising from fears about the change. The organization relies heavily on supervisors—as management's link to operative employees—to carry out this responsibility, for which they need good communication skills (see Chapter 10). The following guidelines may help as well:[19]

- Tell employees about a change as soon as you learn about it.
- Make sure employees understand what the change is, then explain how the change is likely to affect them.

- Be as positive about the change as possible, citing any benefits to the employees. These might include more interesting jobs or bigger bonuses. At the same time, don't get caught up in parroting the company's point of view.
- Describe how the organization will help employees cope. Will there be training in how to follow new procedures? Will the organization provide counseling or other assistance to employees being laid off? What will happen to employee benefits?
- Do not try to hide bad news, including the possibility that some employees will lose their jobs. But be professional and don't needlessly communicate your own worries.
- Give employees plenty of opportunity to express concerns and ask questions. It is better for a supervisor to hear concerns and questions than to let them circulate in the rumor mill, where information may be misleading or incorrect.
- Answer as many questions as you can and get the answers to the rest as soon as possible. If you can't provide complete information, say, "Let me tell you what I know."
- Keep alert to your company's status in the marketplace and let your employees know about it. Are new orders coming in? Are new products or services ready to roll out? Any team will be more productive if members feel they understand what is happening in the company as a whole and if their supervisor is a dependable source of accurate and positive information.
- When employees are upset, listen to expressions of sadness and anger without argument. It is unfair and unwise to tell employees they are overreacting. People experience change subjectively, and one subjective experience is as valid as another.

In listening to and answering questions, remember that some employees will not think of questions until some time has passed. Therefore, provide opportunities for employees to ask questions on an ongoing basis, not just at the time a change is announced.

Changing

When employees appreciate the need for a change and have received any necessary training, they are ready to begin altering their behavior. The key to implementing change is to build on successes. A supervisor should determine those aspects of the change over which he or she has control, then seek to carry them out successfully. A supervisor should point out each success the group achieves along the way. As employees see the change achieving desirable results, they are more likely to go along with it and even embrace it.

Demonstrating practical success was important when New Century Mortgage wanted its managers to ensure that its employees were fully "engaged"—meaning they understand and are able to do what is expected of them and they care about fully contributing. The Irvine, California, mortgage lender worked with a consulting firm to conduct a survey of employee engagement. Despite discussions about the relevance of this change, many supervisors were skeptical. However, the company persisted in having managers and employees work together to develop ways to build engagement where the survey found it was weak. As New Century's people began implementing these plans, the company kept track of each division's earnings. Soon the company could report that revenues were far greater in divisions where employees were fully engaged. Furthermore, by comparing two years' surveys, the company demonstrated that divisions that carried out plans to improve engagement outperformed divisions that failed to emphasize engagement. Seeing these practical benefits, New Century's managers stopped questioning the new program.[20]

New Century tried its program to improve employee engagement without waiting to fully convince its people the program was worthwhile. As in this example, building on successes generally entails starting with basic changes in behavior, rather than beginning with an effort to change values. Values, by their nature, are more resistant to change. To induce changes in behavior, the change effort should include tangible or intangible rewards for the desired behavior. As employees experience positive outcomes, their attitudes become more positive, and their values may shift as well.

A supervisor who has control over scheduling a change should establish reasonable deadlines. As employees meet each deadline, the supervisor can point out their on-time achievements. For example, imagine that an accounting department is installing a new computer system. Instead of focusing simply on whether everyone is using the system properly, a supervisor can establish dates for setting up various pieces of equipment and learning to operate different parts of the system. Then the supervisor can note that the terminals arrived on time, that everyone learned how to log on and enter their password in a single training session, and so on.

A supervisor also might have control over which people are directly involved in the change or the order in which people get involved. The supervisor of the accounting department might recognize that some employees are already enthusiastic about the new system or are flexible and open to change. These people should learn the system first; then they can spread their enthusiasm around and help other employees when it is their turn to learn.

Similarly, if a group of employees works well together and enjoys one another's company, a sensible approach is to keep these employees together. For example, the change of adding another shift might proceed more smoothly if informal groups are not split into different shifts. In contrast, when a change involves bringing together two groups of employees from different organizations, locations, or shifts, a supervisor might build cooperation by teaming up employees from each group.

Refreezing

The change process is complete only when employees make the new behavior part of their routine. However, because new procedures are less comfortable than the old and familiar ones, employees may revert to their old practices when the initial pressure for change eases. In organizations that do not manage change effectively, managers may assume a change effort has succeeded simply because employees modified their behavior according to instructions. But if employees merely fulfill the basic requirements of a change without adjusting their attitudes, and if the organization has not arranged to reinforce and reward the change, backsliding is likely.

That is just what happened to a hospital unit's attempt to start a self-directed work team. The employees of the hospital unit at first seemed to embrace that change when they said good-bye to a 15-year supervisor who had controlled with a strong hand. They agreed to operate as a team and chose a leader with a more low-key personality. Team members quickly stepped in and handled the administrative work their former supervisor had performed, and their new supervisor had no problem delegating. But as time passed, the team members began expecting their leader to handle more and more of the administrative duties, and the team leader allowed the old ways to return.[21]

Backsliding is a natural response among employees, but it can become a problem unless a supervisor acts to get everyone back on track. A supervisor should remind employees about what they have achieved so far and what is expected of them in the future (see the principles of motivation described in Chapter 11). An important part of refreezing is for employees to be rewarded for behavior that shows they have made the desired change.

Proposing Change

In many situations, a supervisor wants to make a change but needs to ask higher-level management for authority to implement it. A supervisor also is wise to ask his or her manager about changes that are controversial, difficult to implement, or of major importance. These situations require a supervisor to make a proposal to higher-level management.

To propose a change effectively, the supervisor should begin by analyzing it. How will it help the organization better achieve its goals? Will it improve quality or productivity? What steps are required to carry it out? How much will it cost? Who will carry it out? What training will be required? Only when the answers to these questions confirm that the change is beneficial and feasible is the supervisor in a valid position to continue with the proposal.

Recall that the change process begins with convincing others of the need for a change (unfreezing, in Lewin's model). Some organizations actively cultivate suggestions for improvement, making it relatively easy for a supervisor to sell a change. In other organizations, management may view change more cautiously. Thus, it is often important for a supervisor to begin by helping management see the situation that gives rise to the need for a change. A supervisor may have to do this before he or she even mentions changing something.

Once a supervisor's groundwork has prepared management for the proposal, a supervisor should have one ready to submit. Except for simple changes, a supervisor should make proposals in writing. The beginning of a proposal should contain a brief summary of what the change is and why it is desirable. Then the supervisor can provide details about the procedure for change and the costs and benefits involved. (For more suggestions about upward communication and reports, see Chapter 10; for guidelines on maintaining good relations with your manager, see Chapter 8.)

ORGANIZATIONAL POLITICS AND POWER

organizational politics
Intentional acts of influence to enhance or protect the self-interest of individuals or groups

Implementing change and resolving conflicts are easier for a person who has a relatively strong position in the organization. Thus, supervisors can most effectively manage conflict and change if they are able to improve their positions within an organization. Together, the activities through which people do this are called **organizational politics.** Improving one's position is not in itself good or bad; therefore, politics also is not innately good or bad. Political skills *are* important, however. They help a supervisor obtain the cooperation and support of others in the organization. A recent survey found that managers spend almost a full day out of every five-day workweek on matters related to organizational politics, including the politically motivated activities of their employees (see Figure 14.7). More about organizational politics is available in the Appendix that follows this chapter.

FIGURE 14.7
Share of Time Spent by Managers on Organizational Politics

Source: "Reducing Conflict in the Office," *USA Today Magazine*, July 2003, downloaded from LookSmart's Find Articles, www.findarticles.com.

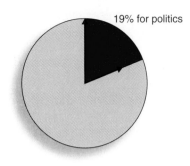

19% for politics

The usual way that people use politics to improve their positions is by gaining power. **Power** is the ability to influence people to behave in a certain way. For instance, one supervisor says, "I wish everyone would be at work on time," yet employees continue to come in late. Another supervisor gets employees so excited about their contribution to the company that they consistently arrive at work on time and perform above what is required of them. The second supervisor has more power than the first.

power
The ability to influence people to behave in a certain way

Sources of Power

Editorial supervisor Stan Bakker has a decade-long track record of turning manuscripts into best-sellers. When he tells one of the editors on his staff how to handle a particular author or manuscript, the editor invariably follows Bakker's directions. Why? Partly because he is the boss, and partly because the editors respect his expertise. Thus, Bakker's power comes both from his position in the company and from his personal characteristics.

Power that comes from a person's formal role in an organization is known as **position power.** Every supervisor has some position power with the employees he or she supervises. Higher-level managers, in turn, have a greater degree of position power.

position power
Power that comes from a person's formal role in an organization

In contrast, **personal power** is power that arises from an individual's personal characteristics. Because a person does not need to be a manager in an organization to have personal power there, employees sometimes view a co-worker as an informal leader of their group. If a supervisor announces a reorganization, one employee may successfully urge everyone to rally around the new plan—or may undermine morale by making fun of the changes. The informal leader in a group could be someone that other employees see as having expertise or being fun to work with.

personal power
Power that arises from an individual's personal characteristics

Supervisors cannot eliminate personal power in subordinates, but they should be aware of it so they can use it to their advantage. A supervisor can watch for problems that might arise when the supervisor and an informal leader have conflicting goals. Perhaps more important, a supervisor can seek ways to get an informal leader on his or her side; for example, a supervisor might announce a decision to the informal leader first or discuss plans with that person.

Types of Power

Because power comes from their personal characteristics as well as their position in the organization, supervisors can have a variety of types of power. A supervisor who has less position power than he or she would like might consider the following types of power to see whether some can be developed. These types are summarized in Table 14.1.

Legitimate power comes from the position a person holds. Thus, a supervisor has legitimate power to delegate tasks to employees. To exercise legitimate power effectively, a supervisor needs to be sure employees understand what they are directed to do and are able to do it.

Referent power comes from the emotions a person inspires. Some supervisors seem to light up the room when they enter; they have a winning personality that includes enthusiasm, energy, and genuine enjoyment of the job. People like working for such a supervisor and often perform beyond the call of duty because they

TABLE 14.1
Types of Power

Power Type	Arises From
Legitimate	The position a person holds
Referent	The emotions a person inspires
Expert	A person's knowledge or skills
Coercive	Fear related to the use of force
Reward	Giving people something they want
Connection	A person's relationship to someone powerful
Information	Possession of valuable information

want the supervisor to like them. A person with referent power is often called "charismatic."

Expert power arises from a person's knowledge or skills. Employees respect a supervisor who knows the employees' jobs better than they do. Their respect leads them to follow the supervisor's instructions. For example, the head of a company's research and development team might be a scientist who is well regarded in the field. Researchers could be expected to ask for and rely on this supervisor's advice.

Coercive power arises from fear related to the use of force. A supervisor who says, "Be on time tomorrow, or you're fired!" is using coercive power. This type of power may get results in the short run, but in the long run, employees come to resent and may try to get around this supervisor. A supervisor who often relies on coercive power should consider whether he or she is doing so at the expense of developing other, more appropriate types of power.

Reward power arises from giving people something they want. The reward given by a supervisor might be a raise, recognition, or assignment to a desired shift. A supervisor who plans to rely on reward power to lead employees had better be sure that he or she is able to give out rewards consistently. Often supervisors are limited in this regard. Company policy may put a ceiling on the size of raises to be granted, or there may be only a few assignments that really thrill employees.

Connection power is power that stems from a person's relationship to someone powerful. Imagine that two supervisors are golfing buddies. One of them gets promoted to the job of manager of purchasing. The other supervisor has connection power stemming from his relationship to the new manager. Similarly, if one of the organization's employees is the daughter of a vice president, she has connection power as a result of that family relationship. Connection power can be a problem for the organization and its managers when the people who have it place the interests of their relationship ahead of the interests of the organization. Nevertheless, it is a fact of organizational life.

Information power is power that arises from possessing valuable information. Someone who knows which employees are targeted in the next round of layoffs or when the department manager will be out of town has information power. The secretaries of top managers have information power as well as connection power.

Political Strategies

A person's political strategies are the methods the person uses to acquire and keep power within the organization. Depending on the particular strategies a person chooses and how he or she uses those strategies, they may be ethical or unethical. The following strategies commonly are used in organizations:[22]

- *Doing favors*—People remember favors and generally are willing to help out or say a good word in return. However, doing favors solely to create an obligation is unethical. For more ideas about the impact of doing favors, see the "Supervision and Ethics" box.

SUPERVISION AND ETHICS

ARE GOOD DEEDS GOOD BUSINESS?

Companies compete for sales, and employees compete for promotions. In a competitive business environment, is there a place for kindness?

Some people think so, at least in certain situations. Helping others can increase the likelihood they will cooperate with you. Also, some organizations encourage helpfulness as part of building teamwork and commitment to the organization.

The accounting firm KPMG has a benefits-sharing program. Under the program, employees (except partners, the top-level employees who share ownership of the company) are allowed to donate some of their own time off to their colleagues. An employee may donate 4 to 40 hours to another employee who needs paid time off to care for a family member with a serious medical condition. During a recent year, KPMG employees donated about 8,000 hours to 32 of their co-workers.

One employee on the receiving end that year was Devon Wzientek, who gave birth to a son with a congenital heart defect. The baby needed three surgeries, starting when he was a few days old. Wzientek went through two weeks of maternity leave, six weeks of short-term disability, and the six weeks of vacation time she had saved up. Still, she needed to stay home to care for her baby, so KPMG co-workers together gave her another 12 weeks of time off with pay. Wzientek's experience made her loyal to the company and committed to her

colleagues. She says, "Eventually, someone will need some vacation time, and I will most definitely be donating my time to them—in a heartbeat." But Wzientek is not the only one who bonded with co-workers. Being the giver strengthens relationships, too. Todd Cameron, a manager who donated 20 hours to Wzientek, says, "There were good feelings all around."

According to Frank Flynn, a Columbia University professor, employees tend to have more positive opinions of co-workers who show generosity. They appreciate co-workers who help by taking on extra work, covering another person's shift, or offering to give advice. But Flynn also notes that people have negative opinions of co-workers who seem to behave this way in order to gain personally. Generosity can backfire if it keeps employees from getting their own work done or is so extreme that co-workers begin to resent the debt they feel toward the generous employee.

This effort to rate other people's intentions produces some patterns in the way co-workers experience generous acts. For example, women tend to gain less credit for generosity than men do, perhaps because people expect their female colleagues to be "nicer." Individual women who are rated as nicer tend to get less credit for generous acts than their male colleagues.

Source: Kris Maher, "Giving Can Be Good for Getting Ahead," *The Wall Street Journal*, August 31, 2004, http://online.wsj.com.

- *Making good impressions*—Those who are skilled at organizational politics know that it is important to create a positive image of themselves. Not only do they look their best, but they make sure their accomplishments are visible.
- *Cultivating the grapevine*—The saying "knowledge is power" applies to one's position in the organization. Therefore, power is greater for those who are connected to the grapevines that carry information in the organization (see Chapter 10). Ways to get connected include serving on committees and developing friendships and informal contacts.
- *Supporting the manager*—The supervisor's manager can be a powerful ally. Therefore, it is important to help the manager look good.
- *Avoiding negativism*—People have more respect for those who propose solutions than for those who merely criticize.
- *Giving praise*—People like to be praised, and written compliments are especially valuable. As long as the praise is sincere, the supervisor can offer it to anyone, even his or her manager.

FIGURE 14.8
Approaches to
Building a
Power Base

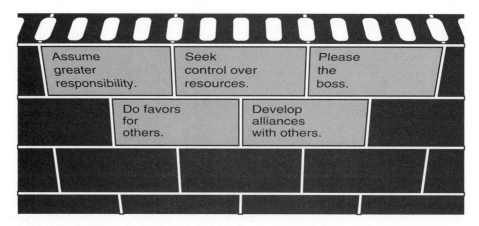

Building a Power Base

At the heart of organizational politics is building a base of power. The particular approach used varies with the kinds of power an employee or manager might acquire. Figure 14.8 summarizes some possible approaches. Some people take on more responsibility in an effort to become needed in the organization. Others seek control over resources; the supervisor with more employees or a bigger budget is considered to be more powerful.

An important way supervisors can build their power bases is to please their managers. Peers and subordinates who recognize that a supervisor has a close relationship with the manager tend to treat the supervisor carefully to avoid antagonizing the manager.

To do favors so that others will be in one's debt is yet another approach. Bribery of course is unethical, but there are many ethical ways to do favors for others. A supervisor might offer to stay late to help a co-worker finish a project or jump-start the co-worker's car on a cold day. When the supervisor needs help or a favorable word from someone, the co-worker probably will be happy to return the favor.

Doing favors can help a supervisor with one of the other techniques for building a power base: developing alliances with others in the organization. A supervisor who has many people on his or her side is able to get more done and build a good reputation. This does not mean supervisors have to hang around with greedy, pushy, or unethical co-workers. Instead, they should identify people they admire as potential allies. Alliances can be built with these people by earning their trust, keeping them informed, and developing comfortable relationships through common interests.

Establishing a Competitive Edge

On the assumption that there are limits to the number of promotions and other goodies available, organization members seek to gain a competitive edge. They try to stand out so that when raises, promotions, and choice assignments are handed out, they will be the recipients. Ethical efforts to establish a competitive edge generally are based on trying to do an exceptional job.

Some unethical approaches to establishing a competitive edge are spreading lies and rumors about peers and taking credit for the ideas and work of subordinates. Trying to look good at the expense of someone else may be effective at first, but when the truth comes out, the person who uses this tactic winds up the biggest loser. Other people learn to distrust such a person. In the long run, the most successful way to look exceptional is to produce exceptional results.

Socializing

At many organizations, part of the game of getting ahead includes socializing with co-workers. Perhaps the people who get promoted the fastest are those who on occasion play golf with the boss or go out for a drink after work. Depending on a supervisor's behavior in these situations, socializing can be helpful, or it can put an end to an employee's career growth.

Common sense can help the supervisor handle socializing appropriately. For example, a supervisor who gets drunk at a party is likely to behave foolishly. Likewise, dating a subordinate is an invitation to trouble. If the relationship lasts, other employees are likely to be jealous of the subordinate and doubt the supervisor's ability to be fair. If the relationship does not work out, the supervisor could be set up—justly or unjustly—for charges of sexual harassment by an angry subordinate. (For an explanation of sexual harassment, see Appendix B.)

In general, the wisest course is to be sensible but natural. For example, a supervisor should not push to become a buddy of the manager or of subordinates. Nor should a supervisor use social occasions as an opportunity to make a big impression; showing off is hardly an effective way to build relationships.

SKILLS MODULE

PART ONE: CONCEPTS

Summary

14.1 List positive and negative aspects of conflict.

When it leads to necessary changes, conflict is a positive force because it signals that a problem exists. However, ongoing conflict puts people under stress and takes up time that could be spent more productively. When conflict involves anger at management or the organization, it may lead to destructive behavior.

14.2 Define types of conflict.

Conflict may be intrapersonal, taking place within one person. Conflict between individuals is called interpersonal. Structural conflict results from the way the organization is structured. Strategic conflict is brought about intentionally to achieve some goal, such as motivating employees.

14.3 Describe strategies for managing conflict.

One strategy is to compromise, or agree to a solution that meets only part of each party's demands. Another approach is to avoid the conflict or pretend it does not exist (smoothing). Forcing a solution occurs when a person with power selects and imposes the outcome. None of these strategies tries to solve the underlying problem, and all assume that the situation is a win–lose for those involved. Confronting and solving the problem, called conflict resolution, assumes that a conflict can be a win–win situation.

14.4 Explain how supervisors can initiate conflict resolution, respond to a conflict, and mediate conflict resolution.

To initiate conflict resolution, a supervisor must begin by understanding what the conflict is. The supervisor then states the problem and listens to the response; when the parties are communicating, they can find a solution and agree upon what each person will do.

To respond to a conflict, a supervisor should listen to the other person and try to understand the problem. Then the supervisor can build cooperation by

394 Part Four   *Skills of the Supervisor*

agreeing with part of the statement and working with the other person to reach a solution.

To mediate conflict resolution, a supervisor begins by establishing a constructive environment, then asks each person to explain what the problem is and state what he or she wants. Next the supervisor restates each position, asks for suggested solutions, and encourages the parties to select a mutually beneficial solution. Finally, the supervisor summarizes what course of action has been agreed upon.

14.5 Identify sources of change and explain why employees and supervisors resist it.

Change can come from management in response to an opportunity or need to do things better. It can come from employees in the form of unionizing or making suggestions. Change can be imposed by external forces such as the government. Employees and supervisors resist change because it typically requires extra effort and sometimes leaves people worse off. Other reasons for resisting change are fear of the unknown and worry that one is incapable of making the change.

14.6 Discuss how supervisors can overcome resistance and implement change.

To overcome resistance to change, supervisors can recognize and respond to employees' feelings. They also can keep employees informed about the change, being realistic but emphasizing any benefits. The supervisor should give employees opportunities to ask questions about the change. To implement change, the supervisor should build on successes. This includes communicating successes as they occur, setting reasonable deadlines for the steps that must be taken, and involving first the people who are most likely to be enthusiastic about the change.

14.7 Describe the types of power supervisors can have.

Supervisors can have legitimate power, which comes from their position in the organization; referent power, which comes from the emotions they inspire in others; expert power, which comes from their knowledge or skills; coercive power, which comes from fear related to their use of force; reward power, which comes from giving people something they want; connection power, which comes from their relationships to people in power; and information power, which comes from the possession of valuable information.

14.8 Identify common strategies for organizational politics.

Political strategies commonly used in organizations include doing favors, making good impressions, cultivating the grapevine, supporting the manager, avoiding negativism, and giving praise.

Key Terms			
conflict, *p. 372*	smoothing, *p. 377*	power, *p. 389*
frustration, *p. 373*	conflict	position power, *p. 389*
conflict management,	resolution, *p. 378*	personal power, *p. 389*
p. 376	organizational politics,	
compromise, *p. 377*	*p. 388*	

Review and Discussion Questions

1. On her first day on the job, Jenna's supervisor introduces her incorrectly to her co-workers, mispronouncing her name. For several weeks after that, Jenna's co-workers, intending to be friendly, pronounce her name incorrectly. Jenna goes

along with it, not wanting to jeopardize her new relationships. Finally, feeling uncomfortable about the situation, Jenna approaches her supervisor about the mistake. Is this a positive or negative conflict? Why?

2. Imagine that you are a production supervisor at a hand-tool manufacturer such as Snap-On Tools. Your manager says, "I know you were looking forward to your trip to Hawaii next month, but we will be stepping up production, and three new employees will be joining your group. I wish you would consider staying to make sure everything goes smoothly."

   a. What is the nature of the conflict in this situation? In other words, what two goals is it impossible for you to achieve at the same time?

   b. List as many possible solutions as you can think of to resolve this conflict.

   c. Which solution do you prefer? How could you present it to your manager?

3. Identify each of the following conflicts as interpersonal, structural, or strategic.

   a. The production department's goal is to make parts faster, and the quality-control department wants slower production to reduce the rate of defects.

   b. A salesperson does not take telephone messages for her co-workers because she believes she has a better chance of being the department's top performer when her co-workers do not return their calls.

   c. One cashier at a supermarket is much older than the others, and he does not spend much time talking to them. The other cashiers criticize him for not being a team player.

4. Why does compromise generally leave both parties feeling frustrated?

5. Rachel Gonzalez supervises servers at a restaurant. She knows that many of them are upset about the hours she has scheduled for them, but she believes that people should not argue. So she avoids discussing the subject, and she posts the following week's schedule just before leaving for the day. What is wrong with this approach to conflict management? What would be a better way to manage this conflict?

6. Ron Herbst is a supervisor in a clinical laboratory. He has noticed that one employee regularly comes to work in a surly mood. The employee is getting his work done on time, but his attitude seems to be affecting other employees.

   a. How can Ron initiate conflict resolution with this employee? How should he describe the problem?

   b. If the employee responds to Ron's statement of the problem by saying, "I'm fine. Don't worry about me," what should the supervisor do and say?

7. The managers of a soft-drink bottling company decide that production workers will each learn several jobs and rotate among those jobs. They have read that this technique improves productivity, and they believe that workers will be happier because their jobs will be more interesting. However, many of the employees and their supervisors are reluctant to make the change. What could explain their resistance?

8. What are the factors that can affect the success of a change?

9. How can a supervisor overcome resistance to change?

10. What is the primary reason that efforts for change within an organization fail? What can a supervisor do to avoid this failure and ensure that change will be successful?

11. What are the two basic sources of power available to a supervisor? Which do you think is more important to the supervisor's effectiveness? Why?

12. Which type or types of power is the supervisor exerting in each of the following situations?

   a. A sales supervisor promises a $50 bonus to the first salesperson to close a sale this week.

   b. One day a month, a supervisor orders in pizza and joins her employees for lunch. The employees look forward to these gatherings because the supervisor joins them in recounting funny stories, and she usually is able to fill them in on some management plans.

   c. A supervisor in the bookkeeping department got his job thanks to a referral from his father, who regularly plays racquetball with the company's president. Since the supervisor was hired, the president has visited the bookkeeping department a couple of times to see how he is doing. The manager of the department is very diplomatic in his criticism of the supervisor.

   d. When the employees in a word-processing department make many errors per page or a particularly glaring error, their supervisor posts the offending pages on the department bulletin board to shame the employees into performing better.

13. A sales supervisor believes she could be more effective if she had more cooperation from the company's credit department. If the credit of potential customers could be approved faster, her salespeople could close more sales. What political tactics would you recommend that the sales supervisor consider to get more cooperation from the credit department?

PART TWO: SKILL-BUILDING

YOU SOLVE THE PROBLEM

Reflecting back on page 371, imagine that the employees in a department at Best Buy's headquarters have been asking to participate in the ROWE program. Working as a group and taking the perspective of the group's supervisor, list the conflicts you would expect to arise if the supervisor doesn't agree to this change. Mark each change on the list with *i* for intrapersonal, *I* for interpersonal, *Su* for structural, or *Sa* for strategic. Then make a similar list for the conflicts you would expect to arise if the supervisor does agree to the change.

Imagine that an employee needs to leave early twice in one week in order to attend parent–teacher conferences. Have one member of your group play the employee and one play the supervisor. Role-play how the employee would arrange for the time under a traditional work arrangement. Then have two group members play the same roles assuming it is three months after adoption of ROWE. Does one arrangement seem more comfortable for the employee? For the supervisor? If you were the supervisor, which arrangement would you prefer?

Problem-Solving Case: *National Conflict Resolution Center Helps Find Win–Win Solutions*

For people embroiled in a conflict, it can be hard to envision a solution that both sides can accept. Anger and hurt feelings may overwhelm their ability to think about the problem and consider everyone's point of view. In those sticky situations, many organizations turn to the National Conflict Resolution Center (NCRC), based in San Diego, California.

The NCRC operates three divisions. Its Business Center offers organizations the services of a panel of experts to mediate disputes among co-workers, employees, and management or between customers and companies. Without choosing sides, the mediator leads a conversation in which the parties to the dispute discuss the problem and develop a solution that all parties agree upon. The Training Institute trains individuals in how to mediate conflict resolution. And the San Diego Mediation Center helps neighborhood and community organizations resolve local disputes. Through these services, the NCRC has taken a lead in resolving thousands of disputes.

Mediation services cost $250 to $400 an hour—a lot of money, but far less than the cost of hiring a lawyer to resolve a conflict in court. Another benefit of mediation in the workplace is that it moves people from thinking of each other as opponents. If an employee has a complaint about a supervisor, both people will be upset at work each day the dispute continues. Productive work relationships become difficult. When the individuals enter mediation, they begin thinking about solving the problem instead of fighting about it. In addition, the NCRC has found that participants gain a feeling of empowerment, because they are contributing to the outcome of the mediation process.

The NCRC's Training Institute has lessons that apply to any supervisor. Most basically, the mediator's job is about listening. Robin Seigle, director of the Business Center, explained, "So often people get into conflicts because of an assumption they make about the other person." When the parties to a conflict sit down with a mediator, they hear each other's description of the situation, and often they learn that their assumptions were not completely correct. Trainer Barbara Filner gives examples of the kinds of questions a mediator asks: "What were you hoping would happen? What were you thinking about?" By understanding what the participants want under ideal circumstances, the mediator can help them work toward a resolution

that helps them. According to one of the institute's trainees, Brandon Moreno, effective listening also helps calm people down. Moreno said that since he has received mediation training, people tell him "that I'm able to engage people, and get them to open up and build rapport."

One of the NCRC's clients is the federal Transportation Safety Administration (TSA). Following the attacks of September 11, 2001, anxiety about the safety of air travel rose, and TSA screeners have been under pressure to keep passengers safe. At the same time, screening procedures can feel invasive and inconvenient to passengers. Under these stressful conditions, conflicts can erupt. Training in mediation skills has helped TSA employees deal with stressed-out coworkers, as well as with nervous and impatient travelers.

1. Based on this description of mediators, what kinds of supervisory skills are needed for mediating a conflict? Consider the various skills described in Chapters 1 through 14.

2. When might a supervisor benefit from using trained mediators, such as NCRC mediators, rather than mediating a conflict him- or herself? Why would the experts be important in these situations?

3. Suppose you are a supervisor of TSA screeners in an airport. You notice that a passenger is visibly upset about having her carry-on bag inspected. As you step near the table where the inspection is taking place, you hear her say, "You're going to make me miss my flight." Would you get involved in this situation? If so, how? What, if any, mediation skills from NCRC might help you?

Source: Pat Broderick, "Defusing Disputes: National Conflict Resolution Center Seeks Solutions to Variety of Problems and Issues," *San Diego Business Journal*, March 7, 2005, downloaded from Business & Company Resource Center, http://galenet .galegroup.com; National Conflict Resolution Center, "Frequently Asked Questions," www.ncrconline.com, accessed September 5, 2006.

Knowing Yourself

What Is Your Conflict-Handling Style?

Everyone has a basic style for handling conflicts. To identify the strategies you rely upon most, indicate how often each of the following statements applies to you. Next to each statement, write *5* if the statement applies often, *3* if the statement applies sometimes, and *1* if the statement applies never.

When I differ with someone . . .

_____ 1. I explore our differences, not backing down, but not imposing my view either.

_____ 2. I disagree openly, then invite more discussion about our differences

_____ 3. I look for a mutually satisfactory solution.

_____ 4. Rather than let the other person make a decision without my input, I make sure I am heard and also that I hear the other person out.

_____ 5. I agree to a middle ground rather than look for a completely satisfying solution.

_____ 6. I admit I am half wrong rather than explore our differences.

_____ 7. I have a reputation for meeting a person halfway.

_____ 8. I expect to say about half of what I really want to say.

_____ 9. I give in totally rather than try to change another's opinion.

_____ 10. I put aside any controversial aspects of an issue.

_____ 11. I agree early on, rather than argue about a point.

_____ 12. I give in as soon as the other party gets emotional about an issue.

_____ 13. I try to win the other person over.

_____ 14. I try to come out victorious, no matter what.

_____ 15. I never back away from a good argument.

_____ 16. I would rather win than end up compromising.

To score your responses, add your total score for each of the following sets of statements:

Set A: statements 1–4   Set C: statements 9–12

Set B: statements 5–8   Set D: statements 13–16

A score of 17 or more on any set is considered high. Scores of 12 to 16 are moderately high. Scores of 8 to 11 are moderately low. Scores of 7 or less are considered low. Each set represents a different strategy for conflict management:

- Set A = Collaboration (I win, you win).
- Set B = Compromise (Both win some, both lose some).
- Set C = Accommodation (I lose, you win).
- Set D = Forcing/domination (I win, you lose).

Source: From *Supervision: Managerial Skills for a New Era,* by Von der Embse. Copyright © 1987 Pearson Education, Inc. Reprinted by permission of Pearson Education Inc., Upper Saddle River, NJ.

Pause and Reflect

1. For which conflict management style is your score highest? Are you surprised?

2. What are some advantages of the style(s) you use most often? Some disadvantages?

3. Do you think you would benefit from becoming more comfortable with conflict management styles for which your score was low?

Class Exercise   **Resolving Conflict**

This exercise is based on role-playing. One class member takes the role of a supervisor, and two class members act as the employees. The supervisor leaves the room for five minutes as the employees act out the following scenario:

Pat and Chris work in a word-processing department, preparing reports and letters on computer terminals. Pat trips on the cord to Chris's computer, shutting it off and erasing the project Chris was working on. Chris is upset. If Chris does not finish the job by the end of the day, the failure to meet a deadline will show up on Chris's performance records and hurt Chris's chances for getting a raise. In addition, the manager who requested the work will be upset, because this is an important project.

This is a basic scenario; the employees should be creative in adding details. For example, they can address the following questions:

- Did Pat erase the files on purpose?
- Has Pat ever done something like this before?
- Do these employees otherwise get along?
- Are communications in general and this conflict in particular complicated by some difference between the employees (age, sex, race, etc.)?

After the two class members have acted out the scene, the supervisor returns to the room, and the role-playing continues as the employees bring their conflict to the supervisor. The supervisor should try to manage the conflict.

When the supervisor is satisfied with how the conflict has been handled (or when 10 minutes have elapsed), the class discusses the following questions:

1. Did the supervisor understand the real problem? If not, what was the real problem?
2. Did the supervisor and employees solve the problem? Was the solution a good one?
3. In what ways was the supervisor effective in resolving the conflict? How could the supervisor improve his or her approach?
4. What other possible solutions might the supervisor and employees have considered?

Building Supervision Skills

Exercising Power to Bring about Change

Divide the class into teams of five or more students. Each student receives a card marked with the type of power he or she possesses: legitimate, referent, expert, coercive, reward, connection, or information. (If the group is small, some students may have two types of power.) Students should not show other team members which card they have. Each team has a goal: to convince the rest of the class that changing something (e.g., holding class in the evening instead of the afternoon) is a good idea.

Using the different kinds of power, each team presents its idea to the class. Afterward, the class should discuss how effective each team was, how effective individual team members were, and what type of power was most effective in getting people to respond positively to the idea of change.

Appendix **A**

Organizational Politics

Most students of supervision find the study of organizational politics intriguing. Perhaps this topic owes its appeal to the antics of Hollywood's corporate villains who get their way by stepping on anyone and everyone. As we will see, however, organizational politics includes, but is not limited to, dirty dealing. Organizational politics is an ever-present and sometimes annoying feature of modern work life.

"According to 150 executives from large U.S. companies, office politics wastes an average of 20 percent of their time; that's 10 weeks a year."[1] On the other hand, organizational politics is often a positive force in modern work organizations. Skillful and well-timed politics can help you get your point across, neutralize resistance to a key project, or get a choice job assignment.

Roberta Bhasin, a district manager for US West, put organizational politics into perspective by observing the following:

> Most of us would like to believe that organizations are rationally structured, based on reasonable divisions of labor, a clear hierarchical communication flow, and well-defined lines of authority aimed at meeting universally understood goals and objectives.
>
> But organizations are made up of *people* with personal agendas designed to win power and influence. The agenda—the game—is called corporate politics. It is played by avoiding the rational structure, manipulating the communications hierarchy, and ignoring established lines of authority. The rules are never written down and seldom discussed.
>
> For some, corporate politics are second nature. They instinctively know the unspoken rules of the game. Others must learn. Managers who don't understand the politics of their organizations are at a disadvantage, not only in winning raises and promotions, but even in getting things *done*.[2]

We explore this important and interesting area by (1) defining the term *organizational politics*, (2) identifying three levels of political action, (3) discussing eight specific political tactics, (4) considering a related area called *impression management*, and (5) discussing how to manage organizational politics.

DEFINITION AND DOMAIN OF ORGANIZATIONAL POLITICS

"*Organizational politics* involves intentional acts of influence to enhance or protect the self-interest of individuals or groups."[3] An emphasis on *self-interest* distinguishes this form of social influence.

Supervisors are endlessly challenged to achieve a workable balance between employees' self-interests and organizational interests. When a proper balance exists, the pursuit of self-interest may serve the organization's interests. Political behavior becomes a negative force when self-interests erode or defeat organizational interests. For example, researchers have documented the political tactic of filtering and distorting information flowing up to the boss. This self-serving practice puts the reporting employees in the best possible light.[4]

Uncertainty Triggers Political Behavior

Political maneuvering is triggered primarily by *uncertainty*. Five common sources of uncertainty within organizations are

1. Unclear objectives.
2. Vague performance measures.
3. Ill-defined decision processes.
4. Strong individual or group competition.[5]
5. Any type of change.

Regarding this last source of uncertainty, organization development specialist Anthony Raia noted, "Whatever we attempt to change, the political subsystem becomes active. Vested interests are almost always at stake and the distribution of power is challenged."[6]

Thus, we would expect a field sales representative, striving to achieve an assigned quota, to be less political than a supervisor working on a variety of projects. While some supervisors stake their career success on hard work, competence, and a bit of luck, many do not. These people attempt to gain a competitive edge through some combination of the political tactics discussed below. Meanwhile, the salesperson's performance is measured in actual sales, not in terms of being friends with the boss or taking credit for others' work. Thus, the supervisor would tend to be more political than the field salesperson because of greater uncertainty about management's expectations.

Because employees generally experience greater uncertainty during the earlier stages of their careers, are junior employees more political than more senior ones? The answer is yes, according to a survey of 243 employed adults in upstate New York. In fact, one senior employee nearing retirement told the researcher: "I used to play political games when I was younger. Now I just do my job."[7]

Three Levels of Political Action

Although much political maneuvering occurs at the individual level, it also can involve group or collective action. Figure A illustrates three different levels of political action: the individual level, the coalition level, and the network level.[8] Each level has its distinguishing characteristics. At the individual level, personal self-interests are pursued by the individual. The political aspects of coalitions and networks are not so obvious, however.

People with a common interest can become a political coalition by fitting the following definition. In an organizational context, a *coalition* is an informal group bound together by the *active* pursuit of a *single* issue. Coalitions may or may not coincide with formal group membership. When the target issue is resolved (a sexually harassing supervisor is fired, for example), the coalition disbands. Experts note that political coalitions have "fuzzy boundaries," meaning they are fluid in membership, flexible in structure, and temporary in duration.[9]

Coalitions are a potent political force in organizations. Consider the situation Charles J. Bradshaw faced in a finance committee meeting at Transworld Corporation; Bradshaw, president of the company, opposed the chairman's plan to acquire a $93 million nursing home company:

> [The senior vice president for finance] kicked off the meeting with a battery of facts and figures in support of the deal. "Within two or three minutes, I knew I had lost," Bradshaw concedes. "No one was talking directly to me, but all statements addressed my opposition. I could tell there was a general agreement around the board table. . . ."
> Then the vote was taken. Five hands went up. Only Bradshaw voted "no."[10]

FIGURE A
Levels of
Political Action
in Organization

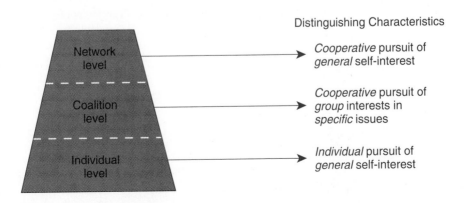

Distinguishing Characteristics

→ *Cooperative* pursuit of *general* self-interest

→ *Cooperative* pursuit of *group* interests in *specific* issues

→ *Individual* pursuit of *general* self-interest

After the meeting, Bradshaw resigned his $530,000-a-year position, without as much as a handshake or good-bye from the chairman. In Bradshaw's case, the finance committee was a formal group that temporarily became a political coalition aimed at sealing his fate at Transworld. Coalitions on the corporate boards of American Express, IBM, and General Motors also ousted the heads of those giant companies.

A third level of political action involves networks.[11] Unlike coalitions, which pivot on specific issues, networks are loose associations of individuals seeking social support for their general self-interests. Politically, networks are people oriented, while coalitions are issue oriented. Networks have broader and longer-term agendas than do coalitions. For instance, Avon's Hispanic employees have built a network to enhance the members' career opportunities.

POLITICAL TACTICS

Anyone who has worked in an organization has firsthand knowledge of blatant politicking. Blaming someone else for your mistake is an obvious political ploy. But other political tactics are more subtle. Researchers have identified a range of political behavior.

One landmark study, involving in-depth interviews with 87 managers from 30 electronics companies in Southern California, identified eight political tactics.

TABLE A Eight Common Political Tactics in Organizations

Source: Adapted from R. W. Allen, D. L. Madison, I. W. Porter, P. A. Renwick, and B. T. Mayes, "Organizational Politics: Tactics and Characteristics of Its Actors," *California Management Review,* Fall 1979, pp. 77–83.

Political Tactic	Percentage of Managers Mentioning Tactic	Brief Description of Tactic
1. Attacking or blaming others	54%	Used to avoid or minimize association with failure. Reactive when scapegoating is involved. Proactive when goal is to reduce competition for limited resources.
2. Using information as a political tool	54	Involves the purposeful withholding or distortion of information. Obscuring an unfavorable situation by overwhelming superiors with information.
3. Creating a favorable image (impression management)	53	Dressing/grooming for success. Adhering to organizational norms and drawing attention to one's successes and influence. Taking credit for others' accomplishments.
4. Developing a base of support	37	Getting prior support for a decision. Building others' commitment to a decision through participation.
5. Praising others (ingratiation)	25	Making influential people feel good ("apple polishing").
6. Forming power coalitions with strong allies	25	Teaming up with powerful people who can get results.
7. Associating with influential people	24	Building a support network both inside and outside the organization.
8. Creating obligations (reciprocity)	13	Creating social debts ("I did you a favor, so you owe me a favor").

TABLE B   Are You Politically Naive, Politically Sensible, or a Political Shark?

Source: Reprinted from J. K. Pinto and O. P. Kharbanda, "Lessons for an Accidental Profession," *Business Horizons,* March–April 1995. Copyright © 1995, with permission from Elsevier.

Characteristics	Naive	Sensible	Sharks
Underlying attitude	Politics is unpleasant.	Politics is necessary.	Politics is an opportunity.
Intent	Avoid at all costs.	Further departmental goals.	Self-serving and predatory.
Techniques	Tell it like it is.	Network; expand connections: use system to give and receive favors.	Manipulate; use fraud and deceit when necessary.
Favorite tactics	None—the truth will win out.	Negotiate, bargain.	Bully; misuse information: cultivate and use "friends and other contacts."

Top-, middle-, and supervisors were represented about equally in the sample. According to the researchers: "Respondents were asked to describe organizational political tactics and personal characteristics of effective political actors based upon their accumulated experience in all organizations in which they had worked."[12] Listed in descending order of occurrence, the eight political tactics that emerged were

1. Attacking or blaming others.
2. Using information as a political tool.
3. Creating a favorable image. (Also known as impression management.)[13]
4. Developing a base of support.
5. Praising others (ingratiation).
6. Forming power coalitions with strong allies.
7. Associating with influential people.
8. Creating obligations (reciprocity).

Table A describes these political tactics and indicates how often each reportedly was used by the interviewed managers.

The researchers distinguished between reactive and proactive political tactics. Some of the tactics, such as scapegoating, were *reactive* because the intent was to *defend* one's self-interest. Other tactics, such as developing a base of support, were *proactive* because they sought to *promote* the individual's self-interest.

What is your attitude toward organizational politics? How often do you rely on the various tactics in Table A? You can get a general indication of your political tendencies by comparing your behavior with the characteristics in Table B. Would you characterize yourself as politically *naive,* politically *sensible,* or a political *shark*? How do you think others view your political actions? What are the career, friendship, and ethical implications of your political tendencies?[14]

IMPRESSION MANAGEMENT

Impression management is defined as "the process by which people attempt to control or manipulate the reactions of others to images of themselves or their ideas."[15] This encompasses how one talks, behaves, and looks. Most impression management attempts are directed at making a good impression on relevant others. But, as we will see, some employees strive to make a bad impression. For purposes of conceptual clarity, we will focus on upward impression management, or trying to impress one's immediate supervisor. Still, it is good to remember that anyone can be the intended target of impression management. Parents, teachers, peers, employees, and customers are all fair game when it comes to managing the impressions of others.

A Conceptual Crossroads

Impression management is an interesting conceptual crossroads involving self-monitoring and organizational politics.[16] Perhaps this explains why impression management has gotten active research attention in recent years. High self-monitoring employees ("chameleons" who adjust to their surroundings) are likely to be more inclined to engage in impression management than would low self-monitors. Impression management also involves the systematic manipulation of attributions. For example, a supervisor will look good if upper management is encouraged to attribute organizational successes to her efforts and attribute problems and failures to factors beyond her control. Impression management definitely fits into the realm of organizational politics because of an overriding focus on furthering one's *self-interests*.

Making a Good Impression

If you "dress for success," project an upbeat attitude at all times, and avoid offending others, you are engaging in favorable impression management—particularly so if your motive is to improve your chances of getting what you want in life.[17] There are questionable ways to create a good impression, as well. For instance, Stewart Friedman, director of the University of Pennsylvania's Leadership Program, recently offered this gem:

> Last year, I was doing some work with a large bank. The people there told me a story that astounded me: After 7 p.m., people would open the door to their office, drape a spare jacket on the back of their chair, lay a set of glasses down on some reading material on their desk—and then go home for the night. The point of this elaborate gesture was to create the illusion that they were just out grabbing dinner and would be returning to burn the midnight oil.[18]

Impression management often strays into unethical territory.

An analysis of the influence attempts reported by a sample of 84 bank employees (including 74 women) identified three categories of favorable upward impression management tactics.[19] Favorable upward impression management tactics can be *job focused* (manipulating information about one's job performance), *supervisor focused* (praising and doing favors for one's supervisor), and *self-focused* (presenting oneself as a polite and nice person). Take a short break from your studying to complete the questionnaire in Table C. How did you do? A moderate amount of upward impression management is a necessity for the average supervisor today. Too little, and busy managers are liable to overlook some of your valuable contributions when they make job assignment, pay, and promotion decisions. Too much, and you run the risk of being branded a "schmoozer," a "phony," and other unflattering things by your co-workers.[20] Excessive flattery and ingratiation can backfire by embarrassing the target person and damaging one's credibility. Also, the risk of unintended insult is very high when impression management tactics cross gender, racial, ethnic, and cultural lines.[21] International experts warn:

> The impression management tactic is only as effective as its correlation to accepted norms about behavioral presentation. In other words, slapping a Japanese subordinate on the back with a rousing "Good work, Hiro!" will not create the desired impression in Hiro's mind that the expatriate intended. In fact, the behavior will likely create the opposite impression.[22]

TABLE C   **How Much Do You Rely on Upward Impression Management Tactics?**

Source: Adapted from S. J. Wayne and G. R. Ferris, "Influence Tactics, Affect, and Exchange Quality in Supervisor-Subordinate Interactions: A Laboratory Experiment and Field Study," *Journal of Applied Psychology,* October 1990, pp. 487–499.

Instructions

Rate yourself on each item according to how you behave on your current (or most recent) job. Add your circled responses to calculate a total score. Compare your score with our arbitrary norms.

Job-Focused Tactics	Rarely Very Often
1. I play up the value of my positive work results and make my supervisor aware of them.	1—2—3—4—5
2. I try to make my work appear better than it is.	1—2—3—4—5
3. I try to take responsibility for positive results, even when I'm not solely responsible for achieving them.	1—2—3—4—5
4. I try to make my negative results not as severe as they initially appear to my supervisor.	1—2—3—4—5
5. I arrive at work early and/or work late to show my supervisor I am a hard worker.	1—2—3—4—5

Supervisor-Focused Tactics	
6. I show an interest in my supervisor's personal life.	1—2—3—4—5
7. I praise my supervisor on his/her accomplishments.	1—2—3—4—5
8. I do personal favors for my supervisor that I'm not required to do.	1—2—3—4—5
9. I compliment my supervisor on her or his dress or appearance.	1—2—3—4—5
10. I agree with my supervisor's major suggestions and ideas.	1—2—3—4—5

Self-Focused Tactics	
11. I am very friendly and polite around my supervisor.	1—2—3—4—5
12. I try to act as a model employee around my supervisor.	1—2—3—4—5
13. I work harder when I know my supervisor will see the results.	1—2—3—4—5

Total score = _____

Arbitrary Norms

13–26   Free agent
27–51   Better safe than sorry
52–65   Hello, Hollywood

Making a Poor Impression

At first glance, the idea of consciously trying to make a bad impression in the workplace seems absurd. But an interesting new line of impression management research has uncovered both motives and tactics for making oneself look bad. In a survey of the work experiences of business students at a large northwestern U.S. university, more than half "reported witnessing a case of someone intentionally looking bad at work."[23] Why? Four motives came out of the study:

(1) Avoidance: Employee seeks to avoid additional work, stress, burnout, or an unwanted transfer or promotion. (2) Obtain concrete rewards: Employee seeks to obtain a pay raise or a desired transfer, promotion, or demotion. (3) Exit: Employee seeks to get laid off, fired, or suspended, and perhaps also to collect unemployment or worker's compensation. (4) Power: Employee seeks to control, manipulate, or intimidate others, get revenge, or make someone else look bad.[24]

TABLE D   Some Practical Advice on Managing Organizational Politics

Source: Reprinted from D. R. Beeman and T. W. Sharkey, "The Use and Abuse of Corporate Politics," *Business Horizons*, March–April 1987. Copyright © 1987, with permission from Elsevier.

To Reduce System Uncertainty

Make clear what are the bases and processes for evaluation.

Differentiate rewards among high and low performers.

Make sure the rewards are as immediately and directly related to performance as possible.

To Reduce Competition

Try to minimize resource competition among managers.

Replace resource competition with externally oriented goals and objectives.

To Break Existing Political Fiefdoms

Where highly cohesive political empires exist, break them apart by removing or splitting the most dysfunctional subgroups.

If you are an executive, be keenly sensitive to managers whose mode of operation is the personalization of political patronage. First, approach these persons with a directive to "stop the political maneuvering." If it continues, remove them from the positions and preferably, the company.

To Prevent Future Fiefdoms

Make one of the most important criteria for promotion an apolitical attitude that puts organizational ends ahead of personal power ends.

Within the context of these motives, *unfavorable* upward impression management makes sense.

Five unfavorable upward impression management tactics identified by the researchers are as follows:

- *Decreasing performance*—restricting productivity, making more mistakes than usual, lowering quality, neglecting tasks.
- *Not working to potential*—pretending ignorance, having unused capabilities.
- *Withdrawing*—being tardy, taking excessive breaks, faking illness.
- *Displaying a bad attitude*—complaining, getting upset and angry, acting strangely, not getting along with co-workers.
- *Broadcasting limitations*—letting co-workers know about one's physical problems and mistakes (both verbally and nonverbally).[25]

Recommended ways to manage employees who try to make a bad impression can include affording them more challenging work, greater autonomy, better feedback, supportive leadership, clear and reasonable goals, and a less stressful work setting.[26]

MANAGING ORGANIZATIONAL POLITICS

Organizational politics cannot be eliminated. A supervisor would be naive to expect such an outcome. But political maneuvering can and should be managed to keep it constructive and within reasonable bounds. Harvard's Abraham Zaleznik put the issue this way: "People can focus their attention on only so many things. The more it lands on politics, the less energy—emotional and intellectual—is available to attend to the problems that fall under the heading of real work."[27]

An individual's degree of politicalness is a matter of personal values, ethics, and temperament. People who are either strictly nonpolitical or highly political generally pay a price for their behavior. The former may experience slow promotions and feel left out, while the latter may run the risk of being called self-serving and lose their credibility. People at both ends of the political spectrum may be considered poor team players. A moderate amount of prudent political behavior generally is considered a survival tool in complex organizations. Experts remind us that

> . . . political behavior has earned a bad name only because of its association with politicians. On its own, the use of power and other resources to obtain your objectives is not inherently unethical. It all depends on what the preferred objectives are.[28]

With this perspective in mind, the practical steps in Table D are recommended. Notice the importance of reducing uncertainty through standardized performance evaluations and clear performance–reward linkages.[29] Measurable objectives are the supervisor's first line of defense against negative expressions of organizational politics.[30]

Part Four Video Cases

MANAGER'S HOT SEAT VIDEO 1: "PERSONAL DISCLOSURE: CONFESSION COINCIDENCE"

Even if a supervisor is talented in leading, solving problems, and motivating the people who work for him or her, sometimes the supervisor still will have to confront "problem employees." While many times the issues experienced by the employees are not work related, their work can be affected. In such a situation, it is appropriate and necessary for a supervisor to step in. Read the following scenario describing the video segment "Personal Disclosure: Confession Coincidence," and then watch the video selection. After this, answer the three questions that pertain to the specific challenges in this supervisor–employee situation.

SCENARIO

Kathleen Doerder has set up a meeting with an employee, Janeen Winthrop, who has a recent record of poor performance. Although Kathleen has met with Janeen on two prior occasions to discuss the issue, her poor performance and frequent absences and tardiness have continued. Janeen's behavior has disrupted work flow, negatively affecting a number of colleagues within the department.

QUESTIONS

1. Pages 322–324 talk about certain counseling techniques a supervisor may use in a discussion with an employee: *directive* and *nondirective counseling*. How does Kathleen use both of these techniques in her meeting with Janeen?
2. Look at the sections "Confrontation of the Troubled Employee" and "Guidelines for Effective Discipline" in Chapter 12. What are four things Kathleen does correctly by the book's standards in regard to handling her issues with Janeen?
3. How do you think Kathleen could have used discipline to help stop Janeen's problems at work earlier?

MANAGER'S HOT SEAT VIDEO 2: "CHANGE: MORE PAIN THAN GAIN"

While supervisors sometimes have to deal with an employee's *personal* problems affecting his or her work, supervisors may also have to intervene in problems *between* employees, especially when company changes occur. The next video, "Change: More Pain than Gain," shows a supervisor discussing a conflict two employees are experiencing after a company merger. Read the following scenario describing the video selection, and then watch the video selection. After this, answer the three questions that pertain to the specific challenges in this supervisor–employee situation.

SCENARIO

A national media communications company, MediaWorld, has acquired a regional communications company, Franklin/Warner. As a result of the merger, the regional marketing department has been reorganized, combining the staff of the two organizations. Carlos Alarcon, the vice president of marketing, is overseeing the restructuring process and having difficulty with people shifting roles, sharing assignments, and adapting to new hierarchies.

The manager meets with two department members, Rita Finch and Juan Rayes, who are very displeased with the new changes. The employees eventually ask the manager to leave the company and head a start-up—funding is already in place.

QUESTIONS

1. Chapter 14 lists four types of conflict that may arise within an individual or between individuals or groups. After listening to Juan and Rita's situation, choose two of the four types of conflict and show how they are present in the dispute the two are having with the company merger.

2. Look at Figure 14.4 and trace Carlos's steps in responding to the conflict. Does Carlos complete all the steps? If yes, why? If no, explain where in the chart his response breaks down.

3. What do you believe Juan and Rita came into the meeting expecting to achieve?

Supervision and Human Resources

Successful Supervisors Select, Train, and Appraise Employees
Digital Vision/Getty Images

Chapter **Fifteen**

Selecting Employees

Learning Objectives

After you have studied this chapter, you should be able to:

15.1 Discuss common roles for supervisors in the selection process.

15.2 Distinguish between job descriptions and job specifications and explain how they help in selecting employees.

15.3 List possible sources of employees.

15.4 Identify the steps in the selection process.

15.5 Discuss how a supervisor should go about interviewing candidates for a job.

15.6 Define types of employment tests.

15.7 Summarize the requirements of antidiscrimination laws.

15.8 Explain how hiring decisions are affected by the Americans with Disabilities Act (ADA).

15.9 Describe the requirements of the Immigration Reform and Control Act (IRCA) of 1986.

You may have a technology or a product that gives you an edge, but your people determine whether you develop the next winning technology or product.

—*Steve Ballmer, CEO, Microsoft*

A Supervisor's Problem: Finding Fun Workers for Cold Stone Creamery

When Amanda S. Kodz opened a Cold Stone Creamery franchise in Spring Township, Pennsylvania, she needed 30 part-time employees. So Kodz held . . . auditions?

Usually, we think of an audition as a way to select entertainers, such as musicians or actors, and in fact, entertainers are just what Cold Stone is looking for too. The employees at a Cold Stone Creamery are expected to do much more than scoop ice cream into bowls or cones. They are supposed to carry out the company's mission to "put smiles on people's faces by delivering the Ultimate Ice Cream Experience." That experience includes employees inviting customers to select a flavor of ice cream and choose from a variety of mix-ins—fruit, nuts, and candies—which the employees add to the ice cream on frozen granite stones behind the display cases, using small spades to blend the mixture together while the customers watch. If customers appreciate their cheerful work enough to deposit a tip in the jar by the cash register, employees break into one of the songs in the Cold Stone Creamery songbook—familiar tunes blended with ice-cream–related lyrics.

In Spring Township, Kodz set out to fill these jobs by holding group auditions. With 5 to 15 applicants (generally young people) at a time, she invites them into a room where they break the ice by taking turns sharing an interesting fact about themselves. Next, they are invited to imitate "something or someone funny."

Finally, they sing from the company songbook, together and in smaller groups. The process is about more than playing around. Kodz says that by watching applicants carry out these activities, she learns "how the kids work together in a team and if they will mesh well."

So far, it is a staffing formula that has helped Cold Stone expand from its first location in Tempe, Arizona, to a chain of more than 1,000 stores throughout the United States.

Finding and keeping employees is particularly challenging for filling the part-time, entry-level jobs that are common in the food-service industry. Yet a supervisor's success depends largely on the supervisor's people.

QUESTIONS

1. What does Kodz need to do to find enough people interested in working for her at Cold Stone Creamery?

2. How can Kodz determine which applicants will truly provide the fun experience that is behind Cold Stone Creamery's success?

Sources: David A. Kostival, "Cold Stone Creamery Opens First Berks County Site," *Reading (Pa.) Eagle*, February 8, 2005, downloaded at Business & Company Resource Center, http://galenet.galegroup.com; Cold Stone Creamery, "Cold Stone Franchise History," www.coldstonecreamery.com, accessed September 7, 2006.

Amanda Kodz uses an elaborate interviewing process because she knows that her franchise's success depends on her employing the kind of people who will maintain Cold Stone Creamery's positive image. In addition to this practical business reason, careful hiring is important because it must meet several legal requirements. Thus, it is in a supervisor's best interests to do a good job in helping select employees. Enthusiastic, well-qualified people are more likely to deliver high quality than indifferent, unqualified people. This is especially true in today's leaner organizations; when fewer employees are getting the work done, each employee has a greater impact on the organization's overall performance. However, a recent survey found that almost half of newly hired employees lose their job within a year and a half. Often, those employees had the necessary technical skills but didn't fit in well—for instance, because they lacked motivation or couldn't accept feedback.[1]

This chapter addresses the supervisor's role in selecting employees, which often entails working with the organization's human resources (or personnel) department. The chapter explains how supervisors define needed qualities of jobs and employees by preparing job descriptions and job specifications. It describes how organizations can recruit candidates and decide whom to hire. Finally, it addresses some legal issues that supervisors and others in the organization must be aware of when hiring.

ROLES IN THE SELECTION PROCESS

A supervisor's role in the selection process can vary greatly from one organization to another. In small organizations, a supervisor may have great latitude in selecting employees to fill vacant positions. Other organizations have formal procedures that require the human resources department to do most of the work, with the supervisor simply approving the candidates recommended. In most cases, a supervisor works to some extent with a human resources department. In this way, a supervisor benefits from that department's skills in screening and interviewing candidates and from its familiarity with laws regarding hiring practices.

As described in Chapter 3, a growing number of organizations expect employees to work in teams. At the least, the use of teamwork requires the selection of employees who will be effective team members. A supervisor might therefore try to identify candidates who are cooperative and skilled in problem solving or who have helped a team achieve good results in the past. In other cases, the use of teamwork dramatically changes a supervisor's role in the selection process. When teamwork takes the form of self-managing work teams, a team generally interviews candidates and recommends or selects new team members. A supervisor, as team leader, needs to understand the principles of selection so that he or she can coach employees in carrying out the process. The organization's human resources staff supports the team, rather than the individual supervisor.

SELECTION CRITERIA

To select the right employees, the supervisor, team (if applicable), and human resources department have to be clear about what jobs need to be filled and what kind of people can best fill those jobs. A supervisor or self-managed team provides this information by preparing job descriptions and job specifications, consulting with the human resources department as needed. Table 15.1 details basic kinds of information to include in job descriptions and job specifications.

job description
A listing of the characteristics of a job, including the job title, duties involved, and working conditions

A **job description** is a listing of the characteristics of the job—that is, the observable activities required to carry out the job. A written job description typically includes the title of the job, a general description, and details of the duties involved. As you will see subsequently in this chapter, it is important for the job description to spell out the essential duties of the job. When appropriate, a job

TABLE 15.1
Contents of the Job Description and Job Specification

Source: From *Modern Management*, 8th edition, by Samuel C. Certo. Copyright © 2000 Pearson Education, Inc. Reprinted by permission of Pearson Education, Inc., Upper Saddle River, NJ.

Job Description	Job Specification
Job title	Education
Location	Experience
Job summary	Availability to work overtime
Duties, including backup functions during peak periods	Skills—technical, physical, communication, and interpersonal
Productivity and quality standards	Training
Machines, tools, and equipment	Judgment and initiative
Materials and forms used	Emotional characteristics
Relationships—supervision and teams, if any	Physical effort
Working conditions	Unusual sensory demands (sight, smell, hearing, etc.)

FIGURE 15.1
Sample Job Description: Maintenance Mechanic

Source: From Raymond Noe, John R. Hollenbeck, Barry Gerhart, and Patrick M. Wright, *Human Resource Management: Gaining a Competitive Advantage*, 4th ed., 2003 Copyright © 2003, The McGraw-Hill Companies.

General Description of Job General maintenance and repair of all equipment used in the operations of a particular district. Includes the servicing of company vehicles, shop equipment, and machinery used on job sites.

1. *Essential Duty (40%): Maintenance of Equipment*
   Tasks: Keep a log of all maintenance performed on equipment. Replace parts and fluids according to maintenance schedule. Regularly check gauges and loads for deviances that may indicate problems with equipment. Perform nonroutine maintenance as required. May involve limited supervision and training of operators performing maintenance.

2. *Essential Duty (40%): Repair of Equipment*
   Tasks: Requires inspection of equipment and a recommendation that a piece be scrapped or repaired. If equipment is to be repaired, mechanic will take whatever steps are necessary to return the piece to working order. This may include a partial or total rebuilding of the piece using various hand tools and equipment. Will primarily involve the overhaul and troubleshooting of diesel engines and hydraulic equipment.

3. *Essential Duty (10%): Testing and Approval*
   Tasks: Ensure that all required maintenance and repairs have been performed and that they were performed according to manufacturer specifications. Approve or reject equipment for readiness to use on a job.

4. *Essential Duty (10%): Maintain Stock*
   Tasks: Maintain inventory of parts needed for the maintenance and repair of equipment. Responsible for ordering satisfactory parts and supplies at the lowest possible cost.

Nonessential Functions
   Other duties as assigned.

description may also describe working conditions. Figure 15.1 shows a sample job description for a maintenance technician.

A **job specification** is a listing of the characteristics desirable in the person performing the job. These include four types of characteristics:[2]

job specification
A listing of the characteristics desirable in the person performing a given job, including educational and work background, physical characteristics, and personal strengths

1. *Knowledge*—Information required to perform the tasks in the job description.
2. *Skills*—Proficiency in carrying out the tasks in the job description.
3. *Abilities*—General enduring capabilities required for carrying out the tasks in the job description.
4. *Other characteristics*—Any additional characteristics related to the successful performance of the essential tasks (e.g., personality characteristics).

A job specification for the maintenance technician's position therefore would include characteristics such as knowledge about the company's vehicles and shop equipment, skills in repairing these things, broad mechanical abilities, and a commitment to high-quality work.

A supervisor (or team with the supervisor's coaching) should provide the information that applies to a particular job. If a job description and job specification already exist for a position, a supervisor should review them to make sure they reflect current needs. Preparing and using these materials helps a supervisor base hiring decisions on objective criteria—how well each candidate matches the requirements of the job. Without them, a supervisor risks hiring people solely because he or she likes them better than others.

RECRUITMENT

recruitment
A process of identifying people interested in holding a particular job or working for the organization

To select employees, the supervisor and human resources department need candidates for the job. Identifying people interested in holding a particular job or working for the organization is known as **recruitment,** which involves looking for candidates from both inside and outside the organization.

Looking Inside the Organization

Many employees are eager to accept a promotion. Less commonly, employees welcome the variety of working in a new department or at a different task even when the transfer does not involve more money or prestige. These changes can be a source of motivation for employees.

Increased motivation is only one way the organization benefits from promotions and transfers. In addition, the promoted or transferred employees start the new job already familiar with the organization's policies and practices. It may be easier to train new people for entry-level jobs than to hire outsiders to fill more complex positions.

To find employees who are interested in and qualified for a vacant position, a supervisor or human resources department recruits within the organization. Internal recruitment is conducted in two basic ways: job postings and employee referrals. A job posting is a list of the positions that are vacant in the organization. Typically, a job posting gives the title of the job, the department, and the salary range. In addition, a supervisor's employees may be able to recommend someone for the job—friends or relatives who do not currently work for the organization or qualified candidates they have met through trade or professional groups. Some organizations pay employees a bonus for referrals if the candidate is hired.

Looking Outside the Organization

A growing organization will especially need to look outside the organization for at least some of its employees. New hires are less familiar with the organization, but they bring fresh ideas and skills that the organization may lack. The basic ways to identify qualified candidates outside the organization are through advertising, employment agencies, online job sites and blogs, and schools.

Help-wanted advertisements are a popular way to recruit candidates for a job. Most people at some time or another read the want ads in their local newspapers to see what jobs are available. Organizations also can advertise in journals and magazines directed toward a specialized audience. For example, a research laboratory looking for a writer might advertise in *Technical Communications,* and a manufacturer looking for an engineer to develop new products might advertise in *Design News.* Advertising in these kinds of specialized publications limits the recruiting to candidates with a background (or at least an interest) in the relevant field.

Employment agencies seek to match people looking for a job with organizations looking for employees. These agencies may be government run, in which case they do not charge for their services, or private. Many private agencies charge the employer for locating an employee, and some charge the person searching for a job. In either case, the agency collects a fee only when someone is hired. Using an agency makes sense when the organization lacks the time or expertise to carry out an effective recruiting effort. (In addition, organizations are increasingly relying on agencies to recruit all types of temporary employees.) Agencies also help screen candidates, a step in the selection process described in the next section.

Online recruiting has become a popular way to match candidates to jobs. Posting job openings online is convenient and inexpensive for reaching candidates around the nation. Employers can list information about job openings on their own Web sites or through job-listing services such as Monster, CareerBuilder, and Yahoo HotJobs. Some companies have supplemented this information with podcasts, allowing candidates to download audio files describing opportunities to work at the company, along with other information such as tips for interviewing. Consulting firm Bain & Company tried out podcasting as an efficient way to reach graduates of the Indian Institute of Management for jobs at its new facility in India. Response was so positive that Bain decided to expand its use of podcasts to recruit from additional schools in other countries.[3] Another Internet tool, the blog (Web log or online personal journal), is becoming a resource for online recruiting. Blogs specializing in a particular industry or company sometimes include links to relevant information about employment. Knowing that Internet users may be looking for jobs online, some recruiters are writing their own blogs to attract these job hunters. At Microsoft, recruiter Heather Hamilton writes about careers at the company; in one week, Hamilton's blog had 25,000 page views. Hamilton commented, "I could be on the phone all day every day and not reach that many people."[4] When companies use these tools, they should have systems in place for responding to applicants.

Depending on the requirements of the job, a supervisor might want employees who recently have graduated from high school, a community college, a trade school, a prestigious university, or some other type of school. In such cases, the organization might seek job candidates through schools of the desired type. Large organizations that expect to hire many recent graduates sometimes send recruiters to talk to students at the targeted schools. Many schools also arrange various kinds of listings of employers who are interested in hiring. Recruiting through schools is a way to limit candidates to those with the desired educational background. A growing number of companies are extending these efforts to internships. Hiring a student for a summer is a way to see how that person handles a variety of situations. In a recent survey, employers said they offer full-time jobs to more than half of their interns.[5]

Humphrey Chen needed to hire employees for ConneXus, a service through which radio listeners can identify the titles and artists of songs using their cell phones. Chen took a novel route to recruiting through MIT, his alma mater. He e-mailed the head administrative assistant in the computer science department and asked her to mention some of ConneXus's current job openings in the next mass e-mail she sent to students alerting them to class and exam schedules. A week later, Chen had hired four MIT students, three as interns and one full-time.[6]

THE SELECTION PROCESS

In recent years, organizations typically have had many more candidates than they have needed to fill their vacant positions. Thus, once an organization has identified candidates for a job, it begins the major work: the selection process. Through this process, the supervisor and human resources department seek the person who is best qualified to fill a particular job. Figure 15.2 shows how the various steps in the selection process narrow the field of candidates. Usually the human resources department does the initial screening, and the supervisor makes the final decision.

FIGURE 15.2
The Selection Process

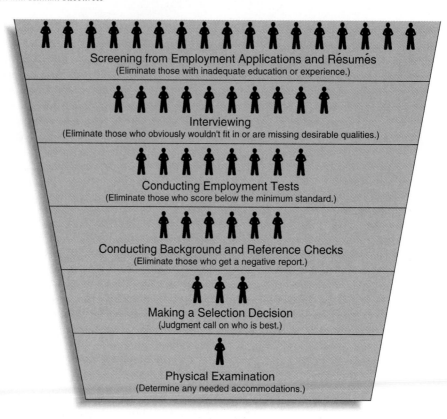

Screening from Employment Applications and Résumés
(Eliminate those with inadequate education or experience.)

Interviewing
(Eliminate those who obviously wouldn't fit in or are missing desirable qualities.)

Conducting Employment Tests
(Eliminate those who score below the minimum standard.)

Conducting Background and Reference Checks
(Eliminate those who get a negative report.)

Making a Selection Decision
(Judgment call on who is best.)

Physical Examination
(Determine any needed accommodations.)

In the traditional approach shown in Figure 15.2, the field of candidates narrows as the organization screens applications and résumés, interviews candidates, and conducts tests and background checks. A growing number of organizations have begun using computer technology to make this process more efficient, as described in the "Supervisory Skills" box. Often, the technology provides testing and automated interviews before any candidates are invited to in-person interviews.

Screening Employment Applications and Résumés

Candidates for a job respond to recruitment by filling out an employment application or sending in a résumé. Figure 15.3 shows a sample employment application. The first stage of the selection process is to review the applications or résumés to screen out candidates who are unqualified or less qualified than others. The objective of screening is to narrow the pool of applicants to the number that the supervisor or human resources department wants to interview for the job.

Usually someone in the human resources department takes care of the screening process, comparing the applications or résumés with the job description prepared by the supervisor and eliminating the candidates who obviously fail to meet the qualifications called for in the job description.

Supervisors seldom participate actively in this process, but sometimes they know of a candidate whom they would like to consider. In such cases, the name of this person is sent to the human resources department with the request that the person be included in the selection process. Rarely does the human resources department screen out a person that a supervisor wants included.

SUPERVISORY SKILLS

SELECTING EMPLOYEES

TECHNOLOGY INNOVATIONS UPDATE THE SELECTION PROCESS

More and more job hunters are likely to interact with a computer before they write or talk to anyone at the company for which they want to work. For example, many supermarkets are installing systems offered by Unicru and HR3 that allow would-be employees to submit applications through the stores' Web sites. Unicru also sets up kiosks in stores so job candidates can apply online while in the store. HR3 supplements its Internet system with a toll-free phone number that candidates can use to submit their background information.

Both systems collect data from applicants and match applicants' characteristics to available jobs. The systems sort the candidates by ZIP code, helping each store in a grocery chain select the nearest qualified candidates. HR3's system emphasizes honesty and drug use, screening out candidates who admit to problem behaviors; the company also measures attitudes toward work, helping employers screen out candidates who resist supervision or hard work.

These automated systems also help with the next step of the selection process. They create a set of interview questions suitable for each candidate, based on the information the candidate provided. The questions are designed to meet the requirements of employment laws, helping supervisors limit interviews to appropriate topics.

For many kinds of jobs, testing may be automated as well. An automated test can be an inexpensive way to narrow the field of candidates and make interviewing more efficient because the company invites only qualified employees. For example, if someone applies for the job of office assistant, the computer that takes the application can provide tests of keyboarding, alphabetic filing, and proofreading skills. The supervisor would then interview only the candidates whose test results show they are the fastest at keyboarding and the most accurate at filing and proofreading. Other widely used tests measure skill at using spreadsheets, carrying out financial tasks, and computing solutions to math problems.

When employers use automated testing to narrow the field, they have more confidence that all the remaining candidates they interview will possess many of the basic skills required to carry out a job. Interviews can focus more on how well the employee will fit with the organization's values and style of working. When used properly, these systems not only are more efficient but also should help the employer make the right choices, hiring people who will make a valuable contribution and be committed to their work.

Sources: Tom Weir, "Primary Candidates," *Progressive Grocer,* February 15, 2004, downloaded from Business & Company Resource Center, http://galenet.galegroup.com; Adam Agard, "How Savvy Employers Interview Only the Most Highly Skilled Applicants," *Supervision,* July 2003, downloaded from InfoTrac, http://web1.infotrac .galegroup.com; Adam Agard, "Pre-Employment Skills Testing: An Important Step in the Hiring Process," *Supervision,* June 2003, downloaded from InfoTrac, http://web1.infotrac.galegroup.com.

Interviewing Candidates

When the human resources department has narrowed the list of candidates to a few people, the next step is to interview them. Objectives of interviewing include narrowing the search for an employee by assessing each candidate's interpersonal and communication skills, seeing whether the supervisor and employee are comfortable with each other, and learning details about the information the candidate has provided on the application or résumé. In addition, each candidate has an opportunity to learn about the organization, which helps him or her make a decision about accepting a job offer.

Learning and carrying out effective interviewing practices sometimes may seem like a lot of trouble to a supervisor. When tempted to look for shortcuts, a supervisor should bear in mind the significance of selection interviews. For any new employee, the organization will spend tens, maybe hundreds, of thousands of dollars on salary, benefits, and training. Thus, collecting the information needed to

FIGURE 15.3   Sample Employment Application

OPTIONAL APPLICATION FOR FEDERAL EMPLOYMENT – OF 612

Form Approved
OMB No. 3206-0219

Section A – Applicant Information

*Use Standard State Postal Codes (abbreviations). If outside the United States of America, and you do not have a military address type or print "OV" in the State field (Block 6c) and fill in the Country field (Block 6e) below, leaving the Zip Code field (Block 6d) blank.

1. Job title in announcement	2. Grade(s) applying for	3. Announcement number

4a. Last name	4b. First and middle names	5. Social Security Number

6a. Mailing address*	7. Phone numbers (include area code if within the United States of America)
	7a. Daytime
6b. City 6c. State 6d. Zip Code	7b. Evening

6e. Country (if not within the United States of America)

8. Email address (if available)

Section B – Work Experience

Describe your paid and nonpaid work experience related to this job for which you are applying. Do not attach job description.

1. Job title (if Federal, include series and grade)

2. From *(mm/yyyy)*	3. To *(mm/yyyy)*	4. Salary per $	5. Hours per week

6. Employer's name and address	7. Supervisor's name and phone number
	7a. Name
	7b. Phone

8. May we contact your current supervisor?   Yes ☐   No ☐
If we need to contact your current supervisor before making an offer, we will contact you first.

9. Describe your duties and accomplishments

Section C – Additional Work Experience

1. Job title (if Federal, include series and grade)

2. From *(mm/yyyy)*	3. To *(mm/yyyy)*	4. Salary per $	5. Hours per week

6. Employer's name and address	7. Supervisor's name and phone number
	7a. Name
	7b. Phone

8. Describe your duties and accomplishments

U.S. Office of Personnel Management
Previous edition usable

NSN 7540-01-351-9178
50612-101

Page 1 of 2

Optional Form 612
Revised December 2002

FIGURE 15.3 (*continued*)

Section D – Education

1. Last High School (HS)/GED school. Give the school's name, city, state, ZIP Code (if known), and year diploma or GED received:

2. Mark highest level completed: Some HS ☐   HS/GED ☐   Associate ☐   Bachelor ☐   Master ☐   Doctoral ☐

3. Colleges and universities attended. Do not attach a copy of your transcript unless requested.			Total Credits Earned		Major(s)	Degree (if any), Year Received
			Semester	Quarter		
3a. Name						
City	State	Zip Code				
3b. Name						
City	State	Zip Code				
3c. Name						
City	State	Zip Code				

Section E – Other Qualifications

Job-related training courses (give title and year). Job-related skills (other languages, computer software/hardware, tools, machinery, typing speed, etc.). Job-related certificates and licenses (current only). Job-related honors, awards, and special accomplishments (publications, memberships in professional/honor societies, leadership activities, public speaking, and performance awards). Give dates, but do **not** send documents unless requested.

Section F – General

1a. Are you a U.S. citizen?   Yes ☐   No ☐   ➡   1b. If no, give the Country of your citizenship

2a. Do you claim veterans' preference?   No ☐   Yes ☐   ➡   If yes, mark your claim of 5 or 10 points below.

2b.   5 points ☐   ➡   Attach your *Report of Separation from Active Duty* (DD 214) or other proof.

2c.   10 points ☐   ➡   Attach an *Application for 10-Point Veterans' Preference* (SF 15) and proof required.

3. Were you ever a Federal civilian employee?   No ☐   Yes ☐   ➡   If yes, list highest civilian grade for the following:

3a. Series	3b. Grade	3c. From *(mm/yyyy)*	3d. To *(mm/yyyy)*

4. Are you eligible for reinstatement based on career or career-conditional Federal status?   No ☐   Yes ☐
    If requested in the vacancy announcement, attach *Notification of Personnel Action* (SF 50), as proof.

Section G – Applicant Certification

I certify that, to the best of my knowledge and belief, all of the information on and attached to this application is true, correct, complete, and made in good faith. I understand that false or fraudulent information on or attached to this application may be grounds for not hiring me or for firing me after I begin work, and may be punishable by fine or imprisonment. I understand that any information I give may be investigated.

1a. Signature	1b. Date *(mm/dd/yyyy)*

U.S. Office of Personnel Management   NSN 7540-01-351-9178   Page 2 of 2   Optional Form 612
Previous edition usable   50612-101   Revised December 2002

421

make the right hiring decision is at least as important as doing the research for making other investments of comparable size. Viewed in this light, carefully preparing for and conducting a selection interview is well worth the time and effort.

Who Should Interview?

The initial interview with a job candidate frequently is conducted by someone in the human resources department. Depending on an organization's policies and practices, a supervisor may participate in later interviews. For this reason, a supervisor can benefit from understanding how to interview effectively.

An organization may support the use of teamwork by having teams (or several team members) interview job candidates. Team interviews provide evidence of how a candidate interacts with a team. At Gates Rubber's plant in Siloam Springs, Arkansas, a job candidate meets first with the personnel department, then with a group of three people from different parts of the plant. Plant manager Burt Hoefs explains, "We're evaluating communications skills, work attitudes, and general confidence levels. Since all the work of the plant is done in teams, we're also focusing on an applicant's ability to respond well in a group setting."[7] When interviews are conducted by teams, a supervisor needs to combine skills in interviewing with skills in facilitating group processes (see Chapters 3 and 9).

Technology also is modifying the supervisor's role as interviewer by automating standard parts of the interview—or even the entire process. Capital One, for example, employs thousands of call center employees for its credit-card operations. To make hiring more efficient, the company conducts automated phone interviews. A candidate for a call center job phones a toll-free number, at which the company provides a series of recorded screening questions. Candidates who pass the screening visit a regional office, where they take tests and provide further information. The tests include a phone simulation during which the candidate listens and replies to problems such as complaints from angry customers. The company's computer system evaluates the background information and test responses to arrive at a hiring decision. This process minimizes the supervisor's role as interviewer but speeds up the process and has selected a more productive group of employees. The supervisor's role in selecting Capital One employees is limited to defining the job requirements that the computer system will incorporate into its automated decision making.[8]

Preparation for the Interview

As shown in Figure 15.4, the interviewer should begin the interviewing process by preparing. To prepare for an interview, an interviewer should review the job description and develop a realistic way to describe the job to candidates. An interviewer also should review an applicant's résumé or job application and consider whether the information given there suggests some specific questions to ask. Suppose the interviewer wants to know why a candidate chose a particular major

FIGURE 15.4   The Interviewing Process

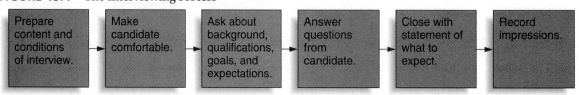

Prepare content and conditions of interview. → Make candidate comfortable. → Ask about background, qualifications, goals, and expectations. → Answer questions from candidate. → Close with statement of what to expect. → Record impressions.

in school or switched fields—say, leaving a job as a salesperson to become a mechanic. The interviewer also will want to inquire about any time gaps between jobs. Finally, the interviewer should arrange for an interview location that meets the conditions described in the next section.

Interview Conditions

Most job candidates feel at least a little nervous. This can make it hard for an interviewer to tell what a person would be like on the job. Therefore, it is important for an interviewer to conduct the interview under conditions that put a candidate at ease. Good interview conditions include privacy and freedom from interruptions. Seating should be comfortable. Some interviewers sit next to the candidate at a small table, rather than behind a desk, to create a less formal, more equal setting. Candidates also can be put at ease by offering them a cup of coffee and taking a minute or two for comments on a general, noncontroversial topic such as the weather.

Privacy is sometimes difficult for a supervisor to arrange. Many supervisors do not have an office with a door to close. If possible, a supervisor should arrange to use a conference room or someone else's office. At the very least, a supervisor interviewing in a cubicle should hang a "Do Not Disturb" sign outside.

Content of the Interview

After making the candidate comfortable, an interviewer should begin by asking general questions about the candidate's background and qualifications. An interviewer also should ask a candidate about his or her goals and expectations concerning the job. The following questions are among those most commonly asked:[9]

- Why do you want to work for our company?
- What kind of career do you have planned?
- What have you learned in school to prepare for a career?
- What are some of the things you are looking for in a company?
- How has your previous job experience prepared you for a career?
- What are your strengths? Weaknesses?
- Why did you attend this school?
- What do you consider to be one of your most worthwhile achievements?
- Are you a leader? Explain.
- How do you plan to continue developing yourself?
- Why did you select your major?
- What can I tell you about my company?

When the interviewer has asked enough questions to gauge the candidate's suitability for the position, he or she should give the candidate a chance to ask questions. Not only can this opportunity help the candidate learn more, but it also can give the interviewer insight into the candidate's understanding and areas of concern. For more guidance on preparing and using interview questions, see the "Tips from the Firing Line box".

The interviewer should close the session by telling the candidate what to expect regarding the organization's decision about the job, such as a telephone call in a week or a letter by the end of the month. As soon as the candidate has left, the interviewer should jot down notes of his or her impressions about the candidate. Memories fade fast, especially when the interviewer meets many candidates.

TIPS FROM THE FIRING LINE

INTERVIEWING JOB CANDIDATES

Duane Lakin, a psychologist in Wheaton, Illinois, says there's a reason most supervisors struggle with interviewing job candidates: "Most people are not very good at interviewing because it is not their primary job." Besides getting some training in how to interview, use the following suggestions to improve your interview technique with applicants:

- Identify the skills and behaviors you want in an employee. If you already have successful employees holding similar positions in your group, think about what qualities and behaviors make them successful.

- Based on the preceding step, ask each candidate to give examples of using those skills or behaviors. For example, if you need someone who is a team player, you might ask, "In your last job, how did you handle disagreements with other members of your team?"

- When applicants give examples, especially when they are vague, use follow-up questions to probe for details. In the previous example of handling disagreements, you might follow up with, "What happened when you tried that? What did you learn from that experience?" If someone says their greatest weakness is "perfectionism," ask how perfectionism caused problems in a previous job.

- When candidates talk in generalities (for instance, "I'm a people person" or "I'm quality focused"), ask what they mean. Ask them to give an example.

That will help you determine whether the candidate's words mean what you hope they do.

- Keep your probing pleasant, and encourage candidates to relax. The idea is to encourage them to be frank and honest about themselves, not defensive.

- Compare candidates against the job description and job specification, not against one another. Choose one who meets or exceeds your requirements, not just the best of an unsatisfactory group. If no one meets your requirements, keep looking.

One company that applies these tips is the Golden Corral restaurant chain. The company has established interview questions based on behaviors that are desirable for its jobs. Golden Corral provides interviewers with follow-up questions that help them compare candidates' work experiences with the core skills the company has identified for each position. On the basis of information provided by the candidates, the company scores them on various traits, including their education level and the restaurant volume they have worked with in the past. According to Golden Corral's senior vice president of operations, Lance Trenary, "We . . . insist that we don't hire anyone below [a preset] level."

Sources: Kathryn Tyler, "Train for Smarter Hiring," *HRMagazine*, May 2005; Steve Weinberg, "Determining the Formula for Hiring the Best People," *Kitchen & Bath Design*, June 2006; Cord Cooper, "Deal with People Effectively: Snare a Top-Notch Team," *Investor's Business Daily*, October 6, 2005, all downloaded from Business & Company Resource Center, http://galenet.galegroup.com.

The questions an interviewer asks must be relevant to performance of the job. This means that an interviewer may not ask questions about the candidate's age, sex, race, marital status, children, religion, or arrest (as opposed to conviction) record. For example, an interviewer may not ask, "So, are you planning to have any children?" or "What nationality is that name?" Such questions violate antidiscrimination laws, described subsequently in this chapter. Table 15.2 identifies many permissible and impermissible questions. A supervisor who is in doubt about whether a particular question is allowable should check with the human resources department before asking it.

Interviewing Techniques

structured interview
An interview based on questions the interviewer has prepared in advance

The person who conducts the interview may choose to make it structured, unstructured, or a combination of the two. A **structured interview** is one based on questions an interviewer has prepared in advance. By referring to the list of questions, the interviewer covers the same material with each candidate. In an

TABLE 15.2 **Permissible and Impermissible Questions for Selection Interviews**

Sources: Richard D. Irwin, Inc., "Management Guidelines," Appendix 2, December 1, 1991; Robert N. Lussier, *Supervision: A Skill-Building Approach* (Homewood, IL: Irwin, 1989), pp. 254–55; Janine S. Pouliot, "Topics to Avoid with Applicants," *Nation's Business*, July 1992, pp. 57–58; Gary Dessler, *Human Resource Management* (Upper Saddle River, NJ: Prentice Hall, 2000), p. 234.

Category	Interviewer May Ask	Interviewer May Not Ask
Name	Current legal name; whether candidate has ever worked under another name	Maiden name; whether candidate has ever changed his or her name; preferred courtesy title (e.g., Ms., Miss, Mrs.)
Address	Current residence; length of residence	Whether candidate owns or rents home, unless it is a bona fide occupational qualification (BFOQ) for the job; name and relationship of person with whom applicant resides
Age	Whether the candidate meets a minimum age requirement set by law (e.g., being 21 to serve alcoholic beverages)	Candidate's age; to see a birth certificate; how much longer candidate plans to work before retiring; dates of attending elementary or high school; how applicant feels about working for a younger (or older) boss
Sex	Candidate's sex if it is a BFOQ (e.g., a model or restroom attendant)	Candidate's sex if it is not a BFOQ
Marital and family status	Whether the candidate can comply with the work schedule (must be asked of both sexes if at all)	Candidate's marital status; whether the candidate has or plans to have children; other family matters; information about child care arrangements; questions about who handles household responsibilities; whether candidate is seeking work just to supplement the household income
National origin, citizenship, race, color	Whether the candidate is legally eligible to work in the United States; whether the candidate can prove this, if hired	Candidate's national origin, citizenship, race, or color (or that of relatives); how candidate feels about working with or for people of other races
Language	List of languages the candidate speaks or writes fluently; whether the candidate speaks or writes a specific language if it is a BFOQ	Language the candidate speaks off the job; how the candidate learned a language
Arrests and convictions	Whether the candidate has been convicted of a felony; other information if the felony is job related	Whether the candidate has ever been arrested; information about a conviction that is not job related
Height and weight	No questions	Candidate's height or weight
Health history and disabilities	Whether the candidate is able to perform the essential functions of the job; how (with or without accommodation) the candidate can perform essential job functions	Whether the candidate is disabled or handicapped; how candidate became disabled; health history; whether the candidate smokes; whether the candidate has AIDS or is HIV positive
Religion	Whether the candidate is a member of a specific religious group when it is a BFOQ; whether the candidate can comply with the work schedules	Religious preference, affiliations, or denomination; name of applicant's priest, pastor, rabbi, or other religious leader
Personal finances	Credit rating if it is a BFOQ	Candidate's credit rating; other information about personal finances, including assets, charge accounts; whether candidate owns a car

(continued)

TABLE 15.2 Permissible and Impermissible Questions for Selection Interviews (*continued*)

Category	Interviewer May Ask	Interviewer May Not Ask
Education and work experience	Job-related education and experience	Education and experience that are not job related
References	Names of people willing to provide references; names of people who suggested that the candidate apply for the job	Reference from a religious leader
Military service	Information about job-related education and experience; whether candidate was dishonorably discharged	Dates and conditions of discharge; eligibility for military service; experience in foreign armed services
Organizations	List of memberships in job-related organizations such as unions or professional or trade associations	Memberships in any organizations that are not job related and would indicate race, religion, or other protected group; candidate's political affiliation

unstructured interview
An interview in which the interviewer has no list of questions prepared in advance but asks questions on the basis of the applicant's responses

unstructured interview, an interviewer has no list of questions prepared in advance but thinks of questions on the basis of an applicant's responses. An unstructured interview gives an interviewer more flexibility but makes it harder to be sure that each interview covers the same material.

A practical way to combine these two approaches is to prepare a list of questions that must be covered with each candidate. Then, an interviewer who wants the candidate to clarify a response to a particular question asks a follow-up question such as, "Please tell me about your reasons for handling the problem that way." An interviewer need not ask the questions in the order written so long as all of them are covered eventually. On the basis of a candidate's comments, an interviewer may want to move to a question further down the list. Even though the format varies somewhat from candidate to candidate, this approach ensures that an interviewer does not omit important topics from some interviews.

open-ended question
A question that gives the person responding broad control over the response

closed-ended question
A question that requires a simple answer, such as yes or no

Within either a structured or an unstructured interview, an interviewer may ask questions that are open-ended or closed-ended. An **open-ended question** is one that gives the person responding broad control over the response. A **closed-ended question** is one that requires a simple answer, such as yes or no. An example of an open-ended question is, "What experiences in your past job will help you carry out this one?" Examples of closed-ended questions are, "Did you use an iMac computer on your last job?" and "Which shift do you prefer to work?"

Open-ended questions tend to be more useful in interviewing, because they lead a candidate to provide more information. For example, to learn how thoroughly a candidate has researched the job—an indication of how serious he or she is about the position—an interviewer might ask, "What would you look for if you were hiring a person for this position?" Loretta M. Flanagan, who directs Westside Future, an organization dedicated to reducing infant mortality, uses open-ended questions to learn about the human relations and problem-solving skills of job candidates. For example, she might pose this question to a candidate for a case worker position:

> A high, drug-using pregnant woman comes into the office, wanting immediate help. She has missed two previously scheduled appointments. The case manager is busy with another client and has a second client arriving in 20 minutes. How do you handle such competing demands?

Of course, there is no single correct answer. Flanagan looks for candidates who show an ability to set priorities and to justify the course of action selected.

Because the candidate decides how to answer an open-ended question, the answer sometimes is not clear enough or specific enough. Then, the interviewer will want to probe for more details, possibly saying, "Can you give me an example of that?" or "What do you mean when you say your last job was 'too stressful'?"

Problems to Avoid

When conducting an interview, a supervisor needs to avoid some common errors in judgment. One of these is making decisions based on personal biases. For example, a supervisor may dislike earrings on men or certain hairstyles worn by women. However, these characteristics are unlikely to indicate how well a candidate would carry out a job. Likewise, being a friend or relative of a supervisor is not a good predictor of job performance. Making a hiring decision on the basis of these and other biases can lead an interviewer to exclude the person who is best qualified.

halo effect
The practice of forming an overall opinion on the basis of one outstanding characteristic

Another source of errors is the **halo effect,** which means forming an overall opinion on the basis of one outstanding characteristic. For example, many people will evaluate someone's personality on the basis of the person's handshake. "She has a firm grasp," an interviewer might think with regard to a candidate. "I can tell that she's energetic, decisive, and gets along well with people," when the candidate might not have any of those desirable traits. An interviewer needs to look for evidence of each trait, not just lump them all together.

A supervisor also needs to avoid giving candidates a misleading picture of the organization. If a candidate seems desirable, the supervisor may be tempted to describe the organization in glowing terms so that the candidate will want to work there. But if the reality is not so wonderful, the new employee is bound to be disappointed and angry. He or she may even quit. On the other hand, within the bounds of realism, a supervisor should give a good impression of the organization and its people. Even a candidate who is not the best person for the job may someday be a customer or be in a position to influence other people's views about the organization.

Administering Employment Tests

From a résumé or employment application, it is relatively easy to see where a candidate worked and went to school, but how can you tell whether a candidate really has the skills to do the job? Just because Pete Wong works for the marketing division at a candy company does not mean he knows how to sell candy (maybe that is why he wants to leave). Just because Ruth Petersen got a college degree in engineering does not mean she can apply her knowledge to working with a team to prepare the layout of an actual plant.

One way to see whether employees have the necessary skills is to administer an employment test. A variety of employment tests are available:

aptitude test
A test that measures a person's ability to learn skills related to the job

- A test that measures an applicant's ability to learn skills related to the job is known as an **aptitude test.**

proficiency test
A test that measures whether the person has the skills needed to perform a job

- An applicant may take a **proficiency test** to determine whether he or she has the skills needed to perform a job. An example is a word-processing test for a secretarial position.

psychomotor test
A test that measures a person's strength, dexterity, and coordination

- For jobs that require physical skills, such as assembling, an applicant may take a **psychomotor test,** which measures a person's strength, dexterity, and coordination.

- Some organizations also use personality tests, which identify various personality traits. Kurt Swogger used personality tests to hire and reassign employees in the research and development group at Dow Chemical's plastics division. By sorting out employees who are inclined to dream up big new ideas, those who see opportunities to modify existing products, and those who are more in tune with customers and markets, Swogger transformed a plodding division into a team of innovators. The focus on personality has resulted in more new ideas from the division as well as a faster pace of development.[10]

- Finally, some organizations test for drug use, especially where the use of drugs by employees poses a serious safety risk, as in the case of machine operators or pilots. Such tests are controversial, but they are legal in most states.[11]

Usually the human resources department handles the testing of applicants.

Some tests contain language or other biases that make them easier for employees of one ethnic group than another. Using these tests could violate antidiscrimination laws, described subsequently in this chapter. Similarly, personality tests can pose a problem if they identify candidates with mental or emotional disabilities.[12] Discrimination laws cover individuals with a disability if they are able to perform the job's required functions. Therefore, if a supervisor wants to use employment tests, the tests should be reviewed by the human resources department or an outside expert to ensure that they are not discriminatory.

Despite these restrictions, employers can be creative in·devising employment tests that focus on job requirements. Candidates for fire-fighting jobs with Central Pierce Fire & Rescue, near Tacoma, Washington, participate in role-play simulations to see how well they handle citizens who are upset. The organization's human resources manager, Karen Johnson, says some candidates handle the role-players beautifully, but "We've had a couple candidates throw [a role-player] out the door"—figuratively speaking, it is hoped.[13] The Chrysler Group of DaimlerChrysler has candidates for assembly jobs undergo tests of how quickly and accurately they assemble parts. Candidates for professional and management jobs are given tests in which they must react to memos and phone calls. They may also engage in role-playing where they coach someone playing the role of an employee with a job-related problem.[14]

Conducting Background and Reference Checks

Many résumés and job applications contain false information. In a recent survey by the Society of Human Resource Management of its members, 90 percent of the respondents said they had discovered falsified information while checking a reference. At the top of the list of things job applicants lie about are their former employers, the length of time they worked there, their past salaries and titles, and their criminal records. According to one expert, "People put their best foot forward on their résumé, but on an application and in interviews, they often forget the image they constructed for themselves."[15]

A basic way to verify that the information on a job application or résumé is correct is to check references. Not only can checking an employee's background save the organization from hiring an unqualified person, but it also can protect the organization from lawsuits. The courts have held employers responsible for crimes committed by an employee whose background at the time of hire was not investigated reasonably, with the result that the organization hired someone with a history of misdeeds for a position where he or she could do harm.[16]

A supervisor or a member of the human resources department may call or write to schools and former employers, or the organization may pay an employee screening company to do a background check. The relatively small fee to use one of these companies can be money well spent by an organization that is too small

FIGURE 15.5
**Examples of
Restrictions on
Background Checks**

Source: Privacy Rights
Clearinghouse,
"Employment Background
Checks," Fact Sheet 16,
rev. June 2004,
www.privacyrights.org.

Do not request:

Bankruptcies after 10 years

Arrest and civil lawsuit records

Accounts placed for collection
  (7 years old or older)

**Do not consider in
hiring decisions:**

Bankruptcies

Workers' compensation

Medical history

**Get permission
first:**

Education records

Certain military
  service information

for a human resources staff. In recent years, heightened security concerns and the easy availability of personal data on the Internet have increased the use of background checks. However, supervisors should be aware that various state and federal laws protect individuals' privacy and limit the types of information employers may use and the way they gather information. For some examples, see Figure 15.5. When there is any doubt, the supervisor should get advice from a qualified expert before initiating a background check.

Applicants may give several kinds of references:

- *Personal references*—people who will vouch for the applicant's character.
- *Academic references*—teachers or professors who can describe the applicant's performance in school.
- *Employment references*—former employers who can verify the applicant's work history.

Most people can think of a friend or teacher who can say something nice about them, so the main use of personal and academic references is to screen out the few cases of people who cannot do so.

Previous employers are in the best position to discuss how an applicant performed in the past. However, to avoid lawsuits from former employees, many organizations have a policy of giving out very little information about past employees. Often a background check will yield only that the applicant did in fact hold the stated position during the dates indicated. Some employers may be willing to discuss the applicant's performance, salary, promotions, and demotions. Because previous employers are cautious about what they disclose, a telephone call to a former supervisor may be more fruitful than a written request for information. People are sometimes willing to make off-the-record statements over the telephone that they will not commit to in writing.

Making the Selection Decision

The final decision of whom to hire is usually up to the supervisor. Typically, more than one person will survive all the preceding steps of the screening process. As a result, the final decision is usually a judgment call.

A supervisor can handle the dilemma of several well-qualified people being considered for a position by looking for additional relevant selection criteria. In practice, hiring decisions often reflect a variety of issues, including the supervisor's comfort level. Supervisors sometimes choose an employee like themselves so that they will feel comfortable; they also might select a person whose strengths differ from and thus balance their own strengths. Research into the success secrets of *Fortune* magazine's "100 best companies to work for" found that these companies emphasized selecting employees whose values and beliefs matched those of the company. This means supervisors should consider not only the technical requirements of the job itself but also such strengths as the employee's enthusiasm and desire to contribute to the team. At the same time, supervisors should keep in mind that people who share the same values will be diverse in other ways. For example, it may benefit the team to have some people who seek compromise and others who challenge old ways by arguing for fresh ideas.[17] A supervisor can improve his or her selections by applying the principles of effective decision making covered in Chapter 9.

When a supervisor has selected the candidate to hire, the human resources department or supervisor offers the job to the candidate. The person who offers the job is responsible for negotiating pay and fringe benefits and settling on a starting date. If none of the candidates a supervisor has identified seem satisfactory, no candidate has to be picked and the recruiting process can be repeated. Perhaps the organization can look in new places or try to attract better candidates by offering more money.

Requesting a Physical Examination

In the past, many organizations have required that job candidates pass a physical examination. However, since Congress passed the Americans with Disabilities Act (described later in this chapter), experts have advised that employers request a physical exam only after a job offer is made.[18] A physical examination after the job offer helps the organization determine whether the person is physically able to fulfill job requirements, yet the timing of the exam reduces the risk that someone will sue the company for refusing to hire him or her because of a disability. Another use of the physical exam is to determine whether the person is eligible for any life, health, and disability insurance that the company offers as benefits.

An illness, disability, or pregnancy may not be used as the basis for denying a person a job unless it makes the person unable to perform the essential functions of the job. If a physical examination suggests a condition that may interfere with the person's ability to perform these essential functions, the company—very likely someone in the human resources department—should ask the candidate how it can adapt the equipment or job to accommodate that person. Because of these limitations on the use of information from physical examinations, most organizations will want the human resources department to handle the exams and the issue of how to accommodate employees with disabilities. A supervisor can then focus on a candidate's experience and talents.

LEGAL ISSUES

Congress has passed laws that restrict employment decisions. Most of these laws are designed to give people fair and equal access to jobs based on their skills, not on their personal traits such as race or physical disabilities. Whatever a supervisor's role in selecting employees, he or she must be aware of the laws affecting hiring to help ensure that the organization's actions are legal.

Antidiscrimination Laws

Certain federal laws prohibit various types of employment discrimination.

- Under Title VII of the Civil Rights Act of 1964 (commonly known as Title VII), employers may not discriminate on the basis of race, color, religion, sex, or national origin in recruiting, hiring, paying, firing, or laying off employees, or in any other employment practices. The government agency charged with enforcing this law is the **Equal Employment Opportunity Commission (EEOC).** The EEOC investigates charges of discrimination and may pursue a remedy in court or arrange for mediation (which means an impartial third party hears both sides and decides how to resolve the dispute).

Equal Employment Opportunity Commission (EEOC)
The federal government agency charged with enforcing Title VII of the Civil Rights Act

- The Age Discrimination in Employment Act of 1967, as amended in 1978 and 1986, prohibits employers from discriminating on the basis of age against people over 40 years old.
- The Rehabilitation Act of 1973 makes it illegal to refuse a job to a disabled person because of the disability, if the disability does not interfere with the person's ability to do the job.
- The Pregnancy Discrimination Act of 1978 makes it unlawful to discriminate on the basis of pregnancy, childbirth, or related medical conditions. A job applicant won a ruling against Wal-Mart for its failure to hire her because she was pregnant.[19] Supervisors should be aware that while such cases are quite rare, they can occur.
- Disabled veterans and veterans of the Vietnam War receive protection under the Vietnam Era Veterans Readjustment Act of 1974, which requires federal contractors to make special efforts to recruit these people. (This is a type of affirmative action, described shortly.) In deciding whether a veteran is qualified, an employer may consider the military record only to the extent it is directly related to the specific qualifications of the job.

Figure 15.6 illustrates the categories of workers protected by the antidiscrimination laws.

FIGURE 15.6
Categories of Workers Protected by Antidiscrimination Law

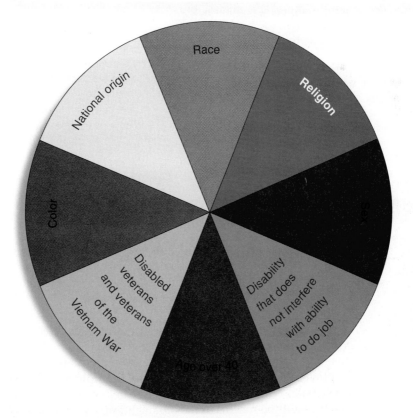

SUPERVISION AND DIVERSITY

DIVERSITY ON THE MENU AT BERTUCCI'S BRICK OVEN RISTORANTE

Bertucci's Brick Oven Ristorante, a restaurant chain with an Italian theme, operates in dozens of locations with 6,500 employees. The company's clientele is diverse, and because management wants its staff to be equally diverse at all levels of the organization, Bertucci's has adopted a policy of "deliberate inclusion." Its diversity policy couples efforts to attract diverse employees with a commitment to developing employees and promoting from within.

Recruitment includes community outreach by supporting local ethnic, religious, and cultural organizations. The company also participates in diversity-related events hosted by community and civic organizations.

Many restaurants are diverse at the entry level, but at Bertucci's, the commitment extends to "internal recruitment," that is, promotion from within. Rahel Yohannes, general manager of the restaurant in Springfield, Virginia, says, "When we hire, we hire not only for that hourly position but for a future in the company." Yohannes—an East Africa native—adds that, from their first day on the job, employees find out that "everyone is welcome and everyone can have a career here."

Bertucci's makes that promise a reality by giving employees a chance to learn skills. The company established a diversity council, which assessed needs and determined that lack of English skills was a primary barrier to career advancement. Bertucci's began offering a course called English as a Working Language to employees identified as having leadership skills but who needed better English skills to advance. Hourly as well as management employees

are eligible to participate in the program, which combines basic English training with lessons on restaurant vocabulary and American culture and history. Employees travel to headquarters for the English as a Working Language classes.

Rick Barbrick, the company's president and chief operating officer, says the program is "daunting" but an excellent investment: "At the end of the day, [the participants] get an incredible skill, and we get a group of people loyal to the company who will go into the community and talk about how Bertucci's paid them to learn to speak English and how they're progressing because of it."

A good example is Carivaldi Santos. An immigrant from Brazil, Santos was hired by Bertucci's after he spent two hours filling out an employment application with the help of his Portuguese–English dictionary. He started out washing dishes in Massachusetts; his supervisor was so impressed with his hard work and dedication that she recommended him for the program. The language barrier was all that was holding Santos back; he had been a professor in Brazil. He successfully completed the English course and soon earned a promotion.

Bertucci's diversity policy means all are valued—even the white males like Barbrick. Of the other white men at Bertucci's, Barbrick says that if he weren't committed to genuine diversity, "They would feel threatened because they'd think I'm just looking for minorities to promote." In fact, he adds, hiring and promotion are based on competency, not quotas. "The [diversity] process is designed to strengthen the company and make it a better place for all of us to work and a better place for the guest to dine."

Source: Donna Hood Crecca, "Setting the Course," *Chain Leader,* August 2004, downloaded from Business & Company Resource Center, http://galenet.galegroup.com.

Although some people criticize these laws as a burden on employers, organizations should benefit from making employment decisions on the basis of people's knowledge, skills, and abilities instead of incidental personal traits such as race, age, or sex.

As the managers of many organizations have observed the growing diversity of the workforce and their customers, they have decided that simply avoiding discrimination is too limited a policy. They have adopted policies called "managing diversity." At an organization that effectively manages diversity, managers and employees create a climate in which all employees feel respected and able to participate. A recent report by the Society for Human Resource Management found that three-fourths of the organizations surveyed said they make diversity a consideration in all of their policies and business initiatives.[20] For an example of such an organization, see the "Supervision and Diversity" box.

Managing diversity implies that the organization is hiring and promoting a variety of people. For this and other purposes, many organizations have established affirmative action programs. **Affirmative action** refers to plans designed to increase opportunities for groups that traditionally have been discriminated against. In effect, these plans are an active attempt to promote diversity in the organization, not just treat everyone the same way.

Some people mistakenly think that affirmative action means setting up artificial quotas that favor some groups at the expense of others. However, organizations can increase opportunities in other ways. In addition to using training to create a pool of qualified applicants, some companies recruit at schools where many students are members of racial minorities.

Ballot initiatives in California and Washington were aimed at curtailing affirmative action programs in hiring by state and local governments. People who favor affirmative action policies argue that because several candidates often have the qualifications to fill any given job, intentionally giving some jobs to people from disadvantaged groups not only is ethical but also supports the achievement of the benefits related to diversity. Whatever your opinion of affirmative action, it is important to note that—except for employers that have federal contracts or subcontracts—organizations are not required by law to set up these programs. Rather, affirmative action programs are one possible response to laws against discrimination.

affirmative action
Plans designed to increase opportunities for groups that traditionally have been discriminated against

Workplace Accessibility

In 1990 Congress passed the Americans with Disabilities Act (ADA), which prohibits employers with more than 15 employees from discriminating on the basis of mental or physical disability in hiring and promotion. A person who can perform the essential functions of a job may not be prevented from doing so simply because the person has a mental or physical disability. Table 15.3 summarizes criteria for disability status under the ADA. Organizations also must avoid discrimination in public accommodations, transportation, government services, and telecommunications.

TABLE 15.3
Disability Status under the Americans with Disabilities Act

Source: From "What Constitutes a Disability?" *Nation's Business,* June 1995, U.S. Chamber of Commerce.

"Disability" Includes	"Disability" Does Not Include
Substantial limitation preventing a person from conducting a major life activity	Cultural and economic disadvantages
Physical and mental impairments	Common personality traits, such as impatience
History of using drugs as the result of an addiction	Pregnancy
Severe obesity (weight in excess of 100 percent of the norm or that arises from a medical disorder)	Normal deviations in weight, height, or strength
	Temporary or short-term problems
	Illegal drug users disciplined for current abuse
	Illegal drug use that is casual (not related to addiction)

Note: People with disabilities are protected from employment discrimination only to the extent that their disability does not prevent them from performing the essential functions of the job.

One benefit to organizations that comply with the ADA is that it encourages employers to take advantage of a large pool of potential workers whose talents are often ignored. The National Organization on Disability estimates that 70 percent of the nation's 49 million disabled people are unemployed.[21] But more and more companies, including Charles Schwab, Ford Motor, Honeywell, Johnson & Johnson, and Wells Fargo, are finding out why a 30-year study by DuPont showed that the job performance of disabled workers was equal to or better than that of their fully functioning peers. When quadriplegic Chris Harmon applied for a job at Crestar Bank, the recruiter who hired him had to put a pen in his mouth for him so he could sign the job application. But now that he has been hired as a telephone customer service representative, Harmon uses voice-activated technology to operate his computer and bring the information he needs to the screen. No one calling the bank ever realizes that he is disabled.[22]

Accommodations for Employees with Disabilities

To comply with the ADA, employers must make accommodations for employees with disabilities if the necessary accommodations are "readily achievable," that is, easy to carry out and possible to accomplish without much difficulty or expense. Businesses may receive a tax credit of up to $15,000 to help offset the cost of making their establishments accessible.

This law extends beyond wheelchair accessibility to require accommodations for any eligible disabled employee, including those with impaired sight and hearing, arthritis, high blood pressure, and heart disease. Thus, accommodations might include door handles that are easy to manipulate and TDD telephones for hearing-impaired employees. For employees with mental disabilities, appropriate accommodations may include speaking more slowly, allowing extra time if possible, providing someone to read application materials, demonstrating (rather than merely describing) application and job procedures, and replacing a written test with an "expanded interview," at which an employee who has difficulty describing abilities may demonstrate them instead.[23] In addition, organizations can head off many problems related to mental disabilities by making extra coaching and counseling available to employees as needed. Grace Louie, who manages a San Francisco Safeway store, says about one-tenth of her 150 employees are disabled. She says some people need to have a supervisor demonstrate the job because they have difficulty reading, but "Once they get going, they're usually fine."[24]

What Supervisors Can Do

Supervisors can take several steps to comply with the ADA. One is to review and revise job descriptions. Because an organization cannot discriminate against those who can perform the essential functions of the job, each job description should indicate what is essential. It should focus on the results the employee must achieve instead of the process for achieving those results. For example, a job description for a telephone lineworker might say "Repair telephone lines located at the top of a pole" but not "Climb telephone poles." In addition, supervisors should make sure that production standards are reasonable; current employees should meet those standards.

When interviewing candidates, a supervisor should be careful not to ask whether they have a physical or mental condition that would prevent them from performing the job. Rather, after making a job offer, the organization will seek to accommodate any impairments the person may have. Similarly, the supervisor should not ask for candidates' health history, including any on-the-job injuries that candidates have suffered.

Immigration Reform and Control Act

By passing the Immigration Reform and Control Act (IRCA) of 1986, Congress gave employers responsibility for helping discourage illegal immigration. IRCA forbids employers to hire illegal immigrants and requires them to screen candidates to make sure they are authorized to work in the United States. At the same time, however, employers may not use these requirements as a rationale for discriminating against candidates because they look or sound "foreign."

This means the employer must verify the identity and work authorization of *every* new employee. To do this, the employer can ask each new employee to show such documentation as a valid U.S. passport, unexpired Immigration Authorization Service document, unexpired work permit, birth certificate, driver's license, or social security card.[25] In large organizations, this law primarily affects the human resources department, giving it an extra task in the hiring process. In small organizations, however, a supervisor may be responsible for verifying that all his or her new employees are authorized to work in the United States.

SKILLS MODULE

PART ONE: CONCEPTS

Summary

15.1 Discuss common roles for supervisors in the selection process.
In most cases, a supervisor works with a human resources department in the selection process. If the organization depends on teams, a supervisor might try to identify candidates who are cooperative and skilled in problem solving or who have helped a team achieve good results in the past. If a team is making the selection, the supervisor as team leader needs to understand the principles of selection so that he or she can coach employees in carrying out the selection process. A supervisor also prepares job descriptions and job specifications, consulting with the human resources department as needed.

15.2 Distinguish between job descriptions and job specifications and explain how they help in selecting employees.
A job description is a listing of the characteristics of the job—observable activities required to carry out the job. A job specification is a listing of characteristics desirable in the person performing the job. The two forms help show how well each candidate matches the job requirements.

15.3 List possible sources of employees.
An organization may recruit inside and outside the organization. Current employees may be promoted or transferred to fill job openings, or they may recommend people for jobs at the organization. Outside the organization, employees can be recruited through help-wanted advertisements, employment agencies, online job sites or blogs, and schools.

15.4 Identify the steps in the selection process.
On the basis of employment applications or résumés, the staff of the human resources department screens out unqualified candidates. Next, the human resources department or the supervisor interviews candidates. An organization may administer employment tests. Background and reference checks are

conducted on candidates in whom the organization is still interested. A supervisor makes a selection decision, after which a candidate may be asked to take a physical examination.

15.5 Discuss how a supervisor should go about interviewing candidates for a job.

First, a supervisor should prepare for the interview by reviewing the job description and each applicant's résumé or job application, planning questions, and arranging for a place to conduct the interview that offers privacy and freedom from interruptions. When a candidate arrives, a supervisor should make him or her comfortable and then ask about the candidate's goals and expectations for the job. Questions must be relevant to the performance of the job and should include both open-ended and closed-ended questions. The interviewer should avoid making common errors in judgment, such as personal biases, or offering misleading information about the organization. Then a candidate should have a chance to ask questions. A supervisor should close the interview by telling a candidate what to expect. As soon as the candidate leaves, the supervisor should make notes of his or her impressions.

15.6 Define types of employment tests.

Aptitude tests measure a person's ability to learn job-related skills. Proficiency tests measure whether a person has the skills needed to perform a job. Psychomotor tests measure strength, dexterity, and coordination. Personality tests identify personality traits. Some organizations also test for drug use. Physical examinations may be required after a job offer is made.

15.7 Summarize the requirements of antidiscrimination laws.

The organization, including the supervisor, must avoid actions that discriminate on the basis of race, color, religion, sex, national origin, age over 40 years, or physical or mental disability, including pregnancy-related disabilities. These laws apply to recruiting, hiring, paying, firing, and laying off employees and to any other employment practice. In addition, federal contractors and subcontractors must use affirmative action to encourage the employment of minorities and veterans of the Vietnam War. When evaluating veterans' qualifications, an employer may use only the portions of the military record that are related to job requirements.

15.8 Explain how hiring decisions are affected by the Americans with Disabilities Act (ADA).

The ADA prohibits discrimination on the basis of mental or physical disability against people who can perform the essential functions of a job. Instead, employers must make accommodations for employees with disabilities if the necessary accommodations are readily achievable. To comply with the law, supervisors should review and revise job descriptions to make sure they indicate what functions of the job are essential. When interviewing candidates, a supervisor should avoid asking about disabilities and a candidate's health history.

15.9 Describe the requirements of the Immigration Reform and Control Act (IRCA) of 1986.

Under IRCA, employers are responsible for helping discourage illegal immigration. They may not hire people who are not authorized to work in the United States, yet they may not discriminate against people who simply appear to be foreigners. Thus, employers must verify the identity and work authorization of every new employee.

Key Terms

job description, *p.* 414
job specification, *p.* 415
recruitment, *p.* 416
structured interview,
p. 424
unstructured interview,
p. 426

open-ended question,
p. 426
closed-ended question,
p. 426
halo effect, *p.* 427
aptitude test, *p.* 427
proficiency test, *p.* 427

psychomotor test, *p.* 427
Equal Employment
Opportunity
Commission (EEOC),
p. 431
affirmative action,
p. 433

Review and Discussion Questions

1. Think of your current job or a job you recently held. Write a job description and a job specification for the job. How well do (or did) you match the requirements of the job?

2. A business executive said that people tend to make the mistake of hiring in their own image. What does this mean? How does this tendency make it more difficult for an organization to build a diverse workforce?

3. In recruiting for each of the following positions, what source or sources of candidates would you recommend using? Explain your choices.

   a. A receptionist for a city government office.

   b. A printing press operator.

   c. A graphic artist for an advertising agency.

   d. A nurse for an adult day care facility.

4. Describe what happens during the screening process. What does the human resources department look for when reading employment applications and résumés?

5. Supervisor Lisa Kitzinger is interviewing candidates for a computer operator job. Kitzinger works in a cubicle, and she has a secretary who could help during the interview process. What can she do to put candidates at ease?

6. Which of the following questions is (are) appropriate for a job interview for the position of office manager for an automobile dealership?

   a. Do you attend church regularly?

   b. Do you know how to use our computer and telecommunications systems?

   c. Are you familiar with our line of cars?

   d. Are you married?

   e. Aren't you close to retirement age?

   f. What skills did you develop at your previous job that you feel would be helpful in this job?

7. How can an interviewer combine the techniques of structured and unstructured interviews?

8. Donald Menck, the supervisor on a boatbuilding line, interviews a male job candidate who comes to the interview dressed in a jacket and tie. Menck is surprised by the candidate's clothing, which is more formal than what is needed on the job; he is also impressed. He assumes that the candidate is intelligent and motivated. What common error in judgment is Menck making? What steps should he take during the interview to overcome it?

9. An airline has a policy that all its employees must receive a physical examination before they start working for the company. At what point in the selection process should the company request the examination? How may the airline use this information?

10. Which of the following actions would be considered discriminatory under federal laws? Explain your answers.

    a. A company creates a policy that all employees must retire by age 65.

    b. A supervisor gives the biggest raises to men, because they have families to support.

    c. A company that recruits at colleges and universities makes at least 20 percent of its visits to schools that are historically black.

    d. In a department where employees must do a lot of overtime work on Saturdays, a supervisor avoids hiring Jews because Saturday is their day of rest and worship.

11. Joel Trueheart supervises customer service representatives for a toy company. The employees handle complaints and questions from customers calling the company's toll-free telephone number. To fill a vacancy in the department, Trueheart has reviewed many résumés and is in the process of interviewing a few candidates. One of the most impressive résumés is that of Sophia Ahmad, but when Trueheart meets her, he is startled to observe that she is blind. What should he do to make sure he is complying with the Americans with Disabilities Act?

12. What steps must employers take to ensure that they are complying with the Immigration Reform and Control Act?

PART TWO: SKILL-BUILDING

YOU SOLVE THE PROBLEM

Reflecting back on page 413, discuss with your group members how you might feel as an applicant auditioning for a job as a server at Cold Stone Creamery. Would you be enthusiastic about this process?

Working together and on the basis of your experiences as customers (and perhaps employees) of ice-cream parlors, list the duties and standards of this job. Then list the qualities you think are important in a person holding this job. Use your lists to develop a job description and job specification for the position.

Which of the requirements from your job description and job specification does the Cold Stone Creamery audition evaluate? What else should a Cold Stone Creamery supervisor do to select qualified, motivated employees?

Problem-Solving Case: *Wanted by Honda: Engineers Who Love Small-Town Living*

Although the U.S.-based Big Three automakers General Motors, Ford, and DaimlerChrysler have announced cutbacks and layoffs recently, some auto companies are still hiring. Toyota, Nissan, Honda, and other companies have set up operations in the United States. While they employ far fewer in the United States than the Big Three, their ranks are growing. Nearly one out of four jobs with auto companies in the United States are with companies other than the Big Three. Honda R&D Americas recently told a reporter that it was adding about 100 employees a year and had 50 positions it was trying to fill with engineers.

To staff those positions, Honda faces a challenge: its location. The Honda research and development facility is located in an out-of-the-way spot in Ohio, the town of Raymond, located about 60 miles northwest of Columbus. Most automotive research facilities in the United States are located near Detroit, because so much of the industry talent lives and works in that area. The Honda plant sits on an 8,000-acre plot of land along with the company's Transportation Research Center, and Honda operates two assembly plants in nearby Marysville and East Liberty. Surrounding this complex are cornfields.

Because of its location, Honda does not seek most of its recruits from other auto companies. It hires local residents to fill manufacturing jobs, and for engineers, it turns to schools in the region to find recent graduates. Carol Hadden, who manages human resources, says one good source of engineering recruits has been Ohio State University.

Knowing that small-town life does not appeal to many recent grads, Honda requires applicants to visit the Raymond site for their first interview. Allen explains, "We make them come here to make sure they know where we are." Those who look around and like the location have a better chance of being enthusiastic about a career at Honda R&D.

1. Suggest three ways Honda R&D Americas could recruit engineers to fill jobs at its research and development facility in Raymond, Ohio.

2. If you were interviewing a candidate for a job at this facility, what would you ask to determine whether the candidate would be satisfied to stay at Honda?

3. How would Honda R&D's emphasis on recruiting recent graduates, rather than experienced automotive engineers, affect your job if you were the supervisor of these employees? Would you want Honda to change its recruiting strategy? Why or why not?

Sources: Lindsay Chappell, "Honda's U.S. R&D Center Looks Locally for Talent," *Automotive News*, March 20, 2006; Lillie Guyer, "Cutbacks Aside, Industry Still Needs Engineers," *Automotive News*, March 27, 2006; Gail Kachadourian, "Auto Jobs: A Big Tilt Away from the Big Three," *Automotive News*, April 25, 2005, all downloaded from Business & Company Resource Center, http://galenet.galegroup.com.

Knowing Yourself

Would You Hire You?

One of the criteria supervisors look for in a job candidate is a good fit with the company culture. Use this quiz to determine what you value in your own work environment, and you'll have a better idea what kind of firm might want to hire you.

The 54 items below cover the full range of personal and institutional values you'd be likely to encounter at any company. Divide the list of items into the 27 choices that would be evident in your ideal workplace, and the 27 that would be least evident. Keep dividing the groups in half until you can rank-order them, and then fill in the numbers of your top and bottom 10 choices in the space provided. Test your fit in a hiring situation by seeing whether the company's values match your top and bottom 10.

Your top 10 choices:

_____ _____ _____ _____ _____ _____ _____ _____ _____ _____

Your bottom 10 choices:

_____ _____ _____ _____ _____ _____ _____ _____ _____ _____

The Choice Menu
You are:

1. Flexible
2. Adaptable
3. Innovative
4. Able to seize opportunities
5. Willing to experiment
6. Risk taker
7. Careful
8. Autonomy seeker
9. Comfortable with rules
10. Analytical
11. Attentive to detail
12. Precise

13. Team oriented
14. Ready to share information
15. People oriented
16. Easygoing
17. Calm
18. Supportive
19. Aggressive
20. Decisive
21. Action oriented
22. Eager to take initiative
23. Reflective
24. Achievement oriented
25. Demanding
26. Comfortable with individual responsibility
27. Comfortable with conflict
28. Competitive
29. Highly organized

30. Results oriented
31. Interested in making friends at work
32. Collaborative
33. Eager to fit in with colleagues
34. Enthusiastic about job

Your company offers:
35. Stability
36. Predictability
37. High expectations of performance
38. Opportunities for professional growth
39. High pay for good performance
40. Job security
41. Praise for good performance
42. A clear guiding philosophy

43. A low level of conflict
44. An emphasis on quality
45. A good reputation
46. Respect for the individual's rights
47. Tolerance
48. Informality
49. Fairness
50. A unitary culture throughout the organization
51. A sense of social responsibility
52. Long hours
53. Relative freedom from rules
54. The opportunity to be distinctive, or different from others

Pause and Reflect

1. Considering your current job or your most recent job, do you think you are (were) a good fit with your organization's culture?

2. Putting yourself in your supervisor's shoes, if you could make the choice again, would you (as your supervisor) hire you?

Source: From Matt Siegel, "The Perils of Culture Conflict," *Fortune*, November 9, 1998. Copyright ©1998 Time, Inc. All rights reserved.

Class Exercise

Preparing to Interview Job Candidates

This chapter has covered the steps involved in making sound employee selection decisions. Finding employees who have the necessary skills to meet today's workplace challenges is not an easy task. Most organizations are facing similar challenges: adapting to technological changes, improving quality, dealing with workforce diversity, reorganizing work around teams, and empowering employees at all levels to improve customer service. This exercise focuses on the skills employers are looking for in today's job candidates, and it provides practice in developing interview questions that will help you in your evaluation of prospective employees.

Instructions

1. Study Table A.

2. Match the letter of each specific skill from Table A with the appropriate descriptor in Table B. (Each answer will be used only once. The first two answers have been done for you in the left-hand column.)

TABLE A
16 Job Skills Crucial to Success

Source: Adapted from Anthony P. Carnevale, *America and the New Economy* (San Francisco: Jossey-Bass, 1991).

Category of Skill	Specific Skills in Each Category
Foundation Competence	*a* Knowing how to learn
	b Reading
	c Writing
	d Computation
Communication	*e* Listening
	f Oral communication
Adaptability	*g* Creative thinking
	h Problem solving
Personal management	*i* Self-esteem
	j Goal setting and motivation
	k Personal/career development
Group effectiveness	*l* Interpersonal skills
	m Negotiation
	n Teamwork
Influence	*o* Organizational effectiveness
	p Leadership

3. In the space after each descriptor in Table B, write an interview question to ask job candidates that will give you insight into their abilities in each area; assume you are interviewing job candidates to fill a job as bank teller. (The first two are already filled in to give you an idea of some sample questions.)

Source: The class exercise was prepared by Corinne Livesay, Belhaven College, Jackson, Mississippi.

TABLE B **Descriptors of Specific Skills**

Answer	Descriptor and Interview Question
i	1. Employers want employees who have pride in themselves and their potential to be successful. *Question: Can you describe a task or project you completed in your last job that you were particularly proud of?*
h	2. Employers want employees who can think on their feet when faced with a dilemma. *Question: If you had a customer return to your teller window and claim, in a rather loud and irritated voice, that you had made a mistake, how would you handle the situation?*
	3. Employers want employees who can assume responsibility and motivate co-workers when necessary. *Question:*
	4. Employers want employees who will hear the key points that make up a customer's concerns. *Question:*
	5. Employers want employees who can learn the particular skills of an available job. *Question:*

(continued)

TABLE B   Descriptors of Specific Skills (*continued*)

Answer	Descriptor and Interview Question
	6. Employers want employees who can resolve conflicts to the satisfaction of those involved. *Question:*
	7. Employers want employees who have some sense of the skills needed to perform well in their current jobs and who are working to develop skills to qualify themselves for other jobs. *Question:*
	8. Employers want employees with good mathematics skills. *Question:*
	9. Employers want employees who can work with others to achieve a goal. *Question:*
	10. Employers want employees who can convey an adequate response when responding to a customer's concerns. *Question:*
	11. Employers want employees who have some sense of where the organization is headed and what they must do to make a contribution. *Question:*
	12. Employers want employees who can come up with innovative solutions when needed. *Question:*
	13. Employers want employees who can clearly and succinctly articulate ideas in writing. *Question:*
	14. Employers want employees who know how to get things done and have the desire to complete tasks. *Question:*
	15. Employers want employees who can get along with customers, suppliers, and co-workers. *Question:*
	16. Employers want employees to be analytical, to summarize information, and to monitor their own comprehension of the reading task. *Question:*

Building Supervision Skills

Interviewing and Selecting New Employees

This exercise simulates an abbreviated version of the selection process. Imagine that the manager of a family-style restaurant such as Denny's needs to hire a server. Working together, the class develops a job description and job specification. The instructor records them on the chalkboard or overhead projector. When in doubt about the details, class members should use their imaginations. The objective is for the class to agree that these two lists are reasonable and complete.

When the job description and job specification are complete, the class develops a list of interview questions that would indicate whether a candidate is appropriate for this job. Besides creating questions to ask, the class also might consider other ways to determine this information during an interview (for example, observing some aspects of the candidates' behavior).

Next, four class members take on the following parts for a role play:

1. Restaurant manager.
2. Candidate 1: a college student with eagerness but no restaurant experience.
3. Candidate 2: a woman who appears to be about 60 years old and who had eight years' experience as a server during the 1960s.
4. Candidate 3: a man with four years' experience as a server in five different restaurants.

The class members taking these roles should feel free to add details to these descriptions of "themselves." The person acting as the restaurant manager interviews each candidate for no more than five minutes each. (A real interview would probably last much longer.)

The role-playing interviews could be videotaped and then played back during the discussion.

Finally, the class discusses one or both of these topics:

1. *Selecting a candidate:* By a show of hands, the class votes for which candidate they would recommend hiring. What are your reasons for choosing that particular candidate?
2. *Interviewing techniques:*
   - Did the restaurant manager interview objectively, based on the criteria determined at the beginning of the exercise?
   - Did the interview cover all the important points?
   - Did the manager use open-ended or closed-ended questions?
   - How did the manager's style of questioning help or hurt the information gathering process?
   - Did the candidates have a chance to ask questions?
   - Did the manager obey the antidiscrimination laws?
   - How did the interviewing experience feel to the candidates? To the manager?

Chapter **Sixteen**

Providing Orientation and Training

Learning Objectives

After you have studied this chapter, you should be able to:

16.1 Summarize reasons for conducting an orientation for new employees.

16.2 Discuss how a supervisor and the human resources department can work together to conduct an orientation.

16.3 Identify methods for conducting an orientation.

16.4 Describe the training cycle.

16.5 Explain how supervisors can decide when employees need training.

16.6 Define major types of training.

16.7 Describe how a supervisor can use coaching and mentoring to support training.

16.8 Discuss how a supervisor can evaluate the effectiveness of training.

Training is important to continuous improvement because of the change that is taking place around us. You need to be aware of that change, and you need to be continually growing to adapt to it.

—*Paul Kortier, plant training leader, Libbey Inc.*

With hundreds of restaurants and tens of thousands of employees, the Cheesecake Factory faces a huge challenge in spreading its values and methods throughout the company. The restaurant chain needs managers at all levels to be committed to training so that employees can learn the company culture along with work procedures. As the company has grown, its top managers have been concerned about preserving the high commitment to customer service that they associate with employees of a small, start-up business.

Training is provided for employees at all levels of the organization. Dishwashers, many of whom are immigrants, may use an interactive learning program to improve their English-language skills. Kitchen staff must be trained in preparing and presenting the hundreds of dishes on the Cheesecake Factory's extensive menu. Servers participate in on-the-job training for two weeks after being hired. During this training period, they work under the guidance of a mentor, who observes their interactions with customers and helps them figure out how to handle tricky situations. Following the two-week training, the servers take a test; they must earn an A before the company will hire them as permanent workers. They receive additional training a month later and again each time the company revamps its menu. Servers who perform well are eligible to receive cross-training in various responsibilities so they can earn certification as a serving trainer at a higher pay level. Candidates for management jobs take a 12-week course

at one of the company's "training restaurants" to develop their skills in managing. These training programs are the same from one restaurant to the next so that the employees will give customers the same high-quality experience at each location.

Training methods include many of those described in this chapter: on-the-job learning, interactive games, coaching, role-playing, and computer-based training. Together, these programs cost the company an average of $2,000 per hourly employee. But the Cheesecake Factory's management believes the money is well invested because employee turnover is below the industry average and customers are loyal and well satisfied.

As they do at the Cheesecake Factory, supervisors at many companies support employee participation in training programs that have been developed for the company as a whole. They also may train employees informally on the job.

QUESTIONS

1. How might a supervisor at the Cheesecake Factory support the company's training efforts?
2. What training skills would the supervisor be able to use?

Source: Gina Ruiz, "Traditional Recipe: Tall Order," *Workforce Management*, April 24, 2006, downloaded from Business & Company Resource Center, http://galenet.galegroup.com.

Supervisors are responsible for making sure their employees know what to do and how to do it. Good selection practices ensure that employees are capable of learning their jobs and perhaps already know how to carry out many of the tasks they were hired to perform. However, especially in view of the intense changes faced by most organizations, even the best employees need some degree of training. In this context, **training** refers to increasing the skills that will enable employees to better meet the organization's goals.

Training is a major expense. Businesses in the United States budgeted more than $51 billion for formal training in 2003, representing hundreds of dollars per employee.[1] And these formal programs may be only a small part of all the training that goes on in organizations. Army nurse Rose A. Hazlett attributes much of her success in the military to informal coaching provided by her supervising officers. During her first duty station, when she was an enlisted Navy seaman, her Navy supervisor recommended that Hazlett go to college and consider health care as a field. Hazlett started with courses at a community college and eventually earned a bachelor's degree (later adding a master's degree and admission to a doctorate program). As a nurse and a young lieutenant following her transfer to the Army, Hazlett reported to the chief nurse. That officer told Hazlett lessons she would take to heart: "As an officer, people would have to respect the bars on my

training
Increasing the skills that will enable employees to better meet the organization's goals

445

FIGURE 16.1   Specific Types of Training Provided by U.S. Companies

Source: Tammy Galvin, "2003 Industry Report: *Training* Magazine's 22nd Annual Comprehensive Analysis of Employer-Sponsored Training in the United States," *Training*, October 2003, downloaded from InfoTrac, http://web1.infotrac.galegroup.com.

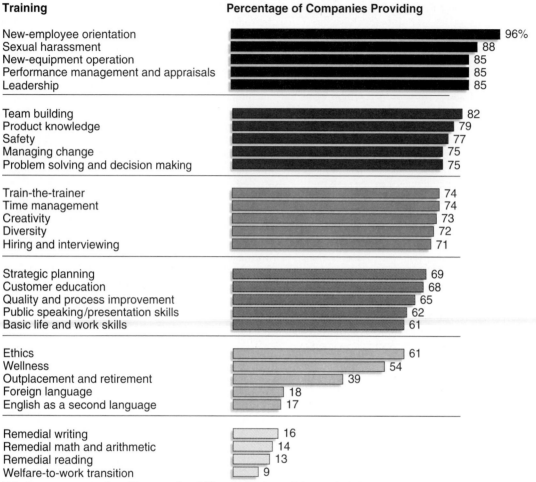

Training	Percentage of Companies Providing
New-employee orientation	96%
Sexual harassment	88
New-equipment operation	85
Performance management and appraisals	85
Leadership	85
Team building	82
Product knowledge	79
Safety	77
Managing change	75
Problem solving and decision making	75
Train-the-trainer	74
Time management	74
Creativity	73
Diversity	72
Hiring and interviewing	71
Strategic planning	69
Customer education	68
Quality and process improvement	65
Public speaking/presentation skills	62
Basic life and work skills	61
Ethics	61
Wellness	54
Outplacement and retirement	39
Foreign language	18
English as a second language	17
Remedial writing	16
Remedial math and arithmetic	14
Remedial reading	13
Welfare-to-work transition	9

Note: Responses were gathered from a number of different industries and job types, including training, human resources, sales and marketing, and customer service.

shoulders, but respect as a person was something I would have to earn . . . the result of my respecting those under my guidance and command." Hazlett credits the informal training of these conversations with more experienced people with helping her become "who I am today—a proud, Hispanic American nurse, patriot, and leader."[2]

At TalentFusion Inc., training in team building, for instance, is about as informal as it can get. A recruitment agency that operates both on and off the Internet, TalentFusion holds weekly soccer games as part of employee training. "The game isn't about proficiency in soccer," explains CEO David Pollard. "It's about proficiency in team building and being goal-oriented, two things that translate perfectly to our work off the field."[3]

Employee training, however it is conducted, meets important needs. New employees need a chance to learn the specific ways things are done in the organization. In addition, employees are best equipped to contribute to a changing workplace when they have an opportunity to learn new skills and improve their existing ones through a variety of training programs. Well-trained employees can deliver higher quality than poorly trained people. Training can improve productivity by holding down a variety of costs: overtime pay for employees unfamiliar with their jobs, workers' compensation and lost time of employees injured when they fail to follow safe practices, lawsuits arising from misconduct such as sexual harassment (discussed in Appendix B), and much more. Finally, well-trained employees are likely to be more satisfied because they know what they are doing and how it contributes to achieving the organization's goals. Figure 16.1 shows areas in which U.S. companies were conducting training, according to a recent survey.

This chapter describes types of training for employees and ways supervisors can participate. It begins by laying out the supervisor's role in orientation, the employee's first learning experience. Next, the chapter discusses types of training available once employees are on board and explains how supervisors can assess when training is needed. The chapter also addresses the growing expectation that supervisors supplement formal training with coaching or mentoring. Finally, the chapter describes why and how to evaluate training efforts.

ORIENTATION OF NEW EMPLOYEES

Do you remember your first day at your current or most recent job? When you arrived, you might not have known where you would be working or where the restrooms were. You probably did not know your co-workers or how they spent their lunch hour. You might not have known the details of how to carry out your job, including where and how to get the supplies or materials you would need.

orientation
The process of giving new employees the information they need to do their work comfortably, effectively, and efficiently

The uncertainty you felt is common to new employees in all kinds of organizations. For that reason, supervisors should assume that all employees need some form of orientation. In this context, **orientation** refers to the process of giving new employees the information they need to do their work comfortably, effectively, and efficiently. As you can see from Figure 16.1, *Training* magazine's recent survey found that 96 percent of companies sampled offered employees a formal orientation program. Even in organizations in which someone else is responsible for carrying out a formal orientation program, supervisors must ensure that their employees begin their jobs with all the information they need.

Benefits of Orientation

An employee who spends the day hunting for the photocopier, trying to figure out how to operate a cash register, or looking for someone to explain how to fill out a purchase order is not working efficiently. The primary reason organizations have orientation programs is that the sooner employees know basic information related to doing their jobs, the sooner they can become productive. They can work faster and with fewer errors, and their co-workers and supervisor can spend less time helping them.

Not only does orientation give new employees the knowledge they need to carry out their work, but it also reduces their nervousness and uncertainty. This frees new employees to focus on their jobs rather than their worries, which boosts employee efficiency and reduces the likelihood they will quit.

Another reason for conducting orientation is to encourage employees to develop a positive attitude. The time spent on an orientation session shows that the organization values the new employees. This will almost certainly add to employees' feelings of satisfaction and desire to cooperate as part of the organization. It can make new employees feel more confident that joining the organization was a good idea. In addition, work is more satisfying when we know how to do it well. The organization benefits because employees with positive attitudes tend to be more highly motivated, so they are more likely to do good work.

Positive attitudes and commitment arise partly from healthy, supportive work relationships. When an orientation shows a new employee that the supervisor and co-workers want him or her to succeed, the new employee has more ability and desire to meet expectations. Nancy Ahlrichs suggests some ways to strengthen positive work relationships during orientation. According to Ahlrichs, the supervisor should be physically nearby on the first day, signaling that the supervisor is glad to have the new employee on board and wants to make the transition smooth. Tours and introductions help the new employee get acquainted with others. A welcoming e-mail message from top management or the supervisor adds a positive touch that shows the company cares. Assigning the new employee to a buddy or mentor (discussed subsequently in this chapter) gives the new employee a valuable resource who can provide information and encouragement. These interpersonal aspects of orientation are important to include along with any written or computerized orientation materials.[4]

At Motorola Semiconductor Products Sector in Phoenix, Arizona, training in Six Sigma methods (discussed in Chapter 2) is now included in every new employee's orientation. The company's quality engineering manager, Craig Erwin, says that Six Sigma, considered a "stretch goal," continues to yield improvements in product reliability and quality, "in spite of increasing product complexity and higher customer expectations." Including the training in employee orientation not only alerts every worker to Six Sigma's importance to the firm but also gives each new hire a head start in achieving the goal of continuous improvement.[5]

The Supervisor's Role

In a small organization, supervisors often are responsible for conducting the orientation. If you are one of those supervisors, look for ways to adapt the principles in this chapter to your group's particular needs.

Large organizations generally have a formal orientation program conducted by the human resources department. Even so, supervisors have a role in orientation. Whereas the formal orientation program focuses on information pertaining to the organization as a whole, supervisors still must convey information about the specifics of holding a particular job in a particular department. If you are a supervisor in these circumstances, learn which of the topics and methods your human resources department already covers, and then consider ways you and your employees can handle any remaining ones. See the "Supervisory Skills" box for some specific ways to manage the "honeymoon" period.

Orientation Topics

When the human resources department and supervisor share responsibility for conducting an orientation, the human resources department typically covers topics related to the organization's policies and procedures, including hours of work and breaks; location of company facilities such as the lunchroom and exercise facilities; procedures for filling out time sheets; and policies regarding performance appraisals, pay increases, and time off. The human resources department also handles the task of having new employees fill out the necessary paperwork, such as enrollment forms for insurance policies and withholding forms for tax purposes. The person conducting the orientation should explain each of these forms to new employees.

A supervisor is responsible for orientation topics related to performing a particular job in a particular department. A supervisor explains what the department

SUPERVISORY SKILLS

PROVIDING ORIENTATION

ORIENTATION IDEAS FROM THE PROS

In the following examples, experienced managers share their thoughts about what has helped them prepare new employees to deliver results.

At Sawhill Custom Kitchens and Design, located in Minneapolis, Minnesota, new employees get information in writing so they can refer to it later. Each new hire receives a handbook spelling out the company's philosophy and policies, as well as a job description detailing the requirements of the position. A new employee also is assigned to a senior designer and "shadows" the veteran, accompanying him or her to see how an experienced person works with customers. Because employees must be familiar with the products they sell, Sawhill also sends employees on tours of manufacturers' facilities, where they learn about the product lines.

Training at Belgrade TrueValue, a hardware store in Belgrade, Montana, starts even before individuals are hired. During job interviews, owner Steve Bachmeier asks candidates to describe their best and worst experiences with customer service. This launches a conversation about Belgrade TrueValue's standards for customer service. After the candidate is hired, that emphasis continues through mentoring and hands-on training. In addition, pamphlets and classroom training provide new employees with information about the store's products. New employees in the store spend their first two days working with a trainer in the checkout area. Because the store has a goal that no customer will stand in a line waiting for a cashier, all employees learn to handle checkout. Following that initial training, employees receive one page of information each week for four weeks and are encouraged to seek out the managers listed on the information sheets, as a way to show initiative and become acquainted with the store's management. The first week's material covers topics such as how to read shelf tags and stock shelves. The following three weeks cover specific departments in the store. The program is designed to build employees' know-how and confidence to ask for help in resolving customers' questions.

At another TrueValue store, Wabash TrueValue, located in Wabash, Indiana, employees spend their first few hours on the job working alongside owner Brian Howenstine. That coaching from the top gives Howenstine a chance to talk about his expectations as well as company policies. Then, so that the new hire doesn't feel overwhelmed, Howenstine has the person spend the rest of the day just wandering around the store and becoming familiar with what is on the shelves.

Sources: "What Do You Find to Be the Most Important Aspects of Effectively Training Employees?" *Kitchen and Bath Design*, June 2006; Darci Valentine, "New-Hire Training Tips: A Guide to Teaching Them the Ropes," *Do-It-Yourself Retailing*, February 2006, both downloaded from Business & Company Resource Center, http://galenet.galegroup.com.

does and how these activities contribute to the organization's goals. A supervisor who covered this information in the selection interview should repeat it during the orientation process. As described subsequently, the supervisor's orientation should point out the locations of facilities the employee will need to use and explain any of the department's own policies and procedures.

A supervisor's orientation also should provide instructions on how to perform the job. A supervisor may be able to explain a simple job at one time, but most jobs are more complex and will require a supervisor to first give an overview of the job's responsibilities and then, over the course of days or weeks, show the employee how to perform different aspects of the job. To build morale while training, a supervisor also can explain why the employee's job is important—that is, how it contributes to meeting department and organizational objectives.

A supervisor should prepare and follow a checklist of the topics to cover during the orientation of new employees. Figure 16.2 is adapted from a checklist distributed to supervisors at Swift and Company; it is printed on a two-by-three-inch card so supervisors can easily refer to it. In preparing a checklist, a supervisor should include items that fit his or her particular situation.

FIGURE 16.2 **Sample Checklist for Orientation**

Source: Adapted from a Swift and Company document.

SUPERVISORS' CHECKLIST
The Right Start for New Hourly Paid Employees

A. Explain (before employee starts the job):
  1. Rate of pay, including overtime.
  2. Pay day.
  3. Initial job or assignment.
  4. Hours—call out—holiday pay—no tardiness.
  5. Starting and quitting time.
  6. Lunch period—relief periods.
  7. Whom to call if unable to come to work (give name and phone number on card).
  8. Work clothes arrangement—laundry.
  9. No smoking areas.
  10. Safety rules—no running—mesh gloves—reporting all accidents, etc.
  11. Sanitation—this is a food factory.
  12. Name benefits (will explain later).
  13. Possible job difficulties—sore muscles or hands, dizziness, nausea, etc. (encourage to stick it out).
  14. Buying of company products.
  15. Nothing from plant without order.
  16. Importance of quality product.

B. Show:
  1. Locker—restrooms.
  2. Lunchroom.
  3. Where employee will work—introduce to supervisor and immediate co-workers.
  4. Explain the job—use JIT.
C. Talk to new employee (to encourage):
  1. Twice first day.
  2. Once each day the next four days.
D. After one week, explain:
  1. Vacation.
  2. Hospitalization.
  3. EBA—Group.
  4. Pension.
  5. Suggestion plan.
  6. Union contract, if organized plant (probationary period).

Orientation Methods

The methods a supervisor uses will depend on the organization's policies and resources. For example, a large organization with a human resources department may provide a handbook of information for new employees and spell out orientation procedures to follow. A small organization may expect individual supervisors to develop their own orientation methods. Some common methods include using an employee handbook, conducting a tour of the facilities, and encouraging the involvement of co-workers.

Employee Handbook

employee handbook
A document that describes an organization's conditions of employment, policies regarding employees, administrative procedures, and related matters

If the organization publishes an employee handbook, a new employee should be introduced to this document during the orientation. An **employee handbook** describes an organization's conditions of employment (e.g., attendance, behavior on the job, performance of duties), policies regarding employees (e.g., time off, hours of work, benefits), administrative procedures (e.g., filling out time sheets and travel expense reports), and related matters. A supervisor should show a new employee what topics are covered in the handbook and explain how to use it to find answers to questions. For example, an employee might use the handbook to learn how long he or she must work to qualify for three weeks' vacation.

Tour of Facilities

Another important orientation method is to give the employee a tour. The tour might start with the employee's own work area, which should already be prepared with the supplies, tools, or equipment the employee will need. The supervisor then shows the employee the locations of physical facilities he or she will need to know about, including restrooms, water fountain, coffee station, fax, and photocopier, and where to get supplies, parts, or other materials needed to do the job.

During the tour, the supervisor should introduce the new employee to the people with whom he or she will be working. Friendly, positive words during introductions can help make the new employee part of the team. In introducing a new nurse to her colleagues in the hospital, a supervisor might say, "This is Janet Strahn. She's one of the top graduates from Northern, and I know we're all going to appreciate her help." In introducing a new maintenance mechanic to a machine operator in the department, a supervisor might say, "Pedro is the guy you'll need if your machine goes down." In both examples, the supervisor is emphasizing the importance of the new employee to the department.

Involvement of Co-Workers

A new employee's co-workers have an important role to play in orientation. Their behavior goes a long way toward making the new employee feel either welcome or like an outsider. Therefore, a supervisor should ask all employees to help welcome newcomers. If the organization tries to build team spirit through activities such as clubs and sports teams, a supervisor should see that these are well publicized so that new employees can participate easily. A supervisor may encourage co-workers to invite a new employee to join them on breaks and at lunch. On the employee's first day, a supervisor can help a new employee feel welcome by inviting him or her to lunch.

Follow-Up

In addition to the initial information provision, an orientation should involve follow-up. A supervisor should check with new employees at the end of the first day and the first week to make sure they understand what they are supposed to be doing and know where to get what they need. At all times, a supervisor should encourage employees to ask questions.

Of course, a supervisor should not stop following up after one week. Regularly checking on the performance and progress of employees is part of a supervisor's control responsibilities, particularly in technical professions.[6]

TRAINING

As mentioned previously, employees need continued training even after they have worked for the organization for years. Training shows employees how to do the basics of their jobs and then helps them improve their skills. It also helps employees adapt to changes in the workplace. Because change occurs in every organization, the need for training continues (see Chapter 14).

The Training Cycle

The process of providing training occurs in a cycle of steps (see Figure 16.3). The first step is to assess needs for training. As described in the next section, assessment of training needs is part of a supervisor's job. In addition, higher-level management or the human resources department may identify a need for various kinds of training. The next three steps involve planning the training. Then someone conducts the training as planned. Finally, the training should be evaluated.

FIGURE 16.3
The Training Cycle

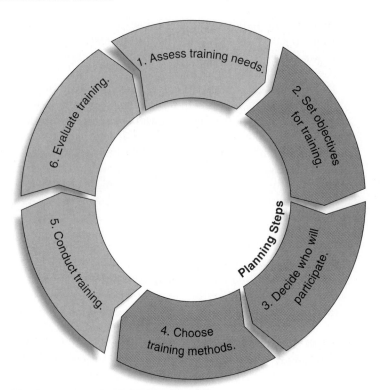

Planning Steps

A supervisor or other person proposing the training begins the planning stage by setting objectives for it. These objectives are based on a comparison of the current level and the desired level of performance and skills. In other words, they specify progress from the current level to the desired level. The training objectives should meet the criteria for effective objectives (see Chapter 6). Thus, they should be written, measurable, clear, specific, and challenging but achievable. Training objectives also should support the organization's goals by helping develop the kind of employees who can make the organization more competitive. At United Technologies Corporation (UTC), business challenges have forced the company to focus on reducing its workforce and making the remaining employees more efficient. Despite the difficult climate that follows cutbacks, UTC has to ensure that the remaining employees know they are valued and appreciate the need to apply their skills more productively than ever. To meet that goal, UTC established a training program for its frontline supervisors, comprising more than 10,000 supervisors whose employees make products as diverse as helicopters, elevators, and fuel cells. The training program emphasizes supervisory skills such as constructively discussing performance with employees.[7]

A supervisor also decides who will participate in the training program. For example, training pertaining to how to prevent and avoid sexual harassment applies to all employees, so everyone in the department would participate. But training on how to operate a new piece of equipment would include only those who might use that equipment. This decision may take into account the interests and motivation levels of employees, as well as their skills. For example, an employee who is eager to advance in the organization will want to participate in many training activities to develop a variety of skills. An employee who is

SUPERVISION ACROSS INDUSTRIES

BANKING

TRAINING IMPROVES CROSS-SELLING AT HOME FEDERAL SAVINGS AND LOAN

When Lynn Sander became senior vice president of retail banking at Home Federal Savings and Loan Association, she took advantage of her newness to the organization and "mystery shopped" at Home Federal's branches. Without revealing her true identity, Sander tried using the various services at each branch of Home Federal, based in Nampa, Idaho. What she found told her that the employees needed more training. They were pleasant and tried to help, but they showed no skill in selling additional products to their mystery customer. A follow-up test of selling skills confirmed Sander's impression; employees scored below the industry average.

Under Sander's leadership, Home Federal set up a training program that focuses on skills training related to selling. This approach makes sense, according to Michael Cherry, who owns a company that offers training for sales skills. Cherry says banks have traditionally focused on teaching employees about various products. This approach assumes that greater knowledge about the products will lead the employees to encourage customers to sign up for the products. However, a more effective way to sell is to focus on customer's needs, so training should teach employees how to listen to customers and help them identify needs for which the bank has services.

Home Federal took this approach and hired outside experts to provide the new training program. The program included instruction in such skills as greeting customers, using the customer's name, asking open-ended questions, and following up with customers. Open-ended questions, for example, are important because they help employees build customer relationships.

Every Home Federal employee took part in this program. Executives as well as frontline employees were included, so everyone would appreciate how the change to a customer focus would affect the institution. After the training, employees' selling skills and performance began to rise above average. In Sander's words, "You could actually see the change happen." Based on the training program's success, Home Federal has continued it, requiring it for all new employees.

Source: Nancy Feig, "The Cross-Sales Puzzle: Putting the Right Pieces in Place," *Community Banker,* July 2004, downloaded from Business & Company Resource Center, http://galenet.galegroup.com.

interested primarily in job security will probably want just enough training to keep up to date on how to perform the job.

The last step in planning training is to choose the training methods. Some training methods are described subsequently in this chapter. If selecting a training method is part of a supervisor's role, he or she may wish to consult with the human resources department or a training expert to learn which techniques will best meet the objectives of the training. To learn how Home Federal Savings and Loan Association planned a successful training program, see the "Supervision across Industries" box.

Implementation

Once the training has been planned, someone must conduct it in a timely manner. In some cases, the trainer may be a supervisor. A department's employees may be qualified to conduct some kinds of training, such as demonstrating how to use a computer system. In other cases, a professional trainer is more appropriate. The choice depends on the expertise of a supervisor or employee, the content and type of training, and the time and money available for training. A supervisor with a big budget and little expertise in a particular area of training is most likely to use an in-house or outside expert. Training topics most often tackled by a supervisor are those about the specific job or department instead of company policies and values, interpreting the company's performance, or working effectively as a team.

When a supervisor is conducting the training, he or she can benefit from applying principles of learning.[8] One of these principles is that adults generally get the most out of training if they are taught a little at a time over a long period, especially if the training is seeking to change behavior rather than merely add to the learner's store of knowledge. Thus, shutting down for a day of training would be less effective than scheduling a half hour every week or so. Another principle is that adults want to see how the training content applies to their everyday problems and needs. Generally, they bring significant experience to the training sessions, and the training program should acknowledge and draw upon what they already know.

Expert trainers also advise that sessions should combine a variety of methods because individuals have different learning styles; they approach a subject and retain information in varying ways. Training methods should include visual and spoken information, as well as a chance to involve employees in trying what they learn, perhaps through role-plays, simulations, or games. The methods should be appropriate for presenting the theory and instruction (procedures, methods, rules, and so forth) of the subject matter, as well as for presenting models of how to carry out the new skill and experiences with trying the new skill. At Kimberly-Clark, for example, employees had trouble learning about the company's supply chain (all the steps to get a product to consumers) from slide presentations and meetings. When training expanded to include simulation games and video presentations, employees began to understand the process and why it affected the company's performance.[9] Figure 16.4 shows major categories of training methods used by U.S. employers.

Finally, motivation is as important to successful learning as it is to other employee activities. Training will therefore be most effective when it reflects the principles of motivation discussed in Chapter 11.

FIGURE 16.4
Use of Various Training Methods

Source: Tammy Galvin, "2003 Industry Report," *Training*, October 2003, downloaded from InfoTrac, http://web1.infotrac.galegroup.com.

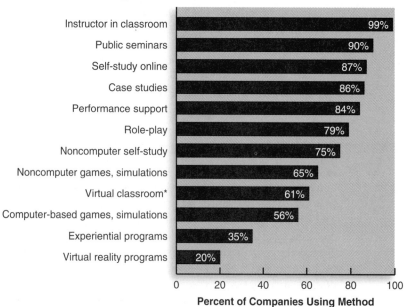

Training Method

Training Method	Percent
Instructor in classroom	99%
Public seminars	90%
Self-study online	87%
Case studies	86%
Performance support	84%
Role-play	79%
Noncomputer self-study	75%
Noncomputer games, simulations	65%
Virtual classroom*	61%
Computer-based games, simulations	56%
Experiential programs	35%
Virtual reality programs	20%

Percent of Companies Using Method

*Instructor at a remote location.

Evaluation

After the training is over, the supervisor evaluates the results. Did it meet the objectives? The last section of this chapter discusses the evaluation of training in greater detail. Evaluation completes the training cycle by helping the supervisor identify needs for additional training.

Assessment of Training Needs

Whether or not supervisors conduct much of their employees' formal training, they are still responsible for recognizing needs for training. With input from the employees, supervisors should determine the areas of training that employees will need and schedule the times for them to receive it.

Needs assessment should be an ongoing, not an occasional, concern of supervisors. Change is such a dominant force today that organizations depend on a workforce that continually learns and develops to give them a competitive edge.

A supervisor has several ways to identify training needs. First, a supervisor can observe problems in the department that suggest a need for training. For example, if a restaurant's customers are complaining about the quality of service, the manager might conclude that some or all of the staff needs training in how to satisfy customers. Or if forms sent from one department to another frequently contain a similar type of error, the department's supervisor should investigate why the people filling out the forms are making this type of mistake. Although frequent questions from employees are not necessarily a "problem," they do indicate that employees may need training in some area.

Certain areas of change also signal a need for training, and a supervisor should pay attention to them and consider what new knowledge and skills employees will need to keep abreast. If an organization encourages employee empowerment and teamwork, employees will need to know how to make decisions, evaluate team efforts, and listen to team members. When new technology (from a competitor, supplier, or elsewhere) affects an organization or the individuals in it, employees will need to learn about that technology and gain skill in applying it. If a department or its customer base is becoming more diverse, employees will need to learn how to respect, communicate with, and achieve objectives with people of different cultures.

Another way to obtain information about training needs is to ask employees. Employees frequently have opinions about what they must learn to do a better job. At a minimum, supervisors and employees should discuss training needs during performance appraisals (see Chapter 17). In addition, a supervisor should encourage employees to communicate their needs as they arise.

Finally, a supervisor can identify training needs when carrying out the planning function. Executing plans often requires that employees receive training in new skills or procedures. For example, if the organization will be introducing a new product, salespeople will have to be able to communicate its benefits to customers, and customer service staff will have to be able to answer questions about it.

In addition to recognizing these signals, a supervisor also should evaluate them. Do they indicate a need for training or for something else? Sometimes poor performance is not a training problem but a motivation problem. Errors or defects may be a symptom that employees lack resources or cooperation from elsewhere in the organization. Frequent questions may signal a need for better communication instead of (or in addition to) training. Before spending money on training, a supervisor should consider whether it is the best response to these signals. A good place to begin may be to ask the relevant employees to help find the underlying issue.

Mandatory Training

A supervisor is not the only one to decide when training is required. Government regulations, union work rules, or company policy may dictate training in certain circumstances. If the state mandates a number of continuing education classes for teachers, if the union requires an apprenticeship of so many months for pipe fitters, or if the company's top managers decide that everyone should take a class in total quality management, the supervisor's job is to make sure that his or her employees get the required training. The supervisor does so primarily through decisions related to scheduling and motivation.

Learning Environment

Along with planning for formal training sessions, supervisors can help organizations meet the need for training by fostering a climate that values learning. This kind of climate has been called a "learning environment." Jack Welch, former chairman of General Electric (GE), says he has learned a great deal from the managers who reported to him and encouraged them to challenge his ideas. "GE has what I like to call a culture of learning," he says, "and that means learning from anyone."[10]

Another way to foster a learning environment is to set a good example. Supervisors should develop their own knowledge and skills through a variety of means, from reading to attending seminars. Also, supervisors should share information generously with employees. They can enable employees to learn from one another by encouraging them to exchange what they have learned through their education, training activities, and experience. When employees request time and other resources for training, a supervisor should view the training as an investment to be evaluated, not merely a distraction from the "real work" of the organization.

Types of Training

A variety of types of training are available for employees (see Figure 16.5). Most organizations use a variety of training methods. At Regions Financial, a banking company based in Birmingham, Alabama, candidates for management jobs rotate through a variety of banking positions and participate in classroom training, computer-based instruction, and on-the-job training guided by a mentor. Verizon

FIGURE 16.5
Types of Training

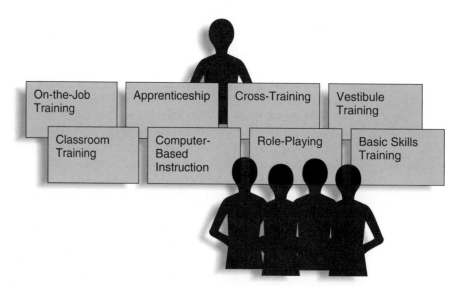

Wireless gives each of its customer service representatives 96 hours of training, including simulations, classroom instruction, and on-the-job learning.[11]

In selecting or recommending a type of training, a supervisor should consider the expense relative to the benefits, the resources available, and trainees' needs for practice and individualized attention. No matter what type of training is used, a supervisor should be sure that the trainer understands the objectives of the training and the ways to carry them out. A supervisor also should counsel employees who seem discouraged and praise them when they show progress.

On-the-Job Training

on-the-job training
Teaching a job while trainer and trainee perform the job at the work site

In many cases, the easiest way to learn how to perform a job is to try it. Teaching a job while trainer and trainee do the job at the work site is called **on-the-job training.** The trainer—typically a co-worker or supervisor—shows the employee how to do the job, and then the employee tries it.

An employee who learns in this way benefits from being able to try the skills and techniques being taught. The results tell immediately whether the employee understands what the trainer is trying to teach. However, on-the-job training carries the risk that an inexperienced employee will make costly and even dangerous mistakes. Thus, this type of training is most suitable when the tasks to be learned are relatively simple or the costs of an error are low. For more complex or risky tasks, it may be wiser to use other forms of training before or instead of on-the-job training.

Apprenticeship

apprenticeship
Training that involves working alongside an experienced person, who shows the apprentice how to do the various tasks involved in a job or trade

Many tradespeople learn their trades through an **apprenticeship.** This involves working alongside an experienced person, who shows the apprentice how to do the various tasks involved in the trade. Thus, an apprenticeship is a long-term form of on-the-job training. (Many apprenticeship programs also require that apprentices complete classroom training.) Most apprenticeships are in the building trades, such as carpentry and pipe fitting.

For example, the National Electrical Contractors Association and International Brotherhood of Electrical Workers (NECA-IBEW) offers three- to five-year apprenticeships that promise on-the-job training, college credits, competitive pay, and health and pension benefits. The organization hopes to train more than 100,000 electricians and information technology system installers through the program.[12]

An apprenticeship program is more complicated to set up than simple on-the-job training for individual tasks. However, it is one way to help a supervisor meet training needs that require months or years of learning.

Cross-Training

As you learned in Chapter 11, an increasing number of organizations are using job rotation, meaning that employees take turns performing various jobs. Job rotation requires that employees learn to perform more than one job. Teaching employees another job so that they can fill in as needed is known as cross-training. Employees who have completed cross-training can enjoy more variety in their work, and their supervisor has more flexibility in making assignments. The resulting flexibility also makes cross-training necessary for many forms of teamwork.

Vanamatic Company, a machine shop in Delphos, Ohio, uses cross-training to enable its employees to work in teams. Each team carries out production tasks for a manufacturing cell, in which various machine tools are used to make a particular product. Through cross-training, each member of a team learns to perform all the jobs in the manufacturing cell, such as operating a screw machine and a machining center. Employees also are tested to identify their strengths and work preferences. Teams allocate the work among their members, trying to assign each worker to a preferred area of operation. But when special needs arise, everyone can jump in and help as needed. According to Adam Wiltsie, the company's manufacturing engineer, "The operators enjoy the change of pace provided by doing different jobs in the cell," and efficiency is much greater than it was under the traditional arrangement of each employee specializing in just one process or machine.[13]

In planning cross-training, a supervisor should make sure that employees spend enough time practicing each job to learn it well. Some jobs are more complex than others and will require more training time. Also, some employees will learn a given job faster than others.

Vestibule Training

While on-the-job training is effective, it is not appropriate as initial training for jobs that have no room for errors, such as piloting or nursing. In those cases, people learn principles or techniques before doing the actual job. A type of training that allows employees to practice using equipment off the job is called **vestibule training.** Employees undergoing vestibule training use procedures and equipment set up in a special vestibule school. For example, a large retail store might set up a training room containing cash registers, or an airline might use a simulated cabin for training flight attendants.

vestibule training
Training that takes place on equipment set up in a special area off the job site

Vestibule training is appropriate when the organization hires people who do not already know how to use its equipment. Employees learn to operate the equipment without the pressure of accidents occurring, customers getting impatient, or other employees depending on a minimum amount of output. The expense of vestibule training or other off-the-job training is higher because employees are not producing goods or services for the organization while they undergo the training. However, if the organization hired only people who already had all the necessary skills, it would probably have to pay more and might have difficulty finding enough qualified candidates.

At Espresso Connection, a small chain of drive-through coffee bars in Washington State, Christian Kar slashed his marketing budget to pay for additional employee training, realizing that impressing customers with good service was the real key to increasing sales. When it came to knowing how to use the firm's equipment and prepare drinks, new employees used to learn by doing. But Kar hired several part-time trainers and developed a special hands-on facility where new employees spend a week using the machines and learning how to make various coffee drinks. Only when they've mastered the basics do recruits go on to another 40 hours of on-the-job training at one of the stores. Under the new program, training also includes the specifics of high-quality customer service. Peak-hour sales have doubled since training began. "The training has definitely helped," says Kar.[14]

Classroom Training

Other than vestibule training, about 69 percent of off-the-job training involves some form of classroom instruction.[15] This training takes place in a class or seminar where one or more speakers lecture on a specific topic. Seminars are available from a variety of sources on many topics, so a supervisor who is considering attending or sending employees to a seminar should first make sure the topic will be relevant to job performance. Classroom training also can occur at the workplace, even if the organization lacks the time or facilities for formal classes.

The main advantage of classroom training is that the person conducting it can deliver a large quantity of information to more than one person in a relatively short time. Depending on the format and trainer, it can be a relatively inexpensive way to convey information. A disadvantage is that most of the communication travels in one direction—from the lecturer to the audience. One-way communication is less engaging and memorable. In addition, classroom training rarely allows the learners to practice what they are learning.

Classroom training therefore benefits from the trainer's ability to maintain a high level of interest, such as by including computer-based instruction and role playing. Randstad North America, a temporary-employment agency, sent its 250 branch managers to a five-day course exploring some of the basics of supervision. The emphasis was on applying the course's lessons, so to learn about coaching, participants were asked to bring in an example: the most difficult employee they needed to coach. Each manager then paired up with another participant for role-playing. In each participant's role-play, the branch manager played him- or herself, and the partner played the problem employee.[16]

Computer-Based Instruction

At a growing number of organizations, computer software is taking the place of classroom-based trainers. In fact, according to *Training* magazine, about 16 percent of training courses are delivered via computer-based training with no live instructor involved.[17] Computer-based instruction typically uses a computer to present information, generate and score test questions, keep track of the trainee's performance, and tell the trainee what activities to do next. This type of training is a common way of learning to use a new computer program; the software comes with a series of lessons that give the user a chance to try using it. Computer-based training that employs the Internet is commonly referred to as e-learning. Table 16.1 lists 10 major advantages that e-learning offers organizations. E-learning is particularly useful when trainees are spread over a wide geographic area. In that case, the organization may use *distance learning*, in which computers and communications technology deliver the course content to participants who are located far away from the provider of the training.

Some firms have already put themselves on the leading edge of integrating technology into workforce training, One innovation is to use the technology of video games to make learning more interesting and enjoyable. Cold Stone Creamery has a custom online game that simulates one of its stores. Players learn portion control by scooping ice cream as the timer runs out; when it does, they see whether they served too much. Almost three out of every ten Cold Stone employees downloaded this learning game voluntarily because they find it so entertaining. Canon trains repair personnel with a game in which they drag and drop parts onto an image of a copier. If they send the part to the wrong place, a light flashes and a buzzer goes off. Canon compared the performance of trainees using the game with performance of trainees who learned from manuals; the gamers' scores were noticeably higher.[18]

interactive multimedia
Computer software that brings together sound, video, graphics, animation, and text and adjusts content on the basis of user responses

Computer-based instruction is becoming more engaging and widespread because of the growing affordability of **interactive multimedia.** This software brings together sound, video, graphics, animation, and text. The best interactive multimedia programs adjust the course content on the basis of the student's responses to questions. Interactive multimedia typically is delivered on DVD or CD-ROM, storage media that many personal computers can use. Accenture uses interactive multimedia to create simulations in which trainees practice answering

TABLE 16.1
**E-Learning Offers
10 Major
Advantages**

Source: From Bray J.
Brockbank, "E-Learning
Offers 10 Major
Advantages," *Executive
Excellence,* July 2001.
Reprinted with permission
of Leadership Excellence.

1. Real-time learning and application of critical knowledge. E-learning is immediate and up-to-date.
2. Learner-centric training. E-learning changes the focus of training from instructor to learner. It is tailored to the learner's responsibilities and capabilities, creating relevant applications.
3. Ability to attract, train, and retain employees. The number one reason for the loss of key employees is that they feel their company has not invested sufficient resources into their professional development.
4. Personalized training. An effective e-learning system learns about its users and tailors its offerings to their learning style, job requirements, career goals, current knowledge, and preferences.
5. Ownership of learning. E-learning empowers people to manage their own learning and development plans. Ownership of learning is crucial for individual growth and the retention of employees.
6. Simulation. We learn by doing. E-learning is an innovative way to simulate each learning experience with content provided by top professionals.
7. Collaboration. This is done through either joint problem solving or the sharing of ideas and experience among study groups and chat rooms. Collaboration is a path to effective learning and innovative processes.
8. Ability to train anytime and anywhere. Training in a virtual information classroom is now possible anytime, anywhere.
9. Cost effectiveness. Costs can be applied to each learner, and results can be measured against costs. And, e-learning is less intrusive into daily work duties, saving time and money through less interruption of employees' regularly scheduled duties.
10. Quantifiable results. E-learning can be effectively measured in terms of knowledge gain and retention. With e-learning, corporations can track progress, report results, and specify additional subject matter. This is where the return on investment will be recognized by the employer and employee.

questions and otherwise interacting with digitized images of clients. Retailer JCPenney uses interactive multimedia to train customer service representatives in its credit-card division. The computer simulates phone calls from customers, so the reps can practice handling irate (and reasonable) customers.

Some computer-based training uses simulations, as in the previous example of Cold Stone Creamery. The computer displays conditions that an employee might have to face. For example, a flight simulator would show pilot trainees the cockpit and the view from the window. Another simulation might be of dials and other readouts monitoring the performance of machinery. A trainee uses the computer's keyboard or some other device to respond to the situation displayed by a computer, and the simulator responds by showing the consequences of the trainee's actions. This enables the trainee to practice responding to conditions without suffering the real consequences of a mistake, such as a plane crashing or a boiler exploding.

Computer-based instruction has a significant cost advantage over other methods when there are many trainees. An organization may not have to pay a trainer. In addition, trainees can work at their own pace, eliminating the frustration that arises from a class moving too fast for them to understand the material or too slow to maintain their interest. A good training program can help trainees learn faster or better than they might through another training technique. At JCPenney, customer service representatives trained with interactive multimedia reach peak proficiency in one-third less time than employees who had more traditional training. Accenture credits interactive multimedia for its employees having "deeper competencies, more skill and knowledge."[19] The lower cost of computer-based training is a likely reason the use of such training has increased even as companies cut their overall training budgets.[20]

Even small companies can benefit from computer-based training. Sherman Assembly Systems of San Antonio, Texas, is a contract manufacturer of electronic cable assemblies. Many of its employees are former welfare recipients who have received job training from Goodwill Industries but who still lack high school diplomas. To help them achieve their general equivalency diplomas (GED), CEO Michael Sherman enlisted the help of a local college to supply a Web-based GED program that runs on a couple of dedicated computers in the company's conference room.[21]

Some people, however, are nervous about using a computer. A supervisor or other trainer must encourage and help these people. Also, some forms of computer-based instruction do not allow employees to work as a team, ask questions, or exchange ideas. When these training features are important, a supervisor should choose software that offers these capabilities, supplement the computer-based training, or select other training methods.

Experts offer the following advice for successfully implementing a computer-assisted training program:[22]

- Tell learners what they will be able to do after the training.
- Include rewards, such as money, time off, better working conditions, new tools and equipment, or career opportunities.
- Minimize noise and interruptions in the learning environment and maximize access, speed, and ease of use.
- "Chunk" instruction into segments of 20 minutes or less.
- Vary the media, including a variety of audio, video, and print materials as well as simulations and interactive tools.
- Give legitimate feedback.
- Remember to incorporate the human touch via chat rooms, e-mail, electronic office hours, audio streaming, or online mentoring.
- Reinforce learning with questionnaires or "alumni" chat sessions.

Role-Playing

role-playing
A training method in which roles are assigned to participants, who then act out the way they would handle a specific situation

To teach skills in working with other people, an organization may use **role-playing.** This method involves assigning roles to participants, who then act out the way they would handle a specific situation. Some of the exercises in this book use role-playing. A technique that enhances the usefulness of role-playing is to videotape the session and play it back so participants can see how they looked and sounded.

Role-playing gives people a chance to practice the way they react to others, making it especially useful for training in human relations skills such as communicating, resolving conflicts, and working with people of other races or cultures. People who have acted out a particular role—for example, the role of supervisor—generally have more sympathy for that person's point of view. The major potential drawback of role-playing is that, to be most useful, it requires a trainer with expertise in conducting it.

At New York–based Internet media company MaMaMedia.com, which produces Web-based "playful learning" products for children under 12, employees learn by doing, but as children do. "We try to approximate the way children learn through exploration, fun, surprise, and imagination," says Rebecca Randall, executive vice president of marketing and brand development. "One of the best ways to provoke thought is by engaging people in games, play, activities, theater, and role-playing."[23]

Basic Skills Training

An often-heard complaint among employers today is that it is increasingly difficult to find enough employees with the basic skills necessary to perform modern jobs. An increasing number of employers are responding to this problem by conducting their own training in basic skills. Organizations that offer such programs not only improve the skills of their workers but also attract and keep employees who are highly motivated. However, basic skills education offers some challenges to the employer. One is that employees may resist attending because they are embarrassed or afraid the organization will punish them if it finds out they do not have basic skills. To address this challenge, an organization should name the program carefully, calling it something like "workplace education" or "skills enhancement." Supervisors and other managers should reassure employees that participating in the program does not place their jobs in danger. In addition, experts recommend rewarding employees for participating in a basic skills program.

COACHING TO SUPPORT TRAINING

coaching
Guidance and instruction in how to do a job so that it satisfies performance goals

After employees have received training, a supervisor should take on the role of coach to help them maintain and use the skills they have acquired. **Coaching** is guidance and instruction in how to do a job so that it satisfies performance goals. The concept comes from sports, where a coach constantly observes team members in action, identifies each player's strengths and weaknesses, and works with each person to help him or her capitalize on strengths and improve on weaknesses. The most respected coaches generally encourage their team members and take a personal interest in them.

In a business context, coaching involves similar activities. As coach, a supervisor engages in regular observation, teaching, and encouragement to help employees develop so that they in turn can help the team succeed. Much of this coaching is done informally to back up the more formal training process.

In this role, a supervisor observes employees' performances daily and provides feedback. To encourage employees, a supervisor should praise them when they meet or exceed expectations. A supervisor should consider whether good performance is evidence that the employees can be given key responsibilities or have strengths that should be further developed. When an employee makes a mistake, the supervisor should work with the employee, focusing on the problem rather than any perceived deficiencies in the employee's character. Together, the supervisor and employee should decide how to correct the problem—perhaps through more training, a revised assignment, or more reliable access to resources. A supervisor and employee should work on only one problem at a time, with the supervisor continually looking for signs of employee progress. Figure 16.6 summarizes the process of coaching.

The process of coaching is different from simply telling employees what to do. It emphasizes learning about employees, then drawing on and developing their talents. (The Knowing Yourself quiz on page 470 can help you evaluate your coaching potential.) Acting as a coach is especially appropriate for supervisors in organizations that encourage employees to participate in decision making and teamwork.

mentoring
Providing guidance, advice, and encouragement through an ongoing one-on-one work relationship

Mentoring

In some cases, a supervisor may focus coaching efforts on one employee. This practice is called **mentoring,** or providing guidance, advice, and encouragement through an ongoing one-on-one work relationship. A supervisor should not use a mentoring relationship as an excuse for failure to encourage all employees in the

FIGURE 16.6
The Coaching Process

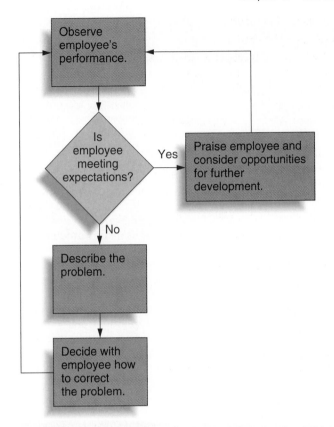

work group. However, mentoring may be an appropriate way to support the training of an employee who has especially great potential, needs extra attention to contribute fully, or has been assigned to the supervisor for that purpose. Some organizations use mentoring of minority and female employees to help them learn to navigate in a setting where communication styles, values, expectations, and so on may differ from those to which they are used. For examples, see the "Supervision and Diversity" box.

At public relations firm FitzGerald Communications, in Cambridge, Massachusetts, new employees work with "buddies" from the client account teams for their first 90 days on the job. They then pick their own mentors, with whom they will meet several times over the course of the next year. The company takes mentoring so seriously that it has produced an 18-page mentoring handbook. The mentoring partners sign a contract to commit to the program, and both give their input in annual employee reviews.[24]

Some of the activities that mentors undertake include listening or acting as a sounding board, sharing knowledge and experience, guiding employees to discover the results of their own behavior, and sharing what they know about opportunities in the organization and its future direction. For example, Dan Boehm once saw that a young salesperson at the software company where they worked was having difficulty closing any sales. By observing and listening to the sales rep, Boehm concluded the young salesperson needed to shift the focus away from his own fears and frustrations and begin concentrating on clients' needs. Boehm coached the salesperson on how to explore each prospect's personality, objectives, and problems. He encouraged the salesperson to set achievable short-term goals. Eventually, the salesperson's confidence returned, and his performance improved.[25]

SUPERVISION AND DIVERSITY

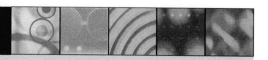

THE MENTOR'S ROLE: "GUIDE ON THE SIDE, NOT SAGE ON THE STAGE"

When organizations' top positions are filled by white men, women and minorities sometimes find that they have to work extra hard to make the desired impression. Many women and minority members of both sexes actively seek out a mentor—sometimes more than one.

Berthenia A. Harmon found a mentor at her school when she decided to make a career change. Harmon, an African American, had been an accounting specialist at an insurance firm but wanted to switch to education. She enrolled at Kean University to earn a master's degree in early-childhood education. There, Harmon's graduate coordinator was a source of encouragement, affirming Harmon's love for her newly chosen career as well as the potential for Harmon to apply her lessons from the corporate world to the bureaucracy of a school system.

As in Harmon's case, successful employees play an active role in the mentoring relationship. These employees identify career goals and seek mentors who can help them with their goals. This means employees may have a series of mentors as their careers progress. Marques T. Crump, for example, had a mentor in his job as a computer programmer, but he determined that he preferred a different kind of work. When he moved to a job as a financial service representative for Primerica, Crump thanked his mentor but declined the offer of a transfer to another computer position.

Many organizations encourage mentoring as a way to make their female and minority employees full participants in the company. Mentors can help employees share their ideas and skills with others in the organization, and they can guide employees to opportunities for developing their skills. Organizations can train their supervisors and other managers in such mentoring skills as asking open-ended questions and identifying opportunities for employees to develop new skills.

Sources: Robyn D. Clarke, "Leading by Direction, Not Dictation: A New Role for Today's Mentor," *Black Enterprise,* April 2003, downloaded from InfoTrac, http://web3.infotrac.galegroup.com; Nancy S. Ahlrichs, *Manager of Choice: Five Competencies for Cultivating Top Talent* (Palo Alto, CA: Davies-Black, 2003), pp. 48–49, 147–48.

EVALUATION OF TRAINING

A supervisor is often in the best position to determine whether training is working. The most basic way to evaluate training is to measure whether the training is resolving the problem. Are new employees learning their jobs? Is the defect rate falling? Do employees use the new computer system properly? Are customers now praising the service instead of complaining about it? Looking for answers to such questions is central to the control process, described in Chapter 6.

Other people, including the employees who have participated in the training, also can provide information to help evaluate training. They might fill out a questionnaire (see Figure 16.7), or the organization might set up a team of people to evaluate the organization's training methods and content.

If the evaluation suggests that training is not meeting its objectives, the training may have to be modified or expanded. The type of training may not be appropriate for the training needs. For example, new employees who are having difficulty learning job skills may not have enough opportunity to practice what they are being taught. To identify what kinds of changes to make, the supervisor can ask questions such as the following:

- Was the trainer well prepared?
- Did the trainer communicate the information clearly and in an interesting way?

FIGURE 16.7
Questionnaire for Evaluating Training

Source: Donald S. Miller and Stephen E. Catt, *Human Relations: A Contemporary Approach* (Lincolnwood, IL: Richard D. Irwin, 1989), p. 330. Reprinted with the permission of the authors.

Title of Program_____

Date _____**Job Title**_____

Directions: Please indicate your response to each question and return this questionnaire to the program leader. Your responses are confidential. DO NOT SIGN YOUR NAME ON THIS EVALUATION INSTRUMENT.

1. In my opinion, this program was: (check one)
   ____ Excellent ____Very good ____Good ____Fair ____Poor
2. Did the program meet the objectives stated in the outline given to you? (check one)
   ____Yes ____No
3. Did the program meet your expectations? (Check one)
   ____Yes ____No If you checked no, please explain _____
   _____
4. Were the training facilities adequate? (Check one)
   ____Yes____No If you checked no, please explain _____
   _____
5. In my opinion, the instructor was: (check one)
   ____Excellent ____Very good ____Good ____Fair ____Poor
6. How important was each of these training elements? (check one for each element)
   Videotapes   ____ Very important ____ Worthwhile ____ Not important
   Role playing   ____ Very important ____ Worthwhile ____ Not important
   Lecture   ____ Very important ____ Worthwhile ____ Not important
   Handouts   ____ Very important ____ Worthwhile ____ Not important
   Group discussion ____ Very important ____ Worthwhile ____ Not important
7. To what extent did you participate in the program? (check one)
   ____A lot ____Just enough ____Somewhat ____Not at all
8. How much will the content of this program help you to perform your job responsibilities? (check one)
   ____ A lot ____Just enough ____Somewhat ____Not at all
9. What other types of training programs are of interest to you? Indicate your preferences. _____
   _____
10. How can this program be improved? Indicate your suggestions. _____
    _____
11. Other comments and suggestions. Please indicate any other comments/ suggestions that you feel will be useful in planning future training programs.
    _____
    _____
    _____
    _____
    _____

- Did the training include visual demonstrations in addition to verbal descriptions of how to do the task?
- Were the employees well enough prepared for the training program?
- Did the employees understand how they would benefit from the training?
- Did employees have a chance to ask questions?
- Did the employees receive plenty of praise for their progress?

To retain experienced managers at a manufacturing plant purchased from General Electric, Gates Energy Products human resource manager Robin Kane conducted a needs assessment to identify necessary skills and critical issues. She then designed a "new manager development program" consisting of courses that met for two days a month for nine months to cover such issues as team leadership skills, goal setting, motivating, delegating and time management, problem solving, decision making, negotiating, and managing conflict and change. Though the plant was later sold again, Kane was able to evaluate the program on the basis of her goal of retaining managers: Turnover remained very low.[26]

Whatever the outcome, training represents a cost to the organization. Consequently, it is worth conducting only when it leads to improved performance, as measured by increased quantity, quality, or both. Training that does not produce results should be changed or discontinued. In organizations in which supervisors and others are selective and use only training that meets evaluation criteria, training programs are not an expense but a valuable investment in the organization's human resources.

SKILLS MODULE

PART ONE: CONCEPTS

Summary

16.1 Summarize reasons for conducting an orientation for new employees.

The primary reason to conduct an orientation is that the sooner new employees know basic information related to their job, the sooner they can become productive. Orientation also reduces the nervousness and uncertainty of new employees, and it helps them develop a positive attitude by boosting job satisfaction.

16.2 Discuss how a supervisor and the human resources department can work together to conduct an orientation.

In a small organization, a supervisor may conduct most or all of the orientation. In a large organization, the human resources department may handle most of the task. In either case, it is up to the supervisor to convey information about the specifics of holding a particular job in a particular department. This includes explaining what the department does and what the new employee's job entails. Typically, the human resources department covers topics related to the organization's policies and procedures.

16.3 Identify methods for conducting an orientation.

During the orientation, a new employee should be introduced to the organization's employee handbook. A supervisor (or someone else) should give the employee a tour of the workplace, pointing out facilities the employee will need to use. During the tour, the employee should be introduced to the people with whom he or she will be working. A supervisor should instruct other employees in their role of welcoming a new employee. At the end of the first day and the first week, the supervisor should follow up to make sure the new employee understands the new job.

16.4 Describe the training cycle.

First, a supervisor (or someone else) assesses training needs. The next three steps cover planning the training: setting objectives, deciding who will participate, and choosing the training method. Then someone (a supervisor, an employee, or a professional trainer) conducts the training. The last step is to evaluate the success of the training. Evaluation sometimes suggests needs for additional training.

16.5 **Explain how supervisors can decide when employees need training.**

A supervisor may observe problems in the department that indicate a need for training. Areas of change may signal training needs. A supervisor may ask employees about the kinds of training they need or identify training needs when carrying out the planning function. Finally, some training may be mandated by government regulations, union work rules, or company policy.

16.6 **Define major types of training.**

The organization may use on-the-job training, which involves learning while performing a job. Related training methods are apprenticeships and cross-training (that is, training employees in more than one job). The training also may take place off-site through vestibule training or in a classroom. Classroom training can be more effective when it includes computer-aided instruction (particularly interactive multimedia) and role-playing. Some computer-aided instruction involves simulations. Finally, in an organization in which employees lack basic skills, such as the ability to read directions or work with numbers, the organization may offer basic skills training.

16.7 **Describe how a supervisor can use coaching and mentoring to support training.**

To help employees maintain and use the skills they have acquired, a supervisor takes on the role of coach, guiding and instructing employees in how to do a job so that it satisfies performance goals. The supervisor observes employee performance and provides feedback on it. Supervisor and employee work together to devise a solution to any problem. Then the supervisor reviews the employee's performance to make sure the employee understood what to do and is doing it. A supervisor may act as a mentor to an employee, providing guidance, advice, and encouragement through an ongoing one-on-one work relationship. Some organizations use mentoring of minority and female employees as a way to help them learn to navigate unfamiliar work situations.

16.8 **Discuss how a supervisor can evaluate the effectiveness of training.**

To evaluate training, a supervisor measures whether the problem addressed by the training is being solved. In addition, participants in the training may fill out a questionnaire in which they evaluate their experience. When training is not producing the desired results, a supervisor should attempt to find out why and then correct the problem.

Key Terms

training, *p. 445*
orientation, *p. 447*
employee handbook,
p. 450
on-the-job training, *p. 457*

apprenticeship, *p. 457*
vestibule training,
p. 458
interactive multimedia,
p. 459

role playing, *p. 461*
coaching, *p. 462*
mentoring, *p. 462*

Review and Discussion Questions

1. Describe a job or activity for which you received training. What was the purpose of this training?
2. Describe a situation in which you received an orientation. What did the orientation consist of? How was the orientation different from training?

3. When Al DeAngelis started his new job as a computer programmer, he arrived in his department at 9:30 a.m., after having spent time in the human resources department filling out forms. Marcia Eizenstadt, his supervisor, shook his hand and said, "Al, I'm so glad you're starting with us today. We need your talents tremendously." Then, explaining that she would be tied up all day in important planning meetings, Eizenstadt showed DeAngelis to his desk and gave him an employee handbook to look at. "Read this carefully," said Eizenstadt. "It'll tell you everything you need to know about working here. By tomorrow or the next day, I hope we'll be able to sit down and go over your first assignment." DeAngelis spent the rest of the day reading the manual, wishing for a cup of coffee, and trying to smile pleasantly in response to the quizzical looks he was getting from other employees passing by and glancing into his cubicle.

    a. What aspects of DeAngelis's orientation were helpful?

    b. How could it have been improved?

4. What are the steps in the training cycle?

5. Who determines when training is needed? What are some indications of a need for training?

6. Phil Petrakis supervises the housekeepers at a hotel in a big city. He has found that the easiest and fastest way to train his staff is to give them a memo describing whatever new policy or procedure he wants to teach. When the employees have read the memo, the training is complete—it is as simple as that. What is wrong with this approach?

7. Which type or types of training would you recommend in each of the following situations? Explain your choices.

    a. Teaching air-traffic controllers how to help pilots land planes safely.

    b. Improving the decision-making skills of production workers so they can better participate in the company's employee involvement program.

    c. Teaching a plumber how to replace sewer lines.

    d. Teaching a receptionist how to operate the company's new telephone system.

8. At a department meeting, production supervisor Lenore Gibbs announced, "Starting next month, the company will be offering a class for any of you who can't read. It will take place after work in the cafeteria." How do you think employees with reading difficulties would react to Gibbs's announcement? How can she phrase the announcement so that employees will be more likely to attend the class?

9. What is coaching? Why is it especially appropriate in organizations that encourage employee involvement and teamwork?

10. What is a mentor? What steps might a mentor take to help a Japanese employee who has been transferred from the Tokyo office to company headquarters in the United States? How might these actions help the employee and the organization?

11. Think back to the training you described in question 1. Evaluate its effectiveness. In what ways might it have been improved?

PART TWO: SKILL-BUILDING

YOU SOLVE THE PROBLEM

Reflecting back on page 445, consider that though employee turnover at the Cheesecake Factory is below the industry average, the restaurant business tends to have very high turnover (that is, many employees quit their jobs each year). Specifically, the industry norm is 106 percent, and turnover at Cheesecake Factory restaurants ranges from about 80 to 95 percent, meaning that a restaurant manager must train new employees for most positions every year.

Suppose that your group is a team of consultants who have been asked to consider whether training could be improved in a way that will bring down the company's rate of employee turnover. The Cheesecake Factory will try your ideas in three of its restaurants. Review the training ideas in this chapter. Prepare a memo recommending changes to the company's training program. Indicate why you think they will improve turnover at the three test restaurants.

Problem-Solving Case: *Training Call Center Employees*

The employees in a call center need to be able to speak to customers politely, but their skill set is more complicated than etiquette. They also need to handle a range of questions and problems about particular products. Whenever their company adds a new line of products or services, the employees have to be prepared to answer a new set of questions. Thus, training is an ongoing concern in call centers. The traditional approach is to present new material in a classroom setting and supplement this learning with other training components.

For efficiency and flexibility, call center training often uses Web-based components. The most common form of these is called asynchronous Web-based training, a set of modules that each agent completes independently at his or her own computer by viewing the course content and then answering questions at his or her own pace. No live instructor is needed. Sometimes the modules include a simulation in which the trainee handles calls from actors posing as customers with questions or problems related to the course content.

Some organizations can afford to customize their training programs to make them more engaging than reading text and answering multiple-choice questions. A call center hired a training company called Resource Bridge to develop online training with the flavor of a video game. Modules for teaching courtesy and professionalism show animated videos of three agents taking a phone call. One agent has a stiff manner, another speaks in pleasant, conversational tones,

and the third is extremely casual, addressing the caller as "hon." When trainees choose the style they think is most appropriate, the training video shows the customer's reaction, rather than just indicating whether the choice is correct. For example, the customer responds to being called "hon" by becoming annoyed at the familiarity. Trainees quickly realize that the approach is ineffective.

When supervisors monitor agents' calls, they can use the recordings to identify training opportunities. If the supervisor observes that an employee is having difficulty handling a particular type of problem or customer, the supervisor can send the employee a Web-based training module that addresses the situation. Envision Click2Coach lets the supervisor select video demonstrations of how to handle a type of problem. The supervisor can record a voice-over explanation of how the employee could have handled a problem more effectively. These and other training programs allow supervisors to select graphics, documents, and audio clips (including recordings of the calls the employee handled) for insertion into the training modules. This capability lets the supervisor efficiently coach individual employees while both remain at their desks.

Electronic coaching is easy and flexible, so supervisors need to be reminded of the importance of face-to-face communication with employees. Personal communication to offer encouragement is essential as a way to reinforce their use of the desired skills.

New employees or employees who have just learned a new set of skills may begin working in a "nesting area." They are seated together in an area of the call center where one or two supervisors are close at hand to provide assistance and answer questions. Also, experienced agents may be assigned to help employees in the nesting area. Placing them in this coaching role may make employees feel more at ease (it can be more comfortable to seek help from a peer rather than from a supervisor). At the same time, coaching others can reinforce the more experienced employees' knowledge and develops them to become supervisors in the future.

Another popular way to train agents is to assign them to a veteran employee who serves as a mentor. For example, if a supervisor at Georgia Power's call center determines that new agents have a weakness in a particular skill, the supervisor assigns those agents to experienced employees who excel in that skill. The agents and their mentors sit near one another so that the mentors are readily available to help. However, Paula Sacks, a Georgia Power supervisor, notes that mentors must be selected carefully. The mentors must be more than skillful at their jobs; they also must be good communicators who are willing to use part of their time for coaching.

1. Imagine that you are a supervisor in a call center, where you oversee 20 employees who handle questions and problems from people who buy your client's products—furniture that must be assembled using basic hand tools. Your client is preparing the launch of new products: rugs and other accessories. Now your agents must be prepared for a new set of issues, such as questions related to fabrics and colors. Which of the methods described in this case will you use to prepare the agents for these changes? Why?

2. Prepare a training plan for your agents. Will you train them all at once or in groups? Which methods will you use first? Will you start the training before or during the product launch?

3. What, if anything, will you need to learn to prepare yourself for these changes? How will you develop your own skills?

Sources: Greg Levin, "The End of Agent Training as We Know It," *Call Center*, July 1, 2006; Kelli Gavant, "Resource Bridge Helps Companies Improve Training," *(Arlington Heights, IL.) Daily Herald*, April 19, 2006, both downloaded from Business & Company Resource Center, http://galenet.galegroup.com.

Knowing Yourself

Could You Coach Someone?

This quiz is designed to evaluate your potential to act as a coach in support of training. Write True or False before each of the following statements.

_____ 1. The best way to get something done is to do it yourself.
_____ 2. If I give someone clear instructions, I know that person will get the job done without my checking on him or her.
_____ 3. I don't mind if someone asks me questions about how to do a job.
_____ 4. If I give someone instructions on how to perform a task, it's that individual's responsibility to complete it.
_____ 5. I like to let people know when they've done something right.
_____ 6. If someone makes a mistake, we focus on solving the problem together.
_____ 7. If someone makes a mistake, I correct the problem myself.
_____ 8. If someone doesn't follow company procedures, I assume he or she hasn't read the company handbook.
_____ 9. I think that interactive multimedia software is the best form of training for everyone.
_____ 10. Training a new employee shouldn't last more than a week.

Scoring: True responses to statements 2, 5, and 6 show good potential for coaching. True responses to the other statements show that you need to become aware of the needs of individuals, then work on drawing on and emphasizing their talents.

Pause and Reflect

1. According to this quiz, how strong are your coaching skills?

2. How might you improve your coaching ability?

Class Exercise

Being a Trainer

One or more students volunteer to teach the class a skill. If possible, the volunteers should have time to prepare their "training session" before the class meets. Some "trainers" might like to work as a team. Suggestions for skills to teach follow; use your creativity to add to the list:

- Folding paper hats.
- Doing a card trick.
- Communicating a message in sign language.
- Making punch for a party.

After the training session or sessions, the class discusses the following questions:

1. How can you evaluate whether this training was successful? If possible, try to conduct an evaluation of what the class learned. What do the results of this evaluation indicate?

2. What training techniques were used? Would additional or alternative techniques have made the skill easier to learn? What changes would have helped?

Building Supervision Skills

Orienting a New Team Member

Divide the class into teams of four or five. Select (or ask for a volunteer) one member of each team to play the role of a newcomer to the school (the newcomer might pose as a transfer student, a student from another country, or the like). The rest of the team will do its best to orient the newcomer to the school. Team members might want to take responsibility for different areas of knowledge; for example, one might draw a map of campus and town for the newcomer, pointing out bus routes and important or useful locations; another might volunteer information about study groups or social activities. At the end of the session, the newcomer should evaluate and discuss how effective the orientation was.

Chapter **Seventeen**

Appraising Performance

Learning Objectives

After you have studied this chapter, you should be able to:

17.1 Summarize the benefits of conducting performance appraisals.

17.2 Identify the steps in appraising performance systematically.

17.3 Discuss guidelines for avoiding discrimination in performance appraisals.

17.4 Compare types of appraisals.

17.5 Describe sources of bias in appraising performance.

17.6 Explain the purpose of conducting performance appraisal interviews.

17.7 Tell how supervisors should prepare for a performance appraisal interview.

17.8 Describe guidelines for conducting the interview.

You have to get ongoing constructive feedback to push you out of your comfort zone.

—*Kevin Sharer, CEO, Amgen*

Steve Nadeau, vice president of human resources for Gwinnett Health System, a hospital with 3,300 employees in Lawrenceville, Georgia, had a problem. "The old-fashioned, paper-and-pencil performance review didn't work well for us," he said. "Evaluations were late, employees said it was too subjective, and managers didn't like the system." The problems snowballed and could even have affected the hospital system's accreditation by the Joint Commission on Accreditation of Healthcare Organizations, which evaluates more than 19,500 health care organizations in the United States.

Then Nadeau purchased a software program designed to support employee evaluations in the health care industry. After a long period of testing and customizing the system with criteria specifically developed for the hospital, the program was implemented. Over the next two months, employees and managers were trained to use the program. The results were truly worthwhile. "Employees have liked it from the start," Nadeau says.

The new system uses five employee ratings based on standards set by the hospital's managers. To keep subjective decisions to a minimum, the system lets managers customize modules, rather than writing criteria from scratch. Although the system supports the hospital's traditional process of having supervisors conduct formal employee reviews once a year, it also allows for input from co-workers. The two-thirds of Gwinnett's employees who don't have regular access to a computer can contribute their input in the form of handwritten responses on evaluation checklists.

These software-based performance appraisals focus on results rather than on personality traits. Employees therefore tend to view the new system as more objective and fair than the old one. That perception is especially important because the results of Gwinnett's performance reviews are linked to pay increases.

Supervisors at Gwinnett Health System don't choose the format for appraising employees' performance, but they have to deliver feedback through the system that the organization has chosen.

QUESTIONS

1. How can supervisors gather the information needed to provide employees with helpful feedback?

2. How can supervisors deliver performance feedback that is objective and fair?

Source: Gail Dutton, "Making Reviews More Efficient and Fair," *Workforce,* April 2001, pp. 76–81.

---

performance appraisal
Formal feedback on how well an employee is performing his or her job

Formal feedback on how well an employee is performing on the job is known as a **performance appraisal** (or a performance review or performance evaluation). Most organizations require that supervisors conduct a performance appraisal of each of their employees regularly, typically once a year. Therefore, supervisors need to know how to appraise performance fairly.

This chapter discusses reasons for conducting performance appraisals and describes a process for appraising performances systematically. It describes various types of appraisals used by organizations today. It also tells how to avoid biases and how to conduct an appraisal interview.

PURPOSES OF PERFORMANCE APPRAISAL

Performance appraisals provide the information needed by employees to improve the quality of their work. To improve, employees need to hear how they are doing. As described in Chapters 7 and 10, a supervisor should provide frequent feedback. Performance appraisals supplement this informal information with a more thought-out, formal evaluation. (Employees who get enough informal feedback probably will not be surprised by the results of the appraisal.) A formal performance appraisal ensures that feedback to an employee covers all important aspects of the employee's performance.

On the basis of this information, the employee and supervisor can plan how to improve weak areas. In this way, performance appraisals support the practice of

SUPERVISION ACROSS INDUSTRIES

MANUFACTURING

WHIRLPOOL APPRAISES ITS APPRAISAL PROCESS

When Whirlpool management learned that employees wanted more feedback from their supervisors, the company started making improvements to its appraisal process. At the heart of the changes was frequent feedback. Whirlpool began requiring supervisors to hold appraisal interviews with each employee at least four times a year, instead of twice. As supervisors and their employees discovered that the reviews were helping the employees improve, some began meeting even more often. Jeffrey Davidoff, whose eight employees are responsible for marketing Whirlpool's products in North America, conducts a review of each employee every two weeks. Those meetings last as long as 45 minutes. You might think that this would become a time waster, but Davidoff said, "I'm noticing much better results."

That attitude reflects a change from what Whirlpool managers had once felt. Before Whirlpool began modifying the review process, supervisors complained about the time required. The company responded by converting most of the process to a computer system. Supervisors would enter comments, and employees would read the ratings on their own computers. However, employees then complained they were missing out on feedback about their performance. They didn't know if they were excelling or falling short of expectations, much less how to improve. Their reaction showed that appraisal meetings were important management tools. Davidoff, for example, has found that when he meets frequently with employees to discuss their performance, he is able to delegate more of the marketing work to them, rather than doing it himself.

Today, along with more frequent meetings, the appraisal process at Whirlpool includes a requirement that employees write performance objectives for themselves. The objectives must include at least one goal that is outside the employee's basic job requirements. The supervisor reviews and approves those objectives. Some employees find that it is difficult to develop objectives, but they appreciate the involvement and clarity about what is expected. Chris Ball, a senior sales manager for Whirlpool, told a reporter, "I feel more ownership" under the new appraisal system. And Davidoff said, "I am pleasantly surprised at how many day-to-day behaviors have changed," now that employees are clearer about what is expected of them.

Source: Erin White, "For Relevance, Firms Revamp Worker Reviews," *The Wall Street Journal*, July 17, 2006, http://online.wsj.com.

coaching, described in Chapter 16. For instance, at Van Kampen Investments in Oakbrook Terrace, Illinois, managers and supervisors use the review process to ask employees about their goals. "If an employee wants to go from customer service to finance, for example," says Jeanne Cliff, senior vice president of human resources, "what's the next step? Managers outline that for them, and give employees written goals and performance development plans."[1]

An appraisal also can help motivate employees. Most people appreciate the time their supervisor spends discussing their work, as well as praise for good performance; just hearing the supervisor's viewpoint can be motivating. Employees also tend to put forth the greatest effort in the areas that get appraised. Therefore, by rating employees on the kinds of behavior it considers important, an organization encourages them to try hard in those areas and keeps skilled workers in the firm. In a 1998 survey of information technology workers, more than 80 percent of those who responded said that receiving feedback and having individual development plans were among the top factors that would make them less likely to leave their firms.[2] And consider the case of Bill Ransom, a union employee who had been with the same aerospace company for 18 years and had received exactly one face-to-face performance review with a supervisor in all that time. "No matter what I did," he says, "nobody reviewed my work and I never got noticed. After a while, I stopped being so concerned about performance."[3]

Above all, supervisors should remember that performance appraisals are part of the ongoing control process. Ron Adler, CEO of Laurdan Associates of Potomac, Maryland, says the purpose of a performance appraisal should not be to mete out punishment or avoid lawsuits. "It's a method of getting action," he stresses, "either asking employees to keep doing what they're doing, or to change."[4] When McKesson Corporation determined that it wanted its call center employees to develop specific skills, the company had the agents and their mentors complete appraisals rating their skill level in each area. For each area in which an employee needed to improve, the employee created a personal development plan, and the company allowed six months for the employee to reach an acceptable level of skill. Some agents initially resisted, but as they saw that the process was fair and encouraged them to develop, they became motivated.[5] To learn how Whirlpool Corporation has adjusted its appraisal process so that it will better support corporate goals, see the "Supervision across Industries" box.

Finally, performance appraisals provide important records for the organization. They are a useful source of information when deciding on raises, promotions, and discipline, and they provide evidence that these appraisals were administered fairly. A performance appraisal also provides documentation on employees whose behavior or performance is a problem. (For more on supervising problem employees, see Chapter 12.)

A SYSTEMATIC APPROACH TO APPRAISING PERFORMANCE

To deliver their potential benefits, appraisals must be completely fair and accurate. Supervisors therefore should be systematic in appraising performance. They should follow a thorough process, use objective measures when possible, and avoid discrimination.

The Appraisal Process

The appraisal process takes place in four steps (see Figure 17.1). A supervisor establishes and communicates expectations for performance and standards for measuring performance. A supervisor also observes individual performance and measures it against the standards. On the basis of this information, the supervisor reinforces performance or provides remedies.

Establish and Communicate Expectations for Performance

During the planning process, a supervisor determines what the department or work group should accomplish (see Chapter 6). Through action plans, a supervisor spells out who is to do what to accomplish those objectives. From this information, it is relatively easy to specify what each employee must do to help the

FIGURE 17.1   The Process of Performance Appraisal

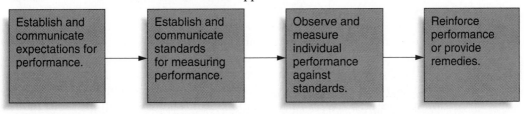

department or work group meet its objectives. One approach is to list the three to five major responsibilities of each position; the appraisal then focuses on these responsibilities.

For example, suppose Francine Bloch supervises the delivery personnel for a chain of appliance stores in Dallas. Each driver is expected to operate the vehicle safely, deliver every appliance without damaging anything, and be polite to customers.

A supervisor must make sure employees know and understand what is expected of them. To do this, the supervisor should make sure that objectives for the employees are clear, and he or she should communicate them effectively (see Chapter 10). Employees are most likely to understand and be committed to objectives when they have a say in developing them. More and more firms now require that supervisors and employees together set mutually acceptable performance goals.

Establish and Communicate Standards for Measuring Performance

Because expectations for performance are objectives, each expectation should be measurable (see Chapter 6). In appraising performance, a supervisor's task includes deciding how to measure employees' performance and then making sure employees know what will be measured. For instance, if the supervisor is looking for effective teamwork, this performance might be defined in terms of attendance (on time) at team meetings, ideas offered to meet the team's challenges, and communication to the team about the progress the person is making on team assignments.[6] With Bloch's employees, the standards would include delivering all appliances without damage, having zero accidents or traffic tickets, and receiving no complaints from customers about service.

Observe and Measure Individual Performance against Standards

Through the control process, a supervisor should continuously gather information about each employee's performance. This is an ongoing activity, not something the supervisor saves to do when filling out appraisal forms. As consultant Carol Booz says, if managers and supervisors can "find a system to keep track of all of the things their employees have done during the review period, they won't view the process as much of a chore."[7] When preparing a performance appraisal, a supervisor compares this information with the standards for the employee being appraised. In the example, Bloch would keep records of uncompleted deliveries, damage, accidents, traffic tickets, and customer complaints (and compliments). When appraising a particular employee's performance, she can see how often those problems arose with the employee.

Reinforce Performance or Provide Remedies

To keep employees motivated and informed, a supervisor needs to tell them when they are doing something right, not just when they are making a mistake. Thus, the final step of the appraisal process includes reinforcement for good performance. This can be as simple as pointing out to employees where they have performed well. For example, Bloch might compliment one of the drivers on a letter of praise from a customer. A supervisor might want to comment that this information will be placed in the employee's permanent record with the organization.

Where performance falls short of standards, an employee needs to know how to improve. A supervisor may state a remedy, but asking the employee to help solve the problem is often more effective. In the case of a driver who has received two traffic tickets for illegal left turns, Bloch might point out this situation and ask the driver for an explanation. The driver might reply that he was confused because he was lost. With that information, Bloch and the driver can work together to get the driver better acquainted with finding his way around Dallas.

Bloch and the driver thus are treating the underlying problem (the driver's difficulty in finding his way around) rather than the symptom (the traffic tickets). Therefore, the driver's performance in this area can improve in the future. In general, to move beyond discussing symptoms to uncover the underlying problems, a supervisor and employee can ask which of the following kinds of causes led to the poor performance:

- *Inadequate skills*—If the problem is the employee's lack of certain skills, a supervisor should see that the employee gets the necessary training, as described in the previous chapter.
- *Lack of effort*—If the problem is a lack of effort on the employee's part, a supervisor may need to apply the principles of motivation discussed in Chapter 11.
- *Shortcomings of the process*—If organizational or job-related policies and procedures reward inefficient or less-than-high-quality behavior, the supervisor and employee may be able to change the way work is done.
- *External conditions*—If the problem is something beyond the control of supervisor and employee (for example, a poor economy, lack of cooperation from another department, a strike by suppliers), the appraisal standards and ratings should be adjusted so that they are fair to the employee.
- *Personal problems*—If performance is suffering because the employee has personal problems, a supervisor should handle the situation with counseling and discipline (see Chapter 12).

In investigating the underlying problem, a supervisor may gain important insights by asking what can be done to help the employee reach goals. Before the appraisal is over, an employee should have a clear plan for making necessary changes.

What to Measure in an Appraisal

Waitress Kelly O'Hara was furious as she walked out of her performance appraisal interview. "Irresponsible!" she muttered to herself, "Lazy! Who does he think he is, calling me those things? He doesn't know what he's talking about." O'Hara's reaction shows that labeling people with certain characteristics is not a constructive approach to conducting an appraisal. Labels tend to put people on the defensive, and they are difficult, if not impossible, to prove.

Instead, a performance appraisal should focus on *behavior* and *results*. Focusing on behavior means that the appraisal should describe specific actions or patterns of actions. Focusing on results means describing the extent to which an employee has satisfied the objectives for which he or she is responsible. If O'Hara's supervisor had noted that he had received several complaints about slow service, he and O'Hara could have worked on a plan to minimize these complaints. Perhaps the problem was not even O'Hara's behavior but recurrent backlogs in the kitchen. The focus on meeting objectives would be more constructive than simply evaluating O'Hara as "lazy," because it tells an employee exactly what is expected. This focus is also fairer, especially if the employee helped to set the objectives. Figure 17.2 summarizes qualities of performance appraisal measures that motivate employees to meet objectives.

FIGURE 17.2
Qualities of Effective Performance Appraisal Measures

Source: Susan M. Heathfield, "Take Those Numeric Ratings and . . .," About.com, http://humanresources.about.com/library/weekly/aa112500a.htm, October 14, 2004.

☺ Objective
☺ Job-related
☺ Based on behaviors
☺ Within employee's control
☺ Related to specific tasks
☺ Communicated to employee

In many cases, a supervisor uses an appraisal form that requires drawing conclusions about the employee's personal characteristics. For example, a supervisor might need to rate an employee's dependability or attitude. Although such ratings are necessarily subjective, a supervisor can try to base them on observations about behavior and results. One approach is to record at least one specific example for each category rated. A rating on a personal characteristic seems more reasonable when a supervisor has evidence supporting his or her conclusion.

EEOC Guidelines

As described in Chapter 15, the Equal Employment Opportunity Commission (EEOC) is the government agency charged with enforcing federal laws against discrimination. The EEOC published the Uniform Guidelines on Employee Selection Procedures, which include guidelines for designing and implementing performance appraisals. In general, the behaviors or characteristics measured by a performance appraisal should be related to the job and to succeeding on the job. For example, if the appraisal measures "grooming," then good grooming should be important for success in the job. Because of this requirement, a supervisor and others responsible for the content of performance appraisals should make sure that what they measure is still relevant to a particular job.

Just as hiring should be based on a candidate's ability to perform the essential tasks of a particular job, so appraisals should be based on the employee's success in carrying out those tasks. The ratings in a performance appraisal should not be discriminatory; that is, they should not be based on an employee's race, sex, or other protected category but on an employee's ability to meet standards of performance. Furthermore, an employee should know in advance what those standards are, and the organization should have a system in place for employees to ask questions about their ratings.

Performance Appraisals and Pay Reviews

Many organizations review an employee's wage or salary level at the time of the performance appraisal. This reinforces the link the company makes between performance and pay increases. An employee with an excellent rating would be eligible to receive the largest allowable increase, whereas someone rated as a poor worker might not get any raise or only a cost-of-living increase.

However, reviewing pay and performance at the same time presents a potentially serious drawback. Employees may focus on the issue of money, so a supervisor has more difficulty using the performance evaluation as an opportunity for motivating and coaching. A majority of companies (68 percent in a recent study by Development Dimensions International) direct their managers to separate performance appraisals from discussions of pay.[8] In those organizations, a supervisor can more readily keep the appraisal focused on the employee's performance. At other organizations, a supervisor who must review pay rates at the same time as performance should make an extra effort to emphasize performance, and it is especially important to provide coaching and feedback about performance throughout the year.

TYPES OF APPRAISALS

Many techniques have been developed for appraising performance. The human resources department or higher-level management usually dictate which type the supervisor will use. An organization that has all supervisors use the same approach establishes a way to keep records showing performance over time, especially when an employee reports to more than one supervisor during his or her employment. Although a supervisor has to use the appraisal format selected for the whole organization, he or she may be able to supplement it with other helpful information. A supervisor can use the "Comments" section of a preprinted form or attach additional information to it.

Graphic Rating Scales

graphic rating scale
A performance appraisal that rates the degree to which an employee has achieved various characteristics

The most commonly used type of appraisal is the **graphic rating scale,** which rates the degree to which an employee has achieved various characteristics, such as job knowledge or punctuality. The rating is often scored from 1 to 5, for example, with 5 representing excellent performance and 1 representing poor performance. Some appraisal forms include space for comments, so that a supervisor can provide support for his or her ratings. Figure 17.3 is a sample appraisal form using a graphic rating scale.

The main advantage of a graphic rating scale is that it is relatively easy to use. In addition, the scores provide a basis for deciding whether an employee has improved in various areas. However, the ratings themselves are subjective; what one supervisor considers "excellent" may be only "average" to another. Also, many supervisors tend to rate everyone at least a little above average. Some appraisal forms attempt to overcome these problems by containing descriptions of excellent or poor behavior in each area. Other rating scales pose a different problem by labeling performance in terms of how well an employee "meets requirements." Presumably, the supervisor wants *all* employees to meet the requirements of the job, but if the scale rates everyone at the top, it is less useful for coaching and rewarding employees. Microsoft tries to address these problems by requiring that only a small percentage of each supervisor's employees be given a rating of "outstanding" in terms of meeting their goals. This requirement forces the supervisor to rate some employees lower than others. In contrast, the City of Fort Worth Equipment Services Department decided its rankings would be based on the collection of hard data, such as the time an employee takes to complete particular repairs. The information about time spent on each project is compared against industry standards to see whether the employee is more or less productive than those standards. The data show whether the employee should be rated a 5 or something less on the agency's five-point scale.[9]

Paired-Comparison Approach

paired-comparison approach
A performance appraisal that measures the relative performance of employees in a group

The **paired-comparison approach** measures the relative performance of employees in a group. A supervisor lists the employees in the group and then ranks them. One method is to compare the performance of the first two employees on the list. A supervisor places a check mark next to the name of the employee whose performance is better, then repeats the process, comparing the first employee's performance with that of other employees. Next, the supervisor compares the second employee on the list with all the others, and so on until each pair of employees has been compared. The employee with the most check marks is considered the most valuable.

FIGURE 17.3 Sample Graphic Rating Scale

Source: John M. Ivancevich, *Human Resource Management: Foundations of Personnel*, 7th ed. (New York: McGraw-Hill, 1998), p. 272. Copyright © The McGraw-Hill Companies.

Name _____ Dept. _____ Date _____		Outstanding	Good	Satisfactory	Fair	Unsatisfactory
Quantity of work	Volume of acceptable work under normal conditions Comments:	☐	☐	☐	☐	☐
Quality of work	Thoroughness, neatness, and accuracy of work Comments:	☐	☐	☐	☐	☐
Knowledge of job	Clear understanding of the facts or factors pertinent to the job Comments:	☐	☐	☐	☐	☐
Personal qualities	Personality, appearance, sociability, leadership, integrity Comments:	☐	☐	☐	☐	☐
Cooperation	Ability and willingness to work with associates, supervisors, and subordinates toward common goals Comments:	☐	☐	☐	☐	☐
Dependability	Conscientious, thorough, accurate, reliable with respect to attendance, lunch periods, reliefs, etc. Comments:	☐	☐	☐	☐	☐
Initiative	Earnestness in seeking increased responsibilities. Self-starting, unafraid to proceed alone Comments:	☐	☐	☐	☐	☐

A supervisor also can compare employees in terms of several criteria, such as work quantity and quality. For each criterion, a supervisor ranks the employees from best to worst, assigning a 1 to the lowest-ranked employee and the highest score to the best employee in that category. Then all the scores for each employee are totaled to see who has the highest total score.

The paired-comparison approach is appropriate when a supervisor needs to find one outstanding employee in a group. It can be used to identify the best candidate for a promotion or special assignment. However, paired comparisons make some employees look good at the expense of others, which can make it ineffective for motivating team performance or coaching employees. In recent years, more companies have used paired comparisons as a way to help them reduce their workforce. These companies must weigh the advantages of identifying the least productive workers against the possible harm to morale and teamwork among the remaining employees.[10]

The downside of the paired-comparison approach sometimes extends even to lawsuits. In the last couple of years, blacks and women at Microsoft, U.S. citizens at Conoco, and older workers at Ford Motor Company have filed class-action lawsuits claiming that these firms discriminated in assigning grades. Microsoft defends the system, which is also used by other major companies such as Cisco Systems, Intel, and General Electric. "We want to give the highest compensation to the very top performers," says Microsoft's senior vice president for human resources, Deborah Willingham. The company says it has checks and balances in the system to ensure fairness and that employees are largely responsible for the rating criteria and can appeal their ratings. Conoco and Ford have also denied any discriminatory intent. Some critics, including David Thomas of Harvard Business School, contend "companies are playing their version of 'Survivor'" however, and Cisco planned to use its grading system as one way to identify the 5,000 workers it said it would lay off.[11]

Forced-Choice Approach

forced-choice approach
A performance appraisal that presents an appraiser with sets of statements describing employee behavior; the appraiser must choose which statement is most characteristic of the employee and which is least characteristic

In the **forced-choice approach,** the appraisal form gives a supervisor sets of statements describing employee behavior. For each set of statements, a supervisor must choose one that is most characteristic and one that is least characteristic of the employee. Figure 17.4 illustrates part of an appraisal form using the forced-choice approach.

These questionnaires tend to be set up in a way that prevents a supervisor from saying only positive things about employees. Thus, the forced-choice approach is used when an organization determines that supervisors have been rating an unbelievably high proportion of employees as above average.

Essay Appraisal

Sometimes a supervisor must write a description of the employee's performance, answering questions such as "What are the major strengths of this employee?" or "In what areas does this employee need improvement?" Essay appraisals often are used along with other types of appraisals, notably graphic rating scales. They provide an opportunity for a supervisor to describe aspects of performance that are not thoroughly covered by an appraisal questionnaire. The main drawback of essay appraisals is that their quality depends on a supervisor's writing skills.

FIGURE 17.4
Sample Forced-Choice Appraisal

Source: John M. Ivancevich, *Human Resource Management: Foundations of Personnel,* 7th ed. (New York: McGraw-Hill, 1998), p. 274. Copyright © The McGraw-Hill Companies.

Instructions	Rank from 1 to 4 the following sets of statements according to how they describe the manner in which _____ performs
	(name of employee)
	the job. A rank of 1 should be used for the most descriptive statement, and a rank of 4 should be given for the least descriptive. No ties are allowed.

1. _____ Does not anticipate difficulties

   _____ Grasps explanations quickly

   _____ Rarely wastes time

   _____ Easy to talk to

2. _____ A leader in group activities

   _____ Wastes time on unimportant things

   _____ Cool and calm at all times

   _____ Hard worker

FIGURE 17.5
Sample
Behaviorally
Anchored Rating
Scale (BARS)

Source: John M. Ivancevich, *Human Resource Management: Foundations of Personnel,* 7th ed. (New York: McGraw-Hill, 1998), p. 277. Copyright © The McGraw-Hill Companies.

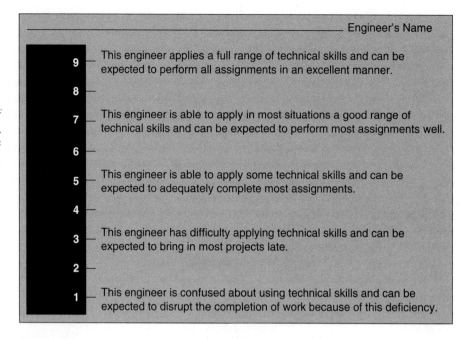

Engineer's Name

9 — This engineer applies a full range of technical skills and can be expected to perform all assignments in an excellent manner.

8 —

7 — This engineer is able to apply in most situations a good range of technical skills and can be expected to perform most assignments well.

6 —

5 — This engineer is able to apply some technical skills and can be expected to adequately complete most assignments.

4 —

3 — This engineer has difficulty applying technical skills and can be expected to bring in most projects late.

2 —

1 — This engineer is confused about using technical skills and can be expected to disrupt the completion of work because of this deficiency.

Behaviorally Anchored Rating Scales (BARS)

Some organizations pay behavioral scientists or organizational psychologists to create **behaviorally anchored rating scales (BARS).** These scales rate employee performance in several areas, such as work quantity and quality, using a series of statements that describe effective and ineffective performance in each area. In each area, a supervisor selects the statement that best describes how an employee performs. The statements in the rating scales are different for each job title in the organization. Figure 17.5 shows a behaviorally anchored rating scale measuring the performance area of engineering competence.

The major advantage of using BARS is that they can be tailored to the organization's objectives for employees. In addition, the BARS approach is less subjective than some other approaches because it uses statements describing behavior. However, developing the scales is time consuming and therefore relatively expensive.

Checklist Appraisal

A checklist appraisal contains a series of questions about an employee's performance. Figure 17.6 shows the format for this kind of appraisal. A supervisor answers yes or no to the questions. Thus, a checklist is merely a record of performance, not an evaluation by a supervisor. The human resources department has a key for scoring the items on the checklist; the score results in a rating of an employee's performance.

Although the checklist appraisal is easy to complete, it has several disadvantages. The checklist can be difficult to prepare, and each job category will probably require a different set of questions. Also, a supervisor has no way to adjust the answers for any special circumstances that affect performance.

Critical-Incident Appraisal

To conduct a **critical-incident appraisal,** a supervisor keeps a written record of incidents that show positive and negative ways an employee has acted. The record

behaviorally anchored rating scales (BARS)
A performance appraisal in which an employee is rated on scales containing statements describing performance in several areas

critical-incident appraisal
A performance appraisal in which a supervisor keeps a written record of incidents that show positive and negative ways an employee has acted; the supervisor uses this record to assess the employee's performance

FIGURE 17.6
Sample Checklist Appraisal

Source: Donald S. Miller and Stephen E. Catt, *Supervision: Working with People*, 2nd ed. (Lincolnwood, IL: Richard D. Irwin, 1991), p. 330. Reprinted with permission of the authors.

	Yes	No
1. Does the employee willingly cooperate with others in completing work assignments?	____	____
2. Does the employee have adequate job knowledge to perform duties in a satisfactory manner?	____	____
3. In terms of quality, is the employee's work acceptable?	____	____
4. Does the employee meet deadlines for the completion of work assignments?	____	____
5. Does the employee's record indicate unexcused absences?	____	____
6. Does the employee follow safety rules and regulations?	____	____

should include dates, people involved, actions taken, and any other relevant details. At the time of the appraisal, a supervisor reviews the record to reach an overall evaluation of an employee's behavior. During the appraisal interview, a supervisor should give an employee a chance to offer his or her views of each incident recorded.

This technique has the advantage of focusing on actual behaviors. However, keeping records of critical incidents can be time consuming, and even if a supervisor is diligent, important incidents could be overlooked. Also, supervisors tend to record negative events more than positive ones, resulting in an overly harsh appraisal. A diligent supervisor can, however, use critical-incident appraisals as a tool for motivating and developing employees. For example, as an adviser to plumbing and mechanical contractors, Paul Ridilla has found that companies can improve performance by identifying and recording the kinds of behavior that add value to the organization: suggesting innovations, working extra hours, training co-workers, and providing the superior service that leads customers to send thank-you notes. Ridilla advises that supervisors keep track of these and other positive behaviors—and recognize and reward them.[12]

Work-Standards Approach

work-standards approach
A performance appraisal in which an appraiser compares an employee's performance with objective measures of what the employee should do

To use the **work-standards approach,** a supervisor tries to establish objective measures of performance. A typical work standard would be the quantity produced by an assembly-line worker. This amount should reflect what a person normally could produce. A supervisor then compares an employee's actual performance with the standards.

Although the work-standards approach has been applied largely to production workers, the principle of objectively measuring outcomes makes sense for a variety of jobs. Work standards are one of the tools that Bank of Newport uses to appraise its tellers' performance. The Rhode Island bank uses "mystery shoppers," who visit each branch once a month. The mystery shoppers observe and record specific behaviors, including whether the employees make eye contact, smile, use the customer's name, and thank them for their business. According to Robert E. Maddock, an executive with Bank of Newport, tellers initially disliked having their behavior recorded in this way, but they appreciated the system more when they saw that they would be recognized for meeting the standards.[13]

Management by Objectives (MBO)

Chapter 6 introduced management by objectives (MBO) as a planning tool. In an organization that uses MBO, a supervisor will also use this approach for appraising performance. A supervisor compares each employee's accomplishments with the objectives for that employee. If the employee has met or exceeded his or her objectives, the appraisal will be favorable. The main advantages of this system are that an employee knows what is expected and a supervisor focuses on results rather than more subjective criteria.

The Police Department of Madison, Wisconsin, recently replaced its traditional appraisals with a system of individual goal setting, leadership training, and employee involvement. A survey of 12 metropolitan police departments conducted by the U.S. Department of Justice later found that Madison's 500-member force had the highest satisfaction level among citizens, and each year it receives more than 1,000 applications for about two dozen job openings.[14]

Assessments by Someone Other Than the Supervisor

Supervisors cannot know how an employee behaves at all times or in all situations. Nor can supervisors always appreciate the full impact of an employee's behavior on people inside and outside the organization. To supplement what supervisors do know, other people might offer insights into an employee's behavior. For this reason, supervisors may combine their appraisals with self-assessments by the employee or appraisals by peers and customers. Appraisals of supervisors and other managers also may come from their subordinates. Combining several sources of appraisals is called **360-degree feedback.** A recent survey found that about one out of five organizations were using some form of 360-degree feedback, including appraisal information from customers or peers.[15]

Several police departments have improved the performance of their officers by using 360-degree feedback as the basis of coaching. These departments use computer systems into which supervisors, the officers themselves, and others who worked with the officers enter evaluations of how well they handled specific incidents or their jobs over a period of time. The officers' supervisors review the ratings and discuss with the employees how to bring the ratings higher. Knowing that others are watching their performance, the employees focus on the behaviors that will make a difference, and then their ratings generally improve.[16] At Trinity Communications Inc., a small marketing firm based in Boston, each employee is reviewed by both colleagues and clients. "It can be scary," founding partner Nancy Michalowski says of the process. "The challenge is to be constructive so that you all can continue to work together."[17]

To use self-assessments, a supervisor can ask each employee to complete an assessment before the appraisal interview. Then the supervisor and employee compare the employee's evaluation of his or her own behavior with the supervisor's evaluation. This can stimulate discussion and insights in areas where the two are in disagreement. At the IKEA chain of home furnishing stores, self-assessment is not just an appraisal tool but also part of a commitment to helping employees develop and earn promotions. Employees complete a self-assessment process that helps them identify their strengths. With their supervisors, the employees review the results of the self-assessment and prepare a plan for achieving their career goals within the company.[18] Supervisors also can use the concept of a self-appraisal to advance in their own careers. For some suggestions, read the "Supervisory Skills" box.

Appraisals by peers—often called **peer reviews**—are less common, but their use is growing, especially in organizations that use teamwork. Employees who work in teams usually appraise the performance of their team members. The teams do this in meetings, in which they discuss each team member's strengths and areas that need improvement. Presumably, employees will react more positively

360-degree feedback
Performance appraisal that combines assessments from several sources

peer reviews
Performance appraisals conducted by an employee's co-workers

SUPERVISORY SKILLS

APPRAISING AND PLANNING

USING SELF-APPRAISAL TO PLAN YOUR CAREER

Taking a position as a supervisor places you on the first rung of the management ladder. This is a significant time to evaluate your abilities and career goals to plan the next phase of your career. A thoughtful self-appraisal is especially important in today's workplace, which rewards creative career planning and lifetime learning.

If your organization offers appraisal tools such as psychological tests and self-assessment tools, take advantage of these. Also start by reflecting on the opportunities you have had so far to exercise leadership on and off the job. Do you naturally seek out positions of leadership? Do group members look to you as a leader? If you have not had much leadership experience, make a commitment to finding leadership roles through volunteer projects and work assignments.

In addition, ask yourself what areas of additional knowledge would help you in your present job and in the career you desire. Identify and participate in classes, conferences, and degree programs that will give you access to the knowledge you will need.

Look for and accept projects that will challenge you and are in line with your goals. But be careful to take assignments in which you can succeed and demonstrate your potential. If you are not ready for a particular assignment, be honest about your limits.

As you set goals and define areas in which you need to strengthen your leadership skills, look for a mentor to guide you in this process. Whose leadership do you respect and admire? Before approaching that person, define some goals for the mentoring relationship, so that your time together will be productive. Identify whether you mainly want encouragement from this person or are more interested in the person's insights about your organization, your industry or field, or a particular problem you face. Be open to learning new ideas and learning from someone who has a perspective that is different from your own.

From these short- and long-term efforts at self-appraisal and personal development, you may determine that you are worth more to your employer. Self-appraisal also can help you prepare to ask for a raise. If you determine you are underpaid—taking into account your organization's salary structure, your boss's openness to discussing pay, and the typical pay for your job—you can use the insights from your self-appraisal to document your value to the organization. Describe the situations in which you have exercised leadership, gained knowledge, and completed challenging projects. If your boss rejects your proposal or criticizes your performance, listen carefully, and use the feedback for your next round of self-appraisal.

Sources: Edward E. Lawler III, *Treat People Right: How Organizations and Individuals Can Propel Each Other into a Virtuous Spiral of Success* (San Francisco: Jossey-Bass, 2003), pp. 223–26; Connie LaMotta, "Career Stalled? Find a Mentor," *Direct,* January 1, 2003, downloaded from LookSmart's FindArticles, www.findarticles.com; Max Owens, "How to Ask for a Raise," AOL Find a Job (2003), http://findajob.aol.com/findajob/articles/article.adp?id=82, September 10, 2004.

to peer reviews in which all employees participate in the appraising on an equal basis than to peer reviews used occasionally for selected employees. A challenge of peer reviews is ensuring that all peers are prepared to give objective feedback. A recent study found that members of a peer group tended to give higher evaluations to group members who had a similar social style (mix of assertiveness and responsiveness).[19] When the organization uses peer reviews, supervisors should prepare group members to apply the principles of objective evaluation described in this chapter. Employees may need training, and the appraisal method should focus on measurable, specific behaviors.

The drive to please customers in a highly competitive market, coupled with a desire for practical information on performance, has encouraged some companies to institute programs in which customers appraise employees' performance. As mentioned previously, one way to obtain objective feedback on customer service is to use "mystery shoppers." Those people contact the organization to make a particular purchase or to ask for help with a predetermined problem. The mystery shopper then records the results of the experience. This type of appraisal is most effective when employees know what specific behaviors are desired and the mystery shopper measures those behaviors. For example, cashiers at Bruster's Real Ice Cream, located in Columbus, Georgia, are supposed to invite each customer to come back again. Mystery shoppers making purchases at Bruster's note whether the cashier they encounter issues this invitation. Bruster's reinforces the effort by awarding cash prizes to cashiers who earn a perfect score from a mystery shopper.[20]

At an increasing number of major corporations, subordinates rate how well their bosses manage. Typically, ratings are anonymous, to protect the workers. The purpose of these subordinate appraisals is to give managers information they can use to supervise more effectively and to make their organization more competitive. The appraisals also support the trend toward giving operative employees a greater voice in how an organization is run.

Subordinate appraisals and other 360-degree feedback can correct some of the appraisal biases described in the next section. They also can provide information that is more useful for problem solving and employee development than the typical results of a traditional top-down appraisal. For example, executive coach John Parker Stewart worked with a sales and marketing manager of five employees, all of whom were nearly ready to quit their jobs in frustration. The manager could not see the problem until Stewart showed him the results of upward appraisals. All five employees indicated this manager failed to give them credit for their work; they felt they received no appreciation when they went the extra mile. After the manager recovered from this blow to his pride, he was able to improve the way he rewarded and recognized his team, and the employees repaid him with their loyalty.[21]

For 360-feedback to be effective, the person managing the review process should ensure that the responses are anonymous. Subordinates especially may be afraid to respond honestly if they think that the person being reviewed will retaliate for negative comments.

SOURCES OF BIAS

Ideally, supervisors should be completely objective in their appraisals of employees. Each appraisal should directly reflect an employee's performance, not any biases of a supervisor. Of course, this is impossible to do perfectly. We all make compromises in our decision-making strategies and have biases in evaluating what other people do. Supervisors need to be aware of these biases so that their effect on the appraisals can be limited or eliminated. Figure 17.7 shows some sources of bias that commonly influence performance appraisals.

harshness bias
Rating employees more severely than their performances merit

Some supervisors are prone to a **harshness bias,** that is, rating employees more severely than their performance merits. New supervisors are especially susceptible to this error, because they may feel a need to be taken seriously. Unfortunately, the harshness bias also tends to frustrate and discourage workers, who resent the unfair assessments of their performance.

leniency bias
Rating employees more favorably than their performances merit

At the other extreme is the **leniency bias.** Supervisors with this bias rate their employees more favorably than their performance merits. A supervisor who does this may want credit for developing a department full of "excellent" workers. Or the supervisor may simply be uncomfortable confronting employees with their shortcomings. The leniency bias may feel like an advantage to the employees who receive the favorable ratings, but it cheats the employees and department of the benefits of truly developing and coaching employees.

FIGURE 17.7
Sources of Bias in Performance Appraisals

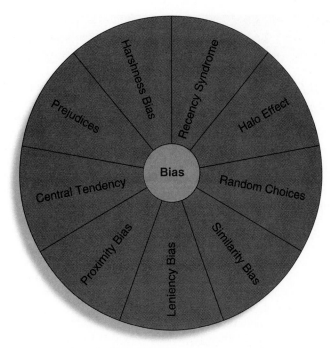

central tendency
The tendency to select employee ratings in the middle of a scale

proximity bias
The tendency to assign similar scores to items that are near each other on a questionnaire

similarity bias
The tendency to judge others more positively when they are like yourself

A bias that characterizes the responses to many types of questionnaires is **central tendency,** which is the tendency to select ratings in the middle of the scale. People seem more comfortable on middle ground than taking a strong stand at either extreme. This bias causes a supervisor to miss important opportunities to praise or correct employees.

Proximity means nearness. The **proximity bias** refers to the tendency to assign similar scores to items that are near each other on a questionnaire. If a supervisor assigns a score of 8 to one appraisal item, this bias might encourage the supervisor to score the next item as 6 or 7, even though a score of 3 is more accurate. Obviously, this tendency can result in misleading appraisals.

When using a type of appraisal that requires answers to specific questions, a supervisor might succumb to making *random choices*. A supervisor might do this when uncertain how to answer or when the overall scoring on the test looks undesirable. For example, if a supervisor thinks an appraisal is scoring an employee too low, he or she might give favorable ratings in some areas about which the supervisor has no strong feelings. Supervisors who catch themselves making random choices should slow down and try to apply objective criteria.

The **similarity bias** refers to the tendency to judge others more positively when they are like ourselves. Thus, we tend to look more favorably on people who share our interests, tastes, background, or other characteristics. For example, in appraising performance, a supervisor risks viewing a person's performance in a favorable light because the employee shares his or her flair for dressing in the latest fashions. Or a supervisor might interpret negatively the performance of an employee who is much shyer than the supervisor.

As described in Chapter 9, the *recency syndrome* refers to the human tendency to place the most weight on events that have occurred most recently. In a performance appraisal, a supervisor might give particular weight to a problem the employee caused last week or an award the employee just won, but he or she should be careful to consider events and behaviors that occurred throughout the

TIPS FROM THE FIRING LINE

AVOID SELF-FULFILLING PROPHECIES OF FAILURE

It may seem obvious that supervisors are supposed to bring out the best performance in all their employees. But surprisingly, research by business professors Jean-François Manzoni and Jean-Louis Barsoux found that management behavior typically is quite different. At the organizations Manzoni and Barsoux studied, managers treated their subordinates differently on the basis of their appraisals of their employees. The treatment of the underperforming employees actually made their performance worse.

The researchers studied the management of employees who were simply less productive and committed than their colleagues, not necessarily the "problem" employees we discussed in Chapter 12. These underperforming employees take up more of the manager's time, because the manager intervenes to try to help them improve. But according to Manzoni and Barsoux, the manager's extra effort instead promotes failure.

The problem begins with appraisal bias. In as little as one week, the boss begins to form opinions about an employee's attitude and performance. The halo of a negative initial opinion then shades the boss's interpretation of future behaviors. As the boss begins to worry about the employee's potential, he or she begins to monitor the employee's every action, delivering specific, forceful instructions. Then every slipup and every failure to follow precise directions confirms the employee's shortcomings. Once the boss has labeled an employee as a "weaker performer," most negative outcomes involving that employee get blamed on the employee, rather than circumstances such as the difficulty of the project or the behavior of others.

Managers also establish lower expectations for an employee who underperforms early. They commu-nicate the lower expectations in various ways. Some are as obvious as giving less important assignments and monitoring the employee closely. Others are more subtle, such as reducing eye contact, sighing to indicate frustration, and sending fewer positive communications such as smiles and banter. As under-performing employees observe how their boss treats them, they become less motivated. They may lose confidence in their own ability or in their chances of making a positive impression. They may focus on preventing trouble with the boss, not on innovating and succeeding.

This pattern of behavior produces a downward spiral of performance. Observing an employee go through the motions on routine assignments, the manager concludes the employee is unmotivated and doesn't "see the big picture." The employee has few opportunities to contribute or chat with the boss, so the employee has difficulty seeing the big picture. The employee may also develop a negative appraisal of the manager as a person who is unfair, stubborn, or unable to appreciate the employee. With that appraisal, the employee may begin to treat the manager in more negative ways. Through this downward spiral, the manager's initial impressions become a self-fulfilling prophecy.

Some managers in the study avoided this self-fulfilling prophecy, and their experience provides valuable guidance. These successful managers fostered two-way communication with their entire team, even the weaker performers. They devoted more effort early to learning about their employees as individuals, not just as workers. The fuller picture of their employees helped the supervisors avoid the halo effect and its consequences.

Source: Jean-François Manzoni and Jean-Louis Barsoux, "Managing Smart: Enabling Under-Performers to Become Valued Contributors," *Ivey Business Journal Online* 67 (March–April 2003), downloaded from Business & Company Resource Center, http://galenet.galegroup.com.

entire period covered by the review. The most accurate way to do this is to keep records throughout the year, as described earlier with conducting a critical-incident appraisal.

The *halo effect*, introduced in Chapter 15, refers to the tendency to generalize one positive or negative aspect of a person to the person's entire performance. Thus, if supervisor Ben Olson thinks that a pleasant telephone manner is what makes a good customer service representative, he is apt to give high marks to a representative with a pleasant voice, no matter what the employee actually says to the customers or how reliable the performance. Possibly more harmful is the impact of a supervisor who develops a broadly negative opinion about an employee, as described in the "Tips from the Firing Line" box.

Finally, the supervisor's *prejudices* about various types of people can unfairly influence a performance appraisal. A supervisor needs to remember that each employee is an individual, not merely a representative of a group. A supervisor who believes that African Americans generally have poor skills in using standard English needs to recognize that this is a prejudice about a group, not a fact to apply to actual employees. Thus, before recommending that a black salesperson needs to improve her speaking skills, a supervisor must consider whether the salesperson really needs improvement in that area or whether the supervisor's prejudices are interfering with an accurate assessment. This is especially important in light of the EEOC guidelines discussed earlier in the chapter.

THE PERFORMANCE APPRAISAL INTERVIEW

The last stage of the appraisal process—the stage at which a supervisor reinforces performance or provides remedies—occurs in an interview between supervisor and employee. At this time, a supervisor describes what he or she has observed and discusses this appraisal with the employee. Together they agree on areas for improvement and development. If you have never been a supervisor, apply the questions in this section to the way your current or most recent supervisor has appraised your performance.

Supervisors often dread conducting appraisal interviews. Pointing out another person's shortcomings can be unpleasant. To overcome these feelings, it helps to focus on the benefits of appraising employees. Supervisors can cultivate a positive attitude by viewing the appraisal interview as an opportunity to coach and develop employees.

Purpose of the Interview

The purpose of holding an appraisal interview is to communicate information about an employee's performance. Once a supervisor has evaluated an employee's performance, the supervisor needs to convey his or her thoughts to the employee. An interview is an appropriate setting for doing so because it sets aside time to focus on and discuss the appraisal in private. The interview is also an opportunity for upward communication from the employee. By contributing his or her viewpoints and ideas, an employee can work with the supervisor on devising ways to improve performance.

Preparing for the Interview

Before the appraisal interview, a supervisor should allow plenty of time for completing the appraisal form. The form should be completed carefully and thoughtfully, not in a rush during the hour before the interview. In addition to filling out the form, the supervisor should think about the employee's likely reactions to the appraisal and plan how to handle them. A supervisor also should be ready with some ideas for correcting problems noted in the appraisal.

A supervisor should notify the employee about the appraisal interview ahead of time. Giving a few days' or a week's notice allows the employee to think about his or her performance. Then the employee can contribute ideas during the interview.

In addition, a supervisor should prepare an appropriate meeting place. The interview should occur in an office or other room where supervisor and employee will have privacy. The supervisor should arrange to prevent interruptions such as telephone calls.

Conducting the Interview

At the beginning of the interview, a supervisor should try to put an employee at ease. Employees are often uncomfortable at the prospect of discussing their performance. An offer of coffee and a little small talk may help to break the ice.

The supervisor can begin by reviewing the employee's self-appraisal, if one was completed, with the employee, asking him or her to give reasons for the various ratings. Then a supervisor describes his or her rating of the employee and how he or she arrived at it. A supervisor can start by describing overall impressions and then explain the contents of the appraisal form. The supervisor should explain the basis for the ratings, using specific examples of the employee's behavior and results. Most employees are waiting for the "bad news," so it is probably most effective to describe areas for improvement first, followed by the employee's strengths. People need to know what they are doing well so that they will continue on that course, realizing that their efforts are appreciated.

After describing the evaluation of the employee's performance, a supervisor should give the employee time to offer feedback. The employee should be able to agree or disagree with the supervisor's conclusions, as well as ask questions. This is an important time for the supervisor to keep an open mind and apply the listening skills discussed in Chapter 10. Hearing the employee's reactions is the first step toward resolving any problems described in the appraisal.

Problem Solving and Coaching

When the supervisor and employee understand each other's point of view, they should reach a decision on how to solve problems described in the appraisal. Together they can come up with a number of alternatives and select the solutions that seem most promising. Sometimes the best solution is for the employee to make behavioral changes; at other times, the supervisor may need to make changes, such as keeping the employee better informed or improving work processes.

Proponents of quality management have criticized performance appraisals for connecting rewards mainly to individual performance. The problem, they say, is that the quality of employees' performance depends mainly on the organization's systems, which give each employee the necessary information, authority, and materials. Still, research has shown that organizations make the greatest strides toward improving quality when employees receive performance appraisals that address their individual performance in meeting quantitative goals. It appears that, at least in American culture, people are motivated by having their individual contributions measured and recognized. Also, measurable results seem fairer as a basis for measuring their performance. Supervisors and their organizations can combine concern for quality improvement with concern for individual performance by identifying ways to measure whether employees are demonstrating teamwork and contributing individually to the quality of the group's output. They may even involve the team in establishing those performance measures.[22]

In addition to problem solving, appraisal interviews often include time for discussion related to coaching the employee and helping the employee develop a career with the organization. Strengths and shortcomings identified in the performance appraisal often provide indications of areas in which the supervisor and employee could work together to develop desirable skills through further training or experience. Discussing employees' potential for growth and improvement is

FIGURE 17.8   The Process of Conducting a Performance Appraisal Interview

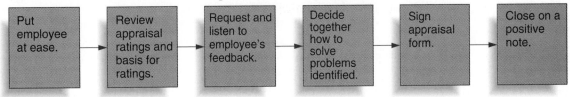

Put employee at ease. → Review appraisal ratings and basis for ratings. → Request and listen to employee's feedback. → Decide together how to solve problems identified. → Sign appraisal form. → Close on a positive note.

essential. Author and consultant Brayton Bowen calls this effort taking "time to educate and communicate as well as evaluate."[23] For example, the supervisor might help the employee identify ways to succeed personally and as part of the team. However, employees may have difficulty shifting their focus away from pay and past performance, especially when performance appraisals are directly or indirectly tied to pay levels. A supervisor therefore should not use performance appraisal interviews as a substitute for coaching on a continuing basis.

Signatures

At the end of the interview, the supervisor and employee usually are required to sign the appraisal form. By doing so, they acknowledge that the interview has been conducted and that the employee has read and understood the form. If the employee refuses to sign, the supervisor can explain that this is all the employee's signature means. If that explanation does not persuade the employee to sign, the supervisor can note on the appraisal form that the employee refused to sign and check with the human resources department regarding what procedures to follow next. The employee should receive a copy of the appraisal form.

The supervisor should close the interview on a positive note, with a comment such as, "You've been doing a great job," or, "I think that with the plans we've made, your work will soon be up to standards." Figure 17.8 summarizes the interviewing process.

Follow-Up

Even after the interview is over, a supervisor continues appraising performance. He or she needs to follow up on any actions planned during the interview. Is the employee making the promised changes? Is the supervisor providing the resources, such as training, that are necessary for improvements to occur? This follow-up should be an ongoing process, not an activity left for the next year's performance appraisal.

SKILLS MODULE

PART ONE: CONCEPTS

Summary

17.1 Summarize benefits of conducting performance appraisals.

Performance appraisals provide information necessary for employees to improve the quality of their work. Appraisals can motivate employees by demonstrating the interest of the supervisor and the organization in them, keeping them informed, and indicating the important areas of performance. Performance appraisals also provide important records for the company, which managers use to make decisions about raises, promotions, and discipline.

17.2 Identify the steps in appraising performance systematically.

First, a supervisor establishes and communicates expectations for performance; second, he or she establishes and communicates standards for measuring performance. Third, a supervisor observes each employee's performance, measuring it against the standards. Fourth, a supervisor provides reinforcement for acceptable or excellent performance and works with the employee to develop remedies for inadequate performance.

17.3 Discuss guidelines for avoiding discrimination in performance appraisals.

As much as possible, an appraisal should focus on objective measures of behavior and results—specifically, how well an employee carries out the essential tasks of the job. The behaviors and employee characteristics measured should be related to the job and succeeding on the job.

17.4 Compare types of appraisals.

Graphic rating scales rate the degree to which an employee has achieved various characteristics, such as job knowledge and punctuality. The paired-comparison approach measures the relative performance of employees in a group. The forced-choice approach presents a supervisor with sets of statements describing employee behavior, and the supervisor chooses the statements that are most characteristic of the employee and those that are least. An essay appraisal includes one or more paragraphs describing an employee's performance. Behaviorally anchored rating scales (BARS) rate employee performance in several areas by using a series of statements that describe effective and ineffective performance in each area. A checklist appraisal consists of a series of yes-or-no questions about an employee's performance. A critical-incident appraisal is based on an ongoing record of incidents in which an employee has behaved positively or negatively. The work-standards approach is based on establishing objective measures of performance, against which an employee's performance is compared. Management by objectives is a system of developing goals with employees and comparing their performance to those goals. In addition, a supervisor may combine several sources of appraisal in 360-degree feedback, including having employees prepare self-assessments, obtaining peer assessments and customer assessments, or asking for appraisals (usually anonymous) of the supervisor.

17.5 Describe sources of bias in appraising performance.

Supervisors who want to prove they are tough may succumb to the harshness bias, rating employees too severely. Supervisors who hate to deliver bad news may succumb to the leniency bias, rating employees too favorably. The central tendency leads some supervisors to give their employees rankings in the middle of the scale. The proximity bias refers to the tendency to assign similar scores to items that are near each other on a questionnaire. Random choices sometimes are made when an appraiser is uncertain about answers or uncomfortable with an overall rating. The similarity bias is the tendency of people to judge others more positively when they are like themselves. The recency syndrome may lead a supervisor to give too much weight to events that have occurred recently. The halo effect leads an appraiser to use one positive or negative trait to describe a person's entire performance. Finally, people are influenced by their prejudices about groups.

17.6 Explain the purpose of conducting performance appraisal interviews.

The purpose of conducting an interview is to communicate the supervisor's impressions of an employee's performance to that employee. In addition, it is an opportunity for an employee to present his or her viewpoint and ideas so that supervisor and employee can work together on improving performance.

17.7 Tell how supervisors should prepare for a performance appraisal interview.
A supervisor should take as much time as necessary to complete an appraisal form thoughtfully. Supervisor also should think about how the employee is likely to react and plan how to handle his or her reactions. A supervisor should be ready with ideas for resolving problems noted in the appraisal. Finally, the supervisor should notify the employee about the interview ahead of time and prepare an appropriate place to meet without interruptions.

17.8 Describe guidelines for conducting the interview.
A supervisor first should attempt to put the employee at ease. Then the supervisor and employee should go over the self-appraisal, if any, and the supervisor's appraisal of the employee. The supervisor should focus first on areas for improvement and next on areas of strength. The employee should have time to give feedback; then the supervisor and employee should work together to develop solutions to any problems identified. The supervisor and employee sign the appraisal form, and then the supervisor closes with a positive comment. After the interview, the supervisor needs to follow up to make sure that planned actions are taken.

Key Terms	performance appraisal, *p.* 473 graphic rating scale, *p.* 479 paired-comparison approach, *p.* 479 forced-choice approach, *p.* 481	behaviorally anchored rating scales (BARS), *p.* 482 critical-incident appraisal, *p.* 482 work-standards approach, *p.* 483 360-degree feedback, *p.* 484	peer reviews, *p.* 484 harshness bias, *p.* 486 leniency bias, *p.* 486 central tendency, *p.* 487 proximity bias, *p.* 487 similarity bias, *p.* 487

Review and Discussion Questions

1. What is a performance appraisal? How do organizations benefit from using performance appraisals?

2. June Pearson was just promoted to supervisor of the bookkeeping department at an insurance company. According to the company's schedule for appraising performance, she needs to conduct an appraisal of Ron Yamamoto, one of the employees, only a month after she started the job. Pearson cannot find any records of goals established for Yamamoto, so she asks his peers and others with whom he has contact to describe his performance. On the basis of this information, Pearson completes an appraisal form and conducts an interview.
   a. Which steps of the systematic approach to appraising performance has Pearson omitted?
   b. How do you think Yamamoto will react to this interview?
   c. Can you think of anything else Pearson could have done to improve this particular appraisal? Explain.

3. Name and describe briefly the five kinds of causes of poor performance.

4. Which of the following are appropriate ways to measure an employee's performance?

    a. Day after day, more than three customers are lined up at Janet's cash register, so her supervisor concludes that she is a slow worker.

    b. Jonathan smiles a lot, so his supervisor assumes he is happy.

    c. Wesley is late to work every Wednesday morning, so his supervisor plans to find out the cause.

    d. Nick habitually takes longer to deliver pizzas than his company promises its customers, so his supervisor notes that he is inefficient.

    e. Production in the group that Caitlin oversees has fallen off somewhat in the last two months, so her supervisor discusses with her the possible reasons.

5. How can a supervisor avoid illegal discrimination in performance appraisals?

6. At a manufacturing company in south suburban Chicago, one policy stated that each manager and employee must be appraised at one-year intervals. At the same time, the company conducts a review of the person's wages or salary, usually giving at least a small raise. In recent years, like many manufacturers, this company has become concerned about reducing costs. The policy regarding performance appraisals has been modified: Managers' appraisals now must be conducted *at least* a year after the manager's salary was last reviewed. One supervisor was reviewed in December of one year, then in February (14 months later), and then in May of the third year.

    a. What reasons do you think the supervisor's manager had for delaying the performance appraisals so that they were more than a year apart?

    b. What effects do you think the delays had on the supervisor?

7. What type of performance appraisal is used most frequently? What are advantages and disadvantages of this approach?

8. What type of performance appraisal was (or is) used at your most recent job? How effective do you think it is? Why?

9. At a company that sells X-ray equipment, an important new sales territory is opening up. Patrick O'Day, the supervisor of the company's sales force, wants to assign the territory to the best qualified salesperson. How can he compare the performance of the members of the sales force to select the best candidate for the job?

10. Give an advantage and a disadvantage of using each of the following types of appraisals:

    a. Essay appraisal.

    b. Behaviorally anchored rating scale (BARS).

    c. Checklist.

    d. Critical-incident appraisal.

11. Which type of bias does each of the following situations illustrate?

    a. Anne Compton is a new supervisor. To make sure that her employees and her manager take her judgments seriously, she gives each of her employees a lower rating than the previous supervisor did.

    b. Ron is late in completing Noreen's written performance appraisal. To finish it as quickly as possible, he looks it over and adds some negative ratings to an overall positive review so that it looks balanced.

    c. Renee really likes her new employee, Joan. Recently, Joan and her family moved to the same town in which Renee lives; their children attend the same school; Renee and Joan even enjoy lunchtime shopping together.

When it comes time for Joan's performance review, Renee rates Joan high in every category.

12. Reginald DeBeers hates conducting appraisal interviews, so he has the process down to a science. Fifteen minutes before the end of the workday, he meets with the employee who is to be appraised. He gets right down to business, explaining what the employee's ratings are and how he arrived at each number. Then the employee and supervisor sign the form. By then, it is quitting time, and DeBeers rises to shake hands with the employee, saying either "Keep up the good work" or "I'm sure you'll do better next time."

What parts of the interviewing process does DeBeers omit? What are the consequences of leaving out these steps?

PART TWO: SKILL-BUILDING

YOU SOLVE THE PROBLEM

Reflecting back on page 473, which steps in a systematic performance appraisal are evident in the Gwinnett Health System story? Imagine that you are a nursing supervisor at Gwinnett, preparing for an annual appraisal interview with one of your nurses. You are concerned about the nurse's interactions with patients. You have occasionally had to resolve problems because this employee has not listened carefully to patients, and the nurse sometimes has an appearance you consider sloppier than the standards you believe are appropriate. You decide to handle the situation by rating the nurse at 3 on a 5-point scale for "professionalism." How might the organization's new computerized system help you with this process?

Have one member of your group play the role of the supervisor and one play the role of the nurse. Have them role-play the appraisal interview in which the supervisor intends to address these concerns.

Afterward, discuss how well the issues were handled in the role-play. What could the supervisor (and employee) done to have addressed the issues more effectively?

Problem-Solving Case: *Appraising Employees in a Dental Office*

Jill Strode supervises the office staff in a dental office. One of Strode's accomplishments was to develop a system for appraising the performance of the employees she supervises.

For each employee, Strode spells out the specific areas of responsibility that will be evaluated. The areas she evaluates match the responsibilities stated in the employee's job description. Thus, for the checkout receptionist, Strode indicates that she will evaluate how that person handles five areas of responsibility, including checkout procedures and telephone communications. In evaluating how an employee handles each area, Strode looks for specific traits, such as knowledge, initiative, innovation, and courtesy. The following excerpts from an appraisal of the checkout receptionist illustrate the format of the appraisals:

JOB RESPONSIBILITY: Checkout Procedures and Folder Routing . . .

Accuracy: Very good overall. Attention to details is superb in all areas. Seldom forgets any part of the "checkout" procedure.

Example: Ability to pick up on errors made in charting, double-checking folders for missed steps (insurance, scheduling, etc.), thoroughness.

Innovation: Below average. This area has remained unchanged since we installed the system. Procedural changes have been suggested by the supervisor and implemented by the checkout receptionist. Needs improvement.

Example: Complaints with folder errors and patient flow have been verbalized; however, no suggestions for changes or improvement in procedures have been offered. Space limitations in checkout area still a concern . . . suggestions for improvements?

To review the performance appraisal with the employee, Strode sets up a formal appraisal meeting. She has developed the following agenda list of topics to cover during the meeting:

1. Review specific areas of responsibility that will be evaluated. Make any changes or additions if needed.
2. Appraisal for each specific area.
   a. Set goals for improvement and change (at least two improvements/changes for each).
   b. Set training dates, if needed.
   c. Get feedback from staff on appraisal from supervisor.
3. Overall appraisal of traits as exemplified in daily activities and actions.
4. Review goals and training dates.
5. Questions and answers from list.
6. Open forum for discussion: employee to supervisor.

Strode then follows up to make sure that the employee and supervisor carry through on the goals and plans they established during this interview.

1. Based on the information given, what type of performance appraisal has Strode developed?
2. Based on the agenda Strode uses for appraisal interviews, what principles of effective appraisals does she follow?
3. Consider whether the examples in this case seem to be useful tools for conducting appraisals of the clerical employees in a dental practice. Suggest additions or improvements by answering the following questions:
   a. In the excerpt from the sample appraisal, what additional information would improve this appraisal?
   b. How, if at all, would you revise the agenda for the appraisal interview?
   c. Why do you think your suggestions would improve the appraisal process?

Source: Jill Strode.

Knowing Yourself

How Well Do You Accept Evaluations?

It can be difficult for any of us to accept judgment or criticism, and sometimes we may become emotional and fail to listen. This little quiz should help you find out how well you are prepared to receive feedback, which is just as important for a supervisor as giving it. Ask yourself the following questions.

1. Do I prepare for my performance review by gathering examples of work I've done well and compliments I've received from colleagues?
2. Have I been accomplishing what my job description calls for? Have I accepted and fulfilled my responsibilities on major assignments?
3. Have I improved on the job, learned additional skills, and/or taken on greater responsibilities?
4. Have I created a list of things about my performance that I can improve? Have I prioritized weaknesses and selected three to work on immediately?
5. Do I tell myself during the review, "I need to listen to this. It will help me grow personally and professionally"?
6. Do I stay tuned in to what I am hearing?
7. Can I remain objective and unemotional as far as possible?
8. Do I hold back from interrupting?
9. Do I summarize and restate what I hear to be sure I have heard it correctly?
10. Do I ask for specific and action-oriented feedback?
11. Have I created an action plan for attaining my goals?
12. Do I follow up to assess my own progress?

Pause and Reflect

1. How can accepting criticism help you in your career?
2. In what areas of accepting evaluations do you want to improve?
3. What will you do to improve in the areas you have identified?

Sources: Susan Vaughn, "Rethinking Employee Evaluations," *Los Angeles Times,* April 8, 2001, p. W1; "Give Yourself a Job Review," *American Salesman,* May 2001, pp. 26–27.

Class Exercise

Using Software to Appraise Employees

Figure 17.1 provides an overview of how supervisors conduct performance appraisals. This exercise elaborates on that model by showing you how you can use *ManagePro* (trademark of Avantos Performance Systems)—the first product of its kind in a new category of business productivity software known as goal and people management (GPM)—to improve your performance management skills.*

Instructions

You are one of 17 supervisors at Tybro, a major toy manufacturer in the Midwest. Place yourself in the following scenario:

Scenario

During a meeting with your boss, he shows you an article from *The Wall Street Journal,* "PC Program Lets Machines Help Bosses Manage People," and says to you, "I want to find out more about whether *ManagePro,* the software program reviewed in this article, could help our Tybro supervisors and managers, and I'd like you to be the one to answer that question for me. Probably the best way for you to find out is to register to attend the one-day *ManagePro* seminar, and then you can make your recommendation when you return, based on your hands-on experience." You attend the seminar and learn a great deal about the performance management process. Following are some of the highlights of what you learned about *ManagePro.*

Overview of ManagePro

The seminar trainer explained that *ManagePro* is based on fundamental, proven management processes that meet the basic performance needs your employees have (see Table A).

Throughout the day you learned how these processes are reinforced throughout *ManagePro* in (1) the way the program is structured, (2) the tools it provides, and (3) the advice available in the Management Advisor.

Program Structure

As you try out the program, you find that information is simple to enter using fill-in-the-blank forms, outlines, and spreadsheet-like tables. Information is also easy to view and manipulate at multiple levels of detail. You find yourself quickly manipulating the program, using your mouse and pointing and clicking at the icons of what you need. Everything is very intuitive and easy to follow. Changes made through any part of the program at any level are reflected automatically throughout the program. For example, if you reorganize your goals in the Goal Planner/Outliner, the changes automatically are reflected in the People Status Board.

* Permission granted by Avantos Performance Systems, Inc., to include the *ManagePro* information contained in this exercise. For further information on *ManagePro,* contact Avantos Performance Systems, 5900 Hollis Street, Suite C, Emeryville, CA 94608, or call 1-800-AVANTOS.

TABLE A
Needs Focused on by *ManagePro*

Employees' Performance Needs	Management Process
"Tell me what we're trying to achieve, and let's agree on what is expected of me."	*Set clear, measurable goals* that support the key business objectives with specific checkpoints and due dates.
"Let's discuss how I'm doing."	*Monitor progress on each goal* at a frequency determined by the capability of the people involved.
"Help me to improve."	*Provide adequate feedback and coaching* to keep people informed and help them improve performance. Surveys consistently show that employees have very little sense of what their boss thinks of their performance. Giving regular feedback to your people and helping them through coaching are critical parts of managing.
"Reward me for my contribution."	*Evaluate, recognize, and reward people's contributions.* If people feel that performance pays off, they will work harder to achieve success.

Some of the key features of *ManagePro* include the following:

- The Goal Planner/Outliner allows you to organize your goals. Goals can be divided into layers of subgoals, given start and due dates, and delegated to a person or team. Click-and-drag movements make it easy to organize and reorganize goals. (See Figure 17.A.)

- The Goal Status Board gives a view of pending goals and their progress. Color-light indicators alert you to items that require action. For example, yellow means at least one subgoal is behind schedule. (See Figure 17.B.)

- The People/Team Planner allows you to organize people, track goals associated with people, and manage information on feedback, coaching, and performance reviews.

- The People Status Board prompts you periodically to consider getting updates on goal progress and consider giving feedback, coaching, and recognition at a

FIGURE 17.A
Stay Organized

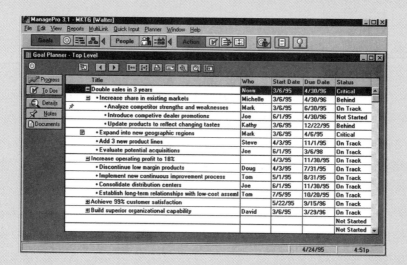

FIGURE 17.B
Stay on Top of Your Goals

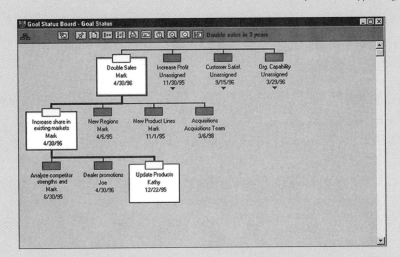

frequency determined by you for each individual or team. For example, you can have *ManagePro* remind you to give a certain employee feedback every three months. This will help you build up your people management discipline so that important activities and processes do not fall between the cracks. (See Figure 17.C.)

Tools

Some of *ManagePro's* support tools include the following:

- The Calendar displays year-, month-, week-, and day-at-a-glance graphic views of events and deadlines.
- The Action List provides a customizable view of action items and status relating to all goals and actions in *ManagePro,* including people management actions such as progress reviews.
- The Reports allow you to generate a variety of standard reports on goals, planning, calendars, action lists, and people management information.

Management Advisor

One other major component of the program is accessed by selecting the Management Advisor button, which allows you to receive context-sensitive management tips and techniques compiled by experts. The Management Advisor helps

FIGURE 17.C
Effectively Manage Your People

	Goals	Progress	Feedbk	Review	Recog	Commit
Mark						
Joe						
Kathy						
Doug						
Tom M.						
Mary						

new supervisors learn and apply management processes on the job; it also provides a refresher and specific diagnostic support for the experienced supervisor.

Conclusion

You return to your office the following day and sit down at your desk to prepare your recommendation to your boss on *ManagePro*. You definitely are sold on the idea that Tybro supervisors (and for that matter, all levels of management at Tybro) would benefit greatly by using this GPM software. In support of your recommendation, you will answer the following questions:

1. What management processes does *ManagePro* support?
2. What three features of *ManagePro* most impressed you as beneficial to improving your performance management and that of your company as a whole? Why?

Building Supervision Skills

Designing an Appraisal

Divide the class into teams of four or five students. Each team will design a performance appraisal intended to evaluate the performance of either the president of the university or the president of the United States (or some other prominent person chosen by the class or the instructor). First, each team should choose which type of appraisal is best suited to evaluate the person's performance. Second, team members decide the content of the appraisal (what questions should be asked). Third, the class as a whole should discuss which types of appraisals were selected and why, and why certain questions were chosen.

Appendix **B**

Supervision Laws: Health and Safety, Labor Relations, Fair Employment

WHERE THERE'S SMOKE . . .

It's becoming common—the sight of workers huddled outside their office buildings, drawing the last bit of smoke into their lungs before they return to work from their furtive cigarette break. According to the National Cancer Institute, U.S. workplaces are rapidly becoming smoke-free, with 69 percent of respondents to a 1999 survey saying they worked in places where smoking is not allowed. In 1993, that number was only 46 percent.

More than three-quarters of states limit smoking in school buildings and health care facilities, but only 24 states limit smoking in private businesses. White-collar workplaces are more likely to be smoke-free than service-oriented or blue-collar workplaces. And there are more smoking bans in the North than in the South. What does it all mean for employees?

Sources: Amy Joyce, "Smoke-Free Workplaces Spreading Like Wildfire," *Washington Post,* November 15, 1998, p. H4; American Cancer Society, "Smoke-Free Workplace Encourages Smokers to Quit," news release, August 28, 2002, www.cancer.org; Minnesota Smoke-Free Coalition, "National Cancer Institute: Up in Smoke: Many States Lag Behind in Workplace Smoking Protections," news release, August 10, 2001, www.smokefreecoalition.org; National Cancer Institute, "Clean Indoor Air: Fact Sheet," State Cancer Legislative Database Program, Bethesda, Maryland, January 2002, www.scld-nci-net.

Some people believe the workplace has become a much healthier environment since the bans started. Even some smokers apparently don't want to be surrounded by smoke all day. Smokers bound by nonsmoking rules at work have been shown to quit at higher rates than in workplaces where smoking is allowed. As they quit, the air becomes cleaner not only for themselves but also for others.

But there may be a persistent backlash from those who cherish the right to smoke. According to the National Smokers Alliance, "Smokers have been unfairly characterized as second-class citizens who don't have the same rights as nonsmokers." The practice of smoking outside the workplace, some feel, forces workers into extreme cold and heat, which is seen as unfair and counterproductive.

Nevertheless, the evidence continues to mount that, in terms of employee health, where there's smoke, there's danger.

Most supervisors today are aware that maintaining the safety and health of employees is a major task. This responsibility is just one of many imposed by the federal government on organizations operating in the United States. Other chapters in this book have addressed additional responsibilities. Chapter 3 discussed labor laws that limit the ways in which organizations can use teamwork. Chapter 11 introduced the impact of the law on the scope of benefits organizations must offer employees. Chapters 15 and 17 explored laws intended to offer equal employment opportunities.

This appendix covers three areas in which federal laws govern the actions of organizations. First, it describes the role of the federal government in regulating safety and health in the workplace. It then describes safety and health hazards, organizational programs for promoting safety and health, and the role of the supervisor in this area. Next, the appendix discusses unions—their impact and the laws governing the interaction of organizations with unions and unionizing efforts. Finally, the appendix examines various ways in which the law has attempted to make the workplace fair and accessible to a diverse workforce. It introduces legal requirements for accommodating disabled employees, providing leave to workers who have family and medical needs, and keeping jobs open for employees who must complete military obligations. Finally, the appendix suggests ways to prevent the harassment of workers and respond when an employee claims harassment has occurred.

GOVERNMENT REGULATION OF SAFETY AND HEALTH

According to the Bureau of Labor Statistics, in 2002, more than 4.7 million occupational injuries and illnesses occurred among the almost 109 million workers in the private sector.[1] These problems are not limited to factory settings. Incidence rates were highest for workers in air transportation, nursing and personal care facilities, and the motor vehicle and equipment industry.[2] Figure B.1 shows the industries that reported the largest number (not rate) of workplace injuries and illnesses in 2002. Not only is the challenge of preventing these problems widespread, but many injuries and illnesses reported today are associated with modern technology—complaints such as injuries related to repetitive motion and the less-than-optimal design of workstations.

Many organizations recognize that safeguarding the well-being of employees in the workplace is not only ethical but also essential to attracting and keeping qualified personnel. Unfortunately, this view has not always prevailed. As a result, the government has stepped in to regulate the safety and health of the workplace.

FIGURE B.1

Industries with the Most Occupational Injuries and Illnesses, 2002

Source: Bureau of Labor Statistics, "Workplace Injuries and Illnesses in 2002," Table 4, news release, December 18, 2003, www.bls.gov.

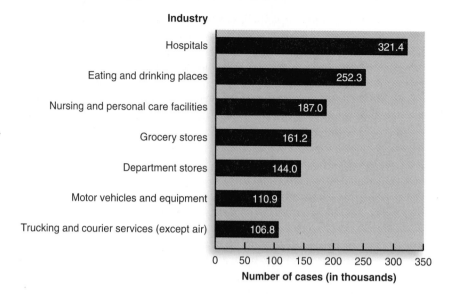

Terrible accidents occurred when the industrial revolution brought together inexperienced workers with new and unfamiliar machinery. Beginning primarily in the early 1900s, state governments passed inspection laws and set up workers' compensation programs to provide benefits for employees injured on the job. In 1913 Congress created the Department of Labor, whose duties include the improvement of working conditions. Despite such actions, however, public sentiment in favor of further protection continued to grow.

Occupational Safety and Health Act (OSHAct) of 1970

The most far-reaching of the laws regulating workplace safety and health is the Occupational Safety and Health Act (OSHAct) of 1970. The law is intended "to assure so far as possible every working man and woman in the nation safe and healthful working conditions and to preserve our human resources." The OSHAct sets up government agencies to conduct research regarding occupational health and safety, set health and safety standards, inspect workplaces, and penalize employers that do not meet standards. Penalties can be severe, including fines of $7,000 per day for failure to correct a violation and jail terms of six months for falsifying records to deceive inspectors.

OSHA and NIOSH

The OSHAct established two federal agencies to see that employers carry out its provisions. The Occupational Safety and Health Administration (OSHA), a part of the U.S. Department of Labor, is charged with setting and enforcing standards for workplace health and safety. People often think of OSHA standards as pertaining mainly to factory-related issues such as personal protective equipment (e.g., gloves, safety shoes) and guards on machinery. However, many OSHA standards pertain to health and safety issues that arise in offices, including recently proposed standards for air quality and the prevention of repetitive-motion injuries. (These topics are discussed later in this appendix.)

To ensure that organizations are meeting its standards, OSHA's inspectors may visit companies but must show a search warrant before conducting an inspection. "Between state and federal [inspections], we do about 85,000 inspections a year total, out of about 6 million workplaces," says former OSHA assistant secretary Charles Jeffress. The agency also hosts a Web site with special areas for small businesses and links to online advisers. It has placed compliance-assistance specialists in its regional offices and also hosts forums and training sessions around the country.[3] OSHA also operates a program of free onsite consultations through which independent consultants evaluate an organization's work practices, environmental hazards, and health and safety program. If an organization follows the consultant's recommendations, it bears no penalties for the shortcomings identified.

The National Institute for Occupational Safety and Health (NIOSH) is responsible for conducting research related to workplace safety and health. It is a part of the Department of Health and Human Services. NIOSH provides OSHA with information necessary for setting standards.

The Supervisor's Responsibility under the OSHAct

Given the extent of OSHA regulations and the thousands of pages interpreting those regulations, supervisors cannot be familiar with every regulation. However, supervisors do need to understand what kinds of practices are required to preserve health and safety in their departments. In addition, the OSHAct imposes some specific responsibilities that apply to supervisors.

The OSHAct requires that supervisors keep records of occupational injuries and illnesses. They must record these on OSHA forms within six working days after learning of the injury or illness. Figure B.2 details which types of accidents and illnesses must be recorded. A supervisor also may have to accompany OSHA officials when they conduct an inspection. These inspections occur in response to a request by an employer, a union, or an employee, or when OSHA's own schedule calls for them. (An employer may not penalize an employee for requesting an investigation or reporting a possible violation.) During the inspection, it is important to be polite and cooperative. This is not always easy because the inspection may come at an inconvenient time, and a supervisor may view it as unwanted interference. However, being uncooperative is no way to foster good relations with the agency and could even lead the inspectors to be tougher than they otherwise might be.

Because chemical hazards are widespread in the modern workplace, OSHA has issued a right-to-know rule requiring that employees be informed about the chemicals used where they work. Each organization must have available information about what chemical hazards exist in the workplace and how employees can protect themselves against those hazards. The information must include labels on containers of chemicals and hazardous materials, as well as Material Safety Data Sheets (MSDS), both of which identify the chemicals, describe how to handle them, and identify the risks involved. A supervisor should make certain that this information is available for all chemicals that are brought into, used in, or produced at the workplace he or she supervises. If a supervisor finds that some information still is needed, the suppliers of the chemicals and other hazardous substances should be able to provide it.

TYPES OF SAFETY AND HEALTH PROBLEMS

Because supervisors have an important role to play in maintaining a safe and healthy workplace, they need to be aware of problems that commonly arise, including health and safety hazards. People tend to associate both classes of hazards with factory settings, but hazards can arise in any work setting, from offices to police cars.

FIGURE B.4
Common Job-Related Injuries and Illnesses and Corresponding Days of Work Generally Missed

Source: NIOSH, *Worker Health Chartbook 2000*, DHHS (NIOSH) Publication No. 2000-127, http://www.cdc.gov/niosh/pdfs/2000-127d.pdf.

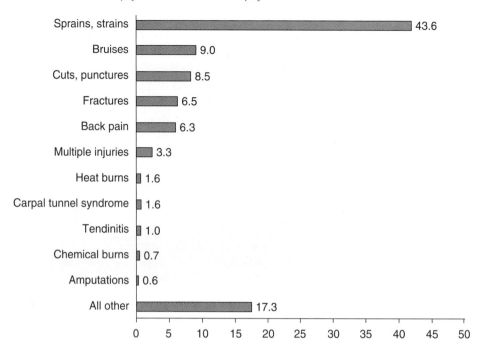

Safety Hazards

A safety hazard is a condition in the workplace that may lead to an injury-causing accident. Common types of injuries include cuts, broken bones, burns, and electric shocks. Figure B.4 shows several common job-related injuries and illnesses, along with corresponding days of work lost. At their most serious, injuries can lead to death. NIOSH reports that each day an average of 9,000 U.S. workers sustain disabling injuries on the job, 16 die from an injury sustained at work, and 137 die from work-related diseases. A NIOSH-funded study of the costs of such injuries and illnesses revealed that the direct cost to businesses is over $40 billion a year, plus about $200 billion in indirect costs.[6] In general, safety hazards arise from personal behavior (that is, unsafe acts) or conditions of the physical environment.

Types of Safety Hazards

Personal behavior as a safety hazard refers to practices by managers and employees that create an environment in which accidents may occur. This behavior may be as basic as carelessness or as obvious as drinking on the job. Sometimes employees cause a safety hazard by refusing to follow proper procedures or use safety equipment such as goggles or gloves. Supervisors and other managers can contribute by failing to enforce safety measures or requiring employees to work such long hours that they do not get enough rest to think clearly. NIOSH's *Worker Health Chartbook 2000* reported that in 1997, motor-vehicle-related incidents were the leading cause of fatal workplace injury.[7] Therefore, supervisors should be especially concerned about encouraging safe behavior among employees who spend work time in vehicles—delivery personnel, salespeople, employees who take business trips, and so on.

Some employees are said to be accident-prone—that is, more likely to have accidents than other people. These employees tend to act on impulse, without careful thought, and do not concentrate on their work. Many employees who are vulnerable to accidents have negative attitudes about their jobs, co-workers, or supervisors. Perhaps they find the work boring. Sometimes people who are otherwise careful are vulnerable to accidents. When people are struggling with personal problems or do not get enough sleep, they may become accident prone. Therefore, a supervisor needs to pay attention to the behavior of all employees to recognize which of them are at risk for causing an accident on any given day. A supervisor may need to restrict the activities of an employee who is temporarily accident prone or even to send that person home. If the problem continues, a supervisor may have to use the counseling and discipline procedures described in Chapter 12.

Hazardous working conditions that can lead to accidents are as varied as a messy work environment, electrical cords where people might trip over them, poor lighting, and a lack of protective devices on machinery. A study by Liberty Mutual that used Bureau of Labor Statistics and workers' compensation data found that falls and slips were the second and third most costly types of worksite injuries in the United States in 1998.[8] Even language barriers can contribute to work hazards, as in the case of a young Hispanic worker who slipped from a wet roof and was paralyzed. His supervisor, who did not speak Spanish, said the worker did not speak English, so it had been difficult to communicate that the roof was dangerously slick.[9]

Responses

A supervisor who observes unsafe conditions should take one of the following actions, listed in order of priority:

1. Eliminate the hazard.
2. If the hazard cannot be eliminated, use protective devices such as guards on machinery.
3. If the hazard cannot be guarded, provide warnings, such as labels on the hot parts inside photocopiers.
4. If you cannot remove or guard the hazard on your own, notify the proper authority. Recommend a solution, and then follow up to make sure that the condition has been corrected.

For Frank Clemente, Cargo Service Center's facility supervisor at Chicago's O'Hare International Airport, one of the busiest airports in the world, safety is especially important. Forklifts often banged and damaged the dock doors at the warehouse, so the doors no longer closed securely. As a result, moisture would form on the floor and around the threshold, making the warehouse floor slippery and hazardous. The company installed "knockout" dock doors, which consist of panels that fit into tracks mounted on the wall. If the doors are dislodged, they can easily be remounted, eliminating the dangerous conditions.[10]

Back and neck injuries account for many workplace injuries, so a supervisor should especially seek measures to prevent and correct safety hazards causing such injuries. Ways to prevent back injuries include designing the job to minimize injuries, training employees to use lifting techniques that minimize strain on the back, reducing the size or weight of objects to be lifted, using mechanical aids, and making sure workers assigned to do a job are strong enough to do it safely. The position that puts the most stress on the back is sitting. Supervisors of office employees should be sure employees have comfortable chairs and enough opportunities to stand up and move around.

Common Concerns

Several common concerns about safety and health in the workplace are especially significant because they are widely occurring, or at least widely discussed. These include smoking, alcoholism and drug abuse, problems related to the use of computers, repetitive-motion disorders, and AIDS.

Smoking

An estimated 57 million individuals in the United States currently smoke cigarettes, risking serious health consequences such as cancer, heart disease, and high blood pressure. With about 440,000 deaths in the United States each year being attributable to tobacco use, smoking is the leading preventable cause of death and disease in the country.[11] Environmental ("secondhand") tobacco smoke contains more than 4,000 chemicals, of which more than 50 are known to be carcinogenic. Secondhand smoke is associated with a greater risk for lung cancer and coronary heart disease, as well as a variety of risks to children, including sudden infant death syndrome, asthma, bronchitis, and pneumonia.[12] As well as a health hazard, cigarette smoking is a safety hazard; lit cigarettes can cause burns, fires, or explosions when handled carelessly or near flammable substances.

Because the consequences of cigarette smoking are potentially serious, many organizations have restricted the amount of smoking allowed in the workplace, as seen in the opening story. In many locations, the restrictions also are required by state or local law. A 1999 survey of 17 states and the District of Columbia conducted by the American Medical Association found that official workplace policies that limited smoking in public, common, or work areas were in effect at 87–97 percent of firms. According to the National Cancer Institute, laws that restrict smoking at some or all work sites are in effect in the District of Columbia and 47 states, with smoking most often prohibited in school buildings and health care facilities.[13]

Supervisors can help minimize the effects of smoking in the workplace by enforcing the organization's restrictions and providing encouragement and recognition to employees who are trying to quit smoking.

Alcoholism and Drug Abuse

Alcoholism and drug abuse are serious problems in the workplace and can be costly to the organization. People who are under the influence of these substances are more likely to be involved in accidents. Many organizational policies therefore call for strong action when an employee is found to be under the influence.

Part of the supervisor's role in promoting safety is counseling and disciplining employees with these problems. (For more information on how supervisors should respond, refer to Chapter 12.)

Problems Related to Computer Use

A sizable majority of U.S. workers now use computers on the job. As computers have become increasingly common in all kinds of work environments, people have attributed some health problems to computer use.[14] Many of the concerns involve the use of video display terminals (VDT), the screens on which computers display information. Users of VDTs have complained that working with or near these screens causes a variety of health problems, including eyestrain and vision problems. Some reports have suggested that VDT use also is linked to pregnancy problems, notably miscarriages, through the radiation emitted by the VDTs, but research currently does not support a link between VDT use and pregnancy risks.

Fortunately, the problems associated with VDT use can be reduced or eliminated. Computer workstations should position VDTs to minimize glare (see Figure B.5), and lighting for screen viewing should be at a moderate level (20 to 50 foot-candles as measured by a light meter). Computer screens should be placed at least 16 inches from the user's eyes. Employees who use computers should

FIGURE B.5
Positioning a VDT for Comfortable Viewing

Source: Courtesy of the Workers' Compensation Board of British Columbia. Illustration used with permission.

16-29"
15°

take rest breaks; a break as short as three to five minutes each hour can alleviate eye discomfort. Occasionally glancing away from the screen toward distant objects relaxes the eye muscles. Those who are concerned about radiation also may wish to install radiation shields on their computers or use only low-emission VDTs.

Typing or staring into computers for long stretches can lead to sore muscles in the back, arms, legs, and neck. Many of these problems are associated with poor posture. The corrections may be as simple as adjusting the height and position of the user's chair, keyboard or mouse, and computer screen. Computer users may also be susceptible to repetitive-motion disorders, discussed next.

Repetitive-Motion Disorders

According to OSHA, musculoskeletal disorders, or MSDs (injuries and disorders of soft tissues include muscles, tendons, ligaments, joints, and cartilage and the nervous system), account for about one out of every three lost-workday occupational injuries and illnesses.[15] MSDs occur in all occupations and industries. In 2002, the main causes of MSDs were worker motion or position. In more than 50,000 cases, injuries occurred from workers performing the same motion over and over in a way that caused damage. Advances in machinery and electronic equipment have enabled workers to perform repetitive functions at an increasingly rapid pace. Unfortunately, the repeated application of force to the same muscles or joints can result in injuries known as repetitive-motion disorders.

An example of these disorders is carpal tunnel syndrome, which involves pain in the wrist and fingers. This is a common complaint among those who type at a keyboard all day or perform other tasks involving the wrist, such as making the same cut in chickens all day at a poultry processor. Some people in the newspaper business have speculated that stiff competition for jobs in that field has forced many reporters and columnists to try to cope with the pain rather than complain about it.

Back problems are another major cost to employees and employers, accounting for an estimated $50 billion per year in workers' compensation. An additional $50 billion is spent each year on indirect costs such as finding and training substitute workers and running physical conditioning and reduced-work programs to help ease employees back into their jobs. Reduced workplace productivity is a cause for concern. "If you look at lost work time," says Professor Alan Hedge of Cornell University's Department of Design and Environmental Analysis, "it's the tip of the iceberg. When you're hurting at work you're not as effective."[16]

To prevent repetitive-motion disorders, an organization can take several measures, including designing jobs and workstations to allow for rests, using adjustable furniture, and avoiding awkward movements and bad posture. This type of response to the problem is an application of ergonomics, the science concerned with the human characteristics that need to be considered in designing tasks and equipment so that people will work most effectively and safely. While supervisors need not be experts in ergonomics, they can cultivate an awareness of these issues. Another measure is to encourage employees who are in pain to seek medical attention right away. Supervisors should never tell their employees to work through pain, as this may aggravate an existing injury.

AIDS

Although other illnesses are more widespread, probably the most feared is AIDS (acquired immunodeficiency syndrome), caused by HIV, the human immunodeficiency virus. The biggest reason for this fear is that AIDS remains incurable and fatal. Fortunately, people cannot catch it from touching a person with AIDS or sharing a drinking fountain or restroom; the HIV virus is transmitted through the exchange of bodily fluids, which can occur through sexual activity, blood transfusions, and the sharing of contaminated hypodermic needles, as well as between an infected mother and a fetus.

Most of the activities involving the transmission of HIV would not occur in the workplace. The major exception is health care institutions where hypodermic needles are used. These institutions should have procedures for the proper handling and disposal of the needles to prevent the spread of AIDS and other serious diseases such as hepatitis.

In most work settings, the major concern about AIDS is how to treat employees who are HIV-positive or who have AIDS. Both fairness and federal antidiscrimination laws dictate treating these employees in the same way as anyone else with a disability. As long as the employees can perform their jobs, they should be allowed to remain. At some point, an organization may have to make reasonable accommodations to allow them to continue working, such as allowing an ill employee to complete job assignments at home.

When an employee has AIDS, a supervisor must confront the fears that other employees are likely to have about working with that employee. With help from the human resources department, a supervisor may need to educate other employees about AIDS and how it is transmitted. Despite these efforts, some employees may shun a co-worker with AIDS. Therefore, the supervisor and others in the organization must do their best to protect the confidentiality of a person with AIDS. If an employee with AIDS or the employee's co-workers are having trouble coping, the supervisor may wish to refer them to the organization's employee-assistance program, if one exists. (These programs are described in Chapter 12.)

WORKPLACE PROGRAMS TO PROMOTE SAFETY AND HEALTH

Many employers have instituted formal programs to promote the safety and health of employees. The program may include training, safety meetings, posters, awards for safe performance, and safety and health committees. A typical committee includes operative employees and managers, perhaps with a membership that rotates among the employees. A recent study of occupational safety and health committees in the public sector in New Jersey found that committees with more worker involvement were associated with fewer reported illnesses and injuries.[17] The duties of a health and safety committee can include regularly inspecting work areas, reviewing employees' suggestions for improving health and safety, and promoting awareness about safety. The committee also might sponsor the organization's contests or awards for safe practices.

Many organizations have extended their safety and health programs to cover off-duty conduct by employees that contributes to health problems. These efforts may be part of a wellness program (see Chapter 13). For example, some wellness programs seek to discourage employees from smoking altogether (not just restricting smoking at work), and others seek to teach healthy eating and exercise habits.

Benefits

By reducing the number and severity of work-related injuries and illnesses, safety and health programs can cut the costs to organizations in a number of areas. These include health and workers' compensation insurance, defense of lawsuits, repair or replacement of equipment damaged in accidents, and wages paid for lost time. The savings can be significant. In addition, safety and health programs can motivate employees, reduce turnover, and help prevent pain and suffering among employees and their families. Finally, an organization that is a safe and healthy place to work is more likely to enjoy good relations with the government and community and should have an easier time recruiting desirable employees.

Characteristics of an Effective Program

A safety and health program is effective when it minimizes the likelihood that people will be injured or become ill as a result of conditions in the workplace, when all levels of management demonstrate a strong commitment to the program, and when employees believe the program is worthwhile. In addition, all employees need to be trained in the importance of safety and ways to promote health and safety in the workplace. This training should give employees an ongoing awareness of the need to behave in safe ways. Finally, an organization should have a system for identifying and correcting hazards before they do damage. In addition to those mentioned elsewhere in this appendix, workplace hazards can include pesticides, loose carpeting, cleaning products, toner, markers, correction fluid, artificial lighting, dark stairways, needles or syringes, lead-based paint (in older buildings), noise, carbon dioxide, radon, X-rays, perfume, radioactive materials and waste, biological waste, poisonous substances, and tools and equipment that don't "fit" the employee.[18]

Role of the Supervisor

Top management's support of safety measures is important; the organization may even have a safety director or other manager responsible for safety programs. Nevertheless, it is up to supervisors to see that employees follow safety precautions. It is the supervisors who observe and are responsible for the day-to-day performance of employees. Unfortunately, some supervisors must witness a serious injury before they appreciate why they must enforce safety rules and procedures. Supervisors who avoid enforcing these rules because they are afraid employees will react negatively are missing the point of why the rules exist. They also are failing to recognize that they have an important role in maintaining a safe and healthy workplace.

Effective supervisors also go beyond simple enforcement of rules. They may encourage their employees to diagnose hazards and help them cut through red tape to improve unsafe conditions. A study of hospitals found that nurses who saw safety-related problems often could not bring about the changes needed to correct those problems.[19] A supervisor can be a necessary ally in this situation.

Training and Hazard Prevention

A supervisor needs to see that employees understand and follow all procedures designed to maintain safety and health. New employees must be well trained in how to do their job safely; more experienced employees need training when they take on new responsibilities or when the organization introduces new procedures, materials, or machinery. In addition, employees need reminders about safe practices. In addition to comments from the supervisor, the reminders could include posters, items in the company or department newsletter, and presentations by one employee to the others. Statistics about the department's performance, such as the number of accidents during the current year compared with last year, can be posted on bulletin boards or reported in the newsletter. In addition, OSHA requires that companies with more than 10 employees display the safety and health poster shown in Figure B.6, which provides information about employees' rights under the OSHAct.

Some special concerns arise with regard to educating workers who are or may become pregnant. A Supreme Court ruling prohibits employers from forbidding pregnant workers from holding hazardous jobs, a policy that, if permitted, could force women to choose between holding a job and having a baby. Nevertheless, women who remain in these jobs may sue an employer for damages if a child is born with injuries caused by hazardous working conditions. The acceptable way to protect female employees of childbearing age is to emphasize information. They should be informed of any pregnancy-related risks of work assignments. A supervisor also may encourage employees to ask for a reassignment to a less hazardous job if they become pregnant. (The organization may not reduce the employee's pay, benefits, or seniority rights.) If the employee cannot be reassigned, the organization can give the employee leave during her pregnancy, including full pay and a guarantee of getting the job back after the baby is born.

Another situation calling for special attention is the supervision of shift workers, who also need additional guidance in safe practices. Employees will be more alert and better able to concentrate if they adapt their overall lifestyle to working night shifts or rotating shifts. They must make an extra effort to get enough quality sleep during the day, seeking out a quiet, dark, cool place for doing so. People who are naturally alert late at night will probably sleep best if they do so right after working at night, whereas others will do better if they sleep just before going in to work at night. People who work a night shift also will be more comfortable if they eat relatively light foods during their shift, avoiding heavy, greasy items.

A supervisor should encourage all employees to participate in the promotion of safe and healthy conditions. One way to do this is to emphasize that employees share in the responsibility for creating a safe work setting. In addition, a supervisor should be responsive to employee complaints related to safety, seeing that the

FIGURE B.6
OSHA Safety and
Health Poster

You Have a Right to a Safe and Healthful Workplace.
IT'S THE LAW!

- You have the right to notify your employer or OSHA about workplace hazards. You may ask OSHA to keep your name confidential.
- You have the right to request an OSHA inspection if you believe that there are unsafe and unhealthful conditions in your workplace. You or your representative may participate in the inspection.
- You can file a complaint with OSHA within 30 days of discrimination by your employer for making safety and health complaints or for exercising your rights under the *OSH Act*.
- You have a right to see OSHA citations issued to your employer. Your employer must post the citations at or near the place of the alleged violation.
- Your employer must correct workplace hazards by the date indicated on the citation and must certify that these hazards have been reduced or eliminated.
- You have the right to copies of your medical records or records of your exposure to toxic and harmful substances or conditions.
- Your employer must post this notice in your workplace.

The *Occupational Safety and Health Act of 1970 (OSH Act)*, P.L. 91-596, assures safe and healthful working conditions for working men and women throughout the Nation. The Occupational Safety and Health Administration, in the U.S. Department of Labor, has the primary responsibility for administering the *OSH Act*. The rights listed here may vary depending on the particular circumstances. To file a complaint, report an emergency, or seek OSHA advice, assistance, or products, call 1-800-321-OSHA or your nearest OSHA office: • Atlanta (404) 562-2300 • Boston (617) 565-9860 • Chicago (312) 353-2220 • Dallas (214) 767-4731 • Denver (303) 844-1600 • Kansas City (816) 426-5861 • New York (212) 337-2378 • Philadelphia (215) 861-4900 • San Francisco (415) 975-4310 • Seattle (206) 553-5930. Teletypewriter (TTY) number is 1-877-889-5627. To file a complaint online or obtain more information on OSHA federal and state programs, visit OSHA's website at **www.osha.gov**. If your workplace is in a state operating under an OSHA-approved plan, your employer must post the required state equivalent of this poster.

1-800-321-OSHA
www.osha.gov

U.S. Department of Labor   •   Occupational Safety and Health Administration   •   OSHA 3165

health and safety committee or the appropriate individual investigates these complaints. Any hazardous conditions should be corrected immediately.

Prompt Responses

A supervisor who observes a violation of health and safety guidelines should respond immediately and consistently. Failure to react is a signal to employees that the guidelines are not really important. First, a supervisor should determine why the violation occurred. Does the employee understand what the proper procedures are? If the employee understands the procedures but still resists following them, the supervisor should try to find out why. For example, if an employee complains that some safety equipment is uncomfortable to use, investigating the complaint may turn up a more effective alternative, such as a greater selection of safety glasses or a way to set up a job so that less safety equipment is required. Despite complaints, however, a supervisor must insist that employees follow safety procedures, even when they seem inconvenient. If the safety rules are violated, a supervisor may have to take disciplinary action. (See Chapter 12 for a discussion of discipline.)

Quality of Work Life

By combating fatigue, boredom, and dissatisfaction, which can make an employee accident prone, a supervisor can promote safety and health. These efforts may include improving the quality of work life by making jobs more interesting and satisfying. Although no one has proved a link between quality of work life and employee safety and health, it seems reasonable to assume that interested, satisfied employees will tend to be healthier and more careful. (Chapter 11 offers some guidelines for expanding and enriching jobs.)

In the case of shift workers, a supervisor can help minimize fatigue by encouraging the organization to place employees on a single shift or rotate shifts so that employees go to work later and later, rather than earlier and earlier or in no steady pattern. Providing bright lighting also will help employees stay alert at night.

Setting an Example

As with any other area in which a supervisor wants employees to behave in a certain way, the supervisor must set a good example and follow safe practices. For instance, a supervisor who uses tools improperly, creates a tower of soft-drink cans on a filing cabinet, or tries to troubleshoot a photocopier without first turning off the power is voiding the effect of even the most eloquent lecture on safety in the workplace.

The following guidelines are some other ways in which supervisors can set an example about safety. Most of these carry little or no financial cost.[20]

1. Be a fanatic about health and safety. Make it a top priority in your factory, shop, or office.
2. Establish a safety committee with responsibility for conducting periodic safety audits.
3. Heighten worker awareness through safety training programs, regularly scheduled safety campaigns, and celebration of National Safety Week.
4. Reward suggestions for improved health and safety measures.
5. Make cleanliness more than a virtue. Make it a requirement.
6. Distribute a safety and emergency procedures and instructions manual.
7. Post emergency phone numbers in prominent locations throughout the workplace.
8. Conduct safety evacuation drills where appropriate.
9. Insist that all hazardous substances and materials be tightly sealed and properly stored.
10. When you say that hard hats are required on the work site, mean it!
11. Install appropriate smoke detectors, alarms, and fire extinguishers.

12. Strictly enforce company no-smoking rules and introduce a no-perfume policy when necessary.
13. Clearly mark all hazardous items and zones.
14. Never condone or encourage safety shortcuts.

LABOR RELATIONS: THE SUPERVISOR'S ROLE

Concerns related to health and safety are among the issues that spurred the formation of unions in the United States during the late 1800s. Employees, who then worked as long as 12 hours each day, banded together to persuade employers to shorten work hours, pay higher wages, and improve safety. Today unions continue to negotiate with organizations over similar issues.

In 1935, the federal government passed the Wagner Act (also called the National Labor Relations Act). This law aims to define and protect the rights of workers and employers, encourage collective bargaining, and eliminate unfair practices (for example, violence and threatening to fire employees who join a union). Following passage of the Wagner Act, union membership tripled (see Figure B.7). As a percentage of the total workforce, union membership peaked in the 1940s.

Union membership has since fallen to less than 14 percent of the workforce during the past decade.[21] This drop has accompanied a decline in the industrial sector of the economy, where union membership was traditionally strongest. The power of unions also has declined along with the numbers. During the 1980s, many unions made major concessions in negotiations with employers.

The processes by which supervisors and other managers work constructively with unions constitute the management discipline of labor relations. Effective labor relations cannot eliminate all conflicts between labor and management, but they do provide a relatively low-cost means of resolving conflict through discussion rather than confrontation. Labor relations occur through activities such as organization drives and collective bargaining.

FIGURE B.7   **Union Membership as a Percentage of the Employed U.S. Workforce**

Source: C. Chang and C. Sorrentino, "Union Membership in 12 Countries," *Monthly Labor Review* 114, no. 12 (1991), pp. 46–53; L. Troy and N. Sheflin, *Union Sourcebook* (West Orange, NJ: Industrial Relations Data and Information Services, 1985); *Statistical Abstract of the United States: 2003* (Washington, DC, 2003), p. 431.

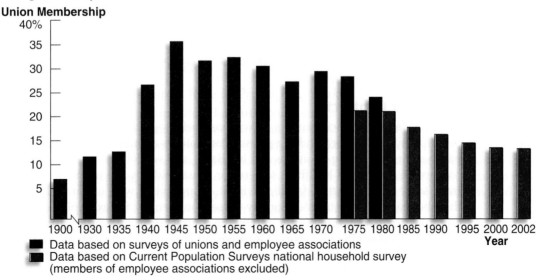

A supervisor must see that the complaint is investigated properly. Generally, the investigation involves a third party, such as a personnel official, interviewing everyone involved. This official, the supervisor, and the parties involved should keep the investigation confidential. The supervisor must avoid expressing an opinion or imposing his or her interpretation on the situation.

Whether harassment occurs depends on how the behavior affects the recipient, not on the intent of the person performing the behavior. Thus, if lewd jokes and pornographic pictures create a climate that feels hostile and intimidating to an employee, it does not matter that the person who told the jokes and hung up the pictures thought only that they were funny. Perceptions vary from one person to another. This principle is especially important to supervisors evaluating their own behavior. Supervisors must appreciate that their position in the organization gives them greater power than the people they supervise. Behavior that might seem merely playful to a supervisor may seem more frightening in the eyes of someone with less power in the organization.

If the investigation indicates that sexual harassment did occur, the problem must be corrected. One approach that does *not* work is ignoring the offensive behavior in the hope that it will go away. The victim telling the offender to stop is effective more than half the time. Because of differences in perceptions, it may be helpful to describe not only the offending behavior but also the kind of behavior that would be acceptable. In addition, a supervisor needs to work with the human resources department to identify a prompt and firm response to charges that are proven. The response might be to move the offending employee to another department or shift or even to fire him or her. Discipline should be appropriate and swift, occurring the same day if possible or at least within a week.

Preventing Sexual Harassment

An employee who harasses another employee hurts the organization in several ways. The person who is being harassed is upset and unable to work as effectively as possible. If that person complains, disciplining the harasser may involve transferring or dismissing him or her, resulting in the loss of an otherwise qualified employee. And if the harassed person sues, the company faces the embarrassment and expense of defending itself in court. It is clearly in the organization's best interests to prevent harassment.

Accommodation of Disabled Employees

As we saw in Chapter 15, the Americans with Disabilities Act requires that employers make their facilities accessible to qualified employees with disabilities. Under this law, supervisors sometimes have to ensure that their company makes reasonable accommodations so that employees with disabilities can perform their jobs.

In the years since the passage of the ADA, the definition of what accommodations are "reasonable" has evolved through administrative decisions and court cases. Deciding what accommodations to make can be complex.[26] Supervisors should work with the human resources department to ensure that any actions taken meet the legal requirements. Supervisors contribute their perspective on which activities are required by the job, while human resource professionals contribute knowledge of what the law requires. Similarly, if an employee's performance seems to be declining and the supervisor believes a disability may be causing the decline, the supervisor should work with the human resources department to avoid discriminatory treatment. In general, supervisors should not convey to an employee their belief that he or she may be disabled; rather, they should focus on the work performance itself. Avoid casually using terms such as "manic" or "crazy," which may be interpreted as references to mental illness.

Family, Medical, and Military Leave

At times, employees must take time off work because they are ill or need to care for family members or fulfill military duties. In some situations, the organization must keep the employee's job available. Supervisors have to plan how the remaining employees will get the work done until the employee returns. They have to help the returning employee make a smooth transition back into the job. These responsibilities require strong leadership as well as good planning skills. Supervisors should be aware of the laws requiring these efforts.

Family and Medical Leave Act

Under the Family and Medical Leave Act (FMLA), employers with more than 50 employees must allow their eligible employees to take unpaid leave for up to 12 weeks for family and medical reasons. Although the law does not require paid leave, it does require that the employer maintain the employee's health benefits during the leave. When the employee returns, the employer must place the employee in the same or an equivalent position.

Reasons for which employees may take leave under FMLA include birth or adoption of a child; the need to care for an ill spouse, child, or parent; and a serious health condition that makes it impossible for the employee to perform his or her job. Employees who wish to take leave under FMLA must give the employer notice—30 days' notice if the reason is foreseeable. They also must comply with the organization's paperwork requirements. The employee's leave may be taken intermittently or in one absence. Each 12 months, the employee becomes eligible for another 12 weeks of unpaid leave. It is up to the employer to determine when each yearlong period begins and ends.

In some states, employers must meet state requirements that are stricter than the federal requirements of the FMLA. California recently became the first state to require paid family leave. Workers can earn up to six weeks of partial income, with the pay funded by a payroll tax of $4 per month per employee. Other states provide paid leave to low-income parents.[27]

The Department of Labor studied data on use of the FMLA during 1999 and the first half of 2000.[28] The department found that 23.8 million workers, or 16.5 percent, took some time off under FMLA. More than half took leave to care for their own health, and almost one-fifth took time off to care for a new child. Of the employees who took a leave, more than half were back at work within 10 days, and one-fourth took their leaves in installments as short as an hour. The main challenge for supervisors is to keep the work group organized when an employee's family or medical needs require time off. Through skillful planning and communication, supervisors can help to keep the organization running smoothly while also complying with the law.

Uniformed Services Employment and Reemployment Rights Act

In addition to family and personal commitments, many employees have made commitments to the military. And military campaigns in Afghanistan and Iraq have required that thousands of these employees serve their country for extended periods. That service has brought renewed attention to a 1994 law, the Uniformed Services Employment and Reemployment Rights Act (USERRA). Under USERRA, an individual who leaves a civilian job for service on active duty or for military training must be reemployed in the job that person would have held if he or she had not been absent for the military service. The law also requires that employers provide returning service members with reasonable efforts for training or retraining if needed, and the employer must make efforts to accommodate disabled veterans when they return. These obligations remain in effect for up to five years of military service. To receive the benefits, the service member must have been released under honorable conditions and report back to the employer in a timely manner.

In contrast to other employment laws, USERRA does not have an exemption for small organizations. Even a family business with a handful of employees is required to rehire returning service members. Complying with USERRA can be particularly challenging for small organizations, which acutely feel the absence of the service member yet may have difficulty affording an additional employee or finding someone to fill in temporarily. Still, most employees can be motivated to do extra because of their appreciation of the sacrifices being made by their co-workers in the military.

An additional challenge of reemploying veterans is that the stress of battle takes a heavy toll on some service members. The recent conflicts in the Middle East have required the largest and longest lasting mobilization of the reserve and National Guard since the Korean War, and the battle conditions have been traumatic for some who served. Some cope, while others experience posttraumatic stress disorder. Remember that supervisors should not even try to diagnose an employee's mental condition. However, if reemployed service members—or any employees—are having difficulty concentrating or getting along with their co-workers, the supervisor may need to intervene as described in Chapters 12 and 13.

One expert who has had plenty of experience with these challenges is Elaine Weinstein, senior vice president of human resources for KeySpan. More than two dozen of KeySpan's employees have been mobilized for military service since September 11, 2001. As they return, Weinstein plans what actions the company needs to take to help them make the transition back to civilian work. Sometimes a flexible work schedule is useful. Weinstein offers advice based on ethics: "Treat them as you would wish to be treated after leaving your family and supporting your country."[29]

Some people have complained about the challenges of complying with fair employment requirements. Family, medical, and military leave all pose hardships on organizations. And the need to avoid harassment feels like a minefield to some people. For example, fear of being accused of sexual harassment leaves some individuals feeling unable to pay friendly compliments. However, respecting the viewpoints, emotional comfort, and personal responsibilities of all employees simply makes ethical and practical sense. The same is true of ensuring employees' safety and health and practicing good labor relations. In each case, a supervisor recognizes that good employee relations is at the heart of cultivating the organization's most important resources: its employees.

Appendix **C**

The Supervisor's Career Path: Finding a Career That Fits

SETTING CAREER GOALS

Many jobs exist, but finding a career that is rewarding and fits your personal needs and preferences can be a challenge. A career is a chosen pursuit; it is all the things you are doing at any given point to create a satisfying life while setting and working toward goals. A job is a regular activity performed for payment. You might have a job as a waiter for money but be interning in a law office and taking political science classes to develop your career.

Careers evolve over time—you will likely hold a series of jobs in a variety of industries that will eventually make up your career. Setting career goals is a crucial part of any job search. It lets potential employers know you are focused and goal oriented. Whether through letters, phone calls, or interviews, every moment of contact with prospective employers must convey that you have goals and that you arrived at these career goals thoughtfully. Determining your career goals involves some soul-searching and research, but it will pay off in a satisfying job that fits.

Step One: Self-Assessment and Your Personality Profile

The first step in finding the right career path is to have a solid understanding of yourself. What do you like? What do you do well? What do you care about? What motivates you? You can access numerous resources to assist you in uncovering your personal interests and values. The Myers-Brigg Type Indicator, mentioned in Chapter 14, is frequently used to assist people with self-assessment. Although you can't take the Myers-Brigg test online, you can access a number of these personality typing tests and get some insights into your preferences. Visit the following Web site for a list: www.jobhuntersbible.com/counseling/ptests.shtml. Formulate lists of your interests, your skills, and the values that comprise your personality profile. This profile will become the foundation for your job search, setting a direction for a career that will match your personality and your interests. Don't forget about your priorities. The Knowing Yourself quiz in Chapter 11, "What Motivates You?" may help you identify issues that are important to your career choice—issues such as work environment, prestige, and job security. In Chapter 15, "Would You Hire You?" helps identify what you value in your work environment. Priorities will help you focus on what is important. While you might have a strong interest in figure skating, you may value security and need money. If so, you'll need a job that is more stable and lucrative—maybe managing an ice rink would meet your interests as well as your needs.

Step Two: Establish Your Skills Inventory

On the basis of your education and job experience, compile a list of all the skills you've acquired. As discussed in Chapter 1, supervisory skills can be broken down into five skill categories:

- *Technical skills*—knowledge of particular techniques/procedures.
- *Human relations skills*—ability to communicate, motivate, and understand other people.
- *Conceptual skills*—ability to see relationship of parts to the whole.
- *Decision-making skills*—ability to analyze information and make good decisions.
- *Knowledge skills*—ability to use e-mail, voice mail, fax, intranet, and Internet to manage data.

Also refer back to Figure 1.4, "Characteristics of a Successful Supervisor," for a reminder of the skill sets demonstrated by successful supervisors.

Think about your skills and strengths in terms of:

- **Personality-related skills.** These are skills that reflect your personal capabilities, talents, and general areas of interest. These would include strengths such

Formats

A résumé is a reflection of you and should showcase your individual style and talents. There are many ways to organize a résumé; the crucial issue is to create a résumé that best highlights your unique strengths and interests. Résumés are typically organized in one of two ways: chronologically or based on functional areas. A chronological résumé is best when your education and experience progress logically for the position you're interested in and you have impressive job titles to highlight. A functional résumé emphasizes skills and qualifications and works well if you are looking to switch fields or if you have gaps in your work history.

Visit job-search Web sites for numerous examples of effective résumé styles and formats. Two helpful sites are http://resume.monster.com/archives/samples/ and www.collegegrad.com/resumes/.

Once you've decided on the format that works best for you, it's time to put it all together. You can use the Dushkin Online Résumé Builder (www.dushkin.com/online/future/resumebuilder.mhtml) to assist you in organizing your information and formatting your résumé.

You will likely need a scannable version of your résumé along with the traditional format you've generated. To increase the chances of your résumé being scanned correctly:

- Use a standard typeface in 12- or 14-point type.
- Use a ragged right margin.
- Do not use italics, underlines, lines, boxes, script, bullets, or borders.
- Do not fold or staple the résumé.
- Use a keywords section to increase the number of "hits"; be sure to include industry buzzwords and jargon.

There are a number of resources for preparing an electronic résumé. Monster.com has some good tips at its Web site: http://resume.monster.com/articles/scannableresume/.

Proofread, Proofread, Proofread

Check and double-check your résumé for typographical and grammatical errors. Have friends and family check it as well. Errors, no matter how minor, are red flags to potential employers because they indicate a lack of attention to detail.

Job Application Letters

A job application letter should accompany any résumé you send and mention the specific position for which you are applying. It should highlight your qualifications and help the reader see how your skills will benefit his or her organization. To adapt your letter to a specific organization, access the organization's Web site and research what the company does, what its goals are, and any other useful facts that might highlight your skills and experience. If the company is launching a new product and you have product development experience, your job letter is an excellent place to highlight this connection. Whenever possible, address your job letter to the hiring manager. A letter that includes a person's name will get more close attention than the standard "Dear Sir/Madam" letter.

Other Useful Job Search Tools

While your résumé is the key tool you'll need for your job search, some other items will come in handy and demonstrate your professionalism:

- **Voice mail:** Whether on your landline or your cell phone, voice mail is the best way to ensure you don't miss that important call. Potential employers confronted with busy signals or unanswered calls might not call back. Be sure your outgoing message is short and professional, and respond to any messages within one business day.

- **E-mail:** A permanent personal e-mail account with a reputable Internet service provider (ISP) is crucial to your job search. You will need an e-mail program that can transmit attachments, such as your résumé, quickly and easily. Make sure the e-mail address you choose is professional and easily recognizable.

- **An information management system:** Throughout your job search, you will access a significant amount of information and contact a number of people. Keep yourself organized by establishing a system for tracking all the information you will acquire throughout your search. You'll likely need a system that will accommodate hard copy as well as electronic information. A set of file folders (both standard paper files and electronic files) will help you keep track of important information as you acquire it. Creating separate files for job hunting tips, your résumé and supporting material (such as work samples), jobs that interest you, and contacts might be a good starting point.

Job Hunting Resources

Once you've set some career goals and prepared your résumé, you can begin your job search in earnest. There are a variety of resources to assist you in this search.

College Career Centers

Most colleges have career centers that can provide job listings and information about companies and set you up with on-campus interviews. They may also have career counselors who can give you feedback on your résumé, assist you with interviewing skills, and advise you about openings. Many of these career centers will work with alumni as well as current students, so don't rule them out just because you've graduated.

The Internet

The Internet is an invaluable resource in your job search. Hundreds, if not thousands, of Web sites can provide advice, information, and opportunities. To avoid being overwhelmed, narrow your use of the Internet to three to five sites that are reliable and pertinent to your specific search. The following are some of the most popular sites on the Web today:

> www.collegegrad.com/jobs/
> www.careerbuilder.com/
> www.monster.com
> http://hotjobs.yahoo.com/
> www.jobbankusa.com/jobs.html
> www.rileyguide.com/

You can also access the Web sites of the companies in which you are interested. More than 1,500 corporate Web sites are accessible through the World Wide Web; most of these sites post job openings that you can apply for directly online.

Classifieds

The proliferation of job-search Web sites has decreased the use of classified advertising significantly. This doesn't mean you should rule out this important source of job openings. Many companies advertise in local papers, trade journals, and industry magazines. As mentioned, reviewing the help-wanted ads can give you insight into local companies and industries that are growing (and hiring).

Job Fairs

Many communities (including your college campus) will host job fairs to help local businesses recruit candidates for openings. These are typically industry specific but also can be more general. Attending job fairs is a good way to learn about companies that are hiring and make valuable contacts with people in your targeted industry.

Headhunters and Recruiters

Professional search firms often are hired by larger corporations to find candidates for open positions. Contacting professional search firms that specialize in your targeted industry can increase your visibility. Recruiters can be a good source of information in terms of trends in the industry and the types of positions available. They also can act as a sounding board, offering feedback on your résumé and advice on your job search.

Networking

In addition to your career center and job-search Web sites, you can use *networking* to boost your chances of finding that perfect job. Networking involves creating alliances and developing your list of professional contacts who may be aware of employment opportunities. An effective networking campaign will focus on connecting with as many associations, trade and industry groups, alumni chapters, and ethnic organizations as possible. Members of these groups are resources you can and should use. Prepare yourself with a simple statement about who you are and what you want: "I am a recent college graduate interested in a career in marketing. I've researched the industry and decided to focus my job search on openings in new product development. . . ." You may then follow up with a request for an informational interview or ask about job openings the individual contact may be aware of in the area you specified.

Be sure to keep track of your contacts. Whether you use index cards or a Palm Pilot, be sure to record names, addresses, phone numbers, and relevant information every time you meet a new contact.

Informational Interviews

Informational interviews are an excellent way to tap into the hidden job market— those unadvertised jobs. In an informational interview, you meet with an individual who works in an industry or occupation you hope to enter. An informational interview can:

- Help you clarify your career goal.
- Uncover employment opportunities that are not advertised.
- Expand your professional network.
- Build confidence for your job interviews.

Look to your network of contacts for potential people to interview. If granted an informational interview, keep these tips in mind:

1. **Do your homework.** Good preparation involves researching the individual, company, and industry. Go to the interview with a goal in mind—are you more interested in finding out about growth areas in the industry or do you need information about the day-to-day responsibilities for a specific occupation?

Come prepared with a list of questions and be sure to ask your contact how much time you have so that you can prioritize your list.

2. **Provide the context.** Remind your new contact which friend, acquaintance, organization, or affiliation you have in common. Then, briefly state your goals for the meeting and offer a brief overview of your background. You can then proceed with the interview, asking your contact the questions you've prepared. Be sure to ask about additional contacts that might be useful to broaden your network.

3. **Don't ask for a job.** Remember this is an informational interview—from the contact's point of view, a plea for work could be uncomfortable. If you impress your new contact and he or she knows of something suitable, that person will mention it.

4. **Follow up.** A formal thank-you is mandatory, but you also should aim to stay in touch with your contacts. If you've met with someone to whom your initial contact referred you, send an e-mail letting him or her know, summarizing the conversation, and thanking that person. If you come across an article that you think might be interesting, forward it. By simply touching base with your contacts every four to six weeks, you greatly increase the number of people who are thinking about you and your job search. Be sure to let your contacts know when you've found a job and thank them again for their assistance.

INTERVIEWING ESSENTIALS

Preparing for Your Interview

Research

The preparation process for a formal job interview is similar to the process for an informational interview. It is crucial that your do your homework. Research the company, individual, and industry as well as the position for which you are applying. The company's corporate Web site is an excellent resource for this type of research, as are industry trade magazines and professional organization Web sites. Find out as much as you can about:

- The company—its corporate goals, financial position, competition, etc.
- The hiring manager—you might find a biography or press releases about this individual by doing a search on the corporate Web site.
- The industry—what trends and challenges is your chosen industry facing?
- The position—see if you can find a job description; do some research on salary ranges at the Bureau of Labor Statistics Web site: www.bls.gov/ncs/.

The interview is about finding a good fit, both for the company and for you. It is your opportunity to demonstrate how your skills and experience will benefit the organization. It is also your opportunity to find out what you need to know about the job and the company for which you might work. Prepare questions that will assist you in the decision process should you be offered the job. Refer back to your personality profile and your priorities, and make sure any questions you have about the responsibilities of the job, the office culture, and so forth get asked. Three to five questions should be about the right number to prepare—more and it may feel like you are doing the interviewing.

Rehearse

Be ready to answer that tried-and-true question: "Tell me about yourself." Determine your greatest strengths relative to the position, and prepare a brief statement about what these are and why they will benefit the company with which you are interviewing. Think about your career goals and how the position for which you are applying fits into these goals. Also be prepared to address the "what is your greatest weakness" question. Practicing answers to common interview questions either in front of a mirror or with a friend will improve your ability to answer these effectively and confidently. Practicing also will give you some insights about your body language, facial expressions, and eye contact—all-important nonverbal clues that seasoned interviewers will pick up on.

Dress Appropriately and Bring the Essentials

If you are not sure about the dress code for the company, call the human resources office and ask. Stick with more conservative styles—avoid anything too trendy—and make sure anything you wear fits well and is clean and in good repair.

- Bring extra copies of your résumé, something to write on, and something to write with.
- If appropriate, bring work samples.
- Bring a list of your references if they are not included on your résumé. The list should include names, addresses, and phone numbers.

The Interview

You've done your homework and practiced responses to the standard interview questions about your strengths, weaknesses, and goals. Each interview you are granted will present its own unique set of challenges, as each is a reflection of the personal style of the interviewer. Your initial interview might be a phone interview or a video interview. It might be with the hiring manager, but it might also be with the team with which you will be working. You might be asked mainly straightforward questions about your skills and experience, or you might be asked more open-ended behavioral questions about how you would react to a variety of situations. The more prepared you are for the interview, the less likely you will get stumped by any of the questions or scenarios you meet. All the work you've done to assess your skills and your appropriateness for the job; the research you've completed on the company, industry, and hiring manager; and the responses and questions you've prepared should make you confident to face whatever challenges lie ahead.

First Impressions

A crucial component of the interview is the first impression. Be on time! Plan to arrive at least 5 to 10 minutes early. Show respect to everyone you come in contact with, whether it is the security guard at the front door, the receptionist, or people you see in the elevator. Smile and make eye contact.

Mirroring is a great way to make a good first impression with your interviewer. Greet him or her with a smile and a handshake that mirrors his or hers—not overly firm or soft. Sit when your interviewer sits and look to him or her for cues on body language. Try not to be overly formal if your interviewer seems to be the more casual type. Sit up a little straighter if you are dealing with someone who seems more formal.

During the Interview

You and your interviewer might engage in small talk to start the interview, but this will likely be limited. The interviewer might begin with a brief explanation of the opening, or he or she might start with a question—let the interviewer lead the discussion. Listen carefully and respond accurately and briefly to each question. Look for opportunities to showcase your skills. Answer questions thoroughly, providing specifics wherever possible. Many successful interviewers use the STAR approach to emphasize not only their skills, but the results (benefits) of their skills:

S: Describe a *Situation* where you relied upon a skill you have highlighted in your résumé.

T: What *tasks* were involved in the situation?

A: What *actions* did you take?

R: What were the *results?*

Don't be evasive; if you don't know the answer to a question, don't try to schmooze your way out of it. Admit what you don't know and ensure the interviewer you will find the answer as quickly as possible.

The salary question may come up, so be prepared to provide your requirements. If you've done your homework, you should know what to expect, and the range of the salary you require shouldn't be a surprise to the hiring manager.

Don't forget to ask your prepared questions. If the interviewer hasn't covered issues that are important to your decision to accept an offer if presented, you'll need to press for time to ask questions. If time doesn't allow, ask if you might follow up with a phone call or e-mail.

Closing

If you feel you are a good match for the position, be sure to make your case before the interview ends. Let your interviewer know you want the job and when you can start. If an on-the-spot decision isn't possible (usually the case), follow up will be needed. It's likely you'll be asked to interview with other members of the hiring team; try to determine who these individuals are and when you might meet with them. Find out what additional information might be useful to the interviewer and when you should follow up. Determine the timetable for filling the position. Make sure you know your interviewer's name, title, and mailing address. Thank the interviewer for his or her time and interest—and don't overstay your welcome.

Postinterview

Make some notes after your interview about the issues you discussed, what went well, and what didn't. Every interview is a learning experience and will enhance your preparation for the next interview. If there was a question that was particularly difficult, note it and make sure you have an answer for it at your next interview. Make sure you have the name, title, and address of your interviewers.

Follow-Up

Thank-you notes for all the individuals you interviewed with are crucial. If you can get them done within 24 hours, it will impress your interviewers and demonstrate your interest. In this e-mail age, a handwritten thank-you note is a nice gesture. Make it brief and courteous. Thank your interviewers for their time and interest, and if you want the job, say so again.

Use the timetable you were given in the interview as a guide for an appropriate amount of time for follow-up. You can follow up by phone or e-mail. Be persistent and keep asking for the next interview or, if appropriate, for the job.

GETTING HIRED

The Job Offer

Your hard work has paid off, and you are offered a job! Remember, impressions still count, so be sure to let your potential employer know how pleased you are to be offered the position. Avoid snap judgments about the offer by making your first question, "When do you need a decision by?" Ask for at least a day or two to consider the offer. Be sure you understand the offer explicitly and that you know:

- The job title and reporting structure.
- The total salary including any potential bonuses.
- The location.
- The hours (not all companies are 9 to 5).
- The expected start date.
- What expenses will be covered (that is, if you have to relocate, will your new employer pay for the cost of moving?).
- The benefits you qualify for—this is an increasingly important issue to consider. Benefits can add a lot to your base pay if they are comprehensive and include health care, tuition reimbursement, and paid vacation time.

A good job offer checklist is available through CollegeGrad.com, at www.collegegrad.com/jobsearch/jobofferchecklist.shtml.

Evaluate the Offer

Once you clearly understand the details of the job offer, you can carefully evaluate its appropriateness. The Bureau of Labor Statistics offers some excellent insights for evaluating job offers at its Web site: www.bls.gov/oco/oco20046.htm. Go back to your personality profile—do the duties and responsibilities of the job fit your interests and values? Does the work environment suit you? Is the position one that will contribute to your overall career goals? Will the salary meet your needs financially? While it may be tempting to accept the first offer, keeping your goals and interests in mind will pay off in long-term satisfaction. Compromises that seem small might grow as your satisfaction declines because the job doesn't match your interests or goals.

Negotiating

If you've decided the position fits within your career goals but there are details about the job offer that concern you, you may be able to negotiate some of these details. The key to successful negotiations is understanding that there is no such thing as "winning." Effective negotiating means reaching a decision that is mutually beneficial. If a company is interested enough in you to have made you an offer, then it likely will consider your reasonable requests for changes to that offer. Reasonable is the key word: Don't ask for a 50 percent increase in the salary that has been offered and expect a positive outcome.

Be respectful when making counteroffers and continue to demonstrate your interest in the company. Explain your rationale and offer alternatives: If you're asking for a higher salary, you might provide statistics on competitive salaries and demonstrate that your request is reasonable. If you need more vacation time for personal reasons, offer to work longer hours or cut back your salary to accommodate your needs. Be prepared for compromises and keep negotiations professional.

Acceptance

Once you have agreed to the terms of your employment, write a letter of acceptance outlining the details of your acceptance. This will ensure you accurately understand the offer and that your employer agrees to the terms. Be sure to reiterate your enthusiasm for the job and the company.

BUILDING YOUR CAREER

Networking at the Office

Your job search may end with your acceptance of a job offer, but your *career search* should not. As discussed, your career evolves over time—the job you have accepted and started is but one step in the development of your career. Use your employment wisely. Search out individuals at your new company who hold positions you are interested in and enlist their assistance in the development of your career. These mentors can be valuable assets as you explore your career possibilities.

Take advantage of every opportunity presented to you to expand your skill set and network with colleagues. Volunteer for task forces, join company groups that interest you, participate actively in meetings—be visible and let colleagues know your goals and aspirations.

Professional Organizations

Every industry has professional organizations or associations. As mentioned in the discussion of networking, these organizations are a great career resource. Membership means opportunities for meetings in which industry trends are discussed and networking abounds. Membership also means access to industry leaders—people making a difference in the industry. There are large, broad associations such as the American Marketing Association (www.marketingpower.com/) with its 38,000 members or the Society for Hispanic Professionals(www.nshp.org/?wf=goto) with its 7,500 members. There are also more specialized organizations such as the New England Direct Marketing Association (www.nedma.com/). You can't join every group, so do some research to find the organizations that have the most to offer you professionally.

Continuing Education

Some industries such as health care and insurance mandate continuing education. To keep professional licenses active, individuals must complete a certain number of continuing education hours. Even if your chosen profession is not one that mandates continuing education, staying up-to-date on the technical skills associated with your position is key to a successful career.

There are numerous resources for continuing education. For more general skills such as computer or software training, your local community is a great place to start. Local libraries, community colleges, and even some school districts offer courses in which you can learn standard software applications such as Power Point and Excel.

Professional organizations are another good source for continuing education and professional development. Most organizations offer seminars and/or training. For example, the American Marketing Association offers a two-day "Marketing Boot Camp" for marketers new to the profession. Find seminars and training sessions that interest you and use these to expand your skill set and network.

Back to the Drawing Board (Sort of)

As you gain experience in your new position and network in your field, your career goals likely will shift. After about six months to a year in your position, you should get out your job-search files and pull your personality profile, skills inventory, and résumé. Review where you were, where you've been, and where you now want to go. What has changed? Updating your résumé on a regular basis will keep you focused on your goals and ensure your career search does not end when your job search does.

RESOURCES

www.collegegrad.com/intv/

www.businessweek.com/careers/content/sep2003/ca2003093_4973_ca009htm?c=bwinsidersep5&n=link18&t=email

www.collegeview.com/career/interviewing/first_impress/sell_yourself.html

www.career.fsu.edu/ccis/guides/negotiate.html

www.bls.gov/oco/oco2003.htm

www.quintcareers.com/STAR_interviewing.html

http://content.monster.com/

www.rileyguide.com/

Part Five Video Cases

MANAGER'S HOT SEAT VIDEO 1: "DIVERSITY IN HIRING: CANDIDATE CONUNDRUM"

When it comes to selecting employees, supervisors must consider many things. An issue that surfaces often in today's business environment is the notion of diversity in an organization and whether or not to hire someone because they are or are not of a certain ethnicity.

Read the following scenario describing the video selection "Diversity in Hiring: Candidate Conundrum," and then watch the video selection. After this, answer the three questions that pertain to the specific challenges in this supervisor–employee situation.

SCENARIO

Robert Gedaliah has interviewed 15 candidates to fill the new customer outreach representative position and narrowed it down to 2. He invited Paul Munez, the customer service team leader, to attend the second interviews of these two candidates. The interviews proceed smoothly, with both candidates demonstrating appropriate levels of experience, skills, and general intelligence. Paul and Robert will discuss the two candidates and reach a decision.

QUESTIONS

1. Chapter 15 talks about the *halo effect*—the practice of forming an overall opinion on the basis of one outstanding characteristic. One could say Robert and Paul have let this error in judgment affect them, though they insist their picks are based on an overall assessment. What are the halo effects for both men?

2. At the outset, Robert seems to have made up his mind about Jacqueline without any help from Paul's input, but this is not exactly true. What one thing does Robert do to consider Paul's thoughts?

3. Robert has told Paul he plans on hiring Jacqueline despite Paul's argument that she might not fit well with the team. What might be some ramifications of this decision in the work environment?

(continued)

MANAGER'S HOT SEAT VIDEO 2: "OFFICE ROMANCE: GROPING FOR ANSWERS"

The selection of employees is an aspect over which a supervisor or manager has substantial control. One thing that is out of a supervisor's hands is the romantic relations two employees could be having outside of work. This video describes how a supervisor might have to step in when a failed relationship crosses over into the work environment.

Read the following scenario describing the video selection, and then watch the video selection. After this, answer the three questions that pertain to the specific challenges in this supervisor–employee situation.

SCENARIO

Abbe Willsby and Randall Keene are co-leaders of a 15-employee team in a retail/fashion company. Soon after Randall separated from his wife, the two began an affair. Six months later, Abbe broke off the relationship after hearing rumors that Randall still had an intimate relationship with his wife. She sends an e-mail to the manager, Bill Schule, with complaints of sexual harassment and insists something be done. Abbe contends that, while they work together, her former boyfriend and co-leader is flirtatious, inappropriate, and constantly discussing past intimate encounters they'd shared. Prompted by the e-mail sent by Abbe, Randall meets with the manager asking for help with the situation.

QUESTIONS

1. According to the discussion of sexual harassment in Appendix B, what things does Bill do correctly in his meeting with Randall?
2. Name two things that Bill needs to do after his meeting with Randall to investigate Abbe's claim.
3. Why do you think Bill wants to talk with Abbe separately? Do you think this is wise? Why or why not?

Notes

Chapter 1

1. Gary Yukl, Angela Gordon, and Tom Taber, "A Hierarchical Taxonomy of Leadership Behavior: Integrating a Half Century of Behavior Research," *Journal of Leadership and Organizational Studies* 9, no. 1 (Summer 2002), pp. 15–32.

2. U.S. Census Bureau, *Statistical Abstract of the United States: 2006*, table 577, p. 387, accessed at www.census.gov.

3. "Women Are Going to the Dogs (and Cats and Birds)," *The New York Times,* April 18, 2001, p. G1.

4. U.S. Census Bureau, "U.S. Interim Projections by Age, Sex, Race, and Hispanic Origin," March 18, 2004, accessed at www.census.gov.

5. Lisa Chin, "The Iron Man of 4th Avenue South," *Seattle Times,* April 4, 2006, downloaded from Business & Company Resource Center, http://galenet.galegroup.com.

6. Brian Grow, "Hispanic Nation," *BusinessWeek,* March 15, 2004, downloaded from InfoTrac, http://web5.infotrac.galegroup.com.

7. "Visible Signs of Relief," *Inc.,* May 2001, p. 67.

8. Timothy P. Henderson, "Retailers Use ESupervision Technology to Manage and Maintain Security at Multiple Sites," *Stores,* February 2001, pp. 64–66.

9. Carl Metzgar, "The Pitfalls of Supervisors Doing Work," *Pit & Quarry,* May 2005, downloaded from Business & Company Resource Center, http://galenet.galegroup.com.

10. See the Management, Business, and Financial Occupations in the Bureau of Labor Statistics, *Occupational Outlook Handbook,* 2006–07 edition, available at http://stats.bls.gov/oco/home.htm.

11. Andrew Park and Peter Burrows, "What You Don't Know about Dell," *BusinessWeek,* November 3, 2003, downloaded from InfoTrac, http://web5.infotrac.galegroup.com.

12. Edward E. Lawler III, *Treat People Right!* (San Francisco: Jossey-Bass, 2003), pp. xiii, 10–13.

13. Ibid., p. 207.

14. Cheryl Dahle, "A Steelmaker's Heart of Gold," *Fast Company,* June 2003, downloaded from InfoTrac, http://web5.infotrac.galegroup.com.

15. Gene Ference, "Coaching Plan Helps Managers Increase Employee Commitment," *Hotel & Motel Management,* April 2, 2001, p. 16.

Chapter 2

1. Louise Lee, "Dell: Facing Up to Past Mistakes," *BusinessWeek,* June 19, 2006, downloaded from InfoTrac, http://web2.infotrac.galegroup.com.

2. Jane Erwin and P. C. Douglas, "It's Not Difficult to Change Company Culture," *Supervision,* November 2000, p. 6.

3. Keith Bradsher, "Ford Has Harsher Words for Latest Recalled Tires," *The New York Times,* June 15, 2001, p. C4.

4. Mary Connelly, "Ford Works with Suppliers to Ensure Quality Standards," *Automotive News,* April 30, 2001, p. 36.

5. "QC Software Cuts Inspection Time 80%," *Manufacturing Engineering,* April 2001, pp. 116–20.

6. Maggie McFadden, "The Quality Is in the Process," *Quality,* June 2006, downloaded from InfoTrac, http://web1.infotrac.galegroup.com.

7. Veronica T. Hychalk, "How Do We Quantify Quality?" *Nursing Management,* March 1, 2001, p. 16.

8. John S. McClenahen, "General Cable Corp. Moose Jaw Plant, Moose Jaw, Saskatchewan, Canada: Prairie Home Champion," *Industry Week,* October 2005, downloaded from InfoTrac, http://web1.infotrac.galegroup.com.

9. "Six Sigma—in Brief," The Quality Portal, www.thequalityportal.com, downloaded July 1, 2004.

10. Gregory T. Lucier and Sridhar Seshadri, "GE Takes Six Sigma beyond the Bottom Line," *Strategic Finance,* May 2001, pp. 40–46.

11. Shawn Tully, "Bank of the Americas," *Fortune,* April 14, 2003, downloaded from InfoTrac, http://web7.infotrac.galegroup.com.

12. Roberto Ceniceros, "Insurance Department Takes Team Approach to Quality," *Business Insurance,* April 30, 2001, p. 92.

13. John P. Walsh, "The Quest for Quality," *Hotel & Motel Management,* May 7, 2001, pp. 36–38.

14. National Institute of Standards and Technology, "Malcolm Baldrige National Quality Award," Fact Sheet, updated November 25, 2003, NIST Web site, www.nist.gov.

15. Walsh, "The Quest for Quality."

16. David Drickhamer, "Beating the Baldrige Blues," *Industry Week,* May 2004, downloaded from InfoTrac, http://web7.infotrac.galegroup.com; National Institute of Standards and Technology, "Baldrige Index Beaten by S&P 500 for Second Year," *NIST Tech Beat,* April 23, 2004, downloaded at www.nist.gov; NIST, "Baldrige Index Beaten by S&P 500 after Nine Winning Years," *NIST Update,* May 15, 2003, downloaded at www.nist.gov.

17. Pallavi Gogoi, "Thinking Outside the Cereal Box," *BusinessWeek,* July 28, 2003, downloaded from InfoTrac, http://web4.infotrac. galegroup.com.

18. John R. Brandt, "Competing beyond Quality," *Industry Week,* January 2003, downloaded from InfoTrac, http://web7.infotrac.galegroup.com.

19. National Institute of Standards and Technology, "2003 Award Winner: Baptist Hospital Inc.," downloaded from the NIST Web site, www.nist.gov, June 28, 2004; Baptist Health Care, "Standards of Performance," downloaded from the Careers page of the Baptist Health Care Web site, www.ebaptisthealthcare.org, June 28, 2004.

20. U.S. Census Bureau, *Statistical Abstract of the United States: 2002,* Tables 605 and 1353, pp. 399, 849, downloaded at www.census.gov.

21. Nancy Morris, "What to Expect When You Relocate," Career-Intelligence.com (2002), downloaded from www.career-intelligence.com, July 1, 2004.

22. Lee Hawkins Jr. and Norihiko Shirouzu, "A Tale of Two Auto Plants," *The Wall Street Journal,* May 24, 2006, http://online.wsj.com. See also John Teresko, "Learning from Toyota—Again," *Industry Week,* February 2006, downloaded from InfoTrac, http://web1.infotrac.galegroup.com.

23. John S. McClenahen, "New World Leader," *Industry Week,* January 2004, downloaded from InfoTrac, http://web7.infotrac.galegroup.com.

24. Julie Flaherty, "Suggestions Rise from the Floors of U.S. Factories," *The New York Times,* April 18, 2001, pp. C1, C7.

25. American Management Association (AMA), "2005 Electronic Monitoring & Surveillance Survey: Many Companies Monitoring, Recording, Videotaping—and Firing—Employees," news release, May 18, 2005, AMA Web site, www.amanet.org.

26. Tonya Vinas, "Spreading the Good Word," *Industry Week,* February 2004, downloaded from InfoTrac, http://web4.infotrac.galegroup.com.

27. James Mehring, "What's Lifting Productivity," *BusinessWeek,* May 24, 2004, downloaded from InfoTrac, http://web4.infotrac.galegroup.com.

28. Raymond Dreyfack, "Treasure Chest: Money-Saving Ideas for the Profit-Minded Supervisor," *Supervision,* February 2006, downloaded from Business & Company Resource Center, http://galenet.galegroup.com.

29. Charles Fishman, "The Toll of a New Machine," *Fast Company,* May 2004, downloaded from InfoTrac, http://web2.infotrac.galegroup.com.

30. Stanley Holmes and Wendy Zellner, "The Costco Way," *BusinessWeek,* April 12, 2004, downloaded from InfoTrac, http://web4.infotrac. galegroup.com.

31. Darnell Little and Adam Aston, "Even the Supervisor Is Expendable," *BusinessWeek,* July 23, 2001, p. 78.

32. Steve Hamm, Spencer E. Ante, Andy Reingardt, and Manjeet Kripalani, "Services: To Stay Competitive, Companies Are Finding New Ways to Automate Operations, Reuse Technology, and Streamline Processes," *BusinessWeek,* June 21, 2004, downloaded from InfoTrac, http://web4.infotrac.galegroup.com.

33. Philip Siekman, "The Struggle to Get Lean," *Fortune,* January 12, 2004, downloaded from InfoTrac, http://web7.infotrac.galegroup.com.

Chapter 3

1. Sonja D. Brown, "Congratulations, You're a Manager!" *Black Enterprise,* April 2006, downloaded from Business & Company Resource Center, http://galenet.galegroup.com.

2. Stevenson Swanson, "Window of Opportunity Opens in N.Y.," *Chicago Tribune,* January 22, 2006, sec. 1, p. 9.

3. Julie Graham, "Hospital Team Works to Cut Cardiac Arrests," *(Rock Hill, S.C.) Herald,* July 4, 2006, downloaded from Business & Company Resource Center, http://galenet.galegroup.com.

4. R. B. Lacoursiere, *The Life Cycle of Groups: Group Development Stage Theory* (New York: Human Service Press, 1980).

5. Fara Warner, "Brains for Sale," *Fast Company,* January 2004, downloaded from InfoTrac, http://web3.infotrac.galegroup.com.

6. Chuck Salter, "When Couches Fly," *Fast Company,* July 2004, downloaded from InfoTrac, http://web4.infotrac.galegroup.com.

7. Patricia M. Buhler, "Managing in the New Millennium: Are You a Team Player?" *Supervision,* March 2006, downloaded from Business & Company Resource Center, http://galenet.galegroup.com; Thomas Capozzoli, "How to Succeed with Self-Directed Work Teams," *Supervision,* February 2006, downloaded from InfoTrac, http://web2.infotrac.galegroup.com.

8. Thomas Capozzoli, "Succeed with Self-Directed Work Teams," *Supervision,* June 2004, downloaded from InfoTrac, http://web4.infotrac.galegroup.com.

9. Charles Fishman, "The Anarchist's Cookbook," *Fast Company,* July 2004, downloaded from InfoTrac, http://web4.infotrac.galegroup.com.

10. Jim Jenkins, "Getting Up to Full Speed," *HRMagazine,* April 2006, downloaded from Business & Company Resource Center, http://galenet.galegroup.com.

11. Dick Gorelick, "What Do Your Meetings Say about You?" *American Printer,* July 2003, downloaded from LookSmart's FindArticles, www.findarticles.com.

12. Salter, "When Couches Fly."

13. Susan Heathfield, "True Empowerment Wins!" About.com Human Resources pages, http://humanresources.about.com, downloaded July 15, 2004; Labor Policy Association, "The Legality of Employee Involvement Teams under the National Labor Relations Act," LPA Legal Compliance Assistance, September 28, 2001, downloaded at www.lpa.org.

14. Michael A. Prospero, "Two Words You Never Hear Together: 'Great Meeting!'" *Fast Company,* June 2004, downloaded from InfoTrac, http://web4.infotrac.galegroup.com.

15. Keisha-Gaye Anderson, "I Can't See You: Getting the Most from Your Off-Site Staff," *Black Enterprise,* August 2003, downloaded from InfoTrac, http://web3.infotrac.galegroup.com.

16. Julia Chang, "The World According to Google," *Sales & Marketing Management,* April 2006, downloaded from InfoTrac, http://web4.infotrac.galegroup.com.

17. Prospero, "Two Words You Never Hear Together."

18. Nancy S. Ahlrichs, *Manager of Choice: Competencies for Cultivating Top Talent* (Palo Alto, CA: Davies-Black, 2003), p. 173.

19. David K. Lindo, "You Can Make It Better," *Supervision,* April 2004, downloaded from InfoTrac, http://web4.infotrac.galegroup.com.

20. Ibid.

Chapter 4

1. Ethics Resource Center, "2003 National Business Ethics Survey: Executive Summary," www.ethics.org, July 19, 2004; Ethics Resource Center, "Major Survey of America's Workers Finds Substantial Improvements in Ethics," news release, May 21, 2003, downloaded at www.ethics.org.

2. Jay Prakash Mulki, Fernando Jaramillo, and William B. Locander, "Effects of Ethical Climate and Supervisory Trust on Salesperson's Job Attitudes and Intentions to Quit," *Journal of Personal Selling and Sales Management*, Winter 2006, downloaded from Business & Company Resource Center, http://galenet.galegroup.com. A survey with similar results is reported in Ethics Resource Center, "National Business Ethics Survey: How Employees View Ethics in Their Organization, 1994–2005," www.ethics.org, July 17, 2006.

3. Gary Dessler, "How to Find-Tune Your Company's Ethical Compass," *Supervision*, April 2006, downloaded from InfoTrac, http://web2.infotrac.galegroup.com.

4. James M. Clash, "Vintage Names," *Forbes*, June 7, 2004, downloaded from InfoTrac, http://web7.infotrac.galegroup.com.

5. G. Jeffrey MacDonald, "A Quest for Clean Hands," *Christian Science Monitor*, February 9, 2004, www.csmonitor.com.

6. T. L. Stanley, "The Ethical Manager," *Supervision*, May 2006, downloaded from InfoTrac, http://web2.infotrac.galegroup.com; Hanna Andersson, "Community Involvement," Fall 2006, www.hannaandersson.com, accessed July 19, 2006.

7. Jim Geraghty, "CIA's George Tenet, the Spy Who Came in with the Gold," *Washington Post*, July 5, 2006, www.washingtonpost.com; U.S. Department of Justice (DOJ), Departmental Ethics Office, Justice Management Division, "Do It Right," www.usdoj.gov/jmd/ethics/generalf.htm, February 9,

2006; DOJ Justice Management Division, "Gifts and Entertainment," www.usdoj.gov/jmd/ethics/gift.html, Feburary 10, 2006.

8. James Cox, "Inmates Teach MBA Students Ethics from Behind Bars: University of Maryland Class Clarifies Moral Consequences," *USA Today,* May 24, 2001, p. B01.

9. Julia Chang, "Codes of Conduct: Ethics Training Shouldn't Be Overlooked in a Down Economy," *Sales & Marketing Management,* November 2003, downloaded from InfoTrac, http://infotrac.galegroup.com.

10. Chan Sup Chang et al., "Offering Gifts or Bribes? Code of Ethics in South Korea," *Journal of Third World Studies,* Spring 2001, pp. 125–39.

11. "Ethics in the U.S., Canada, and Mexico: Who Would You Want to Do Business With?" news release, PR Newswire, June 6, 2006, downloaded from Business & Company Resource Center, http://galenet.galegroup.com.

12. Transparency International, "Transparency International Corruption Perceptions Index 2003," www.transparency.org, July 19, 2004.

13. Paul Klebnikov, "Coke's Sinful World," *Forbes,* December 22, 2003, downloaded from InfoTrac, http://web7.infotrac.galegroup.com; Daniel Fisher, "Dangerous Liaisons," *Forbes,* April 28, 2003, downloaded from InfoTrac, http://web7.infotrac.galegroup.com.

14. Libby Estell, "Think Globally, Give Graciously," *Incentive,* November 2000, pp. 47–50; Dov Seidman, "Across the Border," *American Executive,* March 2006, pp. 34–36.

15. Alexandra MacRae, "More Firms Join UN Push to Be Good Corporate Citizens," *Christian Science Monitor,* July 19, 2004, www.csmonitor.com.

16. "Ethical Conflicts in Ethical Companies: Feeding the Hog," *Management World* (Institute of Certified Professional Managers), February 2003, downloaded from James Madison University Web site, http://cob.jmu.edu/icpm/management_world.

17. Ethics Resource Center, "2003 National Business Ethics Survey: Executive Summary"; Ethics Resource Center, "Major Survey of America's Workers."

18. "Pop Quiz: A Quick Test of Your Managerial Skills," *Sales & Marketing Management,* September 2003, downloaded from InfoTrac, http://web7.infotrac.galegroup.com.

19. Taxpayers against Fraud, "Statistics," www.taf.org, accessed July 18, 2006.

20. Paul Davies, "Gabelli, Affiliates Settle Fraud Suit for $130 Million," *The Wall Street Journal,* July 14, 2006, http://online.wsj.com.

21. Phyllis Plitch, "Blowing the Whistle," *The Wall Street Journal,* June 21, 2004, http://online.wsj.com.

22. Neil Weinberg, "Cops Inc.," *Forbes,* March 17, 2003, downloaded from InfoTrac, http://web7.infotrac.galegroup.com.

Chapter 5

1. Samuel C. Certo, *Modern Management,* 8th ed. (Upper Saddle River, NJ: Prentice Hall, 2000), p. 528.

2. Goodwill Industries International, "Success Story: Night Shift Supervisor Overcomes Obstacles to Learning," What We Do pages, Goodwill Web site, www.goodwill.org, accessed July 25, 2006.

3. Bank of America, "Diversity Fact Sheets," Careers page, Bank of America Web site, www.bankofamerica.com/careers/, downloaded August 9, 2004.

4. Bureau of Labor Statistics, *"Women in the Labor Force: A Databook* Updated and Available on the Internet," news release, May 13, 2005, www.bls.gov.

5. Bureau of Labor Statistics, "Foreign-Born Workers: Labor Force Characteristics in 2005," news release, April 14, 2006, www.bls.gov.

6. See Mitra Toossi, "A Century of Change: The U.S. Labor Force, 1950–2050," *Monthly Labor Review,* May 2002, pp. 15–28.

7. David S. Joachim, "Computer Technology Opens a World of Work to Disabled People," *The New York Times,* March 1, 2006, www.nytimes.com; Grant Gross, "Technology Helps Disabled Workers," *PC World,* May 5, 2005, www.pcworld.com.

8. U.S. Census Bureau, "Facts for Features: Americans with Disabilities Act, July 26," news release, July 19, 2006, www.census.gov. See also K. C. Jones, "IBM Applies Technology for Disabled at Aging Baby Boomers," *TechWeb Technology News,* September 30, 2005, www.techweb.com.

9. Erin White, "Why Few Women Run Plants," *The Wall Street Journal,* May 1, 2006, http://online.wsj.com.

10. Kathy Gurchiek, "Slurs at Work Are on the Rise, Survey Finds," *HRMagazine,* June 2006, downloaded from InfoTrac, http://web2.infotrac.galegroup.com.

11. Mary-Kathryn Zachary, "Labor Law for Supervisors: Religion, Race and Dress Codes," *Supervision,* March 2006, downloaded from Business & Company Resource Center, http://galenet.galegroup.com.

12. Cora Daniels, "Young, Gifted, Black—and Out of Here," *Fortune,* May 3, 2004, downloaded from InfoTrac, http://web5.infotrac.galegroup.com.

13. Rudolph F. Verderber, *Communicate!* 8th ed. (Belmont, CA: Wadsworth, 1996), p. 45.

14. Carol Hymowitz, "Women Swell Ranks as Middle Managers, but Are Scarce at Top," *The Wall Street Journal,* July 24, 2006, http://online.wsj.com; Melanie Lasoff Levs, "Next 20 Female CEOs, 2006," *Pink,* December 2005–January 2006, pp. 67–73.

15. U.S. Census Bureau, "Facts for Features: Father's Day, June 18," news release, June 12, 2006 (revised), www.census.gov.

16. "Training Can Keep Companies out of Court," *BusinessWeek Online,* March 9, 2006 (interview with Eli Kantor), downloaded at Business & Company Resource Center, http://galenet.galegroup.com.

17. C. E. Weller, "Economic Snapshots: Older Workers Staying in the Labor Force," Economic Policy Institute, July 16, 2003, www.epinet.org; Nancy R. Lockwood, "The Aging Workforce: The Reality of the Impact of Older Workers and Eldercare in the Workplace," *HRMagazine,* December 2003, downloaded from InfoTrac, http://web5.infotrac.galegroup.com.

18. Lockwood, "The Aging Workforce."

19. David Raths, "Bridging the Generation Gap," *Info World,* November 8, 1999, p. 84.

20. "Older and Wiser," *BusinessWeek,* May 22, 2000, p. F6.

21. Robert D. Ramsey, "Supervising Employees with Limited English Language Proficiency," *Supervision,* June 2004, downloaded from InfoTrac, http://web5.infotrac.galegroup.com.

22. Patricia Sellers, "By the Numbers," *Fortune,* February 9, 2004, downloaded from InfoTrac, http://web5.infotrac.galegroup.com; Catalyst, "New Catalyst Study Reveals Financial Performance Is Higher for Companies with More Women at the Top," news release, January 26, 2004, www.catalystwomen.org.

23. These examples are taken from Kitty O. Locker, *Business and Administrative Communication,* 6th ed. (New York: Irwin/McGraw-Hill, 2003), pp. 297–300.

24. Donna M. Owens, "Multilingual Workforces," *HRMagazine,* September 2005, downloaded from InfoTrac, http://web2.infotrac.galegroup.com.

25. Gary Dessler, *Human Resources Management,* 7th ed. (Upper Saddle River, NJ: Prentice Hall, 1997), p. 267.

26. Jonathan A. Segal, "Throw Supervisors a Lifeline and Save Yourself," *HRMagazine,* June 2003, downloaded from InfoTrac, http://web4.infotrac.galegroup.com.

27. Equal Employment Opportunity Commission, "Federal Equal Employment Opportunity (EEO) Laws," About EEO pages, EEOC Web site, www.eeoc.gov, last modified April 20, 2004; "New Ripples in the Tide against Job Discrimination," *The New York Times,* March 22, 2000, p. G1.

Chapter 6

1. Jonathan Katz, "Snuffing Out Scrap," *Industry Week,* June 2006, downloaded from InfoTrac, http://web1.infotrac.galegroup.com.

2. Ryan Underwood, "Lighting the GE Way," *Fast Company,* August 2004, downloaded from InfoTrac, http://web6.infotrac.galegroup.com.

3. Joe Mullich, "Get in Line," *Workforce Management,* December 2003, pp. 43–46.

4. Traci Purdum, "The Show Must Go On," *Industry Week,* January 2004, downloaded from Business & Company Resource Center, http://galenet.galegroup.com.

5. William Keenan Jr., "Numbers Racket," *Sales & Marketing Management,* May 1995, pp. 46–66ff.

6. Mark Skertic, "American Airlines Gets into Maintenance Line," *Chicago Tribune,* June 25, 2006, sec. 5, pp. 1, 14.

7. Janet Bigham Bernstal, "The Profit Pursuit," *Bank Marketing,* April 2004, downloaded from InfoTrac, http://web6.infotrac.galegroup.com.

8. Jennifer Taylor Arnold, "Making the Leap," *HRMagazine,* May 2006, downloaded from Business & Company Resource Center, http://galenet.galegroup.com.

9. Joel Levitt, "Active Supervision: Improve Shop Efficiency by 15 Percent," *Fleet Maintenance,* August 2005, downloaded from Business & Company Resource Center, http://galenet.galegroup.com.

10. "Taking the Guesswork out of Customer Satisfaction," *Food Management,* January 2006, downloaded from Business & Company Resource Center, http://galenet.galegroup.com.

11. Ibid.

12. Brad Cleveland, "Reporting Call Center Activity," *Call Center,* December 1, 2003, downloaded from Business & Company Resource Center, http://galenet.galegroup.com.

13. Jennifer Saba, "Galvanizing the PJ Set," *Potentials*, February 2003, downloaded from Business & Company Resource Center, http://galenet.galegroup.com.

Chapter 7

1. Alison Overholt, "Cuckoo for Customers," *Fast Company*, June 2004, downloaded from InfoTrac, http://web2.infotrac.galegroup.com.

2. Christopher S. Frings, "Addressing Management Issues," *Medical Laboratory Observer*, January 2003, downloaded from Business & Company Resource Center, http://galenet.galegroup.com.

3. Thomas Sy and Laura Sue D'Annunzio, "Challenges and Strategies of Matrix Organizations: Top-Level and Midlevel Managers' Perspectives," *Human Resource Planning*, March 2005, downloaded from Business & Company Resource Center, http://galenet.galegroup.com. See also Lonnie Pacelli, "Making Many Units Whole," *Incentive*, January 2005, downloaded from Business & Company Resource Center, http://galenet.galegroup.com.

4. See, for example, Stephen P. Borgatti, "Virtual/Network Organizations," revised February 5, 2001, accessed at www.analytictech.com/mb021/virtual.htm, August 3, 2006.

5. Douglas McLeod, "Insurers Outsourcing Benefits Administration," *Business Insurance*, August 23, 2004, downloaded from Business & Company Resource Center, http://galenet.galegroup.com.

6. Simona Covel, "Eastern Europe Stakes Its Claim as Just the Right Site for Growth," *The Wall Street Journal*, September 8, 2004, http://online.wsj.com.

7. Patricia L. Smith, "Rebuilding an American Icon," *American Machinist*, June 2003, downloaded from Business & Company Resource Center, http://galenet.galegroup.com.

8. Anne Marie Borrego, "Inside Play," *Inc.*, September 2001, pp. 74–80.

9. "Wrong, Wrong, Wrong!" *Computerworld*, May 10, 2004, downloaded from Business & Company Resource Center, http://galenet.galegroup.com.

10. Don Durfee, "Striking a Balance," *CFO*, November 2005, downloaded from Business & Company Resource Center, http://galenet.galegroup.com.

11. "Follow These Leaders," *Fortune*, December 12, 2005; "Advanced Tent Rental Ltd. and Supervisor Fined for Health and Safety Violations," *CNW Group*, May 31, 2006, downloaded from Business & Company Resource Center, http://galenet.galegroup.com.

12. "Dow Jones Announces Business Reorganization," *The Wall Street Journal*, February 22, 2006, http://online.wsj.com.

13. Michael Oneal, "Harley Enjoys Winning Cycle," *Chicago Tribune*, May 14, 2006, sec. 5, pp. 1, 9, 11.

14. "Shhh . . . the Best Kept Secret at The Ritz-Carlton Is . . . ," *Re-designing Customer Service*, May 1995, pp. 1–2.

15. Barbara Davison, "Management Span of Control: How Wide Is Too Wide?" *Journal of Business Strategy* 24, no. 4 (July–August 2003), downloaded from Business & Company Resource Center, http://galenet.galegroup.com; Joseph A. Pegnato, "Federal Workforce Downsizing during the 1990s: A Human Capital Disaster," *Public Manager*, Winter 2003, downloaded from Business & Company Resource Center, http://galenet.galegroup.com.

16. The factors described in this paragraph are based on Harold Koontz, "Making Theory Operational: The Span of Management," *Journal of Management Studies*, October 1966, pp. 229–243; Davison, "Management Span of Control."

17. "Too Much Work, Too Little Time," *BusinessWeek*, July 16, 2001, p. 12.

18. Jill Hecht Maxwell, "One Man, One Computer, 1,431 Lawn Mowers," *Inc. Tech* 2001, no. 2, pp. 46–50.

19. W. H. Weiss, "The Art and Skill of Delegating," *Supervision*, September 2000, pp. 3–5.

20. "When Good Managers Fail: The Law of Problem Evolution," *CioInsight*, May 18, 2005, downloaded from Business & Company Resource Center, http://galenet.galegroup.com.

21. Kirk Johnson, "Rescuers' Mission Remains Steadfast," *New York Times*, July 4, 2001, pp. B1, B7.

22. Joseph A. Raelin, "Growing Group Leadership Skills," *Security Management*, June 2004, downloaded from Business & Company Resource Center, http://galenet.galegroup.com.

23. Michael Bartlett, "The Branch CEO," *Banking Wire*, November 17, 2005, downloaded from Business & Company Resource Center, http://galenet.galegroup.com.

24. Bridget McCrea, "Lightening the Workload," *Black Enterprise*, September 2003, downloaded from Business & Company Resource Center, http://galenet.galegroup.com.

25. Amy Alexander, "Let Yourself Delegate," *Greater Baton Rouge Business Report*, August 19, 2003,

downloaded from Business & Company Resource Center, http://galenet.galegroup.com.

Chapter 8

1. Becky Bright, "Leading through Uncertainty," *The Wall Street Journal*, July 10, 2006, http://online .wsj.com; Deborah Gavello, "Leading versus Managing in the 21st Century," *Western Banking*, March 2003, accessed at the Web site of Western Independent Bankers, www.wib.org; Small Business Administration, "Leading vs. Managing: They're Two Different Animals," *Managing Your Business* pages of the SBA Web site, www.sba.gov, accessed August 9, 2006.

2. Steve Bates, "Baseball Gaffe Provides Leadership Lessons," *HRMagazine*, December 2003, downloaded from InfoTrac, http://web4.infotrac .galegroup.com.

3. Douglas McGregor, *The Human Side of Enterprise* (New York: McGraw-Hill, 1960).

4. Jane Wollman Rusoff, "Portrait of a Branch Manager," *Research*, July 2004, downloaded from Business & Company Resource Center, http://galenet.galegroup.com.

5. Robert D. Ramsey, "Doing the 'Little Things' Right," *Supervision*, April 2006, downloaded from Business & Company Resource Center, http://galenet .galegroup.com.

6. Del Jones, "Business Leadership Book Wins Fans in NFL," *USA Today*, November 28, 2005, Yahoo News, http://news.yahoo.com.

7. Scott Powers, "Disney Executive Lee Cockerell Has a Legacy of Leadership," *Orlando Sentinel*, July 27, 2006, downloaded from Business & Company Resource Center, http://galenet.galegroup.com.

8. Daniel Goleman, "Leadership That Gets Results," *Harvard Business Review*, March 2000, downloaded from InfoTrac, http://web6.infotrac .galegroup.com.

9. Joseph Lipsey, personal correspondence.

10. Susan H. Surplus, "Motivating the Troops: Moving from the Power of 'Me' to the Power of 'We,'" *Supervision*, April 2004, downloaded from InfoTrac, http://web4.infotrac.galegroup.com.

11. Ed Gubman, *The Engaging Leader: Winning with Today's Free Agent Workforce* (Chicago: Dearborn Trade Publishing, 2003), pp. 17–18; James M. Kouzes and Barry Posner, "A Prescription for Leading in Cynical Times," *Ivey Business Journal Online*, July–August 2004, downloaded from Business & Company Resource Center, http:// galenet.galegroup.com.

12. Ed Lisoski, "Courage, Character and Conviction: The Three C's of Outstanding Supervision," *Supervision*, February 2005, downloaded from Business & Company Resource Center, http:// galenet.galegroup.com.

13. Bright, "Leading through Uncertainty."

Chapter 9

1. Quoted by Tom Peters in "Rule #3: Leadership Is Confusing as Hell," *Fast Company*, March 2001, p. 124.

2. Ted Pollock, "Mind Your Own Business," *Supervision*, December 2005, downloaded from Business & Company Resource Center, http:// galenet.galegroup.com.

3. Susan Chandler, "Sense of Entitlement Leads Some CEOs to Plunder Own Firms, Say Experts," *Knight Ridder/Tribune Business News*, September 5, 2004, downloaded from Business & Company Resource Center, http://galenet.galegroup.com.

4. Craig Sutton, "Get the Most Out of Six Sigma," *Quality*, March 2006, downloaded from InfoTrac, http://web1.infotrac.galegroup.com.

5. Kevin Lim, "Turning His Life's Lessons into Corporate Successes," *The Wall Street Journal*, July 24, 2006, http://online.wsj.com.

6. Laith Agha, "Bates Cartoons Return to Walls," *Monterey County [Calif.] Herald*, July 30, 2006; Laith Agha, "Bringing Back Bill Bates," *Monterey County [Calif.] Herald*, July 6, 2006, both downloaded from Business & Company Resource Center, http://galenet.galegroup.com.

7. Sutton, "Get the Most Out of Six Sigma."

8. Roger Von Oech, quoted in W. H. Weiss, "Coming Up with Good Ideas," *Supervision*, December 2005, downloaded from InfoTrac, http://web2 .infotrac.galegroup.com.

9. Deena Amato-McCoy, "Commerce Bank Manages Knowledge Profitably," *Bank Systems + Technology*, January 2003, downloaded from Business & Company Resource Center, http:// galenet.galegroup.com.

10. See Irving L. Janis, *Groupthink: Psychological Studies of Policy Decisions and Fiascoes*, 2nd ed. (Boston: Houghton Mifflin, 1982).

11. Kathleen Melymuka, "How to Pick a Project Team: Tech Skills Are Only the Beginning,"

Computerworld, April 12, 2004, downloaded from Business & Company Resource Center, http://galenet.galegroup.com.

12. Timothy G. Habbershon, "A Little Too Hands-On," *BusinessWeek,* July 5, 2004, downloaded from InfoTrac, http://web4.infotrac.galegroup.com.

13. Keith H. Hammonds, "How Do We Break Out of the Box We're Stuck In?" *Fast Company,* November 2000, pp. 260–68.

14. Ibid.

15. James Webb Young, *A Technique for Producing Ideas* (Chicago: Crain Communications, 1975).

16. Ibid., pp. 59–60.

17. Thea Singer, "Your Brain on Innovation," *Inc.,* September 2002, downloaded from InfoTrac, http://web4.infotrac.galegroup.com.

18. These suggestions are adapted from Weiss, "Coming Up with Good Ideas"; and Pollock, "Mind Your Own Business."

19. Cheryl Dahle, "Natural Leader," *Fast Company,* December 2000, pp. 268–80.

Chapter 10

1. Mary Helen Gillespie, "CEO's Weaknesses Displayed," *Boston Globe,* April 8, 2001, p. J15; "Electronic Invective Backfires," *Workforce,* June 2001, p. 20; Edward Wong, "A Stinging Office Memo Boomerangs," *The New York Times,* April 5, 2001, p. B1.

2. Jennifer Beauprez, "Many Companies Monitor Workers' Web-Surfing Habits," *Denver Post,* March 13, 2000, p. C1.

3. Bruce Vernyi, "An Avenue for Ideas," *Industry Week,* September 2005, downloaded from InfoTrac, http://web1.infotrac.galegroup.com; C. R. Bard, "About Bard," www.crbard.com, downloaded August 22, 2006.

4. T. L. Stanley, "What Would Buzz Lightyear Do?" *Supervision,* March 2006, downloaded from Business & Company Resource Center, http://galenet.galegroup.com.

5. Carl R. Rogers and Richard E. Farson, "Active Listening," reprinted in William V. Haney, *Communication and Interpersonal Relations: Text and Cases,* 6th ed. (Homewood, IL: Irwin, 1992), pp. 158–59.

6. This section is based on Donna M. Owens, "Multilingual Workforces," *HRMagazine,* Sep-

tember 2005, downloaded from InfoTrac, http://web2.infotrac.galegroup.com; Bob Miodonski, "Foreign-Born Workers Deserve Respect," *Contractor,* April 2005, downloaded from Business & Company Resource Center, http://galenet.galegroup.com; Ed Rosheim, "Bridging Language Gap Leads to More Productive Staff," *Nation's Restaurant News,* September 5, 2005, downloaded from Business & Company Resource Center, http://galenet.galegroup.com; Josh Cable, "The Multicultural Work Force: The Melting Pot Heats Up," *Occupational Hazards,* March 2006, downloaded from Business & Company Resource Center, http://galenet.galegroup.com.

7. Leigh Buchanan, "The English Impatient," *Inc.,* May 2001, p. 68.

8. Eve Tahmincioglu, "The 4-Letter-Word Patrol Is in Pursuit," *The New York Times,* June 27, 2001, p. G1.

9. "Clean It Up or Else," *BusinessWeek,* October 26, 1998, p. 8.

10. Ken Fracaro, "Two Ears and One Mouth," *Supervision,* February 1, 2001, p. 3.

11. Richard A. Oppel Jr. and Patrick McGeehan, "Along with a Lender, Is Citigroup Buying Trouble?" *The New York Times,* October 22, 2000, sec. 3, pp. 1, 15 (photo).

12. Linda Dulye, "Get Out of Your Office," *HRMagazine,* July 2006, downloaded from Business & Company Resource Center, http://galenet.galegroup.com.

13. Bill Zollars, quoted in "Follow These Leaders," *Fortune,* December 12, 2005.

14. The ideas in this list are drawn from Harriet Rubin, "Like the King, King David Knew How to Strum a Person Like an Instrument," *Fast Company,* November 2000, pp. 410–13; Belinda E. Puetz et al., "Helpline," *RN,* April 2001, p. 23; Mary Munter, *Guide to Managerial Communication,* 5th ed. (Upper Saddle River, NJ: Prentice Hall, 2000); Edward Bailey, *Writing and Speaking at Work* (Upper Saddle River, NJ: Prentice Hall, 1999).

15. "Indecent Exposure," *Inc.,* 1998, p. 86.

16. Bureau of Labor Statistics, "Computer and Internet Use at Work in 2003," news release, August 2, 2005, www.bls.gov/cps/.

17. Jared Sandberg, "Never a Safe Feature, 'Reply to All' Falls into the Wrong Hands," *The Wall Street Journal,* October 25, 2005, http://online.wsj.com.

18. Eric Benderoff and Mike Hughlett, "Teleconferencing Has Reduced Business Travel for Many

Companies," *Chicago Tribune*, August 10, 2006, downloaded from Business & Company Resource Center, http://galenet.galegroup.com.

19. "E-mail Preferred to In-Person Meetings," *USA Today*, December 2003, www.findarticles.com.

20. Cable, "The Multicultural Work Force."

21. Ann Pomeroy, "Great Places, Inspired Employees," *HRMagazine*, July 2004, downloaded from InfoTrac, http://web4.infotrac.galegroup.com.

22. Peggy Darragh-Jeromos, "A Suggestion System That Works for You," *Supervision*, August 2003, downloaded from InfoTrac, http://web7.infotrac.galegroup.com.

23. Janet R. Waddell, "You'll Never Believe What I Heard," *Supervision*, February 2004, downloaded from Business & Company Resource Center, http://galenet.galegroup.com.

24. Elaine McShulskis, "24-Hour HR," *HRMagazine*, November 1997, p. 22.

25. Based on Mortimer R. Feinberg, "How to Get the Grapevine on Your Side," *Working Woman*, May 1990, p. 23; Ray Alastair, "Profiting from the E-mail Grapevine," *Marketing*, October 11, 2001, p. 27.

26. Siobhan Benet, "Corporate Cues," *Black Enterprise*, March 2004, www.findarticles.com.

Chapter 11

1. Scott Martelle, "Businesses Develop New Take on Giving: More Companies Find That Urging Workers to Volunteer in the Community Boosts Their Image, Staff Morale and Skills," *Los Angeles Times*, April 27, 2001, pp. B1ff.

2. See, for example, Abraham Maslow, *Eupsychian Management* (Homewood, IL: Irwin, 1965); C. P. Alderfer, "An Empirical Test of a New Theory of Human Needs," *Organization Behavior and Human Performance* 4 (1969), pp. 142–75.

3. Jennifer O'Herron, "Don't Miss the Mark: Motivation That Works," *Call Center*, June 1, 2005, downloaded from Business & Company Resource Center, http://galenet.galegroup.com.

4. Kimberly Griffiths, "How to Find 'Em and How to Hold 'Em," *Industrial Distribution*, April 1, 2006, downloaded from Business & Company Resource Center, http://galenet.galegroup.com.

5. Hewitt Associates, "Hewitt Study Shows Work/Life Benefits Hold Steady Despite Recession," news release, May 13, 2002, http://was4.hewitt.com; Society for Human Resource Management, "Rising Health Care Costs Force Employers to Cut Some Non-Essential Benefits," news release, June 22, 2003, www.shrm.org; Madlen Read, "Top Companies Offer More than Maternity Leave to Moms," *USA Today*, September 21, 2004, www.usatoday.com/money/.

6. John A. Byrne, "How to Lead Now: Getting Extraordinary Performance When You Can't Pay for It," *Fast Company*, August 2003, downloaded from InfoTrac, http://web7.infotrac.galegroup.com.

7. Larry Stewart, "Rewarding Teamwork Turns a Shop Around," *Construction Equipment*, January 1, 2006, downloaded from Business & Company Resource Center, http://galenet.galegroup.com.

8. David Dorsey, "Andy Pearson Finds Love," *Fast Company*, August 2001, pp. 78–86.

9. Society for Human Resource Management, "11-Year-Old FMLA in Need of Medical Treatment," news release, February 17, 2004, www.shrm.org.

10. Peter Berg and Ann C. Frost, "Dignity at Work for Low Wage, Low Skill Service Workers," *Industrial Relations*, Autumn 2005, downloaded from Business & Company Resource Center, http://galenet.galegroup.com.

11. Barbara Whitaker, "'Living Wage' Ordinance Both Delights and Divides," *The New York Times*, May 29, 2001, p. A13. The ordinance was passed by the city council but was overturned a year later in a voter referendum. See Alan J. Liddle and Richard Martin, "Santa Monica, Berkeley Reject Private-Sector 'Living Wage' Law, Coffee-Source Restrictions," *Nation's Restaurant News*, November 18, 2002, downloaded from Business & Company Resource Center, http://galenet.galegroup.com.

12. Julia Chang, "Spread the Wealth: Letting Your Salespeople Profit When Your Company Does," *Sales & Marketing Management*, June 2006, downloaded from Business & Company Resource Center, http://galenet.galegroup.com.

13. Dean Foust et al., "Wooing the Worker," *BusinessWeek Online*, May 22, 2000, www.businessweek.com:/2000/00_21/b3682139.htm?scriptFramed, accessed August 13, 2001.

14. Mike Hofman, "Hot Tip: Performance Bonuses with an Extra Kick," Inc.com, www.inc.com/articles/details/0,3532,ART20579,00.html, accessed August 13, 2001.

15. "Leading Dealers Share Tips on Technician Compensation Plans, Managing Cash Flow, Product Line Selection, Marketing the Dealer Advantage, Serving Commercial Customers, and

More," *Yard & Garden*, March 2006, downloaded from Business & Company Resource Center, http://galenet.galegroup.com.

16. Laurence Zuckerman, "Happy Skies of Continental," *The New York Times*, February 27, 2001, pp. C1, C15.

17. Antoinette Alexander, "The Lure: Smart Compensation Plans Can Keep Staff in a Tight Market," *Accounting Technology*, July 2006, downloaded from Business & Company Resource Center, http://galenet.galegroup.com.

18. David Boyce, "Expectations Part of Deal for Gordon," *Kansas City Star*, April 12, 2006, downloaded from Business & Company Resource Center, http://galenet.galegroup.com.

19. Zuckerman, "Happy Skies of Continental."

20. Erika Germer, "Tell Them What They've Won!" *Inc.*, April 2001, p. 70.

21. Alison Overholt, "Cuckoo for Customers," *Fast Company*, June 2004, downloaded from InfoTrac, http://web2.infotrac.galegroup.com.

22. Diane Brady, "Give Nursing Moms a Break at the Office," *BusinessWeek*, August 6, 2001, p. 70.

23. Alan Feuer, "Leading a Porterhouse Ballet," *The New York Times*, June 11, 2001, pp. B1, B4.

24. Ron Lieber, "New Way to Curb Medical Costs: Make Employees Feel the Sting," *The Wall Street Journal*, June 23, 2004, http://online.wsj.com.

25. Dave Marin, "Viewpoint: Rock-Solid Results from Simple Praise," *American Banker*, April 7, 2006, downloaded from Business & Company Resource Center, http://galenet.galegroup.com.

Chapter 12

1. "2003 Unscheduled Absence Survey," *Medical Benefits*, December 15, 2003, downloaded from Business & Company Resource Center, http://galenet.galegroup.com.

2. Ibid.; "Strategies That Can Help You Deal with Excessive Absences," *HR Focus*, December 2003, downloaded from Business & Company Resource Center, http://galenet.galegroup.com.

3. Aaron Bernstein, "Racism in the Workplace," *BusinessWeek*, July 30, 2001, pp. 64–67.

4. Michele Marchetti, "When Salespeople Struggle," *Sales & Marketing Management*, April 2006, downloaded from InfoTrac, http://web4.infotrac.galegroup.com.

5. Judy Swartley, "Coming Clean," *EC&M, Electrical Construction & Maintenance*, April 1, 2006, downloaded from Business & Company Resource Center, http://galenet.galegroup.com.

6. Ibid.; U.S. Department of Labor, Office of the Assistant Secretary for Policy, "2003 National Survey on Drug Use and Health (NSDUH) Reveals the Vast Majority of Drug and Alcohol Abusers Work," Substance Abuse Information Database, www.dol.gov/asp, accessed September 24, 2004; U.S. Department of Labor, Office of the Assistant Secretary for Policy, "General Workplace Impact," *Working Partners: Statistics*, www.dol.gov/asp, accessed September 24, 2004; "Alcohol and Other Substance Abuse: Prevalence, Cost and Impact on Productivity," *Employee Benefit News*, September 1, 2004, downloaded from Business & Company Resource Center, http://galenet.galegroup.com.

7. Swartley, "Coming Clean."

8. "Top Threat: Workplace Violence Remains No. 1 Nemesis," *Security*, June 2001, pp. 9–12; Mike France with Michael Arndt, "Office Violence: After the Shooting Stops," *BusinessWeek*, March 12, 2001, pp. 98–100.

9. "Top Threat: Workplace Violence Remains No. 1 Nemesis."

10. Matthew Flamm, "Domestic Violence Victims Gaining Help in Workplace," *Crain's New York Business*, March 12, 2001, pp. 33, 38; Mike Hofman, "The Shadow of Domestic Violence," *Inc.*, March 2001, p. 85.

11. Flamm, "Domestic Violence Victims Gaining Help."

12. Ibid.

13. France with Arndt, "Office Violence."

14. Jennifer S. Lee, "Tracking Sales at the Cashiers," *The New York Times*, July 11, 2001, pp. C1, C6.

15. Ibid.

16. P. J. Connolly, "Activity Monitors Raise Ethical and Legal Questions Regarding Employee Privacy," *InfoWorld*, February 12, 2001, p. 57E.

17. Caroline Wilbert, "Coke Employee Faces Charges of Wire Fraud, Stealing Trade Secrets," *Atlanta Journal-Constitution*, July 6, 2006; David Gulliver, "Health Care Firm Loses Data," *Sarasota Herald Tribune*, August 17, 2006, both downloaded from Business & Company Resource Center, http://galenet.galegroup.com.

18. Karen Krebsbach, "The Enemy Within," *Banking Wire,* June 16, 2004, downloaded from Business & Company Resource Center, http://galenet.galegroup.com.

19. List of rights provided by Corinne R. Livesay, Liberty University, Lynchburg, VA.

20. Christopher Stewart, "Desperate Measures," *Sales & Marketing Management,* September 2003, downloaded from InfoTrac, http://web5.infotrac.galegroup.com.

21. Rick McLaughlin, "More Than Punishment Involved in Correcting Employee's Poor Performance," *Knight Ridder/Tribune Business News,* August 22, 2003, downloaded from Business & Company Resource Center, http://galenet.galegroup.com.

22. Beth Musgrave, "Some Workers Had Past Problems: Seven Charged Had Been Disciplined Before," *Lexington Herald-Leader,* July 21, 2006, downloaded from Business & Company Resource Center, http://galenet.galegroup.com.

23. U.S. Department of Labor, "Drug-Free Workplace Advisor: Supervisor Training," *eLaws Advisor,* www.dol.gov/elaws, accessed June 26, 2006.

24. See Tamara Cagney, "Why Don't Supervisors Refer?" *Journal of Employee Assistance,* January–March 2006, downloaded from Business & Company Resource Center, http://galenet.galegroup.com.

Chapter 13

1. Robert D. Ramsey, "15 Time Wasters for Supervisors," *Supervision,* June 2000, p. 10.

2. Ted Pollock, "Mind Your Own Business," *Supervision,* March 2001, pp. 17–19.

3. Jared Sandberg "To-Do Lists Can Take More Time Than Doing, but That Isn't the Point," *The Wall Street Journal,* September 8, 2004, http://online.wsj.com.

4. Jason Fry, "A Tale of Two Emailers," *The Wall Street Journal,* January 30, 2006, http://online.wsj.com.

5. Clive Thompson, "Meet the Life Hackers," *The New York Times Magazine,* October 16, 2005, www.nytimes.com.

6. Ibid.

7. Mann quoted in ibid.; White quoted in "Quitting Time!" *Incentive,* October 2000, p. 142.

8. Pace Productivity, "Time Tips," www.getmoredone.com, accessed August 19, 2001.

9. Pollock, "Mind Your Own Business."

10. Pace Productivity, "Time Tips."

11. Ibid.

12. Gail Dutton, "Cutting Edge Stressbusters," *HR Focus,* September 1, 1998, p. 11.

13. Alisa Tang, "Sick or Stressed Out: Workplace Absence, by Job and Gender," *The New York Times,* December 1, 1999, p. G1.

14. Frank Grazian, "Are You Coping with Stress?" *Communication Briefings* 14, no. 1, p. 3.

15. Michael Gelman with Jobert E. Abueva, "The Boss: No Second Chances on Live TV," *The New York Times,* February 14, 2001, p. C8.

16. Margarita Bauza, "Study: More Americans Do Work on Their Vacations," *Detroit Free Press,* August 8, 2006, downloaded from Business & Company Resource Center, http://galenet.galegroup.com.

17. Matt Murray, "Amid Record Profits, Companies Continue to Lay Off Employees," *The Wall Street Journal,* May 4, 1995, pp. A1, A4.

18. Emily Burg, review of *The Procrastinator's Handbook,* www.workingwoman.com/wwn/article.jsp?contentId=5745&ChannelID=212, accessed June 14, 2001.

19. T. L. Stanley, "Balance and Organization," *American Salesman,* August 2004 (quoting Colin Powell's autobiography, *My American Journey*), downloaded from Business & Company Resource Center, http://galenet.galegroup.com.

20. Grazian, "Are You Coping with Stress?"

21. Carol Kleiman, "Turning Stress Control into a Laughing Matter," *Chicago Tribune,* August 6, 1995, sec. 8, p. 1.

22. Claudia Hale-Jinks, Herman Knopf, and Kristen Kemple, "Tackling Teacher Turnover in Child Care: Understanding Causes and Consequences, Identifying Solutions," *Childhood Education,* Summer 2006, downloaded from InfoTrac, http://web2.infotrac.galegroup.com; "Peer and Supervisor Support May Be Critical Coping Strategies for Emergency Medical Services Personnel, Research Indicates," *CNW Group,* January 25, 2006, downloaded from Business & Company Resource Center, http://galenet.galegroup.com.

23. Ann Pomeroy, "Great Places, Inspired Employees," *HRMagazine,* July 2004, downloaded from InfoTrac, http://web4.infotrac.galegroup.com.

24. Dave Simanoff, "Workers' Needs Should Be First in Stress Times, Experts Say," *Knight Ridder/Tribune Business News,* September 18, 2004; Sara Kennedy, "Airline's Dispatchers Weather a Storm," *The New York Times,* September 26, 2004; Jeff Zeleny, "Fourth Hurricane, Jeanne, Slashes into Weary Florida," *Knight Ridder/Tribune Business News,* September 26, 2004, all downloaded from Business & Company Resource Center, http://galenet.galegroup.com.

25. "Employers Increase Wellness Push with New Programs, Incentives," *Employee Benefit News,* July 1, 2006, downloaded from Business & Company Resource Center, http://galenet.galegroup.com.

26. Sara Kennedy, "Physically, Fiscally Fit: Wellness Strategy Can Prove to Be Good Business," *Bradenton (Fla.) Herald,* July 2, 2006, downloaded from Business & Company Resource Center, http://galenet.galegroup.com.

27. Ibid.

28. Emily Berry and Herman Wang, "Wellness Programs Aim to Hold Down Health Costs," *Chattanooga (Tenn.) Times/Free Press,* July 21, 2006, downloaded from Business & Company Resource Center, http://galenet.galegroup.com.

29. Seth A. Berr, Allan H. Church, and Janine Waclawski, "The Right Relationship Is Everything: Linking Personality Preferences to Managerial Behaviors," *Human Resource Development Quarterly* 11, no. 2 (Summer 2000), pp. 133–57.

Chapter 14

1. Cheryl Dahle, "Deflecting the Knife of a Backstabber," *The New York Times,* August 8, 2004, downloaded from Business & Company Resource Center, http://galenet.galegroup.com.

2. Tatsha Robertson, "Between Work and Life There's Balance," *Boston Globe,* June 19, 2005, www.boston.com.

3. Joshua Kendall, "Can't We All Just Get Along?" *BusinessWeek,* October 9, 2000, p. F18; Tony Schwartz, "How Do You Feel?" *Fast Company,* June 2000, pp. 296–313.

4. Jared Sandberg, "Office Democracies: How Many Bosses Can One Person Have?" *The Wall Street Journal,* November 22, 2005, http://online.wsj.com.

5. For an interesting related study, see Catherine H. Tinsley and Jeanne M. Brett, "Managing Workplace Conflict in the United States and Hong Kong," *Organizational Behavior and Human Decision Processes* 85, no. 2 (2001), pp. 360–81.

6. Anne Spray Kinney, "Financial Leadership for the Twenty-First Century: An Interview with Five Public Sector Leaders," *Government Finance Review,* February 2005, downloaded from Business & Company Resource Center, http://galenet.galegroup.com.

7. Dahle, "Deflecting the Knife of a Backstabber."

8. Patricia Kitchen, "Ways to Defuse Conflict at Work," *(Melville, N.Y.) Newsday,* July 2, 2006, downloaded from Business & Company Resource Center, http://galenet.galegroup.com.

9. Belinda E. Puetz et al., "Helpline," *RN,* April 2001, p. 23.

10. See, for example, Dianne Jacobs, "Sharing Knowledge: How to Thrive in Times of Change," *Ivey Business Journal Online,* July–August 2005, downloaded from Business & Company Resource Center, http://galenet.galegroup.com; Marvin J. Cetron and Owen Davies, "Trends Now Shaping the Future," *The Futurist,* May–June 2005, pp. 37–50.

11. Randy Dotinga, "Can Boss Insist on Healthy Habits?" *Christian Science Monitor,* January 11, 2006, www.csmonitor.com.

12. Scott Kirsner, "Designed for Innovation," *Fast Company,* November 1998, p. 54.

13. David Armstrong, "Gillette Will Cut 8% of Work Force, Close Plants under Restructuring Plan," *The Wall Street Journal,* December 19, 2000, p. 1.

14. Richard McCormack, "Service Is an Overlooked Ingredient for Success in Manufacturing," *Manufacturing and Technology News,* March 3, 2006, www.manufacturingnews.com.

15. Claudia H. Deutsch, "Competitors Can Teach You a Lot, but the Lessons Can Hurt," *The New York Times,* July 18, 1999, p. BU 4.

16. Kurt Lewin, "Frontiers in Group Dynamics: Concept, Method, and Reality of Social Sciences—Social Equilibrium and Social Change," *Human Relations,* June 1947, pp. 5–14.

17. "Follow These Leaders," *Fortune,* December 12, 2005.

18. Michael Hammer and Steven A. Stanton, "Beating the Risks of Reengineering," *Fortune,* May 15, 1995, pp. 105ff.

19. Some of the suggestions in this list are adapted from William W. Hull, "Coping with Threatening Change," *Supervision,* May 1, 2001, p. 3; others are from David W. Mann, "Why Supervisors Resist Change and What You Can Do About It," *Journal for Quality & Participation,* May 1, 2001, pp. 20–22.

20. Steve Bates, "Getting Engaged," *HRMagazine,* February 2004, downloaded from InfoTrac, http://web4.infotrac.galegroup.com.

21. Joseph A. Raelin, "Growing Group Leadership Skills," *Security Management,* June 2004, downloaded from Business & Company Resource Center, http://galenet.galegroup.com.

22. Jim Barlow, "The Ins and Outs of Office Politics," *Houston Chronicle,* May 17, 2001, p. C1; Donald S. Miller and Stephen E. Catt, *Human Relations: A Contemporary Approach* (Homewood, IL: Irwin, 1989), pp. 200–2.

Appendix A

1. C. Pasternak, "Corporate Politics May Not Be a Waste of Time," *HRMagazine,* September 1994, p. 18.

2. R. Bhasin, "On Playing Corporate Politics," *Pulp & Paper,* October 1985, p. 175. See also N. Gupta and G. D. Jenkins, Jr., "The Politics of Pay," *Compensation & Benefits Review,* March–April 1996, pp. 23–30.

3. R. W. Allen, D. L. Madison, L. W. Porter, P. A. Renwick, and B. T. Mayes, "Organizational Politics: Tactics and Characteristics of Its Actors," *California Management Review,* Fall 1979, p. 77. See also K. M. Kacmar and G. R. Ferris, "Politics at Work: Sharpening the Focus of Political Behavior in Organizations," *Business Horizons,* July–August 1993, pp. 70–74. A comprehensive update can be found in K. M. Kacmar and R. A. Baron, "Organizational Politics: The State of the Field, Links to Related Processes, and an Agenda for Future Research," in *Research in Personnel and Human Resources Management,* Vol. 17, ed. G. R. Ferris (Stamford, CT: JAI Press, 1999), pp. 1–39.

4. See P. M. Fandt and G. R. Ferris, "The Management of Information and Impressions: When Employees Behave Opportunistically," *Organizational Behavior and Human Decision Processes,* February 1990, pp. 140–58.

5. The first four are based on the discussion in D. R. Beeman and T. W. Sharkey, "The Use and Abuse of Corporate Politics," *Business Horizons,* March–April 1987, pp. 26–30.

6. A. Raia, "Power, Politics, and the Human Resource Professional," *Human Resource Planning,* no. 4 (1985), p. 203.

7. A. J. DuBrin, "Career Maturity, Organizational Rank, and Political Behavioral Tendencies: A Correlational Analysis of Organizational Politics and Career Experience," *Psychological Reports,* October 1988, p. 535.

8. This three-level distinction comes from A. T. Cobb, "Political Diagnosis: Applications in Orgaizational Development," *Academy of Management Review,* July 1986, pp. 482–96.

9. An excellent historical and theoretical perspective of coalitions can be found in W. B. Stevenson, J. L. Pearce, and L. W. Porter, "The Concept of 'Coalition' in Organization Theory and Research," *Academy of Management Review,* April 1985, pp. 256–68.

10. L. Baum, "The Day Charlie Bradshaw Kissed Off Transworld," *BusinessWeek,* September 29, 1986, p. 68.

11. See K. G. Provan and J. G. Sebastian, "Networks within Networks: Service Link Overlap, Organizational Cliques, and Network Effectiveness," *Academy of Management Journal,* August 1998, pp. 453–63.

12. Allen et al., "Organizational Politics," p. 77.

13. See W. L. Gardner III, "Lessons in Organizational Dramaturgy: The Art of Impression Management," *Organizational Dynamics,* Summer 1992, pp. 33–46.

14. For more on political behavior, see A. Nierenberg, "Masterful Networking," *Training & Development,* February 1999, pp. 51–53.

15. A. Rao, S. M. Schmidt, and L. H. Murray, "Upward Impression Management: Goals, Influence Strategies, and Consequences," *Human Relations,* February 1995, p. 147.

16. Fandt and Ferris, "The Management of Information and Impressions" pp. 140–58; W. L. Gardner and B. J. Avolio, "The Charismatic Relationship: A Dramaturgical Perspective," *Academy of Management Review,* January 1998, pp. 32–58; L. Wah, "Managing–Manipulating?—Your Reputation," *Management Review,* October 1998, pp. 46–50; M. C. Bolino, "Citizenship and Impression Management: Good Soldiers or Good Actors?" *Academy of Management Review,* January 1999, pp. 82–98.

17. For related research, see M. G. Pratt and A. Rafaeli, "Organizational Dress as a Symbol of Multilayered Social Identities," *Academy of Management Journal,* August 1997, pp. 862–98.

18. S. Friedman, "What Do You Really Care About? What Are You Most Interested In?" *Fast Company,* March 1999, p. 90. See also B. M. DePaulo and D. A. Kashy, "Everyday Lies in Close and Casual Relationships," *Journal of Personality and Social Psychology,* January 1998, pp. 63–79.

19. See S. J. Wayne and G. R. Ferris, "Influence Tactics, Affect, and Exchange Quality in Supervisor-Subordinate Interactions: A Laboratory Experiment

and Field Study," *Journal of Applied Psychology,* October 1990, pp. 487–99. For another version, see Table 1 (p. 246) in S. J. Wayne and R. C. Liden, "Effects of Impression Management on Performance Ratings: A Longitudinal Study," *Academy of Management Journal,* February 1995, pp. 232–60.

20. See R. Vonk, "The Slime Effect: Suspicion and Dislike of Likeable Behavior toward Superiors," *Journal of Personality and Social Psychology,* April 1998, pp. 849–64; M. Wells, "How to Schmooze Like the Best of Them," *USA Today,* May 18, 1999, p. 14E.

21. See P. Rosenfeld, R. A. Giacalone, and C. A. Riordan, "Impression Management Theory and Diversity: Lessons for Organizational Behavior," *American Behavioral Scientist,* March 1994, pp. 601–4; R. A. Giacalone and J. W. Beard, "Impression Management, Diversity, and International Management," *American Behavioral Scientist,* March 1994, pp. 621–36; A. Montagliani and R. A. Giacalone, "Impression Management and Cross-Cultural Adaptation," *The Journal of Social Psychology,* October 1998, pp. 598–608.

22. M. E. Mendenhall and C. Wiley, "Strangers in a Strange Land: The Relationship between Expatriate Adjustment and Impression Management," *American Behavioral Scientist,* March 1994, pp. 605–20.

23. T. E. Becker and S. L. Martin, "Trying to Look Bad at Work: Methods and Motives for Managing Poor Impressions in Organizations," *Academy of Management Journal,* February 1995, p. 191.

24. Ibid., p. 181.

25. Ibid., pp. 180–81.

26. Ibid., pp. 192–93.

27. Data from G. R. Ferris, D. D. Frink, D. P. S. Bhawuk, J. Zhou, and D. C. Gilmore, "Reactions of Diverse Groups to Politics in the Workplace," *Journal of Management,* no. 1 (1996), pp. 23–44. For other findings from the same database, see G. R. Ferris, D. D. Frink, M. C. Galang, J. Zhou, K. M. Kacmar, and J. L. Howard, "Perceptions of Organizational Politics: Prediction, Stress-Related Implications, and Outcomes," *Human Relations,* February 1996, pp. 233–66. Also see M. L. Randall, R. Cropanzano, C. A. Bormann, and A. Birjulin, "Organizational Politics and Organizational Support as Predictors of Work Attitudes, Job Performance, and Organizational Citizenship Behavior," *Journal of Organizational Behavior,* March 1999, pp. 159–74.

28. A. Drory and D. Beaty, "Gender Differences in the Perception of Organizational Influence Tactics," *Journal of Organizational Behavior,* May 1991, pp. 256–57. Also see L. A. Rudman, "Self-Promotion as a Risk Factor for Women: The Costs and Benefits of Counterstereotypical Impression Management," *Journal of Personality and Social Psychology,* March 1998, pp. 629–45; J. Tata, "The Influence of Gender on the Use and Effectiveness of Managerial Accounts," *Group & Organization Management,* September 1998, pp. 267–88.

29. See S. J. Wayne and R. C. Liden, "Effects of Impression Management on Performance Ratings: A Longitudinal Study," *Academy of Management Journal,* February 1995, pp. 232–60.

30. Rao, Schmidt, and Murray, "Upward Impression Management," p. 165.

Chapter 15

1. Michael Kinsman, "Job No. 1 for Supervisors: Hiring the Right Person," *San Diego Union-Tribune,* October 2, 2005, downloaded from Business & Company Resource Center, http://galenet .galegroup.com.

2. Raymond A. Noe, John R. Hollenbeck, Barry Gerhart, and Patrick M. Wright, *Human Resource Management: Gaining a Competitive Advantage,* 4th ed. (New York: McGraw-Hill/Irwin, 2003), p. 149.

3. Aman Singh, "Podcasts Extend Recruiters' Reach," *The Wall Street Journal,* April 24, 2006, http://online.wsj.com.

4. Kris Maher, "Blogs Catch On as Online Tool for Job Seekers and Recruiters," *The Wall Street Journal,* September 28, 2004, http://online.wsj.com.

5. Margarita Bauza, "A Change in Recruiting: The Long Interview," *Detroit Free Press,* June 5, 2006, downloaded from Business & Company Resource Center, http://galenet.galegroup.com.

6. Donna Fenn, "Scour Power: Smart Recruiters Are Turning the Internet Inside Out in Search of Employees," *Inc.,* November 2000, www.inc.com.

7. "Best Practices: Hiring," *Inc.,* March 1994, p. 10.

8. Jim Romeo, "Answering the Call," *HRMagazine,* October 2003, downloaded from InfoTrac, http:// web4.infotrac.galegroup.com.

9. John M. Ivancevich, *Human Resource Management,* 7th ed. (New York: Irwin/McGraw-Hill, 1998), p. 701.

10. Alison Overhoit, "Are You a Polyolefin Optimizer? Take This Quiz!" *Fast Company,* April 2004, downloaded from InfoTrac, http://web4.infotrac .galegroup.com.

11. "Drug Testing: The Things People Will Do," *American Salesman,* March 2001, pp. 20–24.

12. Rosemary Winters, "Some Companies Use Tests in Criteria for Personnel Decisions," *Salt Lake Tribune,* November 14, 2005, downloaded from Business & Company Resource Center, http://galenet.galegroup.com.

13. Shirleen Holt, "Job Hunters, Simulate This," *Seattle Times,* February 2, 2005, downloaded from Business & Company Resource Center, http://galenet.galegroup.com.

14. Erin White, "Employers Gauge Candidates' Skills at 'Real-World' Tasks," *The Wall Street Journal,* January 16, 2006, http://online.wsj.com.

15. Kari Haskell, "Liar, Liar, You're Not Hired: Even White Lies Hurt Job Hunters," *The New York Times,* May 30, 2001, p. G1.

16. Gary Dessler, *Human Resource Management,* 8th ed. (Upper Saddle River, NJ: Prentice Hall, 2000), p. 173.

17. Ed Gubman, *The Engaging Leader: Winning with Today's Free Agent Workforce* (Chicago: Dearborn Trade Publishing, 2003), pp. 54–55.

18. Dessler, *Human Resource Management,* pp. 49–52.

19. Sue Shellenbarger, "Work and Family," *The Wall Street Journal,* January 27, 1999, p. B1.

20. Robert Rodriguez, "Diversity Finds Its Place," *HRMagazine,* August 2006, downloaded from Business & Company Resource Center, http://galenet.galegroup.com.

21. Bruce Felton, "Technologies That Enable the Disabled," *The New York Times,* September 14, 1997, p. B1.

22. Michelle Conlin, "The New Workforce," *BusinessWeek,* March 20, 2000, pp. 64–68.

23. Equal Employment Opportunity Commission, "Questions and Answers about Persons with Intellectual Disabilities in the Workplace and the Americans with Disabilities Act," last modified October 20, 2004, www.eeoc.gov.

24. David Armstrong, "Building Bridges at Work," *San Francisco Chronicle,* May 4, 2006, downloaded from Business & Company Resource Center, http://galenet.galegroup.com.

25. Dawn D. Bennett-Alexander and Laura B. Pincus, *Employment Law for Business,* 2d ed. (New York: Irwin/McGraw-Hill, 1998), p. 558.

Chapter 16

1. Tammy Galvin, "2003 Industry Report: *Training Magazine's* 22nd Annual Comprehensive Analysis of Employer-Sponsored Training in the United States," *Training,* October 2003, downloaded from InfoTrac, http://web1.infotrac.galegroup.com.

2. Rose A. Hazlett, "A Military Victory," *Minority Nurse,* www.minoritynurse.com, accessed June 14, 2006.

3. Erika Germer, "Not Just for Kicks," *Fast Company,* March 2001, p. 70.

4. Nancy S. Ahlrichs, *Manager of Choice: Five Competencies for Cultivating Top Talent* (Palo Alto, CA: Davies-Black Publishing, 2003), pp. 139–41.

5. Jane Erwin and P. C. Douglas, "It's Not Difficult to Change Company Culture," *Supervision,* November 1, 2000, p. 6.

6. Diane Walter, "A View from the Floor," *Training,* July 2001, p. 76.

7. John S. McClenahen, "The Next Crisis: Too Few Workers," *Industry Week,* May 2003, downloaded from InfoTrac, http://web5.infotrac.galegroup.com.

8. A number of these points are mentioned in Edward Shaw, "The Training-Waste Conspiracy," *Training,* April 1995; Tiffany Potter and Nancy Heineke, "Professional Training: Adult Learning Theory Meets GIS," *GEO World,* July 2006, downloaded from Business & Company Resource Center, http://galenet.galegroup.com.

9. Karl Albrecht, "Take Time for Effective Learning," *Training,* July 2004; Holly Dolezalek, "Pretending to Learn," *Training,* July–August 2003, both downloaded from InfoTrac, http://web4.infotrac .galegroup.com.

10. Claudia Deutsch, "Five Questions for John F. Welch, Jr.," *The New York Times,* March 18, 2001, p. BU7.

11. "Training Best Practices 2006," *Training,* March 2006, downloaded from Business & Company Resource Center, http://galenet.galegroup.com.

12. "High School Grads Find Apprenticeships Hot Ticket to Cool Careers and Big Bucks," *PR Newswire,* June 11, 2001.

13. Chris Koepfer, "Integrating Machining Centers into the Work Flow," *Production Machining,* August 2006, pp. 34–38.

14. Emily Barker, "High-Test Education," *Inc.*, July 2001, pp. 81–82.

15. Galvin, "2003 Industry Report."

16. Jack Gordon, "Movin' 'Em Up, through Effective Training," *Sales & Marketing Management*, June 2006, downloaded from InfoTrac, http://web2.infotrac.galegroup.com.

17. Galvin, "2003 Industry Report."

18. Reena Jana, "On-the-Job Video Gaming," *BusinessWeek*, March 27, 2006, downloaded from General Reference Center Gold, http://find.galegroup.com.

19. Galvin, "2003 Industry Report."

20. See, for example, "Training Best Practices 2006."

21. Leigh Buchanan, "City Lights: In the Bank," *Inc.*, May 2001, p. 68.

22. Jim Moshinskie, "Tips for Ensuring Effective E-Learning," *HR Focus*, August 2001, pp. 6–7.

23. Cathy Olofson, "Play Hard, Think Big," *Fast Company*, January 2001, pp. 64.

24. Anne Marie Borrego, "Using Mentors to Build Loyalty," *Inc.*, February 2000, pp. 121.

25. Betsy Cummings, "Coaching Clinic," *Sales & Marketing Management*, December 2003, downloaded from InfoTrac, http://web4.infotrac.galegroup.com.

26. Leon Rubis, "Mission Possible: Manager Training Helped Company Digest Big Bite," *HRMagazine*, December 1, 2000, pp. 60–62.

Chapter 17

1. Carla Johnson, "Employee, Sculpt Thyself . . . with a Little Help," *HRMagazine*, May 2001, pp. 60–64 (sidebar).

2. Ibid.

3. Carla Johnson, "Making Sure Employees Measure Up," *HRMagazine*, March 2001, pp. 36–41.

4. Ibid.

5. Greg Levin, "Agent Development in Action!" *Call Center*, June 1, 2006, downloaded from Business & Company Resource Center, http://galenet.galegroup.com.

6. Michael M. Grant, "Six Sigma for People? The Heart of Performance Management," *Human Resource Planning*, March 2006, downloaded from Business & Company Resource Center, http://galenet.galegroup.com.

7. Lin Grensing-Pophal, "Motivate Managers to Review Performance," *HRMagazine*, March 2001, pp. 44–48.

8. "Parallels between Performance Management Quality and Organizational Performance," *Supervision*, September 2003, downloaded from InfoTrac, http://web4.infotrac.galegroup.com.

9. Benjamin J. Romano, "Under Pressure, Microsoft Fights to Keep Its Workers," *Seattle Times*, May 19, 2006; Larry Stewart, "Performance Measures Motivate Change," *Construction Equipment*, June 1, 2005, both downloaded from Business & Company Resource Center, http://galenet.galegroup.com.

10. "Parallels between Performance Management Quality and Organizational Performance."

11. Carol Hymowitz, "In the Lead: Ranking Systems Gain Popularity but Have Many Staffers Riled," *The Wall Street Journal*, May 15, 2001, p. B1; Reed Abelson, "Companies Turn to Grades, and Employees Go to Court," *The New York Times*, March 19, 2001, p. A1; Matthew Boyle, "Performance Reviews: Perilous Curves Ahead," *Fortune*, May 28, 2001, pp. 187–88.

12. Paul Ridilla, "'That's Not My Job' Scorecard: Recognize Extra Effort by Your Employees or It Won't Continue," *Plumbing & Mechanical*, July 2004, downloaded from Business & Company Resource Center, http://galenet.galegroup.com.

13. Bill Stoneman, "To Reduce Turnover, Turn the Teller into a Team Player," *American Banker*, July 8, 2003, downloaded from Business & Company Resource Center, http://galenet.galegroup.com.

14. Dayton Fandray, "The New Thinking in Performance Appraisals," *Workforce*, May 2001, pp. 36–40.

15. "Parallels between Performance Management Quality and Organizational Performance."

16. Roger Seiler, "Getting Results with 360 Assessments: Continuous and Periodic Ratings by Superiors and Peers Helps Employees Grow in Their Positions," *Law Enforcement Technology*, September 2005, downloaded from Business & Company Resource Center, http://galenet.galegroup.com.

17. Alison Stein Wellner, "Everyone's a Critic," *BusinessWeek Small Biz*, April 2001, p. 18.

18. Julie Forster, "IKEA's Unusual Benefits, Attitude Scores Hit with Workers," *Knight Ridder/Tribune Business News*, July 14, 2004, downloaded from

Business & Company Resource Center, http://galenet.galegroup.com.

19. Gary L. May and Lisa E. Gueldenzoph, "The Effect of Social Style on Peer Evaluation Ratings in Project Teams," *Journal of Business Communication* 43, no. 1 (January 2006), downloaded from Business & Company Resource Center, http://galenet.galegroup.com.

20. Danee Attebury, "Mystery Shoppers Keep Employees on Their Toes," *Columbus (Ga.) Ledger-Enquirer*, August 1, 2006; Barry Himmel, "Customer Service Impact," *Rental Equipment Register*, January 1, 2006, both downloaded from Business & Company Resource Center, http://galenet.galegroup.com.

21. Julia Chang, "Feedback Needed," *Sales & Marketing Management*, February 2004, downloaded from InfoTrac, http://web4.infotrac.galegroup.com.

22. Richard S. Allen and Ralph H. Kilmann, "Aligning Reward Practices in Support of Total Quality Management," *Business Horizons*, May 2001, downloaded from Business & Company Resource Center, http://galenet.galegroup.com.

23. R. Brayton Bowen, "Today's Workforce Requires New Age Currency," *HRMagazine*, March 2004, downloaded from InfoTrac, http://web2.infotrac.galegroup.com.

Appendix B

1. Bureau of Labor Statistics, "Workplace Injuries and Illnesses in 2002," news release, December 18, 2003, www.bls.gov.

2. Ibid., Tables 1 and 4.

3. Christina LeBeau, "Breakway (A Special Report): Second Thoughts—Not Tough Enough? At Smaller Firms, Less OSHA Oversight and More Deaths and Injuries," *The Wall Street Journal*, March 19, 2001, pp. 14ff.

4. Aerias, "Standards and Guidelines for Indoor Air Quality (IAQ)," 2001, www.aerias. org/c_doc_149.htm.

5. Gayle Hanson, "In-Flight Air Recycling Fouls Friendly Skies," *Insight on the News*, February 17, 1997, p. 18; Julie Flaherty, "Flight Attendants Demand Cleaner In-Flight Air," Reuters, January 4, 2001.

6. National Institute for Occupational Safety and Health, "About NIOSH," www.cdc.gov/niosh/about.html; downloaded October 21, 2004.

7. "Worker Health Chartbook," *Professional Safety*, December 2000, p. 1.

8. "Watch Your Step: Workplace Injuries Cost a Bundle," *U.S. News & World Report*, March 26, 2001, p. 10.

9. Steven Greenhouse, "Hispanic Workers Die at a Higher Rate," *The New York Times*, July 16, 2001, p. A11.

10. "Safety on the Docks," *Warehousing Management*, July 2001, pp. 33–37.

11. U.S. Department of Health and Human Services, "Preventing Disease and Death from Tobacco Use," Fact Sheet, January 8, 2001, www.hhs.gov, downloaded September 20, 2001; U.S. Department of Health and Human Services, "New Surgeon General's Report Expands List of Diseases Caused by Smoking," news release, May 27, 2004, www.hhs.gov.

12. Centers for Disease Control and Prevention, "Secondhand Smoke," Fact Sheet, February 2004, www.cdc.gov/tobacco/factsheets/secondhand_smoke_factsheet.htm.

13. "State-Specific Prevalence of Current Cigarette Smoking among Adults and the Proportion of Adults Who Work in a Smoke-Free Environment, United States, 1999," *Journal of the American Medical Association*, December 13, 2000, pp. 2865–66; National Cancer Institute, State Cancer Legislative Database Program, "Clean Indoor Air," Fact Sheet, January 2002, www.scld-nci.net.

14. See, for example, Oregon Occupational Safety and Health Division, *Evaluating Your Computer Workstation*, publication no. 440-1863, February 2004, www.cbs.state.or.us; Lori Eig and Julie Landis, "MSDs and the Workplace," *Journal of Employee Assistance*, 3rd Quarter, 2004, pp. 12–14.

15. Bureau of Labor Statistics, "Number of Nonfatal Occupational Injuries and Illnesses with Days Away from Work Involving Musculoskeletal Disorders by Selected Worker and Case Characteristics, 2002," Table 11, March 2004, www.bls.gov.

16. Robert J. Grossman, "Back with a Vengeance," *HRMagazine*, August 2001, pp. 36–46.

17. Adrienne E. Eaton and Thomas Nocerino, "The Effectiveness of Health and Safety Committees: Results of a Survey of Public-Sector Workplaces," *Industrial Relations*, April 2000, pp. 265ff.

18. Robert D. Ramsey, "Handling Hazards in the Workplace," *Supervision*, May 2000, pp. 6–8.

19. June Fabre, "Improve Patient Safety and Staff Retention by Mentoring Your Staff," *Healthcare Review*, July 1, 2003, downloaded from Look Smart's FindArticles, www.findarticles.com.

20. These suggestions are excerpted from Ramsey, "Handling Hazards in the Workplace."

21. U.S. Census Bureau, *Statistical Abstract of the United States: 2003* (Washington, DC, 2003), p. 431.

22. Bureau of Labor Statistics, "Work Stoppages Involving 1,000 or More Workers, 1947–2003," Major Work Stoppages: Detailed Monthly Data page, www.bls.gov, downloaded October 25, 2004.

23. Margaret M. Clark, "Employers Fail to Give Required Notice in Majority of Mass Layoffs and Closures," *HRMagazine*, December 2003, downloaded from Business & Company Resource Center, http://galenet.galegroup.com.

24. See Equal Employment Opportunity Commission, "Questions & Answers for Small Employers on Employer Liability for Harassment by Supervisors," June 21, 1999, www.eeoc.gov/policy/docs/harassment-facts.html.

25. Equal Employment Opportunity Commission, "Sexual Harassment Charges, EEOC & FEPAs Combined: FY 1992–FY 2003," March 8, 2004, www.eeoc.gov/stats/harass.html.

26. The cautions in this paragraph are based on Jonathan A. Segal, "Throw Supervisors a Lifeline and Save Yourself," *HRMagazine*, June 2003, downloaded from InfoTrac, http://web2.infotrac.galegroup.com.

27. Jill Elswick, "FMLA Protects Seriously Ill Workers against Job Loss," *Employee Benefit News*, August 1, 2004, downloaded from Business & Company Resource Center, http://galenet. galegroup.com; Burt Helm, "California Offers Paid Leave for All Workers," *Inc.*, October 2004, downloaded from InfoTrac, http://web2.infotrac.galegroup.com.

28. Michael Prince, "FMLA Hasn't Been Big Burden for Employers," *Business Insurance*, September 29, 2003, downloaded from Business & Company Resource Center, http://galenet. galegroup.com.

29. Linda Wasmer Andrews, "Aftershocks of War," *HRMagazine*, April 2004, downloaded from InfoTrac, http://web2.infotrac.galegroup.com.

Glossary

accountability The practice of imposing penalties for failing to adequately carry out responsibilities and providing rewards for meeting responsibilities. 13

action plan The plan for how to achieve an objective. 145

active listening Hearing what the speaker is saying, seeking to understand the facts and feelings the speaker is trying to convey, and stating what you understand that message to be. 260

affirmative action Plans designed to increase opportunities for groups that traditionally have been discriminated against. 433

ageism Discrimination based on age. 123

agenda A list of the topics to be covered at a meeting. 82

apprenticeship Training that involves working alongside an experienced person, who shows the apprentice how to do the various tasks involved in a job or trade. 457

aptitude test A test that measures a person's ability to learn skills related to the job. 427

authoritarian leadership A leadership style in which the leader retains a great deal of authority. 202

authority The right to perform a task or give orders to someone else. 180

average rate of return (ARR) A percentage that represents the average annual earnings for each dollar of a given investment. 55

behavior modification The use of reinforcement theory to motivate people to behave in a certain way. 296

behaviorally anchored rating scales (BARS) A performance appraisal in which an employee is rated on scales containing statements describing performance in several areas. 482

benchmarking Identifying the top performer of a process, then learning and carrying out the top performer's practices. 42

biofeedback Developing an awareness of bodily functions in order to control them. 358

bona fide occupational qualification (BFOQ) An objective characteristic required for an individual to perform a job properly. 124

bounded rationality Choosing an alternative that meets minimum standards of acceptability. 229

brainstorming An idea-generating process in which group members state their ideas, a member of the group records them, and no one may comment on the ideas until the process is complete. 241

budget A plan for spending money. 149

burnout The inability to function effectively as a result of ongoing stress. 355

central tendency The tendency to select employee ratings in the middle of a scale. 487

chain of command The flow of authority in an organization from one level of management to the next. 185

closed-ended question A question that requires a simple answer, such as yes or no. 426

coaching Guidance and instruction in how to do a job so that it satisfies performance goals. 462

code of ethics An organization's written statement of its values and rules for ethical behavior. 99

cohesiveness The degree to which group members stick together. 73

commissions Payment linked to the amount of sales completed. 299

communication The process by which people send and receive information. 255

compromise Settling on a solution that gives each person part of what he or she wants; no one gets everything, and no one loses completely. 377

conceptual skills The ability to see the relation of the parts to the whole and to one another. 5

concurrent control Control that occurs while the work takes place. 160

conflict The struggle that results from incompatible or opposing needs, feelings, thoughts, or demands within a person or between two or more people. 372

conflict management Responding to problems stemming from conflict. 376

conflict resolution Managing a conflict by confronting the problem and solving it. 378

contingency planning Planning what to do if the original plans don't work out. 146

controlling The management function of ensuring that work goes according to plan. 154 Monitoring performance and making needed corrections. 10

corporate culture   Beliefs and norms that govern organizational behavior in a firm. 118

counseling   The process of learning about an individual's personal problem and helping him or her resolve it. 321

creativity   The ability to bring about something imaginative or new. 242

critical-incident appraisal   A performance appraisal in which a supervisor keeps a written record of incidents that show positive and negative ways an employee has acted; the supervisor uses this record to assess the employee's performance. 482

cross-training   Training in the skills required to perform more than one job. 302

decision   A choice from among available alternatives. 226

decision tree   A graph that helps decision makers use probability theory by showing the expected values of decisions in varying circumstances. 237

decision-making leave   A day off during which a problem employee is supposed to decide whether to return to work and meet standards or to stay away for good. 329

decision-making skills   The ability to analyze information and reach good decisions. 5

decision-making software   A computer program that leads the user through the steps of the formal decision-making process. 238

delegating   Giving another person the authority and responsibility to carry out a task. 187

democratic leadership   A leadership style in which the leader allows subordinates to participate in decision making and problem solving. 202

demotion   Transfer of an employee to a job involving less responsibility and usually lower pay. 326

department   A unique group of resources that management has assigned to carry out a particular task. 175

departmentalization   Setting up departments in an organization. 175

detour behavior   Tactics for postponing or avoiding work. 53

directive counseling   An approach to counseling in which the supervisor asks the employee questions about the specific problem; when the supervisor understands the problem, he or she suggests ways to handle it. 322

discipline   Action taken by the supervisor to prevent employees from breaking rules. 324

discrimination   Unfair or inequitable treatment based on prejudice. 119

dismissal   Relieving an employee of his or her job. 326

diversity   Characteristics of individuals that shape their identities and the experiences they have in society. 115

downward communication   Organizational communication in which a message is sent to someone at a lower level. 275

employee assistance program (EAP)   A company-based program for providing counseling and related help to employees whose personal problems are affecting their performance. 332

employee handbook   A document that describes an organization's conditions of employment, policies regarding employees, administrative procedures, and related matters. 450

employee involvement teams   Teams of employees who plan ways to improve quality in their areas of organization. 37

empowerment   Delegation of broad decision-making authority and responsibility. 188

Equal Employment Opportunity Commission (EEOC)   The federal government agency charged with enforcing Title VII of the Civil Rights Act. 431

ethics   The principles by which people distinguish what is morally right. 95

exception principle   The control principle stating that a supervisor should take action only when variance is meaningful. 158

feedback   The way the receiver of a message responds or fails to respond to the message. 256

feedback control   Control that focuses on past performance. 160

financial incentives   Payments for meeting or exceeding objectives. 298

flextime   A policy that grants employees some leeway in choosing which 8 hours a day or which 40 hours a week to work. 292

forced-choice approach   A performance appraisal that presents an appraiser with sets of statements describing employee behavior; the appraiser must choose which statement is most characteristic of the employee and which is least characteristic. 481

formal communication   Organizational communication that is work related and follows the lines of the organization chart. 277

formal groups   Groups set up by management to meet organizational objectives. 67

frustration   Defeat in the effort to achieve desired goals. 373

functional authority   The right given by higher management to specific staff personnel to give orders concerning an area in which the staff personnel have expertise. 181

functional groups   Groups that fulfill ongoing needs in the organization by carrying out a particular function. 67

gainsharing   A group incentive plan in which the organization encourages employees to participate in making suggestions and decisions, then rewards the group with a share of improved earnings. 301

Gantt chart   Scheduling tool that lists the activities to be completed and uses horizontal bars to graph how long each activity will take, including its starting and ending dates. 150

goals   Objectives, often those with a broad focus. 141

grapevine   The path along which informal communication travels. 278

graphic rating scale   A performance appraisal that rates the degree to which an employee has achieved various characteristics. 479

group   Two or more people who interact with one another, are aware of one another, and think of themselves as a group. 65

group incentive plan   A financial incentive plan that rewards a team of workers for meeting or exceeding an objective. 300

groupthink   The failure to think independently and realistically as a group because of the desire to enjoy consensus and closeness. 239

halo effect   The practice of forming an overall opinion on the basis of one outstanding characteristic. 427

harshness bias   Rating employees more severely than their performances merit. 486

homogeneity   The degree to which the members of a group are the same. 74

human relations skills   The ability to work effectively with other people. 4

idle time, or downtime   Time during which employees or machines are not producing goods or services. 53

inference   A conclusion drawn from the facts available. 265

informal communication   Organizational communication that is directed toward individual needs and interests and does not necessarily follow formal lines of communication. 277

informal groups   Groups that form when individuals in the organization develop relationships to meet personal needs. 67

insubordination   Deliberate refusal to do what the supervisor or other superior asks. 317

interactive multimedia   Computer software that brings together sound, video, graphics, animation, and text and adjusts content on the basis of user responses. 459

internal locus of control   The belief that you are the primary cause of what happens to yourself. 201

ISO 9000   A series of standards adopted by the International Organization for Standardization to spell out acceptable criteria for quality systems. 41

job description   A listing of the characteristics of a job, including the job title, duties involved, and working conditions. 414

job enlargement   An effort to make a job more interesting by adding more duties to it. 302

job enrichment   The incorporation of motivating factors into a job—in particular, giving the employee more responsibility and recognition. 302

job rotation   Moving employees from job to job to give them more variety. 302

job sharing   An arrangement in which two part-time employees share the duties of one full-time job. 292

job specification   A listing of the characteristics desirable in the person performing a given job, including educational and work background, physical characteristics, and personal strengths. 415

laissez-faire leadership   A leadership style in which the leader is uninvolved and lets subordinates direct themselves. 202

lateral communication   Organizational communication in which a message is sent to a person at the same level. 277

leading   Influencing people to act or not act in a certain way. 199 Influencing people to act (or not act) in a certain way. 10

leniency bias   Rating employees more favorably than their performances merit. 486

line authority   The right to carry out tasks and give orders related to the organization's primary purpose. 180

Malcolm Baldrige National Quality Award   An annual award administered by the U.S. Department of Commerce and given to the company that shows the highest quality performance in seven categories. 41

management by objectives (MBO)   A formal system for planning in which managers and employees at all levels set objectives for what they are to accomplish; their performance is then measured against those objectives. 146

mentoring   Providing guidance, advice, and encouragement through an ongoing one-on-one work relationship. 462

motivation   Giving people incentives that cause them to act in desired ways. 289

nepotism The hiring of one's relatives. 103

network organizations Organizations that maintain flexibility by staying small and contracting with other individuals and organizations as needed to complete projects. 178

noise Anything that can distort a message by interfering with the communication process. 256

nondirective counseling An approach to counseling in which the supervisor primarily listens, encouraging the employee to look for the source of the problem and propose possible solutions. 323

nonverbal message A message conveyed without using words. 268

norms Group standards for appropriate or acceptable behavior. 71

objectives The desired accomplishments of the organization as a whole or of part of the organization. 141

on-the-job training Teaching a job while trainer and trainee perform the job at the work site. 457

open-ended question A question that gives the person responding broad control over the response. 426

operational planning The development of objectives that specify how divisions, departments, and work groups will support organizational goals. 142

organic structure Organizational structure in which the boundaries between jobs continually shift and people pitch in wherever their contributions are needed. 178

organizational politics Intentional acts of influence to enhance or protect the self-interest of individuals or groups. 388

organizing Setting up the group, allocating resources, and assigning work to achieve goals. 9

organizing Setting up the group, allocating resources, and assigning work to achieve goals. 173

orientation The process of giving new employees the information they need to do their work comfortably, effectively, and efficiently. 447

overhead Expenses not related directly to producing goods and services; examples are rent, utilities, and staff support. 52

paired-comparison approach A performance appraisal that measures the relative performance of employees in a group. 479

parity principle The principle that personnel who are given responsibility must also be given enough authority to carry out that responsibility. 184

payback period The length of time it will take for the benefits generated by an investment (such as cost savings from machinery) to offset the cost of the investment. 55

peer reviews Performance appraisals conducted by an employee's co-workers. 484

perceptions The ways people see and interpret reality. 266

perfectionism The attempt to do things perfectly. 349

performance appraisal Formal feedback on how well an employee is performing his or her job. 473

performance report A summary of performance and comparison with performance standards. 161

personal power Power that arises from an individual's personal characteristics. 389

piecework system Payment according to the quantity produced. 299

planning Setting goals and determining how to meet them. 140 Setting goals and determining how to meet them. 8

policies Broad guidelines for how to act. 144

position power Power that comes from a person's formal role in an organization. 389

positive discipline Discipline designed to prevent problem behavior from beginning. 329

power The ability to get others to act in a certain way. 181 The ability to influence people to behave in a certain way. 389

precontrol Efforts aimed at preventing behavior that may lead to undesirable results. 160

prejudice A preconceived judgment about an individual or group of people. 119 Negative conclusions about a category of people based on stereotypes. 267

probability theory A body of techniques for comparing the consequences of possible decisions in a risk situation. 236

problem A factor in the organization that is a barrier to improvement. 158

procedures The steps that must be completed to achieve a specific purpose. 144

process control Quality control that emphasizes how to do things in a way that leads to better quality. 34

procrastination Putting off what needs to be done. 349

product quality control Quality control that focuses on ways to improve the product itself. 34

productivity The amount of results (output) an organization gets for a given amount of inputs. 31

proficiency test A test that measures whether the person has the skills needed to perform a job. 427

profit-sharing plan A group incentive plan under which the company sets aside a share of its profits and divides it among employees. 300

program evaluation and review technique (PERT) Scheduling tool that identifies the relationships among tasks as well as the amount of time each task will take. 151

proximity bias   The tendency to assign similar scores to items that are near each other on a questionnaire. 487

psychomotor test   A test that measures a person's strength, dexterity, and coordination. 427

punishment   An unpleasant consequence given in response to undesirable behavior. 296

Pygmalion effect   The direct relationship between expectations and performance; high expectations lead to high performance. 303

quality control   An organization's efforts to prevent or correct defects in its goods or services or to improve them in some way. 33

recency syndrome   The tendency to remember more easily those events that have occurred recently. 231

recruitment   A process of identifying people interested in holding a particular job or working for the organization. 416

reinforcement   A desired consequence or the ending of a negative consequence, either of which is given in response to a desirable behavior. 296 Encouragement of a behavior by associating it with a reward. 158

responsibility   The obligation to perform assigned activities. 182

role conflicts   Situations in which a person has two different roles that call for conflicting types of behavior. 71

role-playing   A training method in which roles are assigned to participants, who then act out the way they would handle a specific situation. 461

roles   Patterns of behavior related to employees' positions in a group. 70

rules   Specific statements of what to do or not do in a given situation. 145

scheduling   Setting a precise timetable for the work to be completed. 150

self-concept   A person's self-image. 213

self-managing work teams   Groups of 5 to 15 members who work together to produce an entire product. 76

sexism   Discrimination based on gender stereotypes. 121

sexual harassment   Unwanted sexual attentions, including language, behavior, or the display of images. 122

similarity bias   The tendency to judge others more positively when they are like yourself. 487

Six Sigma   A process-oriented quality-control method designed to improve the product or service output to 99.97 percent perfect. 38

smoothing   Managing a conflict by pretending it does not exist. 377

span of control   The number of people a manager supervises. 185

staff authority   The right to advise or assist those with line authority. 180

staffing   Identifying, hiring, and developing the necessary number and quality of employees. 9

standards   Measures of what is expected. 154

statistical process control (SPC)   A quality-control technique using statistics to monitor production quality on an ongoing basis and making corrections whenever the results show the process is out of control. 36

statistical quality control   Looking for defects in parts or finished products selected through a sampling technique. 35

status   A group member's position in relation to others in the group. 72

stereotypes   Generalized, fixed images of others. 120 Rigid opinions about categories of people. 231

strategic planning   The creation of long-term goals for the organization as a whole. 141

stress   The body's response to coping with environmental demands. 351

structured interview   An interview based on questions the interviewer has prepared in advance. 424

supervisor   A manager at the first level of management. 3

suspension   Requirement that an employee not come to work for a set period of time; the employee is not paid for the time off. 325

symptom   An indication of an underlying problem. 158

task groups   Groups that are set up to carry out a specific activity and then disband when the activity is completed. 67

team   A small group whose members share goals, commitment, and accountability for results. 75

team building   Developing the ability of team members to work together to achieve common objectives. 79

technical skills   The specialized knowledge and expertise used to carry out particular techniques or procedures. 4

Theory X   A set of management attitudes based on the view that people dislike work and must be coerced to perform. 203

Theory Y   A set of management attitudes based on the view that work is a natural activity and that people will work hard and creatively to achieve objectives to which they are committed. 203

Theory Z   A set of management attitudes that emphasizes employee participation in all aspects of decision making. 205

360-degree feedback Performance appraisal that combines assessments from several sources. 484

time log A record of what activities a person is doing hour by hour throughout the day. 342

time management The practice of controlling the way you use time. 342

total quality management (TQM) An organization-wide focus on satisfying customers by continuously improving every business process for delivering goods or services. 39

training Increasing the skills that will enable employees to better meet the organization's goals. 445

turnover The rate at which employees leave an organization. 56

Type A personality A pattern of behavior that involves constantly trying to accomplish a lot in a hurry. 353

Type B personality A pattern of behavior that focuses on a relaxed but active approach to life. 353

unity of command The principle that each employee should have only one supervisor. 184

unstructured interview An interview in which the interviewer has no list of questions prepared in advance but asks questions on the basis of the applicant's responses. 426

upward communication Organizational communication in which a message is sent to someone at a higher level. 275

value The worth a customer places on a total package of goods and services relative to its cost. 42

variance The size of the difference between actual performance and a performance standard. 157

verbal message A message that consists of words. 268

vestibule training Training that takes place on equipment set up in a special area off the job site. 458

wellness program Organizational activities designed to help employees adopt healthy practices. 361

whistle-blower Someone who exposes a violation of ethics or law. 105

work-standards approach A performance appraisal in which an appraiser compares an employee's performance with objective measures of what the employee should do. 483

zero-defects approach A quality-control technique based on the view that everyone in the organization should work toward the goal of delivering such high quality that all aspects of the organization's goods and services are free of problems. 37

Index